AF334925

Virtual Reality Photography

Creating Panoramic and Object Images

SCOTT HIGHTON

**With a Foreword by
Rick Smolan**

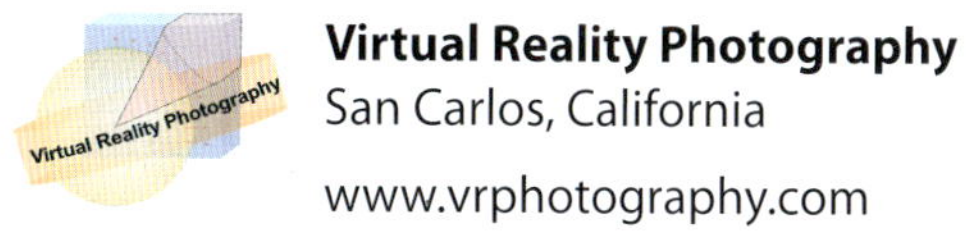

Virtual Reality Photography
San Carlos, California
www.vrphotography.com

Virtual Reality Photography: Creating Panoramic and Object Images
Scott Highton

Copyright © 2010 Scott Highton. World rights reserved. No part of this publication may be stored in a retrieval system, transmitted, or reproduced in any way, including but not limited to photocopy, photograph, magnetic, or other record, without prior agreement and written permission of the author.

All photographs, illustrations, and text herein are the exclusive property and copyright of the author, unless otherwise noted in captions or text.

Library of Congress Control Number: 2009943652

ISBN: 978-0-615-34223-8

TRADEMARKS: All trademarks presented are the exclusive property of their respective owners.

Limit of Liability/Disclaimer of Warranty: The information in this book is presented on an "As Is" basis. While the author and publisher have used their best efforts in preparing this book, they make no representations or warranties with respect to the acccuracy or completeness of the contents herein, and accept no liability of any kind including but not limited to performance, merchantability, fitness for any particular purpose, losses, or damages of any kind caused directly or indirectly from this book. The advice and strategies in this book may not be suitable for your situation. You should consult with a professional where appropriate.

Library of Congress Cataloging-in-Publication Data:
Highton, Scott, 1956 –
    Virtual reality photography: creating panoramic and object images/
    Scott Highton
        Includes index
        ISBN-13: 978-0-615-34223-8
        ISBN-10: 061534223X

Printed in China

10 9 8 7 6 5 4 3 2 1

For purchase and licensing information: **www.vrphotography.com**

Sponsors and Supporters:

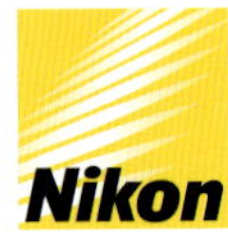

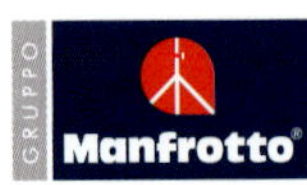
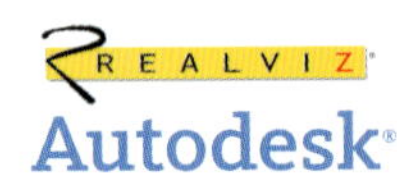
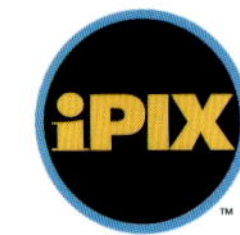
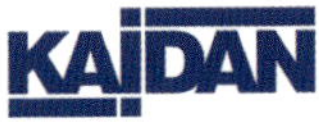
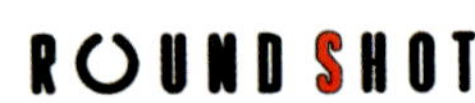
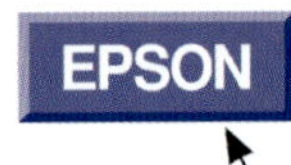
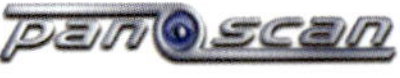
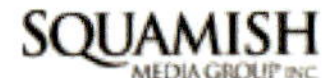

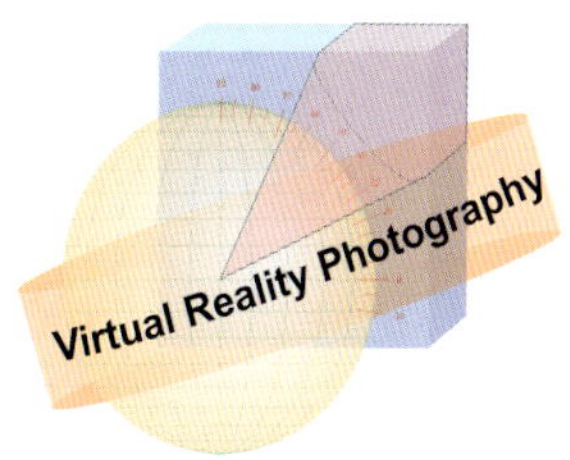

Contents

PHOTOGRAPHY BASICS

Chapter 1: Composition

Chapter 2: Perspective and View

Chapter 3: Exposure

Chapter 4: Sharpness and Resolution

PANORAMIC VR IMAGING

Chapter 9: Panoramic Overview

Chapter 10: Cylindrical Panoramas

**Chapter 11: Cubic and
Spherical Panoramas**

OBJECT VR IMAGING

BUSINESS PRACTICES

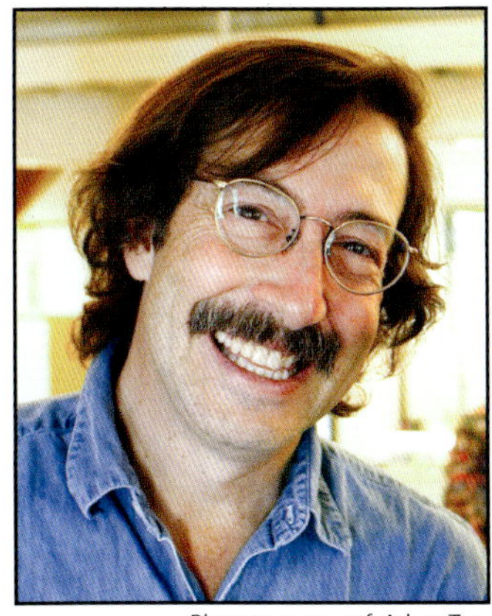

Photo courtesy of Adam Tow

Foreword

by Rick Smolan

Co-Creator of "The Day in the Life" and "America 24/7" book series

Every communication medium is intended to help us tell our stories. This has been the case from stone-age cave drawings, to the now primitive, yet effective hand-written letter. The latest electronic social networks, high end interactive games, television programs, and motion pictures all exist for the purpose of allowing people to tell stories to each other. These are how we share news, education, entertainment, business, and personal communication. The very foundations of commerce and trade depend heavily on our ability to tell each other stories about our products and services.

Human experience today revolves around visual communication. We use images to share almost all aspects of life with one another. Cameras are a daily part of most lives – incorporated into our cell phones, computers, and PDAs. They are included in our cars, on our streets, in our homes, and offices. Many even record our earth from above.

There is an overwhelming glut of visual imagery that results, available for viewing to anyone with access to the Internet – image libraries, webcams, social networks, GoogleEarth, etc. The sheer volume of this increasing imagery is staggering.

The challenge for most of us is in finding the images that show us what we want to know, clearly and simply. For those of us trying to communicate effectively, the challenge is in *producing* imagery that effectively shows what we want. For the most part, the millions of images captured daily around the world are not terribly effective at this.

Technology today offers us cameras that can produce properly exposed, properly focused, and sufficiently detailed images, while requiring little more on our part than aiming and pushing a button – and sometimes, not even that. Yet in spite of this ease, and in spite of the overwhelming volume of images we collectively create, viewers always seem to want more. They want to be able to better share in the experience we try to offer.

If a still photograph is good, perhaps *several* photos, or even a video clip is better. If a written description is good, a conversation might be better. We seek interactivity in our story telling. We learn more about a product or an event when we experience it first hand, or somehow become immersed in the experience ourselves. We want control. Even after a photo has been taken we want to be able to go back in time and turn the camera left and right, to choose our own path through the space or place being photographed.

Interactive imaging and multimedia give us this sense of control, allowing us to find our own path through a photo. Few people would think about buying a new car without first experiencing it with a test drive. Few would ever rent an apartment or buy a house without first seeing it in person. If you were planning a family trip somewhere, wouldn't you prefer to have an interactive preview where you could look around and delve into visual details of lodging, attractions, environment, and facilities before ever leaving home?

Virtual reality photography makes this possible. Panoramic VR images allow viewers to see an environment, a location, or the inside of a new car in its 360° entirety. They allow a viewer to zoom in to examine details, or jump via hot links to other perspectives. Object VR images allow viewers to examine a product, object, or even a rare and precious artifact from any angle, without ever having to touch it themselves. Certainly these experiences are not identical to being there first hand, but they can provide an experience much closer than traditional photography or other media allow.

With this seminal book, Scott Highton, one of the pioneers of virtual reality photography, provides a foundation for both photographers and multimedia designers seeking to learn the techniques of effective visual story telling via interactive imaging. I can't think of a better guide to accompany you on your journey through this fascinating medium.

Acknowledgements

This book would not have been possible without the tremendous support provided by the following people and companies.

Mikkel Aaland planted the idea for this book in my mind a number of years ago, and offered regular encouragement, support, and guidance in helping it come to fruition. Rick Smolan provided valued support, and graciously agreed to write the foreword.

Terry Beaubois and Greg Miller of RDC Interactive were critical in helping to develop the content and structure for the book, as well as providing regular inspiration with their own immersive imaging and interactive media projects. Both have been valued collaborators.

Eric Chen is one of the original authors of QuickTime VR, and H. Lee Martin is one of the minds behind what eventually became IPIX spherical imaging technologies. Both offered invitations that led to me becoming involved in the infancies of these technologies, as did Danny McCall. Jeff Peters and Bruce Cole prompted early sponsorship and financial support from IPIX.

In kind sponsorship was offered by Jim Anders of Kaidan, Frank Casanova and Rhonda Stratton of Apple's QuickTime Group, Kriss Brunngraber and Fabio Prada of Manfrotto, Richard LoPinto and Bill Pekala of Nikon, Fabia Ochoa of Epson, Werner Seitz of Seitz Phototechnik (Roundshot), Richard DiMaio and Liz Tjostolvsen of RealViz (now Autodesk), and Doug DeRusha of Squamish Media Group.

Additional technical support was generously provided by Lewis Knapp of Corybant West, Ted Chavalas of Panoscan, John Borden of Peace River Studios, and Russell Brown of Adobe Systems.

A number of other individuals allowed me to call upon them regularly for advice and information. These include Ken Turkowski, Richard Lyon, Bruce Southwick, Mark Segal, Norbert Wu, Gary Young, Bob Goldstein, Victor Perlman, and Richard Weisgrau.

The assistance and collaboration provided by leading VR photographers over the years has been both inspiring and fun. It is always a pleasure to get together to discuss techniques, projects, business, and unique approaches to our craft. John Greenleigh, Tim Petros, Jook Leung, Pat St. Clair, and Janie Fitzgerald regularly shared details of their businesses and creativity, and willingly served as case study subjects. Each of them also participate as online experts for the **vrphotography.com** web site. Virtual reality pioneer Paul Debevec graciously offered his insights, including his glimpse into the future of VR.

Finally, I want to thank my family – Nancy, Doug, and Melinda – for their amazing love and support of my efforts. Production of this book has been a long journey, and I couldn't have done it without them.

– Scott Highton, January, 2010

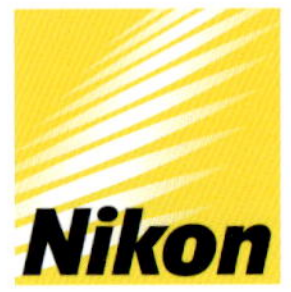
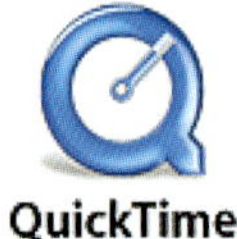
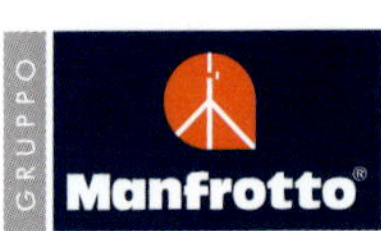
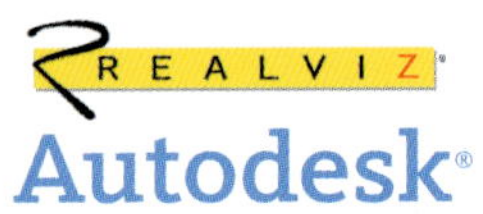
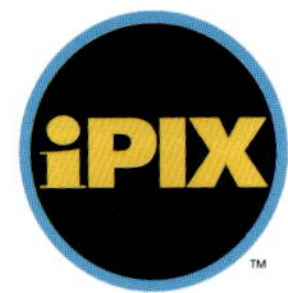
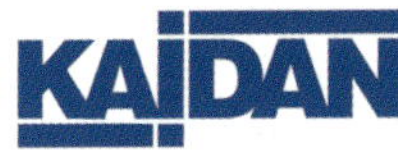
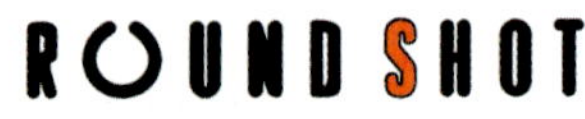

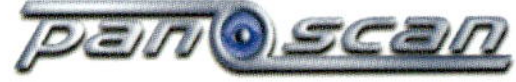
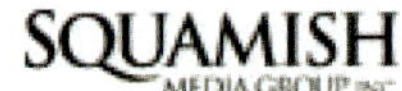

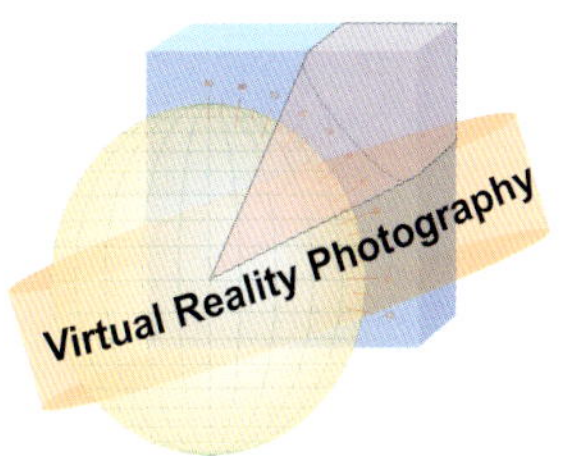

Introduction

Webster's Dictionary:

re·al·i|ty – n. the quality or fact of being real

vir·tu|al – adj. being such practically or in effect, although not in actual fact or name

Virtual Reality and Immersive Imaging

The term "virtual reality" (VR) is, by definition, an oxymoron, since something that exists only in effect, is not itself real. Yet, reality can be represented in many ways, and one of the most realistic of those ways, since its inception over 150 years ago, has been photography.

A traditional black and white photograph is a relatively simple virtual representation of reality. It shows a realistic view of a subject, but is missing many of the elements that would make that subject real, such as color, mass, texture, depth, the occupation of space, or existence over time. Many of these missing elements can be added with more modern recording technologies such as color films and motion picture or video imaging. A three-dimensional view can be displayed using holography or stereo viewing systems. The ability to "feel" a virtual subject can even be simulated with sensory gloves, goggles, and digital systems. Yet none of these technologies creates an absolute true copy of the subject. Instead, such systems are used simply to heighten the viewer's senses and to make the depiction seem, to some extent, "virtually" real.

The proliferation of personal computing has made VR displays of objects and environments a mainstream technology. VR allows a viewer to become "immersed" within a virtual environment without the need for special goggles, gloves, motion sensing suits or room-sized projection systems. Virtual reality experiences are no longer limited to military and high end corporate budgets. Today, there is explosive growth in the use of VR imagery on the World Wide Web and in electronic consumer publishing.

VR imagery allows one to preview a travel destination, tour a home, sit inside a new car, understand the use and functions of a tool, and to get an experience similar to actual immersion in a real location or environment. The use of photographic images for these VR applications has been referred to as "immersive imaging" because the viewer is effectively immersed into a product or scene. Rather than simply looking at a printed brochure of a new car, a prospective buyer can actually view the car from any angle or look around the interior from a virtual perspective within the vehicle.

This virtual driver can zoom in for a closer look in any direction, honk the horn, open the glove box, even start the engine if they so desire, viewing everything from the comfort of their home or office. While the experience isn't quite the same as actually sitting in the car on an actual test drive, it offers a more complete representation of reality from a distance than has ever been available to the general public before.

QuickTime VR

In 1994, Apple Computer introduced QuickTime™ VR, the first significant consumer level technology for creating and displaying VR images. QuickTime VR (QTVR) was the first of many technologies that allowed the photographic creation of virtual environments without the prohibitively expensive camera and computer systems required by earlier VR technologies. QTVR was designed to allow multimedia developers to use off the shelf cameras and lenses, as well as commercially available rendering software, for both the creation and presentation of virtual environments. Display of

QTVR scenes is easily done on most popular computer platforms, as it is a key element of Apple's QuickTime format. Today, QuickTime remains a dominant standard for multimedia authoring and presentation, particularly for web and other electronic content distribution. A number of other VR presentation formats are also available today, but for the most part, they are very similar in appearance and function to QTVR.

QuickTime VR offers two distinct interactive "movie" types. The first is called a **panorama movie**, which is photographed from a central position looking outward – creating a 360-degree panoramic view. A viewer can interactively pan across the image on a computer screen, zooming in and out, looking up or down. One can even "jump" from one panoramic view to another via embedded links. Using a series of these panoramas together, a viewer can experience a virtual tour of an environment, moving throughout it and looking around at will. The link feature can also be used to bring up detailed photos, animations, movies, audio, graphics, or text descriptions of particular subjects within the scene.

The second QTVR movie type is known as an **object movie**. Object movies provide a series of incremental views looking *inward* at an object, rather than outward from a central point like panoramas. This allows viewers to examine an object from any angle, effectively turning that product around or tilting it up and down with their computer mouse. The viewer can also zoom in or out on the object, as well as pan and tilt to highlight a detail of the object in the viewing window.

Photographing a VR panorama can be done using a variety of techniques, but the most popular is to use a standard camera with a wide angle lens to shoot a series of overlapping images around a circle. These individual frames (usually between six and 24) are then blended together using a digital **stitcher** to create a seamless 360° panoramic view. When made into a VR movie, this panorama is displayed on a computer screen, and the viewer has the ability to pan the view continuously to the left and right, look up or down, and zoom in or out at will.

Successful panoramic stitching generally requires that the camera be properly aligned so that the axis of rotation is around what is known as the entrance pupil of the lens being used. This generally requires the use of a tripod and a special VR pan head. Without this, objects in the foreground and distance change their positions relative to each other in the frame as the camera is panned (often known as parallax error). These errors usually prevent the software stitching applications from properly aligning the pixel patterns of the image pairs, and a ghosting effect will result in the blended sections.

A suitable image overlap is also generally required (usually 1/4 – 1/3 of the frame) in order to provide sufficient pixel data for the stitcher to match and blend across. The rotation increment of the camera between adjacent shots in a panorama will depend upon the focal length of the lens being used, and the overlap area desired. A wide angle lens will require fewer shots (and a larger pan increment between shots) than will a longer telephoto in order to make up a full 360° sequence. Ultra-wide rectilinear lenses in the 14mm – 24mm range (35mm format), or high quality fisheye lenses, are generally preferred by most professionals.

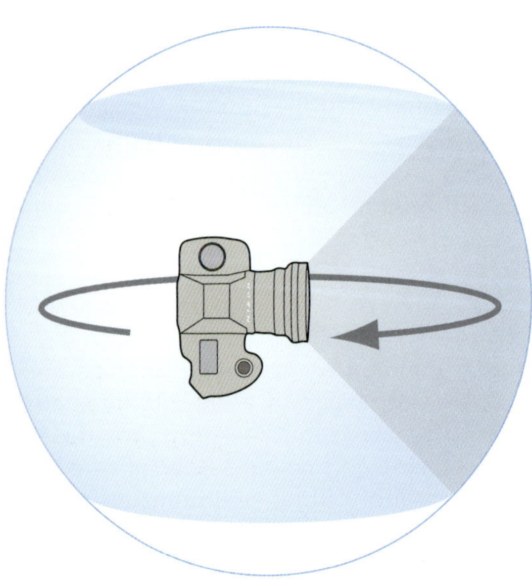

VR Panorama – 360° view outward

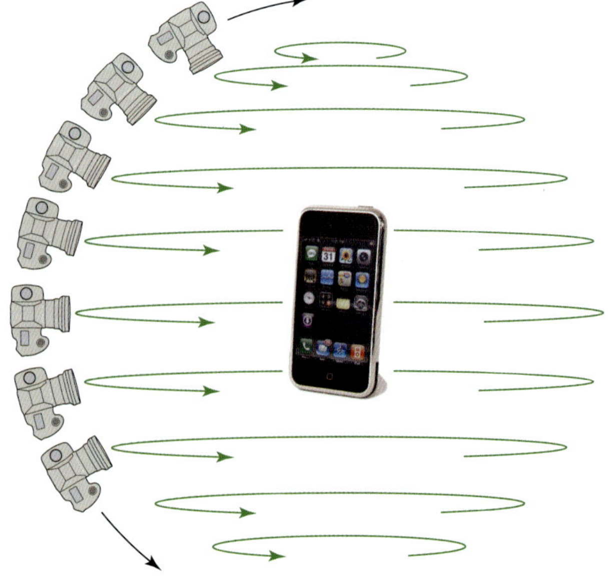

VR Object – 360° views inward

Fig. i-1 VR panoramas capture views looking outward, while VR objects are series of images looking inward.

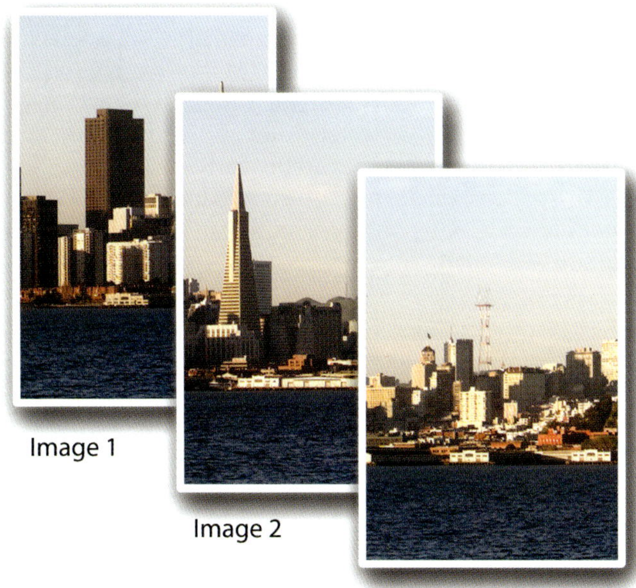

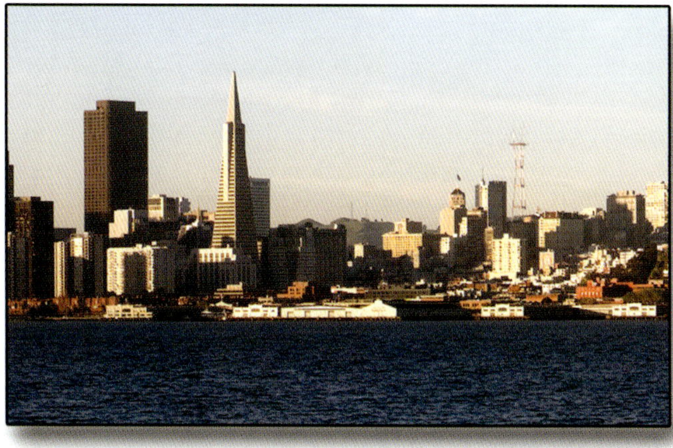

Fig. I-2 The stitching process allows for seamless assembly of multiple photographs into a composited panoramic image.

It is also important to maintain consistent exposures and color balance settings throughout the sequence so that the brightness and colors of each shot closely match those of adjacent shots for smooth blending in the stitching process. This is why cameras with true manual exposure controls (whether digital or film based) are generally preferred for VR photography.

Other camera systems, including traditional slit scan cameras such as RoundShot™ or Panoscan™, can also be used to capture full 360° panoramas without the need for multiple image stitching. However, these systems are far more expensive than traditional 35mm or digital cameras, and only a few models allow use of interchangeable lenses. Digitizing or scanning film images – particularly large panoramic formats – can add significant time and expense to the process. All images must wind up in digital form before stitching can be done on a computer.

Parabolic mirror systems, such as the GoPano™ lens adapter, can enable capture of a full 360° panorama in a single image. These resulting donut or torus-shaped images require processing with a dewarping application in order to be rendered into a flat panorama or VR movie.

The ultimate result of any VR panoramic image capture is to create a seamless image, which can be projected inside a virtual geometric shape (most commonly either a cylinder, sphere or cube) for interactive display on a computer screen. There are numerous tools that can help accomplish this. As with most things in photography, there are tradeoffs in the choice of each. Often, a tool that is the best choice for one job may not be as good for another. The photographer must choose the most appropriate tools for the particular requirements of each job.

While panoramas are most effective for showing a complete view outward from a given spot, **object** movies can serve an equally important role in the presentation of three-dimensional subjects. If you want to show a sculpture, a commercial product, a car, or an airplane from every angle, you may have trouble doing so effectively using panoramic images. Instead, a series of photographs taken from incremental angles surrounding the object will probably work better. These images can then be sequenced or mapped into 3D computer formats so that viewers can view the object interactively from any angle on their computer screens.

The combination of panorama and object movies provides an almost unlimited range of interactivity for multimedia producers and their audiences. Rather than simply watching a linear movie on a given subject, viewers can choose what they look at, in what sequence they view it, and decide for themselves what aspects deserve further investigation.

Planning for Interactivity

Photography for interactive multimedia is generally far more complex than traditional still photography, due in part to the volume of images and content required. There is really no such thing as a "small" interactive multimedia project. Interactivity is only provided by giving viewers multiple options to choose from as they navigate through the project.

Whereas a traditional picture story might contain a dozen images that take a viewer from a beginning of the story to its end, an interactive sequence will involve a geometric increase in images in order to provide "branches" of information for the viewer to explore.

Furthermore, each image linked from the base sequence will probably require supplemental material that can be linked *to*, as well.

Obviously, all these images need to be created during the project's production in order to build even the simplest content structure with sufficient volume to support interactivity. When you add an immersive imaging element, where multiple photos or sequences need to be shot for each single panorama or object movie, the volume of photographs required for even the smallest interactive project can be staggering.

Interactive VR photography is complex work, more like production of a motion picture than traditional still photography or photojournalism. It requires careful advance planning, accurate archiving of photos and sequences, impeccable record keeping, the ability to maintain continuity, and attention to both the project overall *and* its minute details. It is every bit as complicated as shooting a motion picture or television program, perhaps even more so because you are often dealing with multiple story lines (navigation paths) and must maintain continuity and consistency throughout.

The first thing that should be done, well before shooting starts, is to map out the desired navigation structure on paper. This can take the form of an outline, a flow chart, storyboards or an actual map of locations, subjects and specific content needed. Remember that successful interactivity and presentation on screen combines a *variety* of elements, including still and immersive images, moving pictures (animations, videos, movies), sound, illustrations, graphics and text. Even though you may not personally be responsible for creating all of these, you must be aware of how such elements will be used in conjunction with your photography. Photographers working in interactive and immersive multimedia today often need the equipment and skills to not only shoot high quality still and VR images, but to be good cinematographers and audio technicians, as well.

Once the project and its navigation routes have been mapped out, planning for the photography or content acquisition can begin. This is where you plan the depth and detail of the materials you'll create, such as how many different panoramas will be needed – and from what positions they'll be shot, or whether an object movie requires a set of views from a single level or from multiple levels above and below the object. Understanding the entire immersive imaging process will be extremely important in order to plan sufficient time, resources, and budget to complete it all. It doesn't matter whether you are the producer overseeing the entire project or only serving as the photographer. You must be fully aware of the requirements of the production in order to make the appropriate choices of tools and techniques to create the desired content.

Photographing for VR

Photography for VR is as much an exacting science as it is a visual art. Just because a photographer has a good eye for lighting and composition, doesn't mean that he or she will necessarily have the technical skills for capturing a VR scene. Technical skills can be learned. However, the visual and artistic talents of good photographers will generally go farther than technical ability alone in the creation of enticing imagery.

Good photographers will avoid the "snapshot" look unfortunately prevalent in much VR work today. While technical concerns are always important, the effectiveness of any photography, no matter how perfect technically, will be marginal unless the images are visually appealing.

"f/8 and Be There!"

In the early days of photojournalism, when news photographers carried 4"x5" Speed Graphics and an on-camera flash, the old motto was "f/8 and be there!" The assumption was that, with such a large film format and sufficient light provided by the flash bulb, all a photographer had to do was to point the camera in the general direction of the subject and fire. The flash bulbs had enough brightness to light almost any shot. Darkroom printing could correct most exposure problems. The f/8 setting gave sufficient depth of field that everything further than a few feet away would be in acceptable focus. And the large negative could ultimately be cropped to isolate only the subject(s) of interest. It was a crude means for getting acceptable documentation of an event or story, but it rarely provided anything that would appeal to the sophisticated visual demands of today's audiences.

This, unfortunately, is the approach taken by many photographers and producers new to VR work. They simply place their cameras with ultra-wide lenses somewhere in the middle of a scene and take a series of images to assemble into a panorama. They have little concern over composition, lighting, point of view, location of the subject(s), or their relative perspective in the scene. Their concerns are purely technical – camera alignment, frame overlap, and "acceptable" exposure and focus. This is **"f/8 and be there"** all over again. The mistaken assumption is that if you are in the middle of a scene and you're shooting the entire 360° view around, somewhere within that scene should be something that draws the interest of your viewers. This is dull photography, and even when done well technically, does little more than simply document a location.

Good photography draws viewers into the image by providing both a point of view and a perspective. It is visually appealing and evokes some sort of emotion. It is *not* done by simply pointing a camera and firing the shutter. Within every good picture, there must be a story.

All stories, whether written or visual, can be told an infinite number of ways. The trick is to tell *your* version of the story well.

Take a close look at good photography today, whether in photojournalism, corporate work, advertising, motion pictures, or television. A picture is good because the photographer shows a unique and compelling perspective – a particular view from a particular location at a particular moment. The photographer also defines the subject with lighting, framing and composition, and successfully captures the image with decisions of focus and exposure. A good image does not appeal to the viewer simply because the photographer stuck a camera near something of interest and pressed the button.

All these concerns must be addressed to create good VR photography. It is not enough to place a camera on a tripod in the middle of a scene and spin it around. VR imagery requires all the artistic and technical skills of traditional photography, and more.

VR photographers require the ability to compose and light an entire environment so it records properly on film or digital media, and to do so with little or no "off camera" positioning of supplemental lights. (It's a challenge to place lighting outside of the view of the camera when the camera ultimately records everything 360 degrees around itself.) VR photographers must have a technical understanding of every step of the process, including node selection, film / media choice, lens selection, camera alignment, lighting control, subject positioning, digital processing, post production assembly, sequencing and end-user interfaces. They must be systematic and precise in their approach and possess a filmmaker's sense of continuity and story line.

Again, the majority of these skills can be learned, and most people who enter the worlds of VR photography or multimedia production already possess many of them, having come from other visually oriented fields such as traditional photography, publishing, design, and motion picture or video production. The foundations of good *photography* are essential for VR photographers to learn before trying to tackle the more complex matters of producing good VR photography. Hence, the first section of this book is dedicated to these basics.

Part 1

PHOTOGRAPHY BASICS

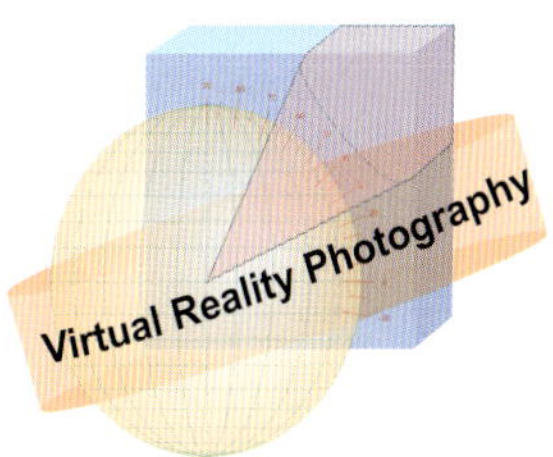

Chapter 1: Composition

With the proliferation of modern, low cost cameras, almost anyone today can take properly focused and well exposed pictures. Gone are the days when you'd get rolls of vacation pictures back from the photo lab only to discover that poor exposure, bad focus, or forgetting to remove the lens cap had eliminated the visual memories of your trip. Today's digital cameras, with their auto-everything systems and immediate display of images, allow even the worst photographers among us to take acceptable photographs of just about any subject.

However, most of us can still tell the difference between the pictures an average snapshooter takes and those shot by professional photographers. There are a lot more elements involved in making good photographs than simply looking through a viewfinder and pushing a button, even when the electronic brain of an automatic camera is making so many decisions for us.

One of these critical elements is composition, or the positioning of the subject(s) within the image frame. Over the years, artists and designers have established a number of rules-of-thumb for composition, which make images more visually appealing. As with most rules-of-thumb, these are not absolute, and can sometimes be intentionally broken for better results. However, they should generally be followed in regular practice for good photography.

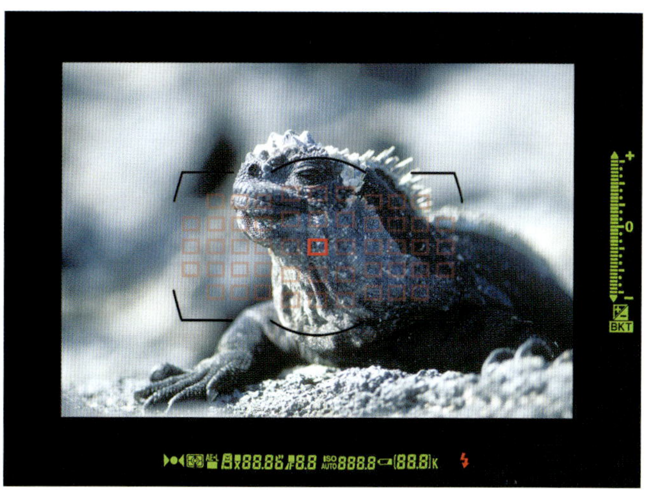

Fig. 1-1 The design of most camera viewfinders tends to encourage the centering of a subject in the frame. This can be a detriment to good composition.

> **RULE #1: The Rule of Thirds**
>
> *Divide your frame into thirds both horizontally and vertically. Compose the image so that your horizon, foreground/background lines and other visual dividers occur on or near these lines. Place your primary subject(s) at or near the intersections of these lines.*

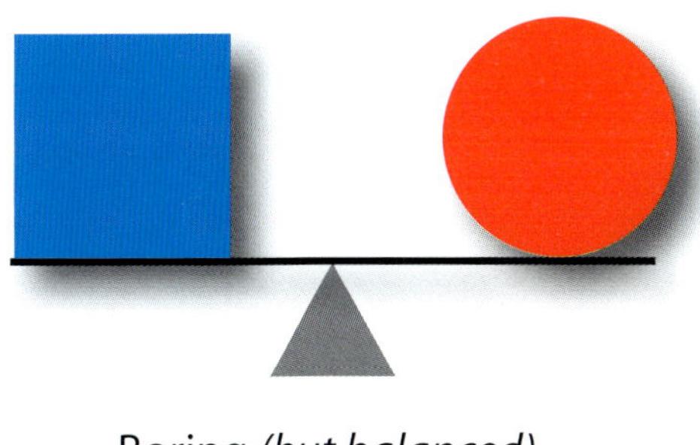

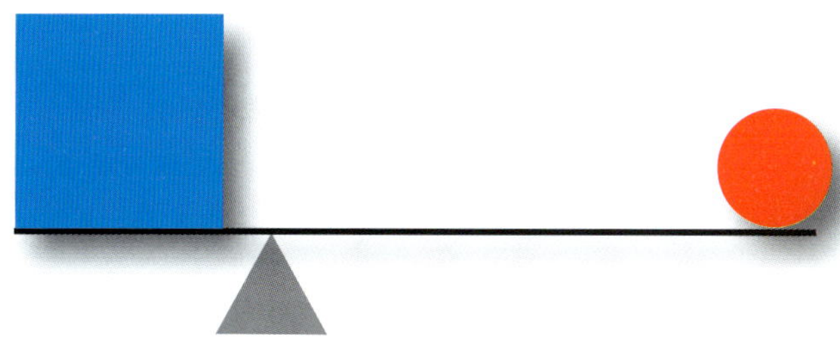

Fig. 1-2 Balance can be achieved visually in different ways.

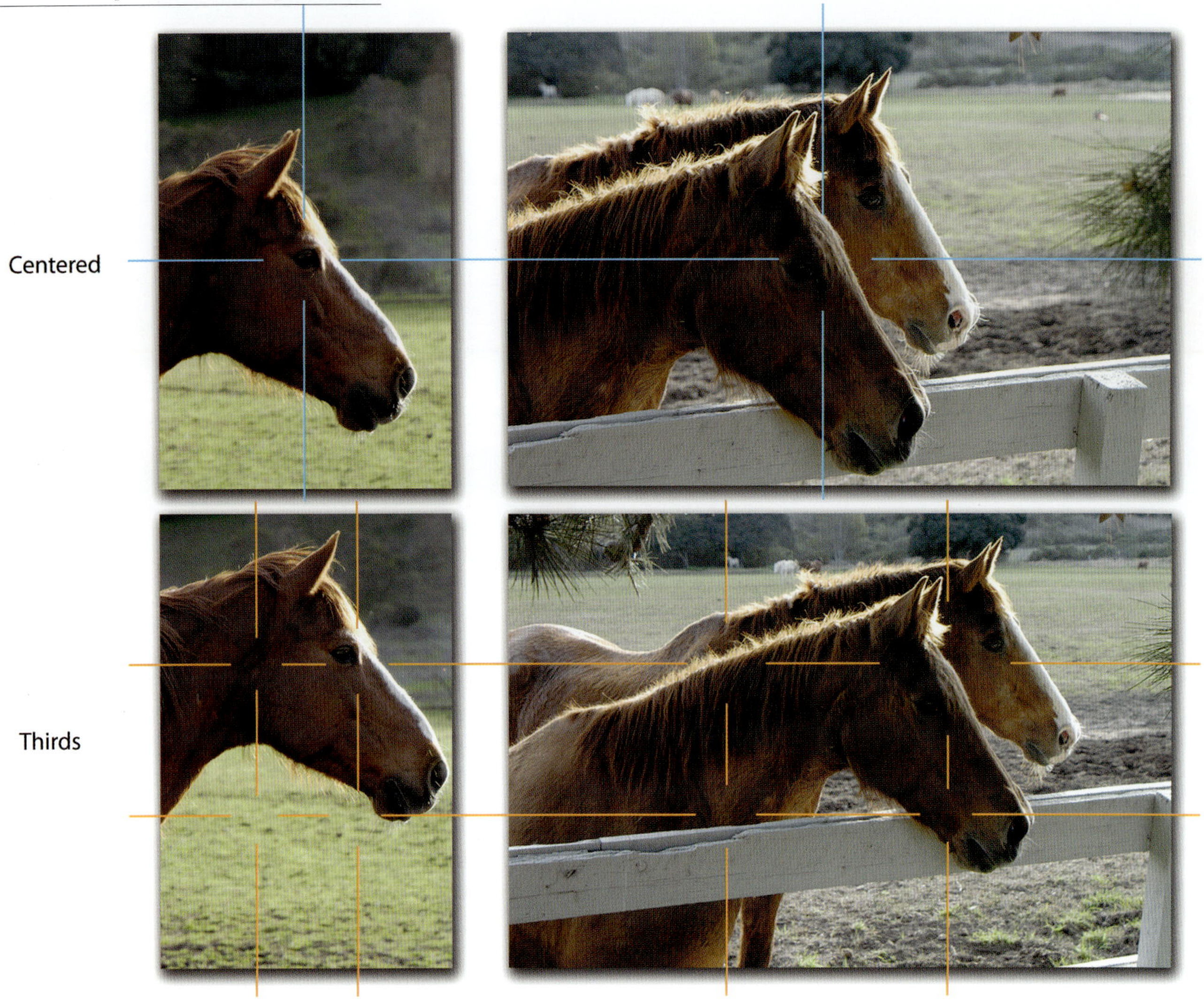

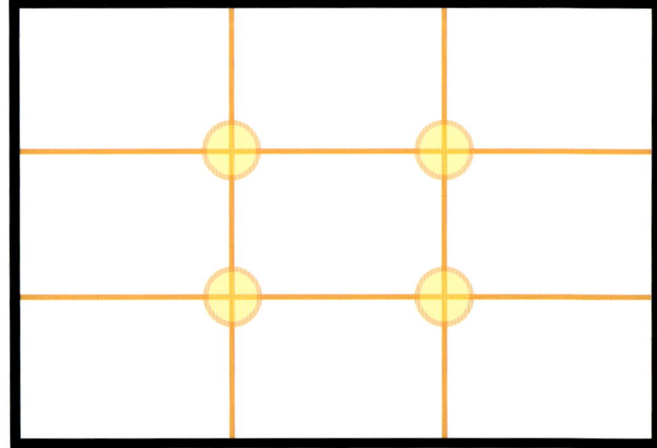

Fig. 1-3 Composition is generally improved by utilizing the Rule of Thirds.

Our natural inclination when looking through a viewfinder is to place our subject in the middle of the frame. This seems to assure us that we won't lose anything that might be important in the picture. Many cameras even have "target" lines or circles in their viewfinders that lead our eye to the center of the frame. However, a centered object appears static and boring to viewers of a photo. Placing the subject(s) or horizon off-center, is the first step in providing a *dynamic balance*, and creates visual interest.

Notice the difference in the photos in Figure 1-3. The top and bottom image sets were shot with the same lens from the same position, but the ones on the bottom that conform to the Rule of Thirds are far more interesting visually than the ones on the top composed with the subject centered in the frame.

There are four intersections of the imaginary lines that divide an image into vertical and horizontal thirds. These are the key spots that should be used in composition of an image, and where one should generally position primary subject(s).

Determining exactly what subject, or even what part of your subject, you want to focus your viewers' attention upon will help you determine its positioning in the frame. Generally, the main subject in your picture should

Fig. 1-4 Dividing the frame into thirds, both vertically and horizontally, provides four intersection points where subjects are best positioned under the Rule of Thirds.

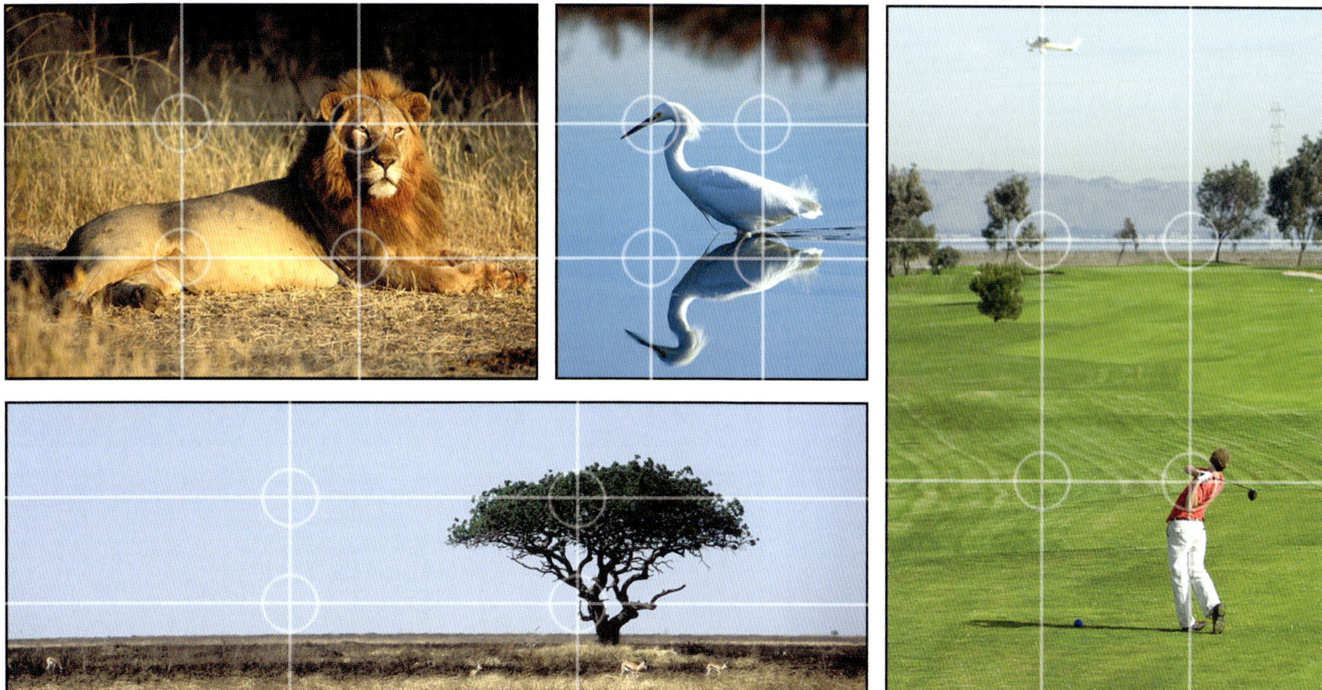

Fig. 1-5 The Rule of Thirds can be applied to images with any aspect ratio – vertical, horizontal, square, and panoramic.

be positioned at one of the four intersections dividing the frame into thirds. If your subject is a person or animal, you will usually want at least one of their eyes to appear at one of these intersections.

Like any Rule of Thumb, there are always exceptions. Rules, after all, need to be broken at times, particularly when pertaining to artistic style. Before you go breaking rules of composition, be sure you have first learned them well and know how they are applied. Once they are second nature to you, then you can experiment outside their bounds.

RULE #2: Converging and Leading Lines

Use converging lines within the image to lead the viewer's eye toward the subject in the photo.

In nature, there are lots of borders or lines that can be used by photographers to point the viewer's eye toward the subject in their photos. These can include the trunks or branches of trees, the edge of a forest, the banks of a river, a line of surf, shapes of animals, the ridge of a mountain, and the line of a valley. Many man-made objects can work similarly, including the edge of a table, patterns in a carpet or floor, walls, ceilings, roads, train tracks, machinery, sidewalks, furniture, and even parts the human body.

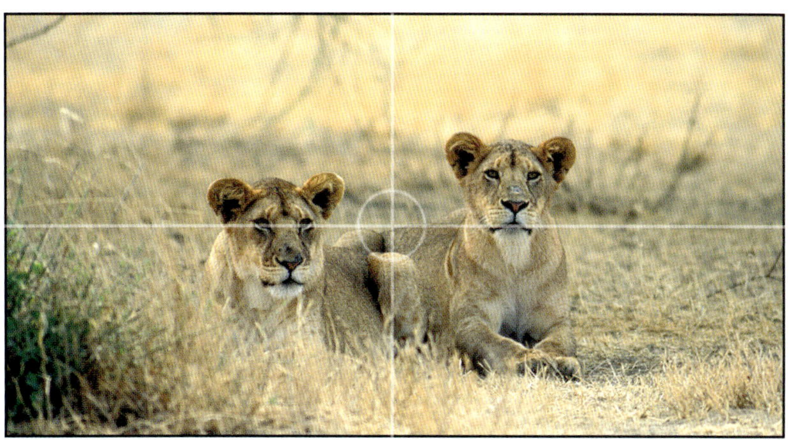

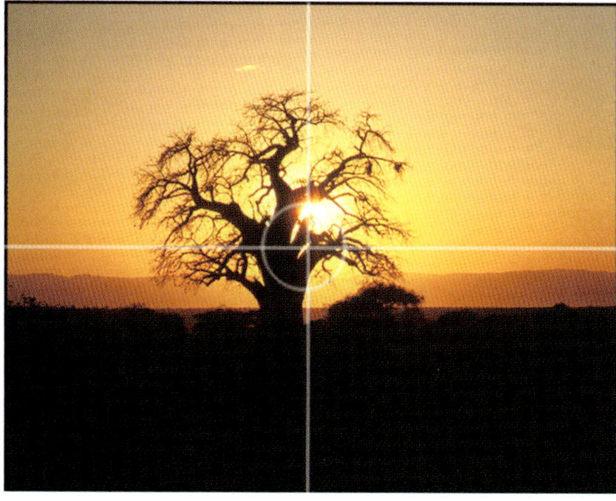

Fig. 1-6 The Rule of Thirds can also be broken effectively at times, but usually it is better not to.

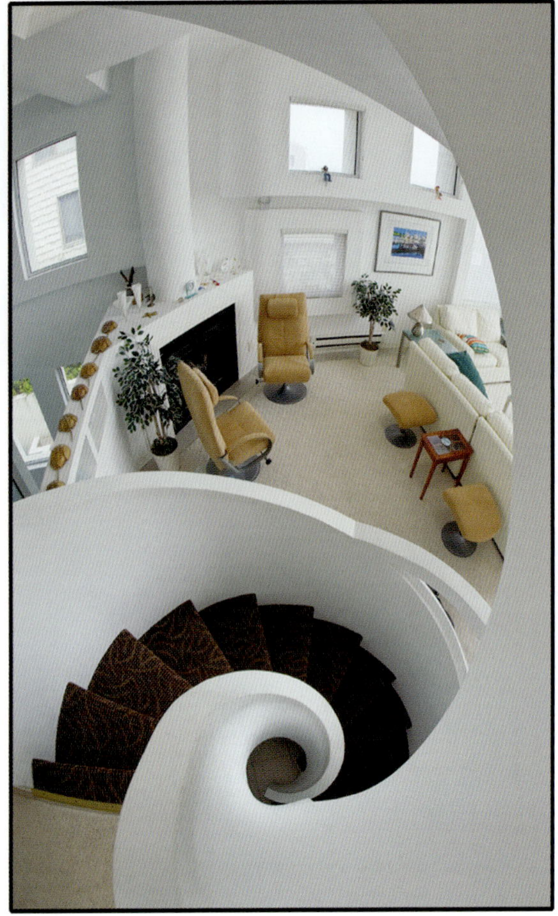

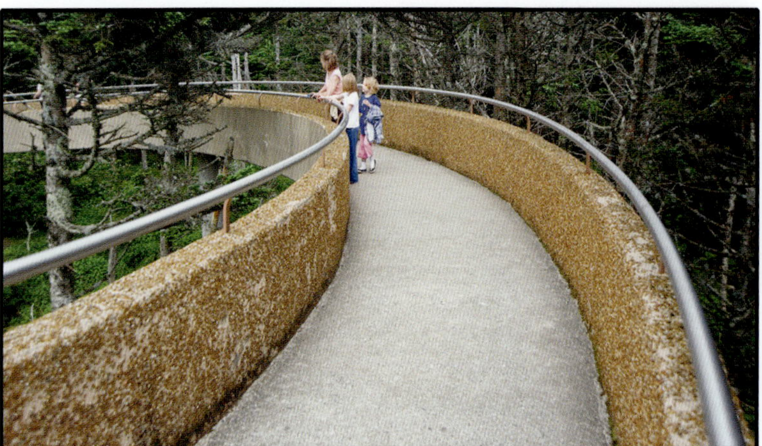

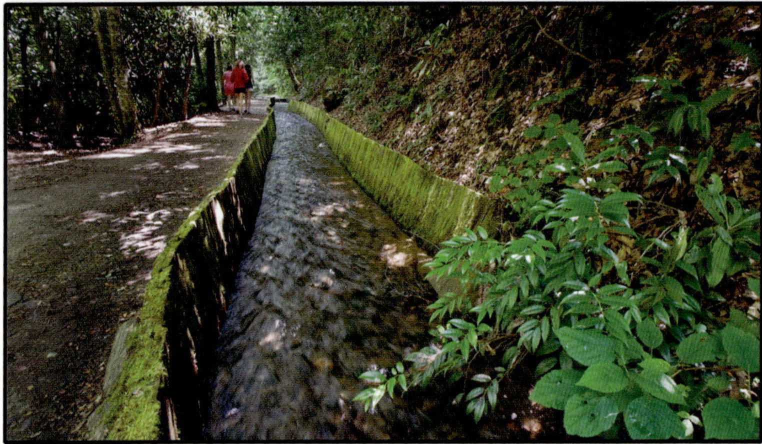

Fig. 1-7 Leading lines draw the viewer's eye toward the part of the image where the lines converge.

When we position the subject of our photos near a spot where these lines converge, our viewer's eyes are drawn from the edges of the photo inward toward the subject. This convergence helps visually define the subject of an image, and also makes the image more pleasing to the eye.

Sometimes, it might be only a single line or edge that leads the viewer's eye toward the subject in the photo. In others, it might be two or more edges converging, such as the sides of a road or pathway that appear to come together at a vanishing point.

Wide angle lenses can exaggerate the perspective of a particular view, and can accentuate the convergence of leading lines in a photograph, particularly if the camera is moved so that the foreground of these edges are very close to the lens.

When you are composing a photograph in your camera's viewfinder, be willing to move around. Notice how sometimes even a slight change of your position can make a tremendous difference in where lines converge in your frame, and can vastly improve your composition.

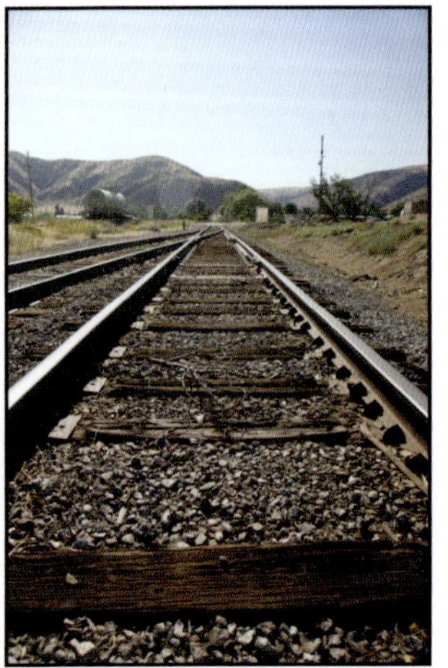

Fig. 1-8 Choice of lens focal length and subject distance both effect perspective.

RULE #3: Scale

Include visual elements to provide reference to relative sizes and scale in a photograph.

Adding an element of scale is particularly useful when photographing subjects that are unusual in size or unfamiliar to the viewer. Scale can sometimes be used in conjunction with leading or converging lines, or with visual transitions between foregrounds and backgrounds.

A photograph of a solitary tree, for example, doesn't really give the viewer a sense of the true size of that tree. However, if another subject is included in the image – particularly something like a person or an automobile that viewers can immediately recognize size-wise, then a visual reference for scale is established.

For macro or microscopic photographs, an old trick for providing scale was to place a coin such as a penny or dime next to the subject. While effective at showing scale, this technique rarely contributes to the quality or visual appeal of an image. Instead viewers are left with a simple documentation, rather than an interesting photograph.

Consider the photographs in Fig. 1-9 showing the same subjects with and without elements of scale. Such elements don't have to look artificial, and can often be found as a part of the natural surroundings of your subjects. Simply adjust your shooting position and composition to take advantage of their presence, when appropriate.

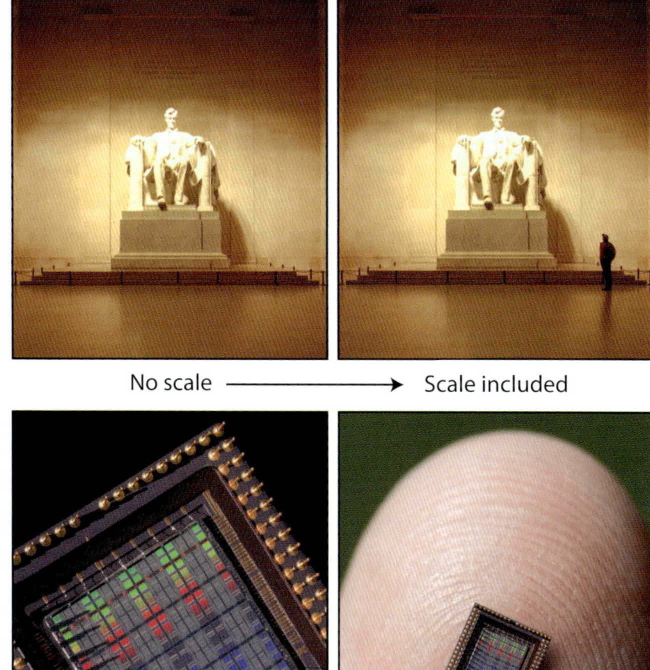

Fig. 1-9 Including a familiar subject can provide a sense of scale within a photograph.

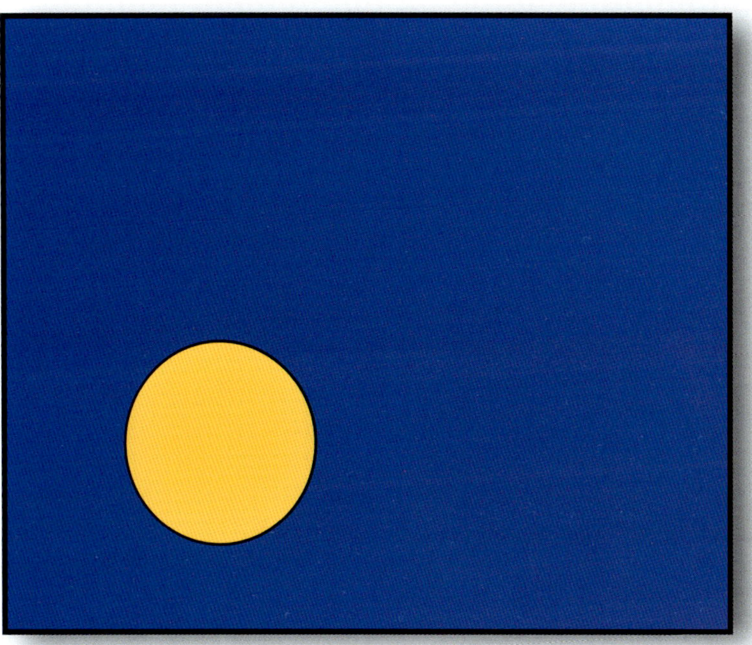

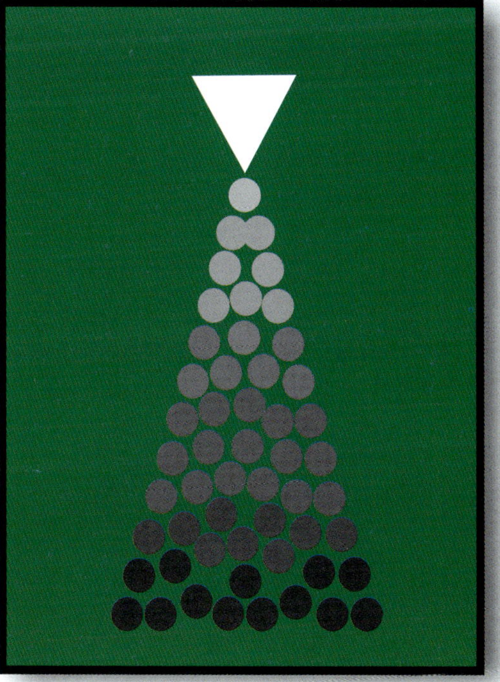

Fig. 1-10 A viewer's eye is usually drawn to the brightest part of the picture.

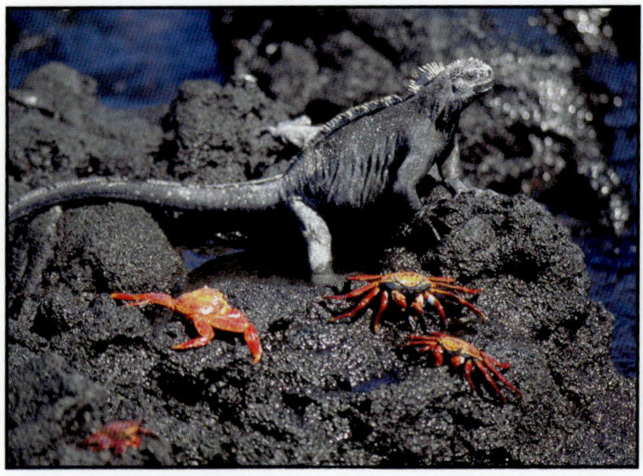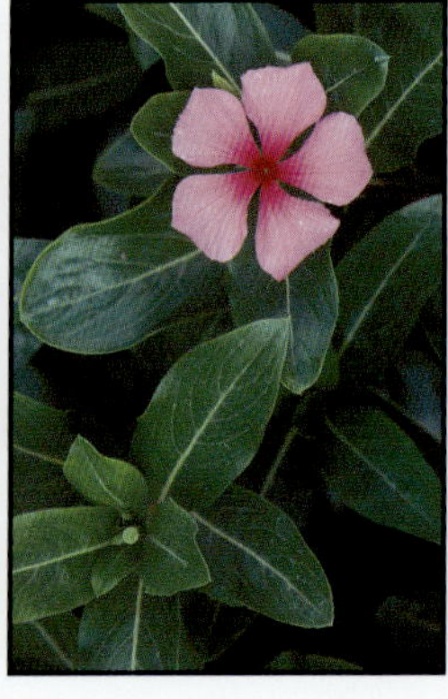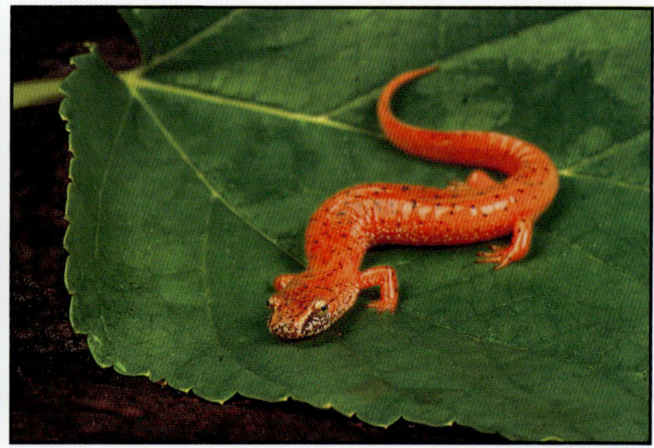

Fig. 1-11 Viewer's eyes are not only drawn to light areas of a photograph, but also to bright or contrasting colors.

Going toward light is basic human nature. Picture yourself in a dark tunnel with light visible at the end. Your eye is naturally drawn toward that light. The same thing happens in a theater or concert hall, where the center of an audience's attention is found where the light is brightest – usually on stage somewhere. Take advantage of this in your photographs, and locate the main subject within a bright area, or make it one of the brighter elements in the picture.

Note that brightness does not always mean lightness. Bold or bright colors can serve a similar effect, even though they are not as light as other parts of an image.

A backlit halo of hair surrounding the face of a model certainly draws the viewer's eye toward that highlighted area. So too does a child wearing a bright red jacket amid a field of green grass, or a yellow beach ball floating on a vast background of blue water.

Isolating a subject within the frame of an image actually requires real work from the photographer, as it means he or she has to move around to view the subject from various angles and distances, constantly looking through the viewfinder. Often, you will find yourself shooting initial pictures of a subject, and then moving in closer to improve your perspective and to simplify the presentation of the subject in your photos.

The lazy way to do this is to simply tell yourself that you can crop out all the unnecessary junk in an image later on. This is the "f/8 and be there" approach of old-time news photographers, who used to carry 4"x5" Speed Graphic cameras and large flash bulbs. With the large size of the 4"x5" negative and the significant amount of light produced by their flash bulbs, these photographers figured that as long as they set their aperture at f/8 (a mid-range exposure) and pointed their cameras in the general direction of the subject or action, they'd have the image they wanted somewhere within that large negative, and they could crop and print it later in the darkroom. Unfortunately, this resulted in lots of bland photographs.

It is your job as a photographer to determine what the photograph is and to create it for your viewers, rather than to just point your camera at a subject and shoot. Your audience will not appreciate having to look for the photograph you *should* have given them within a bland "f/8 and be there" picture you provided. It is too much work, and they will quickly move on

"f/8 and be there"

vs.

Move in closer – fill the frame

Fig. 1-12 Most compositions can be improved simply by moving closer.

to more interesting things. As a photographer, it's your job to simplify and condense your subject into its most basic or interesting elements for your audience.

Cropping out unnecessary and distracting elements in a photo after the fact can assist with this, but this should be used as a tool of last resort by photographers. Changing lenses (focal lengths) or zooming in to crop the image in camera before shooting is better.

But the best way is to move your camera to positions that bring your subject to the forefront. A photographer must "work the scene," moving within it to find the best combination of perspective and angle. Include only the important elements in your pictures. If an image appears cluttered in your viewfinder, move closer! Bring your subject into the foreground.

Allow yourself to make eye contact – to get visually involved with your subject. Good photography is not usually a passive activity. When you sit back and shoot your subjects from a distance, rather than getting up close and personal, you are simply documenting a scene, rather than creating compelling images that tell a story.

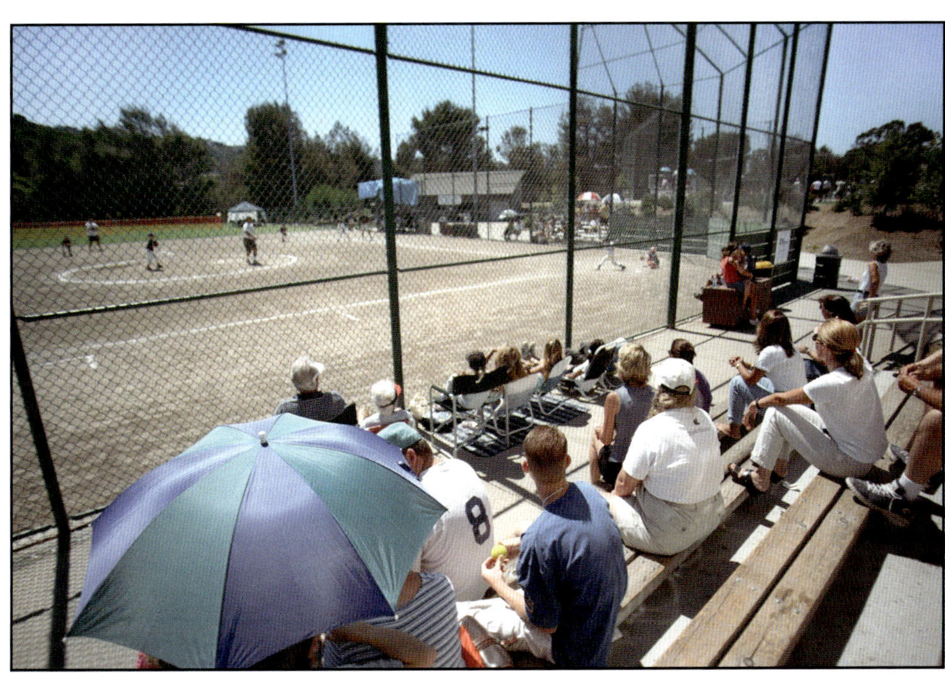

"f/8 and be there" (above)   vs.   Working the scene (below)

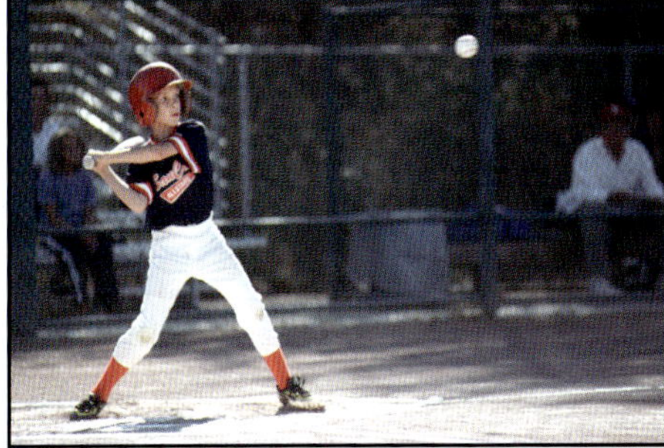

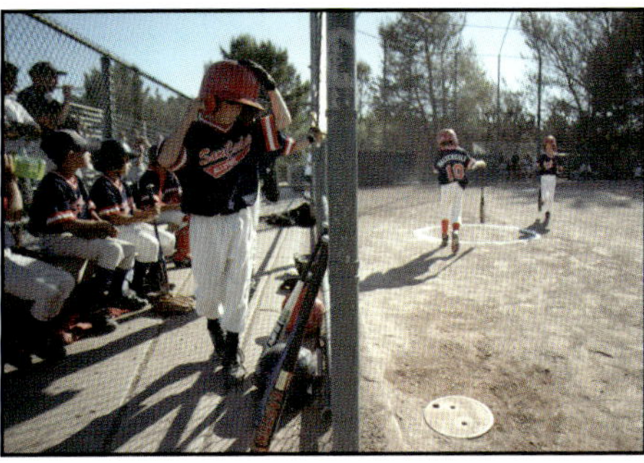

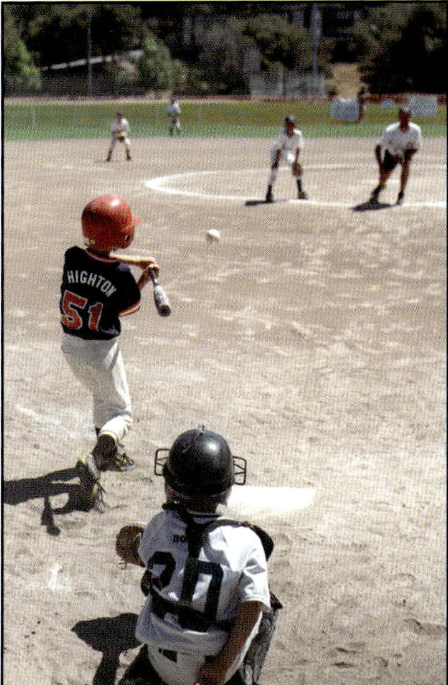

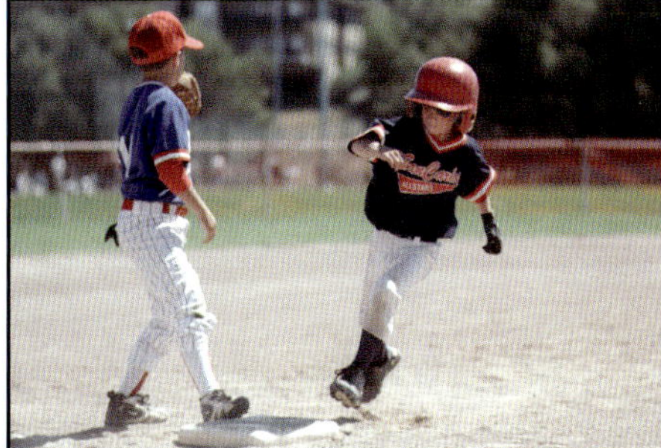

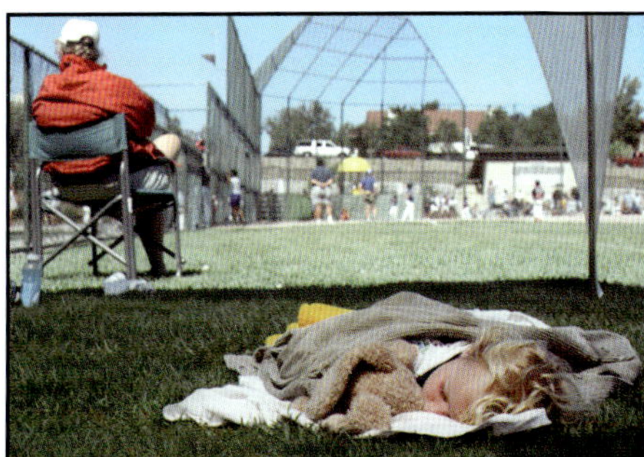

Fig. 1-13 Compare the bland "f/8 and be there" approach that most snapshooters might take (above), to the results (below) from a photographer willing to move around, change focal lengths, and tell a specific story in each shot.

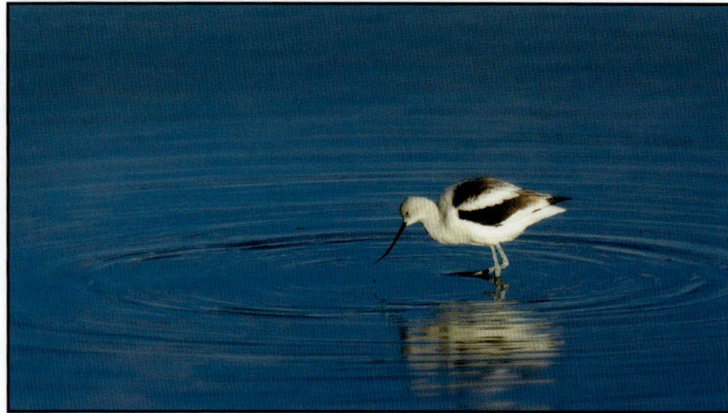

Good negative space isolates subject

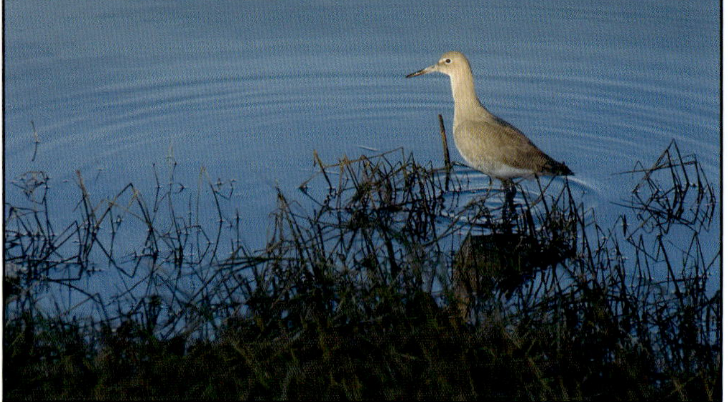

More cluttered negative space – distracts from subject

Fig. 1-14 Use of negative space.

This becomes more critical with immersive imaging and virtual reality photography, which is discussed in detail later on in this book. In panoramic VR, the use of ultra-wide lenses is the norm and your panoramic images encompass an entire scene 360-degrees around you. If you're not in the middle of the action, or truly immersed in the subject, your images will be boring.

The use of negative space may seem like a contradiction to Rule #5 about filling your frame with the subject. But in many situations, a subject can be photographed more effectively with some "breathing space" around it. This "negative" space is simply space in the frame that is void of other subjects or distraction. It might consist of a white wall, a clear blue sky, an extremely dark background, or simply a combination of foreground and background that are so far out of focus as to have no detail. Negative space can be used effectively to aid in overall composition, such as when positioning the subject at the intersection points of the Rule of Thirds.

The use of long telephoto lenses and wide apertures can make this easier, as the shallow depth of fields make everything outside the subject's plane of focus quite blurred. Viewers' eyes are drawn to the in focus parts of an image.

Yet, negative space can be taken advantage of when shooting with just about any focal length lens. Doing so invariably requires (again) that you move around while shooting in order to find the best positions and perspectives.

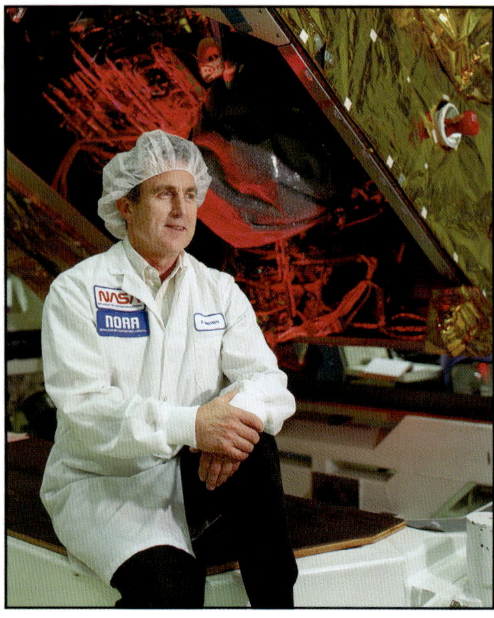

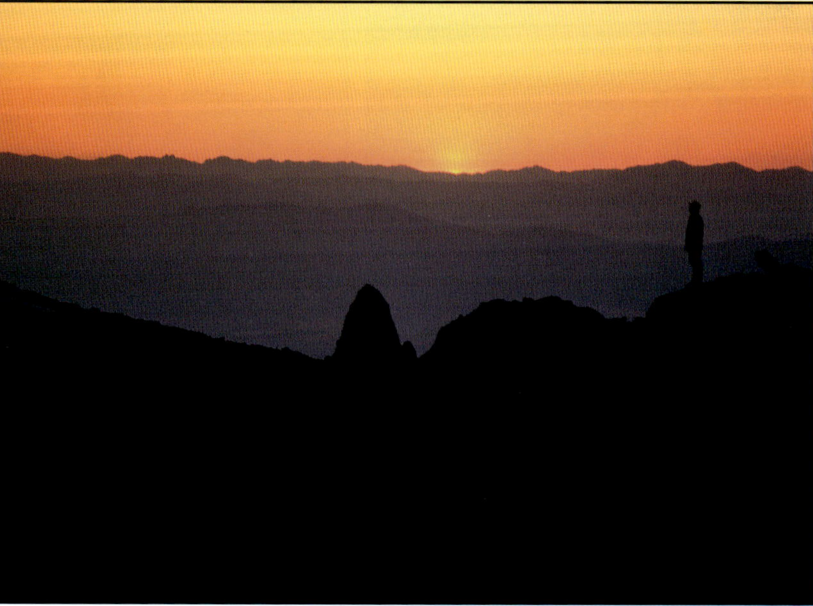

Fig. 1-15 Inward facing subjects.

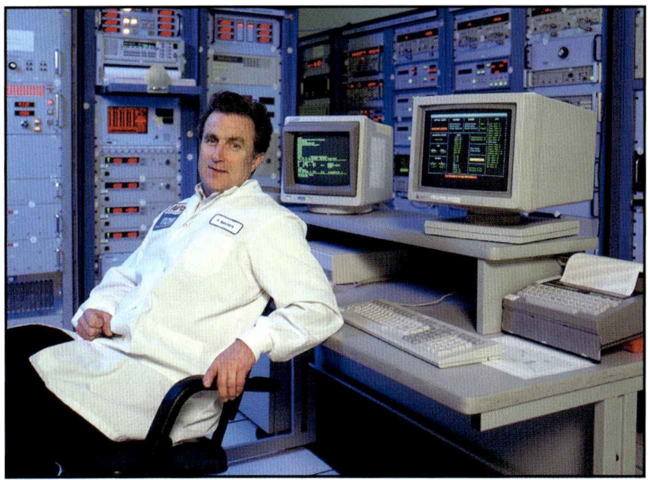

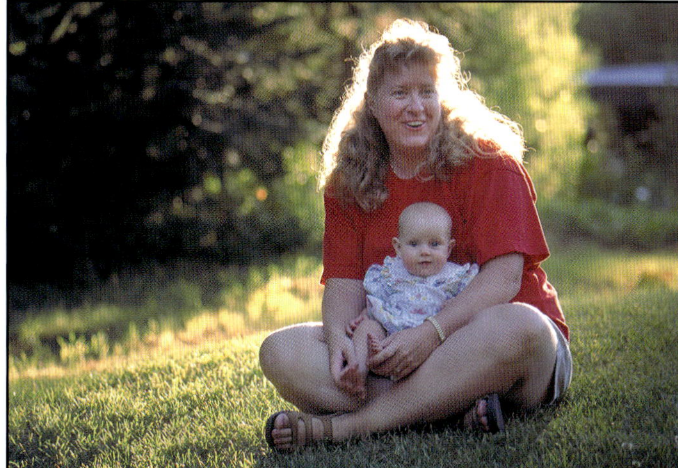

Fig. 1-16 Outward facing subjects.

Generally, when a subject is offset from the middle of the frame (as will be the case if you are following the Rule of Thirds), it is better to have those subjects facing inward toward the middle of the frame, rather than outward toward the edges of the image. This keeps the focus of the viewer's attention within the picture, rather than leading their eyes away from it. Your viewers' eyes will tend to follow the direction that your subject is facing. If the subject is looking toward the edge of the frame, viewer attention will follow it outward away from the photo, rather than remaining within the image as you would hope.

With multiple subjects, it is generally desirable to have them all facing inward. If a subject is on the right side of your frame, it should be facing to some degree toward the left. If on the left side of the frame, it should face toward the right.

This again is a Rule of Thumb that can sometimes be broken for good effect. In fact, rare is the good photograph that adheres to all compositional Rules of Thumb at the same time. However, as with any Rule of Thumb, it should only be broken with good reason, and only after you understand what the purpose and function of the rule is in the first place.

Incorporation of a frame within a frame can very quickly become overused, but can be quite effective when used sparingly. A face looking through a window or a subject in a doorway, are common examples of framing within a frame. Many architectural and natural structures work quite effectively as "frames" around a subject, and naturally focus your viewers' eyes on the subjects within. Other common framing elements include leaves or branches, strong shadow lines, or even shapes that your subject might be reflected in.

It's amazing how many things you can find that work for such framing if you look for them while shooting. Remember however, that if you use the technique too often, your results become trite and you will start boring your viewers. Seize framing opportunities when they present themselves, but don't try to force a frame into every shooting situation. A little goes a long way.

RULE #8: Frame(s) Within a Frame

Use available structures and objects within the scene you are photographing to frame the subject within your frame (i.e. a frame within a frame).

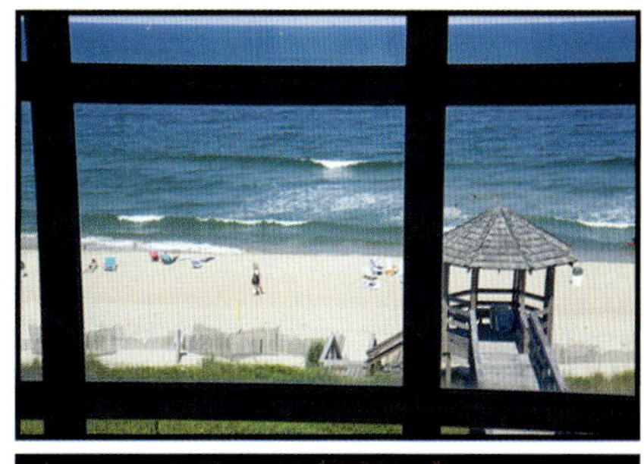

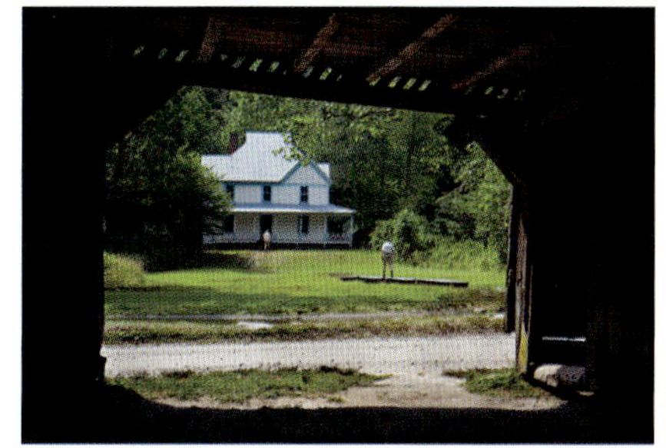

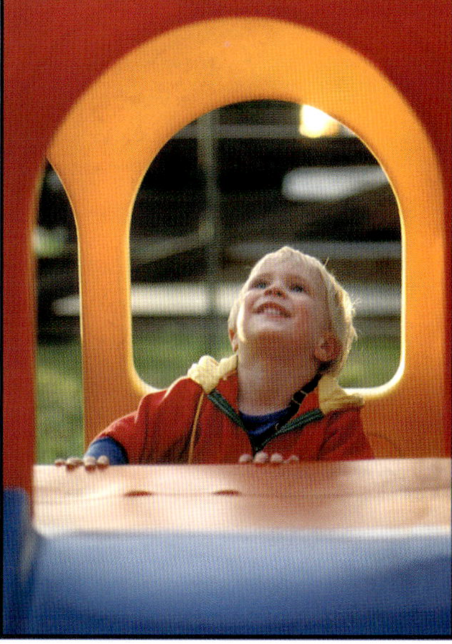

Fig. 1-17 Framing within the image frame.

ASSIGNMENT: COMPOSITION

Find a subject – something familiar, such as a family member, pet, or cherished possession – and shoot an entire 36-exposure roll of film (or digital equivalent) of this subject only. Do this in one session, rather than shooting a few shots and coming back a few hours or days later and shooting more. Set your camera to auto-exposure & auto focus, so the only thing you have to be concerned about is the *composition* of the image in your viewfinder.

Make every shot different, changing your angle, distance, perspective, framing, and composition. Use your zoom lens (if you have one) at both its widest and longest focal lengths. Keep one eye looking through the viewfinder as you move around, and shoot each shot only when you see that your composition has changed significantly – and has become *more* interesting.

Try to isolate as many of the Composition Rules of Thumb as you can, and even intentionally break them on a few shots. Shoot quickly between some shots, and more carefully between others.

When you are finished, process your film or download your digital images to your computer.

Look at your results. Decide what worked and what didn't, reviewing the Rules of Thumb as you do. Could you choose five images that are good enough to enlarge for family or friends?

Repeat the exercise with a different subject (only after you've seen the results of your first attempt).

What you are learning is how to "work the scene." Rarely will your first photo of a subject be your best one. This is one of the reasons why professional photographers take so many pictures. As you see an image changing in your viewfinder, learn to recognize when the situation warrants moving in or out, how to position the horizon or background in the frame, where best to place the subject, or how to change your camera position so that your composition is always improving.

With practice, this will become something you do automatically whenever you look through a camera viewfinder.

Composition Rules of Thumb:

1. Rule of Thirds
2. Converging and Leading Lines
3. Scale
4. Relative Brightness
5. Fill the Frame
6. Negative Space
7. Subjects Face Inward
8. Frame Within a Frame

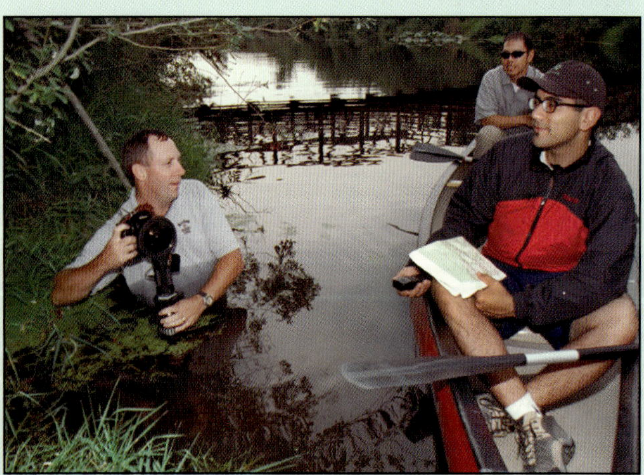

Fig. 1-18 Move around. Find out where your best camera position is for the subjects you are shooting. It's OK to get a little dirty (or wet).

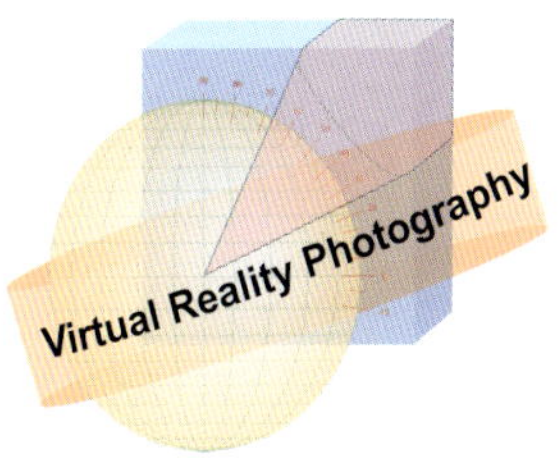

Chapter 2: Perspective and View

As you explore elements of composition in your photography and observe the results in both your viewfinder and images, you will discover that changing your position relative to your subject creates dramatically different results.

This relationship between the camera position and subject is referred to as **perspective**. Perspective is simply the point of view from which a photograph is made. It involves not only the relative positions of the camera and subject, but indirectly the field of view (fov)

Technical Note: Focal Length

Focal length is a measurement of the distance between the rear nodal point of a lens and the point at which the image focuses (the film plane) when the lens is focused at infinity.

If you photograph a subject from a fixed position, the size of that subject projected by the lens onto the film plane is directly proportional to the focal length of that lens. The larger the focal length, the larger the image appears. The smaller the focal length, the smaller the image.

Focal length is the primary characteristic of any lens, as it determines the relative field of view for that lens when used with a given format camera (i.e. 35mm, 6x7 cm, 4x5 in).

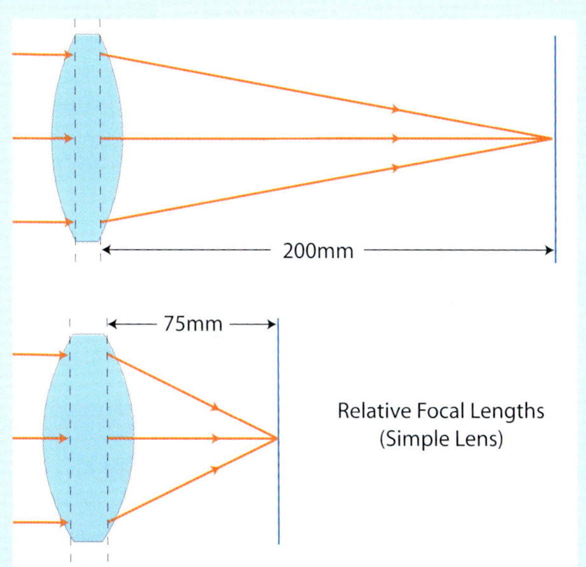

Fig. 2-1 Focal length measurement for simple lenses.

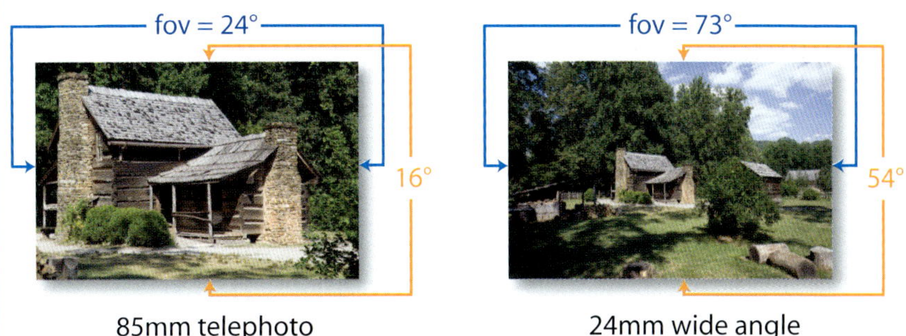

Telephoto lenses are often referred to as "long" lenses because of their longer focal lengths and corresponding physical size, while wide angle lenses are referred to as "short" lenses because of their shorter focal lengths.

Fig. 2-2 Focal length comparison.

represented in the picture as determined by the focal length of the lens.

A wide angle lens provides a wide field of view, and generally requires that the photographer be fairly close to the subject in order to fill the frame. A telephoto lens provides a narrow field of view, and is generally used when a photographer is farther away from a subject.

The field of view for a lens is usually measured in degrees. However, these measurements can become a bit confusing as there are three different figures available for most lenses. These include the horizontal, the vertical and the diagonal fields of view. For simplicity, these are represented by the following terms:

fov(x) – field of view in the horizontal (x) direction

fov(y) – field of view in the vertical (y) direction

fov(d) – field of view in the diagonal (d) direction

Since most camera formats record a rectangular image, the fov(x) and fov(y) figures will replace one another depending upon whether the camera is used in the horizontal (landscape) or vertical (portrait) orientation. The diagonal fov(d) measurement will remain constant though, which is why it is generally used by lens manufacturers in their advertising and promotional materials. Note that if you are using a square format camera, such as a 6x6cm, the horizontal fov(x) and vertical fov(y) fields of view will be the same for a given lens. Yet, the larger diagonal field of view fov(d) will still be used by most lens manufacturers.

Since most camera and lens manufacturers report the field of view of their lenses using the diagonal coverage,

Fields of View: 50mm Lens (6x6cm format)

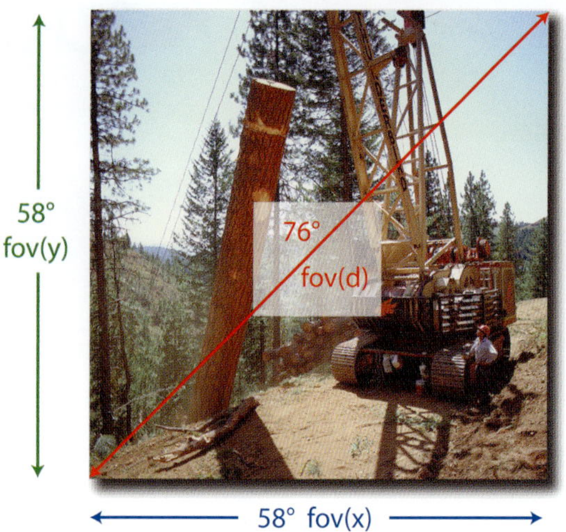

Fig. 2-4 Fields of view – 6x6cm camera format.

we will refer to that dimension through much of this chapter, as well. The other dimensions will become critical later on when we get beyond basics and into VR photography.

Types of Lenses

Wide angle lenses are considered to be those lenses ranging between about 20mm and 35mm in focal length. They offer diagonal fields of view from about 95° (20mm) to 64° (35mm). They are often used to photograph large subjects or scenes when the photographer is in close or working in tight spaces. Wide angle lenses tend to exaggerate the foreground and minimize the background.

Ultra-wide lenses are those in the 13mm to 20mm range, which offer fields of view of 100° and more. They are often expensive and *can* be fairly large in both size and weight. They also exaggerate the perspective of a scene, and tend to distort familiar shapes near the edges of the frame. This happens because most such lenses are designed to be rectilinear, or corrected. This means that straight horizontal and vertical lines, such as walls and ceilings, are rendered as straight lines when projected onto the film plane, in spite of the ultra-wide field of view. This makes round objects near the edge of the frame appear as ovals, and square or rectangular objects appear as polygons (see Fig. 2-5). However, most subjects rendered this way appear natural to the

Fields of View: 50mm Lens (35mm format)

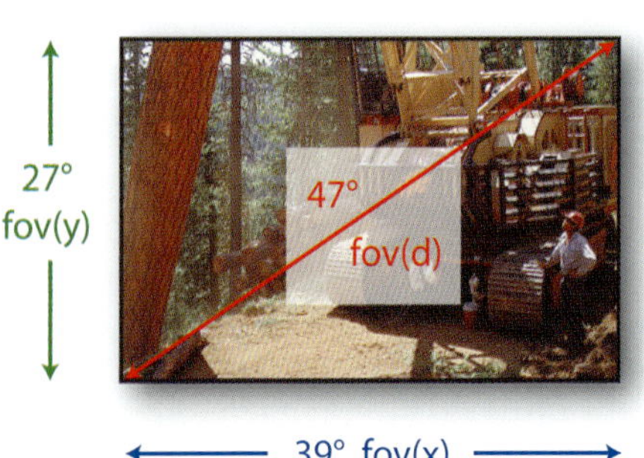

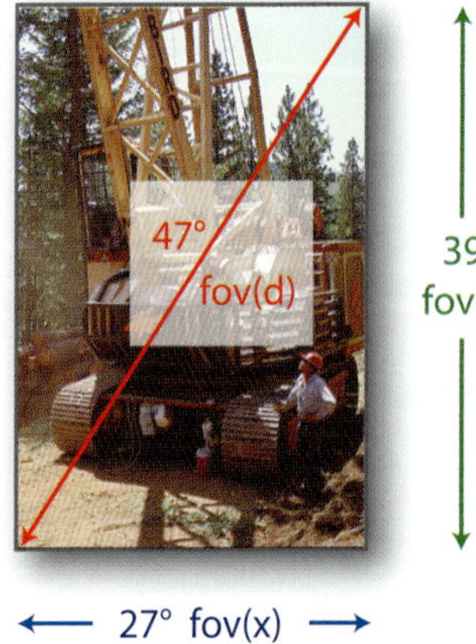

"Landscape" orientation (horizontal)

"Portrait" orientation (vertical)

Fig. 2-3 Fields of view – 35mm camera format.

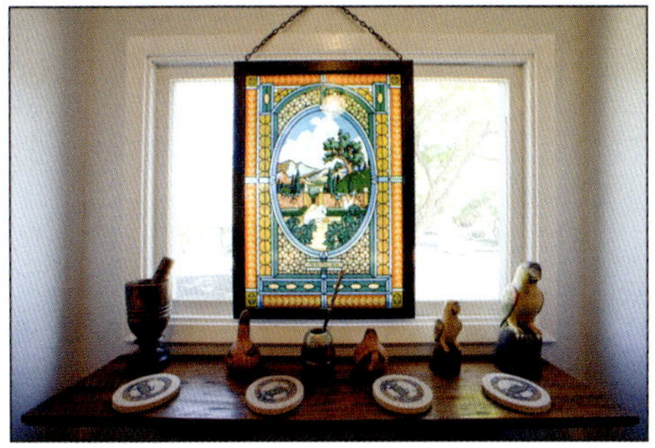

15mm (rectilinear)

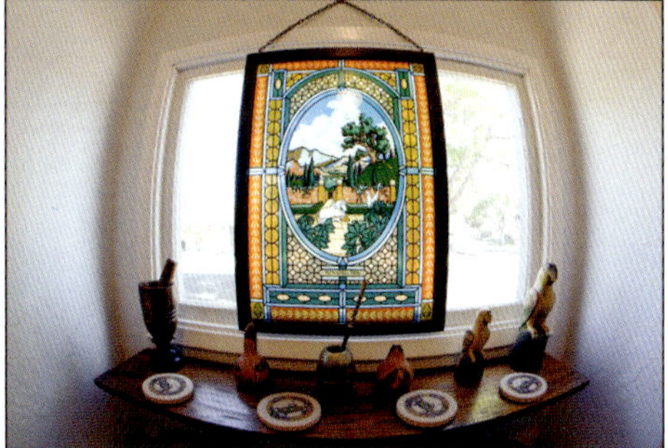

16mm (fisheye)

Fig. 2-5 Rectilinear correction renders straight lines in a scene straight in the photo, but note the "distortions" that result near the edges of the frame. Round objects are rendered as ovals and rectangles become polygons.

human eye. Ultra-wide rectilinear lenses are often used in architectural photography, for extreme wide angle effects and of course, for greater coverage of a scene in virtual reality panoramic photography.

Fisheye lenses are lenses offering extreme wide angle coverage – generally 180° or more. However, they exhibit a characteristic called "barrel distortion" in which the field of view is curved, and both vertical and horizontal lines bow outward from the center of the image. In normal photography, fisheye images offer a unique perspective. They can be quite effective in capturing extremely wide views of confined spaces or for intentional "curve of the earth" distortion. However, too frequent use can appear gimmicky and will likely bore your viewers.

There are two kinds of fisheye lenses. A true fisheye includes the entire image circle, with a view of 180° or more, completely within the film frame or image sensor of the camera. This type of lens captures a full hemispheric view. Such lenses were originally designed for photographing the entire sky from horizon to horizon

for meteorology and astronomy studies. The result is a circular image in the center of the frame with black areas out to the frame edge. For 35mm cameras, these lenses usually entail focal lengths of 8mm or less. A 6mm fisheye lens captures a 220° view, so it can actually see *behind* the camera to an extent.

The second fisheye type is the full-frame fisheye. The barrel distortion is still present in these lenses, but the image circle formed by the lens extends beyond the edges of the frame. The diagonal field of view reaches 180°, with the vertical and horizontal dimensions less than that. Most full-frame fisheye lenses have a 15mm or 16mm focal length in the 35mm format.

Both kinds of fisheye lenses can be used in virtual reality panoramic photography, depending upon the VR technology employed.

Normal lenses were originally defined to be lenses which had a focal length equivalent to the diagonal measurement of the format being used. Thus, for a 35mm film frame (approx. 24mm x 36mm), the diagonal is about 44mm. Thus, a "normal" lens would be about 44mm for a 35mm camera, giving a 53° diagonal field of view.

However, 35mm camera manufacturers have long since abandoned this formula, and today describe "normal" lenses as those in the 50mm range. These tend to have a field of view similar to that of the perceived view of the human eye.

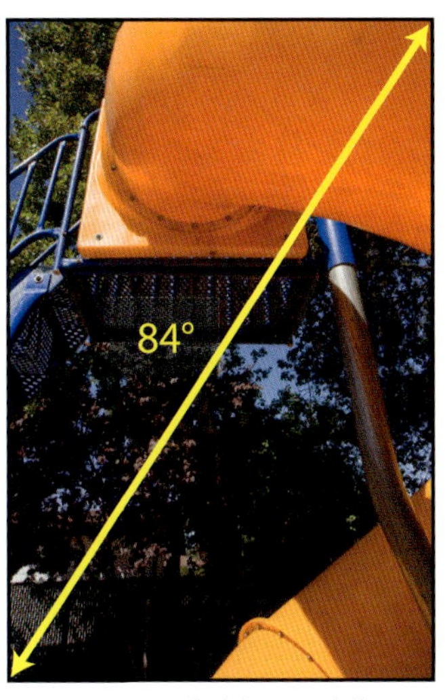

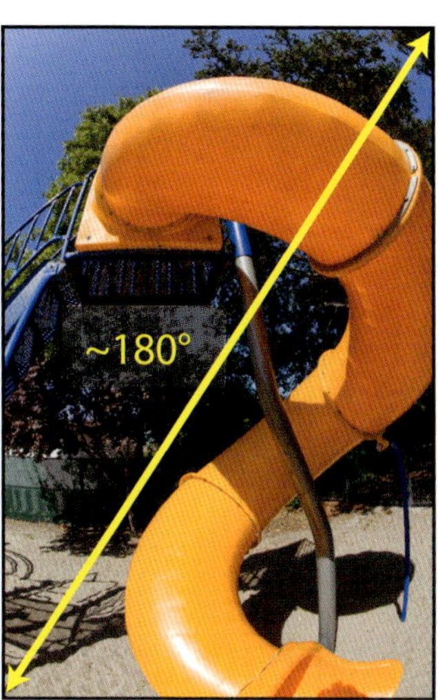

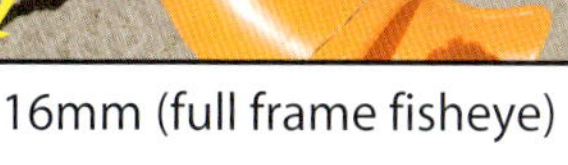

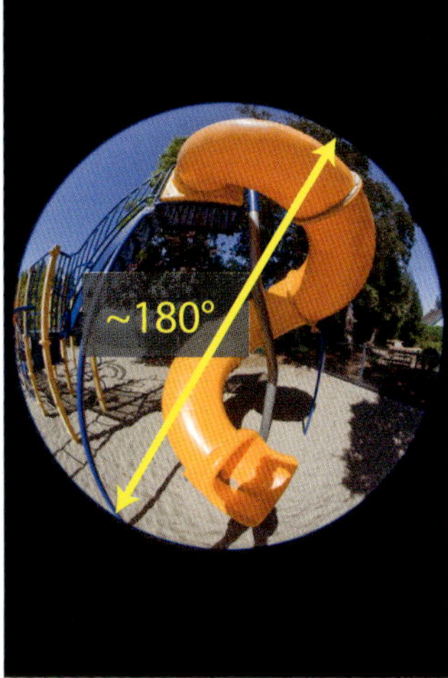

24mm (wide angle)   15mm (ultra-wide angle)   16mm (full frame fisheye)   8mm (true fisheye)

Fig. 2-6 Focal length and view comparison of wide and ultra-wide lenses typically used for panoramic VR photography.

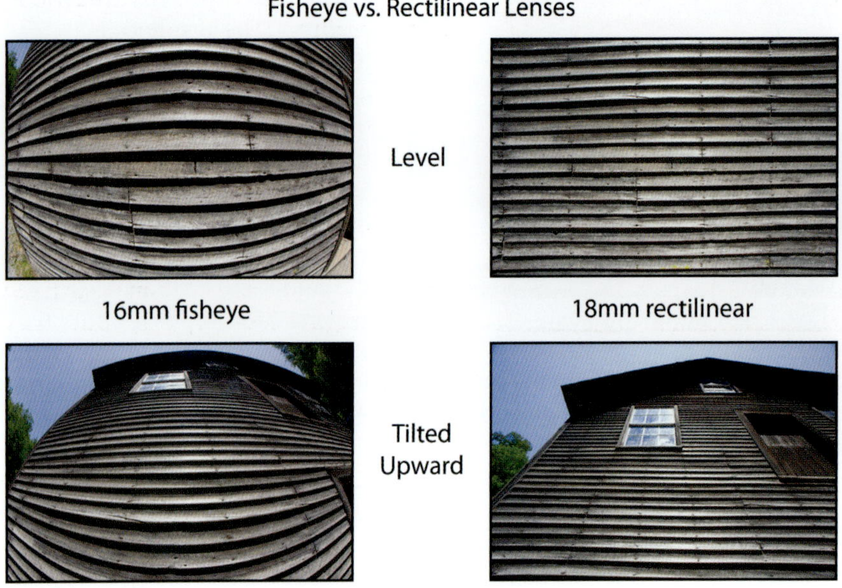

Fig. 2-7 Fisheye distortion vs. rectilinear correction revealed in the patterns of wood planks photographed at a historic mill..

for sports, wildlife, and even news photography, when it is impractical for the photographer to physically get close to his or her subjects.

With standard telephoto lens designs, the longer the focal length of a lens, the longer the physical size of that lens. However, some lower cost telephotos are configured with a mirror (catadioptric) design, which folds and reflects the optical path within the barrel of the lens. This allows the lens to be physically smaller than a "straight" telephoto, saving on both size and weight (as well as cost). The drawbacks to mirror lenses are that they have fixed apertures (a single, preset f/stop) and they render out of focus highlights as hollow donut shapes, which can be distracting at times. (See Fig. 2-9)

Telephoto lenses are those lenses having longer than normal focal lengths, which provide a narrower field of view and tend to make subjects appear closer in the viewfinder than they really are. For 35mm camera systems, telephoto lenses are considered to be those with focal lengths of 70mm and longer. Super telephoto lenses are generally 300mm or longer, often with "fast" or wide apertures. Super telephoto lenses are also often large, heavy, and expensive. They are necessary

Telephoto lenses are also used when photographers want to visually compress separate elements in a scene. The longer the focal length of a lens, the narrower its depth of field – meaning foreground and background elements are further out of focus relative to the subject, than images shot with shorter focal length lenses. Telephotos are often used when photographers want to minimize foreground or background clutter.

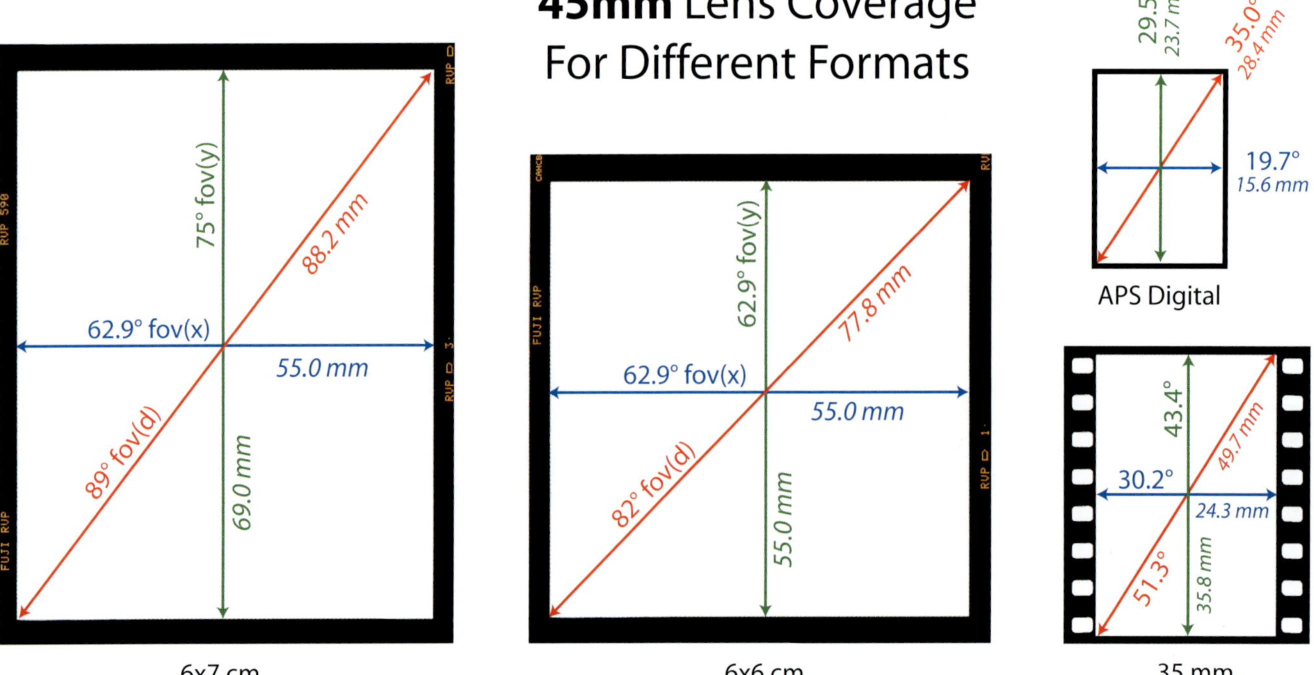

Fig. 2-8 Field of view comparisons (horizontal, vertical, and diagonal) for common camera formats.

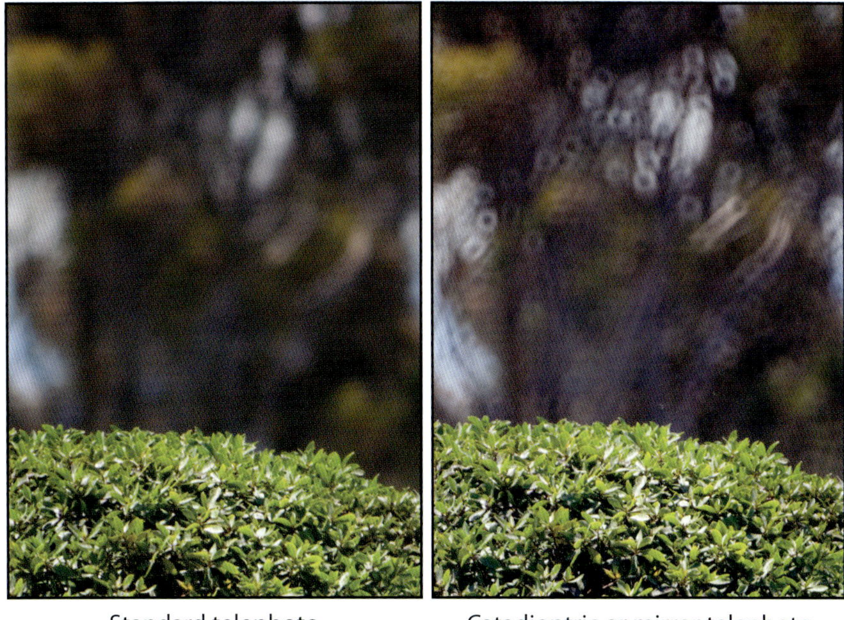

Standard telephoto　　　　Catadioptric or mirror telephoto

Fig. 2-9 Reflex (mirror) telephoto lenses have a noticeably different bokeh, or quality rendered to out of focus areas, than traditional telephoto lenses.

almost every gain involves a tradeoff in either quality or performance.

Today's zoom lenses are far superior to early models. In fact, it has only been in the last 20 years that most professional photographers have even considered using zoom lenses instead of fixed focal lengths. For the most part, zoom lenses are bigger and heavier than their fixed focal length counterparts, but they gather less light and are sometimes not as sharp. There certainly are exceptions to this. In general, you get what you pay for when buying a zoom lens.

The best zoom lenses have limited zoom ranges (i.e. wide angle only, such as 20-35mm; wide-to-normal, such as 35-70mm; or telephoto only, such as 80-200mm), along with wide maximum apertures (f/2.8) which remain constant throughout the zoom range of the lens. Cheaper models have smaller maximum apertures (f/3.5, f/4, f/5.6, etc.), with their maximum apertures varying depending upon whether the lens is zoomed in or out.

A short or moderate telephoto lens would be an 85mm, which has a diagonal field of view of about 29°. An 800mm super telephoto has a diagonal field of view of about 3°.

Zoom lenses are lenses with variable focal lengths. They offer the flexibility of having multiple focal lengths available in a single lens, meaning that a photographer can effectively replace a handful of fixed focal length lenses with a single zoom. While this flexibility is tempting, one has to remember that in photography,

Be wary of low cost zooms that have extreme focal length ranges, such as 28-200mm or 50-300mm. There are physical limits to the optical design of any lens system. Such lenses, often designed to be all things to all people, usually fall short in their optical quality and performance. Cheaper zoom lenses often have noticeable aberrations and distortions at their extreme focal ranges, which can render them unusable for professional photography.

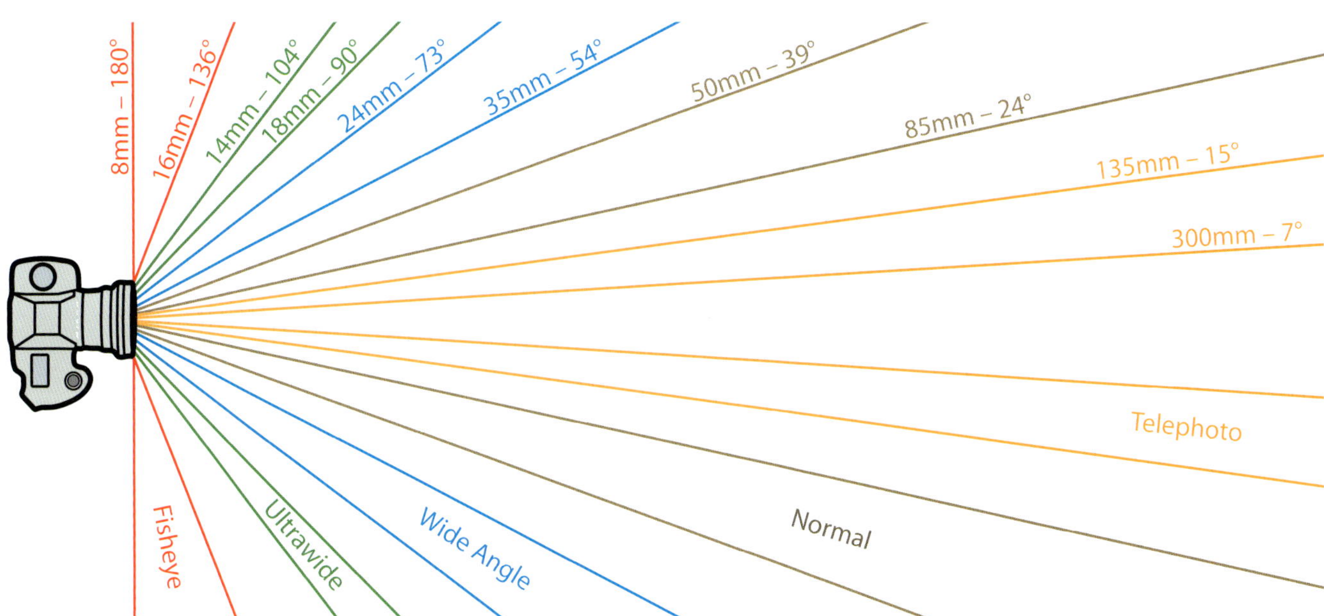

Fig. 2-10 Fields of view or fov(y) for a 35mm format camera in vertical or portrait orientation.

Macro lenses are lenses designed to focus very closely and to allow for life size (1:1) and greater reproduction of the subject. A 1:1 reproduction ratio means that a 1/2" tall subject will actually appear 1/2" tall on the film or imaging sensor of the camera. Focal lengths for macro lenses are usually between 50mm and 200mm. Most are fixed focal lengths. Some zoom lenses have "macro" settings, which allow them to be used at close distances. The longer the focal length of a macro lens, the greater the working distance between the subject and lens – an advantage when shooting closeups of dangerous subjects where a minimum distance must be maintained.

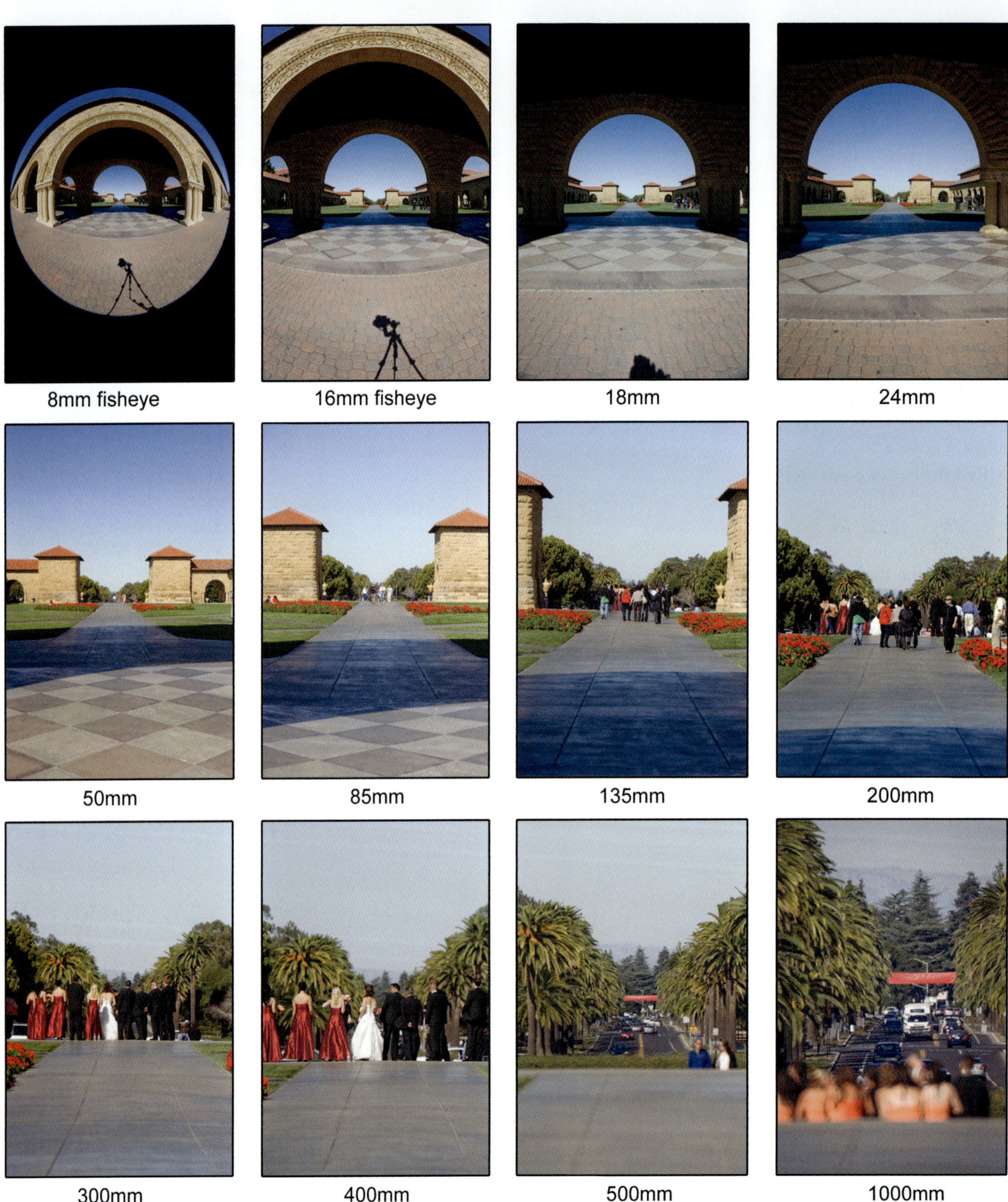

Fig. 2-11 Relative coverage and fields of view provided by different focal length lenses (35mm format).

Perspective Control (PC) or "shift" lenses are specialty lenses, used primarily for architectural-type photography, which allow for minor framing adjustments without tilting or panning the camera. In architectural photography, it is often important to avoid having walls and ceilings appear with converging lines and intersections. One expects walls to be rendered as vertical, and intersecting lines either parallel or perpendicular to each other in architectural imagery. This requires that the camera be squarely facing the subject, since tilting the camera upward or downward results in converging lines and causes walls to look like they're leaning.

Since positioning a camera square to the subject limits composition and framing possibilities, PC lenses allow for the view to be shifted for better composition.

The image circle for a standard lens only needs to extend to the corners of the film frame or image sensor. A PC lens' larger image circle allows for the front of the lens to be "shifted" as needed to allow the framing of the photo to be changed without changing the perspective or parallel line convergence.

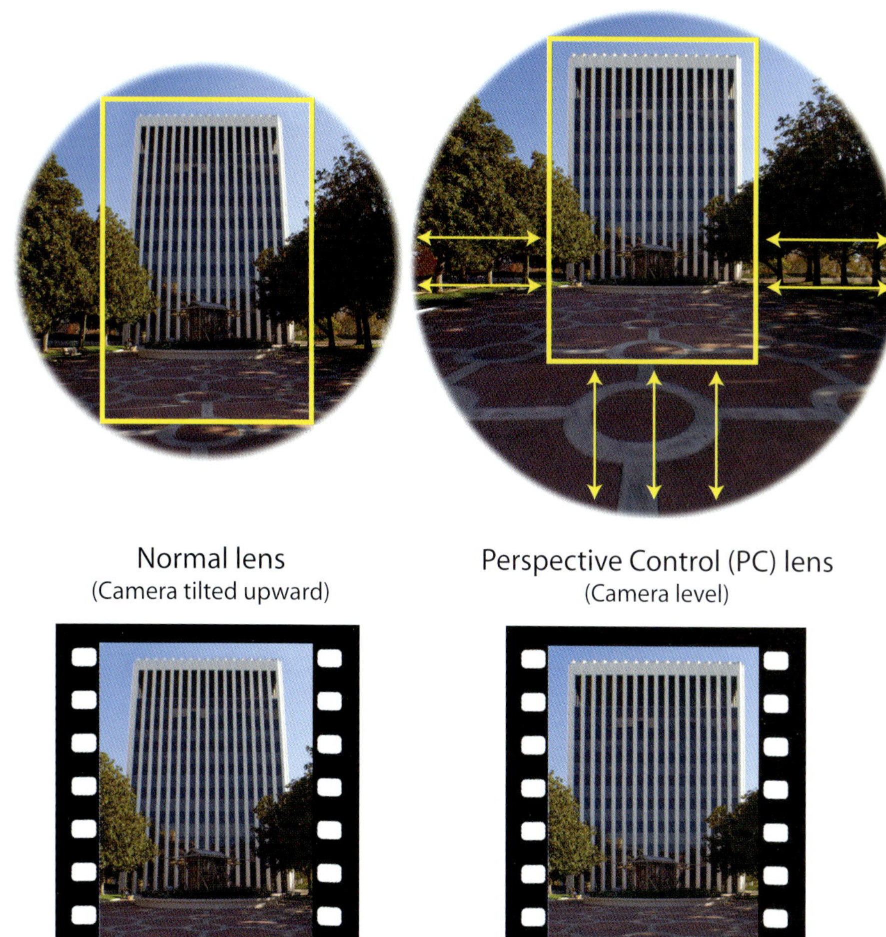

Fig. 2-12 Function of a perspective control (PC) lens.

Landscape and nature photographers can also benefit from use of PC lenses. When shooting a forest, for example, one often needs to tilt the camera upward for better composition. With traditional wide angle lenses, this will cause a convergence of the vertical lines of the tree trunks. Yet viewers generally expect to perceive the trunks as remaining reasonably parallel (at least for trees growing vertically). A PC lens can be used to accomplish this. Landscape photographers also find that PC lenses can be used to more accurately represent the scale and height of distant mountains relative to foreground subjects. Tilting a traditional wide angle lens upward to photograph mountains tends to make mountains appear as though they are leaning backward, and reduces their apparent size in the frame. Proper use of a PC lens can help maintain these visual relationships more accurately.

Most PC or shift lenses fall in the wide angle focal length category, and wide fields of view display more parallel line convergence when tilted or panned off axis. Longer lenses produce less convergence because they have smaller fields of view to start with.

A few PC lenses (depending on the manufacturer) are available with a "tilt" adjustment in addition to the "shift" capability. This also allows the lens to be tilted off the axis of the film plane, a feature generally used to maintain focus between near and far subjects. PC lenses, for the most part, are considered to be specialty equipment, and they add complexity to photography efforts. Most photographers will rarely need them, but it is important to understand their function as it relates to our choices in traditional lenses and their fields of view. Today, it is also possible to accomplish many of the perspective corrections offered by such lenses with digital post production tools, such as Adobe's Photoshop.

Field of View Affected by Camera Format

When you change from one camera format to another, such as from a 35mm film camera to some digital cameras, the field of view provided by a given focal length lens can change, as well.

For example, a 35mm camera captures an image that is approximately 24x36mm in size. A 50mm lens on this camera would provide a diagonal field of view of about 47°. However, most digital cameras today have image sensors which cover a much smaller area than the traditional 35mm frame. This means that the same 50mm lens used on these cameras will provide a significantly reduced field of view. For many digital cameras, the fov(d) of this 50mm lens is reduced to a little over 30°, rather than the 47° of coverage it provides on 35mm film.

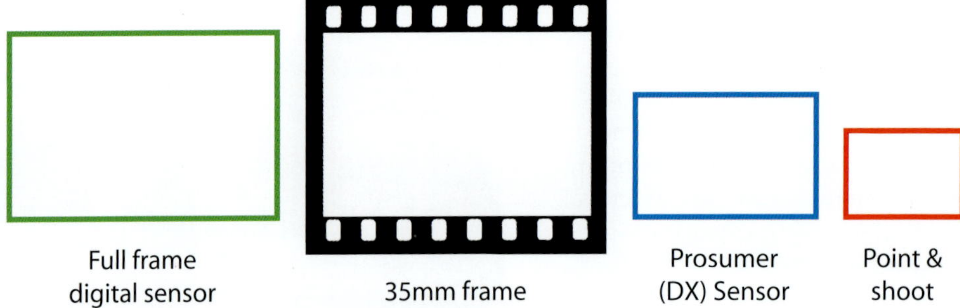

Fig. 2-14 Relative camera format and digital sensor sizes.

Although the physical focal length of the lens does not change, the *effective* focal length in terms of its field of view changes when the size of the *image area* changes. Reduce the image area (format) and you reduce the field of view recorded through the lens. Increase the format size, and you increase the field of view.

This is one of the drawbacks to many digital cameras today. Due to their relatively small image sensors, they simply don't allow for extreme wide angle photography without addition of supplemental wide angle adapters, which usually degrade the quality of the image. An ultra wide 18mm lens becomes the equivalent of a 28mm lens on DX format digital cameras because of the reduced image area of the cameras' sensors. Before selecting a medium or high end digital camera, you should know its effective magnification of lens focal lengths.

Low end and consumer digital cameras have their own zoom lenses built in. Most manufacturers offer corresponding "35mm equivalent" figures for the zoom ranges of these lenses in their product literature.

The magnifying effect of a smaller format can, however, be an advantage when one needs a longer lens for distant subjects. The effective coverage of a 200mm telephoto lens is increased to 300mm when that 200mm lens is used on a digital camera with a 1.5x magnification factor. It is

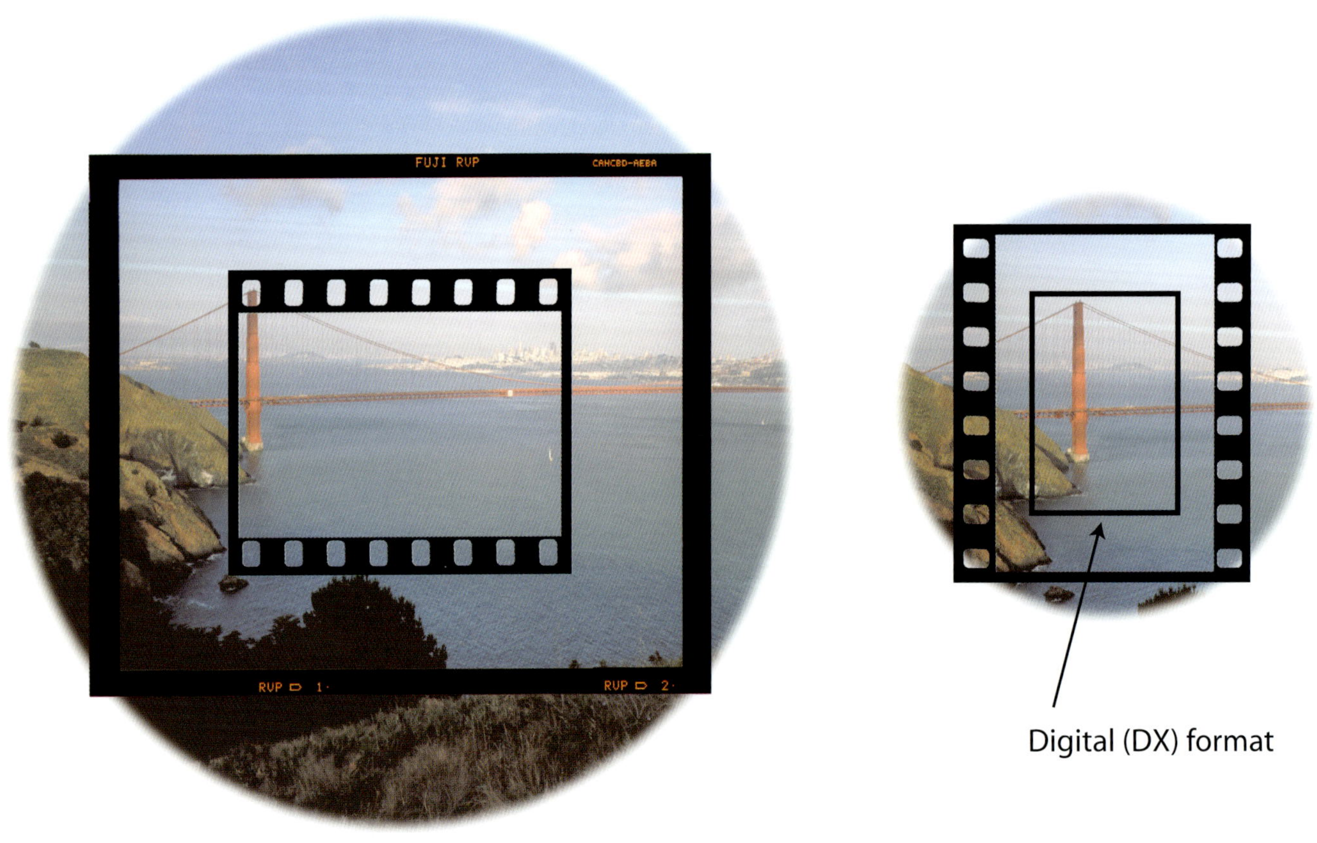

6x7cm format image circle   35mm format image circle

Fig. 2-13 Popular camera formats and the corresponding image circles projected for their lenses.

Technical Note: Field of View Calculations

Field of view calculations can be done with the following formulas.

Rectilinear (corrected) lenses:

fov = 2 * arctan (image size/(focal length * 2))

fov is given in degrees

image size is the dimension of the image frame in mm. This can be the width, height, or diagonal, depending upon which fov you want to calculate.

focal length is measured in mm

Example:

A standard 35mm film frame measures about 24.3mm x 35.8mm (with a diagonal of 43.3mm). If we are using the camera in vertical or portrait mode, and we want to calculate the vertical field of view for a 20mm wide angle lens, we would proceed as follows:

fov(y) = 2 * arctan (35.8mm/(20mm * 2))

= 2 * arctan (35.8/40)

= 2 * arctan (0.895)

= 2 * 41.83

= 84°

Fisheye lenses:

Field of view calculations for fisheye lenses can vary depending upon the projection design of the the lens. However, for *most* fisheye lenses manufactured for the photography market, the formula is:

fov = 4 * arcsin (image size/(focal length * 4))

Example:

A Nikkor 8mm f/2.8 fisheye lens focused at infinity projects an image circle approximately 23mm in diameter.

fov = 4 * arcsin (23/(8 * 4))

= 4 * arcsin (23/32)

= 4 * arcsin (0.719)

= 4 * 45.9

= 184°

Unfortunately, this is not a completely accurate figure for this lens. The Nikkor 8mm actually records a field of view slightly *less* than 180°. The difference is a result of the fact that lens manufacturers commonly round their descriptions for focal lengths to within plus or minus five percent.

The Nikkor 8mm lens is really about 8.2mm in focal length. A Sigma 8mm lens is actually about 7.8mm and produces a fov of between 182° and 186°. However, Sigma lenses have more pronounced light falloff and chromatic aberrations near the edge of their image circles than the Nikkor 8mm.

---

also less costly for manufacturers to design and produce quality lenses for smaller format cameras. Because the image circles of these lenses are smaller, the lenses can be built with more efficiently made optical elements.

As you *increase* the format or imaging area, as in medium and large format cameras, you correspondingly increase the field of view that a given focal length provides. Note however, that lenses designed for 35mm cameras do not work on larger format cameras because the image circle they project onto the film plane is not large enough to fully cover the larger format. Also, the distance between the back of the lens and the film plane (or the "back focus") is much greater for the larger format camera systems. Medium and large format lenses are designed to project larger image circles that fully cover the image area of the format. These medium format lenses generally contain larger optical elements and cost consistently more than their 35mm counterparts.

Field of View and Subject Distance

Field of view has a dramatic impact on the visual relationship between foreground, subject, and background in a photograph. Combined with basic composition, a photographer's choice of lens and shooting position are the foundations of effective photography.

In reality, true perspective depends only on camera-to-subject distance and position. If you take two photographs from the same position using a wide angle and a telephoto lens, the field of view will be greater with the wide angle lens, but the perspective of the (smaller) area covered by the telephoto lens will be identical to

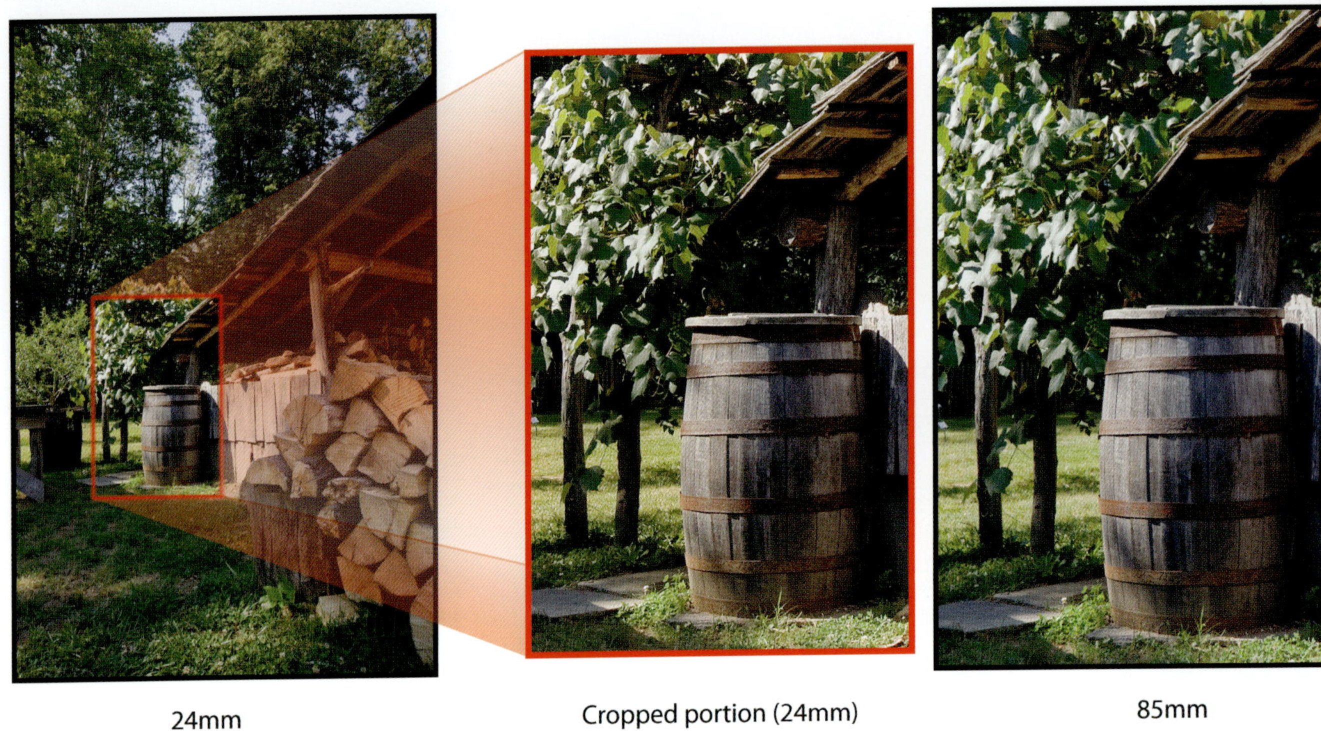

24mm   Cropped portion (24mm)   85mm

Fig. 2-15 Perspective is a function of camera-to-subject distance and camera position, not focal length.

that same subject area for the wider lens. In fact, if you were to enlarge and match the area of the wide angle view to that of the telephoto view, you would find that the images would match perfectly in their perspective. (See Fig. 2-15)

Magnification of the subject from a given camera-to-subject distance is directly proportional to focal length. Doubling the focal length doubles the size of the subject on film. Halving the focal length halves the size of the subject. Thus, a 25mm lens will render the subject half as large as a 50mm lens (if the camera-to-subject distance remains constant). A 200mm lens will render a subject 1/3 the size of a 600mm lens from the same position.

Lens focal length comes into play in changing perspective, however, because a photographer will generally move closer or further away from a subject based on both its relative size and the focal length of the lens chosen. When using a wide angle lens, the photographer will generally be closer to a subject than she would be when using a telephoto lens.

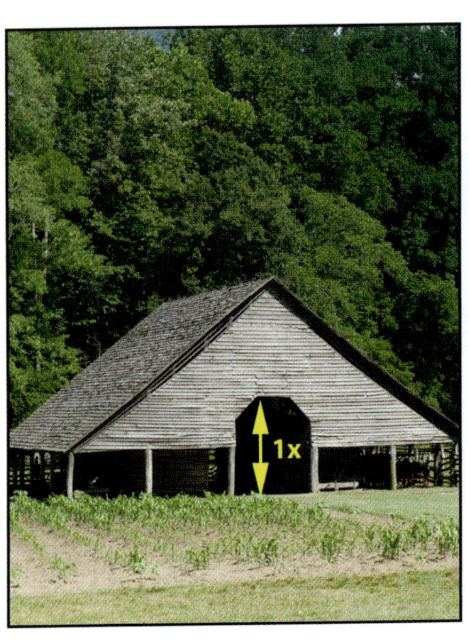

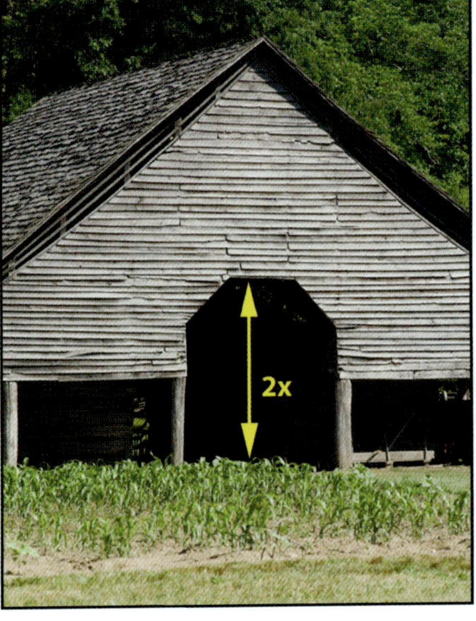

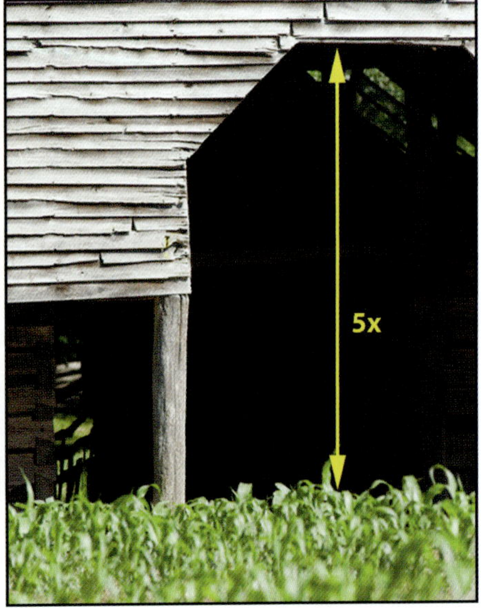

100mm   200mm   500mm

Fig. 2-16 Magnification is directly proportional to focal length.

Changing your camera-to-subject distance will affect the perspective. Focal length simply crops or frames the image differently. The actual perspective is changed only when the photographer changes his distance or relative position from the subject in order to fill or compose the frame.

A wide angle lens with its wide field of view exaggerates the relationship between near and distant subjects. This happens because the relative distance between near and far subjects tends to be greater. Wide angle lenses also tend to amplify the perspective or the sense of depth captured in an image. A subject close to the camera may fill the frame, while an identical subject a few feet further away will be much smaller in the frame. Wide angle lenses are often used to give a sense of large scale, especially to relatively small subjects.

Conversely, telephoto lenses compress the relationship between near and far subjects. This is caused by their narrower field of view. The relative magnification between near and distant subjects becomes more similar when both their distances from the camera are increased.

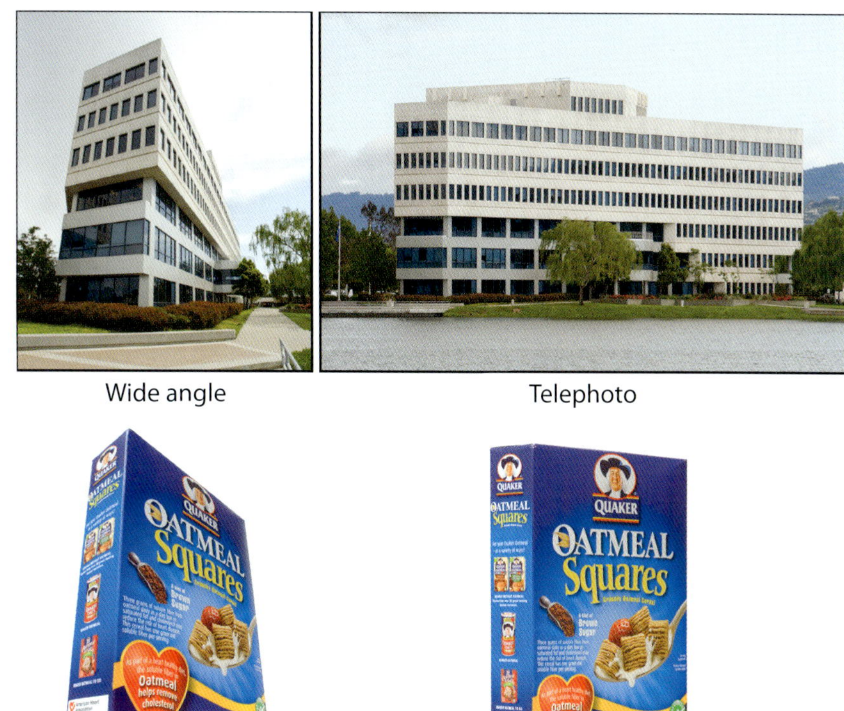

Fig. 2-17 Wide angle views can exaggerate a sense of scale in photos.

Lens Quality

Any discussion of lenses or photographic optics would not be complete without mention of quality issues.

Lens design and manufacture are complicated sciences. Production of good lenses includes challenges of creating high quality optical glass, grinding glass elements to precise dimensions, and mounting those elements on precisely aligned tracks within a lens barrel. Once assembled, all of these precision elements must also be able to stand up to constant use (and abuse).

No lens is perfect, and there are many flaws that can find their way into every lens design, no matter how sophisticated. These include image distortions, susceptibility to flare, astigmatisms, and chromatic abberations, among others. Only the most technically-minded photographers get too involved with such concerns. For these photographers, there are entire technical volumes devoted to such things.

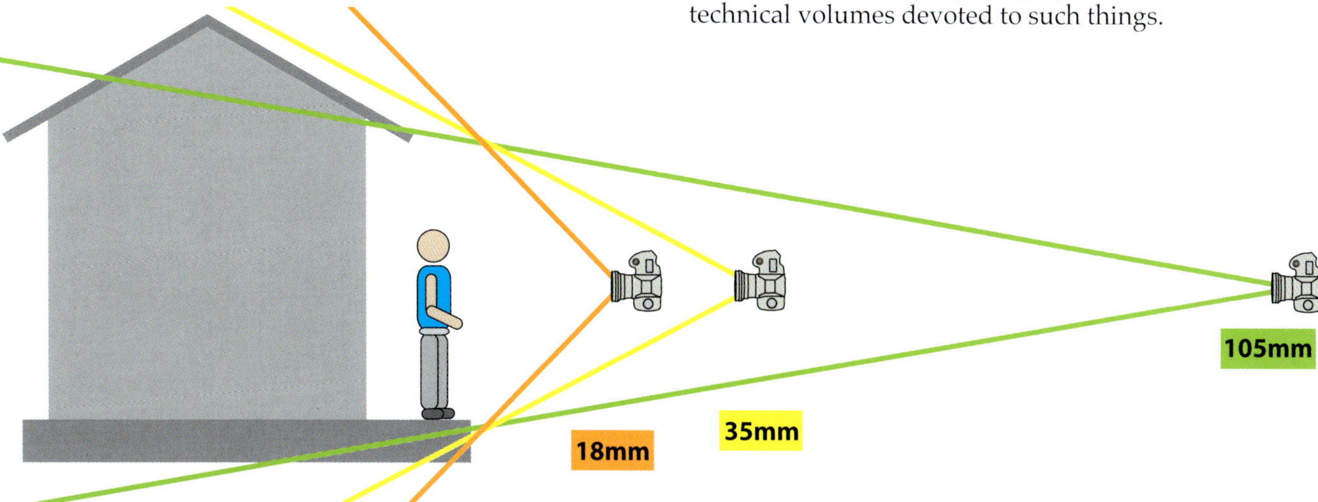

Fig. 2-18 Field of view (from lens focal length) is combined with camera-to-subject distance when choosing a perspective and the relationship between foreground and background subjects.

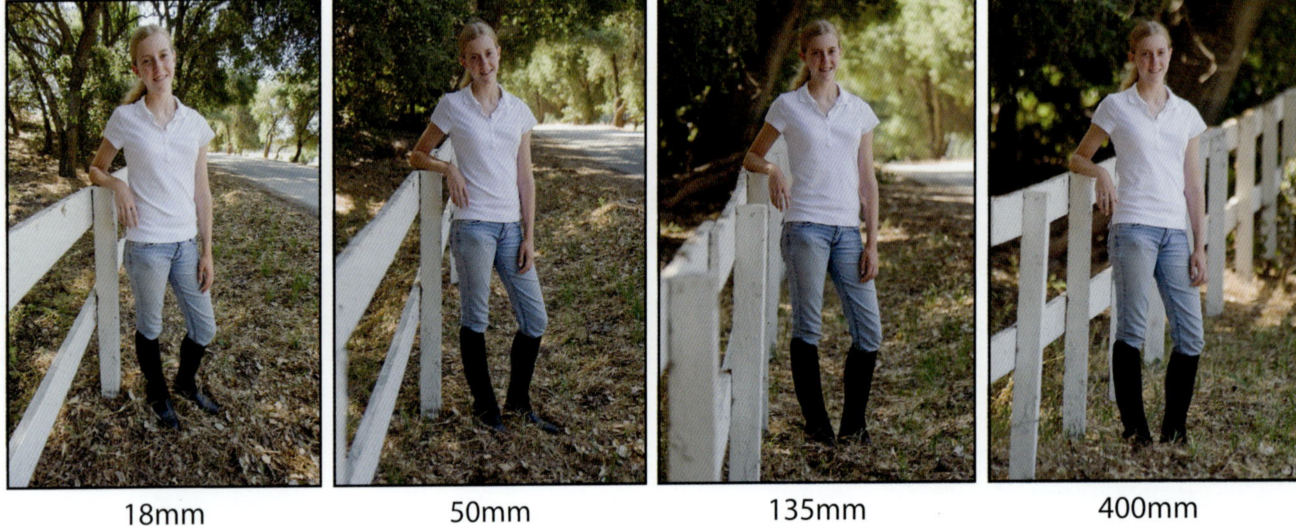

18mm   50mm   135mm   400mm

Fig. 2-19 Changing camera-to-subject distance with focal length in order to keep subject size constant. Changing camera position changes perspective. Lens focal length affects the relative magnification of foreground and background subjects.

For the rest of us, there is really only one thing to remember. You usually get the quality that you pay for. Nikon, Canon, and Leica lenses are usually significantly more expensive than third party lenses. This is generally because they are sharper, have fewer aberrations, and are less prone to flare with their superior design and optical coatings.

Lack of sharpness and loss of color saturation are two of photographers' worst enemies relating to the quality of their photography. As a professional, one needs to minimize as many obstacles as possible in the way of delivering the highest quality of work. Working with less than adequate tools usually costs more in the long run than it would to have started with the right tools in the first place.

ASSIGNMENT: PERSPECTIVE AND VIEW

Find a subject or a location that you are familiar with and can have complete access or freedom to move about. Choose a single lens – it can be wide angle, telephoto or normal – or set your zoom lens to a particular focal length and keep it there.

Shoot an entire roll of film (or digital equivalent) of this subject from varying distances and angles with one focal length. Move in, move out, shoot from a high perspective, then a low one. Get down on the ground and get dirty, climb overhead to shoot downward. Get close, then get even closer. Move back, then move way back. Take a photograph every time you see something interesting happening in your viewfinder until you have made at least 30 or 40 images.

Next, change your lens (or zoom setting) and repeat the exercise. If you started out with a wide lens, switch to a telephoto. If you started out with a telephoto, switch to a wide angle.

Next, study your results. Look at the images side by side and note what works for you in what situations. Notice how certain focal lengths seem to be more effective from certain camera positions relative to your subject (perspectives).

If you have the chance, try repeating the same exercise with an extreme lens of some sort. Rent an ultra-wide 15mm or 18mm, or perhaps a fisheye for a day. Or play with a super telephoto such as a 300mm or 500mm.

Once you have a good feel for the best perspectives for different situations, you will quickly be able to determine an appropriate lens before you even start shooting such subjects. You will be able to previsualize the shot before you ever look through the viewfinder. It's good practice, and keeps you ready for those fleeting opportunities where you may not have time to shoot more than just a few views.

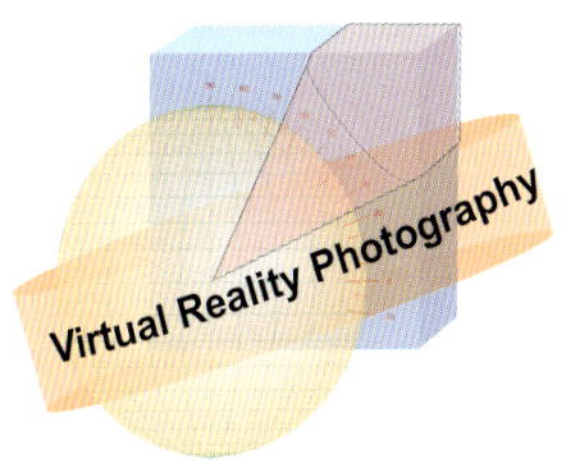

Chapter 3: Exposure

The only math a photographer really needs to know is how to multiply and divide by two.

Photography is the process of recording patterns of light onto film or other media. It is a term derived from Greek roots meaning "to write with light." Without light or illumination of some sort, there can be no photography.

Light is the foundation of everything we do in photography. Using light-sensitive materials, such as film, electronic, and digital sensors, we can record and display patterns of light focused on these media.

This process generally involves a light-tight container (camera) containing film or an image sensor, an optical system to gather and focus the patterns of light (lens), and a portal of some sort (shutter) to allow specifically timed amounts of light into the camera.

Photosensitive media such as film and electronic sensors respond when exposed to light, and within limits, the more light they are exposed to, the greater their response. However, the sensitivity of different media to light can vary widely. Thus, in most photography, it is important to be able to precisely control the amount of light that we expose our film or electronic sensors to.

Exposure is a term used to describe the amount of light reaching a photosensitive material. It is determined by two factors – the brightness (intensity) of that light and the period (time) that the material is exposed. In most cameras, the relative brightness of the light is controlled by the lens **aperture** (also called the diaphragm or iris), while the duration of an exposure is controlled by the **shutter**. The larger the aperture, the more light that can pass through the lens. The longer the shutter remains open, the more light will collect on the film or sensor.

An easy analogy is to simply think of light as if it were water filling a container. Aperture is an equivalent of the diameter of the pipe supplying the water. The larger the pipe, the more water can flow through it at once. The shutter corresponds to a faucet

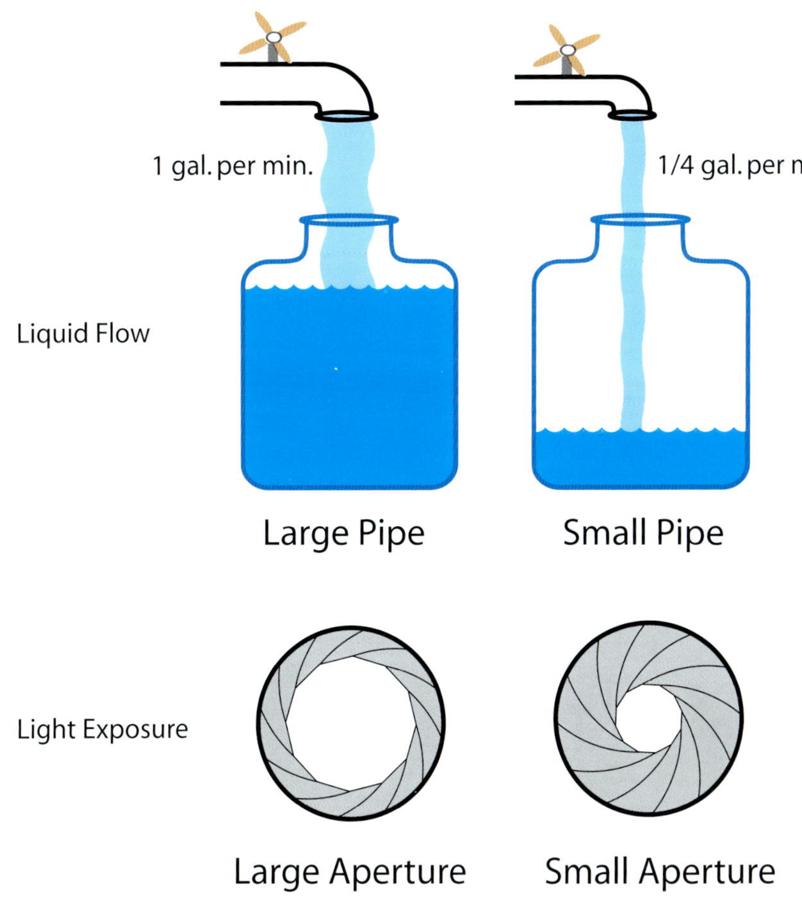

Fig. 3-1 Fluid flow as a model for light passing through a lens aperture.

that simply controls whether the water is flowing or not. The longer a faucet is open, the more water will flow. The longer a shutter is open, the more light will pass through it.

If you need to fill a gallon container, you can do it very quickly if you have a lot of water coming through a large pipe. However, you can also fill the container if you have a lesser amount of water coming through a smaller pipe but you leave the faucet open longer. Photographic exposure works the same way. Aperture essentially changes the size of the pipe, and shutter speed controls the amount of time the faucet is left open.

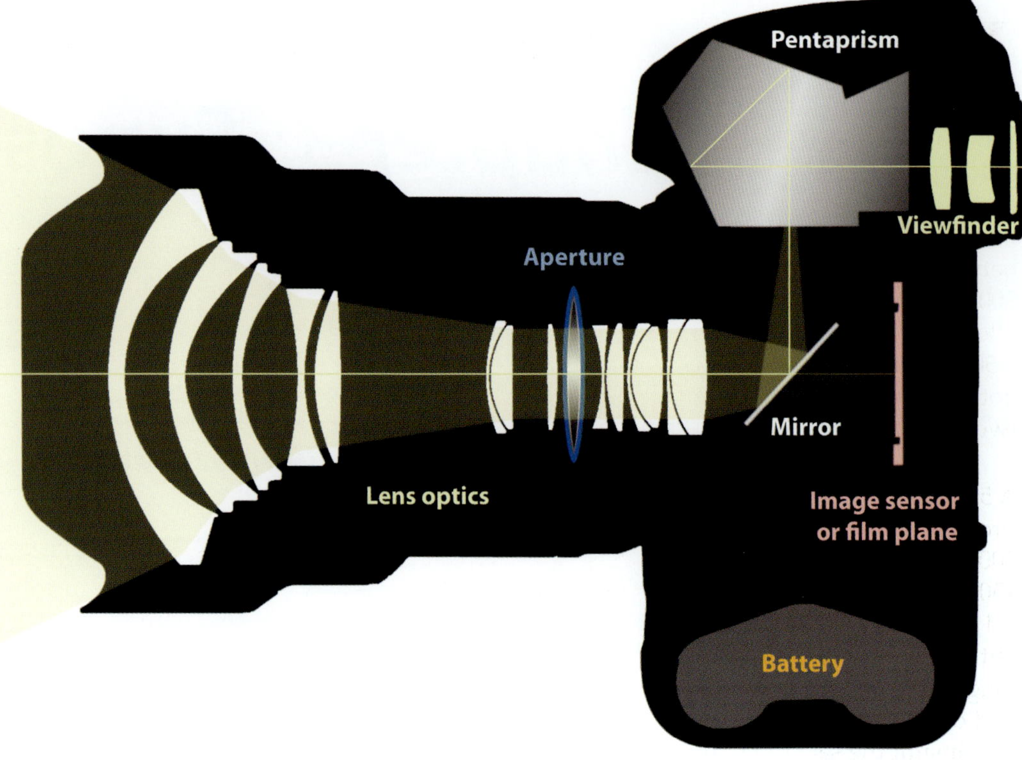

Fig. 3-2 Cutaway view of a modern Nikon digital SLR camera .

The intensity of the light reaching the film plane is a combination of both the brightness of the subject and the amount of light coming from it that can pass through the lens via the aperture. The amount of time the light can collect is determined by the shutter speed. The formula for expressing this relationship is:

$$\text{Exposure = Intensity x Time}$$

Aperture and f/stops

In photography, **aperture** is defined as the size of a lens diaphragm relative to the lens focal length – i.e. the diameter of the aperture divided by the focal length. The result is specified in an **f-number** or "**f/stop.**"

F-numbers are written as fractions, such as "f/2" or "f/16" to properly represent this ratio (diaphragm/focal length). Note that 1/2 is a larger number than 1/16. Thus, f/2 is a larger aperture opening than f/16. Common usage has resulted in photographers saying "f-two" or "f-sixteen" rather than the proper "f-over-two" or "f-divided-by-sixteen," and the result is confusion between what sound like increasing f-numbers representing decreasing lens openings.

Just remember that the f-number is simply a fraction. An aperture of f/2 means that the aperture is 1/2 the focal length of the lens. A setting of f/8 means the aperture has a diameter of only 1/8 the focal length of that lens.

F/stops are generally marked in equal increments on the aperture ring of a photographic lens, with each click or "stop" effectively doubling or halving the size (area) of the aperture opening. When the *area* of the aperture is halved, only half the amount of light can pass through the lens. Doubling the *area* of the aperture doubles the amount of light that can get through.

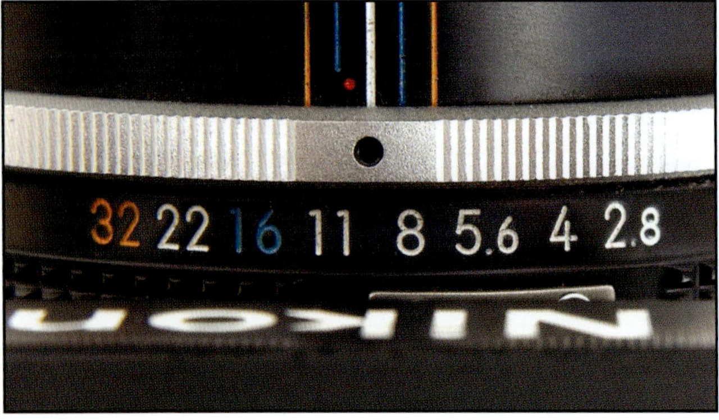

Fig. 3-3 A manual aperture ring on an older Nikkor lens.

Technical Note: Apertures and f/stops

While f-numbers (or f/stops) initially seem to be a complicated means to describe how much light can pass through a lens, they are used because they maintain a constant measure of light transmittance between lenses of different sizes. In principle, a 300mm lens with an aperture setting of f/4 will allow the same amount of light to pass through as a 50mm lens at f/4, even though the dimensions of both aperture and focal length are different for the two lenses.

A 50mm lens with a diaphragm opening of 25mm provides an f/2 aperture setting (25/50 = 1/2). A 300mm lens would require a diaphragm opening of 150mm to provide the same f/2 aperture (150/300 = 1/2). This is what makes long telephoto lenses with wide apertures so large (and expensive). The longer the focal length, the larger the optical surfaces and diameter of the diaphragm need to be in order to transmit the same amount of light as a smaller, shorter lens.

Lens manufacturers usually include the maximum (widest) aperture of a given lens in their product literature descriptions. For example, a 50mm f/1.4 lens is one with a 50mm focal length and a maximum (widest) diaphragm opening of f/1.4. This lens would allow twice as much light to pass through it at its widest aperture than a 50mm f/2 lens. However, the f/1.4 lens will also have f/2 and smaller aperture settings, which will provide the same amount of light transmittance as the corresponding f/2 and smaller settings on the other lens. An f/2 aperture setting will always be f/2, no matter what lens is used.

Remember that the f-number is a fraction – the diaphragm opening divided by the focal length. The f-number for each full stop changes by a factor of 1.414, or the square root of 2, because the light transmission depends upon the *area* of the aperture opening. Thus, if you want to double the area of the circle (the size of the aperture), you multiply its diameter by 1.414. To halve it, you divide the f-number by 1.414.

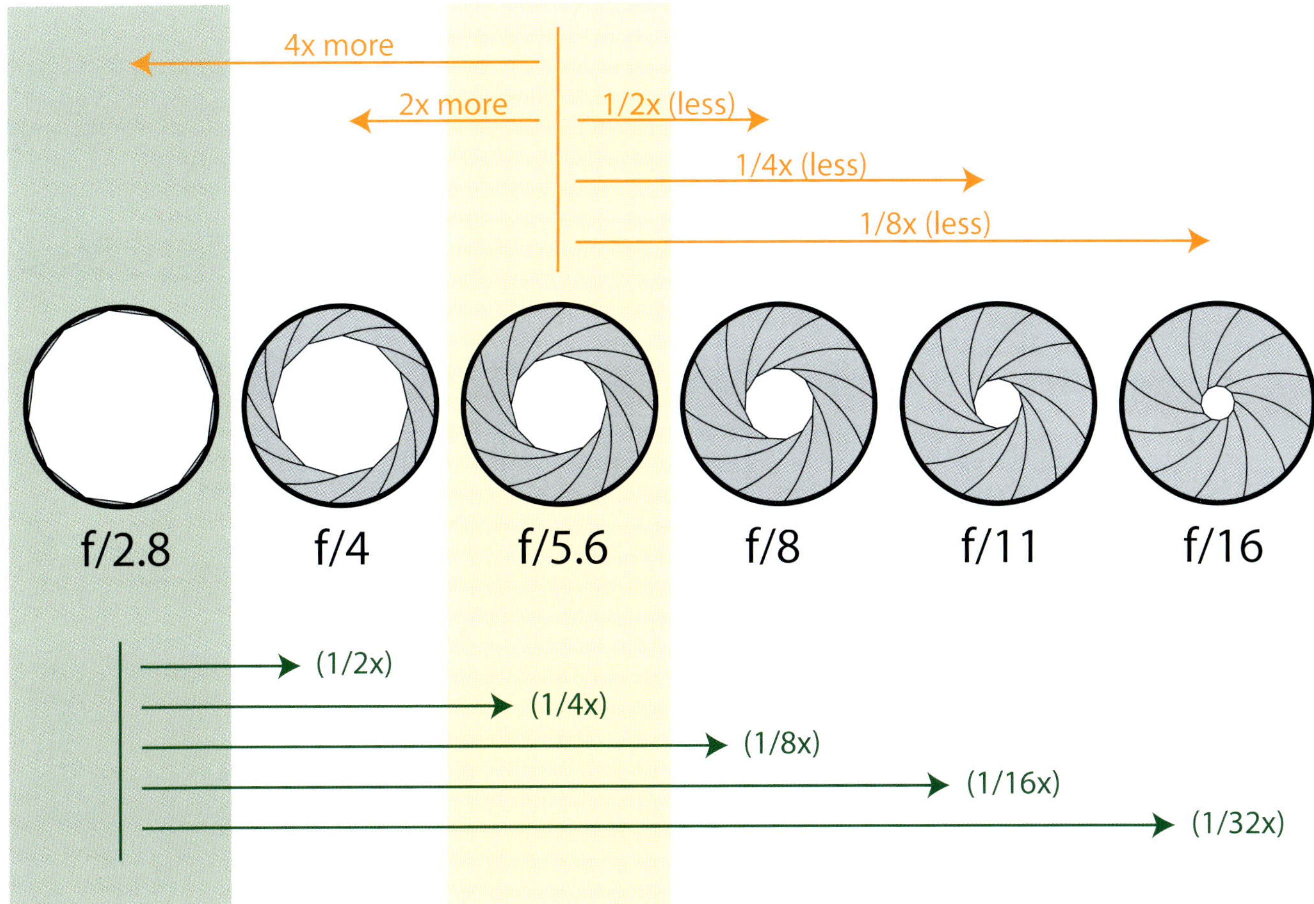

Fig. 3-4 Aperture (f/stop) relationships. A change of a full stop in either direction allows twice or half as much light to pass.

Moving the aperture ring from f/4 to f/5.6 is a one "stop" adjustment, which reduces the area of the diaphragm or iris opening by half. Moving the aperture ring from f/4 to f/2.8 opens the diaphragm one stop, doubling both the area of the opening and the amount of light that can pass through the lens. Note that some lenses include intermediate markings or click stops representing half or third stop increments, rather than only full stop increments. However, even with lenses that have only full stop increments, the aperture can be set anywhere in between the click stops for less than full stop exposure adjustments.

Shutter Speeds

The amount of time the camera's shutter remains open is a second control we have over exposure. The shutter blocks all light from reaching the film plane, except during precisely timed intervals (ranging from about 1/1000 sec. up to several seconds and longer) when it is released.

Most traditional camera shutters have settings adjustable only in 1-stop increments. Much like aperture adjustments, each increment or "click" of the shutter speed either halves or doubles the previous setting. However, most of today's electronic cameras allow for 1/2 or 1/3 stop shutter speed increments, giving more precise exposure control through shutter speed.

If a one-second exposure will allow a given amount of light to reach the film or image sensor, doubling the exposure to two seconds will double the amount of light reaching the film plane. Likewise, decreasing the duration of the exposure to 1/2 second will correspondingly halve the amount of light reaching the film plane. Remember that exposure is a cumulative process combining both

the "volume" or flow of light via the aperture (i.e. the diameter of the pipe) and the duration of the light "flow" via shutter speed (i.e. the time the faucet is "on").

Common shutter speed settings on today's cameras are as follows:

8 secs.
4 secs.
2 secs.
1 sec.
1/2 sec.
1/4 sec.
1/8 sec.
1/15 sec.
1/30 sec.
1/60 sec.
1/125 sec.
1/250 sec.
1/500 sec.
1/1000 sec.

Notice that each shutter speed is half or double that above or below it (some figures are rounded for simplicity). Each of these steps represents a change of one "stop" in the amount of light that will reach the film plane, representing either twice or half as much as the previous shutter speed. As noted at the beginning of this chapter, if you can multiply and divide by two, you have mastered all the math necessary to understand exposure in photography!

If we increase our shutter speed from 1 sec. to 2 secs., we double the amount of light reaching the film. If we increase it another stop to 4 secs., we again double the amount of light, equaling four times the amount of original light – or a two-stop exposure increase. Doubling it yet again

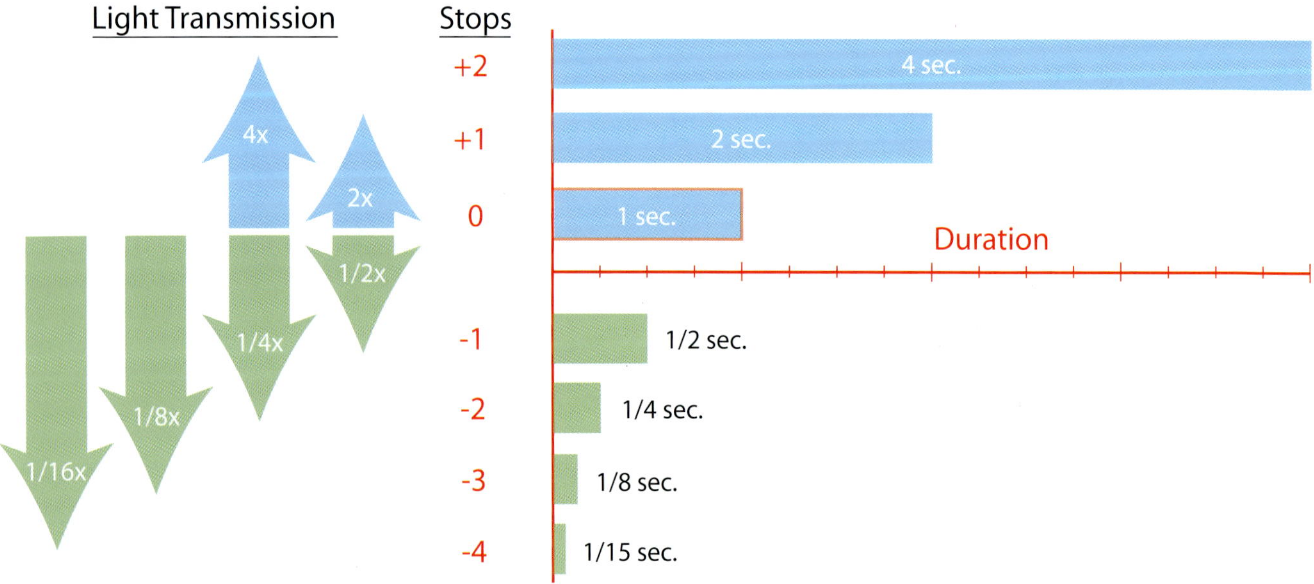

Fig. 3-5 Shutter speed relationships. Like aperture, any change of a full stop allows twice or half as much light to pass.

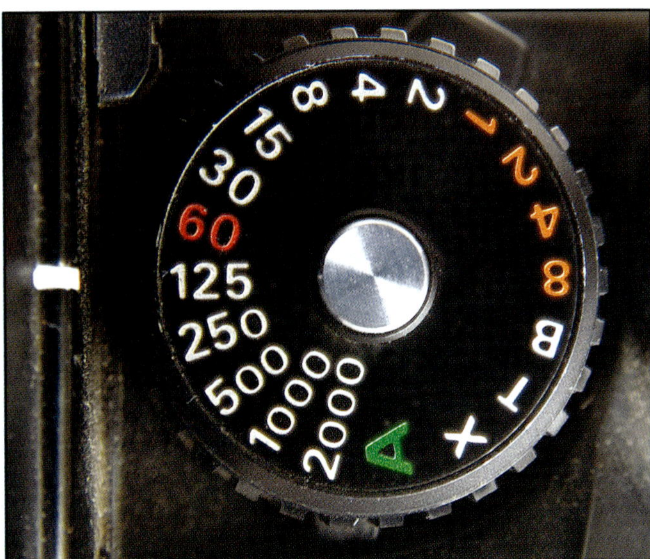

Fig. 3-6 Shutter speed dial on a typical manual camera.

(to 8 secs.) means we've increased the exposure by a total of three stops, or eight times the original amount of light reaching the film or image sensor.

The relationship is reversed when we adjust shutter speed downward.

If you decrease your shutter speed from 1 sec. to 1/2 sec., you halve the amount of light reaching the film. If you decrease it another stop to 1/4 sec., you halve the amount of light yet again. You are now allowing only 1/4 the amount of light to reach the film and have decreased the exposure by two stops. Halving it yet again (to 1/8 sec.) decreases your exposure by a total of three stops, or 1/8 the original amount of light reaching the film or image sensor.

These relationships hold constant no matter where you start out. If your original exposure is 1/500 sec., slowing your shutter speed by three stops (to 1/60 sec.) will allow for 8x the amount of light (2x2x2=8). Slowing your shutter speed to 1/4 sec. will add four more stops (1/30, 1/15, 1/8 and 1/4 secs.) for a total of seven stops of increased light, or 128 times the original light (2x2x2x2x2x2x2=128) transmitted by the 1/500 sec. exposure.

Many camera shutters also have other settings in addition to those listed above. These include a "B" or "Bulb" setting and a "T" or "Time" setting. Both are generally used for exposures longer than are available through the presets. These are used for very low light situations or in unusual lighting circumstances. They almost always require that the camera be stabilized on a tripod in order to prevent blur from camera movement. Use of a cable release or other remote trigger for the shutter is also recommended to prevent small movements of the camera when releasing the shutter.

The "B" setting opens the shutter when the button is first pressed, and closes it when the button is released. The "T" setting opens the shutter when the button is pressed, but does not close it until the button is pressed a second time. The "T" setting is generally used for very long exposures (several minutes and more), where the photographer doesn't want to be stuck holding the shutter release button for the duration of the exposure. Most modern cameras no longer include a "T" setting, but photographers can achieve the same effect by using a locking cable release to lock the shutter open while shooting on "B". Simply releasing the lock closes the shutter and ends the exposure.

Another setting found on some cameras is an "X" shutter speed. This is the "sync" speed, or the fastest shutter speed that will allow proper exposure of the entire frame when using electronic flash with that particular camera. The burst of light from an electronic flash must be synchronized properly with the moment that the camera's shutter is fully open. Otherwise, the light from the flash may be partially blocked from reaching the film plane by the opening or closing curtains of the shutter.

Using Aperture and Shutter Speed Together

Both aperture and shutter speed can be used to control exposure, so why do we need both? In reality, you can fully control exposure using only one, but having both available gives the photographer far more control and an ability to take advantage of benefits offered by one or the other in a wider range of lighting conditions.

For instance, changing aperture allows the photographer to change the depth of field, or the range of acceptable focus in a photo. Shutter speeds allow a photographer to control motion in the picture, either by "freezing" the action at high shutter speeds or blurring it at lower speeds. Long shutter speeds (time exposures) are often the only means to adequately expose a picture in low-light situations.

With two ways to adjust exposure, we can maintain a constant amount of light that reaches the film plane by adjusting either aperture or shutter speed in one direction while adjusting the other an equal amount in the opposite direction. This allows us to control depth of field, motion, or other effect with one, and to compensate for the resulting exposure change with the other. Either shutter speed or aperture can be used to adjust for the brightness of the subject or scene.

Remember how both aperture and shutter speeds are generally marked in full stops – with every click stop either doubling or halving the exposure. This means that you can double the amount of light going through the lens by opening the aperture one stop, while simultaneously halving it by reducing shutter speed duration one stop. The net result is that the same amount of light still

Technical Note: Understanding Shutters

Virtually all consumer and professional cameras today have some sort of mechanical shutter that allows light to enter the camera for precisely timed intervals.

There are two primary types of shutters used commonly today. The first is a **leaf shutter**, which consists of interleaved metal blades that open and close around a central point. When closed, they block all light coming through the lens. Leaf shutters are generally integrated within a lens. Today, they are found primarily in medium and large format camera systems, and in specialty lenses for 35mm and other formats.

The spacing or timing between the two curtains is varied to change the shutter speed.

Focal plane shutters are capable of much faster speeds than leaf shutters (1/1000 sec. and more). At high shutter speeds, the frame is exposed sequentially as the curtains travel across, rather than all at once, as occurs with leaf shutters.

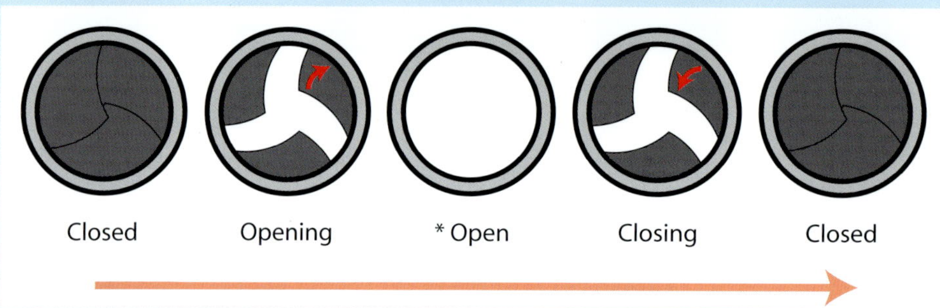

Fig. 3-7 Leaf shutter operation (* is the flash sync moment).

Leaf shutters are limited to a fastest shutter speed of about 1/500 sec. because of the physical mechanics of opening the blades fully and then reversing their directions to close them again. The advantage of leaf shutters is that they allow for flash synchronization at any of their shutter speeds, which focal plane shutters do not.

For longer exposures, the first (opening) curtain will pass completely across the film plane before the second (closing) starts moving. This means that for at least a moment, the gap between the curtains encompasses the entire frame so the whole image area is being exposed at once. In older 35mm cameras, this occurred at shutter speeds of 1/60 sec.

Most modern 35mm and consumer cameras use **focal plane shutters**, rather than leaf shutters. Focal plane shutters are generally built into the camera itself, rather than into the lens. True to their name, focal plane shutters are positioned directly in front of the focal or film plane of the camera, and consist of two or more opaque curtains, which travel in sequence in front of the film or sensor to create a precisely-timed opening for light to pass through.

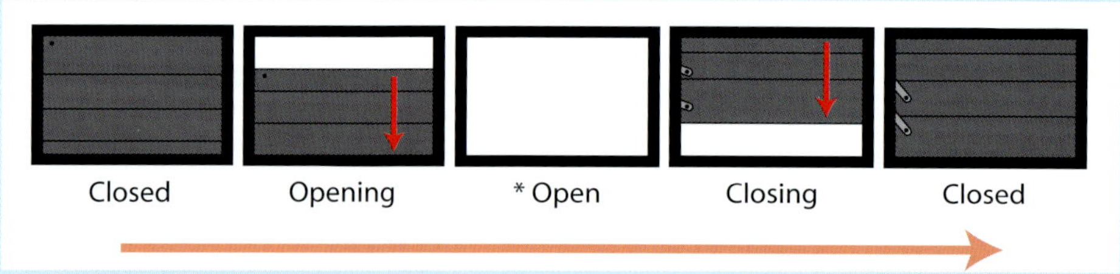

Fig. 3-8 Focal plane shutter operation (* is the flash sync moment).

As the first curtain passes, the shutter is opened and the exposure begins. When the second curtain passes, the shutter is closed and the exposure ends.

and slower. However, modern focal plane shutters are designed more efficiently and they can achieve this full frame exposure capability at speeds of up to 1/250 sec. or more. These speeds are commonly marked as the camera's maximum "sync" or flash synchronization speed. They are important to know about when using electronic flash or "strobe" units.

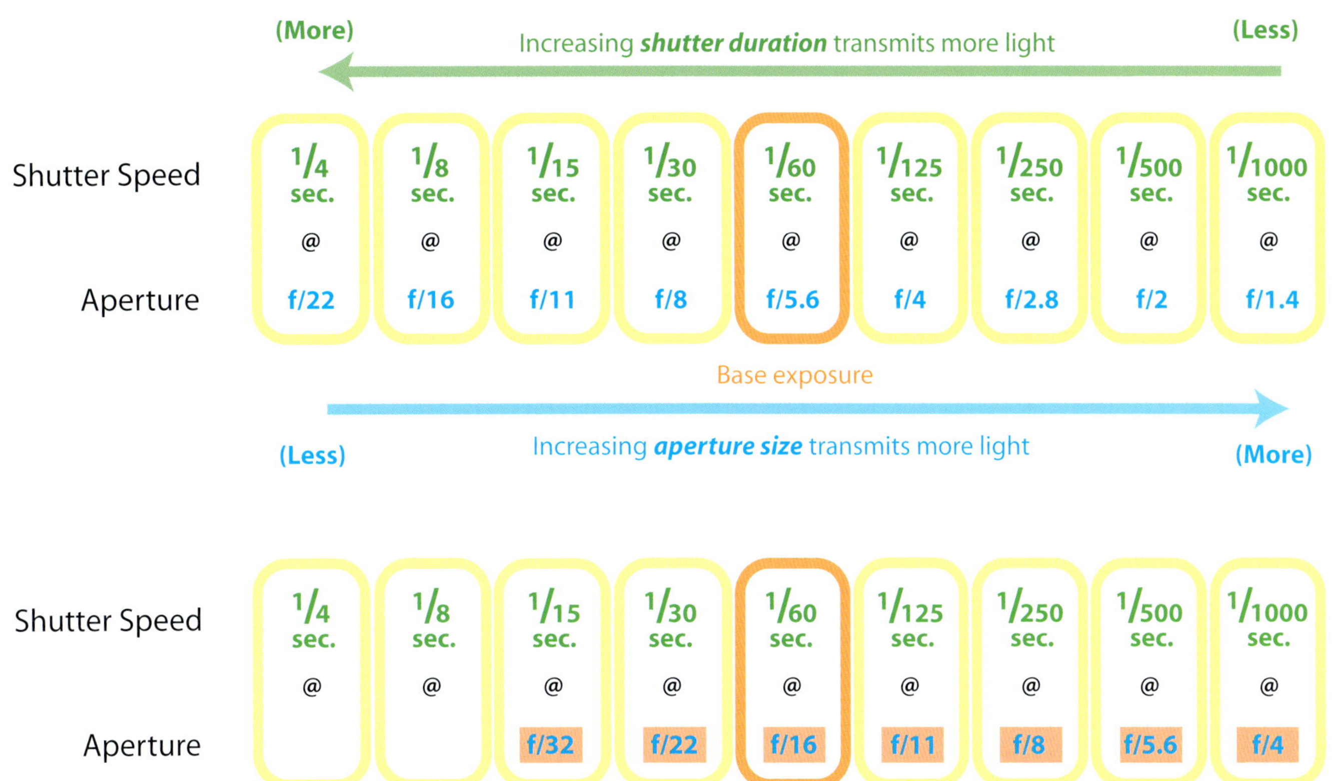

Fig. 3-9 Exposure relationships and equivalents.

reaches the film plane. In our water analogy, this would be doubling the water flow rate while halving the time it is allowed to flow.

For example, if we determine that a proper exposure for a scene is 1/60 sec. at f/5.6, we can also determine many other combinations of shutter speed and aperture that will yield the same amount of light simply by increasing one as we decrease the other.

If we slow the shutter speed from 1/60 sec. to 1/30 sec., we double the light. To compensate for this increase, we could decrease the aperture by one stop, from f/5.6 to f/8. Thus, an exposure of 1/60 sec. @ f/5.6 yields the same amount of light as 1/30 sec. @ f/8. Likewise, 1/4 sec @ f/22 or 1/1000 sec. @ f/1.4 produce the same effective exposure.

Flash Synchronization (Sync)

Often, it is necessary to supplement existing ambient light with additional lighting in order to brighten dark shadow areas or to sufficiently light a scene. Most often, photographers will use a flash or strobe unit to do this. However, because flash is not a continuous light source (like a tungsten lamp or the sun), it presents a challenge to synchronize the timing of the flash burst to the exact moment the camera is exposing the image.

The fastest shutter speed on any camera to which flash or strobe light can be synchronized is referred to as the camera's maximum sync speed. This setting is often highlighted on the camera's shutter speed selector. An "X" often designates this on the shutter speed dial. If faster shutter speeds are used, only a portion of the frame will be exposed at the moment when the strobe or flash is fired, because at least one of the shutter curtains will be partially covering the film plane. These curtains will cast a shadow over whatever parts of the film or image sensor that they cover when the flash fires, preventing flash exposure over the full image area.

Modern photographic flash units (or strobes) fire a sudden burst of light that lasts anywhere from about 1/400 sec. down to 1/50,000 sec. If the camera's shutter is not completely open when this light bursts, only the portion of the frame behind the shutter opening will be exposed by the flash, and the portion(s) covered by the curtains will not. You should therefore use flash or strobe lighting only at the camera's maximum sync (or slower) shutter speed.

Light Sensitivity - ISO and Film Speed

There is a third control that photographers also have over exposure, and that is their choice of film or digital sensor based on its light sensitivity, or **ISO** (formerly **ASA**). ISO is simply a numeric value used to indicate the relative sensitivity of each type of film or sensor setting.

A high ISO number means that the film or digital sensor is more sensitive to light than that of a low ISO number. Common ISO speeds are 100, 200 and 400. A film with an ISO speed of 200 is twice as sensitive to light as a film with an ISO of 100. Thus, the 200 ISO film is a full-stop more sensitive to light. Doubling the ISO number means half the light is required to make the exposure properly. Digital camera sensors are designed with similar ISO sensitivities, although this sensitivity can often be adjusted within the camera's software.

If a scene requires an exposure of 1/250 sec. @ f/8 at ISO 100, it will require one stop *less* exposure (1/500 sec. @ f/8 or 1/250 sec. @ f/11) at ISO 200. Likewise, it would require one stop *more* exposure if shot under half as sensitive ISO 50.

Film is generally rated at a particular ISO, which is commonly referred to as the "film speed." The ISO of film is usually printed on the film packaging and is used by your camera's light meter to help determine proper exposures. Modern film cameras automatically read the ISO information from the UPC code on the film canister when the film is loaded inside the camera. Most digital SLRs allow you to adjust the relative sensitivity of the sensor (some even do it automatically) so you can select different effective ISOs for every shooting situation via the camera's settings menus. With film cameras, you actually have to change to a new roll to get an increase of decrease in ISO sensitivity.

Films with high ISO speeds (more sensitive to light) are called "fast" films because they enable photographers

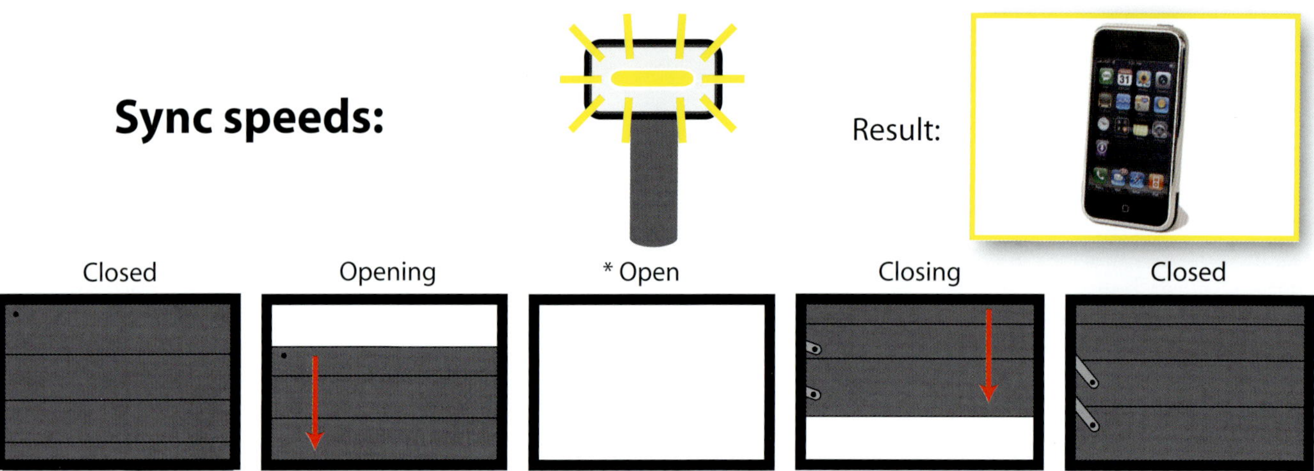

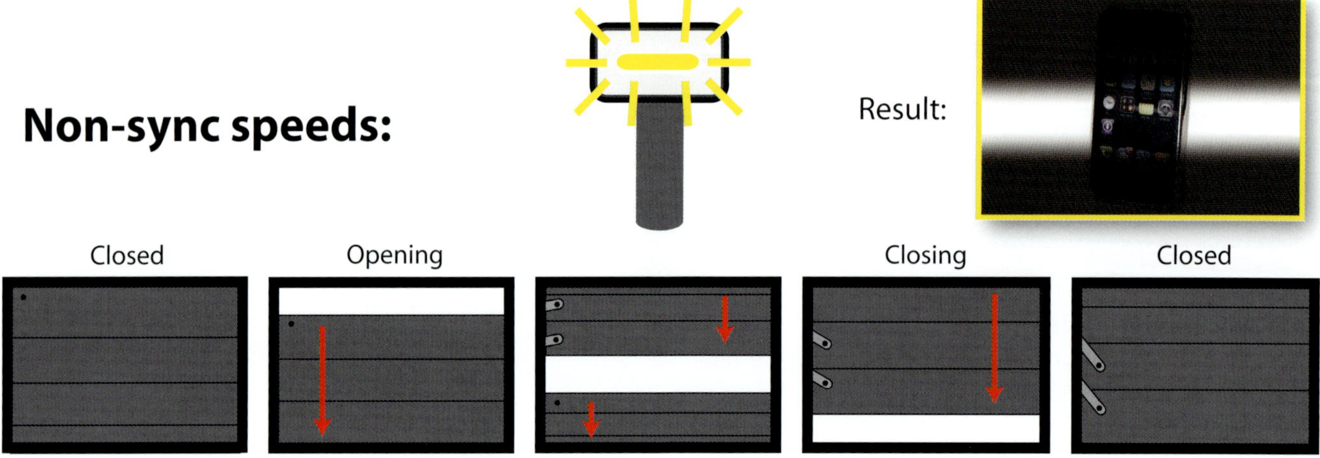

Fig. 3-10 Most modern professional cameras utilizing focal plane shutters have a maximum flash sync speed of 1/250 sec. Consumer and prosumer models may have slightly lower maximums. Some older 35mm cameras have maximum sync speeds as low as 1/30 or 1/60 sec.

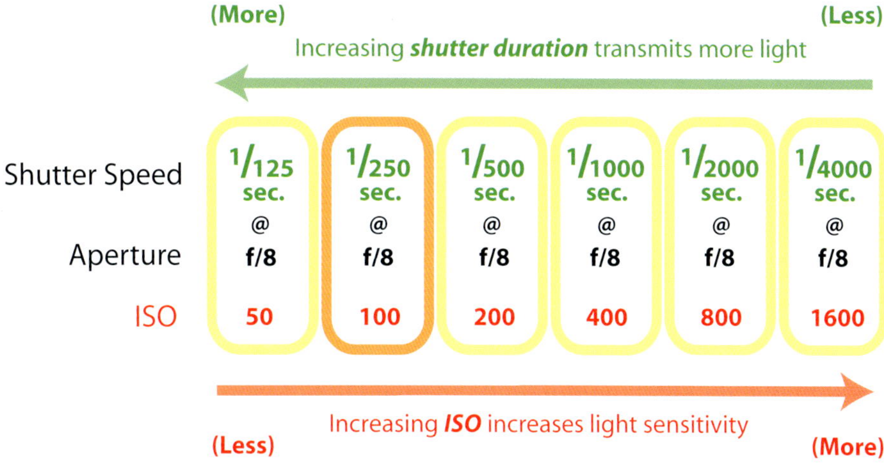

Fig. 3-11 ISO equivalents and exposure.

to shoot at faster shutter speeds. Films with lower ISO speeds are called "slow" films.

As with most things in photography, film speed and digital sensor ISO adjustments involve tradeoffs in other areas. In order to make emulsions that are more sensitive to light, film manufacturers increase the size of the light sensitive silver halide crystals in the film's emulsion. This means that these crystals, or grain structure, become more visible when the image is enlarged than the smaller crystals of less sensitive (lower ISO) films.

Similarly, digital sensors at higher ISO settings tend to exhibit more "noise" than they do at lower ISOs. ISO adjustments on digital cameras are done through on board software and digital data processing, rather than through any sort of physical modification of the sensor.

Often, photographers are willing to make the necessary tradeoffs for a higher ISO, particularly when shooting in low light situations requiring fast shutter speeds, such as indoor sports. Good photography of most sporting events demands fast shutter speeds in order to freeze the action and keep the fast moving subjects sharp. Additionally, this sort of photography often requires the use of telephoto lenses with their smaller maximum apertures. A photographer's best chance at getting properly exposed, sharp images in low-light situations is to use a higher speed film or digital ISO, and to accept the tradeoff of more visible film grain or digital noise.

There are also times when photographers favor a more "grainy" look as an artistic effect in their images, and will choose high ISO media even in brightly lit situations.

Exposure Rule of Thumb – The "Sunny 16 Rule"

Sunlight Exposure = 1/ISO sec. @ f/16

The "Sunny 16 Rule" is a simple rule of thumb that benefits all photographers, particularly when shooting in outdoor situations. This, combined with the understanding that full stop changes in aperture and/or shutter speed halve or double the amount of exposure, will get photographer's very close to the proper exposure almost every time – even without the use of a light meter.

The Sunny 16 Rule is simply a calculation of basic exposure under normal bright sun outdoors. The "16"

"Sunny 16" Exposure Equivalents   1/ISO sec. @ f/16

		(Larger) ←		Apertures	→ (Smaller)		
		f/2.8	**f/4**	**f/5.6**	**f/8**	**f/11**	**f/16**	**f/22**
Bright beach / snow (+1 stop)		1/4000	1/2000	1/1000	1/500	1/250	1/125	1/60
Normal Daylight (Sunny 16)		1/2000	1/1000	1/500	1/250	1/125	1/60	1/30
Slight overcast (-1 stop)		1/1000	1/500	1/250	1/125	1/60	1/30	1/15
Overcast (-2 stops)		1/500	1/250	1/125	1/60	1/30	1/15	1/8
Heavy overcast (-3 stops)		1/250	1/125	1/60	1/30	1/15	1/8	1/4

(Shorter) ←   Shutter speeds   → (Longer)

Fig. 3-12 The Sunny 16 Rule.

refers to an aperture setting of f/16 with a shutter speed of 1/ISO (the film sensitivity).

Thus, if you are using a slow film such as Fuji Velvia, with an ISO of 50, your basic outdoor exposure in direct sunlight would be 1/50 sec. @ f/16, or any equivalent. The closest full stop setting on most cameras would be 1/60 sec. @ f/16, and the equivalents would be 1/30 @ f/22, 1/125 sec. @ f/11, 1/250 sec. @ f/8, 1/500 sec. @ f/5.6, 1/1000 sec. @ f/4, etc., as well as half and third stop increments in between.

A light overcast generally means that you need to add one stop of exposure to the Sunny 16 rule, so your base exposure for the ISO 50 film speed would become 1/60 sec. @ f/11 (instead of f/16).

Heavier overcast or shadowed areas might require a 2-3 stop base exposure increase from Sunny 16 to 1/60 sec. @ f/8 or f/5.6.

Extremely bright scenes, such as sunny beaches and snow scenes would require a <u>decrease</u> of one or more stops from Sunny 16 to 1/60 sec. @ f/22 and equivalent.

Determining Exposure with Gray Card

Today's modern cameras have sophisticated exposure meters which automatically adjust the camera's exposure properly for most situations. These systems measure the total amount of light coming into the camera and generally calculate an exposure average for the scene. This renders mid-tone subjects as mid-tone colors, but does not always work well for bright or dark subjects against contrasting backgrounds. Such exposure averaging does not work well when the subject is strongly backlit, is in a shadowed area of an otherwise bright scene, or is a bright subject on a dark background. In these instances, the photographer may need to override the camera's meter by setting the exposure manually.

One of the best ways to determine proper exposure is to use a neutral gray card. These gray cards (often called 18 percent gray) are designed to reflect a standard medium or mid-tone for exposure meter readings. The photographer places the gray card in the scene and takes a meter reading from it. It is generally best to fill the entire frame with this neutral gray card when taking a meter reading. The resulting exposure is truly a neutral exposure for the scene, rather than being skewed one way or another by overly bright or dark backgrounds (or subjects).

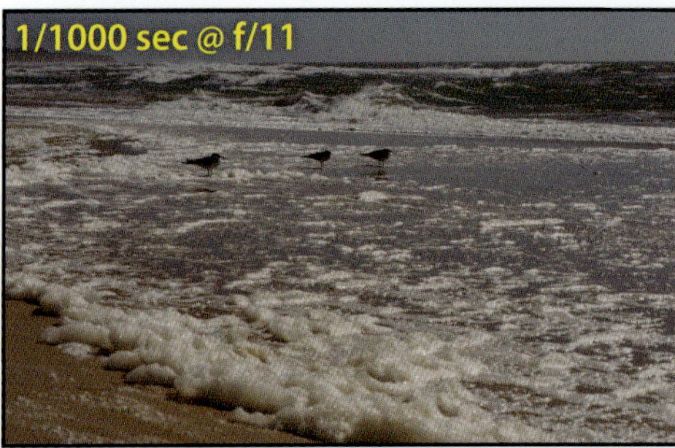

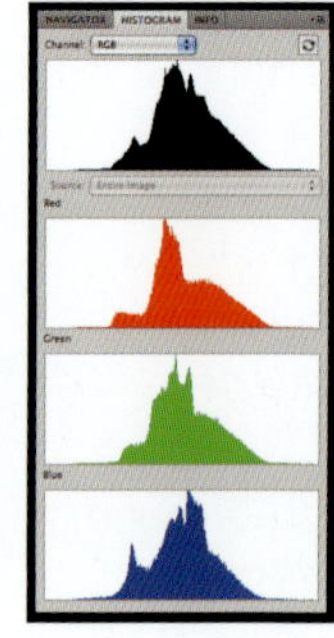

Camera meter underexposes bright scene

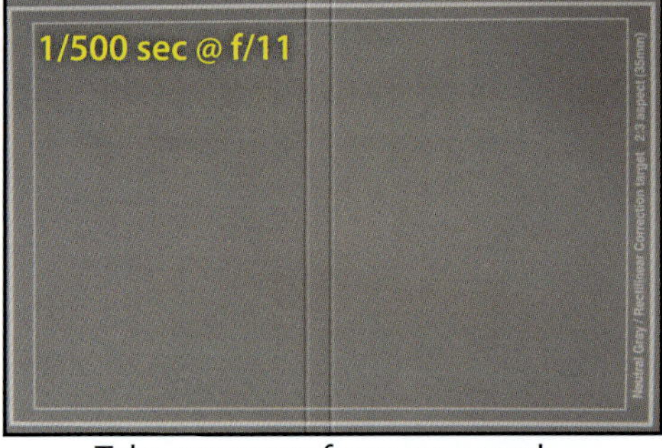

Take exposure from gray card

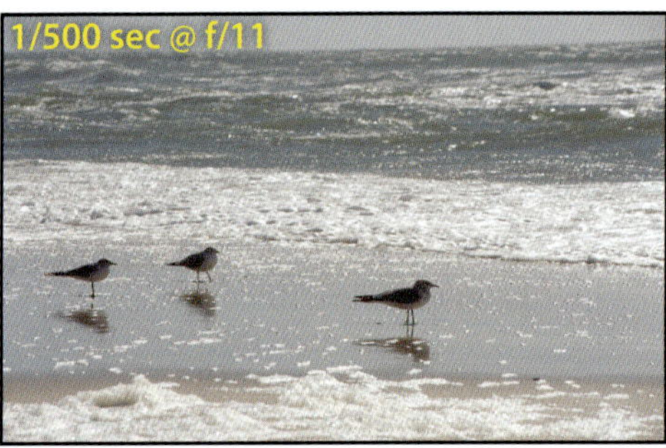

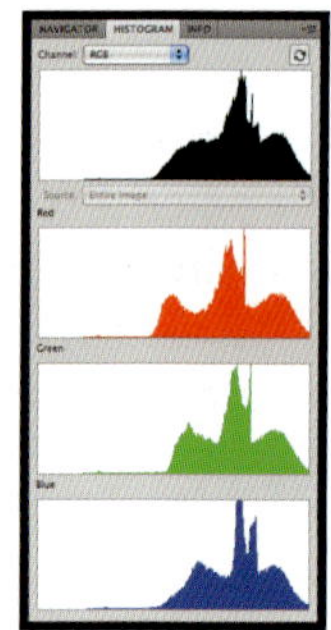

Using gray card exposure gives correction

Fig. 3-13 Using a gray card to determine proper exposure.

This gray card exposure is then used as a starting point for manually exposing the scene. Gray cards are also valuable for auto adjusting color balance when shooting with digital cameras.

Unfortunately, few photographers have an 18 percent gray card with them when they need it. A convenient alternative is to use the palm of your hand instead. Just keep in mind that the skin tone of a Caucasian palm is

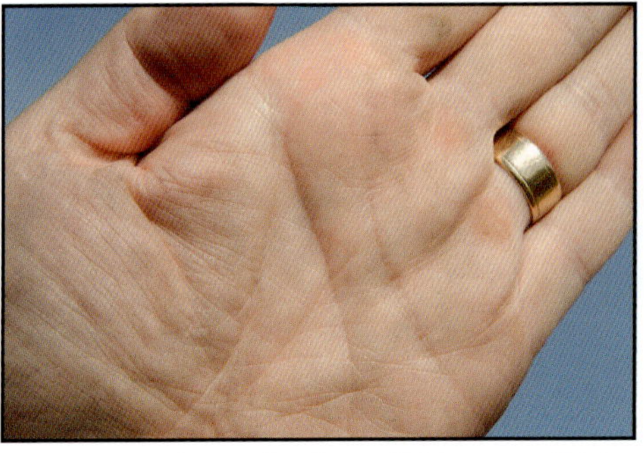

Meter reading of palm: 1/500 sec @ **f/16**   Gray card meter reading: 1/500 sec @ **f/11**

Fig. 3-14 The palm of your hand can be used in place of a gray card if needed.

about a full stop brighter than an 18 percent gray card. This means that you can meter a scene off the palm of your hand and then subtract a full stop from that exposure to get a close approximation of a neutral 18 percent gray card exposure. (Note that the color of your palm is not a "neutral" gray, so it should *not* be used for auto adjusting color balance with digital cameras.)

Finally, one must keep in mind that "proper" exposure in photography can be subjective. Some subjects should be rendered darker than average (such as a black cat or a night time scene) while others should be lighter (such as a polar bear or a snow scene). You don't want either of these to be rendered as a neutral gray or mid-tone color in your photographs. Rather, you want to capture the sense of their lightness or darkness, yet still maintain sufficient detail in highlight and shadow areas. The ability to predict proper exposure adjustments comes through experience and constant critiquing of one's efforts.

Every photographer has their own opinion of how they like their images to be exposed. Some might favor darker exposures, while others favor a slightly lighter look. Every type of film responds differently as well. Each should be thoroughly tested in a variety of shooting situations before a photographer has to rely on it for critical assignments. Transparency or slide films require the most precise exposure as they have little latitude for exposure variation. They also do not handle overexposure terribly well. Overexposed subjects on transparency film tend to result in washed out highlight

details. Negative or print films have significantly more exposure latitude than slide films, and are often a better choice for high contrast shooting situations. However, negative films do not tolerate underexposure very well, and the result is a loss of detail in shadows or darker areas of a scene.

Experienced professional photographers will use a number of tools during a photo shoot in order to accurately determine proper exposures. These include hand held light meters, Polaroid camera backs (for instant film previews) and most often today, digital cameras that allow immediate viewing of the captured images and their exposure histograms. However, even with all these tools available, most photographers will shoot multiple shots of each image or scene, varying the exposure slightly between them. This is called **exposure bracketing**.

Exposure Bracketing
Exposure bracketing is generally best done in 1/3 to 1/2 stop increments. To bracket a set of exposures, you will want to shoot the same scene using incremental exposure settings both above and below that which your camera's light meter indicates.

For instance, let's say the light meter in your camera indicates that the proper exposure for a given scene is 1/250 sec. @ f/11. You will probably want to adjust that exposure up to a full stop in each direction (over and

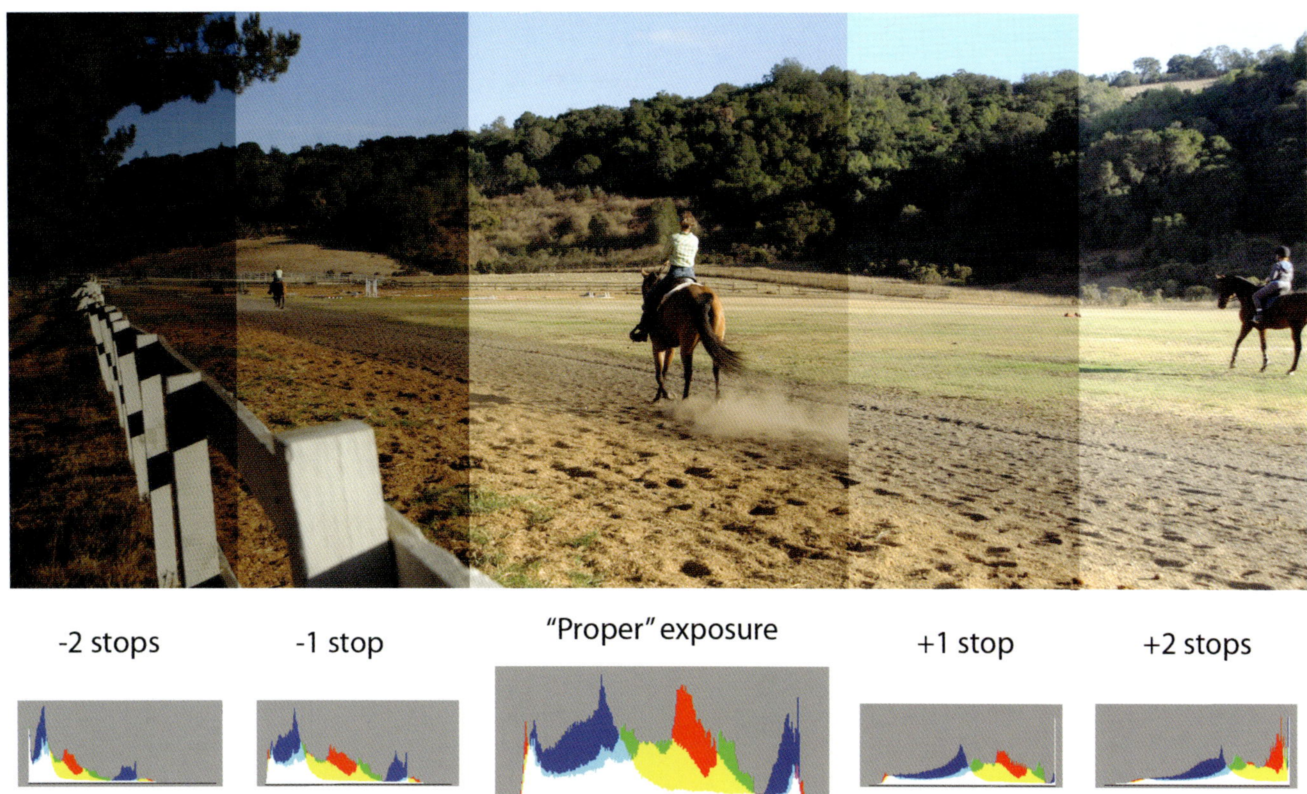

Fig. 3-15 Bracketed exposures and their accompanying histograms showing distribution of pixel values in the image.

under exposing) in 1/3 stop increments. This will result in seven bracketed images as follows:

Underexposed			Base exposure	Overexposed		
-1 stop	-2/3 stop	-1/3 stop	base	+1/3 stop	+2/3 stop	+1 stop

With experience, you can reduce the number of bracketed exposures you shoot. Sometimes, you may feel comfortable only bracketing one or two shots in each direction as you get more comfortable with the performance characteristics of your digital camera, or a particular type of film under specific shooting situations.

Remember that you can bracket these exposures using either adjustments to shutter speed or lens aperture. Older cameras only allow shutter speeds to be adjusted in full stop increments, so it may be necessary to make the 1/3 and 1/2 stop changes using the aperture. Newer cameras allow for 1/3 stop adjustments in both shutter speed and aperture.

ASSIGNMENT: EXPOSURE

Select a favorite transparency or slide film with an ISO of 50 or 100 and load it into a camera with manual exposure controls (see below for digital camera use). Note that most point-and-shoot cameras do *not* offer full manual exposure control. You may have to borrow or rent an older manual exposure 35mm camera, or perhaps a newer professional model featuring both automatic and manual controls.

Now find a scene of interest to photograph. Use the camera's internal light meter to figure the correct exposure for the scene. Note both the shutter speed and f/stop on a piece of paper. Take a picture using this exposure. Next, take three more pictures of the same scene by *increasing* your exposure in 1/3 stop increments (either open the lens aperture or lengthen the shutter speed). Also note these exposures on your paper.

Next, take three more pictures by *reducing* your exposure from the original metered settings in matching 1/3 stop increments. Note these exposures on paper, as well. This will give you a series of seven bracketed images of the scene, ranging from a full stop underexposure to a full stop overexposure, including the reference or "proper" exposure as per to your camera's meter.

Choose several more scenes, including one with strong backlighting, one of a bright subject on a dark background, and one of a dark subject on a light background, and repeat the same exercise above. Be sure to keep written notes on each exposure so you can match them up to the film after processing. (It is often helpful to ask your photo lab to *not* mount your slides, so you can accurately reference the sequence of images on a long strip of film.)

Once you have the film processed, compare the bracketed exposures and observe which of them is best for each situation. This will give you an idea of how your camera's meter performs under various lighting situations and will allow you to make whatever exposure compensation might be necessary for each in the future. Note that every camera's meter (even between identical camera brands and models) may be slightly different from others, as will different emulsions and brands of film. This is an exercise that you will likely want to repeat for every camera and film combination that you use regularly.

You may also want to repeat these exposure tests using an 18 percent gray card to meter your initial exposure, or to compare whether metering off the palm of your hand (remember that it will be about a full-stop lighter than an 18 percent gray card) will help produce consistent exposure results.

These same tests can also be done with a digital camera as long as the camera has manual exposure controls (remember that most automatic consumer digital cameras *don't* have manual exposure controls). Compare the resulting images on your computer screen. With most digital cameras, you will find it is better to slightly *under*expose an image. The same is true with slide or transparency film. However, with negative or print film, it is generally better to slightly *over*expose the image.

Finally, remember that most professional photographers bracket their exposures whenever possible, even though they use a variety of light meters to ensure they start out with good exposures. Bracketing not only provides exposure variations for each shot, but also provides backup images in case an original is accidentally lost or damaged.

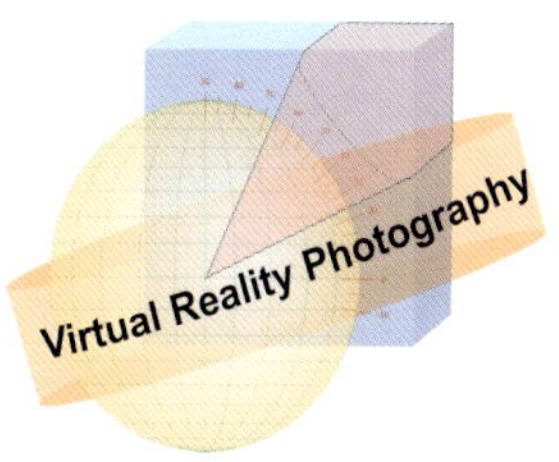

Chapter 4: Sharpness and Resolution

A common attribute of good photography is sharpness of an image. Photographers seem to search endlessly for sharpness, spending money on quality lenses, higher-resolution cameras, better films, and even larger format camera systems. Ansel Adams' landscape photography was renowned for its exquisite detail and sharpness. Similar image quality is the goal of many photographers. While unfocused foregrounds and backgrounds are often used to accentuate a subject, *improperly* focused pictures are generally the first ones to the trash when we edit.

If you show most people similar photographs of the same subject, they will generally choose the one with the sharpest focus as the better image. So it's little wonder that sharpness is a passion for most photographers.

Optical physics specifies that a lens can only focus one point (or distance plane) at a time, and therefore every photograph will only have one focus for subjects located precisely within that plane. The reality, however, is that our eyes do not require *perfect* focus of a scene in order to perceive it to be sharp. Acceptable focus is a matter of degree.

Depth of Field

The range of *acceptable* focus in front of and in back of the focus plane is often referred to as depth of field. It is based on a number of factors including aperture, relative subject-to-lens distances, magnification, and focal length.

Aperture

Perhaps the easiest way to control depth of field is through the use of aperture. Wide (large) apertures give less depth of field while narrow (small) apertures give greater depth of field. If you focus on a subject at a given distance, shooting at a wide aperture of f/1.4 will provide only a very limited range of acceptable or sharp focus. Shooting at a smaller aperture, such as f/16 or f/22, will increase that range of acceptable focus. Depth of field doubles as your *f-number* is halved. This means that an aperture of f/16 will give twice the depth of field as f/8 and four times that of f/4. (Note that this is a different relationship than the change in exposure, which doubles or halves with each *stop* of aperture.)

Remember that you can change your aperture while still keeping exposure constant by adjusting your shutter speed an equal amount in the opposite direction. If you decrease your aperture size by one stop, you can maintain the same exposure by extending your shutter speed by one stop. If a scene calls for an exposure of 1/250 sec. @ f/2, you can also shoot it at 1/125 sec. @ f/2.8, 1/60 sec. @ f/4, 1/2 sec. @ f/22 or any corresponding increments in between. By changing aperture, you can control the

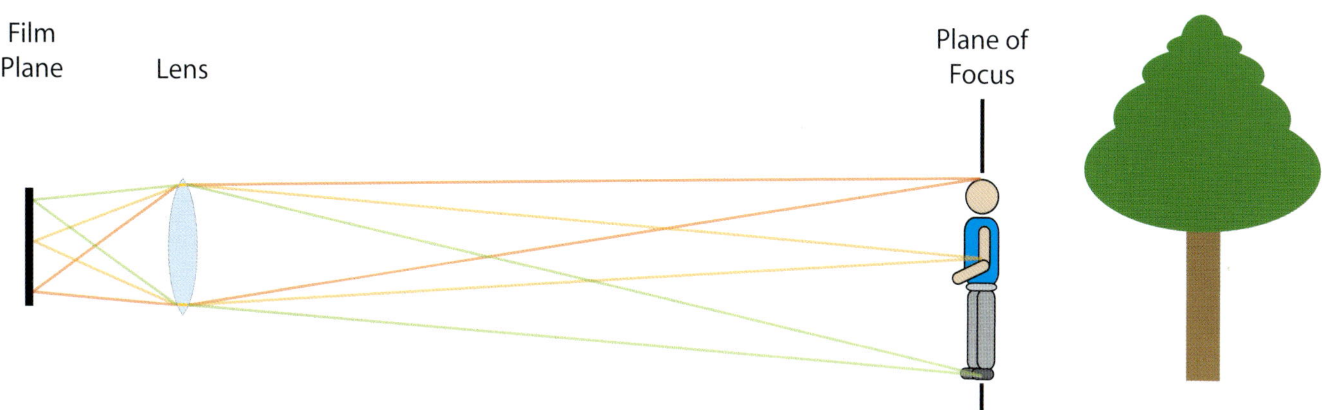

Fig. 4-1 Only a single plane or distance can be in perfect focus at any given time for a particular lens or lens system.

Technical Note: Circle of Confusion

Acceptable sharpness and focus are technically defined by a number of terms, the least understood of which is "circle of confusion." The concept behind a circle of confusion is that if a lens is perfectly focused on an infinitely small point of light, the image of that point projected onto the film plane would be of a minimum size. In reality however, when the subject light source is not located exactly at the plane of focus of the lens, its projected image will be a circle of light somewhat larger (or blurred) than the minimum. The more out of focus this projected circle is, the larger and less well-defined it will become.

Even though a subject may not be exactly at the focus distance, it can appear sharp in the final photo if the circle of confusion is small enough (i.e. if the subject is not *too* far out of focus). Acceptable focus in an image is defined in part by the size of the circle of confusion we are willing to accept. The smaller the size of this circle, the sharper (or closer to perfect focus) the subject must be.

Determining an acceptable image circle will depend upon many factors, including how much detail needs to be seen, the size of the original film image, how large the image will be reproduced or projected, and what the viewing distance will be. An image may appear sharp when enlarged to 5"x7" size, yet may appear too blurred when enlarged to poster size. Thus, the poster sized enlargement would require a smaller circle of confusion, while the smaller 5"x7" print could tolerate a larger one.

A common circle of confusion used by camera manufacturers for depth of field calculations in 35mm photography is about 1/1000 inch (0.0254 mm).

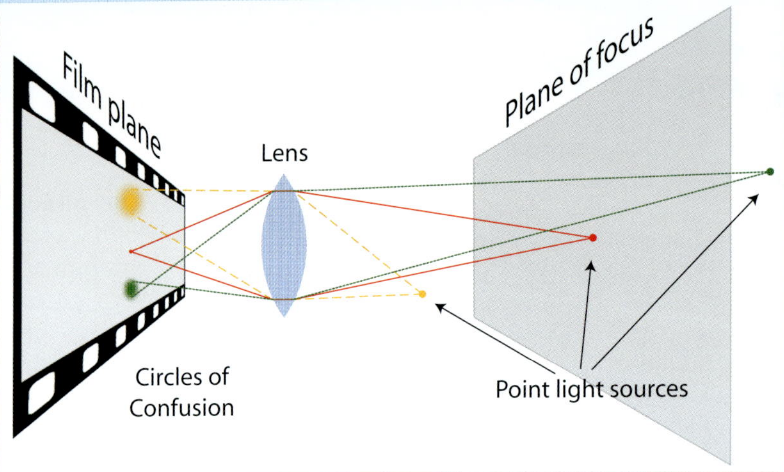

Fig. 4-2 Circle of Confusion size is used to determine "acceptable" focus.

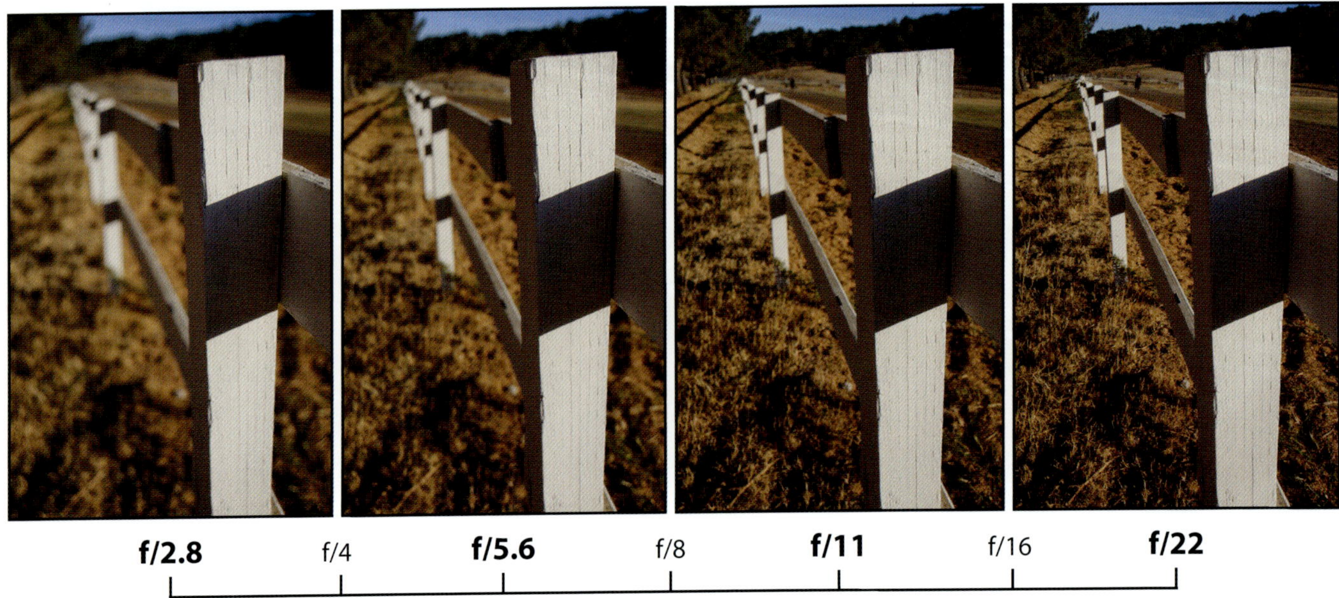

Fig. 4-3 Depth of field increases as aperture size is reduced.

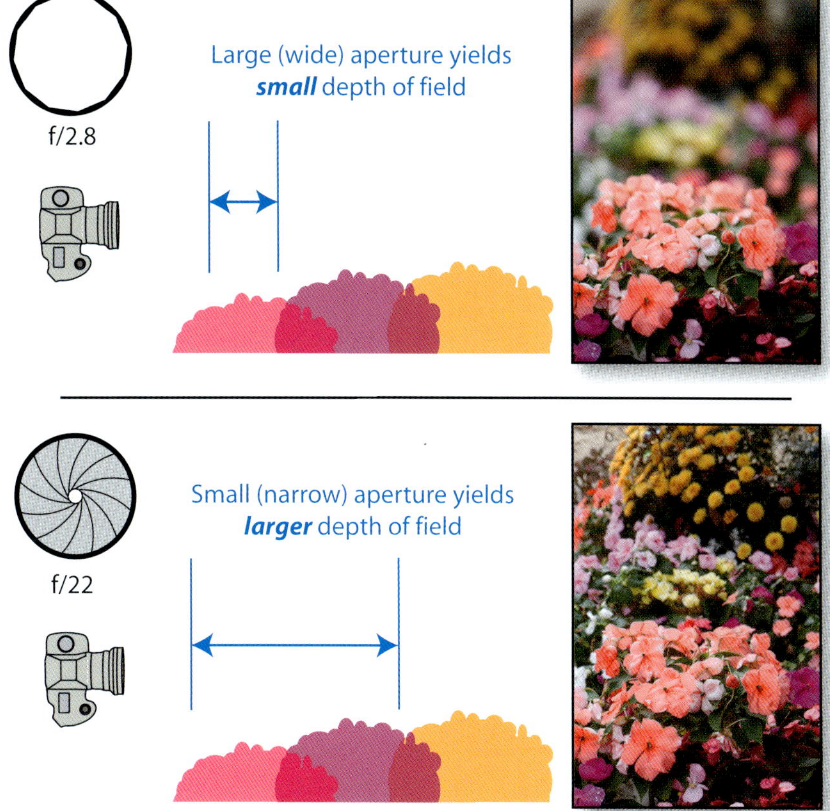

Fig. 4-4 Aperture size influences depth of field. Wider apertures provide less depth of field, while smaller (narrower) apertures provide more.

of acceptable focus) from 11 feet to 24 feet – a total of about 13 feet. However, that same lens (at the same aperture) focused at a subject 4 feet away, would only have a depth of field of about nine inches.

The closer the focus, the narrower the depth of field at a given aperture. Doubling your focus distance increases your depth of field by a factor of four, while halving your focus distance *reduces* depth of field by the same factor.

Magnification

Magnification of a subject within the camera is directly proportional to the subject distance, thus having the same effect on depth of field. If all other factors remain the same, such as the aperture and focal length, the closer the subject is to the lens, the greater its magnification in the camera – and the smaller the depth of field will be. This becomes particularly important in close up and macro photography, where objects are often photographed close to life size.

depth of field or the range of camera to subject distances that will be in acceptable focus.

Subject Distance

The closer a subject is to a given lens and the closer the focus, the smaller the depth of field will be, assuming the same aperture is used. When a subject is focused near the infinity setting on a lens, the depth of field may be many feet. However, if the photographer moves the camera in and focuses closer on the subject, the depth of field will decrease proportionally and may be reduced to a range of inches.

For example, a 50mm lens set at f/8 and focused on a subject 15 feet away will have a depth of field (or range

The greater the magnification of the subject on the camera sensor or film, the smaller the depth of field will be – assuming focal length and aperture remain constant. If you photograph an insect with a 105mm lens at f/11 at life size (a 1:1 ratio), the depth of field will be a small fraction of an inch. If you were to move farther away (and refocus) to decrease your magnification to half life size (1:2), your depth of field will double.

Focal Length

Choosing a lens with a longer focal length will significantly reduce depth of field at a given aperture and distance. When maximum depth of field is needed in a scene, a wide angle lens set at a small aperture will optimize the range of acceptable focus available. Doubling the focal

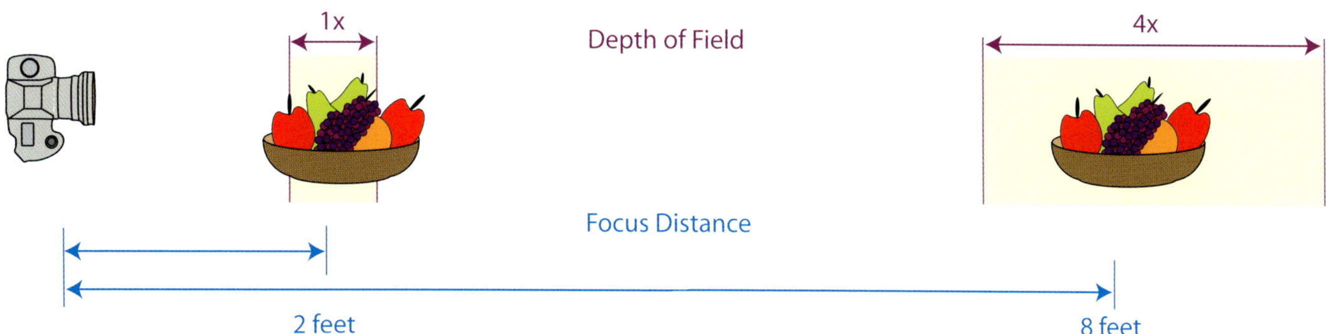

Fig. 4-5 Depth of field becomes smaller as the focus distance is reduced, for a given lens at a given aperture.

length reduces depth of field by a factor of four. If you shoot a scene with a 25mm lens at f/8, and you change to a 50mm lens (focused at the same distance with the same f/8 aperture), you reduce your depth of field to about a quarter of what it was with the 25mm lens.

Likewise, changing from a 50mm to a 200mm lens (four times the focal length) will reduce depth of field about 1/16 the range of the 50mm, assuming the same aperture and focus distance.

Depth of field is a tremendously complex matter, and most formulas for its calculation are simplified approximations. Even calculated depth of field tables published for specific lenses often provide only approximations. From a practical standpoint, formulas

Technical Note: Depth of Field Tables

Changing focal length changes depth of field by roughly an inverse square relationship, assuming that focus distance, aperture, and circle of confusion remain the same. Double the focal length and you get about 1/4 the depth of field. Triple the focal length, and you get about 1/9 the depth of field. Halve the focal length and you get about four times the depth of field.

Example:
Using calculated depth of field tables (which are themselves approximations), we can note depth of field specifications for given focal lengths, apertures, focus distances and circles of confusion. Choosing an aperture of f/8 on a 25mm lens focused at four feet, you will have a depth of field between 2'11" and 6'8" (or 45"). Maintaining all the same settings, but changing to a 50mm lens (doubling the focal length) reduces the depth of field to between 3'8" and 4'6" (10"), or about 1/4 of the depth of field provided by the 25mm lens.

If you wanted to get the same depth of field with the 50mm lens as you had with the 25mm @ f/8, you would need to close the aperture on the 50mm lens <u>four</u> stops to f/32. Remember that halving the f-number doubles the depth of field, so dividing the f-number by four (from f/8 to f/32) would quadruple the depth of field, and would give you back the depth of field you lost when you doubled your focal length.

25mm lens

Circle of Confusion	Aperture		
1/500 in.	f/2.8	f/4	f/5.6
1/710 in.	f/4	f/5.6	f/8
1/1000 in.	f/5.6	f/8	f/11
1/1420 in.	f/8	f/11	f/16
1/2000 in.	f/11	f/16	f/22
Hyperfocal dist.	14'	10'	7'

Focus distance		Extreme distances in acceptable focus		
3 feet	Near	2'6"	2'5"	2'3"
	Far	3'10"	4'4"	5'2"
3.5 feet	Near	2'10"	2'8"	2'6"
	Far	4'8"	5'5"	6'10"
4 feet	Near	3'2"	2'11"	2'8"
	Far	5'7"	6'8"	9'0"
4.5 feet	Near	3'6"	3'2"	2'11"
	Far	6'7"	8'3"	12'1"
5 feet	Near	3'9"	3'5"	3'1"
	Far	7'8"	10'1"	16'6"
5.5 feet	Near	4'1"	3'9"	3'3"
	Far	8'11"	12'4"	23'7"

50mm lens

Circle of Confusion	Aperture		
1/500 in.	f/2.8	f/4	f/5.6
1/710 in.	f/4	f/5.6	f/8
1/1000 in.	f/5.6	f/8	f/11
1/1420 in.	f/8	f/11	f/16
1/2000 in.	f/11	f/16	f/22
Hyperfocal dist.	58'	40'	29'

Focus distance		Extreme distances in acceptable focus		
3 feet	Near	2'10.4"	2'9.8"	2'9.0"
	Far	3'2.0"	3'2.9"	3'4.1"
3.5 feet	Near	3'3.8"	3'2.9"	3'1.9"
	Far	3'8.7"	3'10.0"	3'11.7"
4 feet	Near	3'9.1"	3'8.0"	3'7"
	Far	4'3.6"	4'5.3"	4'8"
4.5 feet	Near	4'2.4"	4'1"	3'11"
	Far	4'10.6"	5'0.8"	5'4"
5 feet	Near	4'7.5"	4'6"	4'4"
	Far	5'5.7"	5'9"	6'0"
5.5 feet	Near	5'1"	4'11"	4'8"
	Far	6'1"	6'4"	6'9"

Fig. 4-6 Depth of field table examples.

Technical Note: Depth of Field Preview

Most professional 35mm cameras have a depth of field preview button, which allows you to see the image in your viewfinder at the actual aperture the lens is set for. This lets you preview the depth of field that will be recorded at the shooting aperture, rather than at the lens' widest aperture (which provides the brightest viewfinder image). Single lens reflex cameras are designed to keep the aperture at its widest opening except when the shutter is actually exposing the film, in order to keep the viewfinder image as bright as possible. It is best to do your critical focusing *without* the preview button pressed so the viewfinder image is at its brightest, and then use the preview button to view the effect of your current aperture setting on depth of field before shooting.

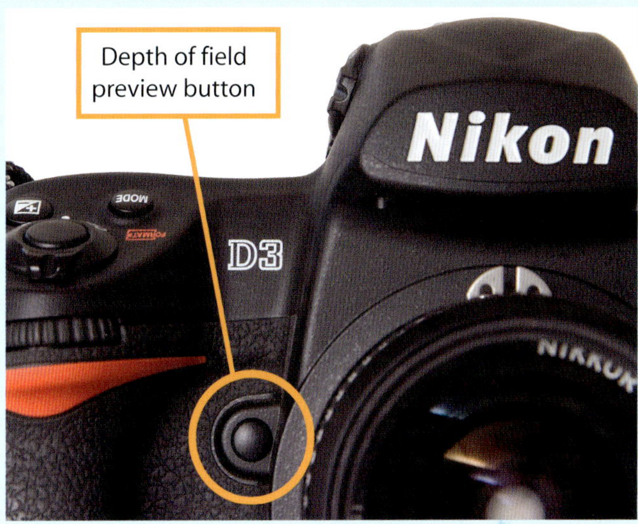

Fig. 4-7 Depth of field preview on a pro digital SLR.

and tables will get you close to what you might need, but in reality, what is deemed sharp or in "acceptable focus" is entirely subjective. The best way to determine what works for your own needs is to actually shoot photos and check your results.

Hyperfocal Distance

Use of hyperfocal distance is one of a photographer's best tools for maximizing depth of field. The concept should be learned by every photographer.

Hyperfocal distance is quite simply the focus setting of a lens (at a particular aperture) which is required to bring everything from infinity to a nearest point into acceptable focus. It is used commonly in landscape scenes shot with wide angle lenses, where the photographer wants to have everything in sharp focus from a prominent foreground to the mountains or skyline in the distance.

Hyperfocal distances are easily read from the scales found on the barrels of most quality lenses. Set the focus of the lens to infinity (∞) and read the hyperfocal distance opposite the index mark for the aperture you are using. Then change the focus setting of the lens to this hyperfocal distance, and you will maximize your total area of focus to range from infinity down to about half the hyperfocal distance.

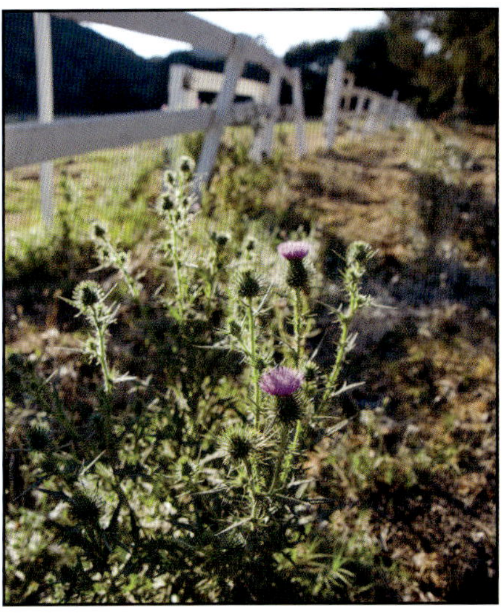
Near focus

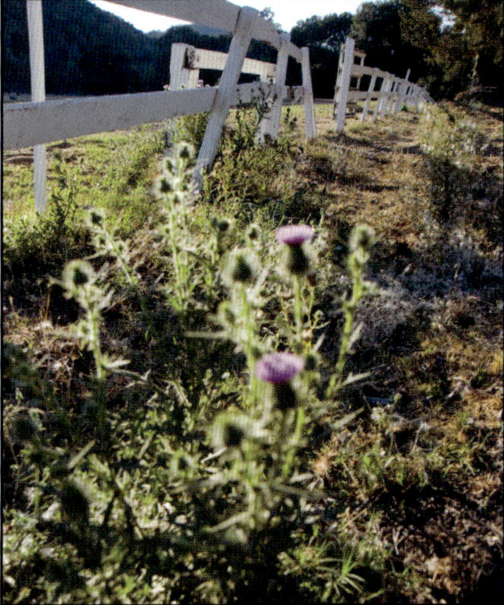
Distant focus

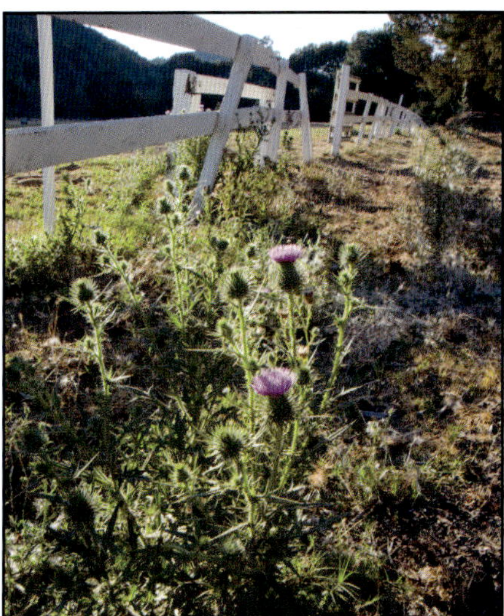
Hyperfocal

Fig. 4-8 Hyperfocal distance focusing comparison. Images were photographed with a 24mm lens.

Technical Note: Hyperfocal Distances and Depth of Field

For most photography, the use of the engraved depth of field indexes on a lens is sufficient for optimizing focus. However, there may be rare occasions when one wants to actually *calculate* hyperfocal distance and depth of field.

The formulas are as follows:

> **Hyperfocal distance = Focal length^2 / (aperture * circle of confusion diameter)**
>
> **Limit of near focus = (Hyperfocal distance * lens focus) / (Hyperfocal distance + lens focus)**
>
> **Limit of far focus = (Hyperfocal distance * lens focus) / (Hyperfocal distance – lens focus)**

These formulas are reasonably accurate for most focusing distances, but do not apply to close up or macro photography. When used for wide angle and normal lenses, calculated distances greater than 30 or 40 feet can be considered infinity focus.

In general, increased depth of field from reducing aperture size is generally gained by about 1/3 in front of the focus point and 2/3 in back. This means that if closing your aperture from f/11 to f/16 gains you 18 inches additional depth of field, you will gain about 6 inches of acceptable sharpness in front of your subject (closer to your camera) and about 12 inches behind it. However, keep in mind that this is only a rule of thumb, and applies to normal focusing distances. As you move into the close up focusing range, depth of field tends to be distributed more equally in front and in back of the focus point.

The concept of hyperfocal focusing can also be used even when there is no need to include distant (infinity) subjects in focus. For example, if your desired subjects only require acceptable focus between 2 feet and 6 feet, you can still use the same method for setting focus on your lens. Simply read the depth of field limits between the proper aperture indexes while focusing the lens at other distances.

These indexes will give you a reasonable idea of the near and far focus limits at any aperture and focus distance. If you want to err on the side of caution, simply close your lens aperture one or more f/stop beyond the index you are using. Remember also to take advantage of your depth of field preview button, when available, to help visually determine how sharp your image will be before shooting.

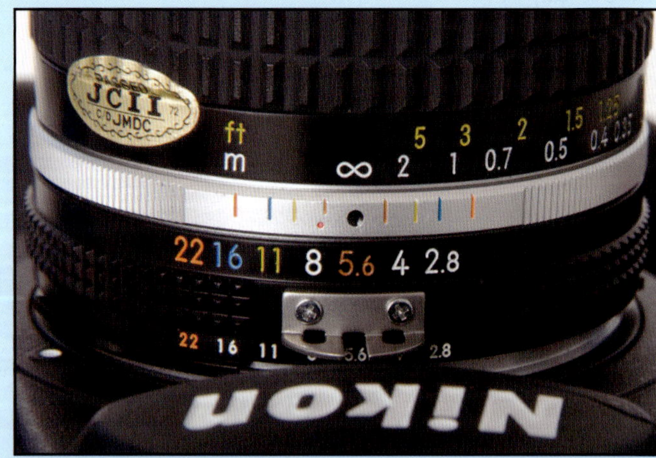

24mm lens @ f/5.6 – focused at infinity (not hyperfocal)

Hyperfocal distance focusing

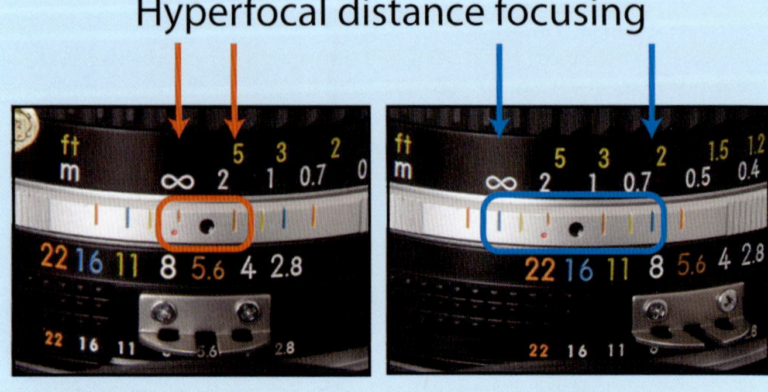

f/5.6 hyperfocal focus   **f/16** hyperfocal focus

Fig. 4-9 Using lens barrel markings for hyperfocal distance.

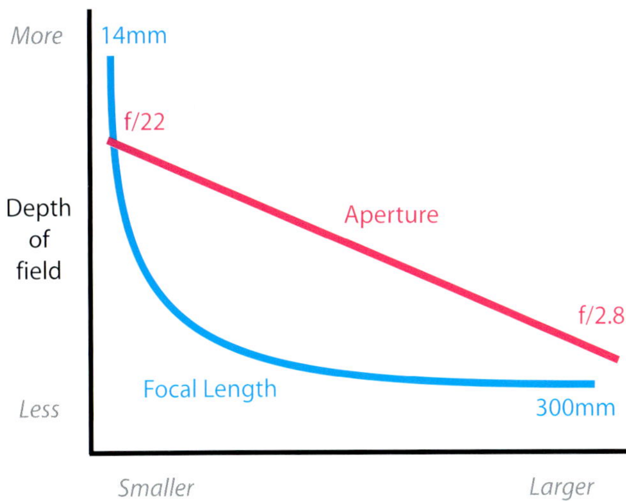

Fig. 4-10 Aperture and focal length affect depth of field.

Using a 24mm lens (see Fig. 4-9) at an aperture of f/5.6, we can read the hyperfocal distance across from the f/5.6 index to be about 10 feet. Changing the focus of the lens to that hyperfocal distance (10 feet), we can now read that zone of acceptably sharp focus from infinity down to about 6 feet.

If we reduce the aperture to f/16, we significantly increase our depth of field. When the lens is focused at infinity, the hyperfocal distance is indicated to be about 4 feet. Changing our focus to the hyperfocal distance of 4 feet now gives us acceptable focus from infinity down to about 2-1/2 feet.

It is important to note that many lens manufacturers determine their hyperfocal indexes based upon maximum image enlargement up to about 8"x10" size. This often is not good enough for professional photographers who may be planning wall-sized prints or anticipating double page spreads in a magazine layout. When sharp focus is critical, photographers will probably want to use hyperfocal settings one or more f/stops wider than the aperture which they are actually shooting. For instance, if you really need the focus range of an f/16 aperture, you might want to stop down to f/22. Alternately, use the f/11 hyperfocal distance for your focus setting if shooting at f/16. Remember to adjust your shutter speed if you change aperture in order to maintain proper exposure.

Some lenses, particularly auto focus zooms and those on consumer point-and-shoot cameras, do not include hyperfocal markings. Many non-professional cameras also do not have depth of field preview capability. These systems are not designed for critical focus and should probably not be used where precise control is necessary. However, with *any* lens, you can maximize your range of sharp focus by remembering that the smaller your aperture, the greater your depth of field will be.

Wide angle lenses used at very small apertures give the most depth of field, while telephoto lenses at large (wide) apertures give the least. On the other hand, when you want to visually isolate a well-focused subject between out-of-focus foreground and background (narrow depth of field), a longer lens set at a wide aperture is a good choice.

Shutter Speeds

Movement of either camera or subject during an exposure can cause blurring of an image, depending upon the severity of that movement relative to the length of the exposure. A fast shutter speed tends to "freeze" movement, while slow shutter speeds record motion as a blur.

It is almost impossible to hold a camera perfectly still in your hands as you shoot a picture. Therefore, it is important when photographing with a hand held camera (as opposed to having it on a tripod or other stable mount), to use a fast enough shutter speed so that the effects of the slight camera movements are minimized. A

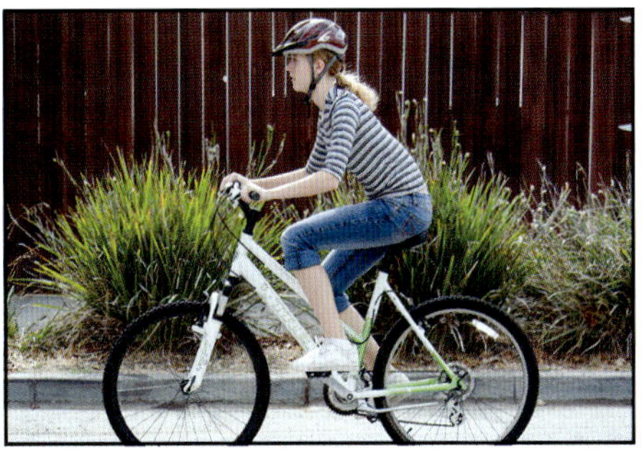
Fast shutter speed freezes everything

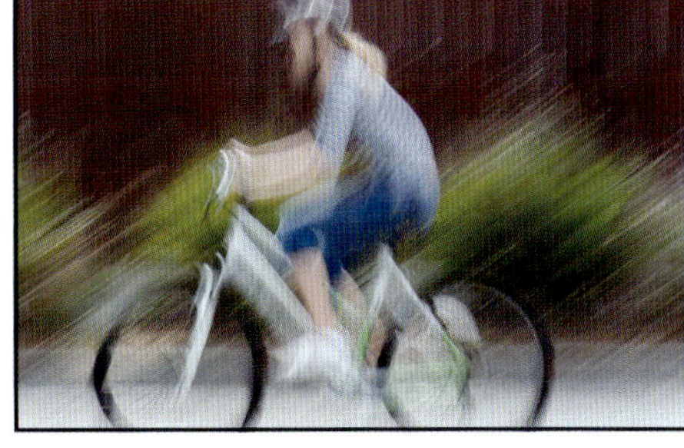
Slow shutter speed blurs everything

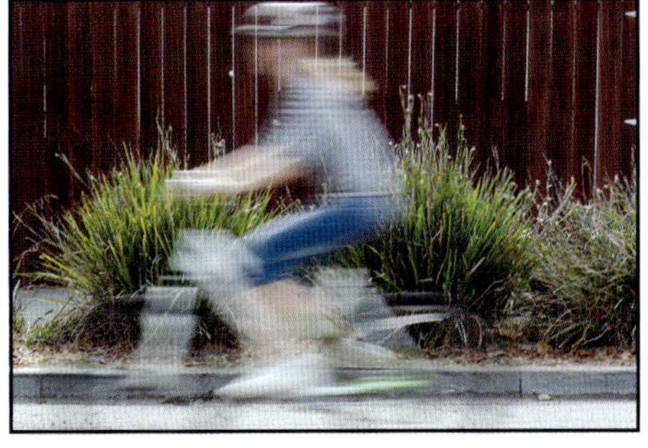
Slow shutter speed, camera on tripod

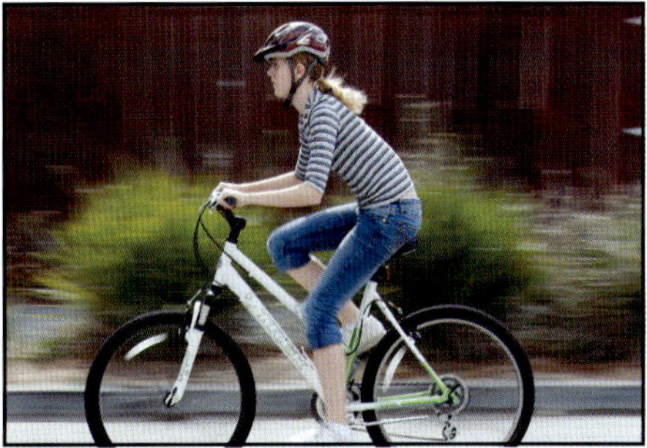
Slow shutter speed, panning with subject

Fig. 4-11 Sharpness is also influenced by camera movement and shutter speed.

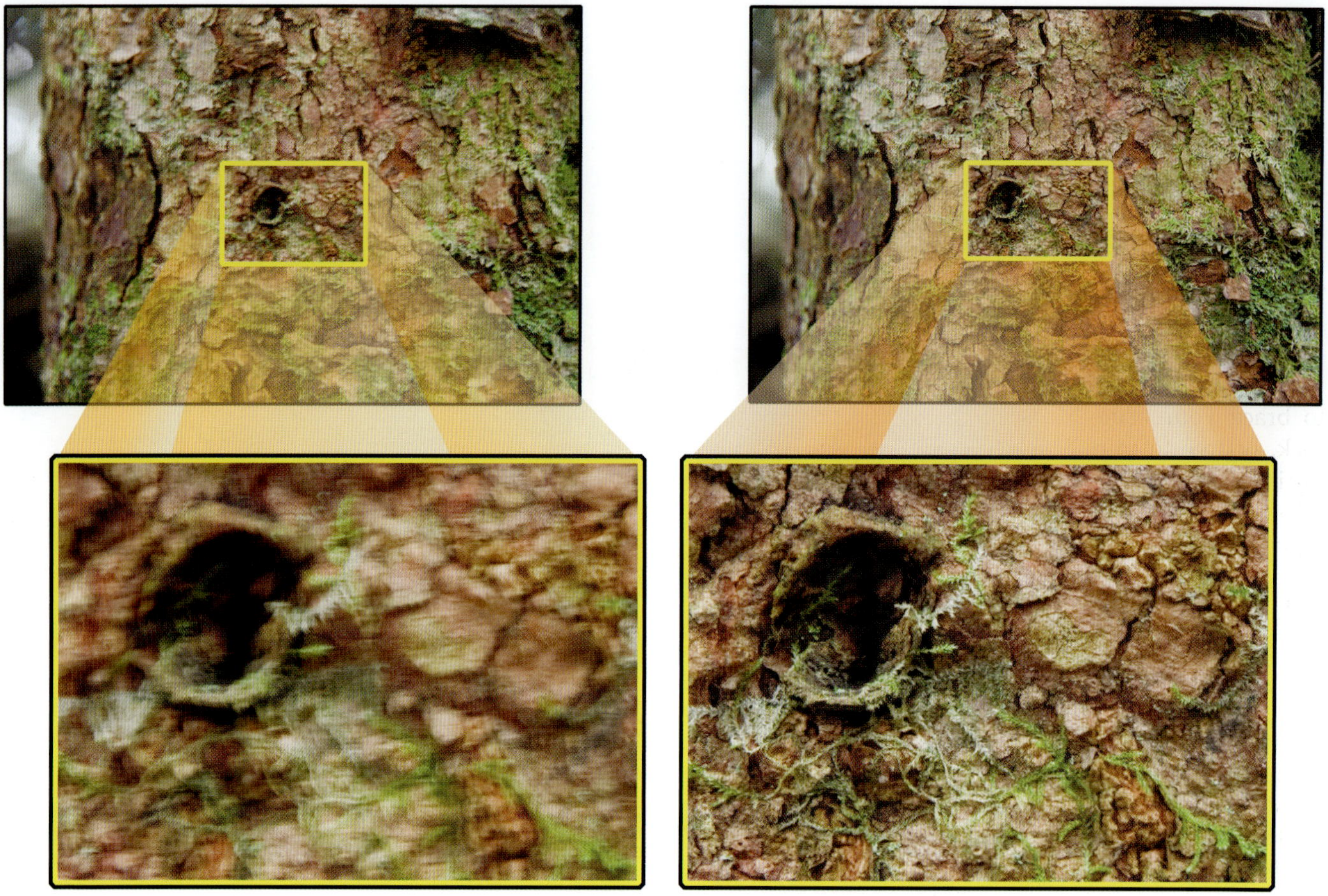

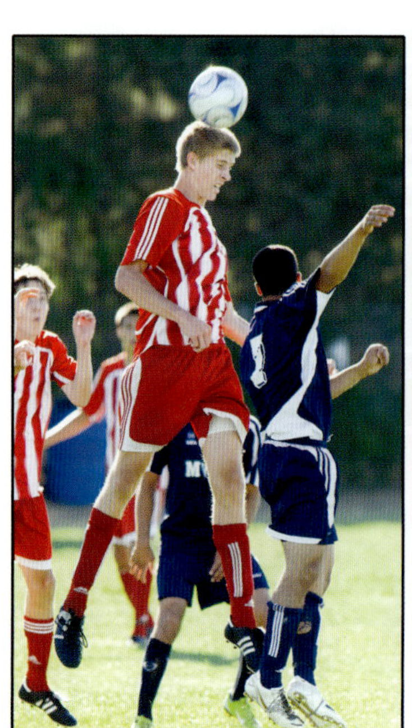

Hand held

Tripod used

Fig. 4-12 Enlarged details can show the difference in sharpness between hand-held and tripod mounted camera exposures.

fast shutter speed provides a shorter period for the image to be exposed, and therefore will reduce the motion recorded during the exposure.

The rule of thumb for hand held exposures is to use a shutter speed that is no slower than 1/focal length of the lens you are using.

For example, if you are using a 28mm lens, your minimum hand held shutter speed would be 1/30 second (1/28 rounded to the closest shutter speed). For a 50mm lens, you would want to use 1/60 sec. or faster. For a 14mm or 15mm lens, 1/15 sec. would be acceptable, while a 200mm lens would demand a minimum speed of 1/250 sec. Keep in mind that this rule of thumb is only in regard to minimizing the effects of hand held camera movement, *not* motion of the subject.

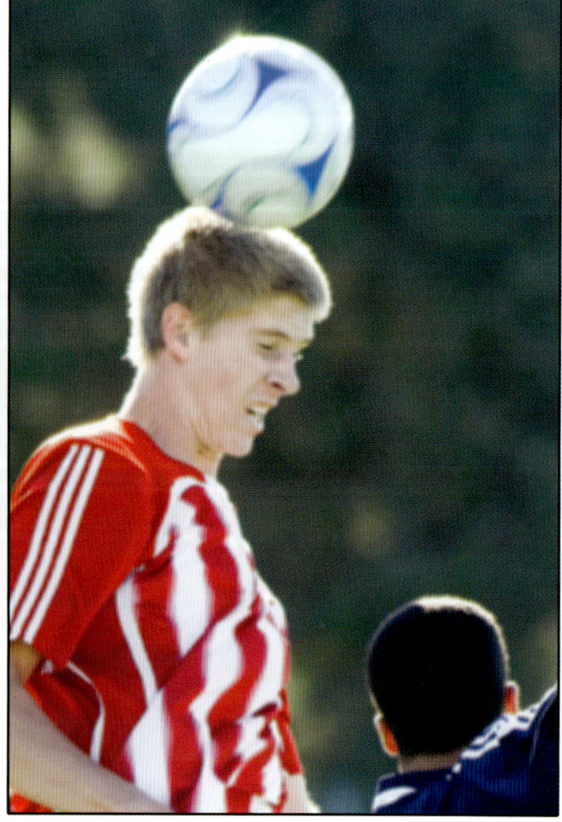

Fig. 4-13 A lack of sharpness may not be noticeable at a small reproduction size, but becomes more obvious when the image is enlarged.

As focal length is increased, magnification of both subject and camera movements are increased. Thus, the longer the lens, the higher the minimum hand held shutter speed must be.

Remember that this is only a rule of thumb, rather than a guarantee. If you are shooting from the back of a truck driving over a bumpy road, a 1/focal length shutter speed may be insufficient because of the increased movement of your camera. Other times, you may be able to brace your camera against a door jamb, rock, or tree to minimize camera movement during an exposure. You might also be able to stabilize it in front of you with your elbows on your knees if you're in a sitting position.

Sometimes, particularly in low light situations, you just have to do the best you can and live with the results. However, the most effective way to eliminate camera movement is to mount the camera on a tripod or other stable support while shooting. This is not always practical, depending upon your shooting situation or subject, but should be done whenever possible, particularly for VR photography.

Understand also that camera movement and slow shutter speeds can be used to your creative advantage. A fast shutter speed may freeze the action of a bicyclist riding

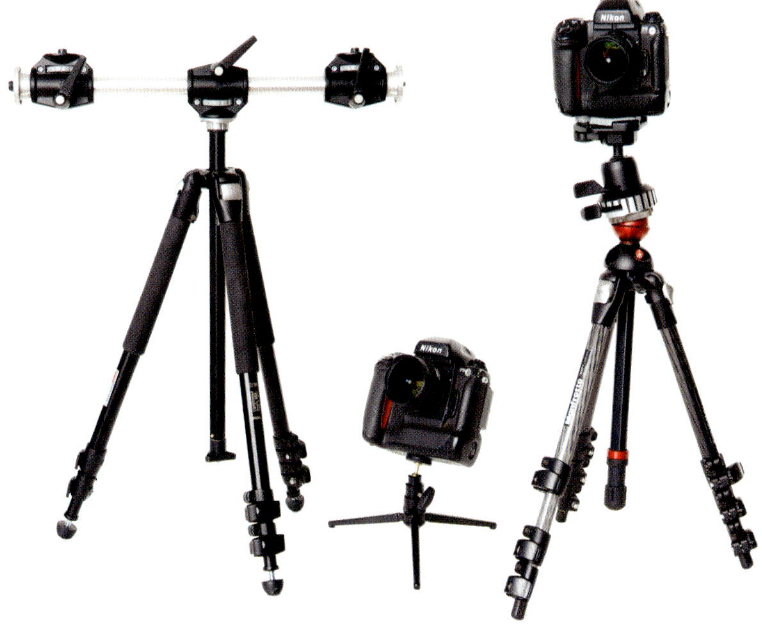

Fig. 4-14 Tripods are available in a wide variety of sizes and styles such as these from Manfrotto.

by. However, a slow shutter speed and panning with the rider as she goes by can result in a sharp image of the rider with a motion-blurred background. (See Fig. 4–11)

Experiment with these kinds of effects, and learn to use shutter speeds for your creative advantage, while also getting an idea of what your own limits and standards are for controlling sharpness. Remember that "acceptable"

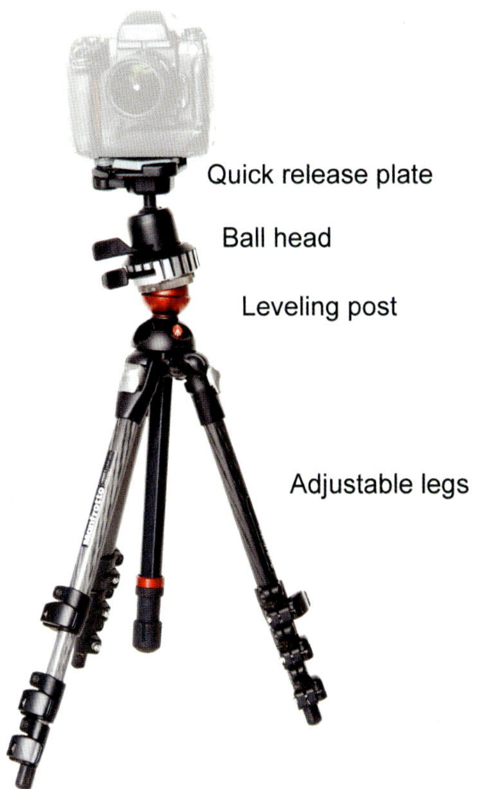

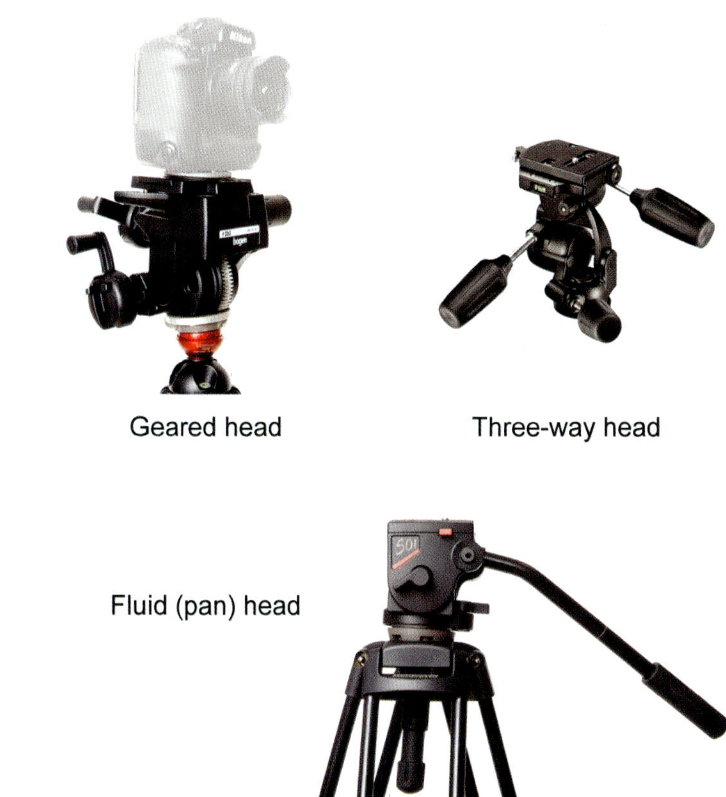

Fig. 4-15 Tripod parts and various tripod head designs. Different heads are intended for different camera weights and uses.

sharpness is dependent on how large your image will be reproduced. A slightly soft image may look fine at thumbnail size, yet may not appear at all focused when blown up onto a large screen or as an 11"x14" print.

Tripods & Camera Supports
The most effective tool for stabilizing any camera is a tripod. Photographers who seek the sharpest images know that use of a tripod is often the only way to achieve them.

Tripods allow you to position your camera and shoot tack sharp photos at shutter speeds of minutes or even hours, rather than small fractions of seconds. A good tripod is an invaluable tool. No photographer should be without one.

They are, however, not always convenient. Tripods can be cumbersome and heavy (although they are available in many sizes and weights), and setting one up generally slows down the sometimes fast-paced process of photography. This can also be a good thing though, as the process can help photographers more carefully consider their compositions, subjects, perspectives, and exposures, rather than simply settling for quick snapshots. The combination of tripod use, depth of field understanding, and focus controls are the keys to consistent image sharpness in photography.

Tripod use is essential for successful VR photography, where precise camera alignment and the sequencing of multiple images provide for the best imagery. A good tripod should be the first accessory every photographer adds after their first camera purchase, and he or she should quickly get into the habit of using it as often as possible.

Tripods are usually constructed with two main elements – a set of three legs and a head, which is the mechanism allowing for position adjustments of the camera without moving the supporting legs. The three legs are independently adjustable in height and angle, so that the tripod can provide level support on uneven surfaces. Tripod heads come in a variety of designs, ranging from geared three-axis models (heavy & relatively expensive) to simple, but effective ball-type heads.

There are other camera supports that photographers can use to stabilize their cameras when shooting to aid image sharpness.

Monopods are one-legged versions of tripods, used most often for extremely long telephoto lenses. These lenses are generally big and heavy, and rather difficult to hand hold. A monopod on a long lens serves as a support column to rest the camera and lens on while shooting. It is nowhere near as solid as a tripod, but can provide a critical difference in image sharpness at most shutter speeds, particularly those near the 1/focal length setting. Monopods are also easier to carry than tripods, and are often acceptable in situations where tripods are not (such as on crowded sports sidelines, or in museums where tripods may be forbidden). Some photographers have been known to utilize canes and walking sticks with screw threads attached as monopods, providing themselves with camera supports where such are normally prohibited.

There are also tremendous numbers of grip mechanisms designed for securing both cameras and lighting equipment in unusual positions. Some of these are commercially made while others are custom pieces – often built from parts available at the corner hardware store and put together by photographers to solve particular problems. Grip equipment from the motion picture and television industry feature a tremendous array of such products, albeit at fairly steep prices sometimes.

One other specialty camera support worth mentioning is a gyroscopic stabilizer. These units consist of a sealed casing a few inches long containing two high–speed weighted gyroscopes aligned on perpendicular axes. The unit connects to the underside of a camera via the tripod thread and is wired to an external battery pack. When the gyros are spinning, their inertia helps dampen sudden camera movements (in pan and tilt

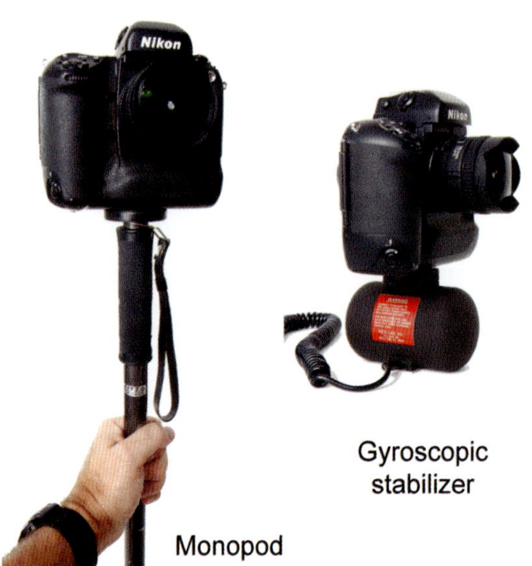

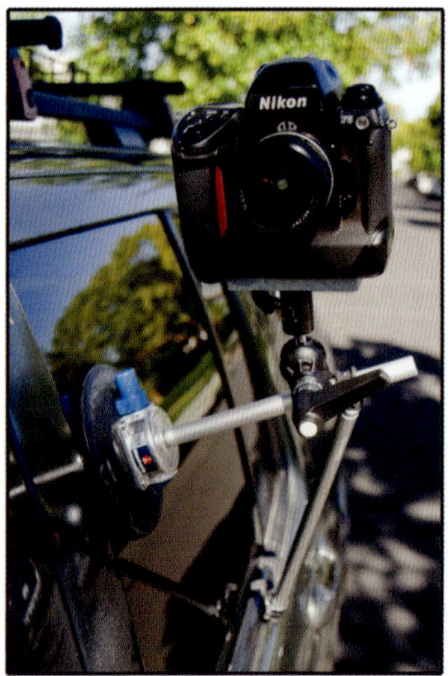

Fig. 4-16 A variety of supports can help stabilize cameras and improve sharpness.

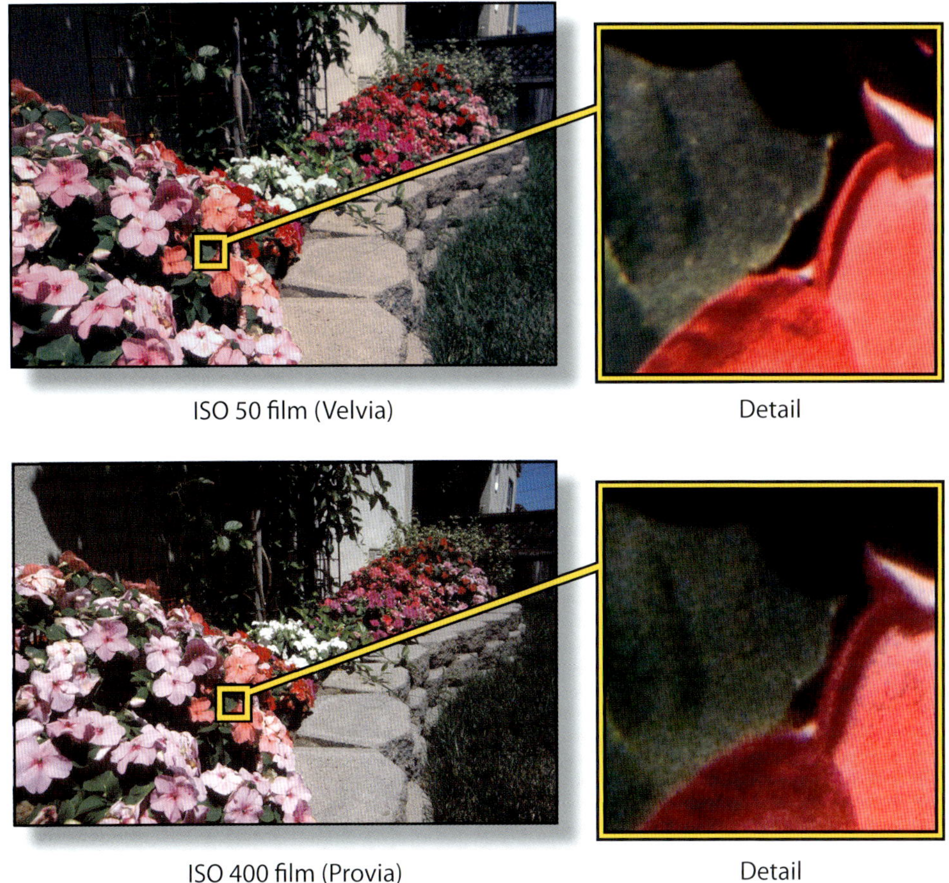

ISO 50 film (Velvia)

Detail

ISO 400 film (Provia)

Detail

Fig. 4-17 Films with lower ISO (light sensitivity) generally have finer grain patterns and can usually resolve finer details than higher ISO films.

can identify the maximum resolving power of the film, sensor, or lens being tested.

The higher the resolution, the more detail you can see and – at least in theory – the sharper the images recorded by it will be.

In film, light patterns are recorded by the tiny silver halide particles that make up the light sensitive emulsion. When the film is developed, the light patterns exposed on the emulsion are revealed and fixed. The smaller these silver particles are, the finer the resolution and detail that can be recorded.

Likewise, digital sensors are made up of tiny electrodes, also known as photosites or more commonly, pixels. The smaller these pixels – and the more of them that are squeezed into the total area of the imaging sensor, the finer the resolution that can be recorded.

directions), thereby stabilizing hand held cameras for use at slower shutter speeds. Gyros are precision instruments costing several thousand dollars, although they can be worth every penny to photographers shooting from aircraft or boats where tripods and monopods may be useless. Gyroscopic stabilization can allow for hand held shooting in rough or bumpy conditions at shutter speeds well below the 1/focal length rule.

Resolution and Grain

One of the subjective measures of image sharpness is how close a viewer can get to the picture, or how big it can be enlarged to see more detail. Resolution is a way to objectively determine the limits of sharpness in this manner.

Every photograph, whether recorded digitally or on film, has a limit to the smallest sized detail it can display. Much of this has to do with the circle of confusion diameter, but it also involves the ability of the film or digital sensor to discern detail.

Lenses and films are tested by their manufacturers using resolution charts and precision optical systems. These charts consist of a series of decreasing sized line pairs. Examining the resulting images at high magnification

However, as with most everything in photography, there are tradeoffs. The smaller the silver halide particles in film are, the less sensitive to light they are and thus, the more light the film needs to be exposed properly. The larger the particles, the more sensitive to light the film will be, but the lower the resolution and detail will be.

Thus, slow films with ISO speeds of 25 to 100, will generally have the highest resolution and potential for sharpness, while faster films, such as those with ISO speeds of 400, 800, and more, will have lower resolving power, but will require less light for proper exposure.

The sensitivities of digital sensors are similar, in that the larger the pixels on the sensor, the higher their sensitivity to light, but the less detail they can resolve. Conversely, the smaller the pixels on the sensor, the less sensitive they are to light, yet the higher the resolution and potential for recording detail will be. Most digital cameras can perform significant post processing of their images, so many digital adjustments affecting relative light sensitivity can be made on the fly as the camera's digital files are being recorded.

There are a variety of other factors that can influence both actual and perceived image sharpness in photography.

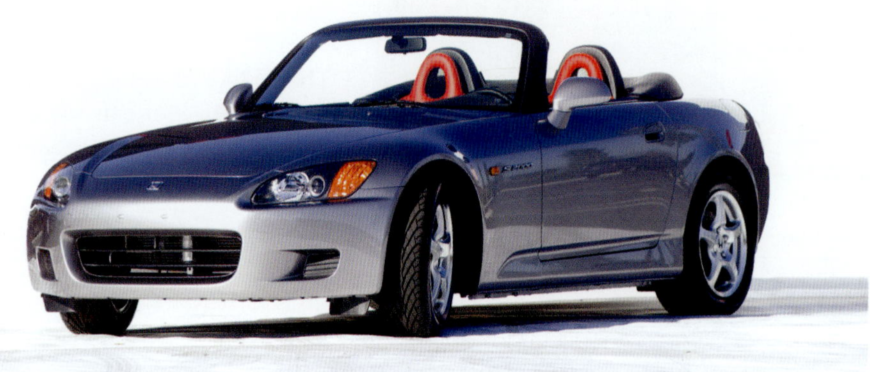

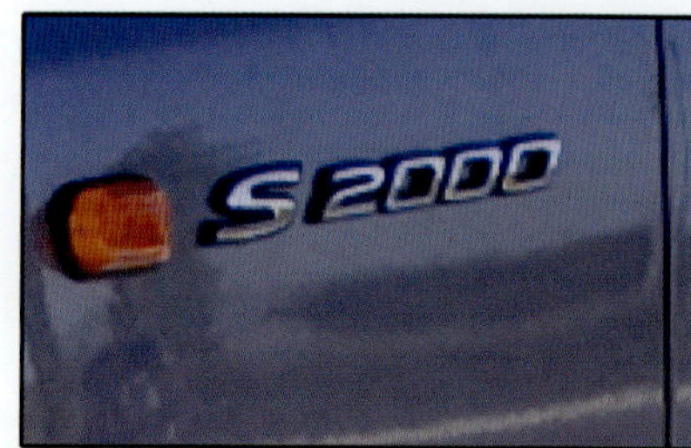

Detail

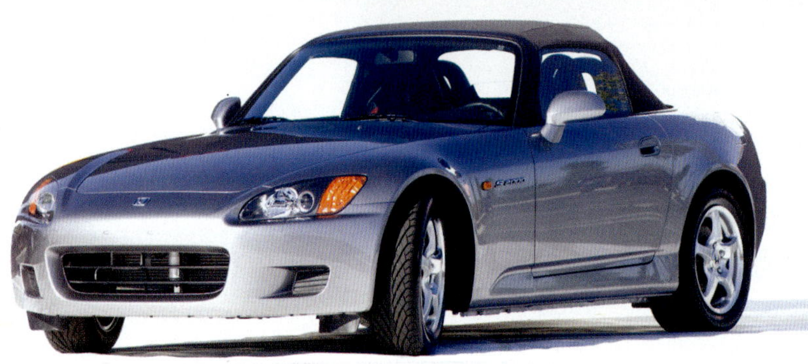

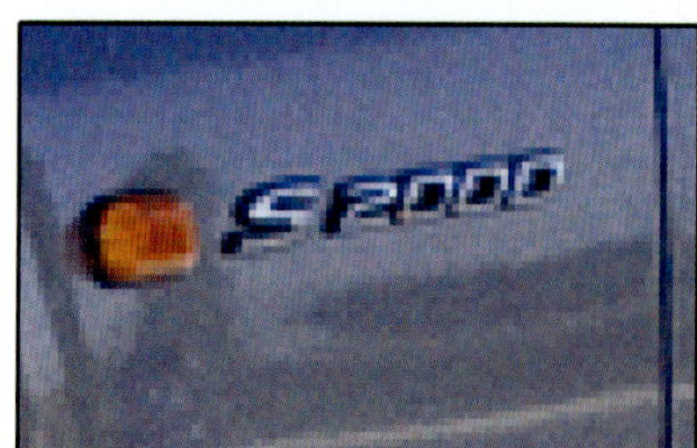

Detail

Fig. 4-18 Resolution comparison between digital camera sensors. Lower resolution provides less image detail.

Lens Quality

In general, you get what you pay for when you buy a lens. The quality of the optical glass, the alignment of the individual elements, and the combination of precision and ruggedness are all factors that affect lens cost.

Although the overall quality of photographic lenses today is far superior to what it was in years past, off-brand (cheaper) lenses will generally have more flaws and aberrations than the more expensive brand name optics. For the average consumer or photo hobbyist, these differences may be barely noticeable. But for those more concerned about image quality and sharpness, a low-cost lens may wind up being more expensive in the long run, when post production "correction" time is factored in, along with the potential cost of reshooting images or returning to locations where the results did not meet the quality needs of a client.

It is very tempting to buy a $250 off-brand lens instead of a seemingly identical $800 brand name lens. Just remember that there are good reasons why one is priced so low and the other so high. Before committing to a purchase, see if you can actually test the lens on your own camera under the shooting conditions you expect to need it. Look closely at the results. Note whether there is color fringing in contrasting areas, whether focus is sharp from center to edges of the frame (at all apertures), whether there are significant exposure differences between the center and edge, and whether the image is distorted in any way (look at straight lines throughout the image to see if they bow or curve).

Dirt and Dust

Even buying the best lenses however, doesn't guarantee sharp images, particularly if the elements of the lens are not kept clean. A layer of dust or fingerprints on the glass of a lens will give a soft look to your images.

Simply having your camera in a smoke-filled room for an hour or so can result in a thin layer of residue on the lens glass. This will produce a slight fogging effect and reduce contrast in your images. A similar problem is encountered when bringing a cold camera into a warm room, where condensation collects on the exposed cold surfaces. This can also happen when bringing the camera from an air conditioned car into outdoor heat and humidity. Give your equipment time to warm up before removing lens caps in these situations, and keep your lenses as clean as possible.

Technical Note: Resolution and Resolving Power

From a technical perspective, resolution and resolving power are measured by the ability to distinguish elements of detail in an image. This ability is affected not only by the quality of the lens and optics used, but by both the size of the light sensitive elements (silver halide crystals in film, or pixels in digital media) *and* the contrast in the subject detail. Resolving power is usually measured in lines per millimeter (lpm).

Higher contrast in the subject's fine detail generally increases a film's apparent ability to resolve that detail. If a test target composed of a series of dark gray lines on a black background is used, a film may only be able to resolve those lines down to a given limit. However, if there is greater contrast between the lines and the background, such as white on black or highly contrasting colors, the film's ability to resolve the details will appear to increase. In lab tests, the resolving power of a chosen film using a high contrast test target can be two to three times higher than when an identically designed low contrast target is used.

It is important to remember that image resolution and perceived sharpness of the image are not necessarily the same, even though they are related. A slightly out of focus, yet contrasty image may appear to our eyes to be "sharper" than a crisply focused, low contrast image, even though the latter is, in reality, the sharper of the two.

Image resolution can also be a factor of the overall size of the film format or the digital image sensor. This is perhaps easiest to illustrate using the symmetrical pixel patterns of a digital image sensor.

If you have a sensor that is 1mm x 1.5mm in size and has a resolution of eight pixels per mm, you will get a total of 96 pixels (8x12). This is illustrated in Fig. 4–19. If you select a lens that will project a particular image into this area, you will only have those 96 pixels to resolve the detail of that subject. However, if you double the dimensions of the image sensor to 2mm x 3mm while keeping the eight pixels per mm resolution, you quadruple the imaging area to 384 pixels (16x24). If you change your lens focal length so that the same subject is projected onto the larger image area, you wind up with a 4x increase in resolution. You could also get the same result by using an image sensor with twice the resolution (16 pixels per mm) at the original 1mm x 1.5mm size and keeping the same focal length of your lens.

This is one of the factors in choosing which camera format you will use for your photography, and why you need to know both the size of an image sensor as well as its total resolution when choosing a digital camera.

Most photographers today are familiar with the 35mm film format, and most professionals have a system of lenses and accessories for whichever

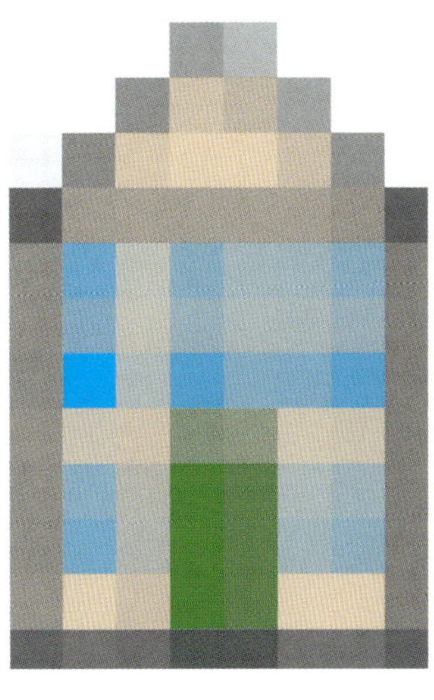

8 x 12 pixels

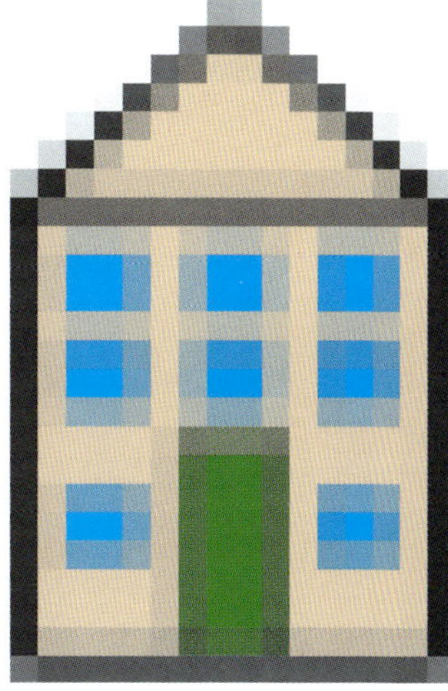

16 x 24 pixels

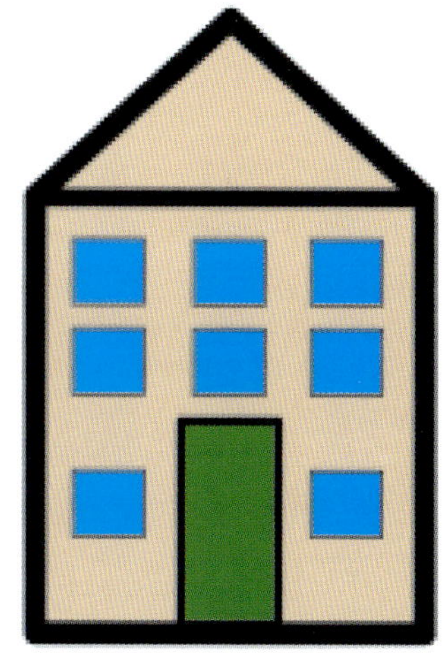

96 x 144 pixels

Fig. 4-19 The ability to distinguish detail in an image is a factor of the image resolution or pixel density.

brand of 35mm camera(s) they own. This is the format standard by which most others are judged in terms of ability to render detail, sharpness and image resolution.

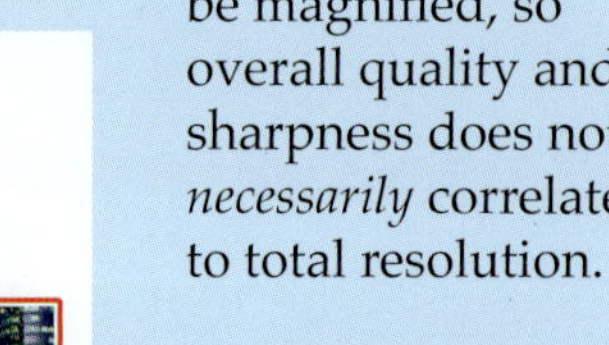

Fig. 4-20 Sizes of digital camera sensor relative to standard 35mm film format.

Smaller digital sensors are easier and cheaper to manufacture than larger ones, and it is possible to squeeze more (and smaller) pixel elements into them than for most larger sensors. However, a smaller sensor or film format requires shorter focal length lenses in order to provide the same image coverage or field of view as a larger format camera. This is why most consumer digital cameras, with their very small sensors, have permanent (non-interchangeable) zoom lenses. One of the problems with the small format, even though it *might* have a higher total number of pixels, is that any aberrations or flaws in the lens optics will be magnified, so overall quality and sharpness does not *necessarily* correlate to total resolution.

On the other hand, larger camera formats and lenses are more expensive, requiring precision manufacture of larger optical and mechanical elements, as well as smaller tolerances in the production of their digital sensors. While they are generally capable of producing better quality images, they also have the drawback of higher image magnification with its consequent reduction in depth of field when shooting.

As with most things in photography, there are always tradeoffs.

Remember to use only a drop or two of cleaning solution when cleaning a lens, and use only photo lens tissue or micro fiber cloths. A clean, soft handkerchief can be used in an emergency, but never use facial tissues, toilet paper, paper towels, or a corner of your shirt to clean the optical surfaces of a lens. These can all leave irreparable scratches. Also, use no more than a drop or two of lens solution when cleaning a lens, and be sure to put the solution on the tissue or cloth first, not directly on the lens. Be gentle. Cleaning too hard will damage the anti reflective coating on a lens, causing unwanted flare and potential color shifts.

Filters

Many photographers will keep a clear skylight or haze filter attached to the front of their lenses to help protect the front glass element from damage. While this is generally a good idea, keep in mind that a filter adds yet another optical element to a lens, and should be of good quality. That expensive lens you bought in pursuit of the best quality imagery is quickly degraded when you put a cheap filter in front of it. Remember also to keep your filters clean, and to replace them when they get scratched or damaged.

Shooting through a glass or plastic window will degrade the quality of an image, both in sharpness and in color.   Opening the window or moving it out of the way will generally produce sharper images with more accurate color. While this may not always be practical, such as inside an airplane or boat, you can

Fig. 4-21 Atmospheric conditions, particularly over longer distances, can reduce sharpness.

often find a better position that gives a less obstructed view if you look around a bit. Window glass also reflects the camera and photographer – something which we rarely notice while looking through the viewfinder, but which becomes a serious distraction when we see the resulting images.

Atmospheric Conditions

Fog and haze between camera and subject will reduce both the contrast and sharpness of an image. This is not only a concern in outdoor situations, but in indoor locations where rooms are smoky or steamy. Extreme temperatures and temperature changes cause visual disturbances in the air which can be detrimental to image sharpness (think of how heat forms mirages in the desert).

Atmospheric conditions are more pronounced over large distances. The more air between your camera and your subject, the less image clarity you'll generally have. To minimize the effects of haze and smoke, avoid using telephoto lenses from long distances, and instead, move in closer to your subject using a shorter lens if you can. The less smoke or haze you shoot through, the clearer your images will be.

Digital Sharpening

Most of today's photo editing software programs offer an ability to "sharpen" images digitally. This leads to the question, "why be concerned about sharpness and resolution in camera if I can always 'fix' the focus of my images digitally later on?"

The fact is that digital sharpening is limited in what it can do. It will not allow you to add detail that is not already there, and it won't make images that are poorly focused truly sharp. It is best suited for improving good images and making marginally focused images somewhat more acceptable.

Digital sharpening (such as with "sharpen" and "unsharp mask" filters in Photoshop) does not really sharpen an image at all. Rather, it increases the contrast (at the pixel level) on the edges between different colors in a photograph, giving an appearance of increased sharpness through increased contrast. While this can, in a limited way, improve the perceived sharpness of an image, it does not actually improve detail and is a poor substitute for a properly focused original.

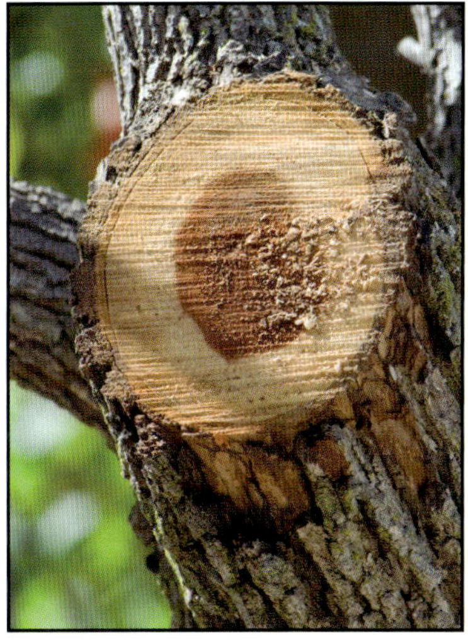

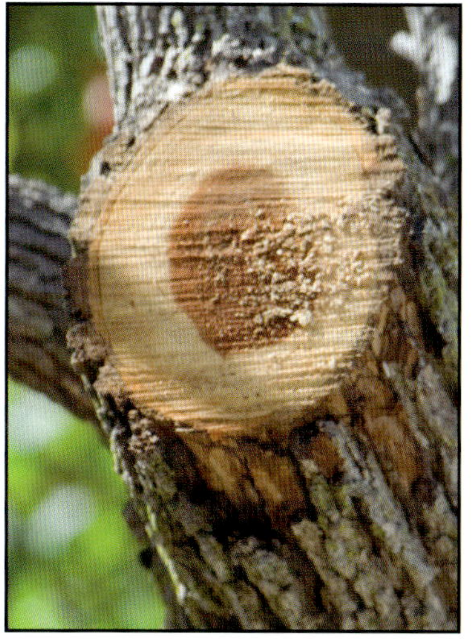

Properly focused   Slightly out of focus   Digitally sharpened (USM)

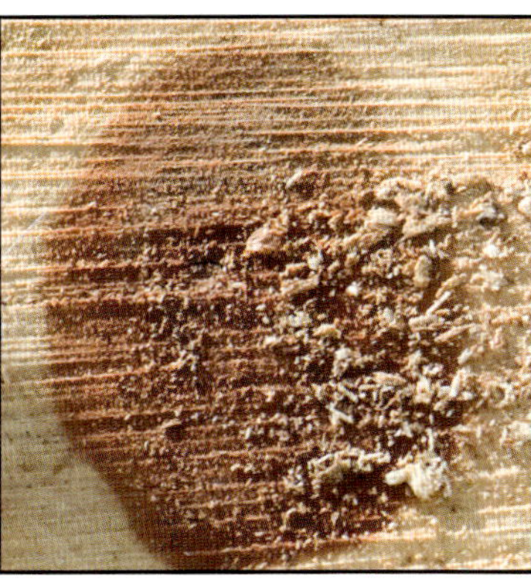

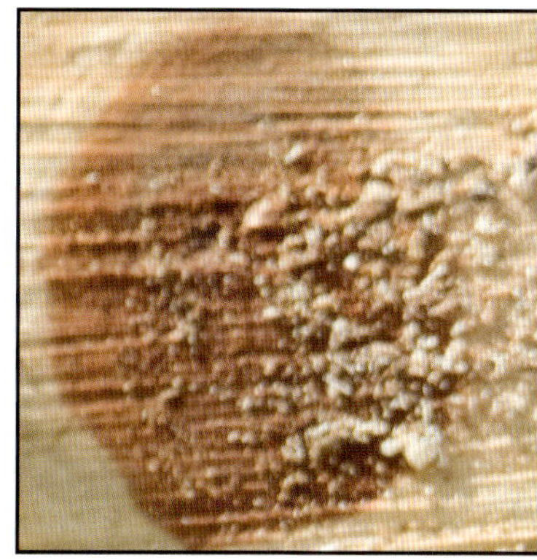

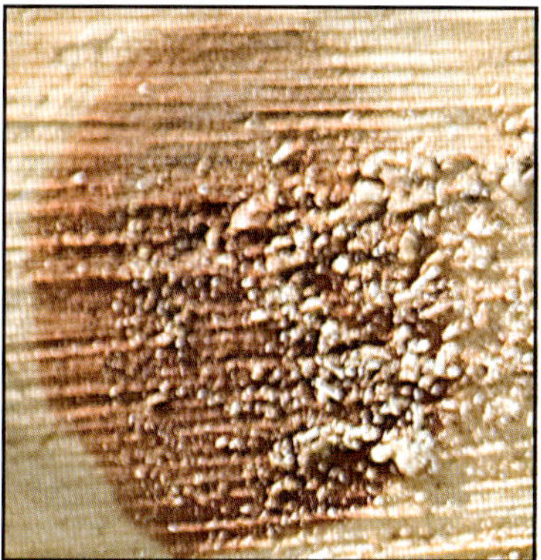

Fig. 4-22 Digital sharpening does not provide sharpness where there is none, but rather, provides the *appearance* of increased sharpness by increasing contrast between adjacent colors at the pixel level. It is best applied to images that are only slightly out of focus to start with. It does not create new detail where there is none to begin with.

Digital sharpening works best on high resolution images that already have good focus and lots of detail. It can make a good image better when used sparingly, but should never be relied upon as justification for using poor technique in the field.

There is a well-known saying in the motion picture and television industries that the five most expensive words are "we can fix it in post." Years before digital technology ever reached the hands of consumers, motion picture guys had the most powerful special effects and post production tools at their disposal. Yet these producers – often working with multi-million dollar budgets – learned quickly that it's cheaper to create quality imagery from the start, rather than trying to "fix" inferior images after the fact.

The extra time it takes to set up a tripod, or the additional money spent on a quality lens, will generally be offset many times over by the costs of trying to correct preventable problems in post production. Unfortunately, most of us learn this lesson the hard way, because we somehow believe that our images will still be good when we make the same mistakes that have ruined the efforts of countless others before us. The good news is that it usually only takes one critical failure on assignment to drive this lesson home. Recognize that this will probably happen to you someday (if it hasn't already). Prepare for it, and try to get it out of the way early in your career. From then on, you will truly understand the importance of focusing your efforts on doing things with the best quality possible at every step along the way.

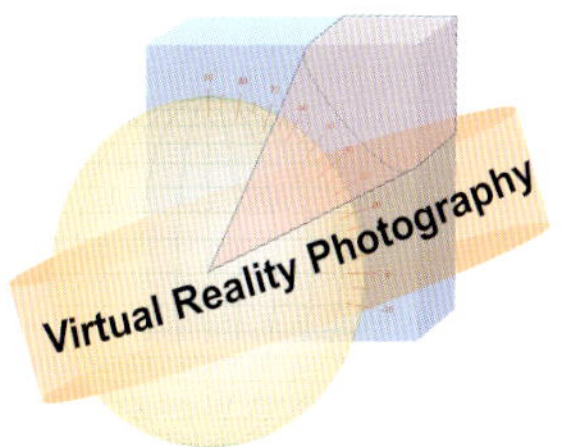

Chapter 5: Lighting

Light is the very essence of photography. The difference between a mediocre photograph and one that is visually stunning can often be simply a difference in lighting – the play between light and shadow, the direction from which the light originates, its overall harshness, softness, and even color. While the subjects we photograph are infinitely varied, the true subject of every photograph is light. Without light, there would be no photography.

Professional photographers spend their entire careers learning how to use light effectively. While the challenges of using it well in traditional photography are significant, doing so for panoramic and VR photography can be an order of magnitude greater. Imagine trying to effectively light and photograph a 360° scene, where the camera captures not only what's in front of it, but everything to the sides and behind, as well. There are few places to position any sort of lighting that won't be seen by the camera. The solution is often to keep lighting as simple as possible – which happens to be the best approach for traditional photography, as well.

Understanding the principles of good lighting is a key to good photography whether in traditional stills, VR, or even in motion picture and video.

The two main elements of light, from a photographer's perspective, are quantity and quality. Even today's simplest point-and-shoot cameras allow us to take

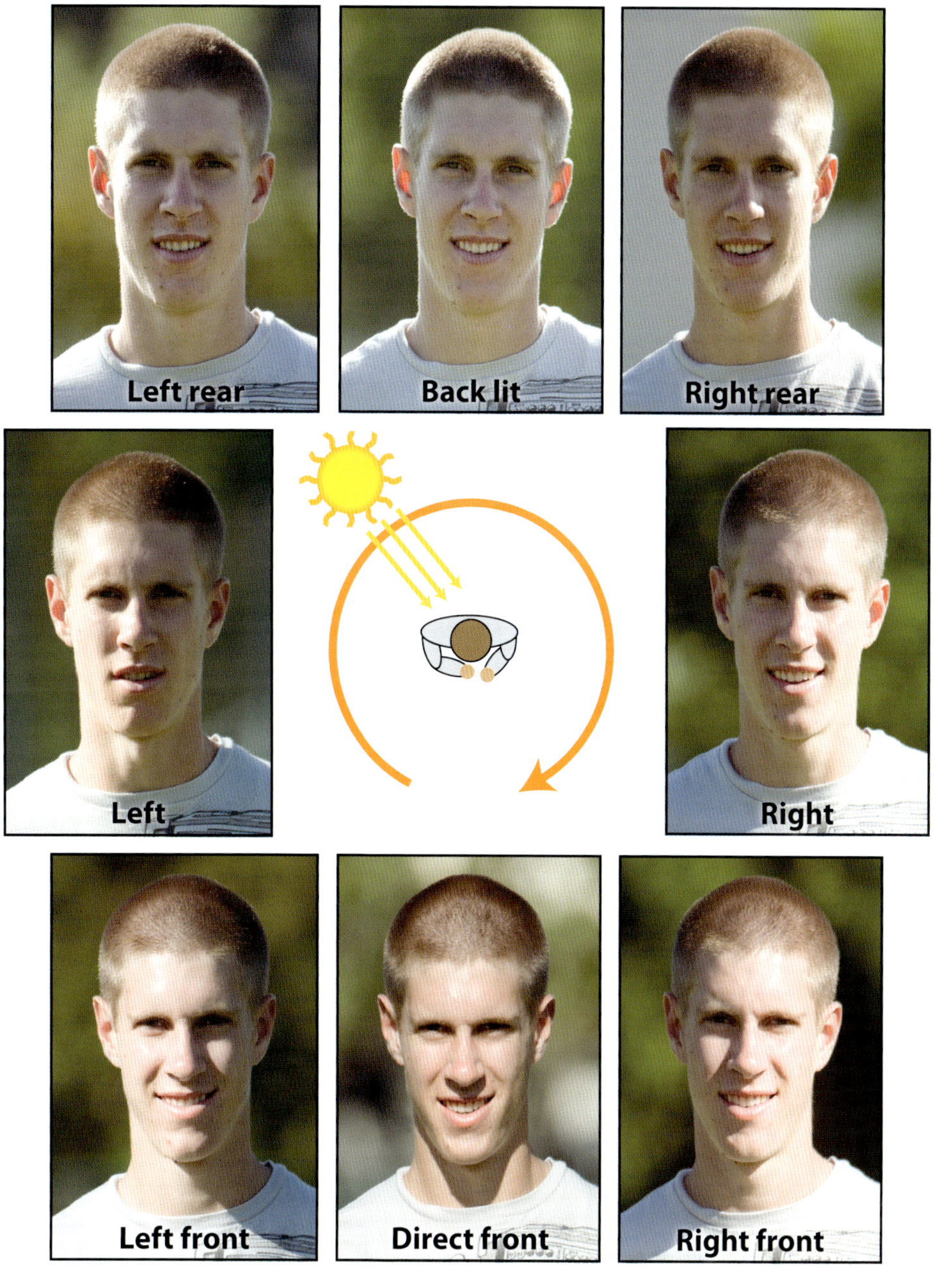

Fig. 5-1 Variations in the angle of a primary light source (the sun) on a human subject.

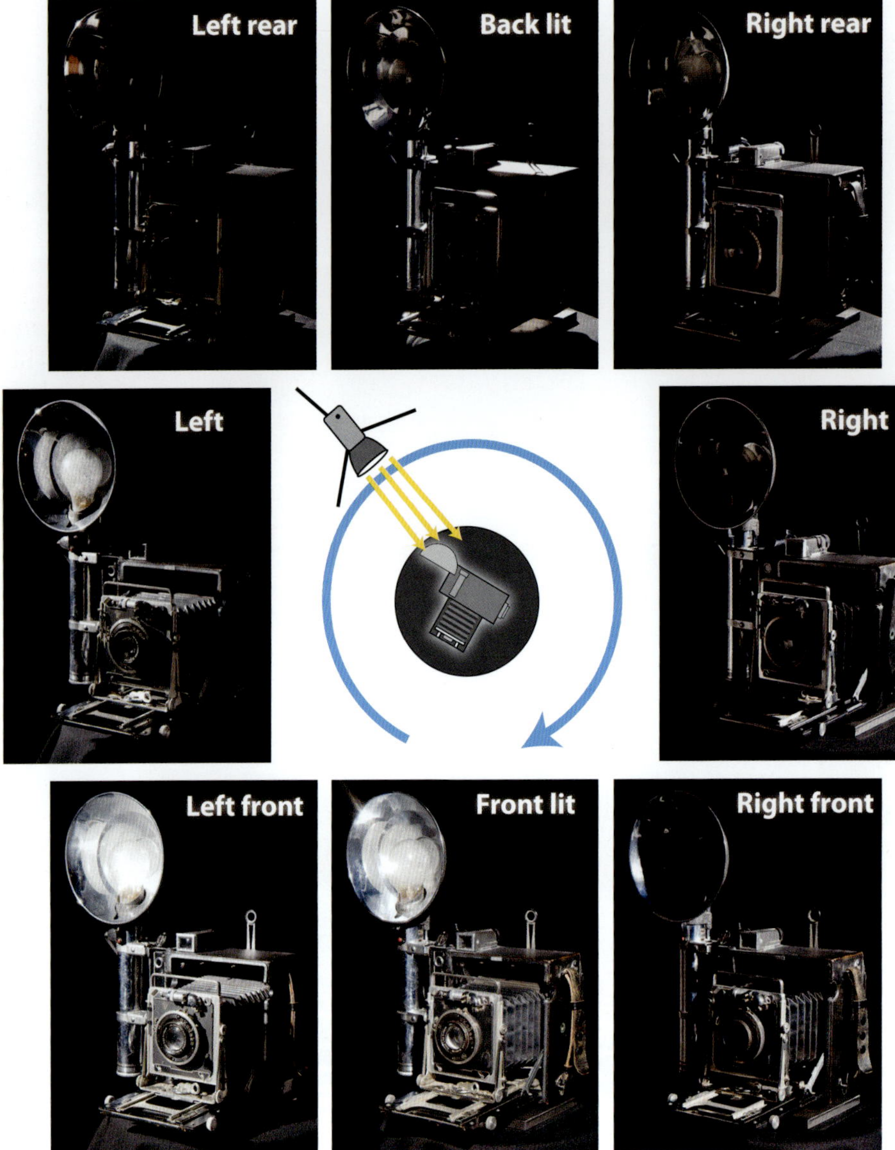

Fig. 5-2 Variations in the angle of a primary light source on a studio subject.

light – most often sunlight – with an addition of a small supplemental light source to help better record an image as the human eye perceives the scene.

A single available light source – when used well – can be just as effective as the most complex studio lighting system. Many photographers, particularly landscape and nature specialists, shoot the vast majority of their photographs using only the light of the sun. Much of this work is absolutely stunning. The trick is learning how to use light to your advantage, rather than just taking snapshots of what you see before moving on. Never assume that there is nothing you can do to alter the light of the sun, or that you have to live with whatever light it happens to be producing at a given moment. Understand how to utilize or control sunlight effectively in your photography, and you will have the foundation for mastering the use of artificial light, as well.

Direction of Light

In general, one of the worst positions from which to light a subject is "over the photographer's shoulder," as used to be recommended by film manufacturers in the instructions that were packaged with their films. While such lighting provides even illumination throughout the frame, it's also very flat, minimizing the texture, detail, and character of the subject. Indeed, it is a combination of highlight and shadow that best defines a subject visually. To accomplish this, the direction of the light should be somewhat off the axis of the camera from the subject.

In panoramic photography, the same lighting principles apply. The difficulty however is that as the camera pans, it will be capturing the scene from a variety of different angles relative to the principal light source. Subjects between the sun and the camera will be backlit, while those opposite the sun from the camera will be front lit. Subjects perpendicular to the camera-sun axis will be lit from the side.

well-exposed and focused images simply by pushing a button. If good photography were as simple as getting our subject in focus and exposing the image properly, almost every picture would be perfect. Of course, we understand that other elements such as composition, perspective, and timing also play an important role, but lighting is critical.

Simply changing the angle of a light or modifying its harshness/softness can make the difference between a flat, dull photograph and one which shows the depth and character of a subject. A good photographer can create quality images using even the cheapest point and shoot camera – simply by using light to his or her advantage.

Good lighting technique does not require expensive studio strobe equipment, giant soft boxes, or the latest "must have" accessories. Often, the best light at a photographer's disposal is natural or "available"

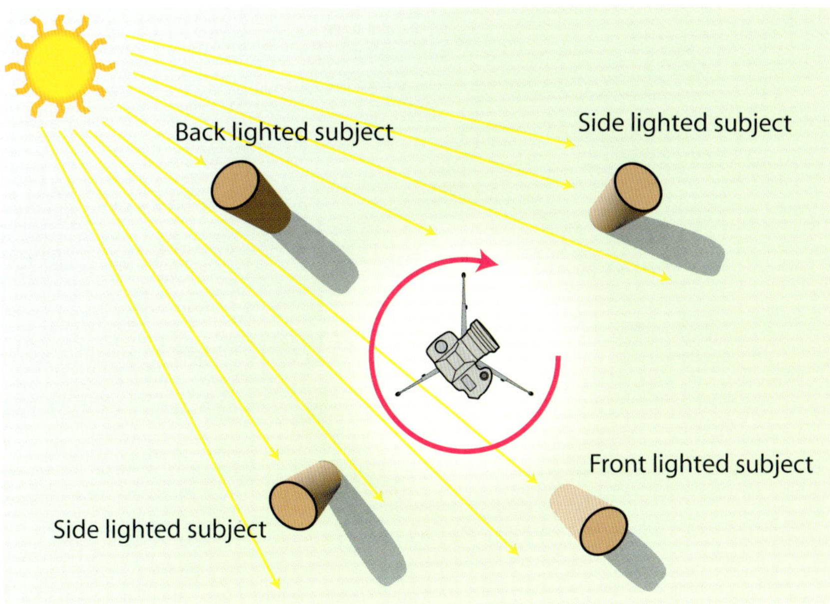

Fig. 5-3 Lighting directions vary from the camera viewpoint on subjects within a 360° panoramic scene.

Obviously, when shooting a 360° panorama, it is difficult to have every subject lit from an optimal direction. However, a photographer can choose his or her shooting position within a panoramic scene based on optimizing the light falling on select subjects within that scene. You can also choose to photograph the scene at different times of the day when the sun might be positioned at a better angle for your subjects.

Some photographers will choose to shoot panoramic scenes during mid-day light, when the sun is directly overhead. This provides relatively even illumination for an outdoor scene and shadow angles vary only slightly between viewing directions. The problem with this is that it generally makes for visually boring imagery, since the sun directly overhead creates flat and harsh light,

and the shadows it produces are often unflattering or distracting.

Some photographers will choose instead to use a camera flash or strobe to light their pictures, particularly indoors. One drawback to using flash is rooted in modern camera design. Most cameras are built to have portable flash units mounted directly on top of the camera's viewfinder, or even included as a part of the camera itself. This means that the light these flash units cast hits the subject from essentially the same axis as the camera lens, and the result again is rather flat looking.

In order to produce images that show three-dimensional depth, the primary light source *must be off axis from the camera*. This means that the light, whether portable flash, studio strobe, tungsten/fluorescent lamps, window light, or the sun, needs to be positioned *off the camera*. Certainly there are exceptions to this, and flat, direct lighting can be used at times for creative effect. However, if you find your photographs lack pizzazz because of uninteresting lighting, the first thing you should try is to move your principal light source 60° to 90° off the subject-to-camera axis. Experiment with further light direction changes from there.

Quality of Light

When we speak of the "quality" of light, we are usually referring to a combination of its color and its hardness/softness. For now, let's consider only the hardness/softness of various light sources and how this effects the subjects of a photograph.

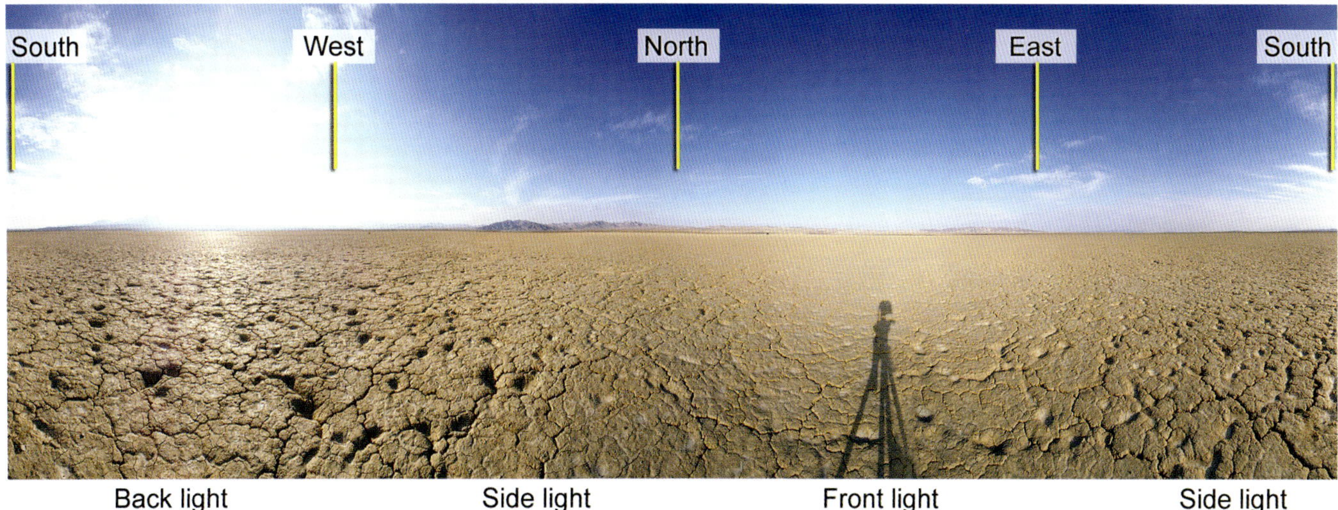

Fig. 5-4 A 360° panoramic image shows how the direction of light on a subject can change depending on view direction. Note the pronounced difference in texture of the dry lake bed revealed by the sun's angle relative to camera and subject.

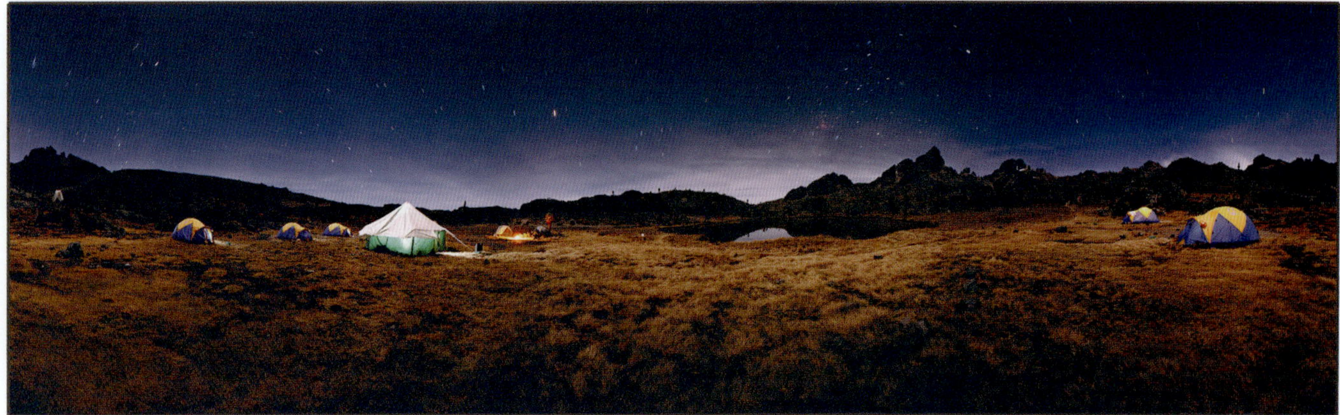
Night time – moon light

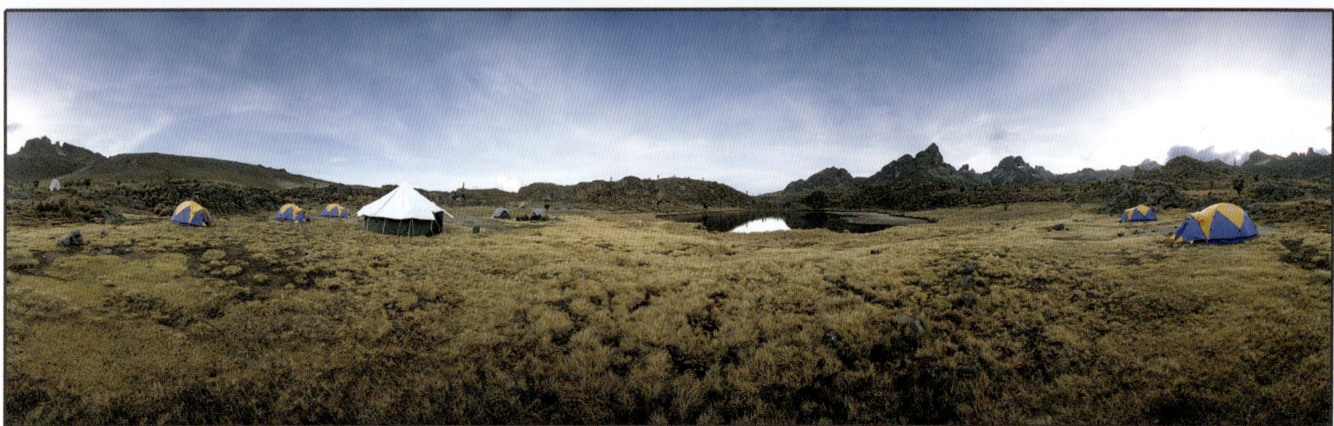
Late afternoon

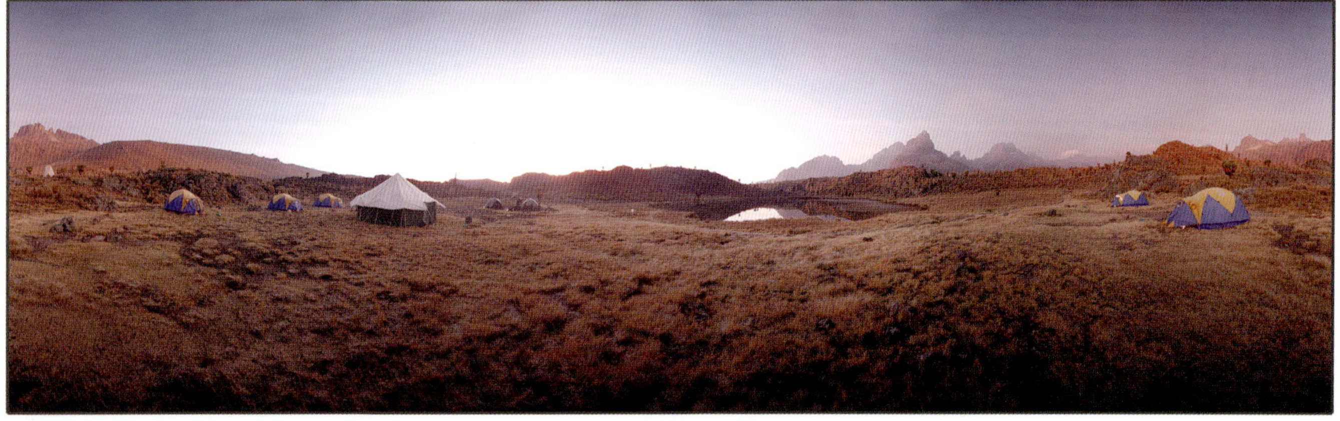
Dawn

Fig. 5-5 Simply changing the time of day in which you shoot a naturally lit outdoor scene can result in radically different lighting and overall look, as in these 360° panoramic examples of a high climbing camp on Mt. Kenya in Africa.

A "hard" light refers to any light that produces crisp shadows with distinct edges. This requires a relatively small point source for the light. Our sun, while thousands of miles in diameter, actually appears from our perspective on earth to be a fairly small round light, occupying only about 1° of our field of view in the sky. On clear days, when its light is not diffused by clouds or haze, the sun casts a fairly hard light resulting in strong, distinct shadows. Spotlights in theaters and other "bare bulb" types of lighting cast similar harsh light, resulting in hard-edge transitions between light and shadow.

If we place any sort of diffusion between a light source and its subject, we "soften" that light by increasing its relative size. This scatters the light so that it strikes the subject from more angles, thereby softening the edges between light and shadow. The transition between the highlight and shadow areas becomes more gradual the more the light is diffused.

This is easily seen in the difference between ambient daylight on a bright sunny day versus on a cloudy or overcast day. Fog and clouds act as giant diffusers for the sun. Above the clouds, the light from the sun is still just as harsh as always. But when that light passes through the clouds, it is reflected and scattered in all directions.

One or more clouds diffuse the sun light. While reducing the amount of light actually reaching the ground, clouds makes the sun light appear softer, since the light is now emanating from the entire cloud area rather than from the small point source of the sun. On a fully overcast day, the light is diffused across the entire sky. Light finally reaching the surface of the earth is actually coming from many different directions above, rather than from a 1° wide unobstructed sun source. Shadows become almost non-existent because the light is coming from so many directions, and the difference in light intensity between open and shaded areas can be negligible.

The quality of artificial lighting can be controlled similarly, whether using portable flash units, studio strobes, tungsten, or fluorescent lighting, and even daylight through windows or skylights.

Most electronic flash units have very small light tubes which act as brilliant point light sources. The light they produce is therefore fairly harsh. The advantages of electronic flashes are that they can be bright enough (albeit only for a moment) to adequately light many scenes, and depending upon their distance from the subject, can match or even surpass the brilliance of sunlight. They are also color balanced to produce a white light closely matching that of the mid-day sun.

The disadvantages to using portable flash, however, are that their unmodified light produces harsh shadows, and because the duration of their light pulse is so brief, we cannot see what it looks like on our subjects without actually recording an exposure on film or digital media. An average burst of light from a portable flash lasts about 1/400 sec., which is nowhere near enough time for our eyes to recognize patterns of light and shadow that are cast upon our subjects.

The good news is that it is possible to alter the quality of the light produced by flash/ strobe units by using light modifiers. The simplest of these would be a translucent white cloth, such as a handkerchief or a piece of tracing paper, placed in front of the light to diffuse or soften it somewhat. The larger size of the material that the light passes through, the

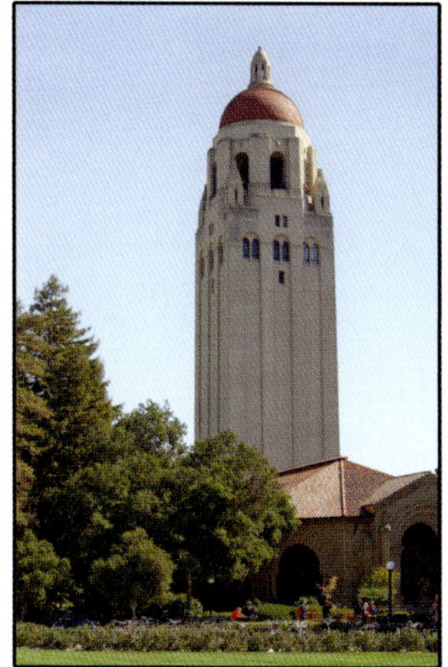
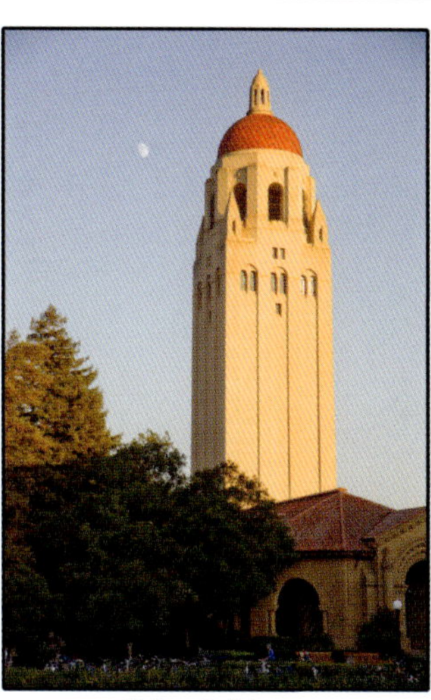

Early afternoon   "Magic" hour

Fig. 5-6 Mid-day lighting on an architectural subject compared to "magic" hour lighting.

more diffuse or softer the light will be when reaching the subject.

Some materials will diffuse light more than others, just as a thick layer of clouds will diffuse and soften sun light more than a thin layer will.

While diffusion fabric and other materials can be used to soften the light falling on a subject, we can also use other large surfaces such as walls and ceilings to "bounce" or reflect light for even greater effect. Keep in mind that the light reflected off these surfaces will take on the color of that surface, so it's usually best to use a walls and ceilings painted white in order to maintain accurate colors on the subject.

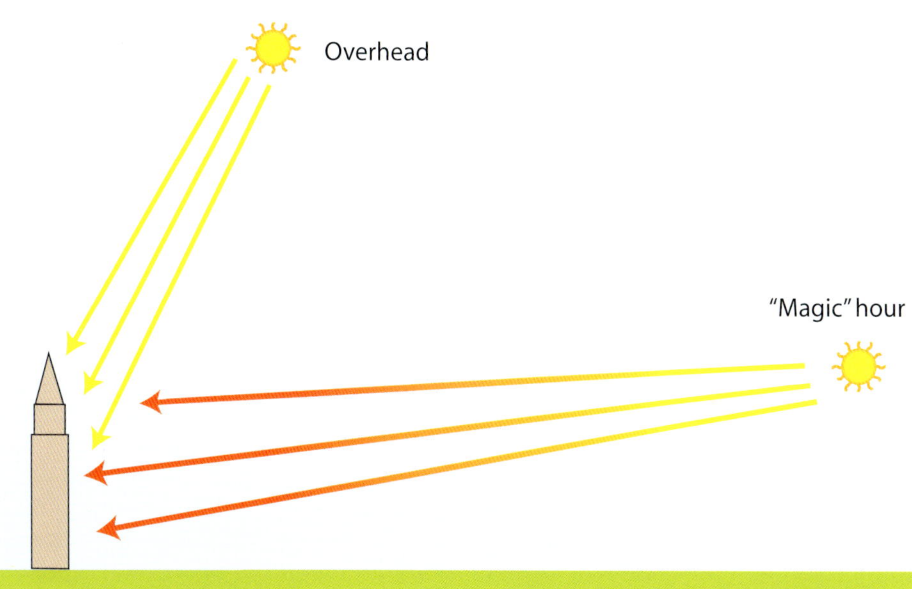

Fig. 5-7 The golden light of "magic" hour is caused by the absorption of more blue wavelengths as sun light travels a longer passage through the earth's atmosphere.

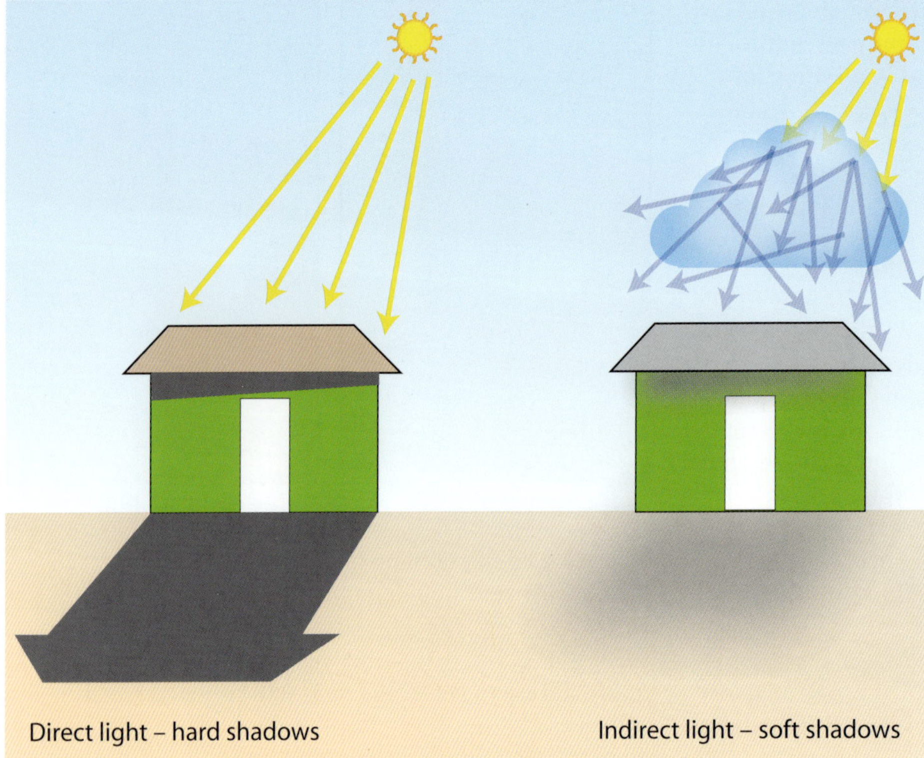

Fig. 5-8 Clouds or haze block and diffuse light from the sun.

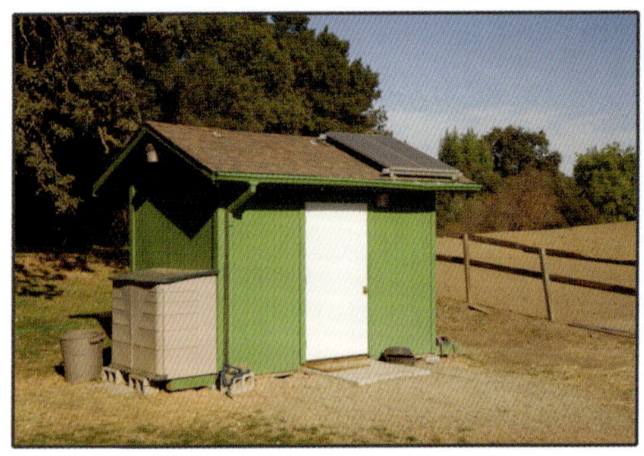
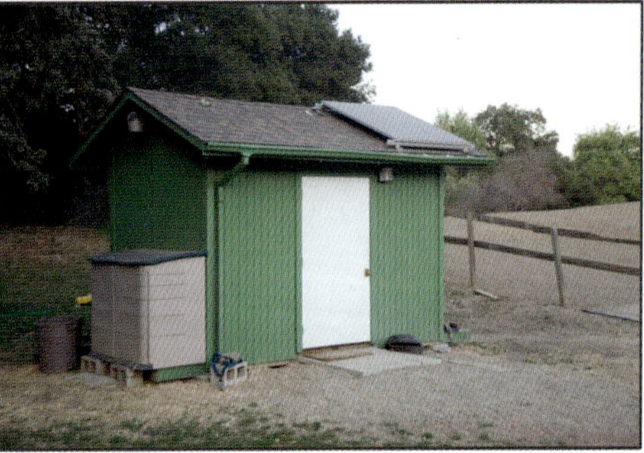

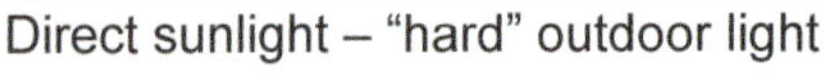

Fig. 5-9 A comparison of direct sun and diffused lighting resulting from a cloudy day.

is outside the camera's field of view. It is also wonderful for shooting interiors and architectural subjects.

Note that with panoramic photography, there can still be significant exposure differences between the inside of a room and the views that might be visible through the window(s). The photographer will have to cope with these. There is much less difference in exposure when the exterior light is soft and indirect than when it is from direct sun. You will find it far easier to properly light and expose panoramic interiors when the room you are photographing is on a shaded side of the building.

"Bounce" lighting can be used effectively either as a main light source or as "fill" light. Fill lighting is used to brighten shadow areas and better balance contrast in an image. It is usually directed at a subject from a direction opposite the main light source, and can be done using reflectors, white boards, nearby bright surfaces, or even secondary lights.

In general, it is better to use a soft or diffuse light for fill lighting, especially when the key (or principal) light is hard. Otherwise, a hard fill light will produce another set of shadows around the subject in addition to those produced by the key light. A softer fill light will brighten the shadow areas in a more subtle manner.

Fill lighting techniques are critical for a VR photographer to master. Since it is so difficult to place fixed lighting within 360° panoramic scenes, the use of subtle fill lighting for foreground subjects becomes a frequent necessity, and can make the difference between quality VR images and mediocre ones. Of course fill lighting techniques are easier to experiment with and learn with traditional photography – within the confines of a fixed frame where there are lots of positions for off-camera lights and reflectors. Once this is mastered, you will find your techniques can be expanded for use in multiple image and panoramic sequences.   We'll discuss fill lighting in more detail later on in this chapter.

The matte (non-shiny) finish of most painted surfaces means that light reflected off of them is scattered in many different directions. The reflected light will be soft and diffuse. A shiny surface, such as a mirror or the paint on a new car, tends to reflect light at more precise angles, meaning that the reflected light will be more similar to the original light source.

Other sources of soft natural interior light are windows and skylights. At certain times of the day, and depending on which directions these windows face, the sun will shine directly through them, casting a hard light with strong shadows. However, most of the rest of the day, they allow only indirect daylight to come into a room. In this manner the window or skylight serves as a large softbox, which the creative photographer can utilize to his or her advantage. This type of light source can be beautiful for portraiture, particularly if the window itself

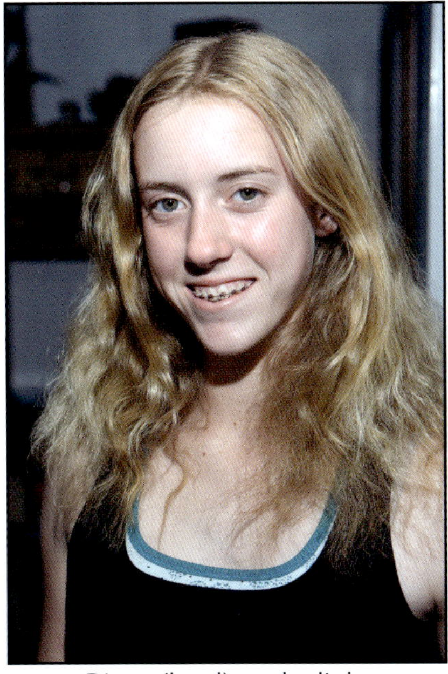

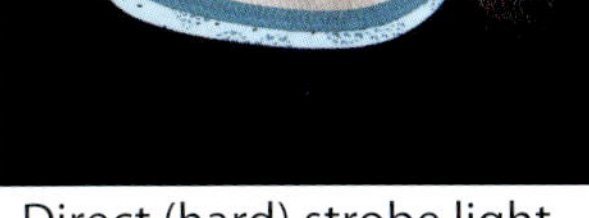

Direct (hard) strobe light

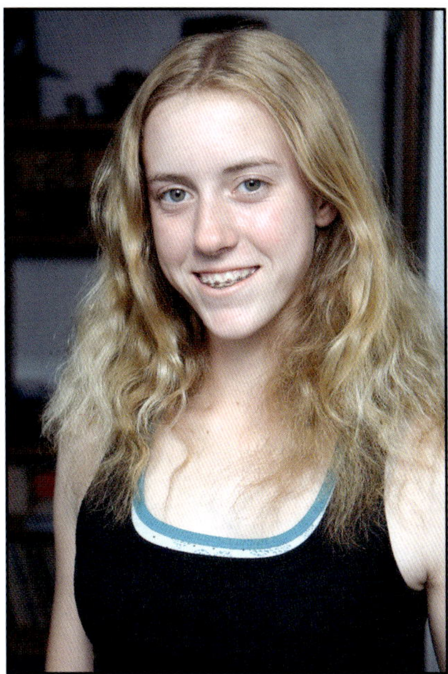

Indirect bounced (soft) light

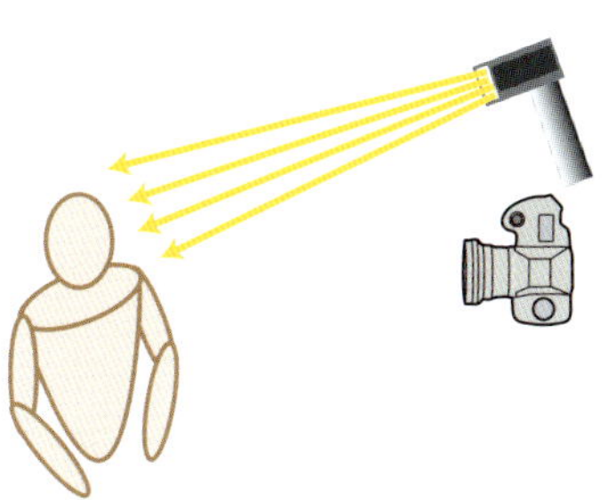

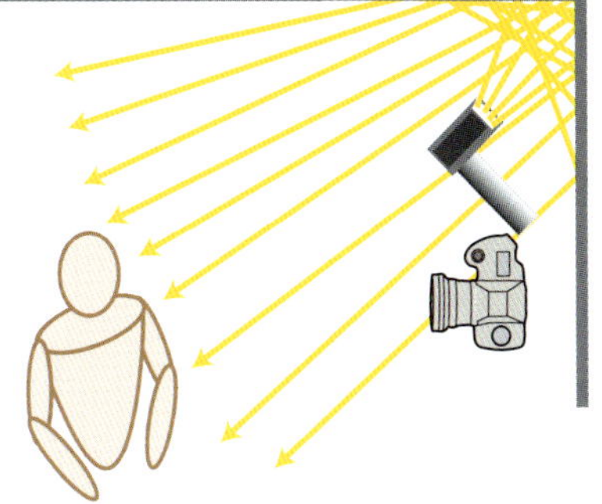

Fig. 5-10 Direct vs. indirect strobe (flash) lighting.

The ability to control the quality of light and its direction relative to subject and camera, is both a necessity, as well as a long–term passion for photographers. Such control does *not* require complex lighting setups and equipment, but often can be done simply by positioning one's subjects in a different location or even photographing them during a different time of day.

For film and television production, where schedules are tight and every hour that a crew is on location can cost thousands of dollars, entire truck loads of lighting and grip equipment are kept on hand. Such gear includes huge diffusion silks, reflectors, stands, weights, generators, and HMI or hot light systems. These tools are used because filming *has* to take place at certain locations and at specific times, and it's the crew's job to make sure that the scene looks good on film, no matter what the existing lighting is. Under these sorts of pressures, VR and still photographers often resort to the same tools and techniques. But for the most part, the simpler and more effective you can keep your lighting efforts, the easier your job will be.

Quantity of Light

The intensity or brightness of light is what we base photographic exposure on. From a photographer's standpoint, the more light we have, the better off we are – most of the time. As we have learned in previous chapters, more light allows us to use smaller apertures resulting in greater depth of field. More light allows us faster shutter speeds and better ability to freeze motion. More light also allows use of slower ISO films or digital sensor settings for better sharpness and resolution. (Even though resolution remains constant with a given digital camera no matter what the ISO setting, digital cameras are optimized to provide the best image quality at their lower ISO settings.)

The human eye is an amazingly sophisticated optical instrument, which automatically adjusts to allow us to see well throughout a wide range of light intensities. We can navigate our cars down a busy road while facing directly into the late afternoon sun, yet can also see our way along a dark trail at night lit only by a partial moon. Our range of vision and light sensitivity are far beyond that of any film or digital media.

Yet remarkably, actual intensity of light is difficult to judge accurately with our eyes. While we can easily determine relative brightness (knowing that the light in one room is brighter than

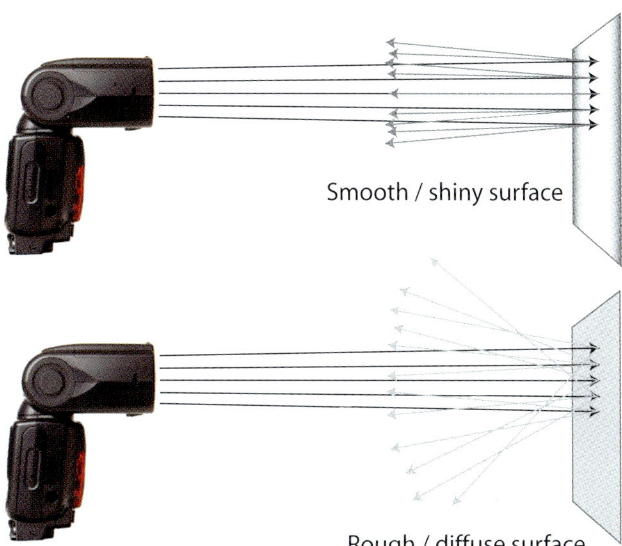

Fig. 5-11 Reflected light becomes more diffuse when bounced off a rough or matte surface than off of a smooth or shiny one.

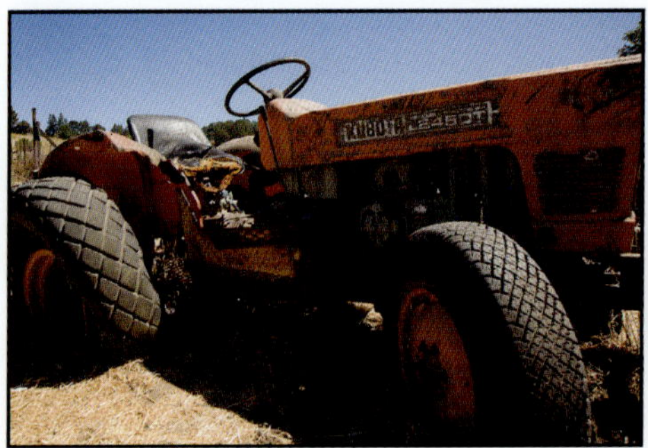
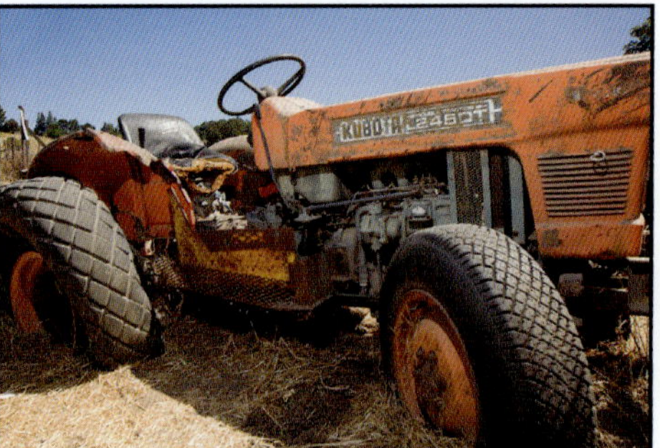

Available light only   With "fill" light added

Fig. 5-12 Fill lighting can be used to better balance shadow and highlight exposures.

another, or that it's darker inside a building than it is outside), it is quite difficult to know exactly how *much* brighter one subject is over another without some way to measure light quantitatively. Since film and digital media are more limited in sensitivity than our eyes, it is important for us to be able to accurately measure light intensity in order to determine proper photographic exposures.

Light meters are the tools we use to measure light quantity. Today, light meters are integrated directly into our cameras, and can determine exposure settings for us automatically. Most point and shoot cameras have internal meters, which set proper exposures without the photographer even knowing what they're doing. Older cameras, as well as modern pro models, allow for manual light readings within the camera's viewfinder for precise photographer control over exposure.

Internal meters are ideal because they calculate exposures based on the light that actually reaches the film (or digital sensor) plane. Because they are positioned behind the camera's lens, they compensate for any light loss from filters or from lens extension due to close focusing.

Up until a few decades ago (before in-camera meters became common), a hand held light meter was a necessity for photographers. Many pros still use them today. These meters measure continuous light levels in two ways – either directly from the light source (incident light) or reflected from the subject (reflected light). Modern hand held light meters can measure both incident and reflected light from almost any light source, including flash or strobe systems.

Incident light readings are best used for overall exposure calculations and on mid-tone subjects, while reflective readings are often useful for overly bright or dark subjects. In-camera meters are reflective meters, since they measure only light reflected from the subject entering the camera thorough its lens.

A hand held light meter is extremely helpful in determining proper exposures between highlight and shadow areas, as well as in balancing levels of more than one light source.

For example, on a bright, sunny afternoon, there can be a five to six stop lighting difference between two sides of a subject – one facing the sun and the other in shadow. This difference is beyond the exposure latitude of many films and digital sensors, so *any* exposure you choose will either optimize the shadow or the highlight areas, but not both. An exposure setting based on the shadow may make the shadow areas look good, but will "blow out" the highlights. An exposure setting based on the sun lit side will make the highlights of the subject look good, but will likely "block up" the shadow areas, so detail there may be lost.

Splitting the difference between the exposures *may* yield acceptable results, but more often than not, will produce images that are both too dark in the shadows and too light in the highlights. Good results will require that the highlights and shadows be controlled so that the balance of light intensity is within the exposure latitude

Fig. 5-13 For motion picture and television work, truck loads of lighting and light control equipment are used on location in order to give subjects a natural, yet polished look on camera. Most of these same lighting principles can be used by other photographers with simpler equipment on a smaller scale.

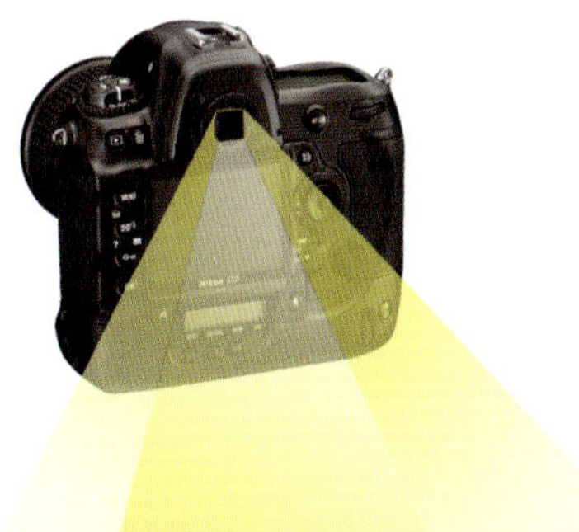

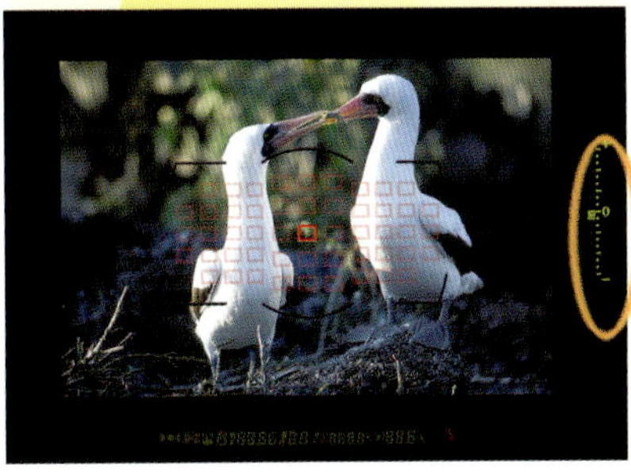

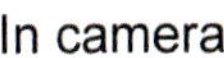

In camera

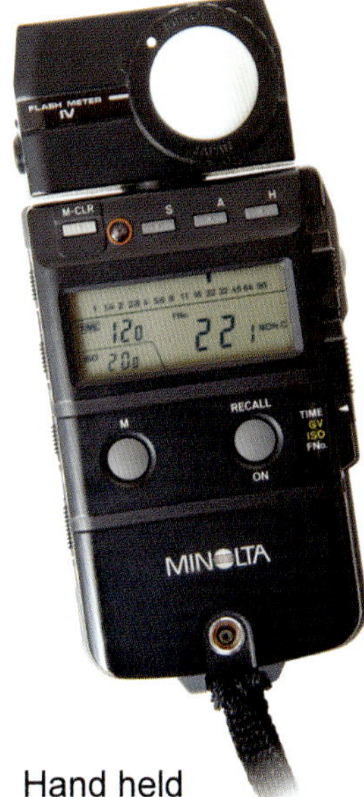

Hand held

Fig. 5-14 Light meters measure the *quantity* of light available for exposure.

shadows and neutral tones, with sufficient detail visible in each. Different types of film and digital sensors have different ranges of acceptable exposure under which they can reveal detail in both highlight and shadow areas. This is called **exposure latitude**.

Slide or transparency films generally have the narrowest exposure latitudes – as little as four to five stops between their rendering of darkest and lightest densities. While this generally means they produce more contrasty and brilliant colors – which are pleasing to the eye, it also makes them the most difficult to use. Traditional negative or print films offer a seven to eight stop exposure latitude. The sensors found in digital cameras vary tremendously. Some cheaper ones can have effective exposure latitudes as narrow as some slide films, while others, particularly in high-end studio systems can have 10-11 stop exposure latitudes. (Note that many pro digital cameras have a much greater exposure latitude when images are captured in their native RAW modes, rather than in JPEG or other formats.)

The trick to "balancing" light levels is to know what differences in exposure your chosen film or camera sensor will tolerate, as well as knowing your own preferences for what looks natural.

From a practical standpoint, it's not always easy to balance the lighting ratios in a scene when shooting on location. Bringing shadow light levels up to within a stop or less of main light levels is usually the goal for natural looking fill light. Addition of a reflector or portable flash positioned off camera may offer the best look for this fill light, but both often require the help of an assistant. It is possible for a photographer to do this alone by setting up a light stand and running a cable or slave system from

of the film or digital sensor being used. This is usually accomplished using light modifiers or supplemental lighting equipment, such as reflectors or flash units. Use of a light meter to measure the exposure differences within a scene will allow you to precisely determine where your exposure should be set, as well as the range of exposure throughout your scene.

In panoramic VR photography, the difference in brightness between one direction of the scene and another can change dramatically, further compounding exposure problems. When the camera faces the sun, the scene will be much brighter than when the camera faces away from it. When shooting panoramic images, your in camera meter may give vastly different exposure readings as you pan around.

Similar difficulties are found when shooting interiors, especially where only one wall of a room contains windows. The window side of the room will be very brightly lit, while the opposite corners may be much darker. A good VR photographer needs to know how to take proper light readings, modify or supplement the existing light accordingly, and calculate an exposure that works throughout the entire 360° scene.

Balance of Light

A well-exposed photograph will usually include highlights,

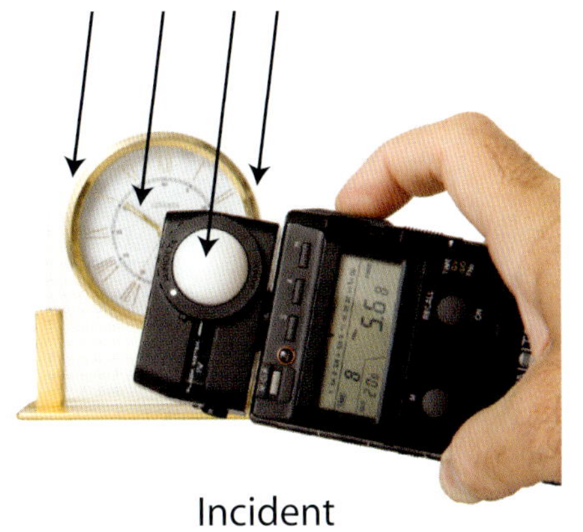

Incident

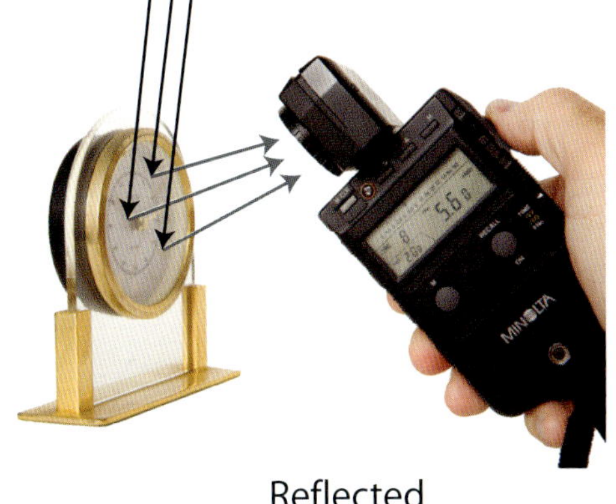

Reflected

Fig. 5-15 Incident vs. reflected exposure. measurement with a hand held light meter.

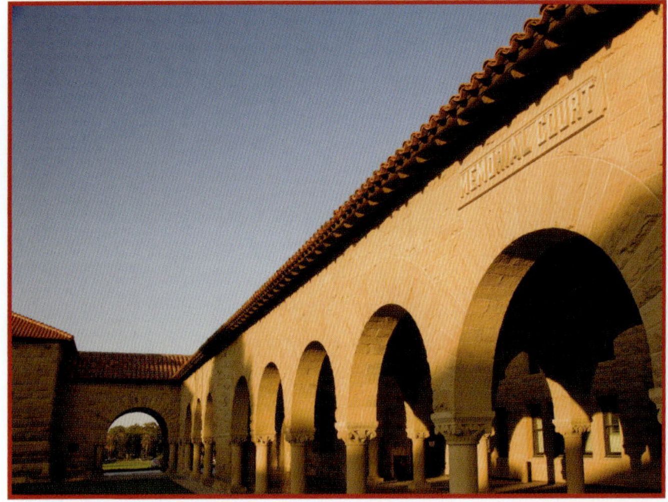

Result: Angle A – Light source behind camera

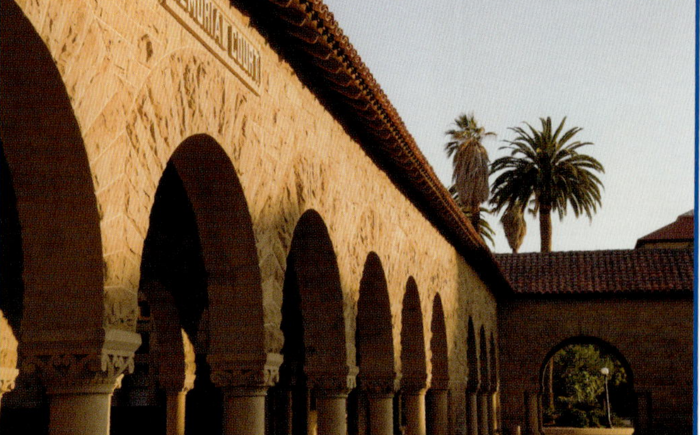

Result: Angle B – Light source to side of camera

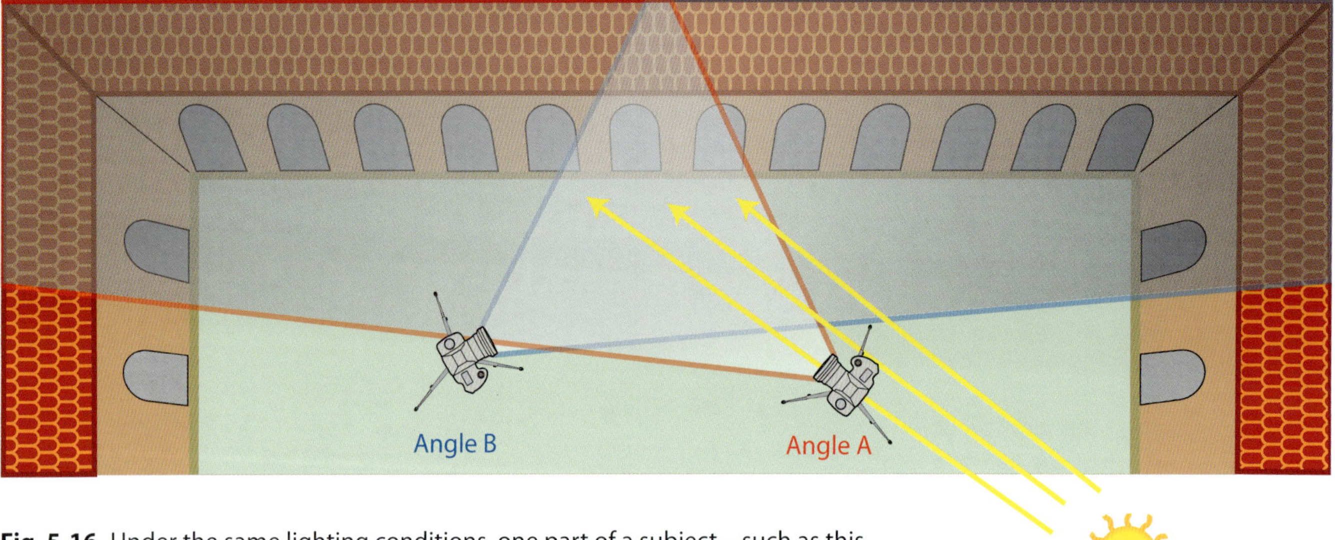

Fig. 5-16 Under the same lighting conditions, one part of a subject – such as this stone wall – can be front lit, while another is backlit. Panoramic photographers need to be aware of these varying angles as they're composing their images.

camera to the remote flash, or by clamping a reflector to a light stand and directing it at the subject. (Don't forget sandbags to hold things down, especially when working outdoors. Even the smallest reflector acts like a sail in the slightest breeze, and invariably tips over anything it's attached to, including tripods with expensive cameras or lenses.)

For simplicity's sake, it is often easiest to attach a portable flash unit to the hot shoe on top of the camera, even though we know this is not the best position to light from. When things are moving fast, and there simply isn't time to deal with more elaborate lighting control, a flash on top of the camera set to fill at 1/2 to a full stop less than the main (or ambient) light level may be an

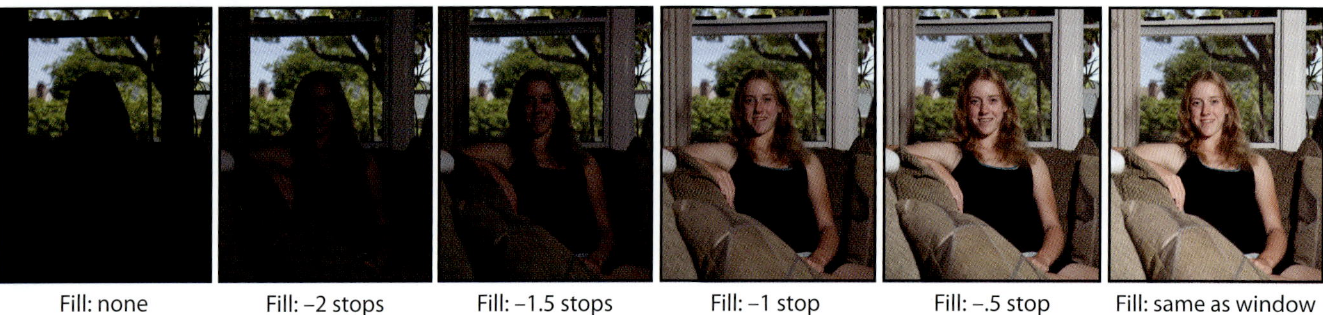

| Fill: none | Fill: –2 stops | Fill: –1.5 stops | Fill: –1 stop | Fill: –.5 stop | Fill: same as window |

Fig. 5-17 Fill lighting. The camera's exposure was set to properly expose the view outside the window. Fill light, as provided by a portable strobe near the camera, was added in amounts indicated (relative to the window exposure) for each shot.

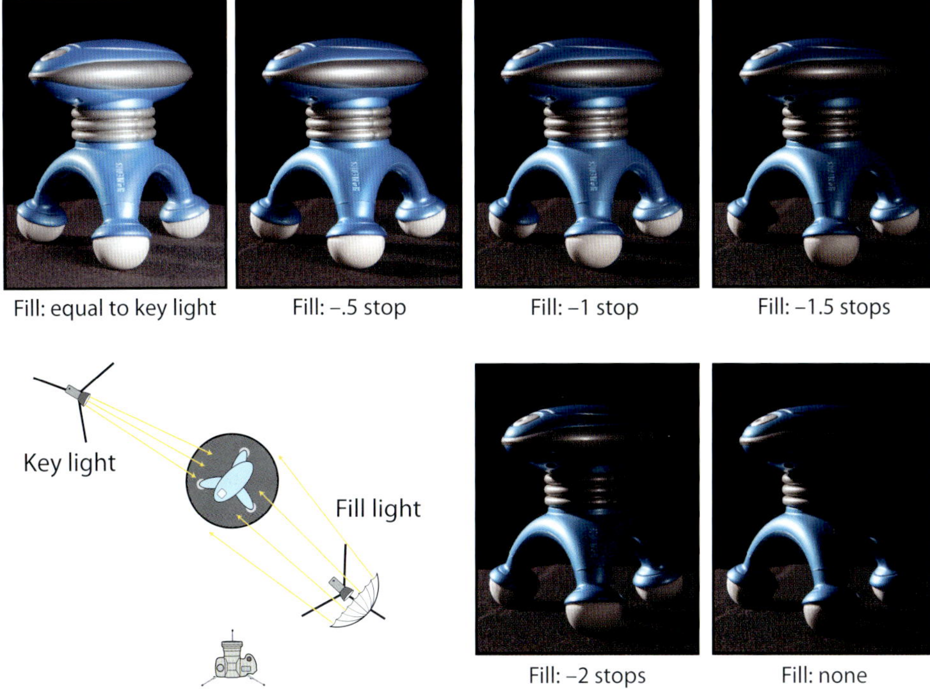

Fill: equal to key light | Fill: −.5 stop | Fill: −1 stop | Fill: −1.5 stops

Fill: −2 stops | Fill: none

Fig. 5-18 Fill lighting can be used just as effectively in studio as on location.

that 360° view they will be perpendicular to the camera and will reflect an on-camera light back into the lens. Getting your fill light off the camera will help prevent this glare, but will create more challenges in keeping your lighting even and consistent. An off-camera light will need to be moved repeatedly as the camera pans in order to remain out of view.

There are no firm rules about lighting ratios, nor how many stops difference there should be between main light, fill light, back light and other lights for effect. Most of the choices you will make will depend upon the media you are using, the subject's shape and color, the mood you are trying to evoke, and your own tastes. However, as you experiment with and explore different lighting techniques, try the following as starting points:

effective choice. Many photographers find that a small diffuser over this on-camera flash reduces the harshness of fill light.

One of the problems in using any on-camera light, whether as a main or fill light source, is that the light gets reflected directly back into the camera lens when shooting subjects with flat or reflective surfaces. This results in distracting glare. Unfortunately, such subjects are common in photography. They include windows, mirrors, semi-gloss painted walls, anything metal, plastics, vehicles, people wearing glasses, and just about anything that is wet. Getting your fill light as far off the camera axis as you can will reduce the likelihood of such glare.

When shooting 360° panoramic scenes, remember that if there are reflective surfaces, at some point around

1) Let the main or key light determine your overall exposure.

2) Set your fill lighting at 1/2 to a full stop *darker* (underexposed) than the main light.

3) Set back lighting at one to two stops *brighter* (more) than the main light.

There will of course be times when you cannot fully control the light you have to work with, but having a solid grasp of the basic principles of lighting and exposure, will help you make the best of what's available. Take exposure notes as you're shooting. Look at your results and review them with your shooting notes, so you recognize what works and what doesn't based on

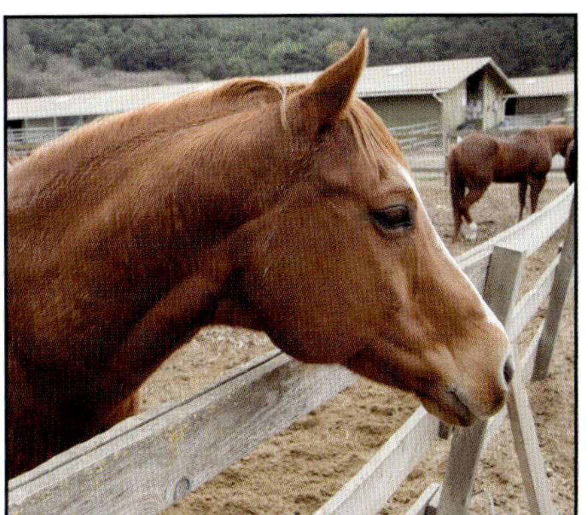

Overcast – no fill

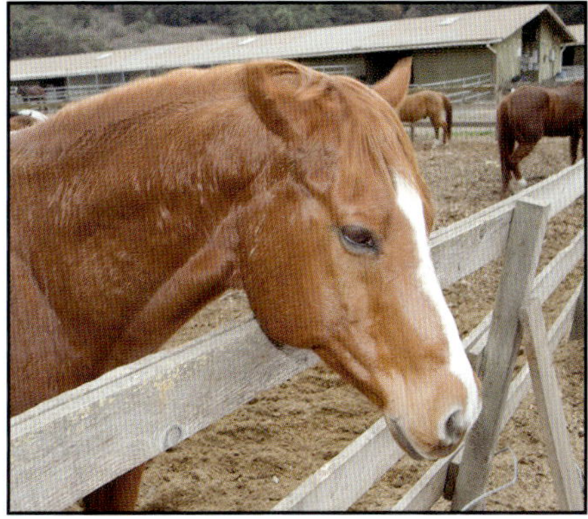

On-camera fill

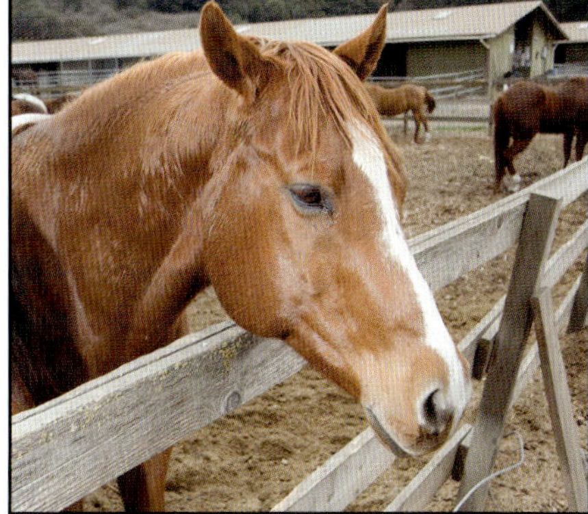

Off-camera fill

Fig. 5-19 Positioning a fill light off the camera axis can better define a subject, since some complementary shadows remain.

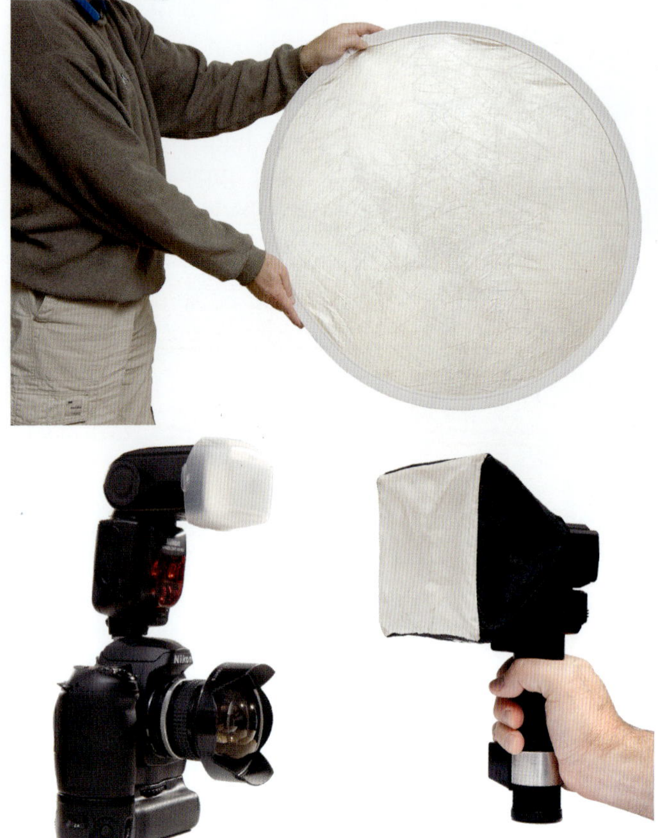

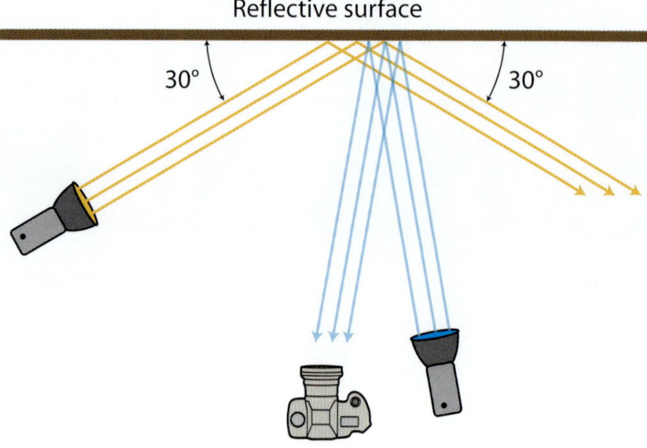

Fig. 5-21 Light is reflected off a surface at the same angle it hits it. Moving a fill light source further off the camera axis can help minimize reflections in polished or shiny surfaces.

Fig. 5-20 Fill lighting equipment can include on-camera flash, hand held strobes, or any type of light reflector.

your own experiences. Today's digital cameras let you see your results almost immediately, and many of them even provide the ability to look at histograms as you're reviewing your images on the camera's screen.

Inverse Square

All of this talk about balancing light levels is great in theory, but how do you actually adjust the amount of light falling on a subject, particularly when using artificial lighting or trying to get the perfect "fill"?

Most flash units have adjustable power settings that allow for modification of their light output. Many even have adjustable automatic settings so you can specify that you want the flash to produce enough light to give you a particular exposure even as you change distance from a subject. These power settings can be used to vary your lighting balance quite effectively, but may not always be the best method. Some only allow full stop increments between settings. Many only offer limited manual adjustments.

The most effective way to control light intensity and brightness, particularly from artificial light sources like photo lamps and flash units, is by altering the distance between the light and your subject.

The intensity of light falling on a subject changes in an inverse square relationship to the distance the subject is from the light source. Don't panic at the implied math here. Remember… if you can multiply and divide by two, you probably know enough math to understand photography.

The inverse square relationship means simply this – if you double the distance between subject and the light, you will get 1/4 as much light falling on the subject. If you triple the distance, you will get 1/9 the light on the subject. Halve the original distance and you will get 4 times as much light.

For example, let's consider that you have a light source 5 feet away from a subject, which provides an exposure of f/8. If you double the distance of the light to 10 feet, you will have only 1/4 the light reaching the subject, meaning you will have to open your aperture to f/4 (two stops) to compensate. If you halve the distance to 2.5

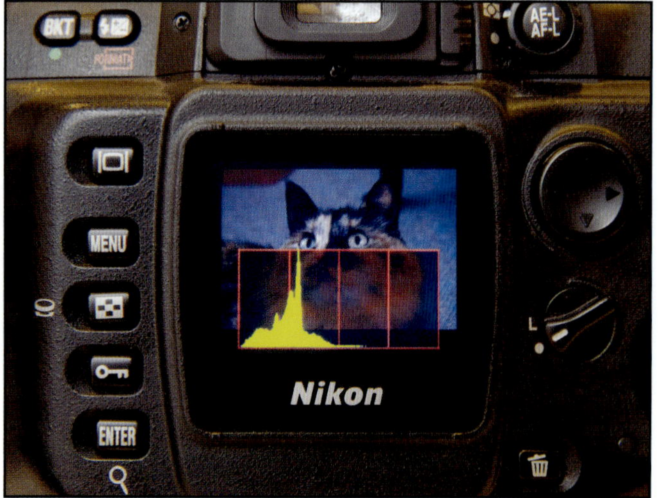

Courtesy of Melinda Highton

Fig. 5-22 Display of a histogram on the viewing screen of a digital camera can aid in determining good exposure.

Technical Note: When Fill Lighting Overpowers Main Light

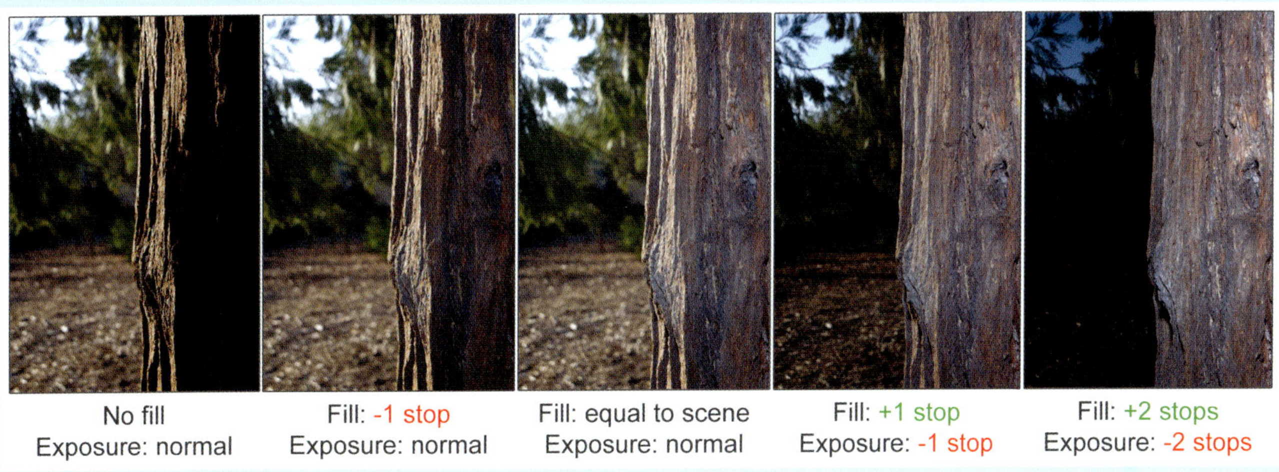

Fig. 5-23 If the brightness of fill light equals or exceeds that of the main light, the results start to look unnatural. This can be used for creative effect when done by choice. However, it most often happens by mistake with automatic exposure systems that haven't been set quite right for fill lighting purposes. Remember that "fill" light is only supposed to *fill* in the shadow areas with enough light to bring out their details – generally 1/2 to one stop *less* than the main light intensity.

feet, you will get four times as much light on the subject, so you will have to close down your aperture by two stops to f/16.

This relationship can be used to your advantage when you need to control the lighting balance between multiple light sources. If you have determined an exposure for your main or key light (often ambient daylight), but your fill light is not quite bright enough, simply move the fill light in a little closer to the subject. The brightness of the fill light will increase corresponding to the inverse square rule.

For example, if your fill light is 8 feet away from your subject, but you need it to be 2 stops brighter (4x as much light), simply halve its distance from the subject to 4 feet. If you only need it to be one stop brighter (2x as much light), move it in to about 71 percent of its original distance (1/SQRT (2) = .71x) or to about 5.6 feet.

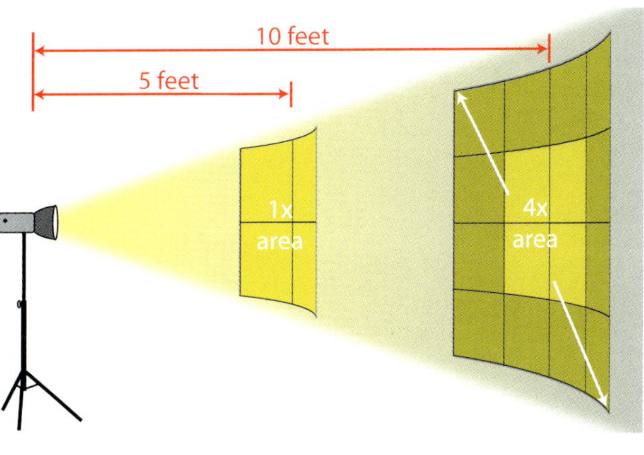

Fig. 5-24 Light dissipates over distance in an inverse square relationship. Doubling the distance spreads the light over four times the area, yielding only 1/4 the illuminance over a given area.

Changing the distance between a light source and subject is often the quickest and simplest way to adjust a light level. For the most part, such adjustments will have a relatively minor effect on the quality of the light being cast.

However, keep in mind that as a light moves farther away from a subject, it does becomes smaller in its relative size. A large softbox 5 feet away from a subject will cast a very soft, diffuse light, but when moved to 20 feet will only appear 1/16 as large from the subject's perspective, and will start to take on the characteristics of a more focused or point source light.

In a similar manner, a small light source, such as an undiffused portable flash, will become relatively large when moved to within a few inches of a subject, as often happens in macro photography. Keep this in mind when making large changes in your lighting setups.

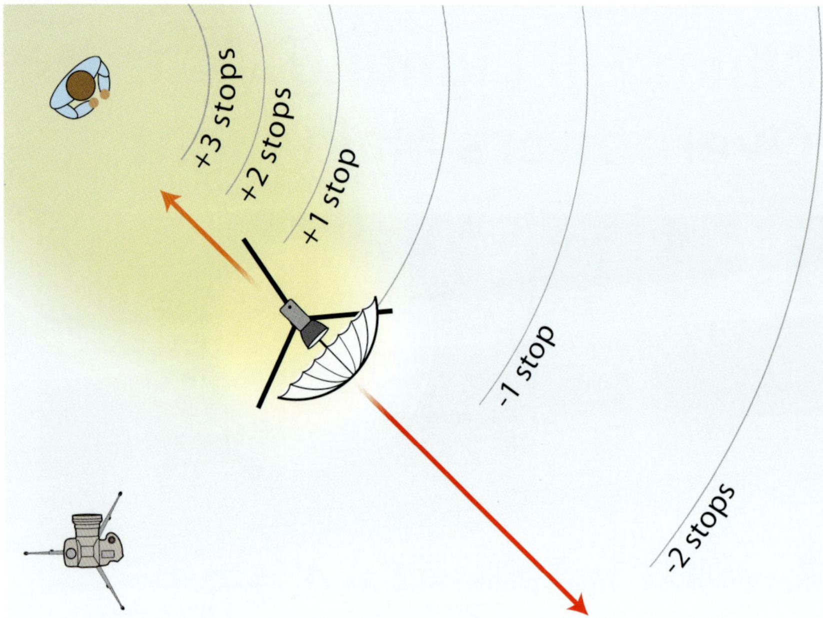

Fig. 5-25 The light illuminating a subject can be adjusted simply by changing its distance from the subject.

Color of Light

To the human eye, most of the light around us appears white in color, whether coming from the sun, an overhead fixture, a table lamp, or a flashlight. Our brains process the information received from our eyes, allowing us to perceive color reasonably accurately under a tremendous range of lighting conditions.

However, true white light is considered to be the combination of equal amounts of every color of the visible spectrum. If the actual combination of light in a particular location contains more blue wavelengths, then the light will appear more bluish in color, rather than perfectly white. Similarly, if there is more yellow, then the overall color cast will be yellowish. The greater the imbalance, the more noticeable the dominant color becomes.

Technical Note: The Inverse Square Law

Assuming that the intensity of a light source is constant and that the light shines equally in all directions, the amount of light falling on any point at a fixed distance from the source should remain constant. Thus, a sphere surrounding a light, with a diameter of 10 feet (5 foot radius), will have equal illumination throughout. The light will be spread equally over the interior surface of the sphere.

However, if we increase the size of the sphere, we increase the surface area that the light covers, so any given point will receive less light. The area of a sphere increases by the square of its radius (area = $4\pi r^2$), so the amount of light reaching any given point decreases by the inverse of the distance (radius) squared.

If you double the distance (radius of the sphere), your light source is spread over an area four times the size of the original surface. This means that any point on the larger

sphere receives only 1/4 the amount of light as a corresponding point on the smaller sphere.

Halving the distance results in four times as much light reaching a given point. Quadrupling the distance means that only 1/16 the amount of light will reach that point.

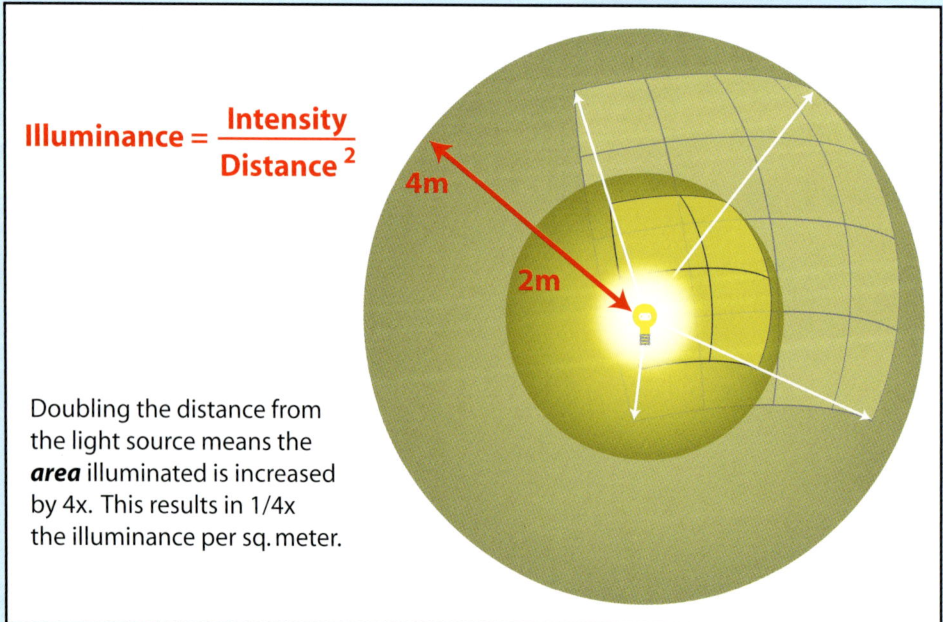

Doubling the distance from the light source means the **area** illuminated is increased by 4x. This results in 1/4x the illuminance per sq. meter.

Fig. 5-26 The inverse square relationship between distance and illuminance.

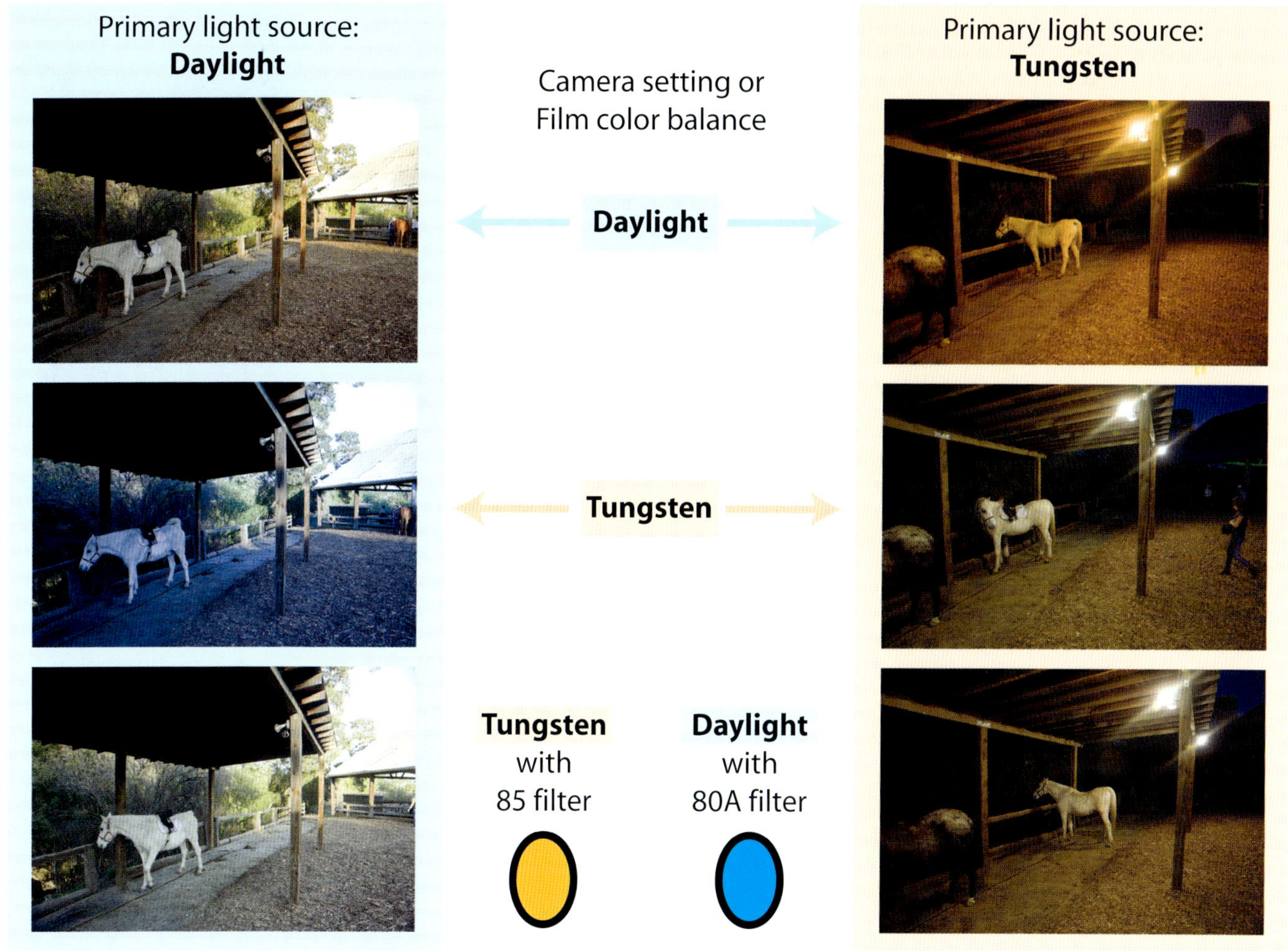

Fig. 5-27 Color balance can be adjusted through choices in film, digital white balance settings, or lens filtration.

The human brain compensates well for color imbalances our eyes see, which is why we can accurately judge a wide range of colors under many different lighting conditions. Without thinking about it, we perceive most of the standard light sources around us to be white, whether they contain the yellowish cast of a tungsten bulb or a blue-green cast of fluorescent tubes. We adapt our perception of "neutral white" to include strong mid-day sunlight, metal halide street lamps, colored lighting in a night club, or even light from a candle.

Photographic film and digital image sensors do not have the same ability that our brain does to adapt and neutralize color casts. They are, in fact, quite literal in their rendering of the colors projected by our lenses. A slight change in the color of light on our subjects often results in a noticeable change in the colors rendered in our photographs.

Therefore, "white" light needs to be standardized for photographic purposes. The method by which this has been done was to utilize our most available light source – the sun – and correlate it to the color of light produced by normally non light-emitting "blackbody" material (such as iron) when heated to a certain temperature. In the case

of the mid-day sun, this "color temperature" would be about 5,500 degrees Kelvin (5,500°K), which corresponds to the white-hot glow that a material like iron would produce at that temperature. When heated to a lower temperature, such as 2,000 degrees Kelvin (2,000°K), the iron would glow more of a yellow or reddish color, and when heated to a higher temperature such as 8,000°K, it would produce a bluer light.

Film and digital image sensors are calibrated to reproduce colors accurately under light of a specified color temperature. For daylight film, this is usually 5,500°K. For tungsten films (designed for use under incandescent lamps), this is usually 3,200°K. The same thing happens with digital camera sensors set for specific lighting temperatures.

Using a daylight film under tungsten light will cause an overall shift in rendered color towards yellow, because the tungsten light sources (at 3,200°K) are more yellow than the 5,500°K daylight that the film is balanced for. Similarly, using a tungsten film under daylight will result in colors being rendered more blue than they really are, since the 5,500°K daylight is more blue than the 3,200°K color temperature that the tungsten film is calibrated for.

Every light source has its own color balance or "color temperature." A common light type that photographers encounter on location is the fluorescent lamp. These fixtures are found in industrial, office, retail, restaurant, corporate, and even home environments, due to their relatively high light output, low energy requirements, and low cost.

One problem with these lights, however, is that they produce a variety of color temperatures, varying with brand, model, and even individual bulbs (or tubes). Fluorescents also do not emit a smooth curve of spectral energy (distribution of colors) as most other lights do. Rather, they emit a spectrum that has spikes at several different wavelengths. This makes the lights difficult to use for accurate color rendition in photography.

Typically, fluorescent lights impart a blue-green or green color cast on film. They usually require some level of magenta filtration to offset this greenish cast, either over the light itself, or over the camera lens.

There are several standard color correction filters that work fairly well to "correct" fluorescent lighting when used with daylight balanced films. They are often

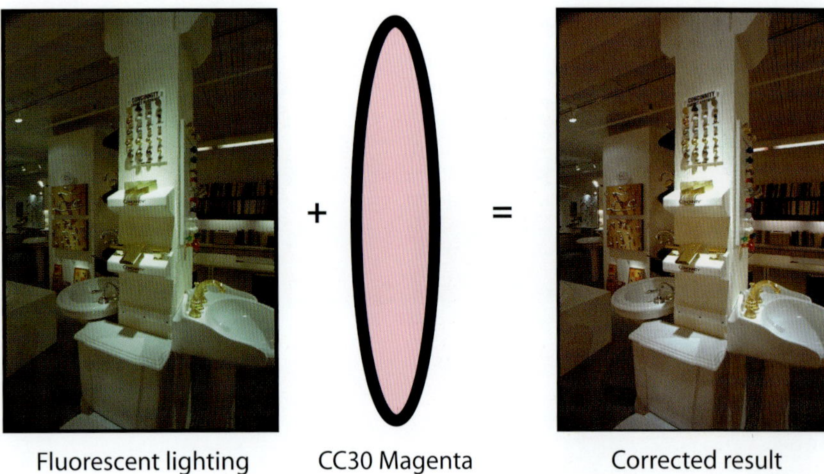

Fig. 5-28 Color correction is needed when shooting under fluorescent lighting with daylight film or a daylight white balance setting on a digital camera.

labeled CC30M (Color Correct 30 Magenta) or FL-D (Fluorescent to Daylight). These filters will produce better color rendition under fluorescent lights than you'd get without them, but the results may still not be too accurate. It is best to test the actual light, film, and filter combinations before doing a critical film shoot. Fluorescent tubes come in a variety of colors, from "Cool White" to "Daylight" and "Warm." Each have different correlated color temperatures, and they are often found installed randomly – and in combination – at locations where there are multiple fixtures in use.

Technical Note: Fluorescent Lights and Shutter Speeds

Most fluorescent light fixtures actually flicker on and off about 60 times (cycles) per second, corresponding with the speed of the alternating (AC) electrical current. While not noticeable to the human eye, this flickering can cause inconsistent exposures when shooting at shutter speeds higher than 1/60 second. If you shoot at 1/250 sec. under fluorescent lighting, that particular 250th of a second moment could occur when the flicker of the fluorescent tube is at its "dark" phase, thus causing underexposure. The exact moment of manual shutter release is impossible to repeatedly match to the brightest phase of the fluorescent on/off flicker. Thus, every shot could occur at a different moment in the flicker sequence, and inconsistent exposures may result.

If you use exposures of 1/60 sec. or longer, every image will include at least a full bright/dark sequence of the fluorescent flicker, and will be exposed more consistently.

There are fluorescent lights designed specifically for photography which can be used at higher shutter speeds. They either utilize ballasts that have a higher frequency of cycles per second, or they sequence the timing of the flicker between adjacent tubes in the light fixture so that at least two of every three tubes are at full brightness at all times. Most of these specialized lighting units also utilize fluorescent tubes that are specifically color balanced to approximate daylight, or 5,500°K.

As a standard precaution, it is safest to use shutter speeds of 1/60 sec. or slower when photographing under fluorescent lights, and to do exposure and color balance tests before shooting critical assignments.

When possible, avoid using fluorescent lighting for photography, particularly when there is a mixture of lighting types present. Such mixed lighting is often found in corporate and real estate locations. Rotating the fluorescent tubes slightly in their fixtures will turn them off (don't rotate them too much or they may fall out and break). However, you can often find one or more wall switches that control banks of the fixtures. There will be times when you have no choice but to include fluorescent lighting in your location shooting strategy, particularly when these fixtures are the dominant light source at your location.

Today's digital cameras make color balancing a much simpler matter compared to shooting with film. Most of these cameras have presets that you can choose, which provide onboard color compensation when shooting under common lighting conditions. These generally include: daylight, outdoor shadow/overcast, tungsten, fluorescent, and automatic white balance (AWB). The automatic white balance setting is usually the best choice for most traditional photography, but it should be _avoided_ for VR photography – where it is essential to have every image in a panoramic or object sequence match. The camera's automatic setting will make small adjustments between every frame you shoot. These will be very distracting when the images are assembled into a panorama or object movie, and may be impossible to effectively re-match in post production.

Mixed Lighting

Color balance can generally be "corrected" through either the use of color correction filters over the lens when shooting, via subsequent color filtration in the printing process (for negative film), or via digital color modification on a computer. It should be noted that most of the image sensors in today's digital cameras are color balanced for daylight shooting. However, these cameras often provide excellent color rendition under a wide variety of lighting conditions, including tungsten, fluorescent, and even mixed lighting. On board software automatically alters overall color shifts digitally when the image is captured.

Mixed lighting situations are the most difficult for a photographer to deal with. Mixed lighting is where two or more dramatically different types of lighting are present. Frequently, photographers will be faced with combinations of daylight, tungsten, and fluorescent light sources on an assignment.

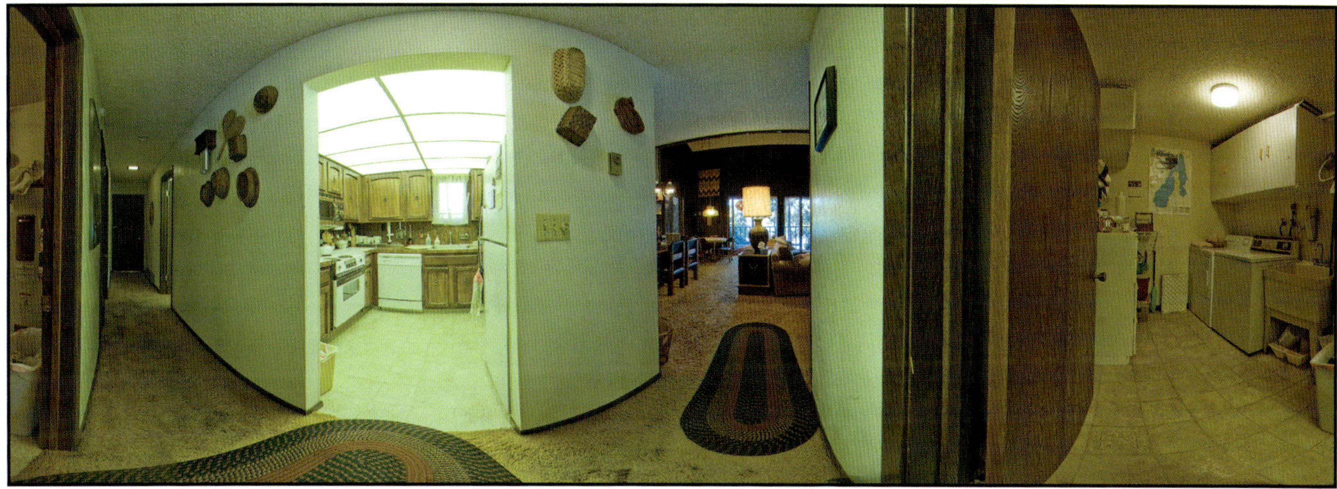

Mixed lighting panorama including fluorescent (kitchen), tungsten (dining & laundry rooms), and daylight (windows)

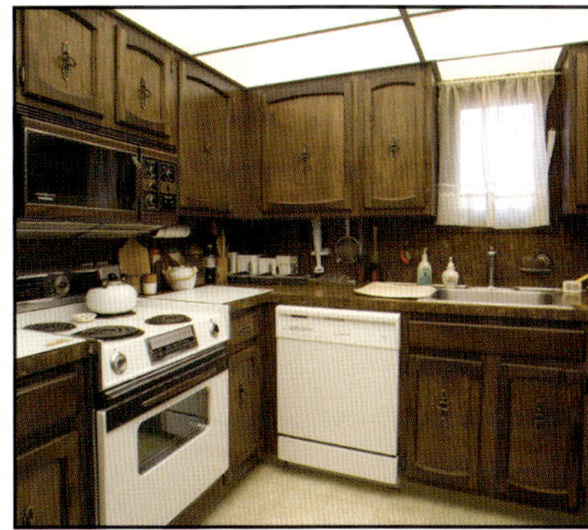

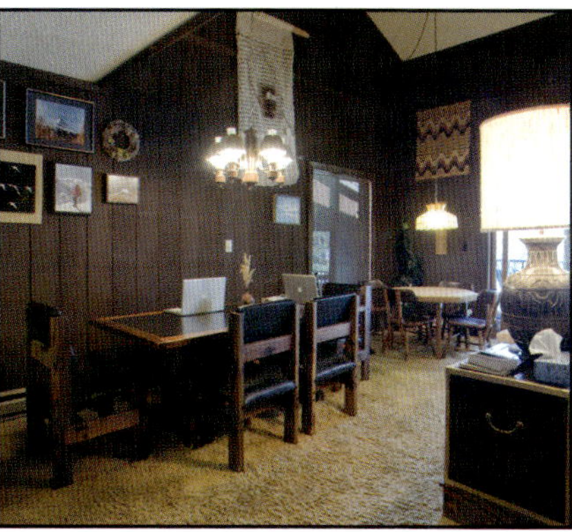

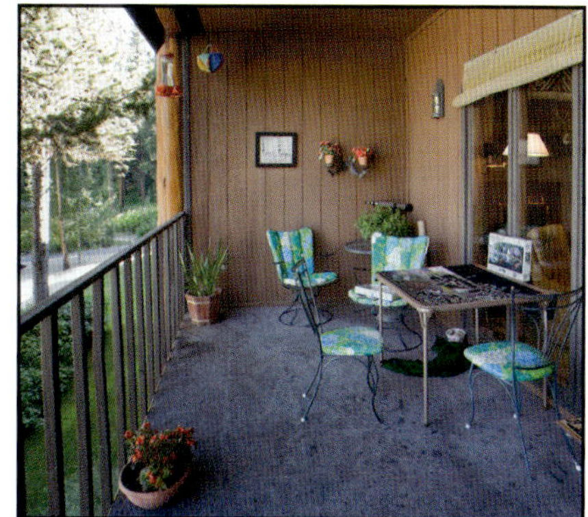

Kitchen balanced for fluorescent   Dining area balanced for tungsten   Exterior balanced for daylight

Fig. 5-29 A combination of lighting types in a panoramic scene can present a real challenge for proper color balancing.

A photographer's job is often one of making a mediocre scene look good, and to properly record that image. Clients don't appreciate their CEO looking green because you photographed him under fluorescent light. Nor do they like seeing the nice white walls of their office appear yellow or blue because you used the wrong light and filtration combination.

When shooting traditional photographs with their limited fields of view, you can often isolate the subject into an area lit by a single dominant lighting source. This allows you to match the type of film or digital white balance to the color temperature of this light, or else to use an appropriate color correction filter on your lens, or even to filter the lights themselves to match.

However, with VR panoramic photography, your view is expanded and it becomes critical to deal with mixed lighting effectively. You are not just shooting a photograph toward the window on one side of a room, but your panorama might also include overhead fluorescent lighting dominating the rest of the office, as well as tungsten desk and floor lamps scattered throughout the scene. In a retail environment, tungsten fixtures are often used for accent lighting, while fluorescent tubes are used in recessed overhead fixtures. Daylight also might come through the store front windows. Your panoramic images have to show all of these areas with natural looking lighting and properly rendered color throughout. It can be quite a challenge.

There are several approaches you can take to mixed lighting situations. In most cases, you are better off choosing the simplest possibility.

Your first step is to determine which type of light is dominant, and choose the proper color filtration and/or film based on that. If the view you are shooting has window light as a dominant foreground in more than one direction, then balancing everything for a daylight color temperature is probably best. If tungsten and fluorescent lighted sections of this panorama are relatively minor in the overall scene, you might be able to leave them uncorrected, as they will only appear as small parts of the image. Slight yellow or green color shifts will not call the attention of the viewer.

Filter Table – Color Correction (CC)

CTB = "Color To Blue" – makes an orange (tungsten) light source appear bluer, correcting it to daylight (5500°K). CTB and CTO filters or gels are rated by how much they shift the color of a light source from one temperature to the other (full, 1/2, 1/3, 1/4, 1/8). They can also be identified in Color Correction (CC) terms, with letter designations indicating more or less correction. An 80A filter converts 3200°K tungsten light to a color temperature matching 5500°K daylight. 80B, 80C, and 80D filters are less blue, converting 3400°K, 3800°K, and 4200°K to 5500°K respectively.

CTO = "Color To Orange" – makes a bluish light source (daylight) more orange, correcting it to tungsten (3200°K).

Plus Green (CC) – "Color Corrects" bluish or orange light sources (daylight or tungsten) to one of several fluorescent light types. CC filters and gels are rated by the amount of green or magenta shift they provide.

Minus Green (CC) – "Color Corrects" greenish fluorescent light sources to daylight (5500°K) color temperatures.

Fluorofilter (CC) – "Color Corrects" greenish fluorescents to tungsten (3200°K) color temperature.

Description	Camera filters (Wratten)	Rosco ID	Lee ID	Color
Daylight to Tungsten	85 (also 85B, C)	3411	204	*Orange*
Daylight to Fluorescent	n/a	3304	244	*Green*
Tungsten to Daylight	80A (also 80B, C, & D)	3202	201	*Blue*
Tungsten to Fluorescent	n/a	3304	241	*Green*
Fluorescent to Daylight	FL-D or 30CC Magenta	3308	247	*Magenta*
Fluorescent to Tungsten	n/a	3310	n/a	*Orange-Magenta*

Fig. 5-30 There are a variety of color correction gels and filters available for converting the color temperature of almost any light source into that of another. Two of the better known manufacturers are Rosco and Lee.

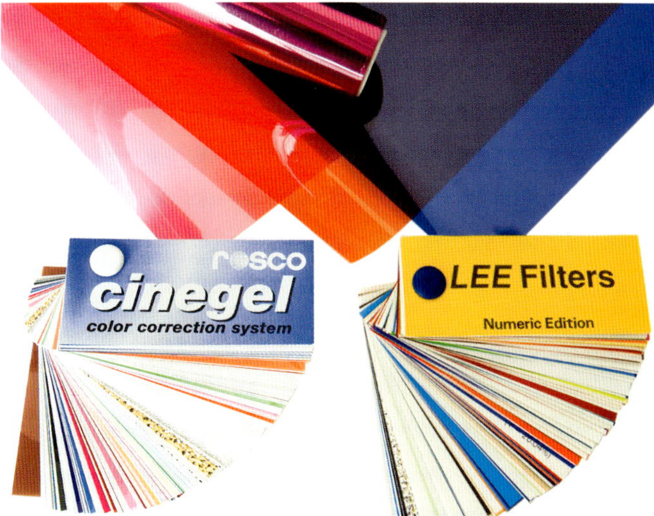

Fig. 5-31 Color correction and other color gels are available in sheets, rolls, and sample books.

Similarly, if you are shooting in a location that is predominantly lit by tungsten or fluorescent sources, simply filter the camera lens (or set a digital camera's color balance) for the necessary color correction and let the other less prominent areas shift color as they will.

If this simple approach doesn't work, then you must either eliminate one or more of the differing light sources, replacing them with properly matching light, or modify them with on-lamp filtration so that all light sources in the scene have similar color temperatures.

Global color correction is most easily done with filters mounted on the camera lens. It is always better to set exposure and color correction properly when shooting, rather than trying to fix major problems in post. Save digital post production efforts for minor tweaking and perfecting of an image, or for salvaging problems that absolutely can't be resolved during the shoot. Remember that the most expensive words in any creative process are, "we can fix it in post."

Eliminating light sources that are the wrong color temperature within a scene can be as easy as turning them off, closing a door, or pulling a curtain across a window. However, this is not always to your advantage, as these light sources may be needed in the scene. For instance, if you need to show a luxurious hotel room with a beautiful view out the window, it won't suit your client to close the curtains just to get rid of the daylight coming through that window. Neither will your client be happy if you leave half the room dark because you didn't want to turn on the tungsten room lights.

Often, you will be faced with having to mix your light sources. In such instances, you may need to use color correction gels over some of your lights in order to

"correct" them to a color temperature similar to that of the predominant light within the scene. Two companies in particular, Rosco and Lee, manufacture low cost color correction "gel" materials, which are used extensively by the motion picture and video industry. They offer gels for almost every color conversion.

Lighting gels can be placed in front of, over, or even around virtually any light source in order to more closely match its color temperature with that of another light. Most often, photographers will shoot with daylight balanced film or camera white balance (WB) settings. So it is usually necessary to gel tungsten and fluorescent lights to match daylight color temperatures.

However, every shooting situation requires its own consideration for what will be the most effective choice for the base color correction. If your scene is primarily lit by tungsten lights (such as many interiors), then you will probably want to color correct any other light source, such as daylight or fluorescents, to a tungsten color balance, and then use a tungsten balanced film or camera WB correction.

If you are photographing a factory or warehouse that is lit predominantly by fluorescent lighting, you may want to use a magenta filter over the camera lens (or a fluorescent WB setting on a digital camera) to correct for the greenish cast the fluorescent lights produce. Then, if there are tungsten lights mixed in, you would put tungsten-to-fluorescent gels over each of them to bring them to the same color temperature as the fluorescents. If there were daylight coming through a window, you could put daylight-to-fluorescent gels over the window to give the daylight a color temperature close to the predominant fluorescents. In this way, you can make mixed lighting color balances match fairly closely.

The difficulty with all this is that it can take a significant amount of effort, and although the sheets and rolls of color correction gels are relatively inexpensive, their cost can escalate if you need to buy large amounts in many combinations. Motion picture and professional photography supply houses generally sell individual sheets (20 x24 inches) for $7-$10 each, while larger rolls (4 x 25 feet) cost between $120 and $150 each. While the gels are reusable, they are generally cut to size to fit a particular lighting fixture or holder, and are often considered "expendable" or thrown away after a shoot is completed.

You will usually want to choose the simplest combination of filtration when working in mixed lighting situations. It might take you and an assistant the better part of a day to install gels over a wall of windows or an atrium (and could cost thousands of dollars in materials), when it might be faster and cheaper to simply put tungsten-to-daylight gels over the interior lights instead.

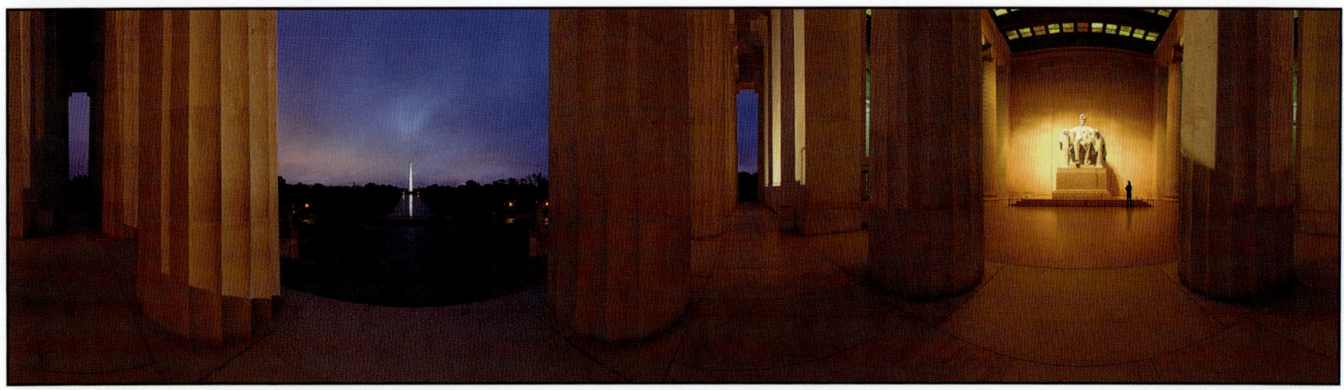

Fig. 5-32 Mixed lighting conditions can often work to the photographer's creative advantage. In this case, the combination of early morning overcast light, combined with interior tungsten and fluorescent lighting, shot unfiltered on daylight film, made for a striking 360° panoramic image of the Lincoln Memorial in Washington, DC.

Certainly, knowing how to color correct mixed lighting is important, but it can be over emphasized. Often, a "perfectly" color balanced mixed lighting scene will not look quite as natural as one where the photographer recorded "unbalanced" colors instead. There are times when a slight yellowish cast of tungsten light shot on daylight film (or digital camera WB setting) can give the scene a feeling of warmth. Similarly, a blue cast of daylight shot on tungsten balanced film or camera WB can give a feeling of coolness to those areas of the image. Even a green shift where fluorescent lights appear can be used for effect.

Take advantage of whatever existing light you can when shooting on location. The less you have to add in supplemental lighting, the simpler your life will

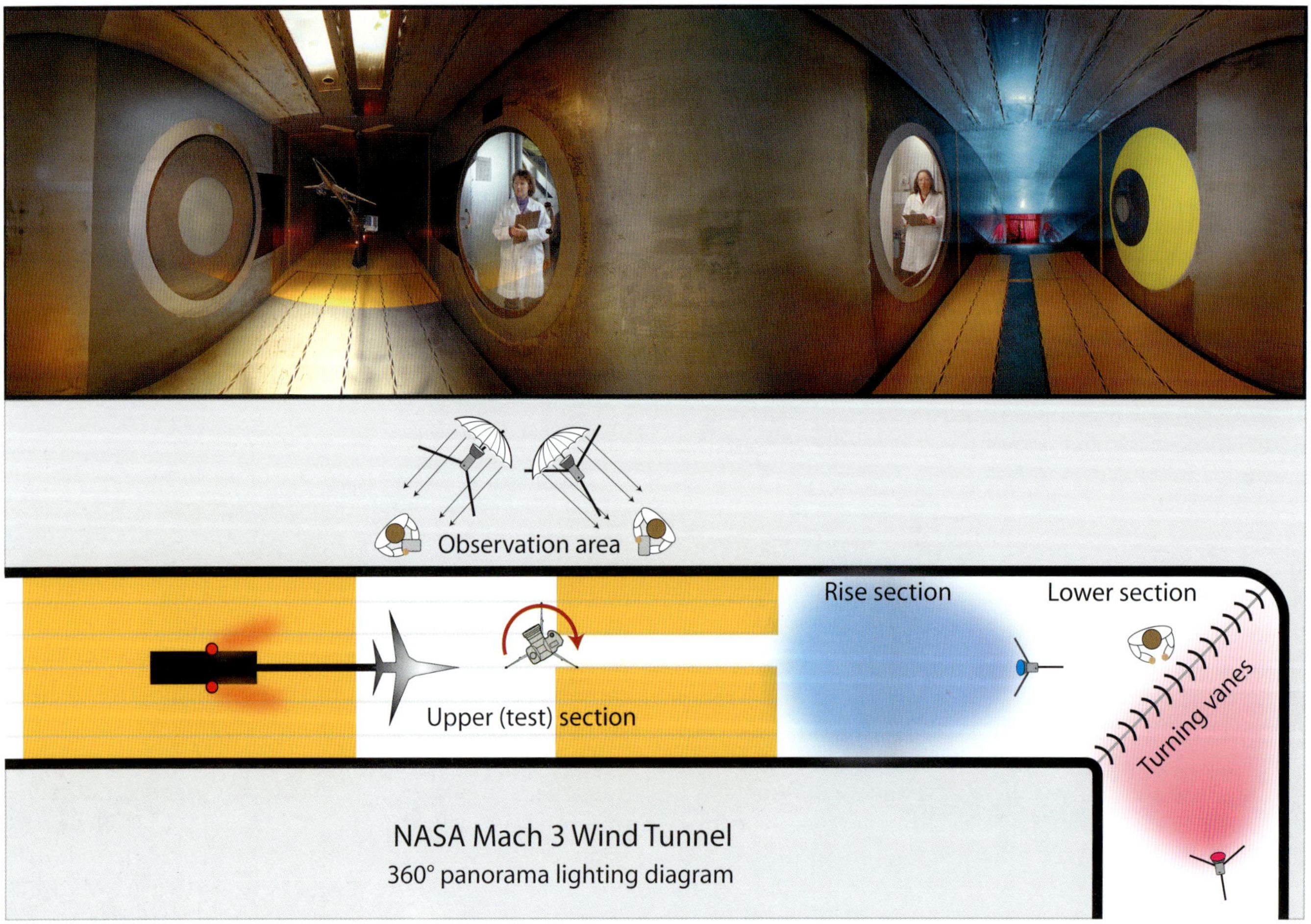

Fig. 5-33 This 360° panorama, photographed inside a decommissioned NASA wind tunnel, took about three days of lighting and preparation in order to shoot effectively.

be. That being said, remember also that there are very few shooting situations, particularly in panoramic VR photography, where lighting corrections or additional lighting will not improve the quality of the resulting imagery. But remember the KISS (Keep It Simple, Stupid) principle. There will be enough other situations where you have no choice but to bring in full studio lighting equipment and spend multiple days doing setups or testing before you are ready to shoot.

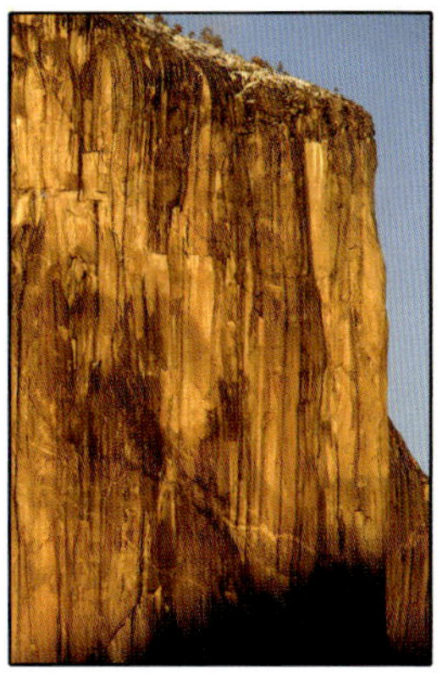

"Magic hour"

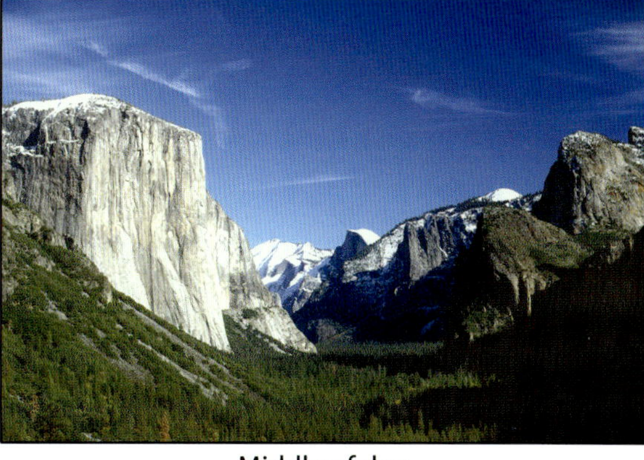

Middle of day

Fig. 5-34 The effects of "magic hour" – the hour after sunrise and the hour before sunset – on the landscape of Yosemite Valley and El Capitan.

There are times when we want to record the color of light in our images without color correction. A beautiful red sunset would not appear quite so beautiful if it were "corrected" to a neutral white color. Similarly, the warmth of a campfire is better visualized when it appears with yellow or orange tones in our photos, rather than as a neutral white. So too, both the "cool" blueness of a clear sky and the aqua green of a tropical reef would be far less attractive if "corrected" to a neutral white or gray.

The light cast by the sun during the hour after sunrise and the hour before sunset generally has a warm, saturated effect on subjects. This, combined with the sun's low angle in the sky, tends to do wonders for photography. Shadows are longer and the intensity of the sunlight is diminished compared to the ambient light in the shadow areas, so highlight and shadow exposure levels fall closer within the exposure latitudes of our film and digital sensors. Experienced photographers refer to the first and last sunlit hours of the day as "magic hour," because the natural lighting does such wonderful things for our photographic subjects.

Dust and moisture in the earth's atmosphere tend to filter out light in the blue end of the spectrum, so the more air the light passes through, the more yellow, or "warmer" it appears. When the sun is low in the sky, its light passes though a significantly longer segment of our atmosphere than it does when it shines from directly above at mid-day. This means that as the sun gets lower, the light reaching us loses more of its blue colors (since they are absorbed faster than the yellow and red end of the spectrum), and the result is the golden light of sunset. The same thing, of course, happens in reverse at sunrise.

This effect is taken to its extreme when sunlight passes through the earth's atmosphere at a shallow angle. In geographic areas where high mountains are in close proximity to lowlands, the rising or setting sunlight can actually pass all the way through the atmosphere and skim over the lowland areas, continuing on its tangential path upward on the opposite side of the earth until it

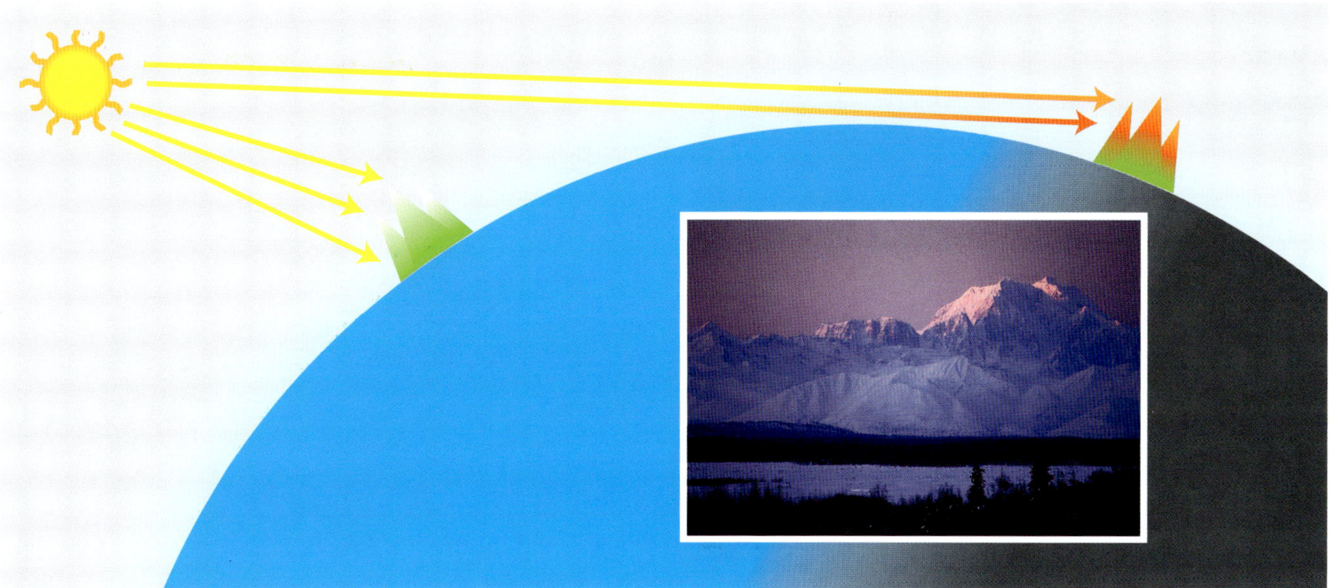

Fig. 5-35 Alpenglow, often seen on high mountain peaks at sunrise and sunset, is caused by the passage of light through the earth's atmosphere. The air filters out shorter blue wavelengths while longer red wavelengths penetrate further.

strikes the tops of the mountains. By the time this light reaches the mountain tops, it often contains only rich orange and red colors because it has passed through so much blue-filtering air.   This effect is known as "alpenglow" and is the source for exquisite high altitude landscape imagery. It is also the cause for brilliant red clouds at sunrise and sunset.

Notice how sunrises and sunsets are often so dramatic when you are aboard an airliner flying at 35,000 feet. It's the same effect – the light from the sun is actually passing through the atmosphere twice as it skims over the surface of the earth and back up toward space before it reaches your window in the aircraft.

ASSIGNMENT: FILL LIGHTING

Using either a film or digital camera with manual exposure controls, along with a portable flash unit that you can control manually, conduct a series of test exposures to learn proper use of fill lighting technique. If using film, choose a relatively slow slide or transparency film, since slide films require more accurate exposures.

The easiest way to do this is using a friend or model as a subject, and to first determine a proper exposure using your camera's internal light meter. The tests will be most effective if you have the sun or your principal source of light coming from the side or from behind the subject. Determine your camera's exposure based on the brightest part of your scene. Make sure that the shutter speed you choose is acceptable for flash photography (the camera's sync speed or slower – 1/60 sec. is safe for most cameras).

Once you've determined the proper aperture setting, make your first shot without any other light added. Be sure to keep notes on your exposure and lighting for every shot.

Next, set your flash unit to produce enough light to equal the ambient light exposure, and place it either directly on top of the camera, or so that its light falls on the subject from the opposite direction of the main light. Keep the flash in this same position throughout the tests.   Now, shoot a picture of your subject with the flash intensity equally balanced to that of the ambient light exposure.

Next, shoot a series of images while decreasing the flash output by 1/3 or 1/2 stop increments (you may need to consult your flash's user manual for instructions). Be sure to maintain the same camera exposure throughout. The result will be a series of images with fill lighting from your flash provided at varying levels, ranging from a 1:1 ratio all the way down to three stops under for the fill. Most photographers will find that fill lighting 1/2 stop or a full stop less than the ambient light looks most natural, yet brings out details in the shadow areas.

You can do similar tests with other types of fill lighting, such as continuous lights (tungsten, fluorescent, flood lamps, etc.), as well as with different light modifiers over your fill lights to soften the light. Remember that you can adjust the amount of fill light reaching your subject by moving the light fixture closer or further away (the amount of light falls off in an inverse square relationship to the distance). If your fill light starts out 8 feet away from your subject, moving it to 11 feet will reduce the amount of light on the subject by a full stop. Moving it to 16 feet away will reduce it by two stops. Bringing it closer to 5.6 feet will increase it by one stop. Use a light meter to measure the exposure changes precisely.

However, keep in mind that for most location photography, particularly for panoramic VR, consistent and repeatable fill lighting using a single portable flash, will be the photographer's most valuable lighting skill. Practice it often, and learn it well. Good fill lighting technique, and the ability to repeat it consistently throughout VR exposure series, needs to be second nature for successful VR photographers.

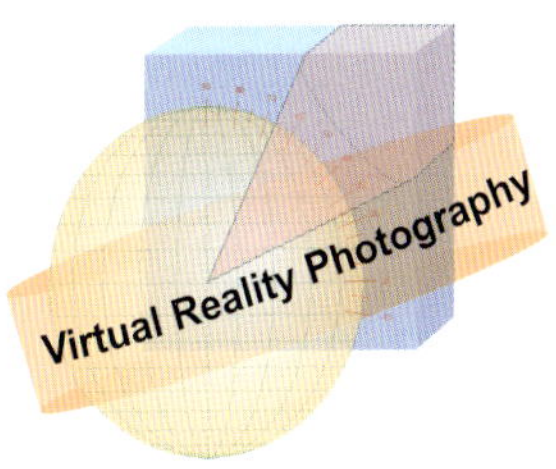

Chapter 6: Film and Digital

If light is the true subject of every photograph, then film (or a digital sensor) is the canvas upon which photographers paint. While such an artistic analogy works to a point, the reality of photography today is that the light illuminating the subjects in front of our lenses is what is *recorded* on our films or digital media. Understanding the mechanics of how film and digital sensors work provides a photographer with the knowledge necessary to choose the best tools for whatever job is at hand.

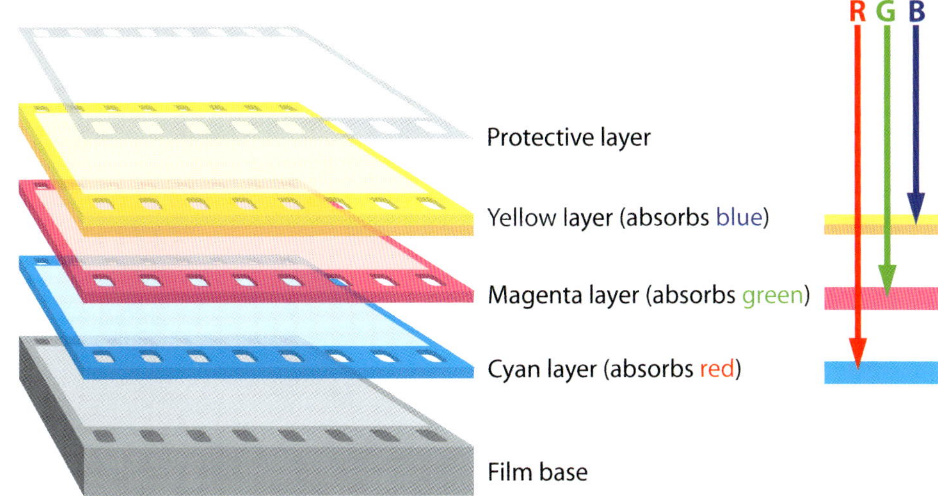

Fig. 6-1 Enlarged view showing structure of color transparency (reversal) film.

Film Construction

Film allows us to focus and capture patterns of light on a two dimensional medium. Photographic film is produced by bonding one or more layers of light sensitive emulsion onto a transparent acetate or polyester base. These light sensitive emulsions are generally made from silver-halide crystals, which become brighter or darker when chemically developed after exposure to varying intensities of light.

In the simplest sense, the most basic black and white films have only one or two emulsion layers, allowing monochromatic recording of light and dark. Colors are rendered as either black, white or some level of gray.

Color films however, have multiple emulsion layers, each of which is designed to record light patterns for a particular subtractive color (cyan, magenta, or yellow). The layers are exposed simultaneously and when developed, allow varying color combinations to pass through. This provides them with the potential to render a significant range of visible colors.

There are two primary types of color films available. The first is called slide or **transparency** (reversal) film, which renders color on film much as we see it with our

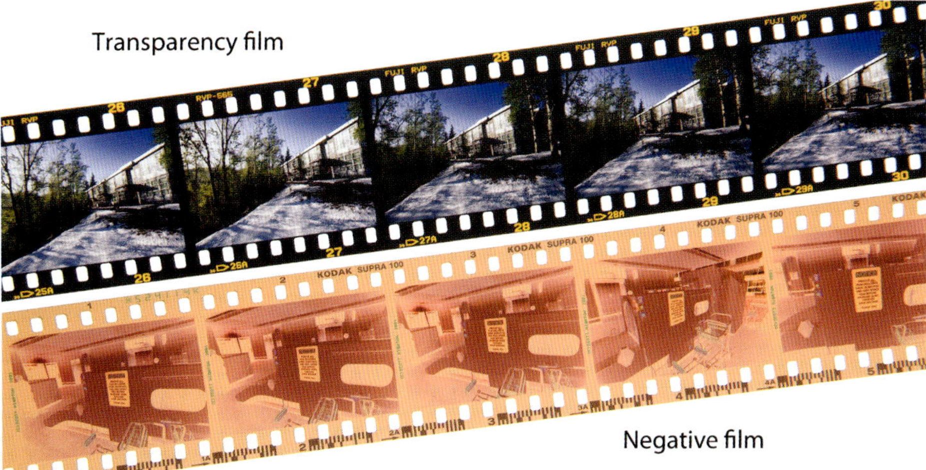

Fig. 6-2 The two primary type of color film are transparency and negative.

eyes. Transparency films are designed to be projected or viewed with a light source behind them. The second is **negative** (print) film, which renders colors opposite of what we see with our eyes, and is designed to be printed in a secondary step that reverses the negative tones back to their positive colors.

Transparency films were long favored for magazine and other print publications due to their rich color rendition and more accurate color reproduction. However, their tolerance for exposure and color temperature is relatively low. Transparency films have narrow exposure latitudes – as little as five stops (a 32:1 ratio). This is the difference between the film's ability to record the most and least light. Transparency films also show significant color shifts when used under lighting with color temperatures other than those specified by the film's manufacturer.

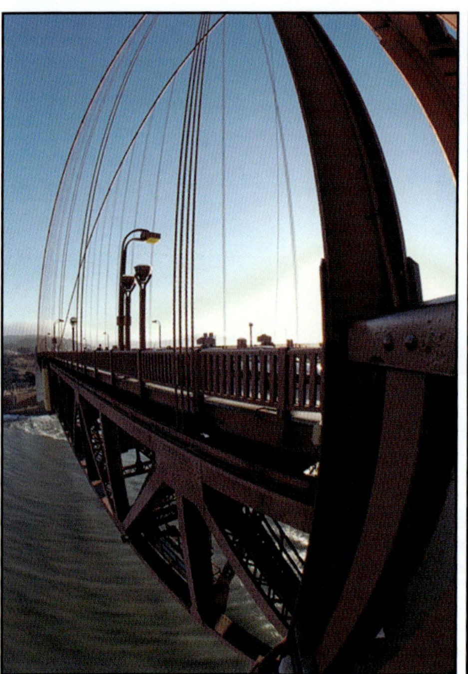
Negative (print) film

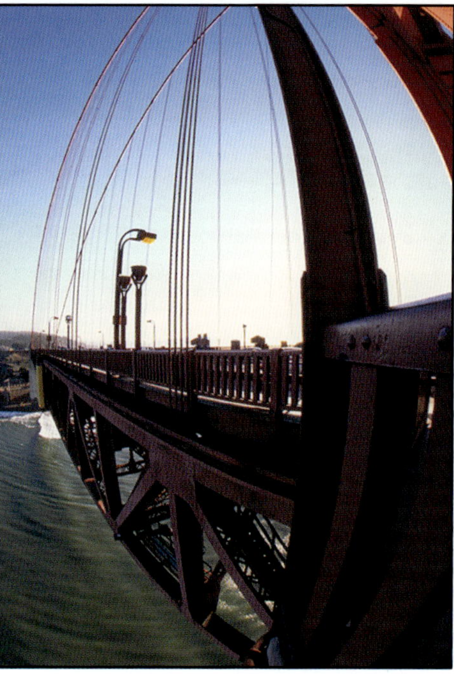
Transparency (reversal) film

Fig. 6-3 Negative films tend to provide greater exposure latitude than transparency films. Transparency films tend to provide more saturated and visually appealing color rendition, but require more precise exposures and lighting control.

Negative film is far more forgiving of exposure and color temperature errors, and the fact that it generally involves a second (printing) process, allows an opportunity to correct exposure and color *after* the original film has been developed. Negative films tend to have exposure latitudes of nine stops and more (a 500:1 ratio), and have a broader tolerance for color temperature variations than do transparency (slide) films. In fact, some negative films, such as certain Fujicolor stocks, are designed specifically for mixed lighting. They include an extra color layer in their emulsion, which is designed to improve color rendition particularly under fluorescent lighting.

This makes negative films far more attractive to photographers needing to shoot in mixed lighting situations, or in situations where available lighting is the only viable option for a photographer to use. Negative films are more "forgiving" of the exposure and lighting discrepancies which panoramic VR photographers face constantly.

It is always better to properly light and expose any scene, but this is not always possible when shooting 360-degree views, where the light on a window side of a room may be many stops brighter than it is on a dark or shadowed side of the room. Similar lighting discrepancies are also found outdoors, where one direction of a 360-degree panorama will be front lit by the sun while others will be in shadow or backlit. The use of fill lighting will often help, but having the extended exposure latitude of negative film at your disposal can aid considerably in maintaining useful exposure levels throughout the panorama.

Today, film photographers have digital scanners, computers, software, and even desktop color printers available, which allow for digital modification and adjustment to any photograph. These tools can be used on any image, whether shot on transparency film, negative film, or even with a digital camera. The fact is that almost all virtual reality photography will wind up in digital form, and will necessarily be tweaked and manipulated with these tools at some point.

While these digital tools are wonderful additions to the photographer's arsenal, remember that they too have their limitations, and should not be viewed as a magic wand to fix any lighting, exposure or color correction problem. These tools are best used for minor corrections, and combined with proper lighting and exposure technique during original image capture.

Digital Sensor Construction

Digital sensors used in today's digital cameras capture color somewhat differently than film, but the end result is similar – a full color rendition of the scene focused on them by the camera's lens.

There are a number of image sensor technologies available today in the broad array of digital camera offerings. For the sake of simplicity, we'll explore only the most common types – the CCD (charge coupled device) and CMOS (complementary metal oxide semiconductor). CCD and CMOS sensors are used in both consumer and professional digital cameras, as well as in most video cameras.

Digital image sensors are electromechanical devices which convert light into electronic signals. They are generally made from silicon compounds, which can be etched into extremely small electronic circuits.

A digital sensor inside a camera serves the same function as film, in that it can record patterns of brightness and darkness that are focused onto it by the camera's lens. The sensor is divided up into a grid array of millions of individual picture elements, or **pixels**. Each pixel transmits an electrical signal corresponding to the intensity of the light reaching it. The image processor then formats and stores the signals from all the sensor's pixels so that the combined data can be used to display the image on a viewing screen or digital printer. The more picture elements the sensor is divided into, the greater the resolution or image detail the sensor can resolve.

Color information is captured by aligning microscopic red, green, and blue filters over alternating pixels on the sensor, and then processing the combinations of RGB color intensities together.

Digital sensors are designed to have a prescribed sensitivity to light, just as photographic films are. In fact, most digital camera manufacturers specify that their cameras have an "equivalent ISO" to that of photographic film. Much like silver-halide films, the faster or more

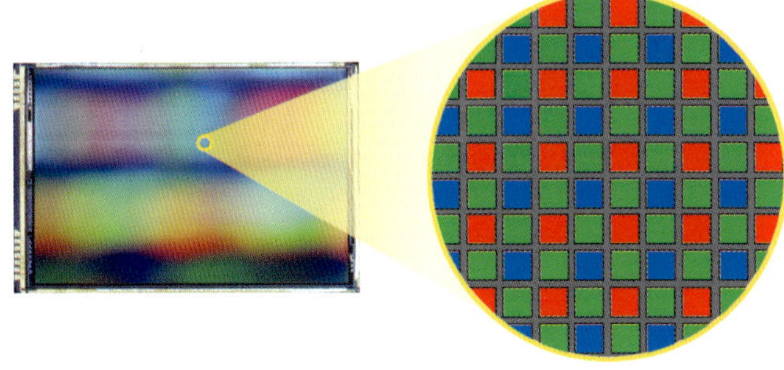

Fig. 6-4 The sensors used in digital cameras align microscopic red, green, and blue filters over individual photo sites, which collectively are used to record full color images.

light sensitive a sensor is, the larger the individual pixel size, and correspondingly, the more pixelation tends to be seen in the resulting images. Larger pixels mean fewer total pixels on the sensor and lower overall resolution. Smaller pixels generally yield higher overall resolution but lower light sensitivity to light.

There are always physical limitations to the effective manufacturing of digital sensors – in particular, how many pixels they can include. However, these limitations continue to diminish with improved manufacturing processes. Today, image sensors in consumer level digital cameras commonly have six million pixels (six megapixels) and more, while high end professional cameras can offer 12 million or more.

Exposure latitudes for digital cameras can vary tremendously, with the cheaper consumer-level cameras generally having narrower ranges than those of the higher end professional cameras. Many professional cameras have as much or more exposure latitude than negative films.

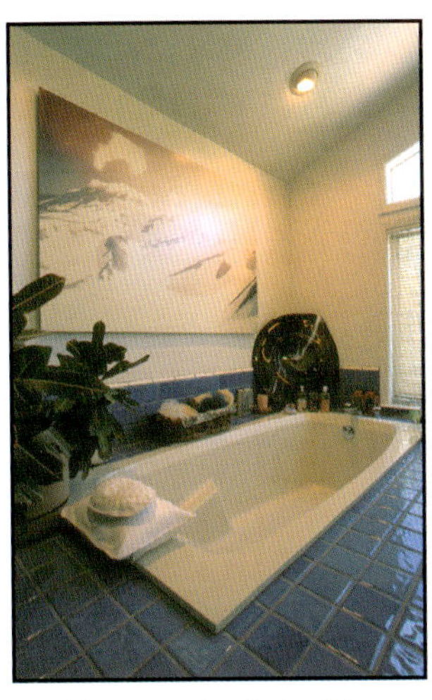
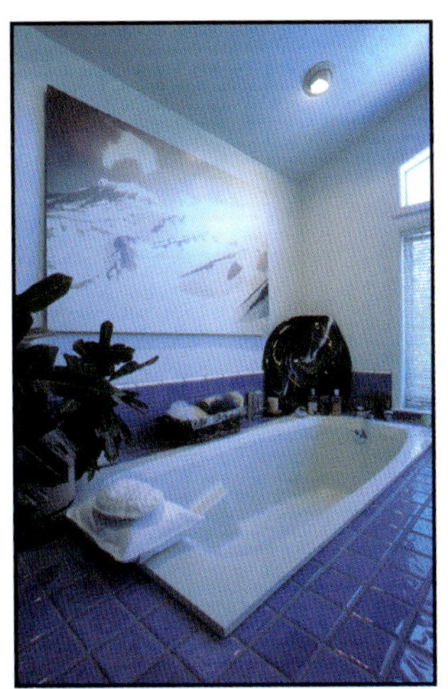
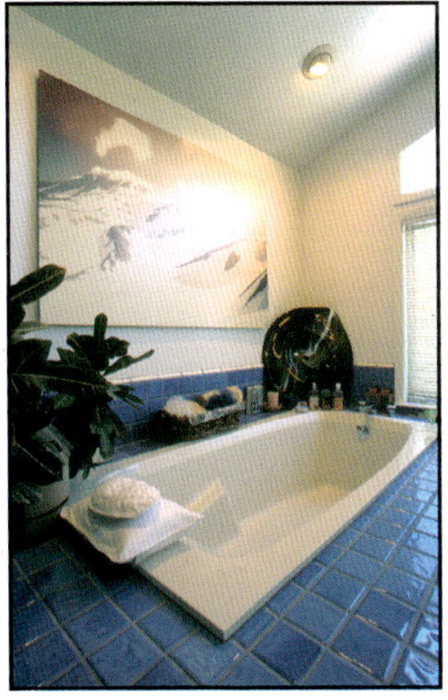
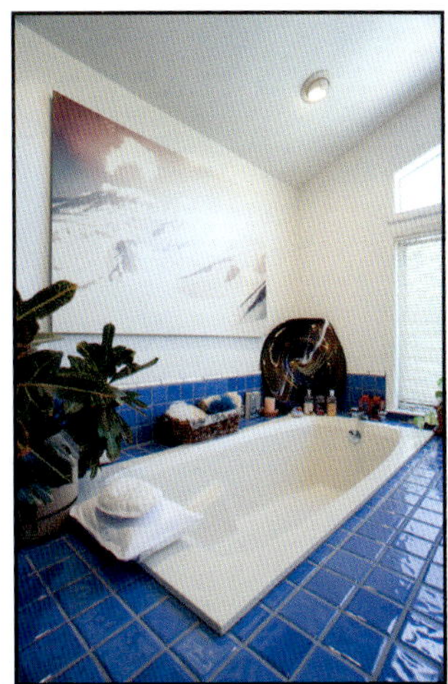

Fig. 6-5 In a mixed lighting situation such as this daylight-and-tungsten lit bathroom, shooting transparency film requires a color correction filter and digital post production adjustments. The auto white balance (AWB) capability of a modern digital camera simplifies the process, and can yield a more accurate and pleasing result.

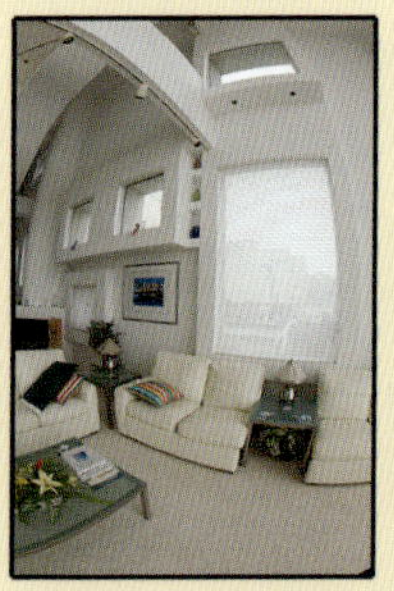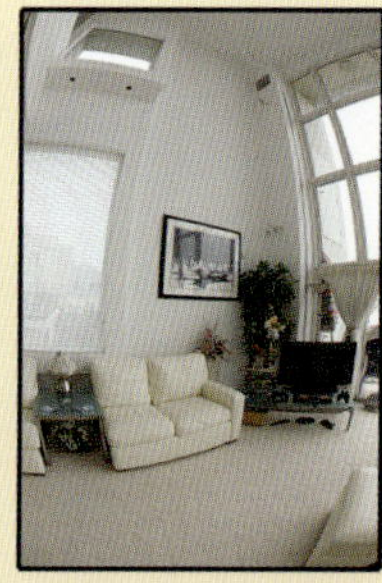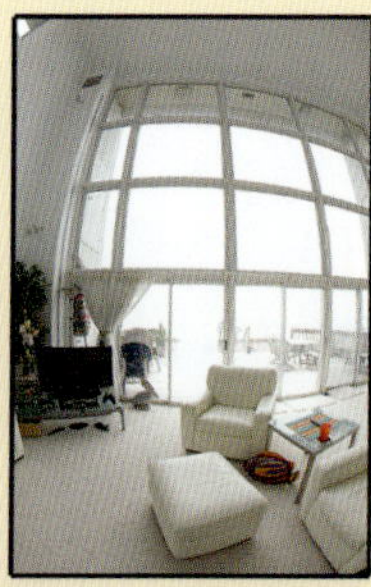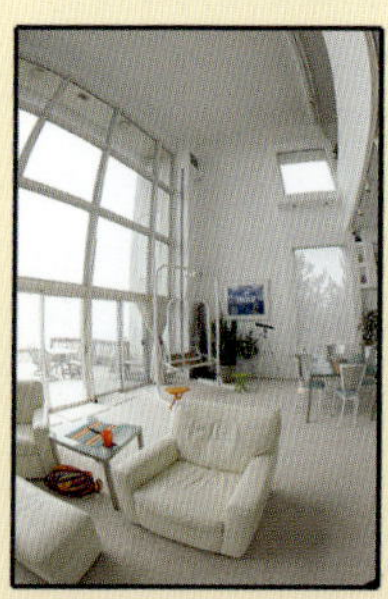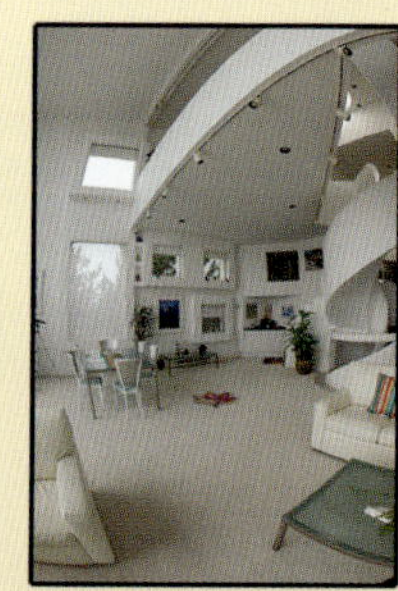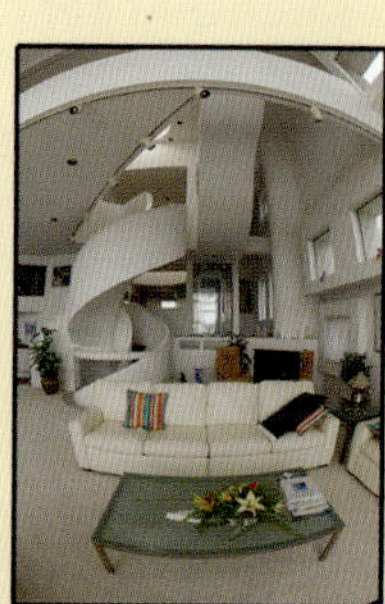

Manual exposure and white balance settings – every image consistent

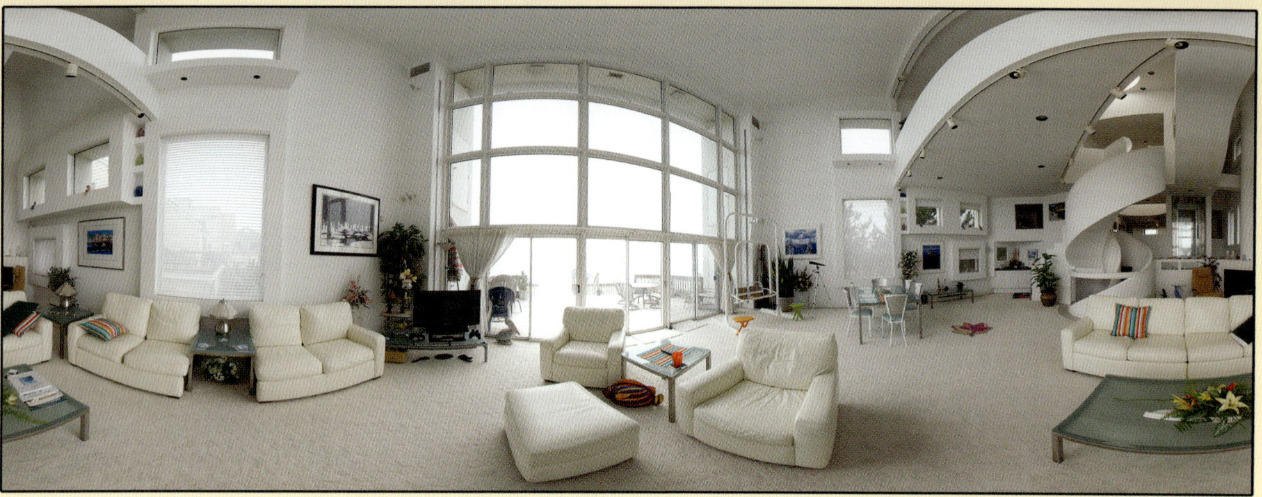

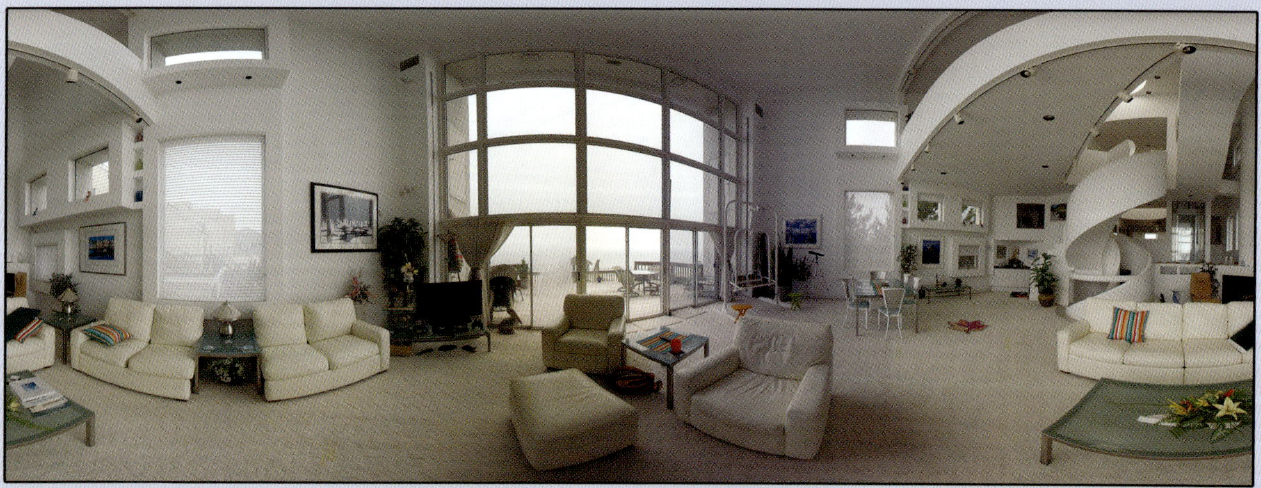

Automatic exposure and white balance - camera auto adjusts for each shot

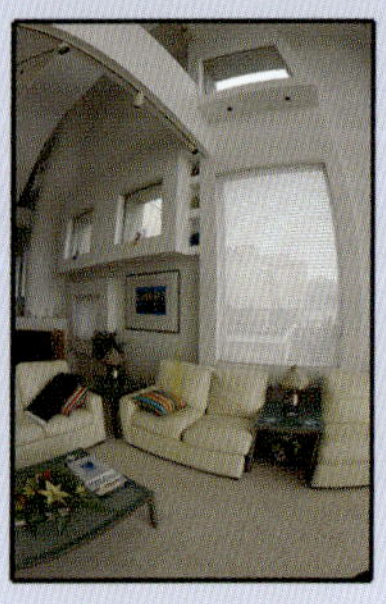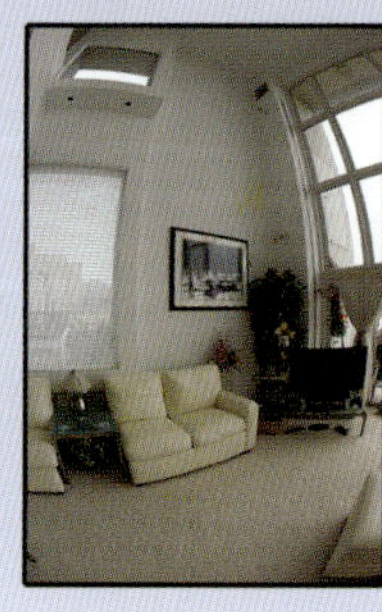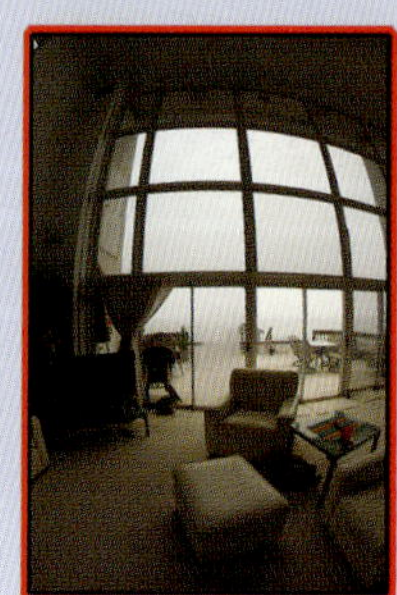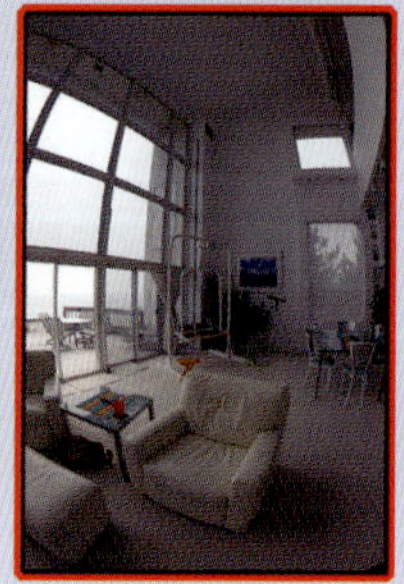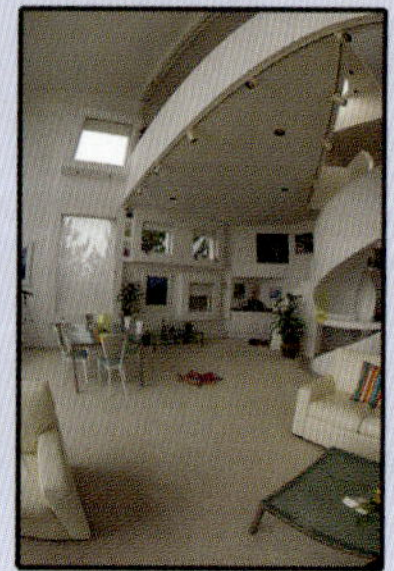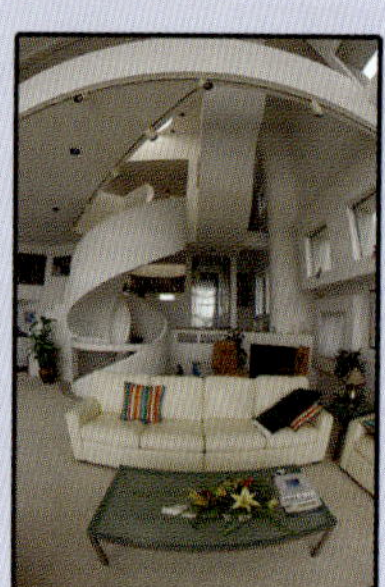

Fig. 6-6 Auto exposure and white balance adjustments can be a problem for photographers shooting stitched panoramic images. Compare the consistency of manually set exposures above with the results of AE and AWB camera settings below.

One area in which today's digital cameras truly excel is in automatic color balancing, particularly under mixed lighting situations. Since all image information is contained within the digital data for an image, it is possible for the camera's on-board processor to optimize that data as it is recorded. This means that both exposure and color information can be adjusted on the fly. The overall color of an image can be balanced toward an approximation of "white" light in a digital process, rather than via color correction filters on the camera's lens.

This "white balancing" is done automatically in digital cameras, sometimes with limited control by the photographer. For the most part, the automatic adjustments work well – and in fact, can provide better overall color correction to a mixed lighting situation than a photographer can do with manual filters and film selection.

However, for the panoramic VR photographer shooting a series of images that will be stitched together to make a panoramic view, the automated adjustments can cause consistency problems yielding image sequences that are difficult, if not impossible, to stitch together seamlessly. It is similar to problems encountered when exposure is changed between images in a sequence. The images may align properly when stitched, but the changes in relative brightness or color balance between shots will cause very noticeable blends between the images.

While it is possible to make selective adjustments to a stitched panorama in Photoshop, the process is much more straightforward when you start out with consistent image sequences.

Consistency and repeatability are also critical when shooting image sequences for object VR. Even slight changes in exposure or color balance between images will show up as flickering when the images are presented in the rapid sequence of an object movie. Almost all object VR photography is done with digital cameras, primarily because the alignment of the images is more consistent (a digital or video image sensor doesn't move within the camera between frames, whereas film is advanced after every exposure). But unless

exposure and color correction can be kept constant during shooting, automatic adjustments will be done by the camera in response to lighting reflections or even different colored sides of an object coming into view as the object rotates.

ISO

Both digital image sensors and film are designed to have a prescribed sensitivity to light. This is generally referred to as the film's **ISO** (formerly ASA) or "film speed." Digital camera manufacturers usually offer an "equivalent ISO" figure to represent the light sensitivity of the image sensors in their cameras.

The larger an ISO, the more sensitive to light that recording medium is. A common ISO for daylight film is 100. A "faster" (more sensitive) film might have an ISO of 400 or higher, while a "slow" film might have an ISO of 50 or even 25. Doubling the ISO means that a film is twice as sensitive to light, or is one stop "faster," while a halving of the ISO means that a film is one stop slower. Thus, an ISO 50 film is one stop *less* sensitive to light as an ISO 100 film. An ISO 400 film is two stops *more* sensitive to light than an ISO 100 film. Relative ISOs on digital cameras work the same way.

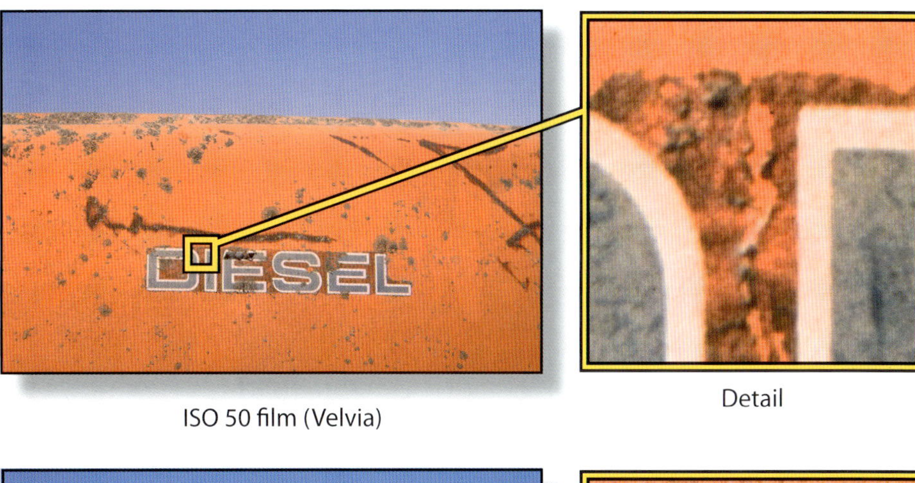

ISO 50 film (Velvia)   Detail

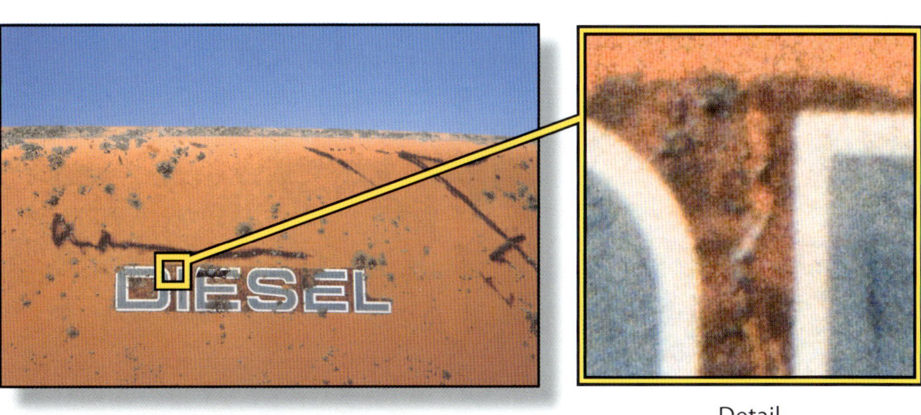

ISO 400 film (Provia)   Detail

Fig. 6-7 Film stocks with a lower ISO tend to have finer grain structure but are less light sensitive. Higher ISO films are more sensitive to light due to their larger grain structure.

A faster ISO speed allows the use of faster shutter speeds (to stop or freeze action), or smaller apertures (for greater depth of field), or a combination of both. Faster ISOs also allow for more successful photography in low light situations, where lower light sensitivity might require impractically long shutter speeds in order to gain correct exposure.

So why don't photographers always use fast films and why don't digital camera manufacturers supply only high ISO image sensors in their cameras? The reason is that increased light sensitivity comes at a price – both financial and in image quality.

As we discovered in **Chapter 3** (Exposure), most everything in photography involves a tradeoff of one sort or another. Increasing light sensitivity in either film or digital sensors generally comes at a cost of reduced resolution, reduced exposure latitude, reduced color accuracy, and increased grain or digital "noise."

With film, increased light sensitivity requires that the light sensitive silver halide crystals be larger. That means that the crystals or "grain" of the film will become more noticeable to the viewer at lower magnifications. The film's ability to resolve fine detail will be limited by the size of the grain. Thus, the smaller the silver grain in the emulsion, the greater the potential resolution of the film will be, but the less sensitive to light it is.

Pixel sizes in digital sensors follow a similar relationship. The larger the pixel area, the more sensitive to light it is, but the fewer pixels a digital sensor can include – thus, the lower the overall resolution.

Some digital cameras (generally the professional models) provide a range of ISOs that the photographer can choose from, offering the photographer a certain amount of flexibility when shooting in varying lighting conditions. This flexibility does not come from any sort of physical modification of the image sensor itself, but rather from on-board digital processing of the pixel data, much as might be done to an image file in a computer application such as Adobe's Photoshop. The digital camera's on board CPU includes algorithms for boosting overall pixel brightness, much as it does for correcting color and white balance.

Photographers using film, rather than digital cameras, also have several options for varying their ISO film speed. The first and easiest, is to simply change the film that your are using in your camera(s).

If you are shooting an exterior scene, you might use a slow speed, fine-grain film for best quality. When you need to move inside to shoot darker interiors, you can simply load a new higher ISO film into your camera. There will probably be slight quality differences in the resulting images, however these may go unnoticed by most viewers because there will be an acceptable change to the look simply due to the fact that you are moving from one environment (outdoor) to another (indoor).

Consistency and continuity are critical to most virtual reality photography, so we generally avoid changing things like film types, lighting conditions, and movement within a scene during shooting. Most virtual reality photography is best done with the camera on a tripod or fixed support in order to maintain consistent alignment between images. Use of a tripod allows for much slower shutter speeds without image blurring from camera movement, as well. This means that slow (or low ISO) speed films can be used quite effectively even in low light situations, simply by choosing longer shutter speeds, which allow more light to reach the film during exposure. So unless there is movement within a scene, which needs to be frozen by fast shutter speeds, it is often possible to use the same films for both indoor and outdoor VR photography, maintaining consistency through both. Remember however, that the color temperature of indoor lighting will often differ from that outdoors, and so color correction filters may be required to achieve a similar look.

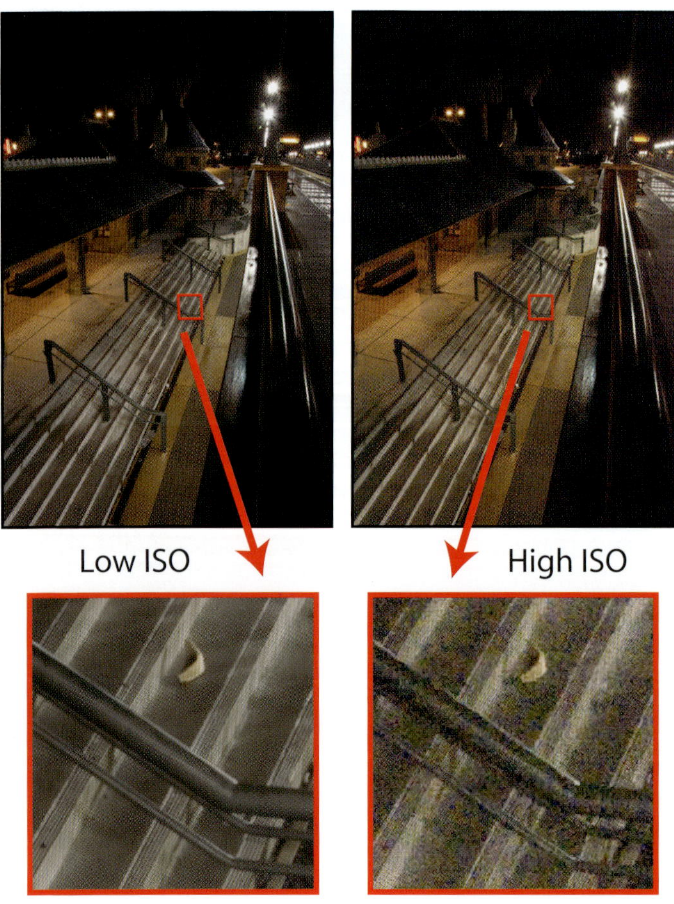

Fig. 6-8 Digital cameras with adjustable ISO settings show similar tradeoffs to film performance. Higher ISOs provide greater light sensitivity, but with increased noise.

A second option for changing film speed is available in the chemical processing of exposed film. **Push processing** involves increasing the length of time a film is developed in order to increase that film's effective ISO or light sensitivity. This can be a useful option when a photographer does not have the proper speed film available at the time of the shoot, and may wind up using a film that is too slow for the available lighting. The film will actually be exposed as though it were a higher ISO, and then push processed to compensate for the underexposure. The photographer must specify to the lab how many stops the film is to be "pushed" before processing. The entire roll of film will need to be processed the same way, so it's not practical to expose part of a roll at its normal ISO while "push processing" selected fames or sequences on that roll.

Push processing is a less-than-perfect solution. It is almost always better to use the proper film for the lighting condition prescribed. But when you have no other choice, push processing can save a shoot. Be sure to clearly mark all rolls of film immediately after their exposure if they are to be push processed. Otherwise, they will invariably get mixed up with film designated for normal processing. Also, make sure to indicate how many stops the film needs to be pushed, or what its desired ISO is.

Push processing most films one stop or less will not noticeably affect image quality. However, pushing the film beyond one stop can cause significant degradation. Pushed film generally yields an increase in contrast and the size of the film grain. The exposure latitude of the film usually decreases, as does overall sharpness.

The effective ISO of a film can also be *reduced* by **pull processing**, where the chemical development time is reduced by the lab. However, both push and pull processing should be limited, outside of intentional artistic effect, to those occasions when no other lighting options are available, and the photographs cannot be made using the proper exposures for a given film ISO.

One would normally assume that a one second exposure at f/2.8 would be equivalent to a 32 second exposure at f/16, since you've lengthened the shutter speed by five stops while decreasing the aperture by an equivalent five stops. Yet because of reciprocity effects, film is not quite as sensitive to light under long exposures, so the 32 second exposure may wind up being underexposed by one or more stops. This "failure" rate will differ for every film. Some type of exposure compensation is usually necessary when using extremely long or short shutter speeds. Most of us will only encounter this when using "Time" or "Bulb" exposures on our cameras, although the phenomenon can also be encountered when using extremely high-speed flash.

In addition to the broad selection of color transparency and negative films a photographer can choose from, there are a number of other specialty films that can be used for both traditional single image photography, as well as for virtual reality imaging.

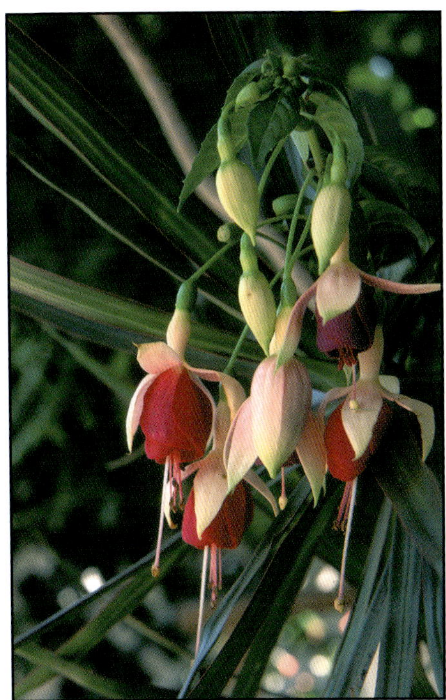

ISO 50 film (Velvia) – Normal process

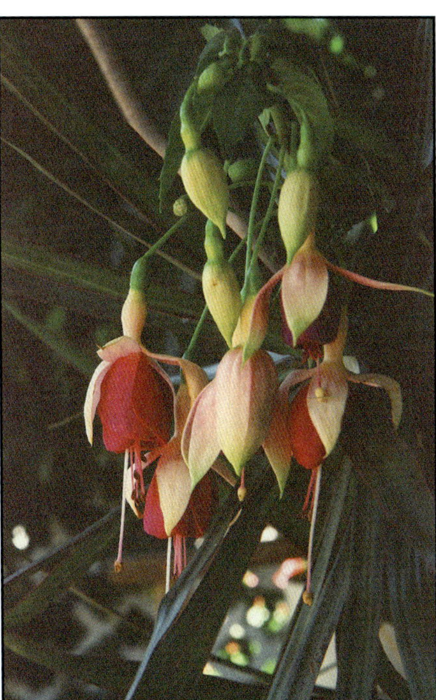

ISO 50 film ***pushed*** to 400 (3 stops)

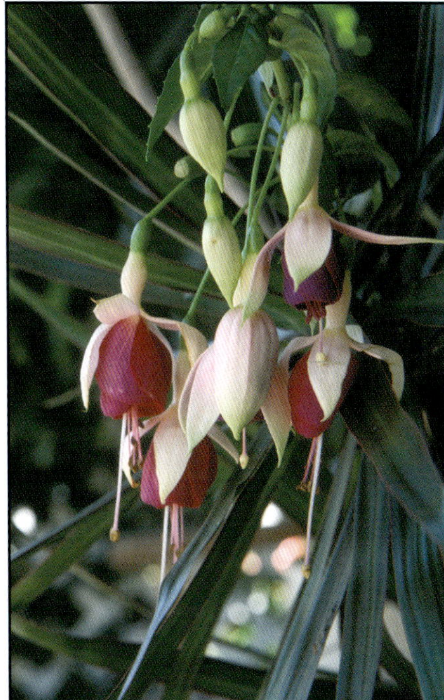

ISO 400 film (Provia) – Normal process

Fig. 6-9 Comparison of "push" processing of an ISO 50 film to 400 with a true ISO 400 film. Push processing is best limited to no more than a single stop (i.e. ISO 50 to 100, or ISO 400 to 800).

Technical Note: Reciprocity Effects

Most films are designed to be used for exposure durations within the normal range of most cameras – usually between one second and 1/4,000 second. Within this range, films generally maintain their published ISO sensitivity and color balance quite adequately. However, at more extreme exposure durations (longer or shorter), most films exhibit incremental shifts in their color balance and / or relative light sensitivity. This is known as **reciprocity effect**.

Along with light sensitivity changes, films exhibit a reciprocity *shift* in color balance when used with long or short shutter speeds. Again, these will vary with each film, as well as with how extreme the shutter speeds are. In general, the color shifts are minor – usually drifting toward green. Corrections can be made either with color correction filters over the lens, or during post production (the printing of negatives, or during scanning and digital color adjustment). Most reciprocity color shifts that accompany time exposures are visually acceptable in the final image.

Film is usually packaged with a data sheet from the manufacturer that provides recommended exposure and filtration corrections for reciprocity effects. These are simply reference points, however. Prepared photographers will always personally test the effects of such exposure changes on a given film before committing to its use on a critical assignment.

The image sensors in most of today's digital cameras yield lesser quality results when used for exposures longer than several seconds, although on-board processing algorithms have been significantly improved. Many professional digital cameras can produce excellent results in low light situations with exposures as long as 30 seconds. Long exposures on digital cameras tend to produce significant digital "noise" and images often of inferior quality. It can, therefore, be better to use film cameras when very long or short exposures are necessary, rather than digital cameras. As digital camera technologies continue to evolve, this shortcoming will surely be overcome, however.

VR photographers will often encounter a need for long exposures when photographing dark interiors with small lens apertures (for increased depth of field) or when shooting outdoors at night.

Reciprocity Adjustments

Film	Shutter speeds	Correction(s)
Fuji Velvia (RVP)	1/4000 sec. – 1 sec.	None
	4 sec.	5M + 1/3 stop
	16 sec.	10M + 2/3 stop
	64 sec. & longer	Not recommended
Fuji Provia 100F (RDPIII)	1/4000 sec. – 128 sec.	None
	4 min.	2.5G + 1/3 stop
	8 min. & longer	Not recommended
Fuji Provia 400F (RHPIII)	1/4000 sec. – 32 sec.	None
	64 sec.	5G + 2/3 stop
	2 min. – 4 min.	7.5G + 1 stop
	8 min. & longer	Not recommended

Courtesy Fuji Photo Film Co., Ltd.

Fig. 6-10 Sample table of reciprocity adjustments for Fuji transparency films.

Most photographers over the age of 30 got their start shooting black and white film, and can remember countless hours spent in the darkroom processing film and making prints. The acrid smells of stop bath and fixer, Dektol stains on our fingers, and countless late nights printing furiously in order to make yet another deadline, remind most of us of the days when almost everything in photography was black and white. We learned the basics and refined our photography skills this way.

Today, black and white photography maintains a certain allure because it is no longer common. The home darkroom has long since been replaced by the one-hour photo lab on the corner. And even these are fast disappearing in today's all-digital age. Almost everything is photographed in color these days, with black and white seemingly reserved for fine art and custom portrait photography.

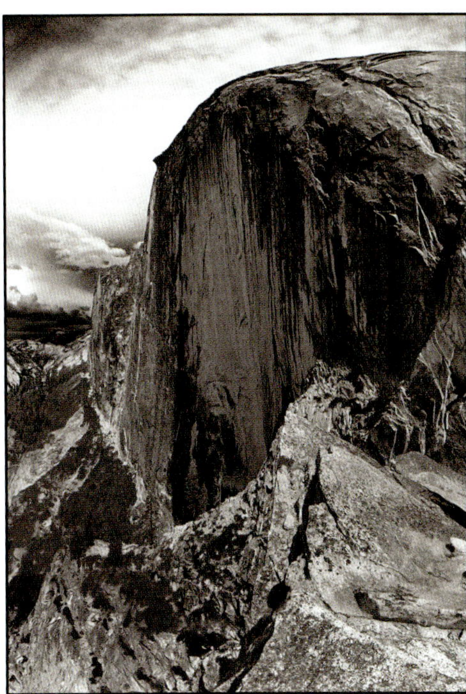
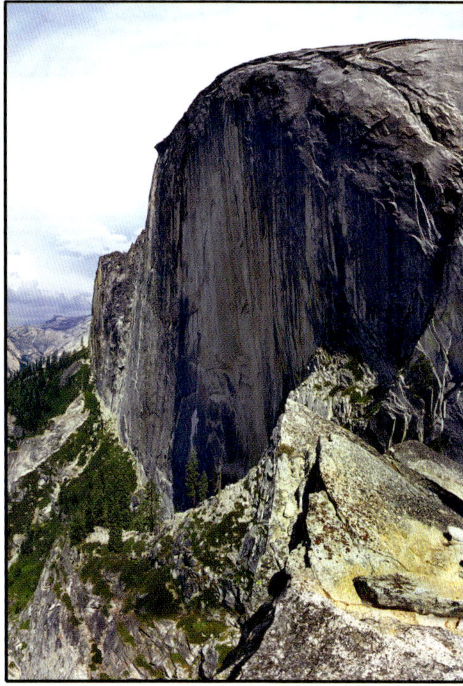

Fig. 6-11 The artistic choice between shooting in black and white or color has become simpler with digital imaging technologies. Capturing a color image allows for a tremendous variety of conversions to black and white in digital post production.

green channel information into individual black and white images.

The classic look of black and white can certainly be used for creative advantage in both traditional and virtual reality photography.

There are additional creative palettes that photographers might want to explore, including capture of light beyond the visible spectrum – such as ultraviolet and infrared. For many years, film manufacturers offered specialty emulsions – such as Kodak's Professional Infrared film. Unfortunately, most of these have been discontinued.

Film manufacturers such as Kodak and Fuji still sell black and white films in a variety of formats, and these should not be overlooked by the creative photographer, even for VR work. However, digital technologies easily allow conversion of color images to black and white (grayscale), even to the point of separating red, blue and

However, most digital camera sensors are sensitive to a light spectrum far greater than what the human eye can see, and are usually covered by special infrared (IR) filters specifically to block this light. This helps render more visually similar colors to what the human eye perceives. It is possible to have these filters removed by specialized camera technicians in order to make a digital camera's sensor capture its

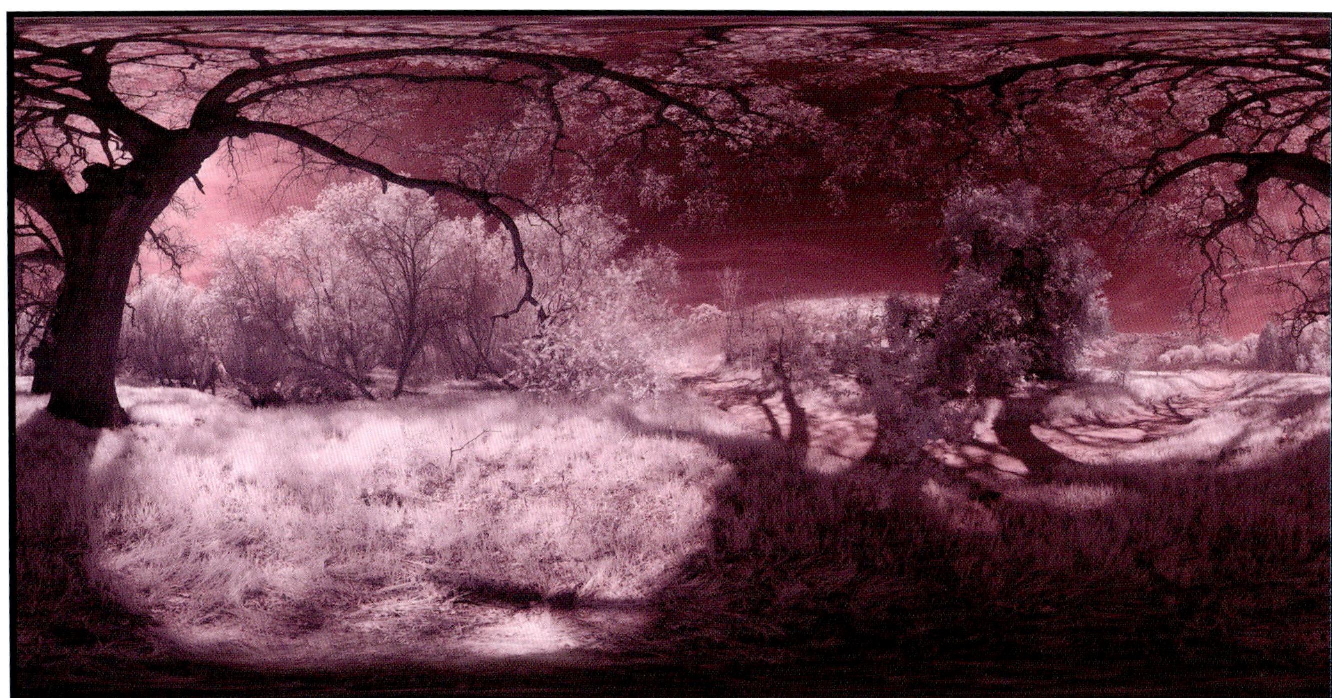

Courtesy: Panoscan Inc.

Fig. 6-12 An "extended spectrum" panoramic image, including infrared and ultraviolet wavelengths, as shot with a high-end Panoscan MKIII camera.

full light spectrum, or a modified portion, such as only infrared wavelengths.

Keep in mind that doing this means your camera will no longer be usable for "normal" photography, and of course, this will probably void any warranty you might have. Yet some photographers find this a new outlet for their visual creativity – including for panoramic VR photography. If you want to pursue this, consider converting an older digital camera with an expired warranty, rather than risking a newer (expensive) one.

An online search for "digital camera IR conversion" will yield a fair number of technicians and service companies who can make such modifications.

There are also high-end professional cameras, such as the Panoscan MKIII, which allow the capture of normal, as well as "extended spectrum" images, that include additional wavelengths extending into both the ultraviolet and infrared regions.

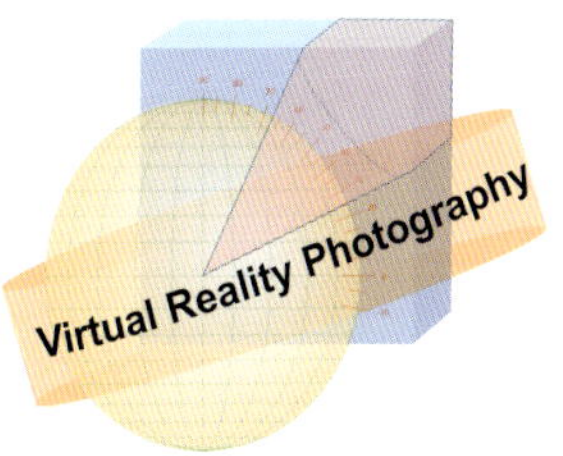

Chapter 7: Digital Basics

Digital technology has revolutionized the world of photography, from the way we create photographs all the way to how photographers run their businesses. Digital systems have changed the face of publishing, as well as the very nature of how we communicate with each other today. Without digital imaging or the ability to display photographic images on a computer screen, virtual reality photography and most other forms of interactive media would not even exist.

Before we delve too far into digital imaging basics, it is important for the reader to understand that digital technologies, by their very nature, involve a certain amount of math. The good news, however, is that very little of this is actually necessary for the photographer to understand in detail. Most digital systems are designed to make their math functions transparent to the user. However, in order to realize both the limitations and the tremendous potential of digital technology, the photographer will need to understand a few basic math concepts.

If you can calculate f/stops, shutter speeds, and can handle inverse square lighting relationships, you can understand the basics of digital imaging.

Digital Components

There are three components of digital imaging: Input, Processing and Output. Input involves digital cameras or film scanners that convert recorded light patterns into digital data that computers can work with.

Processing components are the computers or other electronic systems that we use to manipulate the digital data for stitching, color correction, compositing, sharpening, blurring, and creative effects.

Output components are the desktop printers, printing presses, monitors, and recording devices that we use to display the images after digital processing. These devices convert the ones and zeros of digital data back into analog images that we can view with our eyes.

The Basics

Digital data is a numeric representation of the world around us – otherwise known as tangible or analog information. Digital information can represent the colors and shapes in a photograph, sounds, music, graphic illustrations, or even combinations of text, numbers and calculations.

10x15 pixels

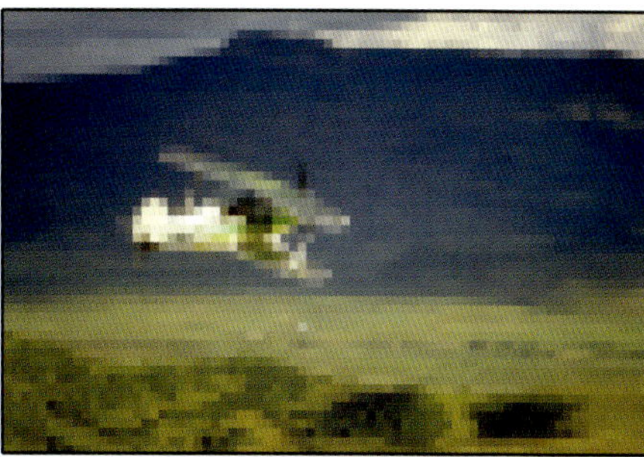

50x75 pixels

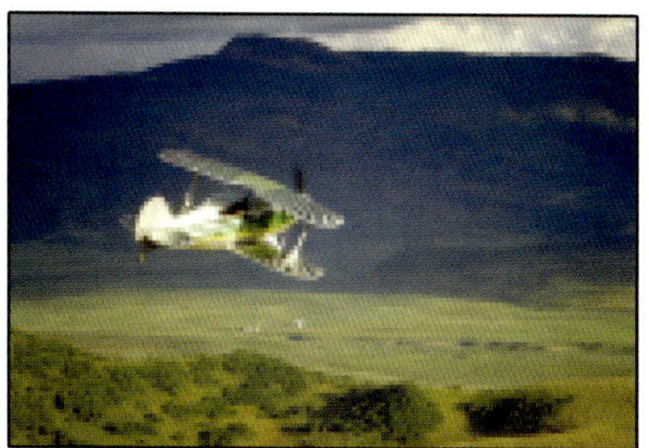

100x150 pixels

Fig. 7-1 The more pixels used to represent an image (resolution), the greater the detail that can be shown.

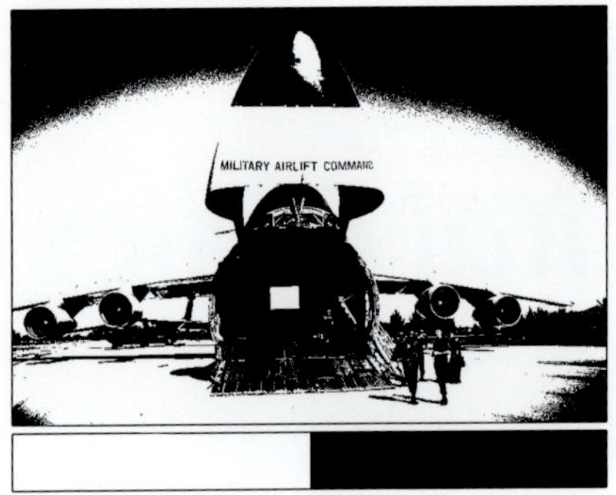

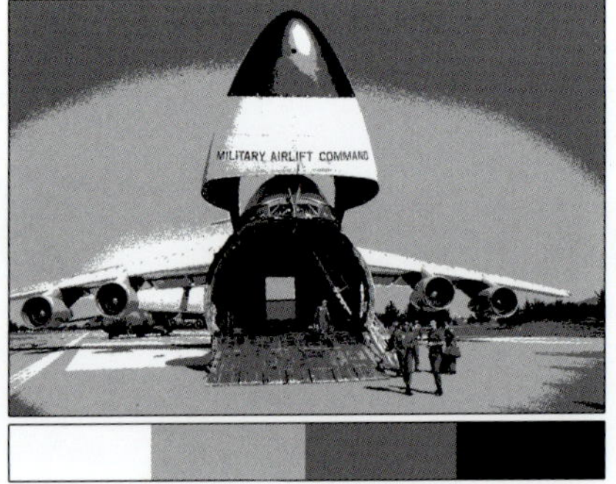

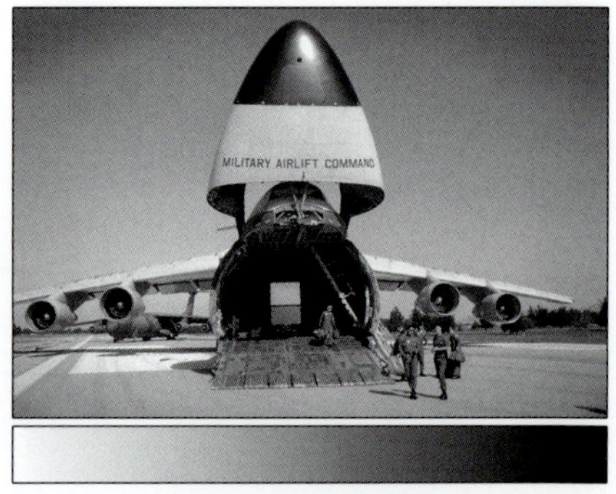

Fig. 7-2 Grayscale bit depth. More data space available to describe each pixel means more tones, or shades of gray can be represented.

In digital imaging, photographs are broken down into minute elements known as pixels. Pixels have been likened to individual grains in silver-based film. Although the analogy is less than perfect, it does illustrate the concept in a reasonably simple way. Each pixel in an image is identified by its two dimensional location within the picture, as well as by the color it represents. The more pixels contained within an image, the greater the resolution and the more digital information is available.

If a digital image contains only a few hundred pixels, the resolution will be quite low and its overall subject may not even be recognizable. There is simply not enough information available for our eyes to make sense of the result. Even with several thousand pixels, we still may not be able to recognize the content of an image. As we increase the number of pixels however, we can increase the resolution and detail of what we can see.

The numeric representation of digital data is done using a binary system, which consists simply of ones and zeros. Each 1 or 0 is referred to as an information **bit**. Simply put, bits work like light switches, which are either on or off at any given moment. One is on, zero is off. The bit is the foundation of digital information. For the photographer, one bit of information at a particular point (pixel) in a photograph would mean that that point is either black (off) or white (on).

By combining groups of these bits together to describe a single pixel, we can represent levels of gray in between the extremes of white or black. If we assign two bits to describe shading or color for each pixel, we can represent four (2^2=4) different light levels (off-off; off-on; on-off and on-on). Thus, instead of having only black or white available, we now also have two levels of gray in between.

If we group three bits together to represent a single pixel, we have eight (2^3=8) combinations possible. These would include black, white, and six levels of gray in between.

With eight bits per pixel, we get 256 possible combinations (2^8=256). This is the minimum standard for digital imaging systems today. Using grayscale (also called two-tone or black & white), eight bits of information allows us to represent 256 levels of gray per pixel, which is quite adequate for photo realistic representation of traditional black and white images.

Coincidentally, eight bits of information is known as a **byte** in computer jargon. A byte is the amount of computer memory required to represent one pixel of 8-bit grayscale information in a digital photo.

Adding color information to a digital image requires more data for each pixel. Using the standard RGB (Red, Green, Blue) color model, most visible spectrum colors can be created by combining different amounts of the primary additive colors – red, green and blue. Computer monitors display these colors by combining 256 levels (8 bits) of *each* of the three primary colors (totaling 24 bits of color per pixel).

For each pixel, if you have only one bit of information per color, you can represent eight colors (2^{1*3} colors = 2^3 = 8). These would be as follows:

Red	Blue	Green	Result
Off	*Off*	*Off*	**Black**
On	*Off*	*Off*	**Red**
Off	On	*Off*	**Blue**
Off	*Off*	On	**Green**
On	On	*Off*	**Magenta**
On	*Off*	On	**Yellow**
Off	On	On	**Cyan**
On	On	On	**White**

If we have two bits per color per pixel, we get four brightness levels for each of the three colors, giving us 64

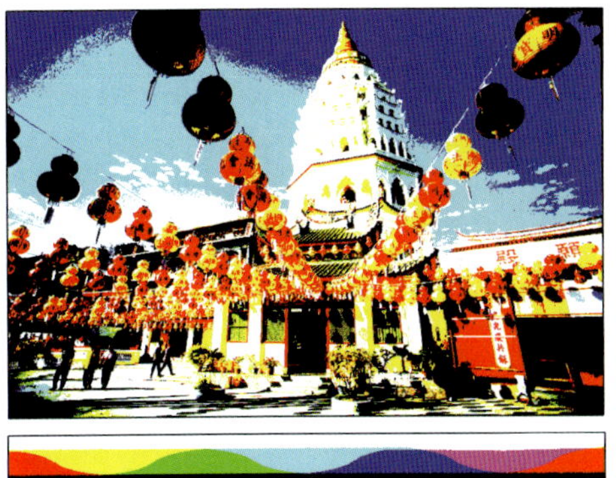

1-bit per color (8 colors)

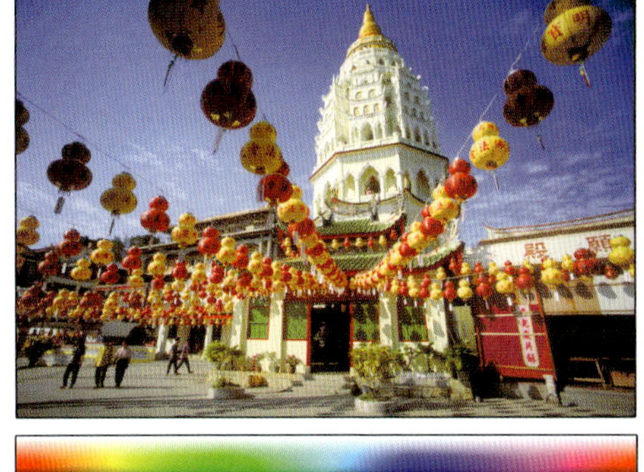

8-bit per color (up to 16 million colors)

Fig. 7-3 Color bit depth. More data space available to describe each pixel means more color tones can be represented.

possible color combinations ($2^{(2*3)}$ colors $= 2^6 = 64$). This is referred to as color depth and, in this case, would be referred to as "2 bits per color."

Expanding this to 8-bits per color, we can have more than 16 million possible colors ($2^{(8*3)} = 2^{24} = 16,777,216$ colors). This is generally considered to be the minimum standard for today's color digital imaging systems. It provides similar color rendition to the range of most films, and is referred to as "24-bit color" or a color depth of "8 bits per color."

Higher end digital imaging systems provide even more color depth. Many digital camera manufacturers tout their equipment's capabilities, claiming 10, 12, and more bits per color. A billion different colors can be represented with 10 bits of RGB color ($2^{(10*3)} = 2^{30} = 1,073,741,824$). Sixty eight billion colors are available with 12-bits per color (2^{36}). Keep in mind however, that this increase in color information results in a corresponding increase in processing power and digital storage required to work with the digital files.

With memory and storage concerns in mind, digital camera and scanner manufacturers often build their equipment to "capture" the image with greater-than-24-bit color and then "optimize" it to 24 bits. These systems can recognize billions of colors, but when storing the image file, save it with the "best" 16 million colors.

If this seems a bit confusing, don't worry. Even an experienced photographic eye will have difficulty telling the difference between a 24-bit and a 32-bit image. The main advantage of larger bit depths is that they offer increased exposure and color latitudes. The range of colors which can be rendered by traditional transparency films is fairly similar to the range of 24-bit color on most computer systems.

Storage and Memory

Manipulation of digital data requires that we be able to perform calculations and record the results for each pixel. This requires both sufficient digital processing and storage capability.

As an example, consider a small digital image measuring 1,000 pixels wide by 1,000 pixels high (one megapixel), with each pixel containing 24 bits of color information. Our image would contain one million pixels, or 24 million bits of information (1,000 x 1,000 x 24). Computer memory and storage are generally measured in bytes, so with 8 bits per byte, this one megapixel image requires three million bytes of memory.

If this image is black and white (grayscale) rather than color, the memory or storage required is only 1/3 of that of a similar color image. A color image would require eight bits of information *per pixel* for red, green and blue, whereas a grayscale image needs eight bits of only black. Thus, a 1,000 x 1,000 pixel grayscale image contains about eight million bits of information (1,000 x 1,000 x 8), requiring only about one million *bytes* of memory.

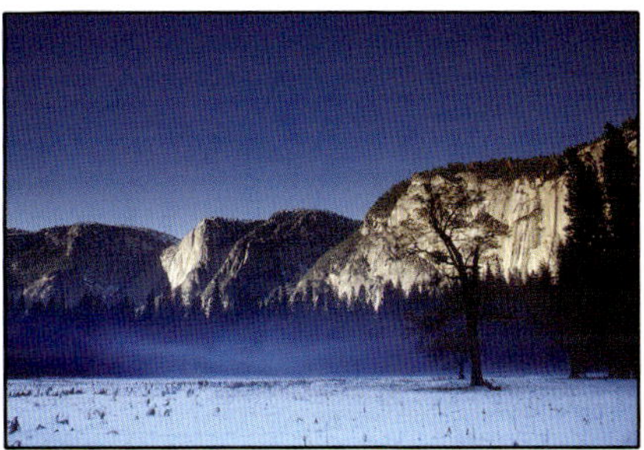
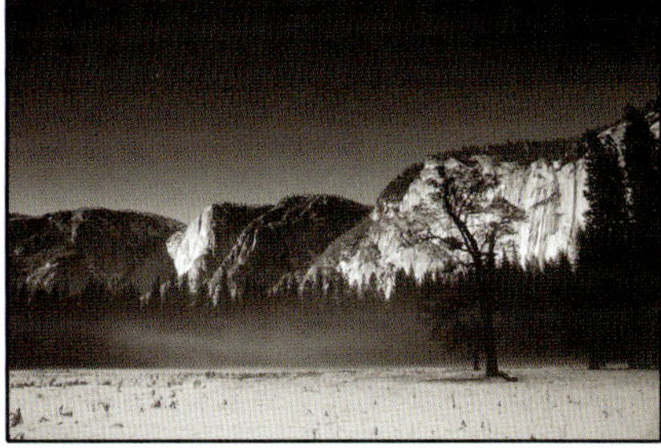

Color (RGB) file = 3MB   B&w (grayscale) file = 1MB

Fig. 7-4 Full color images generally require three times more data than those in black and white. Brightness values for each pixel are stored for each of three color channels (red, green, and blue), rather than just one (black).

A **kilobyte** (KB) is equal to 1,024 bytes, and a **megabyte** (MB) is equal to 1,024 kilobytes. (Kilobytes are often abbreviated as "K", such as "an 800K file" and megabytes are often called "megs", as in "it's saved as an 18 meg file.") Therefore, our 1,000 x 1,000 24-bit color image would be a digital file of 2,930 KB or 2.86 MB. This will be important later when we look at the usability of digital files.

In general, the larger a digital file is, the more detail it contains and the larger it can be successfully reproduced.

Reproduction

One of the benefits of digital data is the fact that it can be perfectly copied. Since a digital photograph is a long series of ones and zeros, duplicating these number strings with a computer is quite simple. Every copy of a digital photograph can be as perfect as the original. There are no inherent contrast, grain, sharpness, or color shift problems that we encounter when duplicating photographs traditionally on film or other photosensitive media.

This obviously has advantages for photographers because it allows us to submit digital files to clients and associates without our original images ever leaving our possession. Since digital data can be transferred electronically, we can transmit our images via online networks and the Web.

On-Screen Presentation

Most VR photography is destined for publication on a computer or video screen, either via the Web, CD/DVD, or video kiosks. Such displays are usually considered to be relatively low resolution, since the traditional computer monitor has a resolution of only 72 dots per inch (dpi). Of course, modern monitors can display at varying resolutions greater than 72 dpi. However, the 72 dpi figure is still used as a standard for screen resolution calculations. With this in mind, consider that every square inch of an image displayed on a computer or video screen will require 72x72 pixels (5,184 pixels). In order for an image to measure 8"x12" on a computer screen at 72 dpi, it will require (8x72) x (12x72) or 497,664 pixels.

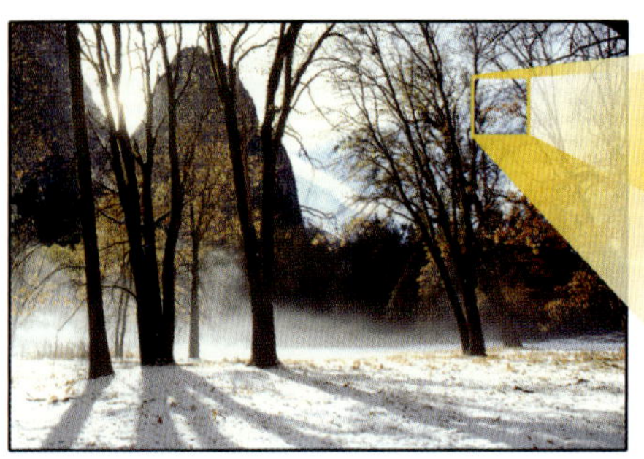
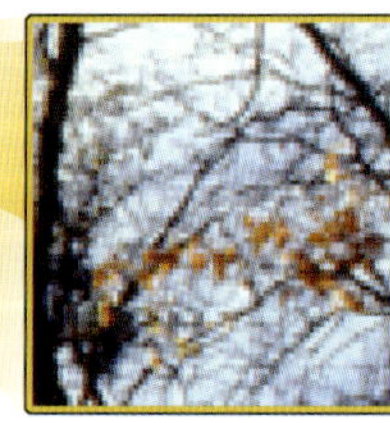

8"x12" @ 72 pixels per inch (ppi)

Fig. 7-5 Detail of a 1" square section of a 72 dpi image.

If the above image were an 8-bit grayscale image (meaning each pixel is displayed as one of 256 monochrome shades from black to white), then it would require one byte of data (8 bits) for each pixel, for a total of 497,664 bytes (486K). If it were a 24-bit color image, it would require three bytes of data for each pixel (one each for the colors red, green and blue), totaling 1,492,992 bytes (1.42MB).

The original standard for a full-screen display on a computer monitor was 640x480 pixels. This was established when most computer monitors measured 13" diagonally. Monitors today are much larger and can display higher resolutions, but the old 640x480 pixel dimension is still often referred to as "full screen." This size also corresponds reasonably closely with traditional NTSC video screens and TV sets (525 vertical lines).

A 640x480 pixel full color image file will require 921,600 bytes (900K) of data (640x480x3). The size that the image is displayed on the computer screen is often referred to as the **window size**. This becomes important in the presentation of VR photography, when we need to determine how large we want an interactive VR movie to be viewed on screen.

A larger window size requires more image data, or more pixels of image information to be available to fill it. Remember also that most virtual reality movies allow the user to zoom in to see more detail within the movie window. So VR images generally require more data than what would be needed to simply fill the movie window at 72 dpi. Otherwise, zooming simply enlarges the limited pixels that *are* available, rather than revealing further detail in the scene or object.

For object movies, one should usually plan a window size that is equal to the dimensions of each photograph in the sequence. A color object movie presented at 640x480 pixels will require 900K of data (640x480x3 bytes) for *every frame* in the object sequence. If the movie contains 36 frames – one shot every 10 degrees around the object – the complete movie will require 31.6 MB of image data (36 x 900K = 32,400K or 31.6MB). Various compression systems can reduce this significantly, but you can see how quickly file sizes can grow, causing playback and delivery problems, particularly for limited bandwidth Web use.

Note that if you were to halve each dimension of that movie window (320x240 pixels), you would wind up needing only 1/4 of the image data (225K per image or 7.9MB total data). Again, post production compression algorithms can significantly reduce the overall file sizes of object movies, but your movie window dimensions will usually be the most significant factor in controlling object movie files sizes.

With panoramic VR movies, you will need to determine whether the content of the panorama will entice the viewer to zoom in for a closer look, and how much of a zoom is likely to be desired. This will help determine how much additional resolution (or pixel data) the image should contain. A good rule of thumb for panoramic VR movies is to provide *twice* the resolution needed for the window size being presented. If the movie window is planned to be 240 pixels high, the panoramic image should be at least 480 pixels high to allow for limited zoom detail.

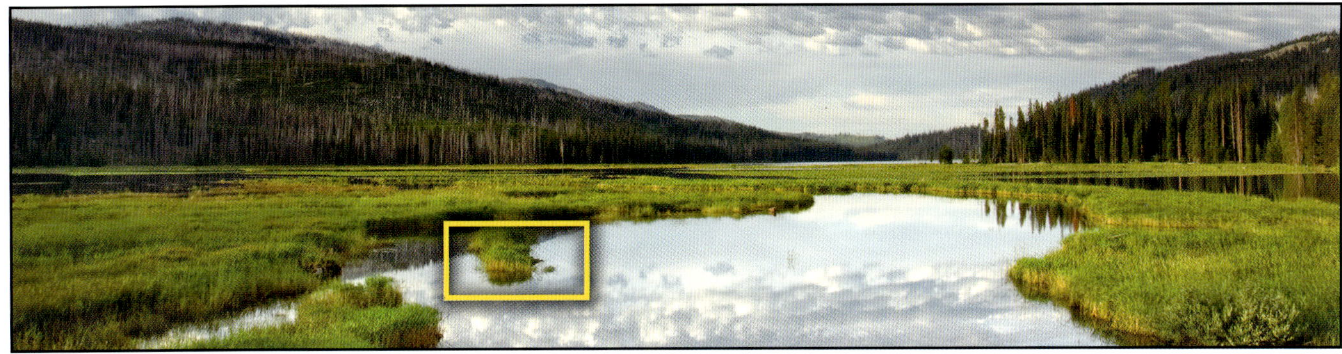

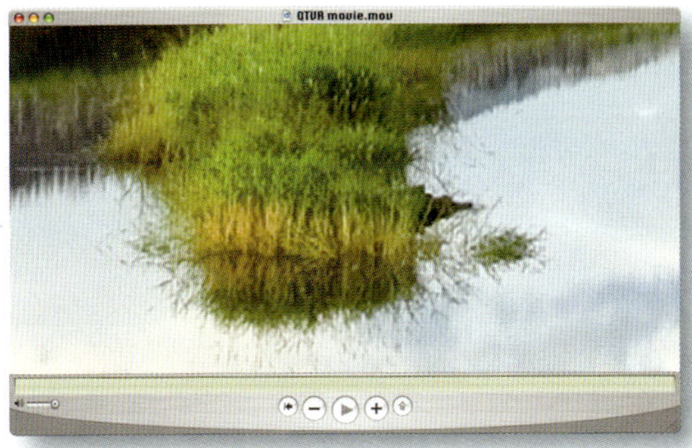

Movie detail: 4000 x 1000 pixel original

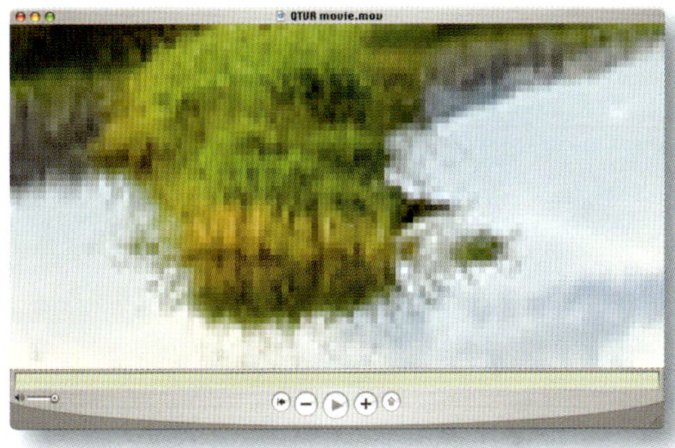

Movie detail: 1000 x 250 pixel original

Fig. 7-6 For panoramic VR images, it is important to have enough resolution in the source panorama to provide reasonable detail for users to zoom in when navigating the panorama's interactive movie window.

A good way to understand and compare panoramic image detail is to use a measurement of **pixels per degree** of view. Let's consider a 360-degree panoramic source image that is 3,600 pixels wide. Each degree of horizontal view comprises 10 pixels (3,600 pixels / 360 degrees = 10 pixels/degree). If the panoramic image is mapped to a sphere, the vertical measurement will correspond similarly. In this instance, a 90° vertical field of view (45° above through 45° below the horizon) would be 900 pixels high, while a 180° vertical field of view would be 1,800 pixels high.

Recommended VR panorama sizes

Movie window	360°x180° source image
320 (h) x 240 (w) pixels	1440 x 720 pixels (2.95 MB)
480 x 360 pixels	2160 x 1080 pixels (6.67 MB)
640 x 480 pixels	2880 x 1440 pixels (11.86 MB)
800 x 600 pixels	3600 x 1800 pixels (18.54 MB)

Fig. 7-7 Recommended minimum panorama file dimensions for presentation in VR movie windows.

A 360-degree panoramic image that is only 1,800 pixels wide will be limited to five pixels per degree of view, while one that is 7,200 pixels wide will have 20 pixels per degree, offering significantly more detail for zooming.

Keep in mind the tradeoffs of increased file size and increased resolution. A panoramic image that is twice the dimension both vertically and horizontally, will contain *four* times as much digital data, and its file size will be four times larger. Even with compression algorithms, VR movie files will retain their sizes proportionally. Added resolution is always nice, but processing, storage and delivery speeds can increase quickly in the VR authoring environment, particularly when you start multiplying these increased file sizes by multiple panoramic nodes in large VR scenes.

Print Publication

One of the advantages of many VR formats is that they can be used not only for electronic and on-screen display, but also for publication in traditional print media. Images from an object movie might also be used by a client for product shots in print catalogs, magazines or even billboard ads. Panoramas can be used as magazine gatefolds, wrap-around book covers, wall prints, billboards, or even as interactive backgrounds for multimedia presentations and in film and television projects. These large reproductions will be impossible to yield from small 72 dpi movie files, so it's often a good idea to plan for these potential uses as we shoot and assemble our VR imagery.

Printed color reproduction is a combination of both art and a science. For decades, it has required the experience of technicians in prepress and printing houses in order to yield accurate color reproduction on paper. Every press is different, as are the performance of different inks on different papers. Knowledge of separation, screen angles, dot gain, trapping, screen resolution, under color removal (UCR), registration, and a plethora of other concerns particular to the print business have been a necessity for successful color printing. Photographers never really concerned themselves with this in the past, since commercial color printing was done by large publishing companies well staffed with prepress and production specialists.

However, with the rise of digital technologies, much of this work is now done on the computer desktop, so a basic understanding of color processes becomes more important for photographers. Most of us also print our work on desktop printers, so a knowledge of color gamuts, screen gammas, and basic color management becomes necessary.

Color Management

Entire books have been written on color management. It is not a subject that most of us want to deal with. In theory, we shouldn't *have* to deal with it. In an ideal world, color management would be automated – done in the background by our digital cameras, computers, monitors, scanners, and printing devices. Unfortunately, we don't yet live in that ideal color management world.

The concept behind color management is a simple one. Every device that records or displays color does so with its own bias. The exact same red paint chip will appear as a slightly different color when viewed under different lighting conditions. A supposedly "pure" red will generally appear as one hue on one computer monitor, yet may be markedly different on another. A piece of color transparency film can include colors that cannot even be recorded in the scanning process. Colors displayed with combinations of red, green and blue light (RGB) on a computer or video screen cannot necessarily be reproduced accurately in print using cyan, magenta, yellow, and black (CMYK) printing inks. Color management is a means to provide numeric measurement of color rendition by any device, whether scanner, printer, monitor, etc., in order to allow for calibration of that device with others.

Color management requires that we create a color *profile* for every device (digital camera, scanner, monitor, and printer) that we use, using a standardized color target containing hundreds of specific color samples. Measurements are then made of the device's actual rendering of each of these colors using a precision color tool called a colorimeter. These measurements are then saved as a **device profile**, which accompanies any image created, displayed or rendered by that device. When moving the file from one device to another, such as from a scanner or camera to a monitor, or from a monitor to

a printer, or from one printer to another, the respective device profiles can be compared and the devices calibrated with one another – allowing colors displayed on one to match on any of the others.

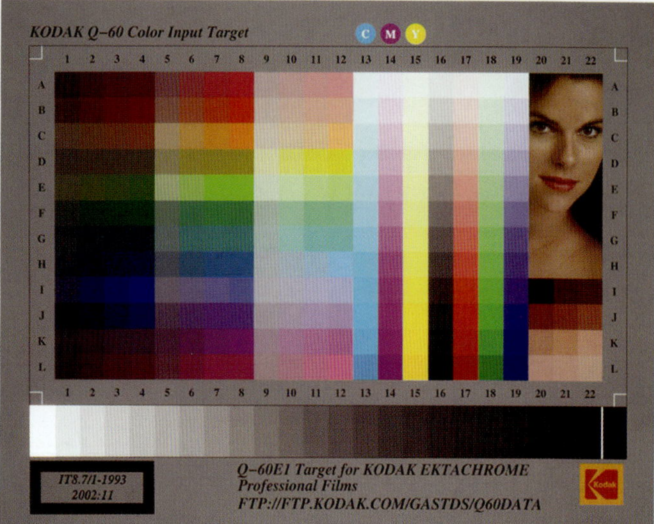

Fig. 7-8 A color target used for generating color profiles.

While the concept is quite simple, the actual practice is not... yet. Part of the problem is that profiling a given device today takes time and special tools, such as an expensive colorimeter and color profiling software. Few computer owners outside of imaging pros even consider a need for color management at all, so there are millions of devices out there that have no published color profiles. Yet all these cameras, scanners, monitors and printers are used to create color images that others hope to duplicate with accurate color rendition. Additionally, every computer monitor may be set to different gamma (contrast) and brightness levels, so the task of universal color management seems somewhat impossible.

Today, the best color management takes place within closed systems, where the same cameras, scanners, monitors and printers are used consistently, and are profiled *and* calibrated regularly. Images coming into the system from outside devices should include profiles of the devices used to create them, so that color matching can be done within and between the respective systems.

Unfortunately, this does little good when images are published electronically (such as for web viewing), where every viewer's monitor may be different, and there is no way to color match or calibrate them all to a single source profile.

Modern digital imaging software, such as Adobe's Photoshop™, provide for color management and the inclusion of device profiles within every image file. This is a good direction. However, color management remains more complicated than the average user is usually willing to deal with. If color accuracy is critical for your work, consider further reading, research, and expense to successfully engage full color management into your systems.

Commercial Printing

Commercial print reproduction of grayscale (black and white) images is relatively simple, as it only requires one ink (black) and one impression of a printing plate on the paper. This printing requires that we use a halftone screen, which optically converts the subtle gradations and tones of a photograph into small dots. The larger the dots, the more ink goes on the paper and the darker that portion of the image is printed. Likewise, the smaller the dots, the lighter that portion of the image prints.

Converting data from the pixels of a digital image into a line screen for reproduction is relatively simple, at least for computers. Most page layout and image manipulation programs include this utility. However, it is important for the photographer to understand the relationship between the amount of data in their digital files and the data necessary to reproduce their images on an offset printing press.

If you have too little information, or too few pixels, the printed piece shows jagged pixel edges (as the individual pixels are enlarged and become visible to the naked eye). If you have too much information, you waste unnecessary processing time and put undue demands on the prepress system, which generally means higher production costs.

Thus, it is advantageous to know what the size and resolution the final printed output will be before you determine how much information you need in your digital image files.

The first rule of thumb is that you will generally want about **twice the resolution** in your digital file than you will need for your printed output. This is not an absolute figure by any means. In fact, some publishers claim you need as little as 1.5 times the resolution. However, twice the output resolution (2X) is the norm. This is often called a "sampling" or "scaling" factor.

Example:
If we want to reproduce a black and white photograph 4" x 6" in a typical

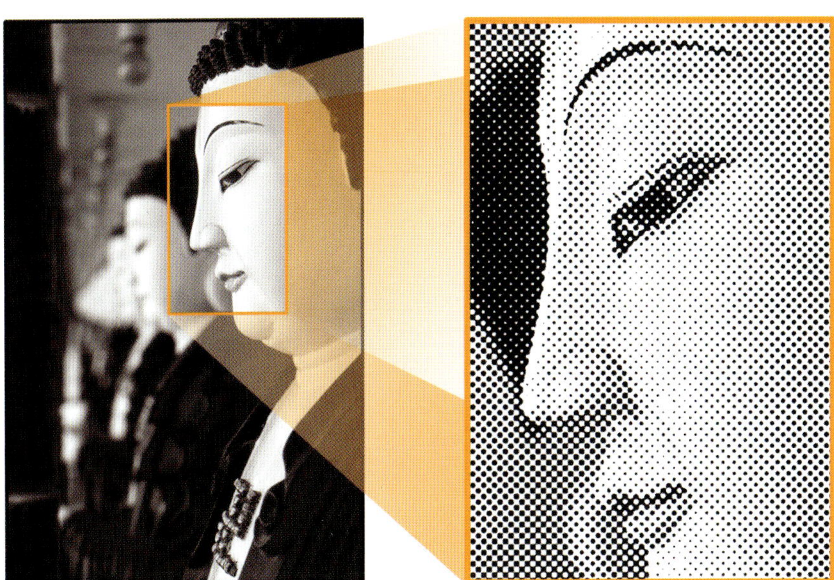

Fig. 7-9 Detail of halftone screen used for black and white printing.

Halftone printing resolution is dependent primarily upon the frequency or number of halftone dots in the image – just as the resolution of a digital image is based upon the number of pixels available.

Halftone screens are available in many resolutions and are measured in lines per inch (lpi). For our purposes, lpi and dots per inch (dpi) can be thought of as essentially the same thing. Typically, newspaper reproduction is done with an 85 or 100 line screen (lpi). Most magazines use 133 line screens, while books are usually printed at 150 or more lines.

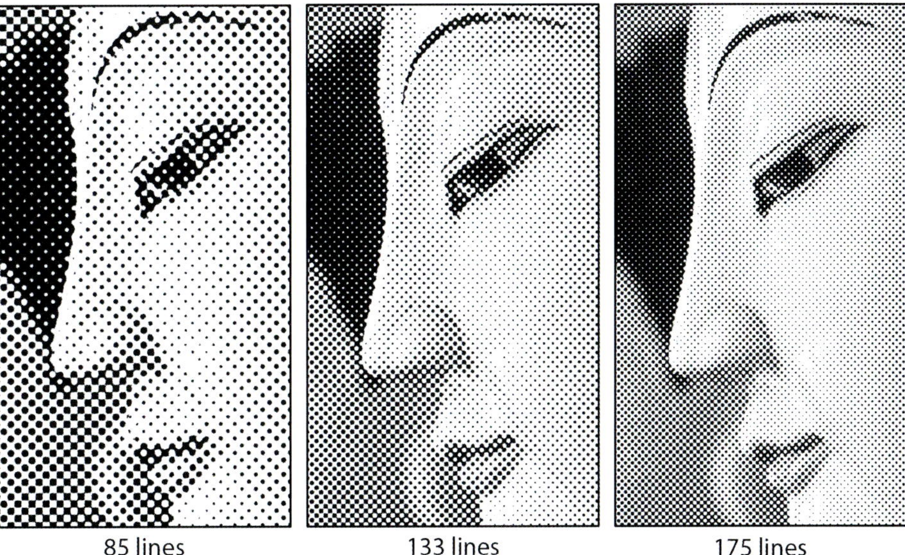

Fig. 7-10 Relative screen frequencies for haltone reproduction.

magazine, we can calculate the digital file needed through the following formula:

$$\begin{array}{rl} & 2 \text{ x screen resolution x reprod. height} \\ x & 2 \text{ x screen resolution x reprod. width} \\ \hline = & \text{file size (bytes)} \\ & (2 \text{ x } 133 \text{ (lines) x } 4 \text{ (inches))} \\ x & (2 \text{ x } 133 \text{ (lines) x } 6 \text{ (inches))} \\ \hline = & 1{,}698{,}144 \text{ bytes (1.6 MB)} \end{array}$$

Thus, we would need a file size of 1.6 MB. This would be an image containing 1,064 x 1,596 pixels (8-bit grayscale). If we were reproducing the same photograph in color, we would need to triple the file size, because we would need the same amount of data for each of the three RGB colors (24-bit color).

1,698,144 bytes *x* 3 colors = 5,094,432 bytes (4.9 MB)

The size and resolution of a digital file limits our successful publication of it.

Halftone reproduction sizes (133 line screen)

Reproduction size	File size (8-bit grayscale)
2" x 3"	**415 K** (532 x 798 pixels)
4" x 6"	**1.6 MB** (1064 x 1596 pixels)
5" x 7"	**2.4 MB** (1330 x 1862 pixels)
8" x 10"	**5.4 MB** (2128 x 2660 pixels)
11" x 14"	**10.4 MB** (2926 x 3724 pixels)

Fig. 7-11 File size requirements for halftone reproduction.

Electronic printing technologies are sufficiently advanced today that most everyone with a computer also owns a fairly good desktop color printer. Many commercial photo labs even make high-end color prints or other display media with electronic printers, rather than with traditional optical enlargement and photochemical processes.

Technical Note: PPI vs. DPI

Many people mistakenly use the terms PPI (pixels per inch) and DPI (dots per inch) interchangeably. While the two terms both refer to resolution, using one in place of the other is not usually accurate.

Pixels per inch (PPI) refers to the resolution of a digital image, while dots per inch (DPI) refers to the resolution at which an image or other content is printed.

Most desktop photo printers use proprietary software algorithms to interpolate data from digital files into the printer's native output resolution. The manufacturers' published resolution figures can be misleading, as they are often specified as "effective resolutions" rather than true resolutions. Trying to calculate needed file sizes based on these published resolution figures is almost an exercise in futility. For most purposes, using a reference of 300 dpi for photo printers will get you good results when calculating how large your image files need to be for various reproduction sizes. If you are considering the purchase of a digital camera, knowing how big you want to print your images will help you determine how much resolution (megapixels of image data) you should be looking for in your camera.

For example, if you want to be able to print your photos up to 8"x10" in size, you will need an RGB color image file about 20.6 MB in size. It would take a digital camera with a sensor of about seven megapixels to capture this much digital data. (A megapixel is commonly defined as one million pixels, and each RGB color pixel represents three bytes of data. So every megapixel in a digital camera sensor represents about three MB of RGB color data.)

Color printer reproduction sizes (300 ppi)

Image size	File size (24-bit RGB)	Megapixels
2" x 3"	**1.5 MB** (600 x 900 pixels)	.54 Mpix
4" x 6"	**6.2 MB** (1200 x 1800 pixels)	2.2 Mpix
5" x 7"	**9.0 MB** (1500 x 2100 pixels)	3.2 Mpix
8" x 10"	**20.6 MB** (2400 x 3000 pixels)	7.2 Mpix
11" x 14"	**39.7 MB** (3300 x 4200 pixels)	13.9 Mpix
16" x 20"	**82.4 MB** (4800 x 6000 pixels)	28.8 Mpix

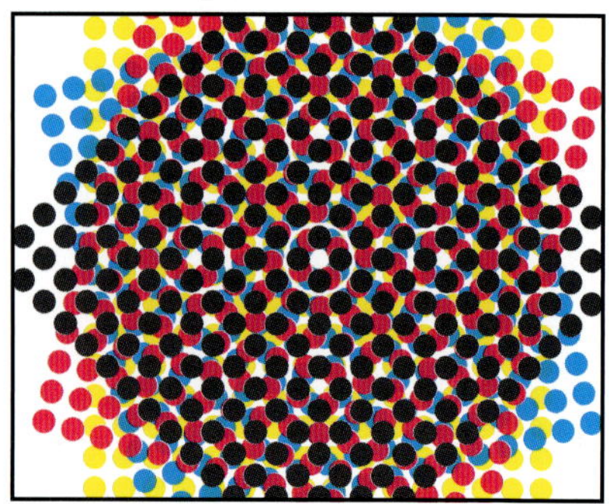

Enlarged color separation pattern

Fig. 7-12 Sample color reproduction file size requirements and a typical color screen alignment pattern for color printing.

Many people will make the mistake of scanning or acquiring every image at the highest possible resolution, thinking that it's better to have too much information that too little. While this approach does provide more options for the use of an image, there is little point to having to deal with multiple 30 MB files when you're only reproducing 2"x3" photos in a catalog. The excess data demands more computing power, more memory, more storage and slows down every step of the computing and printing processes. There is little point in making digital systems work harder (and slower) than necessary by demanding millions of unnecessary calculations at every step along the way. This is a critical concern when dealing with the many images necessary for stitching VR panoramas or for assembling VR object movies. If your source images are too large, they can grind your computer and VR software applications to a crawl.

As with most other aspects of photography, resolution choices involve tradeoffs. Yet the bottom line is that the larger the reproduction size or the higher the resolution in which we want to display our work, the more digital data we need.

File Compression

Most digital photo files can be reduced in size through a variety of mathematical algorithms or compression schemes. These systems, which have acronyms such as JPEG, LZW, MPEG, etc., allow a computer to effectively store more data in a smaller memory space. Some are called "lossless," which means that there is no loss of quality or data in the compression/decompression process. The most efficient compression algorithms compress digital files into their smallest sizes, but are known as "lossy" systems. Generally, the more a file is compressed, the more information is lost and the greater the degradation of the image.

Compressed images need to be decompressed (or uncompressed) before they can be opened or used again. The decompression process either replaces the data removed during compression with the exact same data (lossless) or with approximations of the removed data (lossy). For the most part, photographers don't need to be too concerned with the complexities of compression, except to understand the difference between lossless and lossy systems.

For those using lossy compression schemes, the tradeoff in quality is often worthwhile because of the value of reducing file sizes so significantly. Some compression schemes can reduce file sizes by as much as 30:1, with little noticeable loss of image fidelity. Compressing the file reduces transmission time and storage space. Of course, with the increased availability of high speed internet services, bandwidth limitations seem to be less of a concern. Remember that even though a compressed file may take less storage space, it must be decompressed to its full size before it can be used for stitching in VR panorama or object movie authoring applications. It's the sizes of these *decompressed* files that will affect the performance of these tools.

For VR photography, the most common compression system currently used, both for image assembly and for VR movie preparation, is JPEG. JPEG appears to remain the most universally accepted format in the foreseeable future, as well.

Copyright and Security Concerns

Well over 20 years ago, the United States Office of Technology and Assessment (OTA) presented results of their survey about America's perceptions of right and wrong when it came to copying the work of others. The report, entitled "Intellectual Property in an Electronic Era," indicated that 70 percent of the general population thought it was acceptable to copy other people's work. Forty percent of the American business population did, too.

In the years since that report, the public's apparent willingness to "borrow" or copy the work of others seems to have only increased. The tremendous popularity of web sites such as YouTube, MySpace, Facebook, and others, where copyrighted content is so freely distributed by those who don't own or have license for the work, illustrates this. There are misconceptions that anything posted publicly on the World Wide Web is fair game for copying and reuse, even though there are strict legal penalties (up to $150,000 per infringement in the U.S.) for unlicensed copying of copyrighted works.

In the U.S., copyright is automatic from the moment that a work is fixed in a tangible form (such as being exposed on film, saved as a digital file, etc.) until 75 years after the author's death. Unless specified otherwise in a written contract or the work is done as an employee, the copyright belongs to the author of the work. When it's created, it's copyrighted.

Some photographers mistakenly believe that if they only publish "low resolution" copies of their work on their web sites, that the small files sizes will keep others from reusing that work. However, almost every image processing software application today offers the ability to "rez up" just about any file for effective use at much larger sizes. Some of these work better than others, and there are still limits to how much new useful data can be drawn out from smaller files. However, publication of "low resolution" files in and of itself is not likely to provide sufficient protection against unauthorized use.

Better Security

The first line of defense for protecting your images from unauthorized copying is to ALWAYS include a copyright notice with them. This essentially keeps the honest people out there honest, and provides full warning that your images are indeed protected by copyright. For digital files, your copyright notice should be included as part of the file name when possible, and most certainly in the metadata information. Adding a copyright notice to the bitmapped or pixel data of the image is also useful. When published, either in print or electronic from, your images should include a written copyright notice, either as a part of the image or immediately adjacent to it on the page or screen.

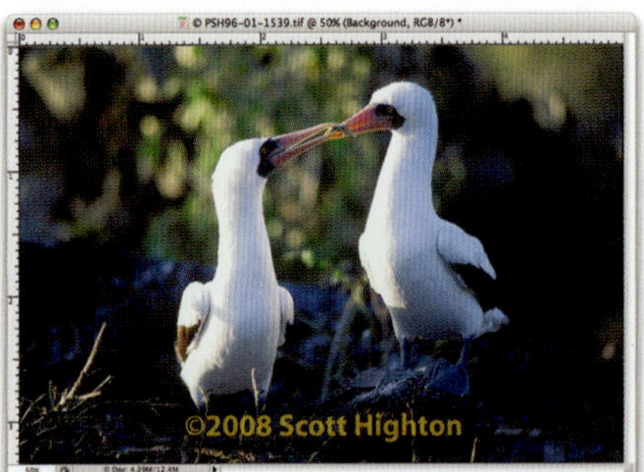

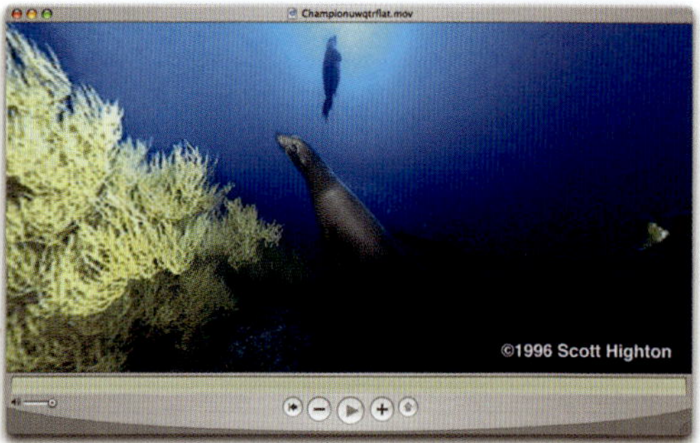

Fig. 7-14 Bitmapped copyright notices via watermark and overlay in a movie window.

The copyright notice should read as follows:

> **© (year) (your name)**
> **All rights reserved**

An example would be:

> **© 2010 Scott Highton**
> **All rights reserved**

Some authors also insist on inclusion of a web site URL or contact information in their copyright notices, so that potential clients who see their work also have a quick way to contact them.

Example:

> **© 2010 Scott Highton**
> **All rights reserved**
> **www.vrphotography.com**

It is important to keep a photographer's credit, copyright notice, and reference information with his or her photographs once those images have been stored as digital files. Newer image cataloging programs provide text files that accompany every digital image. These are called IPTC headers (International Press Telecommunications Council), IIM metadata elements (Information Interchange Model), or the more recent XMP metadata (Extensible Metadata Platform). These files can contain text about each photo, including copyright, captions, file numbers, model releases and other information. Such fields are often used for database searches. Unfortunately, they can also be stripped away from the image when the file is opened or saved with alternate software applications.

Including the photographer's name and copyright notice as a visual part of the image itself helps. This can be added as a credit bar above or below the actual image area, or as a watermark within the image, using most image processing software. Watermarks can still be cropped or retouched out by the end user. However, watermarks offer more assurance that potential users will see and note the copyright information, and will think twice before copying the image.

There are a handful of image encryption systems such as Digimarc™, that actually embed an *invisible* watermark, tracking data, or copy prevention controls into the pixels patterns of an image. So far, these have met with mixed success. They can be quite effective for certain kinds of publication, but often don't hold up terribly well to digital manipulation of an image. Since stitching and assembly of VR image sequences involves so much digital manipulation, these encryption schemes, for the most part have been unusable.

However, with the advances that continually come along in digital imaging, it may well be that more successful systems are on their way.

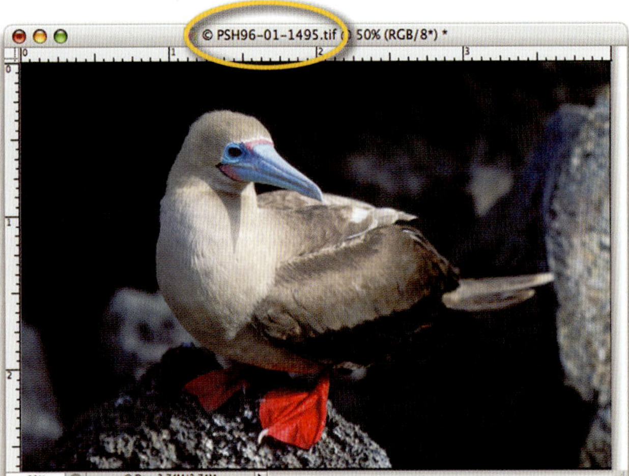

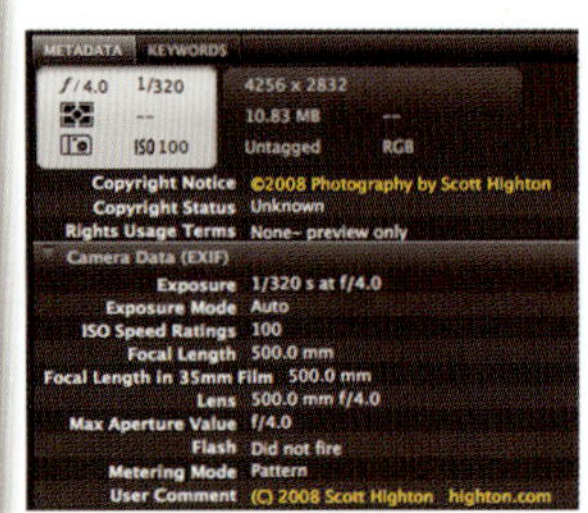

Fig. 7-13 Copyright information embedded into the metadata of an image file.

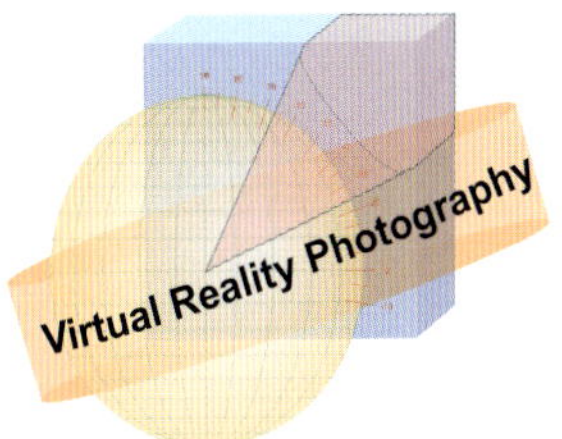

Chapter 8: Practical Shooting

Chronology of a photography career

1) First decade – build most of your equipment (because you can't afford to buy it).

2) Second decade – buy everything (because you can afford it now).

3) Third decade – build or modify everything (because what you need probably doesn't exist commercially).

4) Fourth decade – get rid of most of the equipment you've collected over the first 30 years (because you're not as young as you used to be to carry it all, and you have the skills to do so much more with much less).

The photographic equipment you choose will depend entirely upon what sort of photography you want to do. There are dozens of questions you will need to answer about the work you want to do, and there will invariably be many different options to choose for each.

Do you shoot on location or in a studio (or both)? Will you shoot object VR (primarily product-type shooting) or panoramic VR? Is digital capture your only option, or does film still hold promise? What are the advantages and disadvantages of each for the kind of work you'll be doing? What quality level do you need (high-end, low-end or something in between)? Can you justify the costs against your expected income? What are the hidden costs, such as computer hardware, software, lighting, grip equipment, ongoing fees, etc.? Can you "dabble" for a while with minimal expense, and then move up to something more professional later on? Can VR photography fit in to the other kinds of work you already do? Can your existing equipment be used for VR?

Photographers are notorious for purchasing new equipment in a constant search for better results and innovative techniques. Many pros wind up with closets or studios packed full of equipment, only a fraction of which they use regularly. The biggest mistake any photographer can make is to spend good money in hopes of following a fad or copying what someone else is doing.

Fads and popular styles are short lived. The use of fisheye lenses became popular in the '70s, and quickly became overdone in advertising and editorial work. The same thing occurred with catadioptric (mirror) telephoto lenses, which render unique donut-shaped highlights in out of focus portions of the image. It was an interesting look at first, but it became old after everyone started doing it.

Some will remember the "light painting" fad among studio photographers in the '80s. Many photographers spent thousands of dollars for various light wand or hose devices with spinning filters for their lenses. The fad lasted a year or so, and then most clients tired of it. Tilted horizons came next. In the mid '90s, it seemed you couldn't open up a magazine without wondering if all the photographers in the world were suddenly drinking on the job. It became "cool" to shoot everything from a crooked angle. Buildings looked like they were toppling over. CEO's and other executives appeared to be falling off of their desks. Sure it was a creative look in the beginning, but like all fads, it quickly got old.

Choosing photographic equipment is something that should be considered for the long term. Good cameras and lenses are expensive for the most part, and their long term usefulness should be addressed *before* a purchase is made.

In the world of digital photography, one should remember that the quality and capabilities of the latest equipment increase almost exponentially over time, while prices decrease at almost the same rate. Gordon Moore, a former CEO of Intel, once observed that the processing power of microchip technologies doubles every 18-24 months, while their prices are reduced by half. Moore's Law, as his observation has come to be known, has been manifest repeatedly in digital imaging technologies. Examples range from the highest end professional gear to the cheapest point and shoot models.

With digital and electronic equipment, the rules of thumb for purchase are:

1) Wait as long as possible before buying. Don't buy something until you absolutely need it.

2) Buy only if you're sure the product will pay for itself (and generate added profit) within a year. Beyond that, no matter how much you paid for it, the product is likely to be obsolete in short order.

3) When possible, rent or borrow the equipment before you buy. It's amazing how often the manufacturers' promotional literature fails to mention what might be a critical flaw for the type of work you do. Test the product in your own environment and under conditions that you expect to use it. Then make your decision on whether to purchase or not. A $150/day rental fee is a small price to pay if it helps you avoid spending thousands of dollars for a piece of equipment that ultimately doesn't serve your needs.

Choosing Equipment – Panoramic VR

The first rule of successful VR photography is to try to keep your life as simple as possible. Use the least amount of equipment you can, and choose your gear so its operation is simple. There is enough to think about when trying to create good photography in the first place. The technical demands of VR photography add further complexity to the process.

There have been times when I have found myself carrying 80 pounds and more of VR camera equipment in a backpack to remote locations, either because the client was unsure of what they really wanted, or because I was unsure of what I'd need to do the job properly.

It is not unusual for a professional photographer to arrive on a location shoot with a van or truck loaded with equipment – not because he or she will use every piece, but because he or she *might* need something. This is mainly done for security and backup reasons. Unfortunately, having too many options available also makes choosing the best approach or technique more difficult. When you have more options available to you, you have more decisions to make, and life can become more complicated.

It is usually better to select a core set of equipment and use it consistently. That way, you remain familiar with everything and can quickly pinpoint sources of problems when they arise. Some photographers find it is easiest to assemble their photo gear into specific kits, each in their own case or camera bag, just to keep things simple. This can be done on either a large or small scale.

For example, you may have a small digital camera that you use for family snapshots and personal photos. You could keep this in a small pouch or belt bag that you can grab at a moment's notice. However, if this camera is also part of a panoramic VR kit, you might want to place all the additional VR equipment, such as a tripod, pan head, supplemental lens, additional storage cards, batteries, etc., in another kit which you can grab along with your small camera when needed.

This approach is helpful with high-end equipment, as well. You might keep a kit assembled with a fisheye lens,

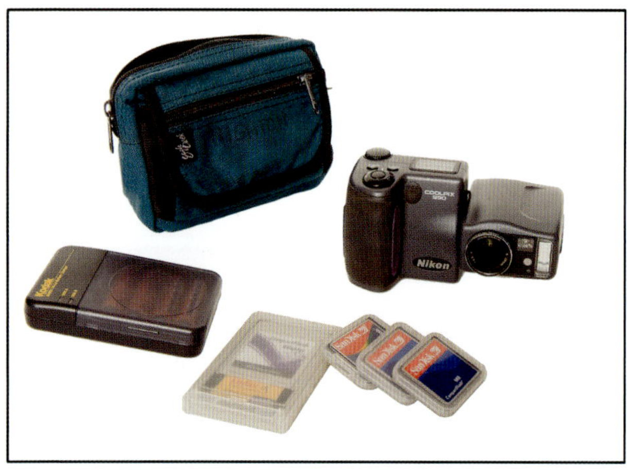

Personal point & shoot kit

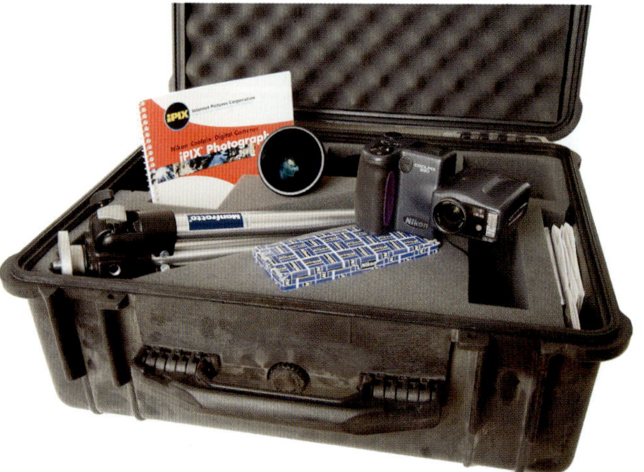

Point & shoot fisheye panorama kit

Fig. 8-1 Simplify your location photography equipment by packing separate kits for each type of photography you do.

rotator, and camera for spherical photography, while having another similarly equipped for QTVR cylindrical or cubic shooting. The difference would be that the latter might include a rectilinear lens or two, rather than the fisheye, and perhaps a different pan head.

For the most part, every VR shoot will be different. If you can comfortably transport everything you might need to your shoot location, then it's probably a good idea to bring it all along. Keep the equipment you're most likely to want within the easiest reach, and relax knowing that you have backup systems and other options available close by if you need them.

However, you will generally be faced with limitations on the amount of gear you can bring to location shoots, whether because of airline restrictions, the size of your shooting crew (most often the photographer will be alone), or your own physical ability to carry what you need where you need it.

Location photographers (whether doing VR or traditional photography) should find a good photo backpack that will allow them to carry the minimum equipment that they might need for a range of shooting situations. Having carried my share of 70-80 lb. photo backpacks, I will warn you to choose the smallest backpack you can get away with for your minimum equipment set. The larger the pack, the more gear you'll put in it (all of which will *seem* essential)... and the more you'll swear at yourself for having to lug it around on location.

Essential Equipment: Tripods

If you are planning to shoot panoramic VR, your choices of equipment are fairly broad. Most of these however, will depend upon what panoramic VR technology you intend to author your work with, as well as what quality limitations you can accept.

Panoramic VR photography almost always requires a tripod or some other stable camera support, which will allow the camera to be held in a consistent shooting position during and between exposures. The size and sturdiness of this tripod will dictate the weight of the camera and lens that you place upon it, as well as how easily you can move with it. While it is wonderful to have a heavy duty tripod with a geared head for quick leveling, the size and weight of such a system makes it prohibitive in many instances.

Personally, I favor the Bogen/Manfrotto line of tripods, primarily for three reasons. The first is that they are sturdy, strong, and well made. Second is that Bogen/Manfrotto offers a huge product line, including tripods, heads, clamps, stands, boom arms, and more grip accessories than most of us can imagine. Much of this equipment is designed with interchangeable parts. Third, their products are fairly reasonably priced. You tend not to worry so much about putting your tripod in salt water, or making custom modifications like cutting down the legs in order to save on size and weight, when you know that you can replace it for reasonable cost.

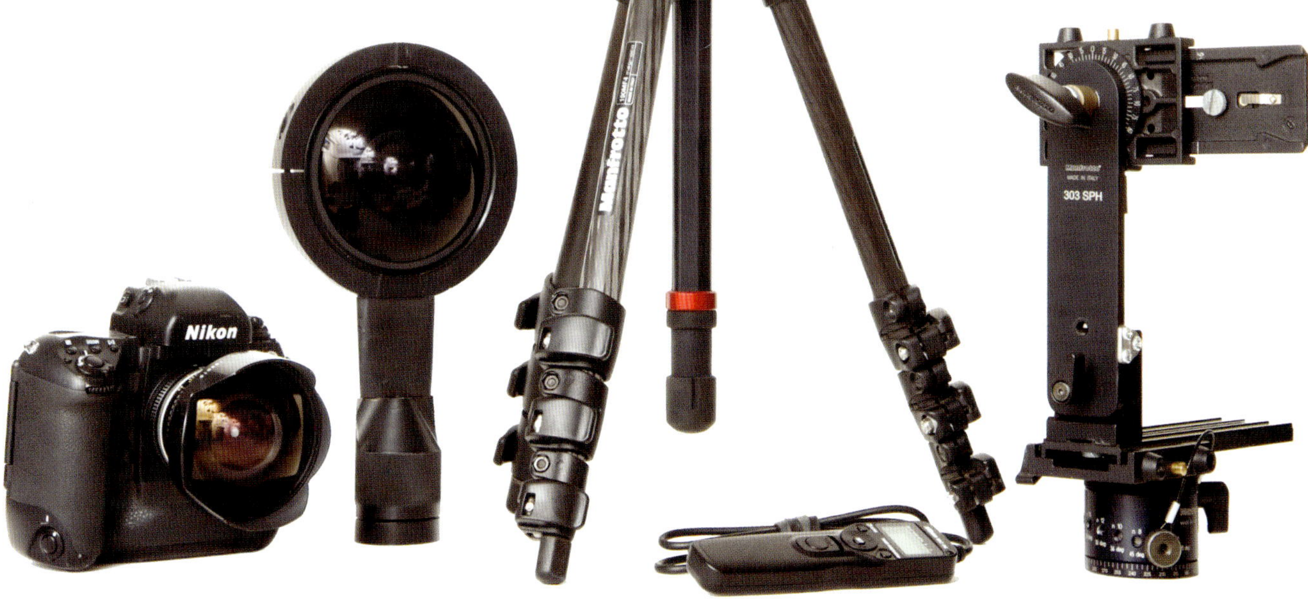

Fig. 8-2 A basic pro panoramic shooting kit, with Nikon pro SLR camera, ultrawide rectilinear and fisheye lenses, tripod, remote release, and Manfrotto 303SPH pan head.

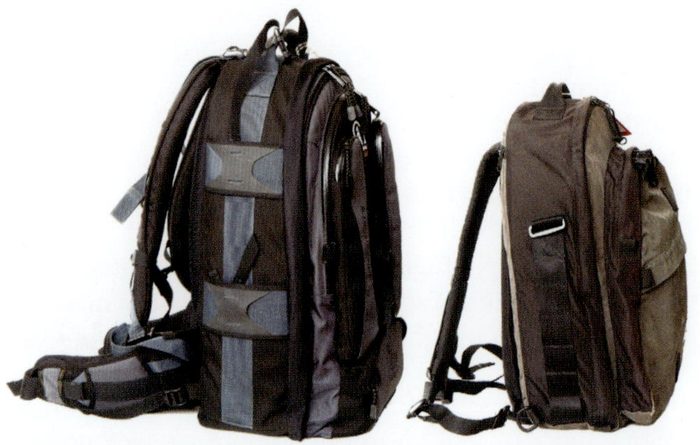

Fig. 8-3 Photo backpacks are available in a variety of sizes, and can simplify packing and transporting camera equipment on location.

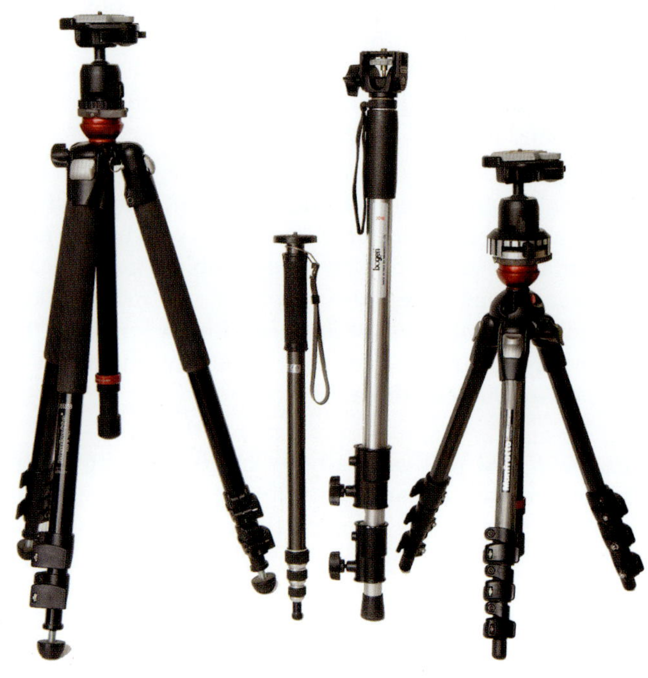

Fig. 8-4 A selection of Manfrotto tripods and monopods.

Bogen/Manfrotto also distributes the Gitzo line of tripods and camera supports. Gitzo tripods tend to be a little stiffer than the Manfrotto line, which provides better stability. However, Gitzos are usually more expensive. Both Manfrotto and Gitzo offer extremely lightweight carbon fiber tripods, which are excellent for backpacking and other shooting situations where minimal weight is critical – and worth paying for. Carbon tripods are generally two to three times more expensive than the standard aluminum models.

As you get more experience shooting virtual reality images, you will probably find yourself wanting to position your cameras in locations where they cannot effectively be supported by standard tripods. Good panoramas often require that we position a camera close in to our subjects, into tight locations, or in places where there may be nothing to support them from below. This is where you'll find yourself cannibalizing tripods

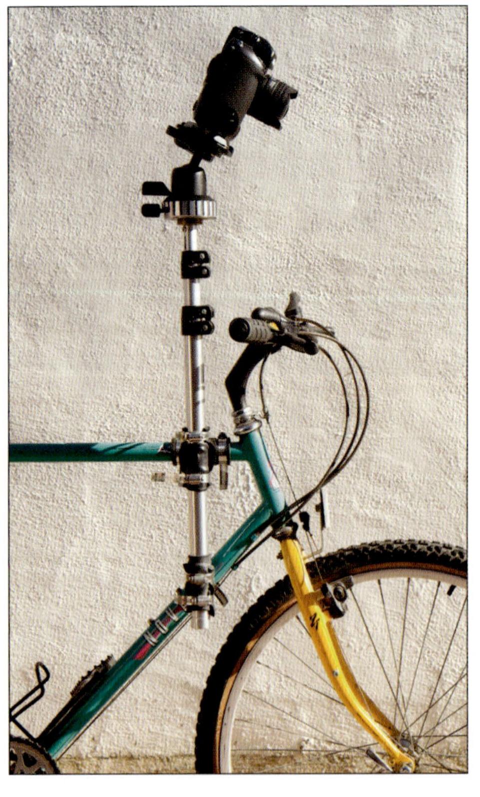

a) Bike mount

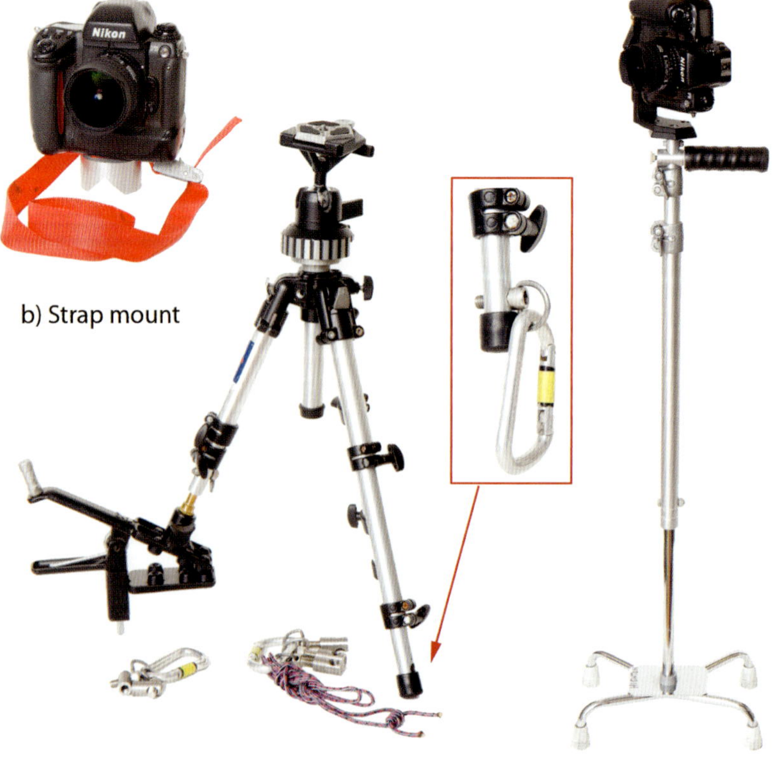

b) Strap mount

c) Clamp adapters - tripod legs

d) "Cane" pod

Fig. 8-5 Simple modifications and customization of camera mounts allow photography in unique locations. or positions.

or other grip equipment, and spending lots of time at your local hardware store in search of clamps, springs, nuts, bolts, tools, and other hardware to customize the needed solutions. Creative problem solving and a little mechanical ingenuity can make your photographic life truly fun! Making friends with a local machinist can be beneficial, as well.

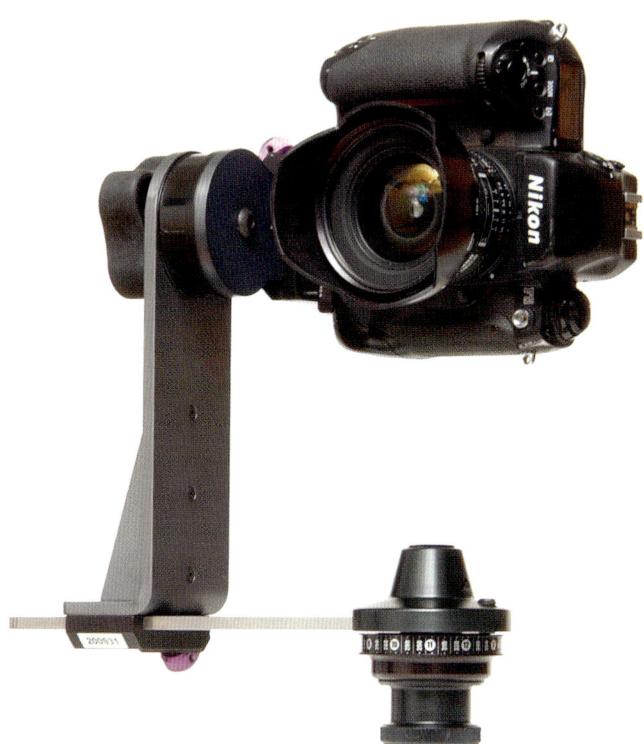

Fig. 8-7 A modern VR pan head from Kaidan incorporating mechanical panning detents and entrance pupil alignment for dual axis (multi-row) panoramic photography. Note the significantly smaller size.

Essential Equipment: Pan Heads

Most panoramic VR photography requires some type of calibrated pan head, such as those from companies like Kaidan, Bogen/Manfrotto, and Peace River Studios. These pan heads allow for precise alignment of the entrance pupil of the camera's lens with the axis of rotation, providing the most effective assembly or stitching of the VR image sequences later on. These heads also provide click stops for consistent pan increments between photos. Some versions also include incremental tilt settings, which are necessary for shooting multi-row panoramas for the newer generation of multi-row stitchers.

Commercially available VR pan heads are often a far better option than trying to make your own rig, as they have been refined by engineers after extensive field testing by working VR pros. However, once you understand how to properly align a camera and lens for VR photography, it is possible to build your own VR pan head using off-the-shelf products from a local camera or hardware store.   Before the first commercial pan heads were available, every photographer shooting VR had to build their own rig. Some of them were actually quite creative in their approaches.

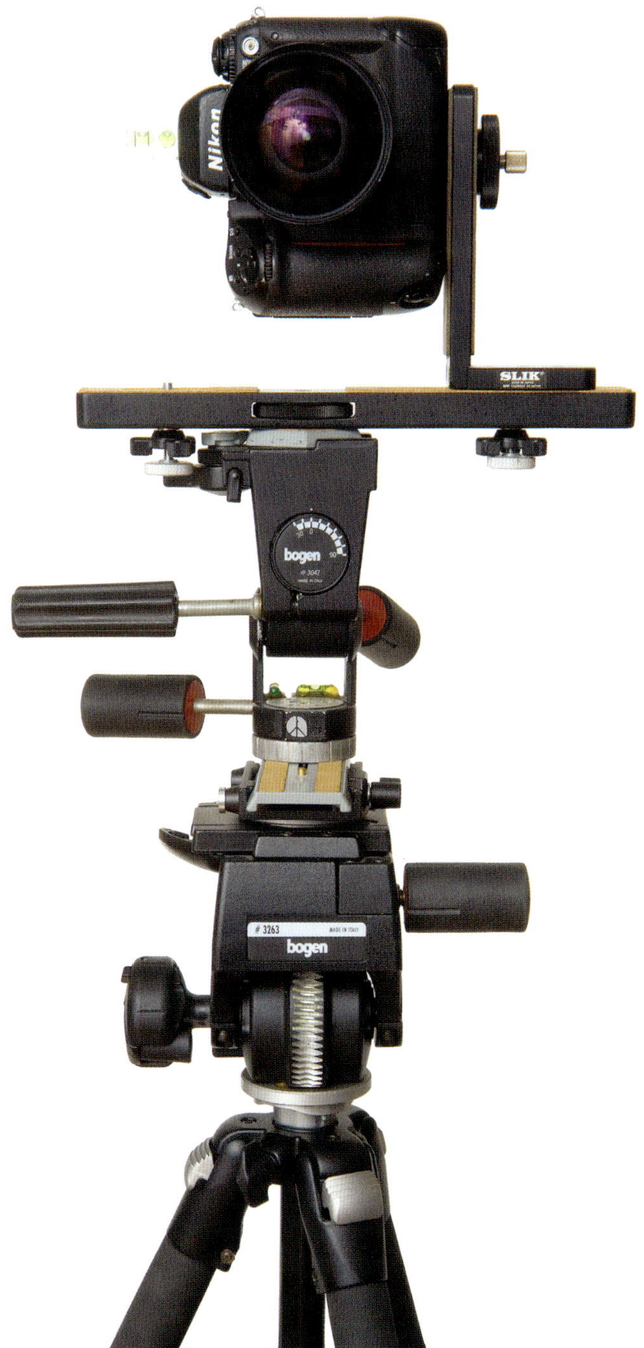

Fig. 8-6 An original QTVR pan head from 1994, built using readily available off-the-shelf photo gear, as specified by Apple. In this case, it included two Bogen / Manfrotto tripod heads, a dual camera adapter, sliding plates, and a Slik L-bracket. This was all necessary in order to align the entrance pupil of the lens over the camera's single panning axis.

Slit scan panoramic cameras, such as the high end Panoscan, BetterLight, and Roundshot models, generally include self-contained pan mechanisms within the camera, and don't require these third party pan heads.

Essential Equipment: Cameras and Lenses

The biggest choice in cameras today is not which brand or model to select, but whether you want to consider traditional film or digital models. Digital cameras have long since overtaken film cameras in popularity, quality, and overall usefulness in most regards. However, there are concerns that are unique to panoramic VR photography, which will remain important in your decision.

Image quality is the first concern. The resolutions of today's consumer digital cameras, generally priced at $1,000 or less, are very similar to those of 35mm film cameras. Ten to 12 megapixels (a megapixel is 1,000 pixels) is the current upper limit for these consumer digital cameras, which closely matches the equivalent resolution of most 35mm films.

Professional digital cameras (most of which now cost between $1,500 and $8,000) offer resolutions of 12–24 megapixels per image. These models offer advantages of accepting existing 35mm lenses, faster frame rates (the minimum time needed between shots), better color rendition, wider exposure latitudes, and better exposure control.

Digital cameras have the advantage over film of providing immediate results. You can see your images right away, and you don't face the risk of film being damaged during transport or processing, or of discovering a major problem with the images after its too late to reshoot them. Digital cameras save the cost of film and processing, although there are added costs of storage media, as well as the computer hardware and peripherals that will be needed if you want to post produce your image files in the field. Extended digital photography on location may require a laptop computer, card reader, plus a DVD writer or other storage device, along with backup equipment in case any of the above units fail.

Digital media are not susceptible to X-ray damage like film is (a major consideration when traveling via airlines), although magnetic media, such as hard drives and compact flash cards, are more prone to damage from electrical fields and dynamic shock from being bumped or dropped.

Digital cameras usually don't tolerate environmental extremes as well as film cameras do, such as high/low temperatures, high humidity, or rough handling. There are more electronic components and things that can go wrong in electronic cameras, which can render them useless in the field. Repair usually requires a trained technician and new parts. Field repair is not generally an option, as is sometimes possible with 35mm film cameras.

For panoramic VR photography, the biggest drawback of many digital cameras is their limited field of view relative to 35mm film cameras when using identical lenses. (Pro models with full-frame sensors are an exception.) Since the digital sensors in most cameras are smaller than the full 35mm film frame, the field of view that can be captured is cropped, thus increasing the effective focal length of a lens.

This is a critical issue when shooting in tight spaces, or where the vertical fields of view need to be maximized – particularly with interiors or other locations when a view upward or downward is important.

Shooting with an expensive 18mm or 14mm ultra wide lens (perhaps costing $1,500 or more) will provide a vertical field of view of between 90° and 104° when used in portrait orientation on a 35mm camera. This would allow you to capture a view 45-50° above *and* below the horizon. However, those same lenses, when used on a Nikon D300, will restrict the view above and below the horizon to 3/4 of that, because the sensor does not cover the full 35mm frame. Less expensive lenses with

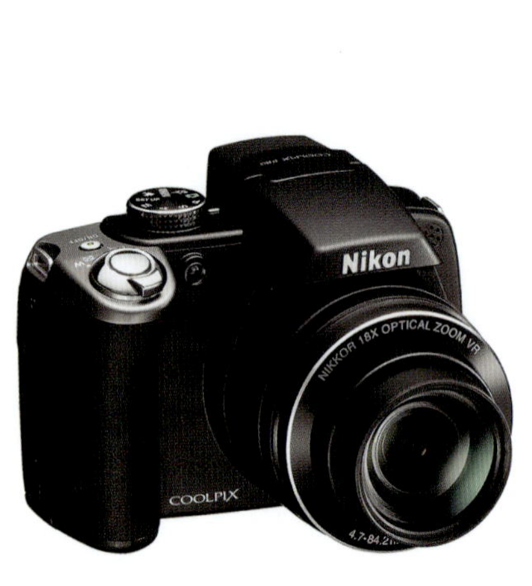
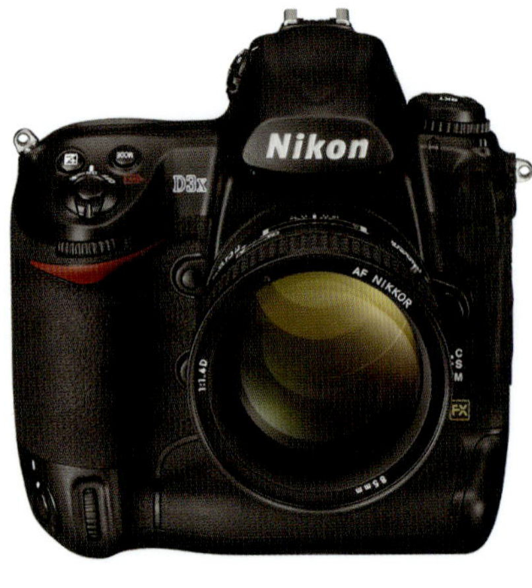
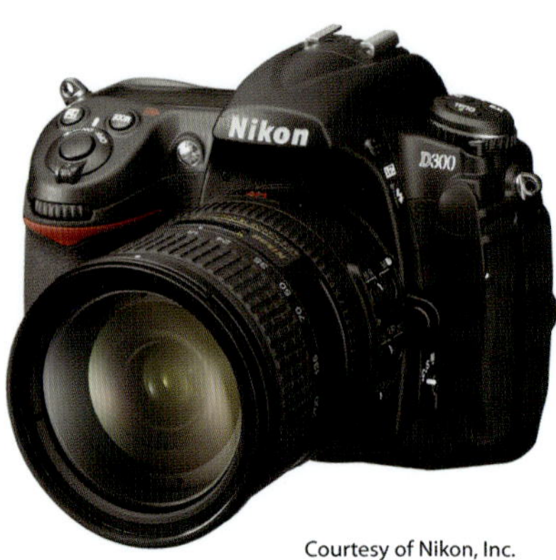

Courtesy of Nikon, Inc.

Fig. 8-8 There are a variety of consumer and professional digital cameras avaiable, such as these examples from Nikon.

longer focal lengths, such as a 24mm or 28mm, could be used instead, but the smaller size of the digital sensor effectively increases their focal lengths as well, reducing the vertical field of view even further.

Nikon specifically has tried to address this by offering a line of DX lenses that are designed for the smaller sensors in their mid-range and consumer SLRs. These include a full frame fisheye (10.5mm), as well as an ultra-wide zoom (12-24mm). However, these lenses can only be used on Nikon's DX format digital SLRs, and are considered by many photographers to be of lesser quality than Nikon's highly regarded optics for traditional 35mm photography.

Newer generations of panoramic stitching software, such as those offered by Autodesk, PTGui, and others, get around this field of view limitation by allowing you to assemble multiple rows of images shot with the camera tilted up or down for added vertical coverage. While solving one problem, this creates another in that each panorama now requires more images to assemble and increases the complexity of the shoot. Shooting takes longer (causing more problems due to changing light or subject movement within overlap areas), post production and assembly is more complex, and the source images require more digital storage space and handling time.

Unique parabolic mirror systems offer another alternative. An example is the GoPano™ from EyeSee360°, which captures an entire 360° panorama in a single exposure. The resulting images are recorded as torus or donut-shaped projections, and must be dewarped using software such as PhotoWarp from EyeSee360°. These mirror systems have somewhat lower image quality. However, they *do* offer the unique ability to capture a full 360° panoramic view (with limited vertical range) at a single moment, which no other one-camera VR system can offer. They are necessary when there is a need to freeze motion throughout a 360° view. They also show considerable promise for use with 360° full motion video systems.

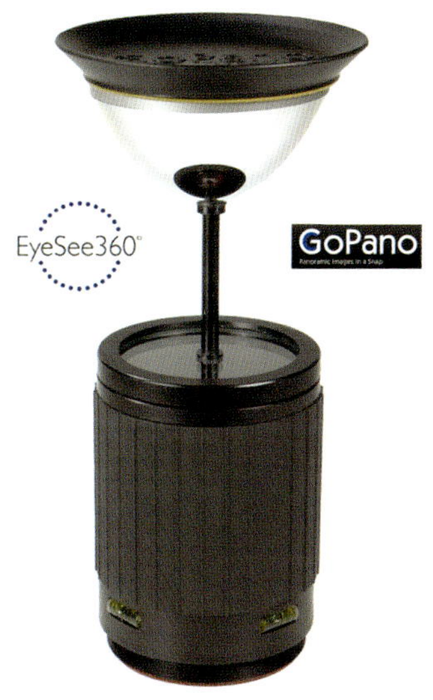

Courtesy of Kaidan, Inc. and EyeSee360, Inc.

Fig. 8-9 The GoPano parabolic mirror attachment allows capture of a full 360° panorama in a single image.

Choosing Equipment: Object VR

While the options for panoramic VR photography are numerous, the equipment approaches for object VR photography are more limited.

Object VR is very similar to motion control photography for film or video, where the camera and subject need to maintain precise and repeatable alignment throughout a series of images that make up a sequence. This generally demands both a turntable mechanism to rotate the object, as well as a stable camera support mechanism that can maintain precise alignment of the subject within the frame over many shots.

While 35mm film cameras can be used quite effectively for panoramic VR photography, they are rarely a good choice for object VR. This is because the film has to move within the camera in between every shot, and does not align with the necessary precision each time. The slight difference in spacing between frames, or a fraction of a degree change in orientation, is not a critical factor for traditional photography, but these misalignments will cause jumpiness or jitter between frames when image sequences are displayed in an object movie. It's also difficult to maintain repeatable positioning of the film during scanning. Frame misalignments will occur while scanning even if the original film is precisely pin registered in the camera and the camera itself anchored to a rock-steady support.

Therefore, in order to maintain consistent image alignment, it is necessary to use a digital, or perhaps even a video camera. Since the image sensors in digital and video cameras remain in a fixed position from frame to frame, the only requirement for stable image sequences is keeping the camera steady. There is no scanning process to introduce misalignments, as the images are digitized directly.

In the early days of object VR, video cameras tethered to desktop computers were the most popular way to shoot. However, as the VR industry has grown and bandwidth increased, the limited resolution of video cameras has become a drawback. They are still practical for object movies that do not need to show much detail, or for low resolution efforts. However, today's digital cameras are a far better choice. Most video cameras also have very narrow exposure latitudes compared to digital still cameras, so they require more care with lighting technique.

Essential Equipment: Object Turntables

The first piece of equipment needed for most object photography is some sort of turntable mechanism which your subjects (objects) can be rotated upon in front of the camera. Object movies enable you to show an object from many angles. We need to photograph such objects from all sides, and then sequence the images together so that

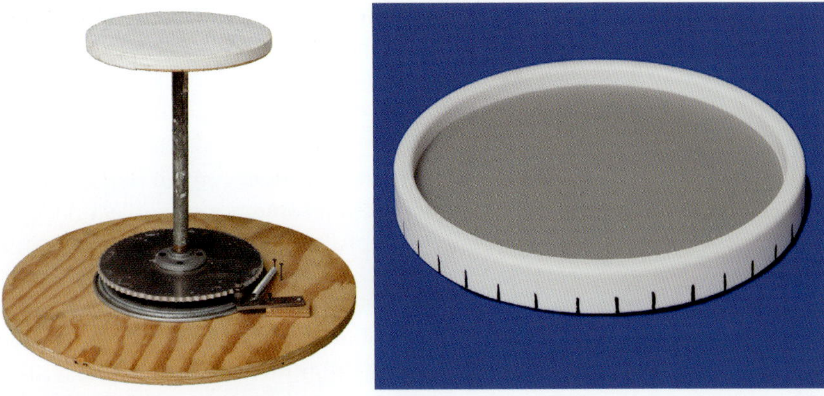

Fig. 8-10 Object turntables can be made with low cost equipment from kitchen supply and hardware stores.

the viewer can interact virtually on screen. A turntable allows us to move an object in front of the camera, rather than having to move the camera around the object (which makes frame alignments more difficult).

A simple turntable can be built from low cost materials found at your neighborhood hardware store. A Lazy Susan mechanism can work well for small objects, and can be found in varying sizes. Simply mark the edges of the turntable in 10° increments and manually rotate the object in front of the camera. With a little imagination, you can design a click-stop mechanism into this rig for further functionality.

Companies like Kaidan, Corybant West, and Peace River Studios offer commercial VR turntables, designed specifically for object photography. These range from low cost, manual table top mechanisms to large, computer controlled rigs capable of holding hundreds of pounds. Companies specializing in industrial and automotive turntables offer even larger systems that a high-end object photographer can use.

Essential Equipment: Camera Support Rigs

The most basic QuickTime VR object movie is a "single row" movie, where the object is rotated in front of the camera and viewed from a single level or position. Photographing these types of movies requires only a turntable mechanism and a simple means of supporting the camera in a fixed position, such as a tripod.

However, object movies are capable of displaying image sequences shot from more than one level (or row), so that the viewer can see an object from any angle around its perimeter, as well as from multiple angles above and below.

Photographing "multi-row" object movies requires more than just a tripod to support the camera, because the camera needs to move up and down in precise increments *while* maintaining both its orientation and distance relative to the subject.

If a single row object movie contains an image shot every 10 degrees of object rotation, it will consist of 36 individual frames (360°/10° per frame = 36 frames).

If we want to show all 36 of those views from multiple rows, then we have to repeat all 36 shots from each of those rows. Thus, two rows of 36 frames each would total 72 images. Ten rows would mean 360 frames. If we were to shoot in 10° increments from 90° above the object through 90° below, we would have 19 rows of 36 images each, for a total of 684 individual frames.

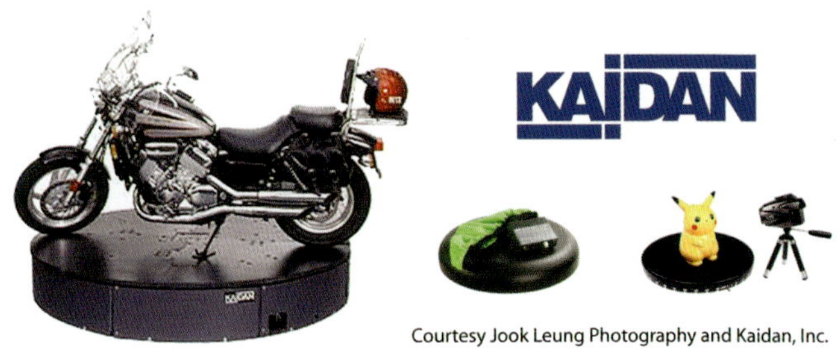

Courtesy Jook Leung Photography and Kaidan, Inc.

Fig. 8-11 Commercial object VR turntables from Kaidan.

VR object rigs are required for the consistent and repeatable positioning of a camera for multi row object photography. There are three different designs for such rigs offered commercially by Kaidan, Corybant West, and Peace River Studios. A number of photographers have built their own rigs using these designs, as well.

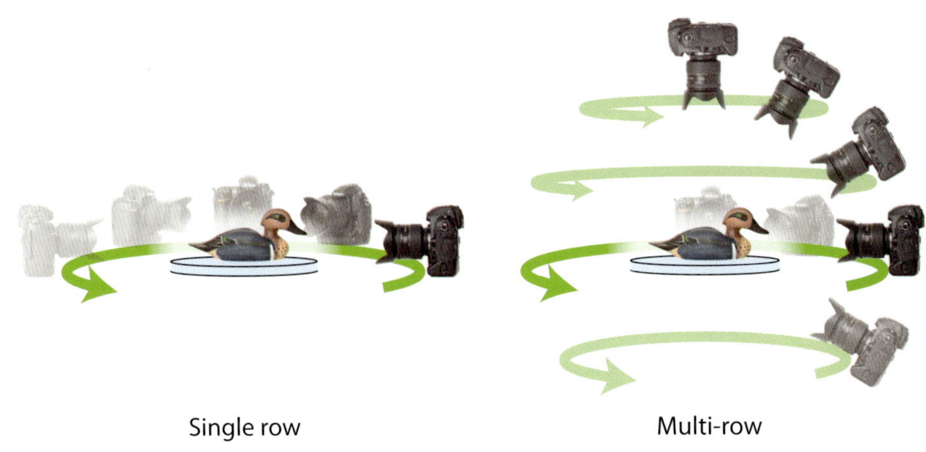

Fig. 8-12 Single row and multi-row object movie shooting perspectives.

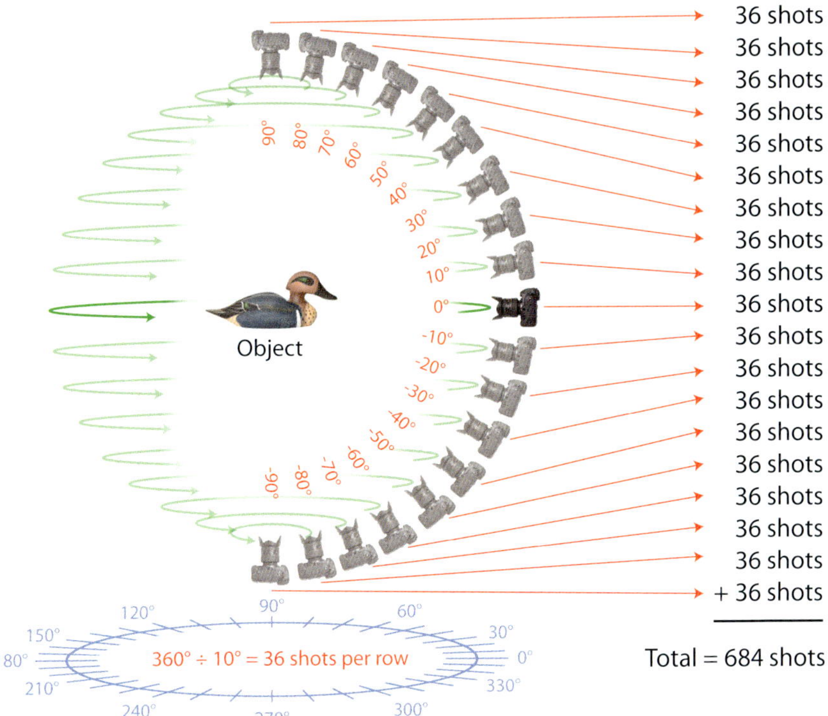

Fig. 8-13 A full 360° x 180° object movie using 10° increments for both horizontal and vertical directions would require a total of 684 photographs.

The first is perhaps the simplest and least expensive. It involves mounting the camera on a counterbalanced boom or swing arm system, which rotates about an axis centered on the object. One advantage of this system is that the boom can be extended so that the camera-to-subject distance can be varied, while the camera can move up or down along the varying arcs.

The disadvantage of this system is that it requires support from two sides in order to be reasonably stable. Some small units utilizing very small (low resolution) web cams are effectively supported on only one end. The boom arm(s) also tend to get in the way of lighting equipment and are easily bumped when working around the set, causing misalignment problems. Depending on lighting, the boom arm(s) can also cast shadows or show up as reflections on the subject.

The second type of multi row camera rig is the fixed arc type, where the camera is mounted to a head that moves up and down a curved rail. The object on a turntable is centered within this arc. This type of system is favored for large object work, because of its structural stability and the fact that there are no boom arms to get in the way of lighting or studio activity. Its disadvantage is that it has a fixed radius or shooting

distance, requiring lens or focal length changes for different sized objects.

The third type of object rig is a cantilevered or folding arm system. This is the most flexible and capable design, but also tends to be expensive. It requires a computer controller to calculate combinations of angles for the arm sections, but allows the camera to be positioned anywhere along infinite arcs at varying distances from the object. It can be used effectively for both large and small objects. Its cantilever arms extend from behind the camera, so there are no booms interfering with lighting from the side. Newer designs are reasonably stable, although accidental bumping of the unit during shooting will still cause image alignment problems.

It should be noted that more recent software technologies for rendering object imagery via projection mapping may minimize the need for the large numbers of photographs currently required for object movies. Companies such as Autodesk and Kaon have systems that use a small number of photographs, shot from each side of an object, and map these images onto a virtual 3-D model. This provides a photo realistic model, which can be interactively viewed from any angle in a virtual 3-D space, much like a QTVR object movie, but requiring a fraction of the number of source photographs. Use of object rigs like the ones above will still be necessary, because the camera needs to be positioned above, below and around the object for proper registration and mapping of the images.

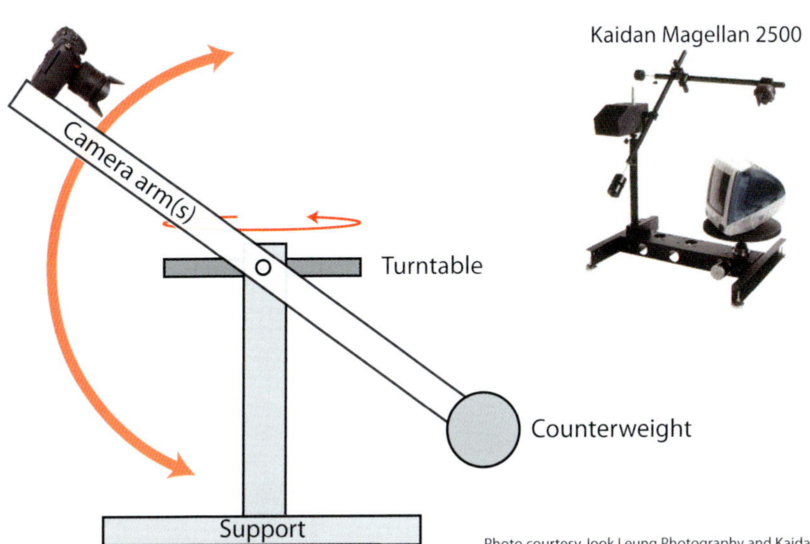

Fig. 8-14 The design concept behind a swing arm object photography rig.

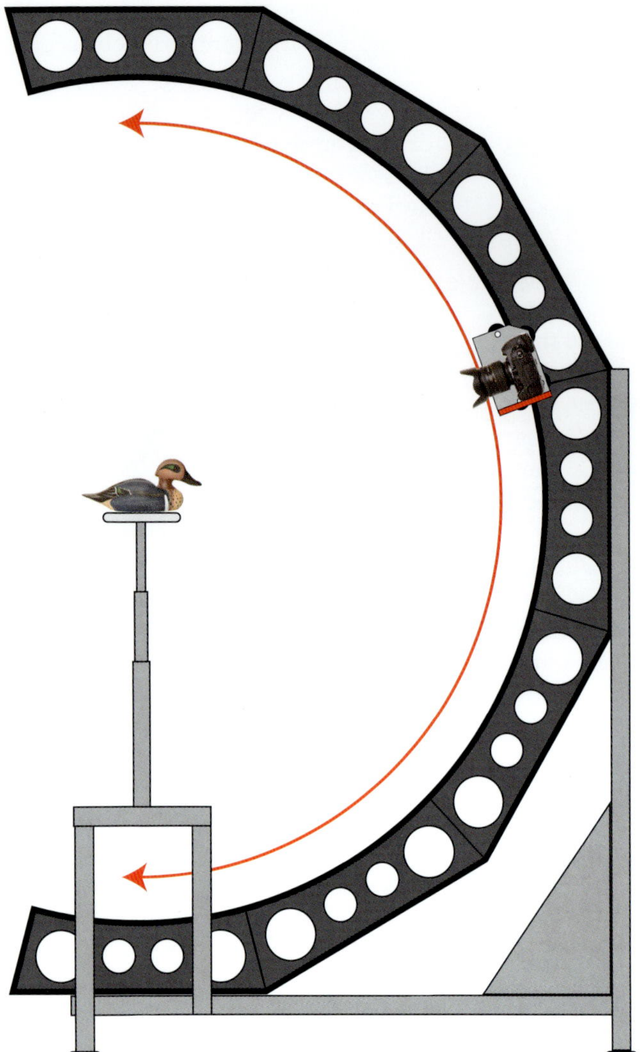

Fig. 8-15 A fixed arc object photography rig design.

Essential Equipment: Cameras and Lenses

Since precise image alignment is usually required for object movie photography, digital cameras are the preferred choice. It is certainly possible to use traditional 35mm film cameras, but you will face added complexity and cost in post production. You are usually better off using the consistent frame (sensor) alignment within digital and video cameras, and thus saving the time and costs of film scanning. The main concern is to make sure that whatever camera you are using has sufficient resolution for all the needs you might have (remember that print reproduction usually requires far greater resolution than the 72 dpi needed for most computer or video displays).

If you do a lot of object photography, a good digital camera will probably pay for itself quickly. It will be necessary to set up an efficient work flow in your studio in order to handle the large number of digital files that you'll be creating.

Many photographers find it best to have a dedicated computer for their object movie capture, connected directly to the camera in use. Kaidan, Corybant West, and Peace River Studios offer software specifically for automated photography of object sequences using their object rigs. Other software applications, such as VR Worx from VR Toolbox can do this, as well.

Your choice of lenses for object photography will depend upon both the size of your subject and your shooting distance. In general, products are best photographed with longer focal length lenses from longer distances, unless a wide angle distortion is desired for some reason. A more distant perspective is usually preferred for product-type photography (which is what most object movies are), as the telephoto views more accurately portray the relative sizes, angles, and parts of the product.

Essential Equipment: Lighting

Good product photography is generally done in the studio, where lighting can be controlled to show a product at its best. The same applies to object photography, which can be thought of as animated product photography. Therefore, studio lighting should be considered essential equipment for object movie photography.

If you are using a video camera for your image capture, you will need to use continuous light sources, such as incandescent flood lamps (hot lights), fluorescent tubes, or daylight balanced HMIs. If you are shooting with a digital or film camera, you can use any of these lights, as well as studio strobe (flash) systems. Since most studio photographers already own strobe equipment, they find it easiest to use

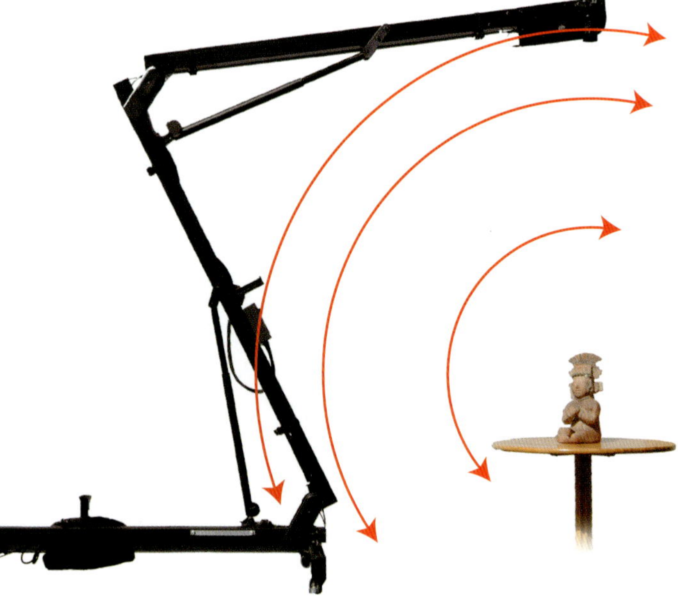

Fig. 8-16 Folding arm or cantilever object rig design.

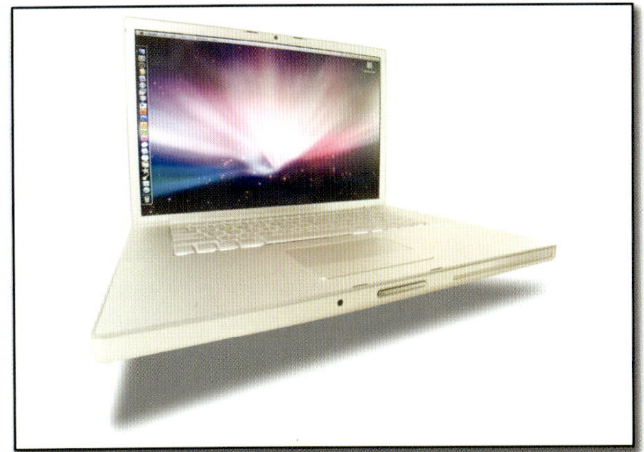

Wide angle (18mm) view close to subject

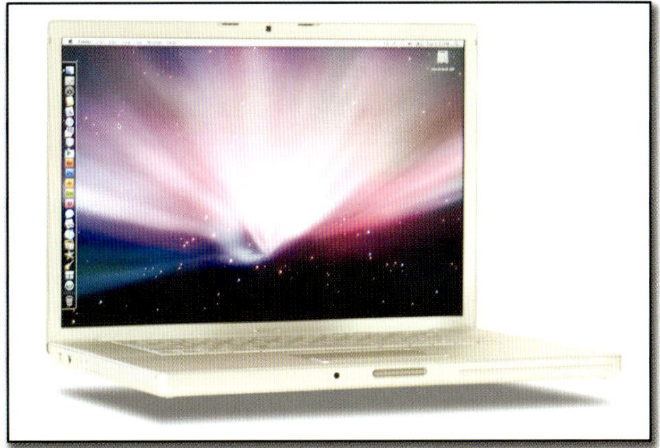

Telephoto (135mm) view distant from subject

Fig. 8-17 Lens focal length and camera-to-subject distance help define the perspectives chosen for object photography.

this for their object photography. Strobe lighting offers greater illumination levels than any of the continuous lighting sources, allowing smaller apertures to be used and providing greater depth of field – all of which are assets when you're trying to make a client's product look as good as possible.

Since every object should be lit to its best advantage, it is important to check your lighting throughout the range of views you are shooting. Your light should remain consistent as the object rotates. As the angle of view changes, lighting problems may reveal themselves, including reflections, glare, and even poor light balance. Set your lighting and preview it from all angles the camera will capture before actually starting the image recording process.

Every photographer's lighting style is different. Yet, for object and product photography, soft, diffuse lighting often works best. A large overhead soft box, either directly above or coming from a 3/4 front angle, is usually a good choice when combined with a fill light from the opposite side. Once you've figured out the basics, and can produce a full sequence of well-lit images throughout an object's rotation, then you can start playing with the addition of other light sources or lighting techniques.

Packing for Travel

Every photographer, particularly those doing panoramic VR, will find themselves traveling to shoot on location. These travels may be as near as the

other side of town, or as far as the opposite side of the earth. Traveling will take you away from a studio or office where all of your camera and computer equipment resides, and will force you to choose specific equipment for the job at hand.

These choices are not always easy. When traveling, we are faced with deadlines, schedule restrictions, and quite often, a lack of facilities to repair, replace, or restock our gear. We must be self contained, self reliant, and fully prepared for anything that might come our way.

This does *not* mean that we have to pack a studio full of equipment into dozens of cases and ship them off to our destination. More often, we need to pare our equipment down to the barest of essentials, and pack it so it is both well-protected and quickly accessible.

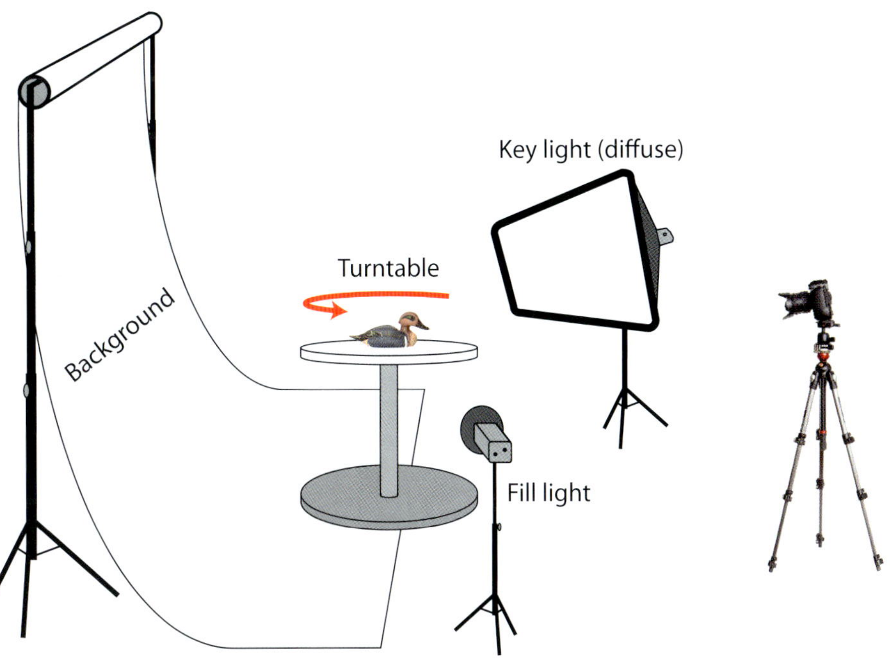

Fig. 8-18 A basic soft lighting setup can often be used for object VR photography.

I've found that the best approach is to pack my gear into several small, task-specific kits, rather than putting everything into one big one. For instance, in one bag, I may have a 35mm camera, several lenses and small strobe unit, while in another I have a digital camera kit. A tripod can be carried separately, or perhaps included with a pan head as part of a VR kit. When you can afford redundancies, pack and carry backup gear separate from the originals. That way, if one or more bags get lost or damaged during your travels, you're still able to continue working with what you have, rather than being completely shut down by the loss.

You may find it convenient to put several small kits into a larger case or backpack for transport, particularly when faced with tight carry-on restrictions by commercial airlines.

Traveling on Airlines

One of the biggest nightmares facing working photographers today is traveling on the airlines. Heightened security worldwide and increasingly restrictive carry-on regulations have made it very difficult to carry more than the most minimal amount of photo equipment with any assurance that it will arrive intact at your destination. In the past, most airlines had special baggage rates for film crews and professional photographers, but most have eliminated these in recent years. If you need to carry a lot of equipment on location, be prepared to pay excess or overweight baggage fees. Also, be aware that most airlines will not cover loss or damage to photo equipment during their transport, so be sure to have your own insurance coverage in place.

Again, the best way to travel on the airlines with photo gear is to take only the minimum amount you need. Carry anything that you absolutely cannot afford to lose as part of your carry-on luggage. Most airlines still allow at least one carry-on bag, plus a brief case, camera bag, or purse. You may need to get creative, but it is possible to transport a fair bit of essential photo gear with you this way.

I have a Tamrac Expedition 8 photo backpack that I can load with a wide variety of equipment. It fits fairly well in the overhead bins of most planes and through the sizing templates at security stations, as long as it's not completely full. I usually try to put less in it than it will hold, just to keep the weight down and to minimize the risk of it hurting another passenger if it were to fall from an overhead bin.

Cameras and lenses go into the main compartment, protected by modular dividers, while personal toiletries and a minimal change of clothing go in the outside pockets, along with containers of film (if I'm shooting film) that can be quickly removed for hand inspection at the x-ray machines.

I also have a Lowe Super Trekker backpack, which is a bit larger than the Tamrac Expedition 8, but which really doesn't work as carry-on baggage any more since the airlines reduced their carry-on size limits. I use my Super Trekker more for location work now. It is particularly suited for hiking and wilderness photography.

Different airlines have different limits on the maximum carry-on size that they allow. Enforcement of these restrictions can also be selective. Be sure to check with your particular airline on what their limits are before you start packing. For reference, many airlines currently specify maximum dimensions of **22"x14"x9"** or **45 inches** total for each carry-on.

In a soft briefcase, I carry a laptop computer and other business necessities, travel documents, a hat, sunglasses, and a lightweight jacket. With the backpack and the briefcase, I can carry everything I usually need to get me through the first day and night of the shoot. Additional less critical photo equipment, plus clothing and other baggage gets checked. I generally try to put everything in soft duffel bags using clothing, sleeping bags, or jackets for padding. I will use hard cases for fragile equipment such as underwater camera housings and studio strobe equipment. I find it better to pack in old, beat up looking cases, rather than shiny new ones, which beg the attention of thieves.

My large photo backpack has come in handy on a few occasions when a flight has been crowded and carry-on allowances are strictly enforced. The limit is usually one piece plus a briefcase, camera bag, or purse. I have

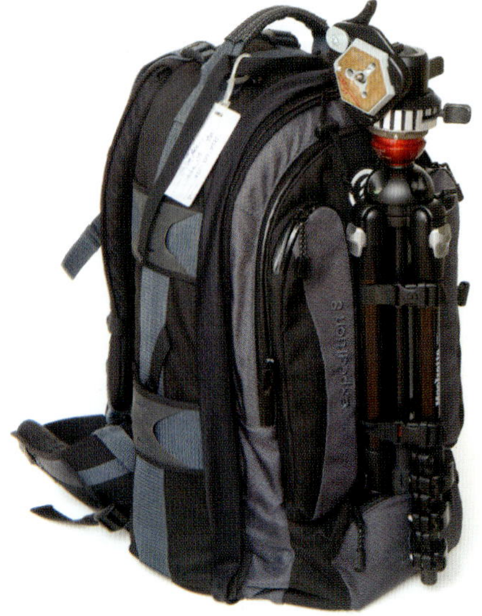
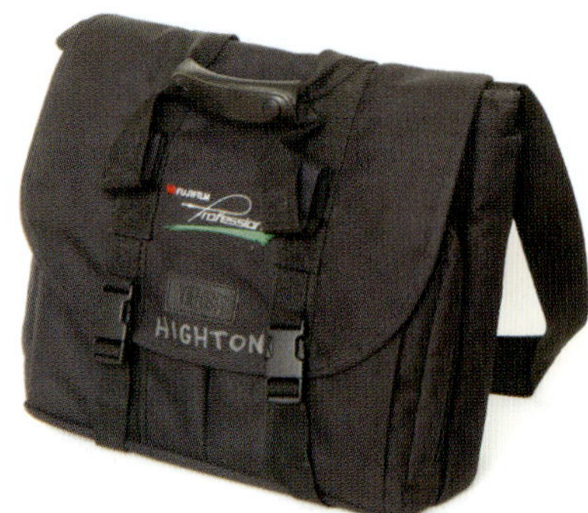

Fig. 8-19 The author's airline carry on combination – a Tamrac Expedition 8 photo backpack and soft briefcase.

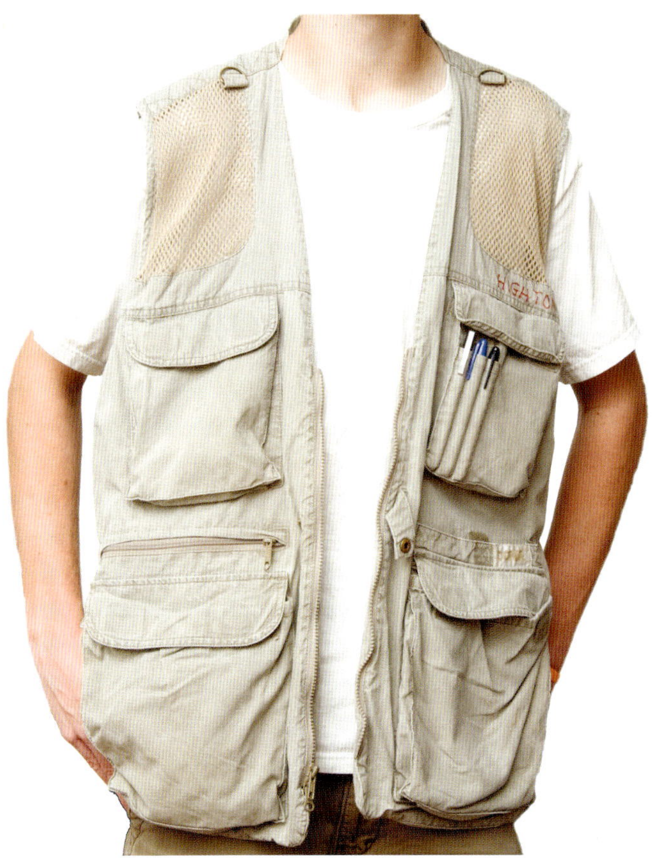

Fig. 8-20   The classic photo vest, such as this one by Domke, can be invaluable in getting equipment safely through airports in some situations. It is also favored by many photographers for location photography.

simply explained that the backpack is a camera bag. If the airline staff questions it, opening the main compartment reveals nothing but photographic equipment, and I am usually allowed to board the plane with it.

On rare occasions, you may be stopped because of the apparent weight of your backpack, and will be asked to check it. Wearing one of the popular "photo vests" has helped a number of photographers get through this situation. They simply remove a camera or lenses from their backpack, and place them in the pockets of their photo vest. They hand the backpack back to the airline staff for a weight check again and are cleared through, wearing the vest on their body. Since the vest and its contents are considered clothing, they are usually exempt as carry on items. Once on board, photographers simply remove their vest and place the equipment back in the backpack, or stow the vest with gear in the overhead bin with their pack. While I've never done this personally, I know a number of other photographers who have.

Avoid carrying your equipment through airports in the pockets of a photo vest unless you absolutely have to, as the vest pockets offer little padding or protection for your gear. This look can also identify you as a lucrative target for pickpockets and thieves.

The best approach is to limit the equipment that you travel with, and to do everything possible to both abide by airline regulations and cooperate with airline employees. This means getting to the airport early. An already stressed ticket agent is unlikely to do you any favors when you show up late and demand special treatment while trying to board the plane with 100 lbs. of carry-on luggage. Get to the airport with plenty of time to spare. Then, be friendly and courteous.

Ticket agents are sometimes willing to discount fees for excess baggage by charging you for fewer than your total number of extra bags. However, this is a courtesy on their part, and they will be much less inclined to extend it to you if you are rushing them, or if you get testy with them. Be prepared to pay the excess baggage fees (often $100 or more per bag). Then, be grateful (and gracious) if the ticket agent charges you less.

The same thing goes for the attendants at the gate with your carry-ons. Be courteous and offer any solution you can if your bags present a problem, rather than getting defensive or raising a fuss. The airline staffers have a difficult enough job as it is. They have no reason to do favors for passengers who make their lives more difficult.

Also, consider traveling with a companion or assistant, or buying an extra seat on the flight if you have lots of equipment and excess baggage. The cost of an extra ticket can sometimes be less than what the excess baggage fees might be (they can add up fast). Furthermore, an extra set of eyes and hands can be invaluable when moving lots of equipment through public places such as terminals and rental car centers. With two or more of you, there will always be one person who can stay with the gear while the other goes to get food, pick up reading material, or visit the restroom.

X-Ray Hazards

If you travel anywhere in the world today on airlines, you are going to face the problem of x-ray machines and exposure of your film to this harmful radiation. The good news for digital photographers is that x-rays pose no real threat to digital media, cameras, and memory cards.

There is good news for film shooters, however. In the U.S., security personnel will generally provide a hand inspection of your film, rather than requiring that it go through the x-ray machines with all your carry-on camera equipment. However, it is best to allow plenty of time for them to do this (again, be early and be courteous).

Exposure to x-rays has a cumulative effect on film. The higher the film's ISO, the more susceptible it will be to x-ray exposure. For most films of ISO 400 or less, a few small doses of U.S. airport x-ray machine exposure will have negligible effect. European airports may differ.

The best approach is to keep all your film in a ZipLock™ bag or other container, which can be removed from your camera bag and handed to the security officers for a hand check, along with your keys, coins, pens, and other objects. That way, you can put the rest of your camera equipment through the x-ray machine without worry, since only the film is at risk from x-ray exposure.

Security officers will generally need to see and inspect every roll of film, so have the rolls clearly visible and out of their original packaging. Inspectors will usually open every film canister to swab each roll for explosives residue.

Some photographers have good success by removing film from its plastic film canisters and packing it in Tupperware™ or other durable plastic food containers. This allows the airport security officers to open the container and see all the film at once, rather than having to open the individual plastic canisters for every roll.

Personally, I prefer to keep my film in individual plastic film canisters, as these provide better moisture and dust protection during travel and shooting in the field. I also find that the loose film leaders sticking out of unexposed rolls of film tend to get snagged on each other, and either get pulled out of the film cartridge or get pushed too far in to retrieve. If you use the Tupperware type containers for your film, I recommend that you also pack a handful of empty film canisters for protection of your film while it's loose in your pockets or vest in the field.

Many photo stores sell lead lined film bags that supposedly protect your film from airport x-rays. Unfortunately, these are fairly ineffective, primarily because the x-ray machine operators will simply back

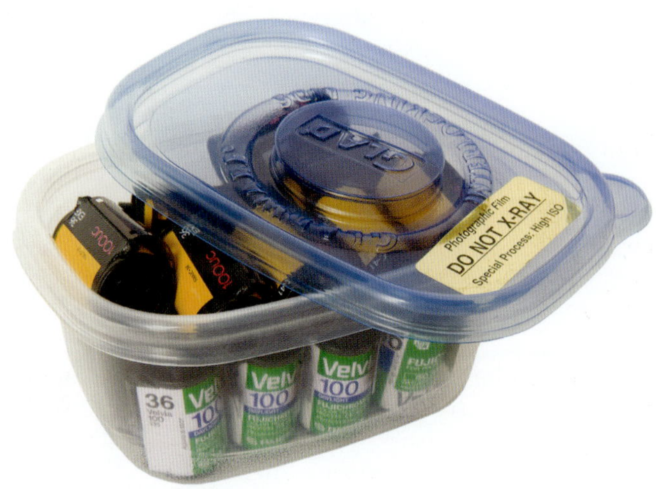

Fig. 8-22   Removing 35mm film from its canisters and repacking it in Tupperware or other see-through containers can help speed the hand inspection proocess for airline security personnel.

up the conveyor belt when they can't see through these bags, and rescan them with a higher doses of radiation until the contents are revealed.

In many foreign countries, hand inspections are *not* an option for film or any other hand carried luggage. You must either submit the contents of your bags to the x-ray machine, or you don't get on the plane. In these instances, you may have to accept the exposure and hope for the best. Remember that for the most part, a few passes through carry on luggage x-ray machines will *not* have a noticeable effect on most films. Just try keeping these to a minimum.

I once discovered a loose roll of unexposed ISO 100 film that had fallen to the bottom of my camera bag and been left there for a while. I was able to determine that it was about a year old, and that it had probably been run through airport carry-on x-ray machines more than 20 times. I shot a series of test exposures with it, and then shot identical exposures with a brand new roll of the same film to compare the effect of the repeated x-rays. After processing, the results were virtually identical. I could tell no difference between the two.

Checked Baggage – X-Ray Warning

In years past, photographers would hand carry only a small amount of their film with them, and then spread the rest (sometimes hundreds of rolls) throughout their checked baggage. The idea was that you'd have enough with you to get started on a shoot if one or more of your checked bags was delayed or lost. Checked bags were not x-rayed, so your film avoided the x-ray risk of security checks.

Unfortunately, **this practice is disastrous today.** Most airports have installed high dose CT-scan x-ray systems

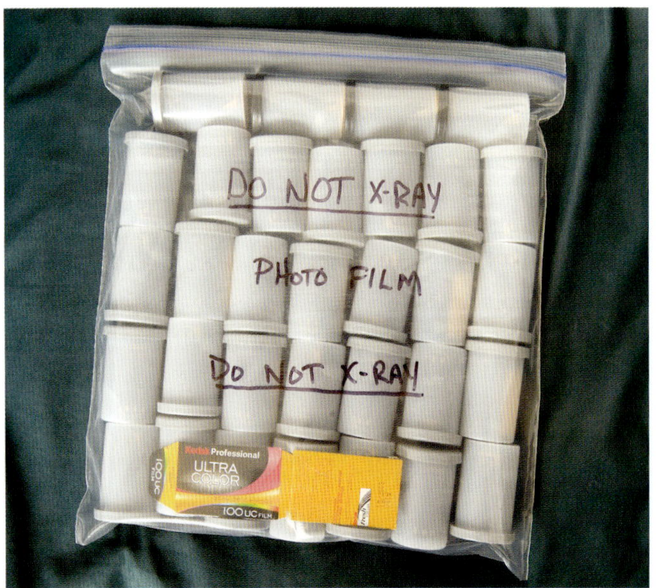

Fig. 8-21   Film should be unboxed and ready for hand inspection when traveling on airlines.

to scan ALL checked baggage. These machines will damage virtually all photographic films, and should be avoided at all cost.

Your film now has a much better chance of surviving the lower exposure systems of the carry on x-ray machines, or by avoiding x-ray exposure altogether with a hand check, than it does surviving exposure from the CT-scan systems. Bottom line today is **NEVER pack your film in your checked baggage**.

Purchasing film at your destination may be a better option than trying to carry it with you via the airlines. However, for most location photographers, this not usually a good option, as it's hard to predict the availability (and cost) of film in the volume that might be needed, particularly in other countries. Some photographers have also found it useful to ship their film ahead via FedEx or other shipping courier. Be sure to confirm ahead of time that they won't x-ray your shipments, though.

Of course, the safest solution today is simply to shoot digitally, rather than having to worry about *any* of the hassles of film any more.

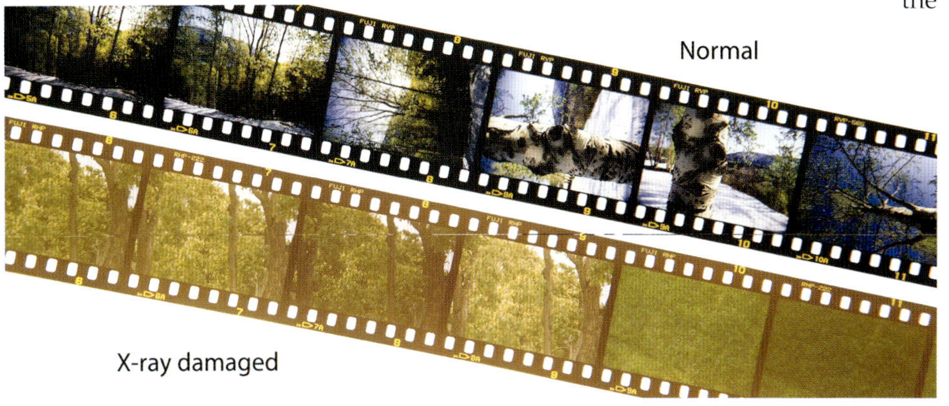

Fig. 8-23 Putting undeveloped film of any ISO (whether exposed or unexposed) inside checked baggage usually means it will receive high-dose x-ray radiation, which will ruin any images.

Packing Equipment

You have a significant investment in camera equipment. Don't risk it unnecessarily by failing to pack it in padded camera bags or cases when you travel. Professional cameras and lenses will stand up to the occasional bumps, a little rain or moisture, and their share of dust and dirt. However, anything you can do to minimize these hazards will extend the life of your equipment and prevent its failure at a critical time.

If you don't have a good camera bag or proper cases for your equipment, wrap each item individually in clothing or other soft materials and pack it near the center of your regular suitcase. Everyone has their own preferences for how they like to pack their gear. Find a system that

works well for you. Think about the possibility of your bag being dropped onto a concrete ramp from a 10-foot high platform. That's a common occurrence for checked baggage.

I personally prefer large, heavy duty duffel bags when possible, because they can carry both large or small amounts, and don't have the look of "expensive camera equipment" among all the other baggage in an airport. I pack tripods inside these duffels, well wrapped by clothing or other padding. If you do this, be sure to loosen all the leg and head locking mechanisms so that there is some movement allowed in case of a hard drop or bump.

I also find that I frequently return from my travels with more than I started with. Souvenirs, extra clothing, and odd sized items you pick up along the way can be easily added to soft duffel bags, whereas they might not fit easily inside hard cases. Duffel bags can also be rolled up and stowed in small spaces once you're on location. Hard cases take up the same amount of space whether empty or full. Duffels don't offer the same protection as hard cases do, so you might prefer one over the other in different situations. I find that a combination of the two will work for most travels requiring extensive equipment transport.

You can place a small TSA-approved lock through the zipper loops of most duffels and other baggage for security. However, inexpensive plastic cable ties can be used for similar effect. Carry a handful of these ties with you when you travel, and every time you check a bag or equipment case, seal it shut with one of the cable ties. Make sure you also have a pocket knife along so you can cut through the plastic ties once you arrive at your destination. (Don't carry the knife with you on the plane, as these are prohibited and will be confiscated at security screenings.) Most baggage thefts are crimes of opportunity. If you place simple obstructions in the way, all but the most determined thieves will move on to easier pickings. Of course, if you put too big a lock on a case, it will again call attention to itself, sending the message that your bag contains something of value, which might be worth stealing.

I know several underwater photographers who use Rubbermaid™ or Igloo™ ice chests for transporting their underwater camera equipment and housings. They surround everything with foam padding inside, and then secure the chests with unobtrusive strapping tape or rope. In an airport, the chests look like they belong to a tourist headed for a fishing trip. The chests also serve as good storage containers aboard a dive boat, protecting against sea spray and rolling objects on decks. They're also relatively cheap, and can be replaced easily when they wear out.

Equipment Maintenance

Keeping photographic equipment in good working order can be a simple job in the protected environment of a home, office, or studio, particularly when you have a minimal amount of gear in the first place. However, once on location, your equipment becomes far more prone to failure due to harsh environments and the fact that your gear is being bumped and jarred as you move around. In particular, digital cameras and computers are very sensitive to rough handling, so an ability to do basic maintenance or repairs in the field is invaluable.

While always seeking to simplify the equipment you travel with, keep in mind that having backup systems can mean the difference between failure and success on a shoot when something goes wrong. Extra cameras or lenses should be a priority, if you can afford them. A digital camera can be used as a backup for a film shoot, or a film camera can be used as a backup to your digital equipment. Extra memory cards for your digital camera are a must, and a laptop computer with a DVD writer can be invaluable for backing up the day's digital images.

There are several items that should be carried by every photographer in your primary camera bag. They include:

The mini screwdriver set is invaluable for repairing camera problems and tightening loose screws, including those on your glasses.

A micro fiber lens cleaning cloth can be carried inside a plastic envelope (to keep it clean) or inside an empty film can. These are wonderful for cleaning optical surfaces, as they absorb oil (from fingerprints) and avoid scratching. There may still be occasions when you need to use old fashioned cleaning fluid and lens tissue, but micro fiber cloths are effective 95% of the time.

The blower brush should be used to remove heavy dust or dirt from your equipment, particularly lenses, before wiping with a lens cloth. The bigger particles of dirt and dust can get trapped under the lens cloth and be pushed into the glass as you clean it, leaving scratches. Some photographers will try to blow dust and dirt away with their breath. This is a bad habit to get into, as the air coming from your mouth contains a significant amount of moisture. This combines with dust or dirt to form a thin layer of "mud" on your lens. Even worse, you will someday accidentally blow on a lens in cold weather, and the moisture from your breath will form a layer of ice on the lens surface, rendering it completely useless until you can warm the entire camera, thaw the ice, and wipe the moisture away.

A small notebook and pen are a necessity, particularly for VR photography, where it is important to note lens focal lengths, number of shots per panorama, and any unusual lighting or image sequencing notes that might

1) **Swiss army knife (put in checked baggage for air travel)**
2) **small screwdriver set**
3) **lens cleaning cloth**
4) **blower brush**
5) **notebook and pen(s)**
6) **cable or remote camera release**
7) **small flashlight**
8) **set of ear plugs**
9) **bubble level for your camera's hot shoe (for VR shooting)**
10) **shower cap (free in many hotel rooms) for protecting camera from rain**

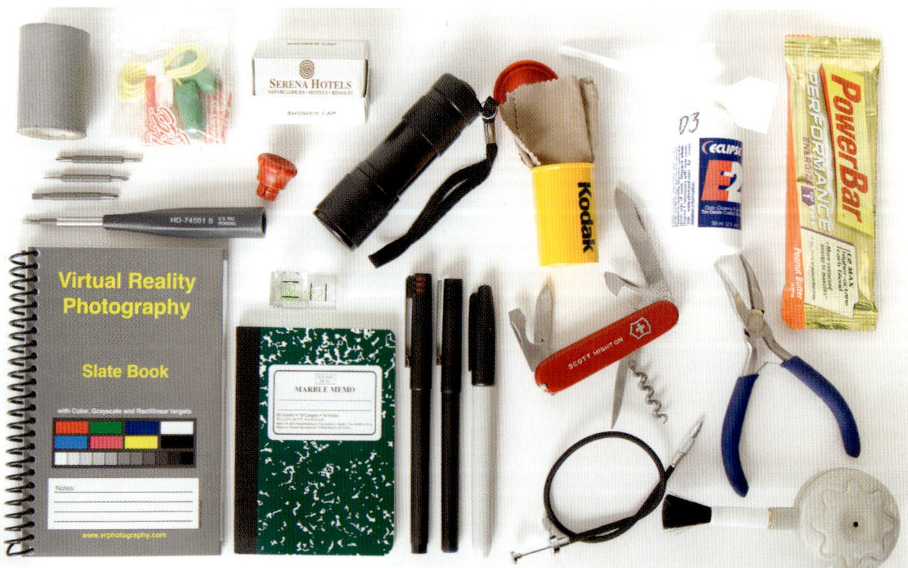

Fig. 8-24 Camera bag essentials. Note that some items (screwdrivers, knife, pliers) cannot be hand carried on airlines and should be packed in checked baggage.

The basic Swiss army knife is almost as important to a photographer as a camera. It has thousands of uses (including cutting those cable ties on your checked baggage once you arrive on location), and should be carried in your pocket at all times (except on airlines).

be important for post production and assembly. The notebook can also be used to write out slate information (much like a motion picture slate used to mark the beginning of each take), which you can photograph as the first image on each roll of film or digital sequence. This "slate" will help you keep accurate notes and information as a part of the source image files, in case the paper notes are misplaced along the way.

A cable or remote release is essential for triggering your camera on long exposures, so that the pressure of your finger on the shutter button doesn't shake the camera and blur your images. Get in the habit of using a cable release to maximize image sharpness whenever your camera is mounted on a tripod.

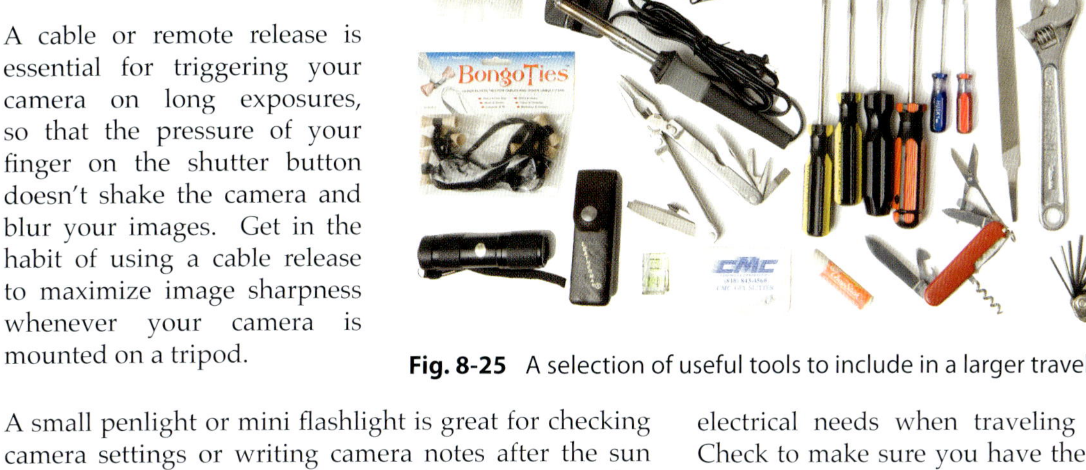

Fig. 8-25   A selection of useful tools to include in a larger travel photo tool kit.

A small penlight or mini flashlight is great for checking camera settings or writing camera notes after the sun has gone down. It's also good for finding dirt or other problems inside your camera, even during daylight hours. It can also be a life saver in emergencies. Mini flashlights are relatively cheap and small, so put one in every camera bag. Check the batteries once a year if you haven't used it recently.

Ear plugs are wonderful when you are shooting around industrial areas or in a location where there is loud machinery in use. While not always a necessity, these take up virtually no space. The biggest benefit I've found to carrying them is during long airplane flights, boat trips, or when trying to sleep in noisy hotels. I recommend seizing every opportunity to sleep during "down" times when traveling, so you are fresh and well rested when the pressure of the photo shoot begins on location. A set of ear plugs can make the difference between getting good sleep or not.

Spare batteries and enough film or digital media to cover your entire shoot should also be a priority. These are items that can be difficult, if not impossible to find in remote or foreign locations. Many digital cameras use batteries fast. Rechargeable batteries are fine when you have power available for recharging, such as in a hotel at night. But don't count on it always being accessible. The same thing goes for laptop computers and their batteries. Voltage converters should be carried for all your

electrical needs when traveling in foreign countries. Check to make sure you have the right adapters before you leave.

Finally, if you are shooting with digital cameras, invest in a good sensor cleaning system, and learn how to use it properly. Dust and dirt will invariably build up on your camera's image sensor, particularly as you travel, change lenses, and simply use your camera (the movement of optical elements inside a zoom lens creates small currents of air that suck dust and dirt into the camera body, where they are further attracted by the electromagnetic charge of the image sensor).

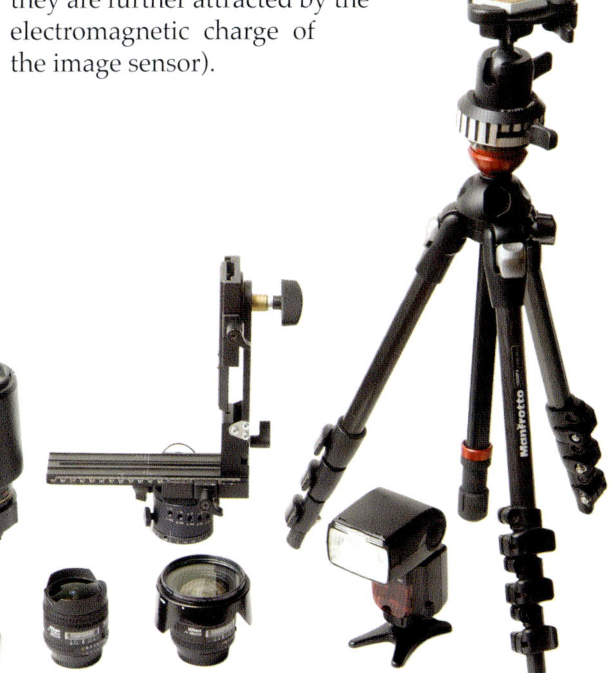

Fig. 8-26   A basic all around digital photography and VR equipment kit with camera, strobe, several lenses, VR pan head, spare battery, charger, and tripod.

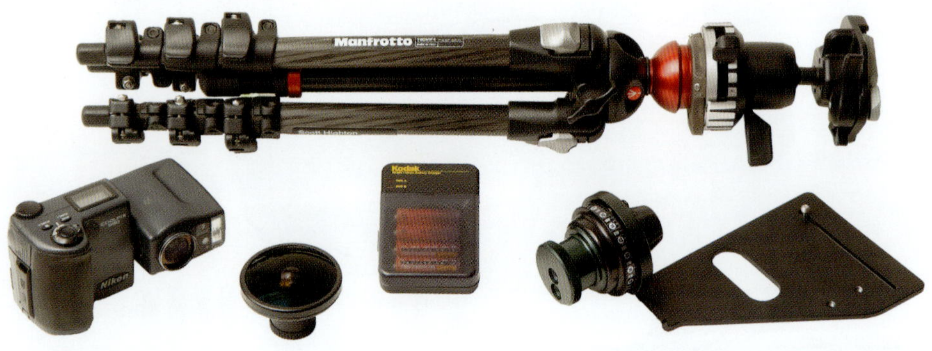

• Supply of digital media or film
• Spare batteries
• Tripod and VR pan head
• Misc. cleaning cloths, tools, mini flashlight, cable release, filters, etc. (Optional)
• Macro lens (60mm or 105mm) or a wide-to-normal (24-85mm) zoom lens with macro capability

Fig. 8-27   Consumer digital shooting kit with fisheye lens adapter and VR pan head.

I highly recommend the Arctic Butterfly brush system. When properly used, it seems to remove almost all dust and dirt from the sensors of most digital SLR cameras.

The addition of sensor swabs (with the cleaning fluid specific to your particular camera) is useful for removing persistent particles and the occasional light smearing of shutter oil on the sensor.

Other items useful in a small tool bag include:

- **Leatherman™ or other multi function tool**
- **Spare Swiss army knife w/scissors**
- **Larger screwdrivers (Phillips & slot head)**
- **Small crescent wrench**
- **Small roll of gaffer's tape (duct tape leaves a sticky residue – avoid it)**
- **Extra tripod plate for your camera**
- **Plastic garbage bag and several ZipLock bags**
- **Selection of plastic cable ties for securing baggage and equipment cases**
- **Spare keys for any baggage locks you may have**
- **Sharpie pen(s) or permanent markers**
- **Small Allen (hex) wrench set**
- **Small metal file**
- **Tweezers**
- **Rubber bands**
- **Q-tips**
- **Sample sizes of aspirin, Chap Stick™, sun lotion, bug repellent, etc.**

A simple all around camera kit that allows you to do both traditional still photography, as well as VR, might include the following: (Cost: $3,500 – $5,000)

- **Nikon film or digital SLR camera**
- **Nikkor ultrawide or fisheye lens (for VR)**
- **Medium telephoto zoom lens (80-200mm)**
- **Hand-held flash unit for fill-lighting (w/diffuser)**

A low-end digital camera kit could include the following: (Cost: approx. $1,500)

- **Nikon Coolpix camera**
- **2-4 digital storage cards**
- **Fisheye lens or converter**
- **Batteries & charger**
- **Pan head bracket**
- **Tripod**

A high-end digital camera kit might include the following: (Cost: $37,000 - $40,000)

- **Panoscan™ digital camera system w/lens**
- **Camera battery & cables**
- **Apple Macbook Pro with software**
- **Heavy duty tripod**
- **Tool kit, etc.**

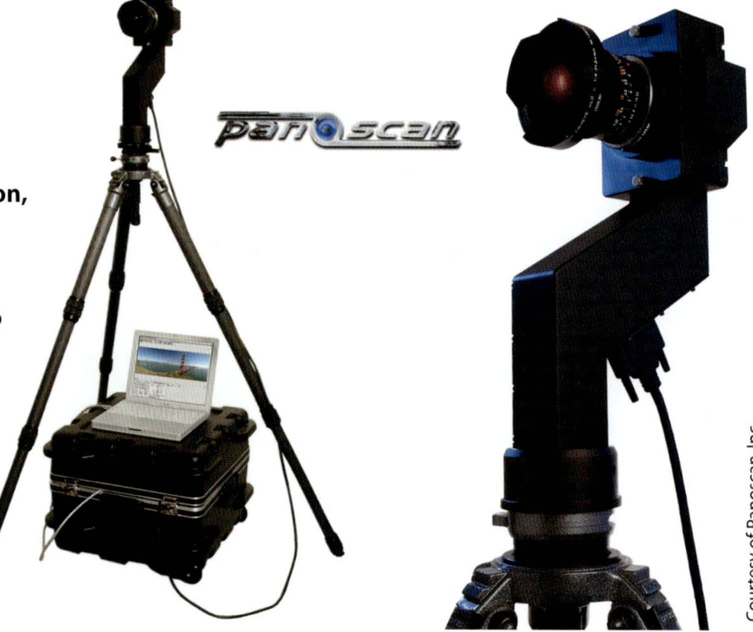

Courtesy of Panoscan, Inc.

Fig. 8-28   A high end Panoscan MKIII scanning digital panorama camera.

Part 2

PANORAMIC VR IMAGING

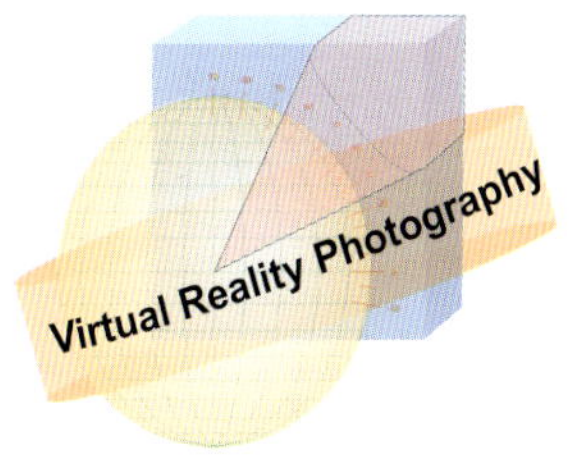

Chapter 9: Panoramic Overview

A 360-degree panoramic photograph is probably the image most readily identified with virtual reality (VR) today. Most people are first exposed to VR on the internet when they encounter a panoramic tour, either of a home for sale, an automotive interior, a travel destination, a virtual store, showroom, or an internet portal.

Panoramic images are perhaps the essence of virtual reality, for they allow us to interact with a location on our computer screens. These views provide us with the ability to look up, down, and 360 degrees around – just as we could if we were there in person. The computer allows us the freedom to zoom in for a closer view, and even to instantaneously "jump" to other 360-degree views that might be linked.

Even though panoramic virtual reality is a somewhat recent technology, panoramic photography has been around for many decades. Dozens of specialty cameras have been developed over the past century, and until recently, these were a requirement for panoramic photography. However, today's digital VR software has changed that. Now, photographs shot with just about any camera can be assembled into seamless panoramas with the use of stitching programs.

Good panoramic photography requires that the photographer develop new ways of looking at an environment and pre-visualizing his or her images. It requires an expansion of one's view to include everything around, rather than only what falls within the traditional rectangular frame of a camera's viewfinder. Many photographers welcome the change to a wide panoramic view from the traditional 2:3 aspect ratio of 35mm cameras. The change in visual perception is much the same as seeing High Definition (HDTV) television for the

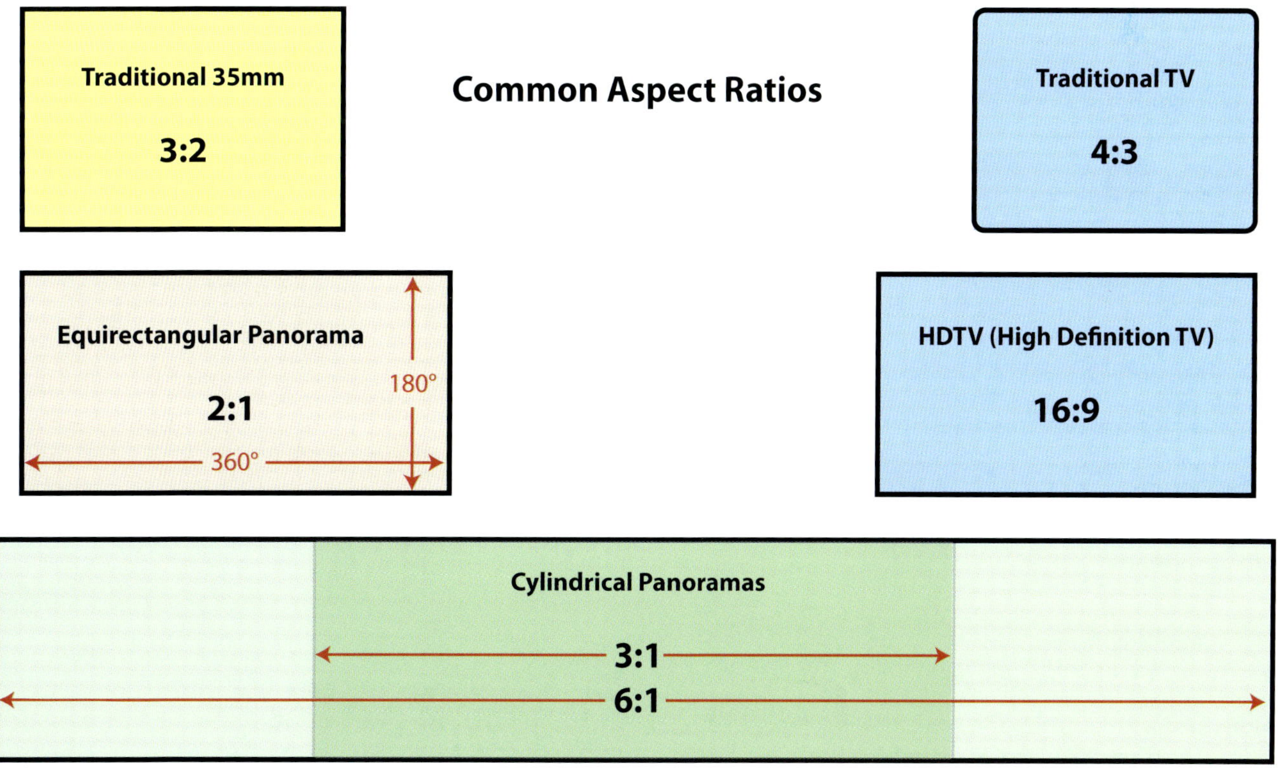

Fig. 9-1 Common aspect ratios (horizontal vs. vertical dimension) for movie and image presentation.

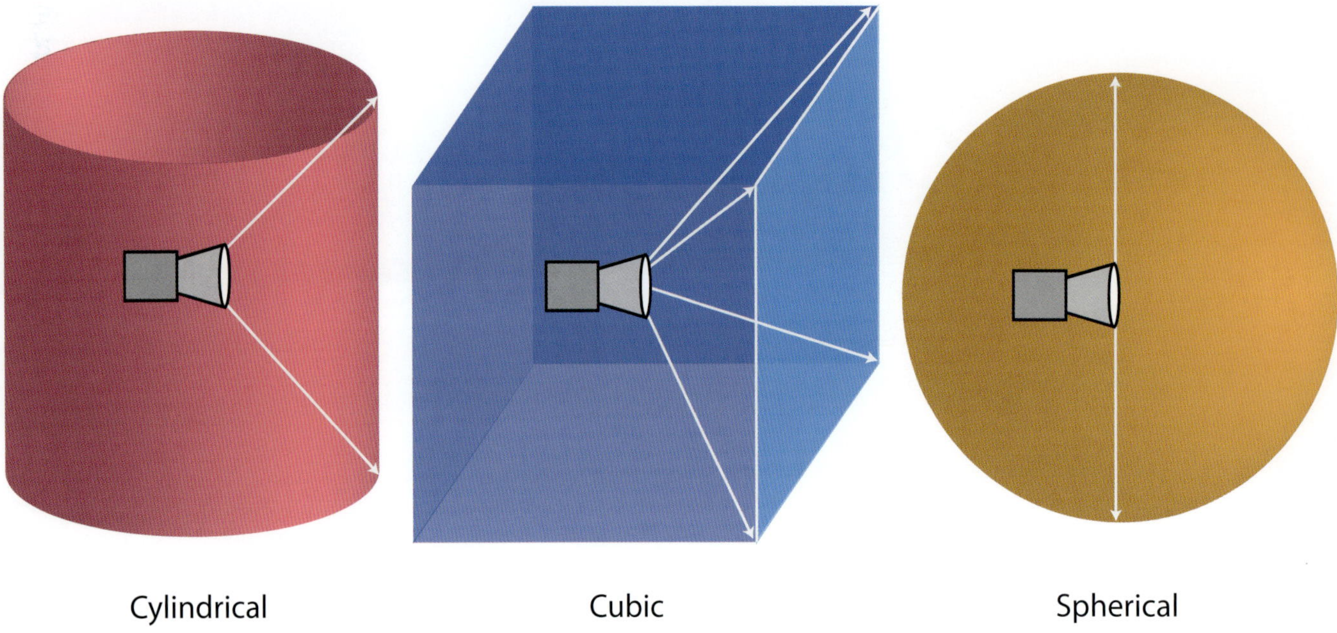

Fig. 9-2 Virtual "projection" geometries most commonly used for the presentation of VR panoramic images.

first time, with its long 16:9 aspect ratio, instead of the traditional 4:3 video frame we were so used to watching over the years.

Displaying panoramic images in a virtual reality format gives users control over where they look and how they navigate within a scene. In order to do this, images must be projected or mapped onto a virtual screen. This is done by rendering a virtual projection of the image to mimic the effects of standing inside a round room with the panorama appearing seamlessly on the surrounding walls. While technical details of this are of little interest to most people, an understanding of the basic geometry involved is important for the photographer wanting to shoot panoramic VR.

Today's mainstream VR technologies use three primary geometric shapes for panoramic projection: **cylinders**, **cubes,** and **spheres**.

Cylinders

The **cylindrical** projection model was the first, and remains perhaps the most common model used today for panoramic VR. It was an integral part of Apple's QuickTime VR when it was released in 1994, and has remained the default standard for the industry. Cylinders have distinct advantages, both from photographic and digital processing standpoints.

In 1994, the processing power of most desktop computers was not nearly as robust as it is today. Algorithms for displaying a cylindrical panorama within a QuickTime movie window require simpler calculations than do those for other geometries. The less complex the calculations, the more responsive the interactivity can be, meaning

that panning is smoother and more realistic on older computers. If a computer's processor can't keep up with the calculations needed to display an image, the refresh rate of the picture slows dramatically. This results in jumpy sequences of static images, rather than a smooth, continuous motion during a pan or zoom by the viewer.

The cylindrical model also enables the photographer to use a variety of traditional cameras and lenses, rather than requiring specialized (and expensive) panoramic photo equipment. A series of overlapping images can be assembled using digital stitching software. Lenses of almost any focal length can be used for the photography. For the most part, the more images assembled, the greater the resolution and detail there can be in the completed panorama.

The primary disadvantage of a cylindrical projection is that it has a limited vertical field of view. This is because the height of a virtual cylinder defines the limit of the vertical view that can be displayed. An infinitely high virtual cylinder (one that extends up and down to infinity) *could* display a 180° vertical field of view, but the amount of picture data required to fill the cylinder wall would become infinite, as well. In theory, the practical limit of a QTVR cylindrical vertical field of view is about 140°. However, in reality, even the widest (non-fisheye) lenses are limited to capturing somewhere between 110° and 120°.

Cubes

The **cubic** projection model was added to QuickTime in 2000. Its advantage is that it represents a reasonably efficient way to display VR panoramas with full vertical (180°) fields of view. Today's faster and more powerful

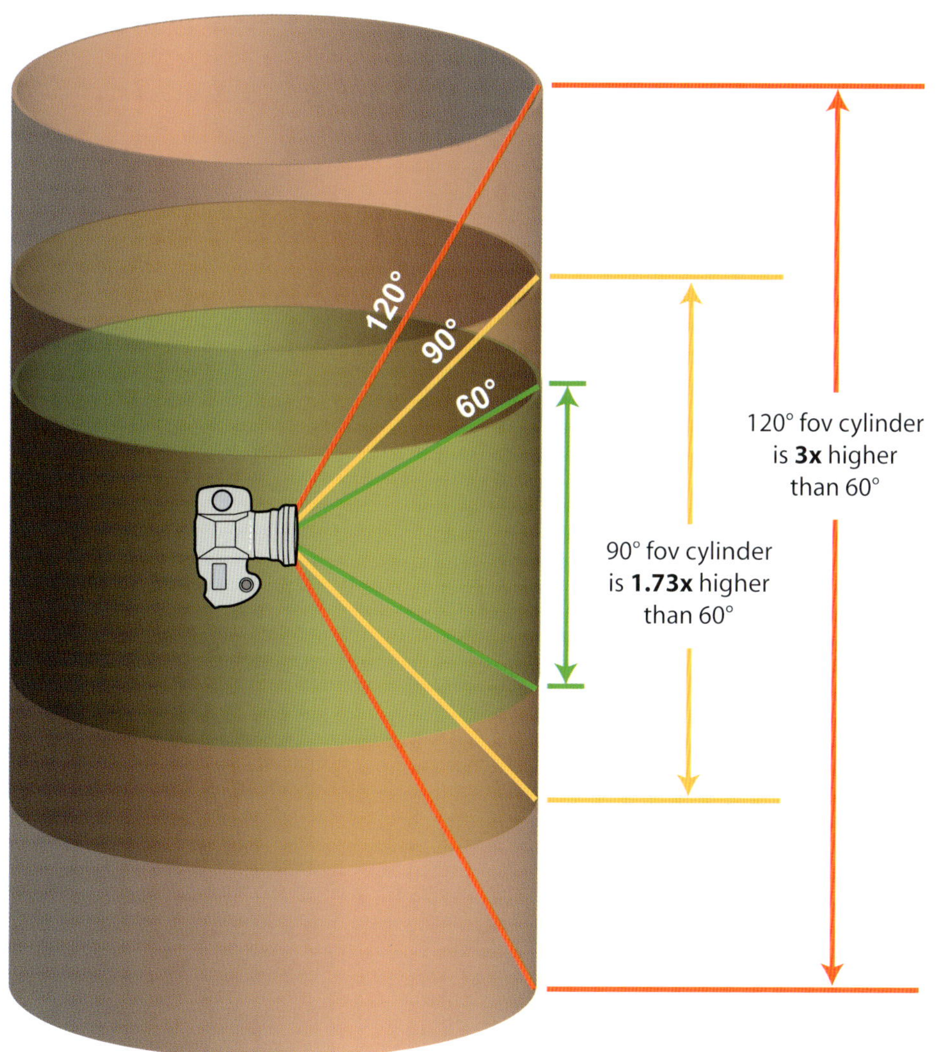

Fig. 9-3 Vertical fields of view are limited for cylindrical panoramas, as the amount of image data needed to fill in the increasing heights of the projected cylinders nears infinity as the vertical field of view approaches 180°.

defunct IPIX Corporation. IPIX's aggressive stance on protecting its patents in the early years of consumer VR development meant that spherical projection has only recently become common in other applications today.

Keep in mind that VR panoramas are not physically projected onto these various geometries inside our computers. The projections described above are performed by a computer to map the panoramic images onto *virtual* surfaces. The resulting image maps are used to display portions of a panoramic image within a viewer window on our computer monitors. Think of it as a virtual process similar to what a painter does when painting a diorama on a curved wall.

Armed with this understanding of today's VR models, we can now explore the methods and equipment used to photograph panoramic VR images.

computers are better able to keep up with data processing required for smooth playback using this more complex projection algorithm.

The views straight up and straight down are centered on the top and bottom faces of the cube, so there is no need for the massive amounts of pixel data necessary to fill in excessively high walls of a virtual cylinder. Although the cubic projection is done upon the six square faces of the inside of a cube, it is rendered so that there is virtually no perception by the viewer of corners or intersections.

Spheres

The most logical way to project a complete panorama is within a virtual sphere. With **spherical** projection, the virtual projection surface is continuous with no corners or intersections, and every mapped pixel is the same distance from the central projection point. This method was originally used most extensively by the now-

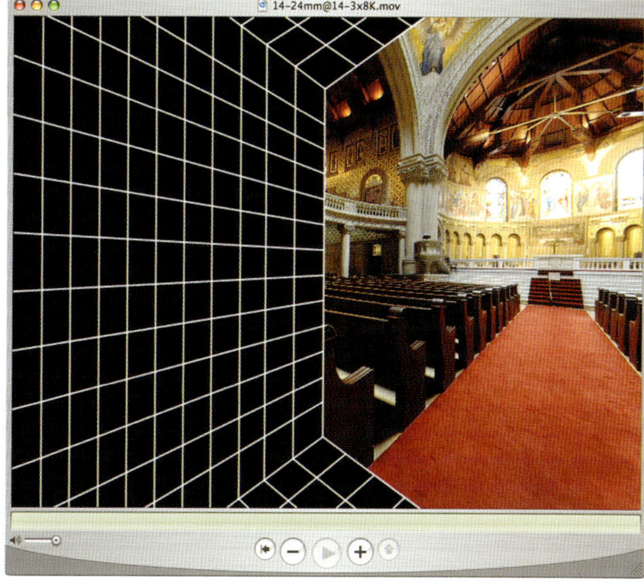

Fig. 9-4 Cubic and spherical projections are most commonly used for 360°x180° panoramic movie presentation today. Both allow the viewer to look straight up and straight down, as well as 360° around. The differences between the two cannot be noticed by most viewers or end-users.

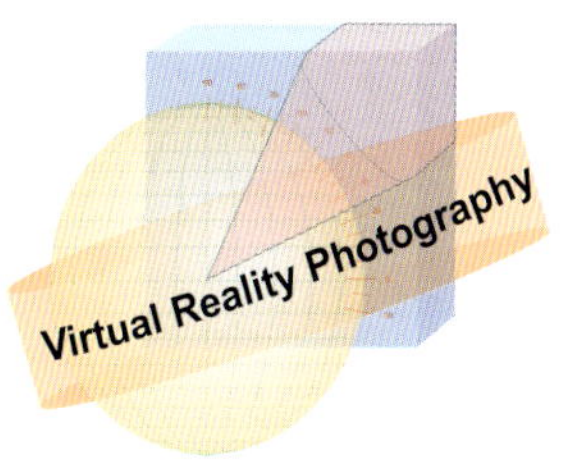

Chapter 10: Cylindrical Panoramas

Single Row Cylindrical Panoramas

There are three primary approaches to photographing and assembling the traditional cylindrical QuickTime VR panorama. They include:

1) Shooting a sequence of overlapping images and using stitching software to blend them together into a seamless panorama.

2) Shooting with a panoramic scanning camera that records a full panorama in a single progressive scan.

3) Shooting with a 360° parabolic mirror lens to capture the entire scene in a single frame, followed by the use of special software to "dewarp" or convert the image to a traditional panorama.

Method 1 – Stitching a Series of Images

The most commonly used (and most affordable) of the above methods is to shoot a series of photographs and stitch them together into a seamless 360° panorama. Once this panorama is assembled, it can be processed into a QuickTime VR or other interactive movie. During post production, links between this panorama and others can be made, allowing for user navigation throughout an entire scene. Other elements such as sound, text, and video can also be added.

Generally, a 35mm or digital camera on a panning tripod head is used to shoot the series of overlapping images. The number of images required will depend upon the focal length of the lens used. The longer the focal length, the more shots will be necessary, since the fields of view for longer focal length lenses are smaller than those of shorter (wide angle) lenses.

Basic stitching applications require that the source images be shot with rectilinear or "corrected" lenses, as opposed to fisheye lenses. This becomes an important consideration when choosing the camera and lens that you'll use. Fisheye lenses, such as the Nikkor 16mm full frame fisheye, offer very large fields of view and are generally less expensive than rectilinear lenses of similar focal length. However, rectilinear lenses are required when using certain stitching programs, although more and more of these stitchers provide for the use of fisheyes, today. For this reason, it is important to be familiar with

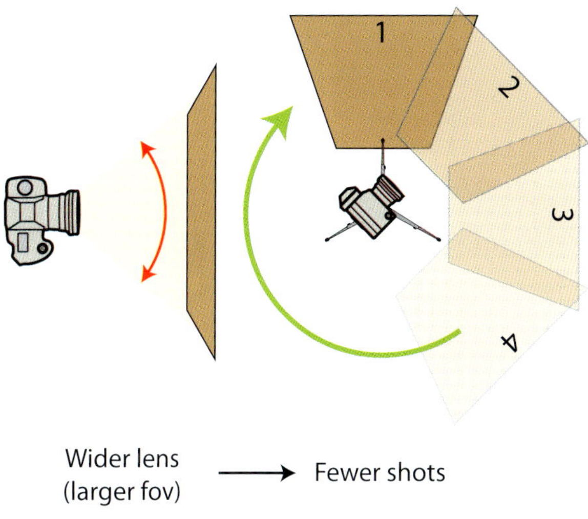

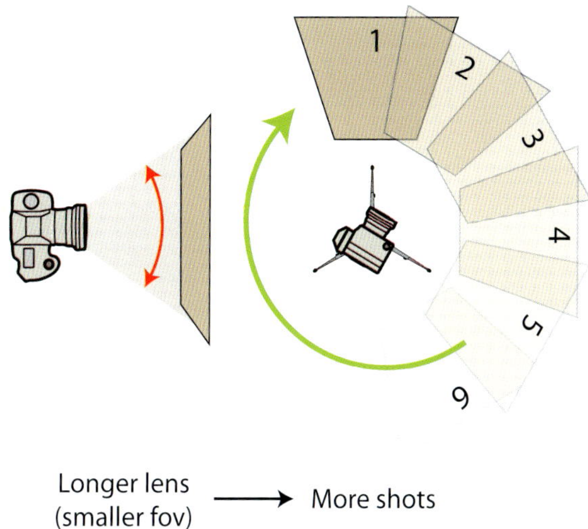

Fig. 10-1 The larger the field of view for a lens, the larger the pan increment between images can be, and the fewer images are needed to create a complete panorama.

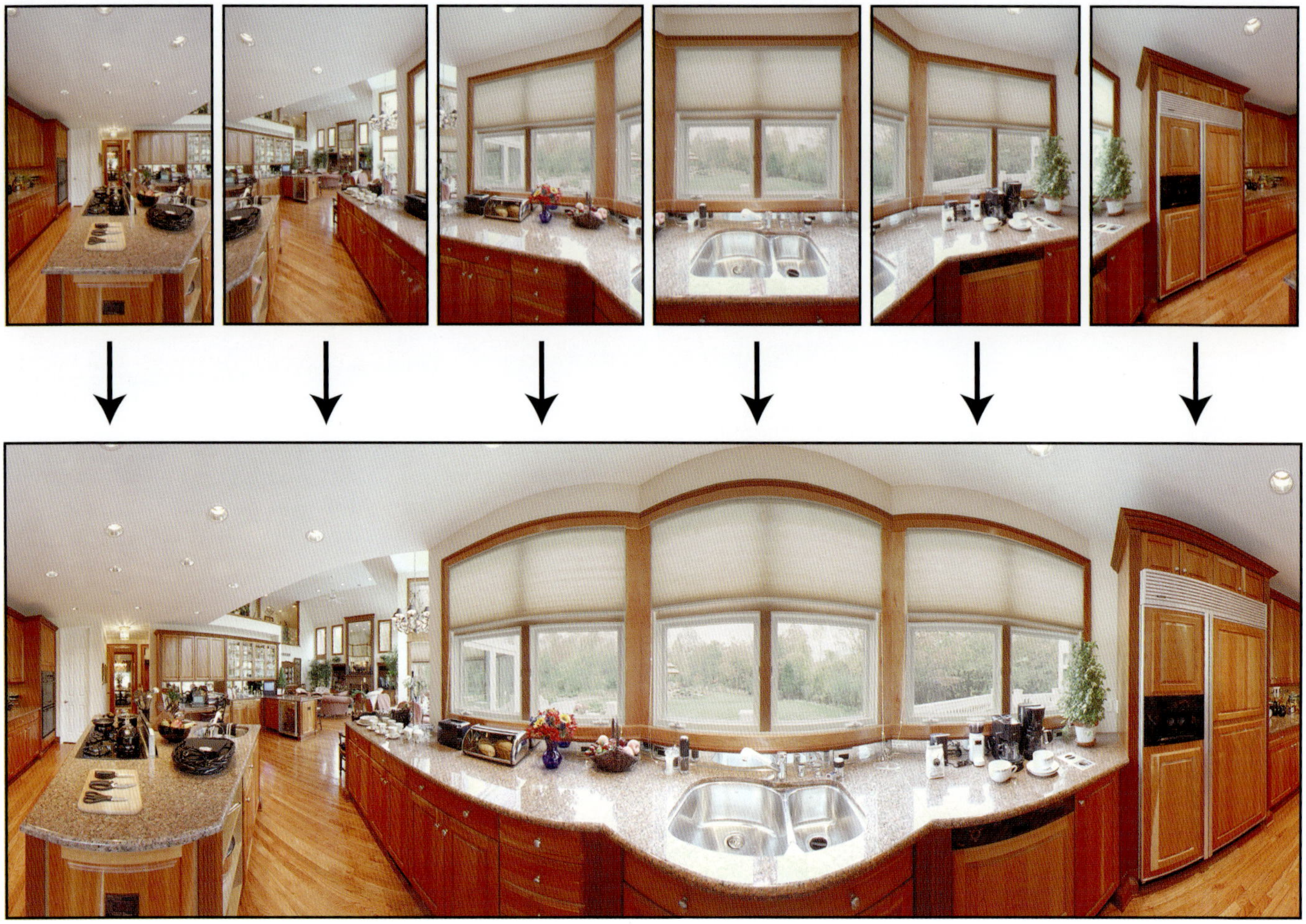

Fig. 10-2 The stitching process takes a series of overlapping images and blends them into a seamless panoramic image.

the requirements and limitations of whatever software stitcher you will be using *before* you plan your shoot.

When shooting an image sequence for a panorama, you'll generally want to orient your camera vertically (in portrait or vertical orientation), rather than in a landscape (horizontal) orientation. Portrait orientation allows you to maximize the vertical field of view that is captured in each image. Shooting with the camera vertically means that the pan increment between overlapping shots will be smaller than it would if the camera were turned horizontally, and more shots will be required for the full 360° coverage. However, greater vertical coverage is generally more desirable for VR panoramas than saving a few shots per panorama.

For example, an 18mm rectilinear lens used on a 35mm camera provides a 90° field of view along the long axis of the frame, with a 67° field of view along the short axis. If we allow for 1/3 to 1/2 image overlap between sequential frames, a complete 360° panoramic sequence will require 8-12 shots in portrait orientation, compared to 6-8 shots in landscape orientation. However, the portrait orientation of the camera will provide us with a 90° vertical field of view throughout the panorama (45° above through 45° below the horizon), as compared to 67° of vertical coverage (33.5° above through 33.5°

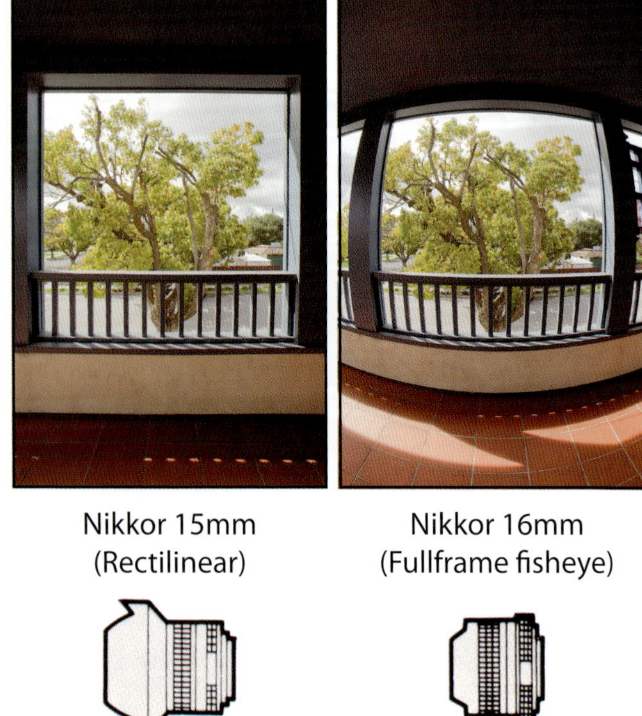

Fig. 10-3 Lens choice: rectilinear vs. fisheye.

Fields of View: 18mm Lens
(35mm format)

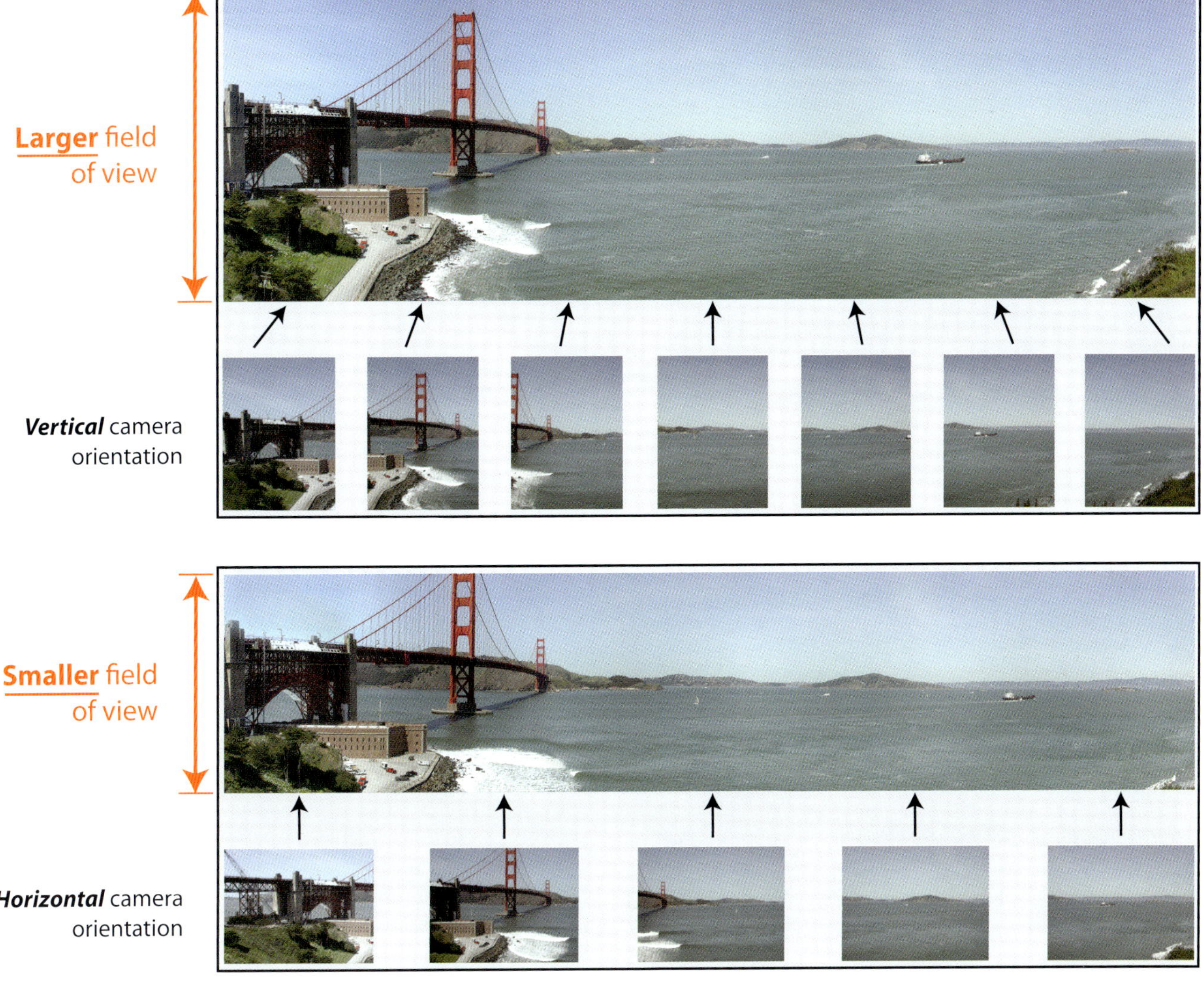

Fig. 10-4 Portrait (vertical) vs. landscape (horizontal) camera orientation.

below the horizon) for the landscape orientation. (Note that actual coverage will be slightly less due to cropping that occurs during the stitching process.)

Maximizing your vertical field of view is critical in most situations, particularly when shooting interiors or other confined spaces. You will want to choose the widest lens possible. For exterior scenes where the need for large vertical coverage may not be as necessary, you may find it better to use a longer lens (requiring more shots to cover the entire 360°) or to shoot in landscape orientation.

Most VR photographers find that it is best to shoot consistently and use portrait orientation for all of their panoramic shooting. Some commercial pan heads designed for VR camera

Fig. 10-5 Portrait (vertical) orientation of the camera increases the vertical field of view of a stitched panorama.

Technical Note: Choosing a Panorama Lens

Choosing a lens for panoramic photography is generally done based upon the subject matter and environments in which you plan to shoot. As with traditional photography, no one lens can do everything, and serious photographers usually rely on one or two primary focal lengths for most of their work.

The first concern is how much vertical field of view you need for the locations you will be shooting. Interiors usually require greater vertical coverage (shorter focal lengths) than exteriors. The confined spaces of car, aircraft, and boat interiors often require vertical fields of view beyond those available with rectilinear lenses, so VR software that allows for multi-row stitching or the use of fisheye images may be needed.

Good ultra wide rectilinear lenses (20mm and shorter) are available for most professional camera systems. Unfortunately, they also tend to be fairly expensive, often costing $1,000 or more. There are third party lenses available for lower cost, as well as wide angle adapters, which are added on to the front of existing lenses to increase their fields of view. However, a common problem with both adapters and "cheap" lenses is that they introduce barrel distortion, causing stitching problems. Be sure to test any lens or add-on optics with your preferred stitching software before committing to its purchase. Many photographers invariably wind up buying the more expensive lens anyway after they discover that the "cheaper" model didn't do the job adequately.

Fixed focal length lenses usually incorporate better rectilinear correction than zoom lenses do. Lens

Interiors

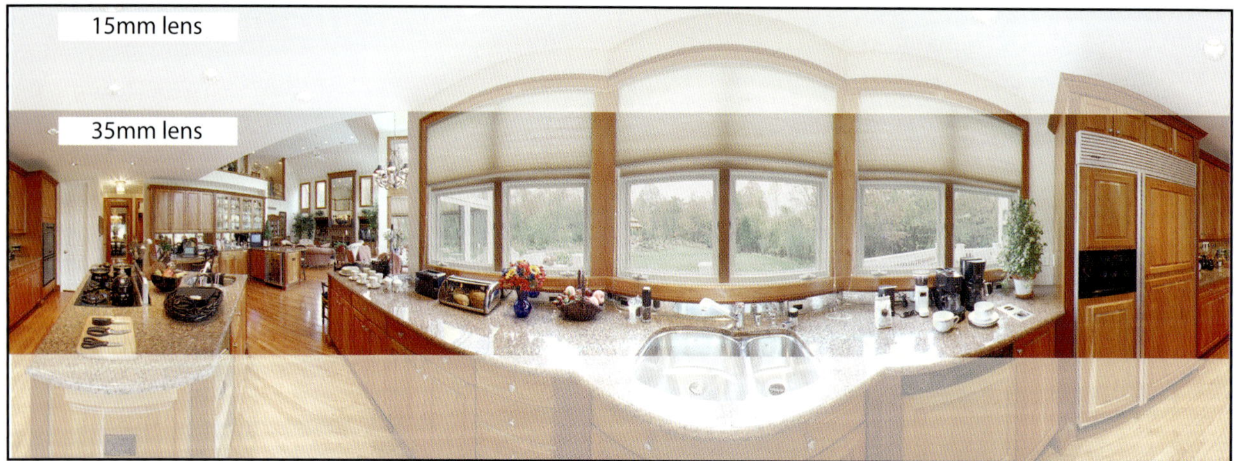

Exteriors

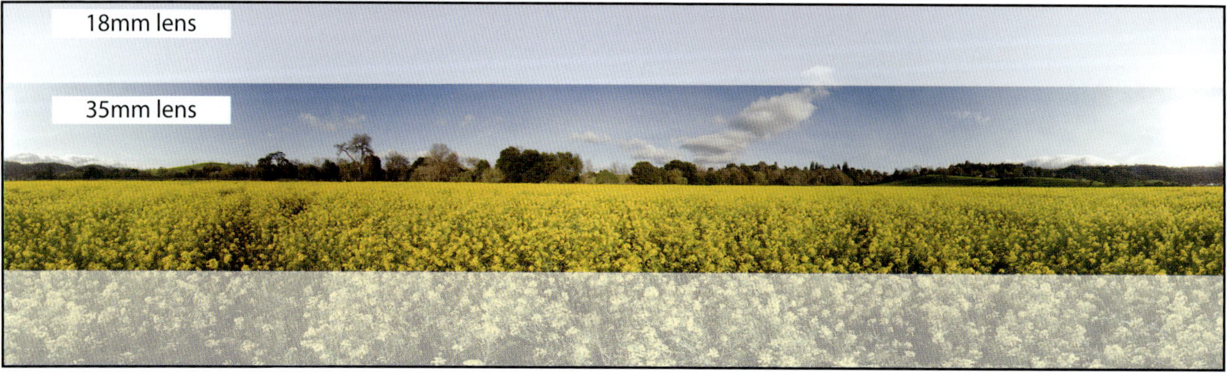

Fig. 10-6 Wider focal lengths provide greater vertical coverage in stitched panoramas, and require fewer source images.

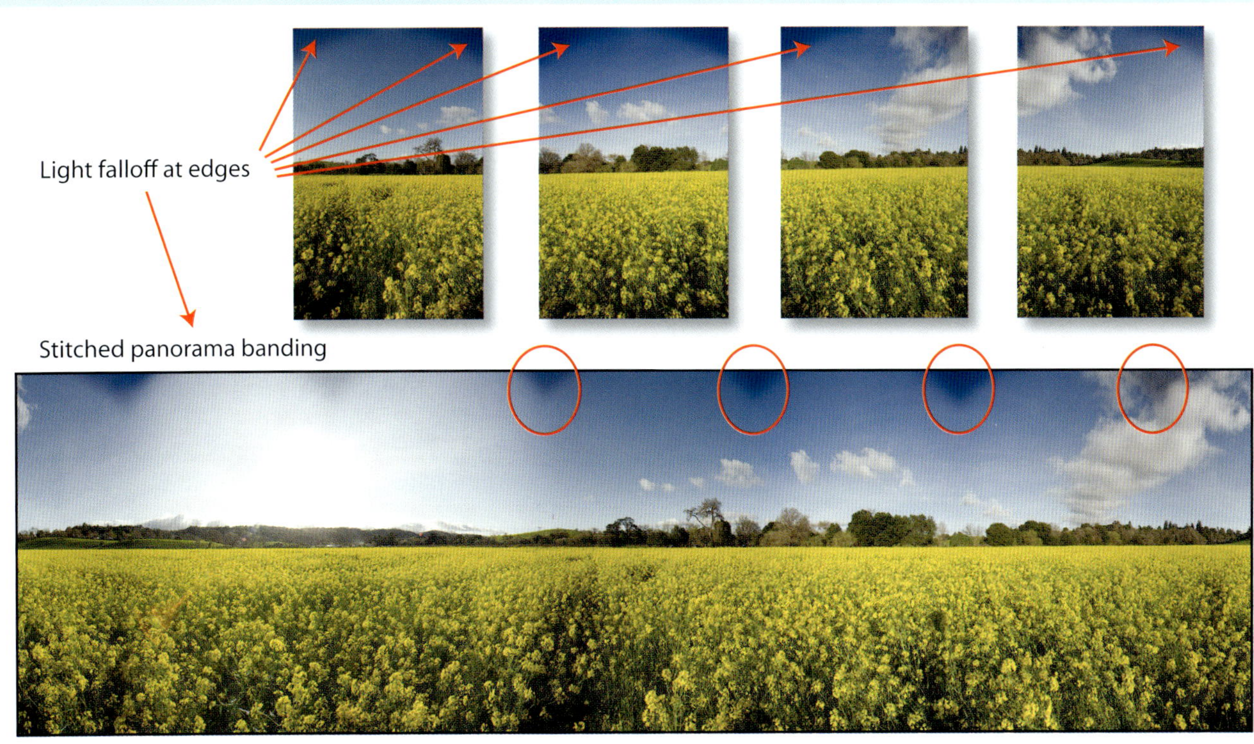

Fig. 10-7 Even minor vignetting, hardly noticeable in single images, can cause problems when stitching panoramas.

design, like most everything in photography, involves tradeoffs and compromises. Designing a lens that can zoom through a range of focal lengths requires even more tradeoffs. Perfectly rendered straight lines on film are not critical for most photography, so limited barrel distortion in the widest focal lengths on zoom lenses is considered one of the acceptable tradeoffs by most lens manufacturers. Be careful, and do plenty of testing before choosing any zoom lens for panoramic VR photography.

Another thing to check with any lens is consistent exposure throughout the image, particularly near the edges or corners of the frame. Lower cost lenses tend to have increased light fall off between the center and the edges of the frame – otherwise known as vignetting. Vignetted images produce a light-to-dark banding effect when images are stitched together. The shorter the focal length, the more pronounced this vignetting will usually be.

Vignetting can also be caused by the filters or lens shades mounted on the front of a lens. Ultra wide lenses are particularly susceptible because of their extreme angles of view. Photographers often add clear skylight or haze filters to the front of their lenses in order to protect the front glass elements, reasoning that it's far cheaper to replace a filter than

it is to replace an entire lens if that front element were to become damaged. Color correction filters are also often needed to correct mismatched lighting and film.

Minor vignetting is almost impossible to detect simply by looking through the viewfinder. Of course, it is rarely a concern in traditional photography where subtle differences in brightness between the center and the edges may even enhance an image. However, when shooting sequences for panoramic stitching, even minor vignetting can become a serious problem. Unfortunately, this is usually not discovered until *after* the shoot when the images are being stitched together, and it's too late to go back and reshoot. Sometimes the problem can be corrected in Photoshop – but this can require significant time and skill.

Unless absolutely necessary for color correction or to protect the lens, remove all filters from the front of your lenses (particularly ultra wides) when shooting panoramic VR sequences.

Fields of View: 18mm Lens

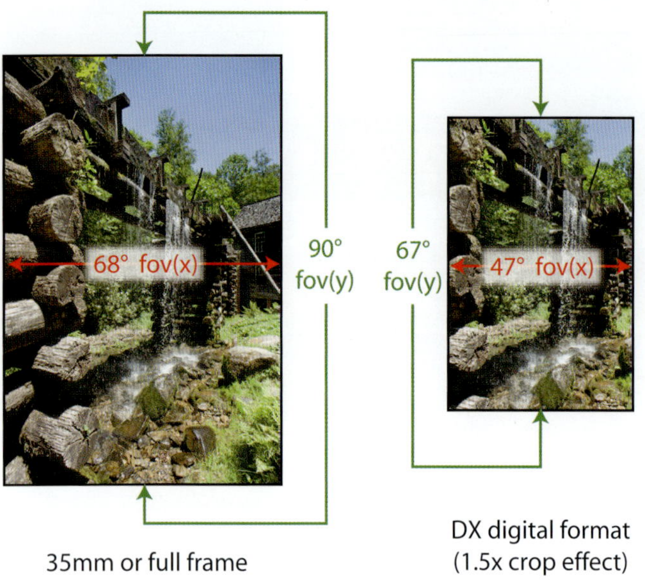

Fig. 10-8 Cameras with smaller format digital sensors crop both horizontal and vertical fields of view of a lens.

alignment can accommodate the camera in either portrait or landscape orientation, but this is something to check before deciding on one for purchase.

When shooting with digital cameras, all of the same principles apply, even though vignetting can be less problematic if the full width of the lens is not utilized due to cropping factors. For cameras that do *not* have full frame sensors, the field of view for the same focal length lens will be smaller than it is for 35mm film. Professional digital cameras generally allow for the use of interchangeable 35mm format lenses. This is a great advantage to the photographer who already has a significant investment in a pro camera system, in that you can use the same lenses and accessories you may already own with both your 35mm and digital cameras.

However, the main drawback to smaller digital sensors is that the precious vertical fields of view that you've paid so much for in expensive, ultra wide rectilinear lenses, is reduced by the cropping effect of the smaller sensor size. You can always shoot more images to cover the full 360° view horizontally, but you cannot recover the lost vertical field of

view, unless you use a multi-row stitching application or fisheye lenses and software (discussed later).

Consumer digital cameras generally have even smaller image sensors than the professional models, and often, the only lens that can be used is their own built-in zoom. These built-in lenses are generally of lower quality than professional lenses, and aren't as wide as ultra-wide fixed length pro lenses. They also tend to have more optical flaws and aberrations, particularly barrel distortions, that cause straight lines near the edges of the image to bow outward. These flaws are usually most pronounced at the widest focal lengths. Wide angle adapters added onto the front of a lens tend to exacerbate these distortions even further, and significantly reduce the potential quality of resulting panoramas.

In spite of these limitations, many consumer digital cameras are used quite successfully in creating VR panoramas.   Stitching software is becoming more sophisticated and better able to compensate for image distortions. Digital photo software such as Photoshop allows for corrective compensation and retouching of panoramas as a part of the stitching process. Many problems can also be repaired after the fact, although usually with significant time and effort.

There are VR markets, such as low-end real estate tours on the Web, that historically have had little concern for quality, and where the low cost of mediocre imagery justifies the throw away nature of much of the work. The limited capabilities and inherent flaws of low cost digital cameras can be more than adequate for this sort of work. However, as concerns for quality and the need for VR images to hold their value over time become

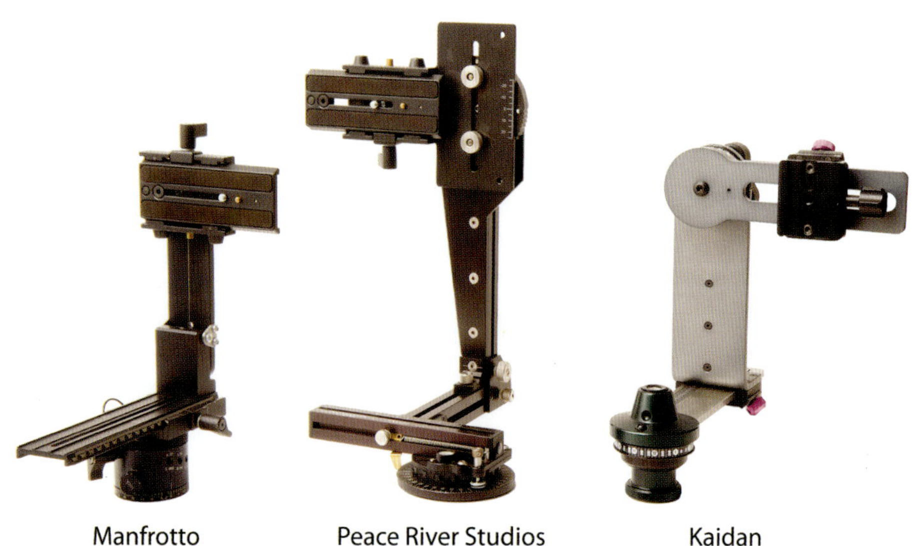

Fig. 10-9 Commercial VR pan heads allow the camera to be mounted vertically while also maintaining the important alignment of the lens' entrance pupil over the pan axis.

more critical, photographers will be better off choosing equipment that is perhaps more expensive, but that will be less likely to limit the future quality and value of their work.

Creating good VR panoramas is as much an exacting science as it is a visual art. The ability to maintain consistency throughout a shooting sequence is a critical requirement. To do this, certain equipment is necessary.

The most important of these is a VR pan head, which is used to provide precision entrance pupil alignment and leveling of a camera, as well as repeatable pan increments between shots. While most early VR photographers had to build their own pan heads from cumbersome off-the-shelf grip equipment, today there are many companies that manufacture and sell commercial VR heads. These include Kaidan, Manfrotto, and Peace River Studios.

Entrance Pupil Alignment

The entrance pupil of a lens is the point about which a lens is rotated, where close and distant subjects focused on the film plane maintain their relative positions to one another. Successful stitched panoramic photography requires that the axis of the camera's rotation be positioned at the entrance pupil of the lens. Otherwise, foreground and background subjects change their relative positions when the camera pans, causing misalignments between shots, and resulting in stitching errors.

The position of this entrance pupil can be different for every individual lens. For most wide-angle lenses however, it can often be found somewhere between the aperture ring and the midpoint of the lens barrel.

Unfortunately, lens manufacturers do not mark entrance pupils on their lenses, so VR photographers have to determine these themselves before shooting. This is done by mounting camera and lens on an adjustable VR pan head and observing the relationships of foreground and background subjects through the viewfinder as the camera is panned. Alignment of the panning axis with the entrance pupil of the lens can be achieved fairly precisely this way. Note however, that this only works if the camera has a reflex or through-the-lens viewfinder, such as on SLR (single lens reflex) systems.

If your camera is *not* an SLR, or the viewfinder does not show exactly what the lens sees (as is the case with rangefinder, twin lens reflex, point and shoot, and most consumer digital cameras), then your entrance pupil alignment will probably need to be done by trial and error. Some digital cameras have video output capability, or can display a live video image on their LCD screen. Since this live image is generated by the sensor inside the camera, it is possible to use this quite effectively for entrance pupil alignment.

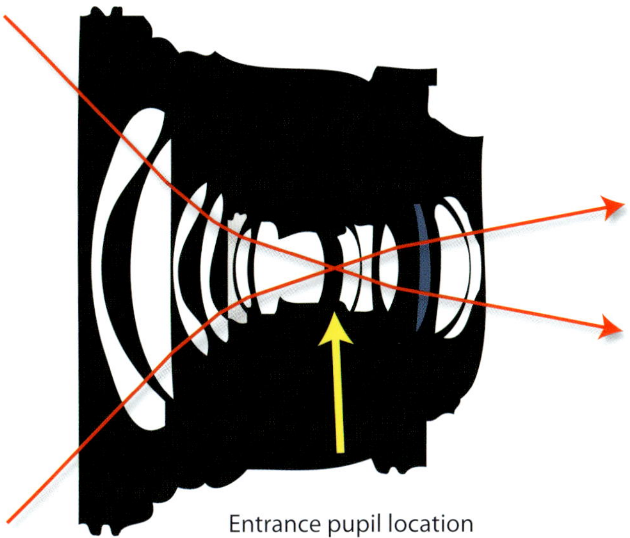

Fig. 10-10 The entrance pupil of a lens is the no-parallax point around which it is rotated for stitched panoramic photography. It is the pan axis point where foreground and background objects remain in their same relative positions on the film or image plane as the camera is panned.

Accurate entrance pupil alignment is critical for the best quality results. However, this becomes less important the further away your subjects are from the lens. As long as your closest foreground subject is four to five feet (or more) away from the camera, entrance pupil misalignments cause few, if any, stitching errors – particularly when using very wide lenses. One should always avoid sloppy shooting technique, but a knowledge of the degree of forgiveness involved can be a tremendous help when you find yourself unable to use a tripod or pan head at all. Entrance pupil misalignments increase in significance the closer your foreground subjects are to the camera.

There is a rule of thumb that the time, care and expense that you *don't* devote to proper technique during shooting, will be multiplied 10 times over attempting to correct in post production. While today's digital imaging technologies make it possible to fix just about anything after the fact, you are usually far better off doing things right while shooting than you are trying to "fix them in post."

Shooting a Single Row Panorama

1) Choose a location within the scene you are shooting that will provide you with interesting foreground subjects throughout the full 360° view.

2) Mount your camera on a tripod with a VR panoramic head. For most panoramas, you will want the camera oriented in a vertical or portrait mode

Technical Note: Entrance Pupil Alignment

To find the entrance pupil of a lens, first mount the camera and lens on an adjustable VR pan head. The camera should be mounted in a portrait (vertical) orientation with the center of the lens positioned directly over the pan axis of the VR head.

You can check the leveling by using a twin bubble level attached to the camera's hot shoe. These bubble levels are available from many camera stores. Be aware, however, that your camera's hot shoe may not necessarily be perfectly aligned with the film gate or sensor inside the camera, especially if the viewfinder has been bumped hard or is dented at all. Ideally, you'll want both the bubble levels on the camera and the VR pan head to remain centered as you pan around.

Step 2: Next, align the optical center of the lens directly over the axis of rotation of the pan head. This is usually done by looking at the front of the camera and adjusting the camera on the pan head so that the center of the lens is directly over the center of the panning mechanism.

Step 3: Once you have the lens centered over the head rotation axis, you can find the entrance pupil by adjusting the camera forward or

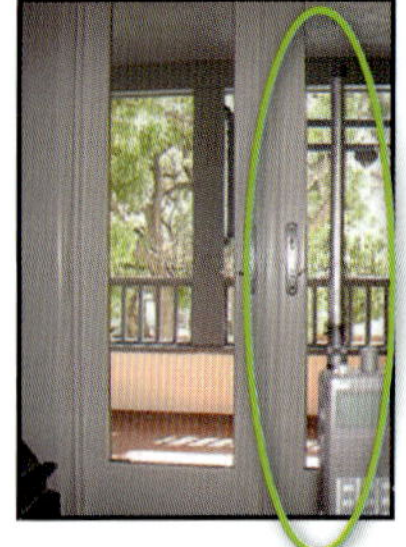
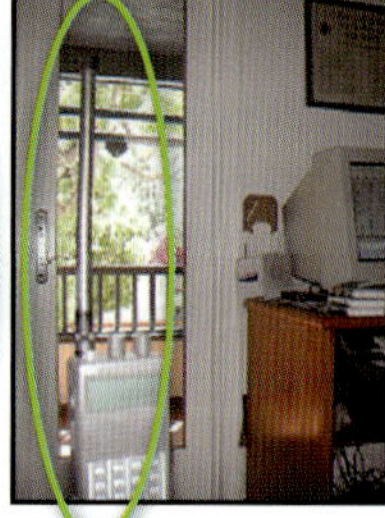
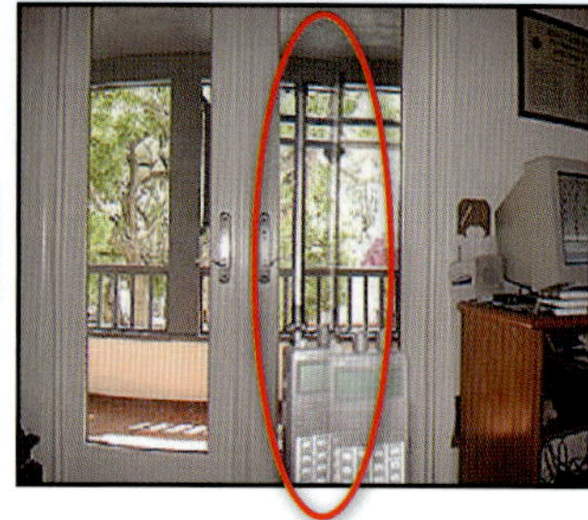

Foreground & background alignment variations during panning

Stitching error

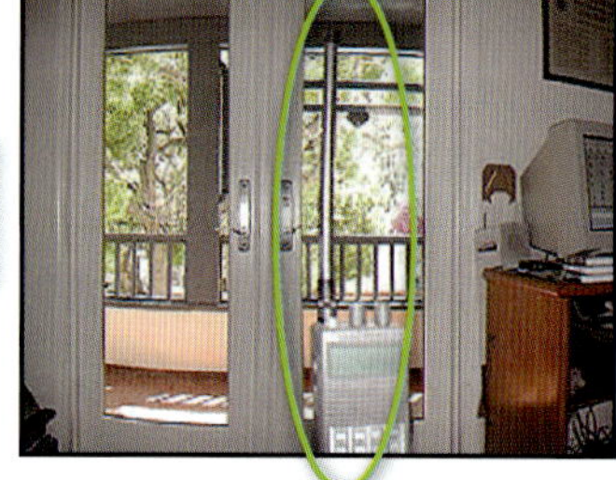

Consistent foreground & background alignment during panning

Good stitch

Fig. 10-11 The importance of entrance pupil alignment.

Step 1: Make sure that the VR pan head is level on top of the tripod. Most VR heads include one or more bubble levels that you can use. Check to make sure the head remains level by watching the bubble as you pan the camera and head 90° or more.

Double check that the camera is mounted squarely on the VR head, so that it is neither tilted up nor down, nor crooked in relation to the head. You can do this by looking through the viewfinder after the head is leveled. Make sure that vertical lines in the scene are vertical in the viewfinder, and that the horizon appears in the middle of the frame.

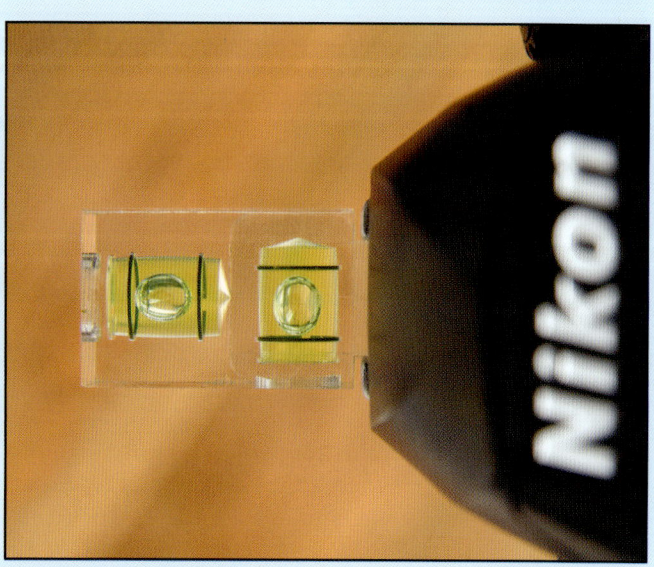

Fig. 10-12 A hot shoe mounted two-axis bubble level.

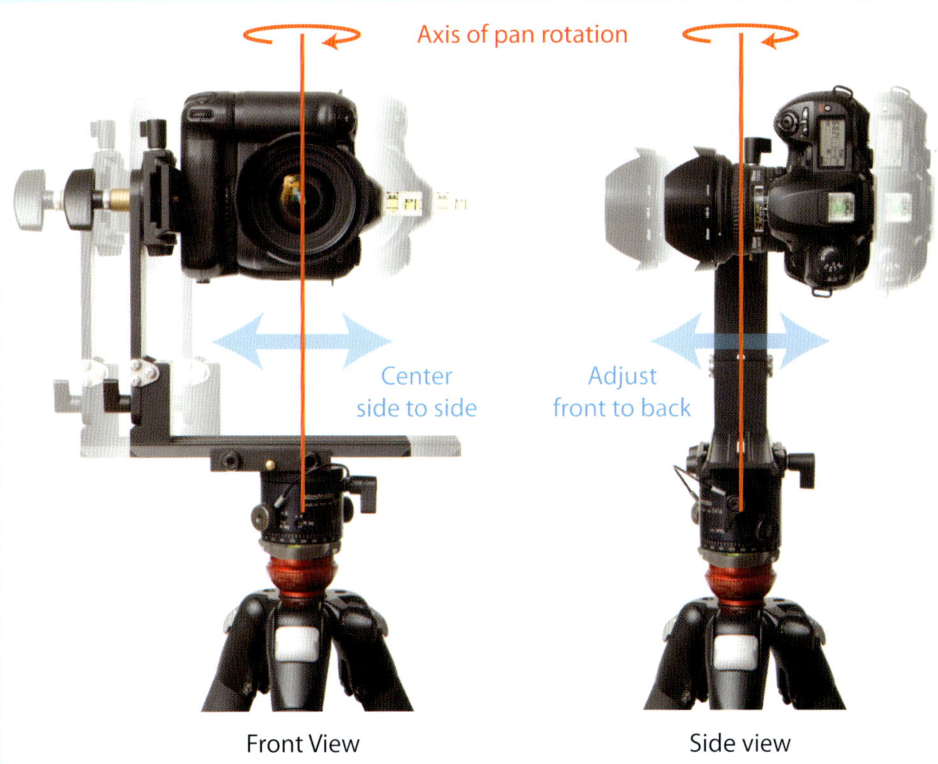

Fig. 10-13 Center entrance pupil front-to-back and side-to-side over the pan axis.

backward on the head. This process is a visual one, and will require you to have a vertical edge of some sort in your foreground that you can line up with another vertical edge in the background. Adjust the camera forward or backward while looking through the viewfinder as you pan the camera back and forth, trying to find a position over the rotation axis that keeps the foreground and background subjects consistently aligned.

Optimally, you'll want a foreground subject less than a foot away from the front of the lens, and a background subject at or near infinity focus. Good vertical background lines include edges of buildings, windows, door jambs, etc. (assuming the structure is plumb). Foreground subjects should be easily moved and as close to vertical as possible. Examples can include the edge of a hardcover book standing upright on a table, a light stand, or the side of a box.

If the foreground subject moves in the same direction as you are panning *relative to the background object* (i.e. the foreground subject moves toward the left as you pan to the left), then the lens is mounted too far *behind* its entrance pupil. The camera needs to be adjusted forward. If the foreground subject moves in the opposite direction relative to the background as you are panning (i.e. the foreground subject moves to the right

as you pan left), then the lens is mounted too far in front of its entrance pupil and needs to be adjusted *backward* on the pan head.

Once you have the entrance pupil of the lens positioned properly over the center of rotation of the pan head, the foreground and background objects will remain in the same position relative to one another when you pan the camera while watching through your viewfinder.

Finding the entrance pupil for other camera or lens combinations is the same. However, the process can be more difficult with consumer or non-SLR digital cameras if you can't see the actual image from the sensor when you look through the viewfinder. With most of these cameras, the viewfinder contains its own miniature optics that roughly approximate what the lens of the camera records. These viewfinders therefore cannot be used for entrance pupil alignments.

Some of these digital cameras allow for use of their LCD screens as a "live" video monitor, showing the image that is captured through the camera's lens by the image sensor inside the camera. You can use this "monitor" ability to align the entrance pupil, panning back and forth while watching the relationship between foreground and background subjects, just as you would looking through the viewfinder of an SLR camera.

For digital cameras that don't have the monitor capability, you will have to shoot a series of foreground/background images on a trial and error basis, and perhaps even download them to your computer in order to determine the proper alignment of the entrance pupil. Kaidan, a popular manufacturer of VR photography equipment, makes a number of preset pan heads for specific digital cameras. If they have one available for your particular camera, the entrance pupil alignment will already be incorporated into the head design, so you

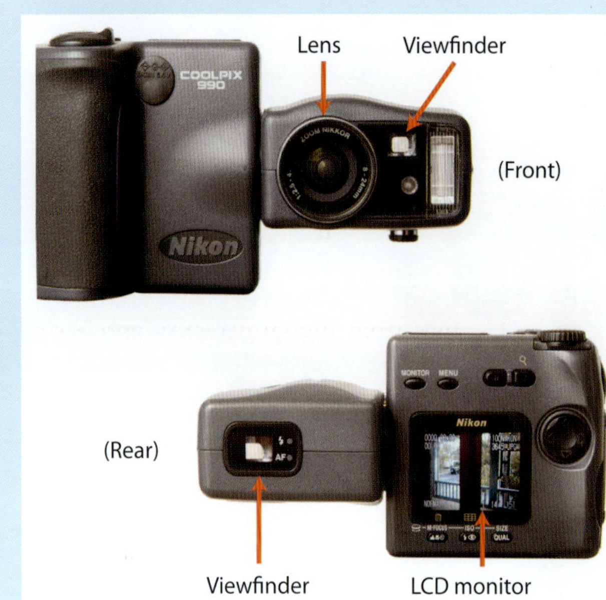

Fig. 10-14 With non-SLR cameras, use the camera's LCD monitor to check entrance pupil alignment.

can simply mount your camera and shoot without even thinking about entrance pupil adjustments.

Once you have the entrance pupil aligned, you should carefully mark its position on the VR head so that you can quickly return to it every time you shoot with that camera and lens combination. You will need to align *each* camera and lens that you use for panoramic photography in this manner. The entrance pupil is likely to be different for every lens,

and sometimes even between lenses of the same focal length from the same manufacturer. I have two ultrawide 18mm Nikkors, one an autofocus f/2.8 lens and the other an older manual focus f/3.5 lens. They have different entrance pupil positions, and thus require different alignments, even when using the same camera.

Many VR photographers simply use a single camera and lens combination with a VR head that is pre-aligned, rather than having to realign their setup each time they want to use it.

Some photographers will dedicate separate heads, each to a specific camera/lens combination used regularly. There is a definite weight and bulk disadvantage to this method, since one has to carry a different pan head for every combination of camera or lens you might use. Yet those who do this tend to pack them in separate kits. For example, one kit might include a pre-aligned head with a camera and ultrawide 14mm lens for shooting interiors, while another might include a 24mm lens, more suitable for outdoor and landscape panoramas.

The best approach I've found seems to be to commit a single camera and lens as your principal panoramic VR kit. I shoot 95 percent of my work with the same Nikon camera body, 16mm lens, and custom modified preset pan head. Having too much equipment can be almost as problematic as having too little. When in doubt, keep your equipment choices as simple as possible.

3) Choose a lens that gives you sufficient vertical field of view to adequately cover the scene and its subjects. From the table in Figure 10-15, determine how many photos will be required and the necessary pan angle between them.

4) Level the VR head and camera.

5) If not done previously, align the entrance pupil of the lens over the axis of rotation of the pan head.

6) Set your camera's exposure to manual mode. Set the lens aperture to f/8 or smaller to maximize depth of field. Then determine the best exposure (shutter speed) for the scene. You can do this using the camera's built in meter and panning throughout the entire 360° as you look through the viewfinder. An average exposure for the scene is often the safest setting to start with, particularly with digital cameras. If you're shooting with negative film, you may want to set the exposure based on the shadow or darkest parts of the scene. Do not change the exposure settings once you have started shooting the panorama sequence.

7) Shoot a single frame at the beginning of each panorama (or node) with a slate of information noting the exposure, the lens focal length, and the number of shots per 360° panorama. This information may be needed by your stitching software later, and it's best to record it as part of your original image sequence in camera. Other helpful information to include is the date, location, node ID (if shooting multiple nodes), film roll ID (for larger projects), project name, and copyright information.

8) Refocus the lens on the scene and select the starting position for the pan sequence. Remember that consistency in your shooting technique minimizes errors. It's usually best to start every panoramic sequence facing the same direction (when possible), such as toward a particular side of the building or toward a certain compass heading. I find it best to square the camera perpendicular to a wall or doorway for the first shot, rather than at some odd angle. Remember that individual source images from panoramic sequences can sometimes be useful as stand alone shots, if well composed and properly oriented.

Fields of View (Fov): 35mm camera and lenses

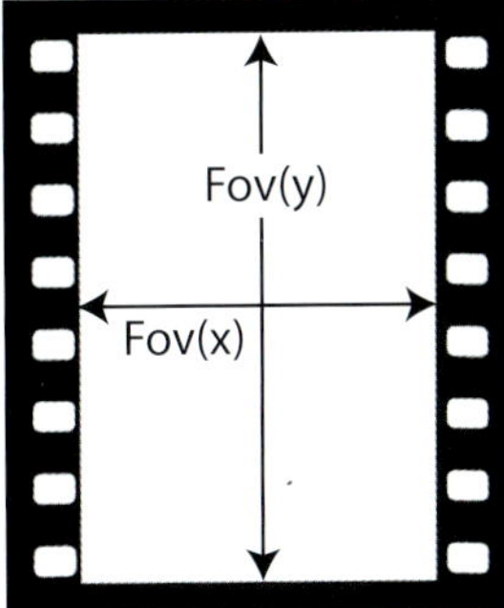

Fov is the Field of view provided by a lens within a 35mm film frame.

Shots/360° represents the *minimum* images needed for a 360° horizontal panorama with 1/3 (or more) overlap between images.

Focal length*	Fov(y)	Fov(x)	Shots/360°
13mm	**108°**	86°	6
14mm	**104°**	82°	6
15mm	**100°**	78°	8
18mm	**90°**	68°	8
20mm	**84°**	63°	9
24mm	**73°**	54°	10
28mm	**65°**	47°	12
35mm	**54°**	38°	15
50mm	**39°**	27°	18
85mm	**24°**	16°	36
105mm	**19°**	13°	40
135mm	**15°**	10°	60
180mm	**11°**	8°	72
200mm	**10°**	7°	72
300mm	**7°**	4.6°	120
400mm	**5°**	3.5°	180

* Rectilinear (non-fisheye) or "corrected" lenses only

Fig. 10-15 Field of view table for 35mm and full frame digital cameras.

9) Shoot the panoramic image sequence, panning to the right between each shot (you *can* pan to the left as you're shooting, but most software applications stitch the images from left to right). Be sure to look through the viewfinder as you're shooting so you will see any lens flares, confirm sufficient overlap, and make sure that focus doesn't change or that subjects don't move between frames.

10) After shooting the complete panorama, shoot a blank frame (cover the lens with your hand or a lens cap). This serves as a visual marker at the end of the sequence, which can be helpful when scanning film or cataloging digital files in post production. A blank frame can also be helpful to mark the restart of a panoramic sequence when necessary.

11) It's a good idea to stop and write your shooting notes in a small notebook after you complete each panorama. These notes should be filed with your processed film or digital files. They will help you remember what you did during the shoot, along with corrections that you might have planned for post production. They will also be useful in identifying shooting errors.

12) If shooting film, remove the film from the camera and label it with a VR roll number. You can shoot multiple panoramas on a single roll of film, but don't try to start a panorama sequence on one roll of film and finish it on another. It's better to waste the last exposures on a roll and keep your shooting well organized, than it is to squeeze every last frame out of a roll. It's too easy to inadvertantly disrupt your shooting sequence or thought process while changing film.

13) Process and scan film (or download files from digital camera), and assemble digitally using your selected VR stitching software. If shooting on film, make sure to instruct your photo lab *not* to cut your film when they process it. You may need it in a single continuous strip for scanning, or you may want to cut it into sections of your own preferred length for filing.

Method 2 – Slit Scan Panoramic Cameras

There are a variety of cameras on the market that are designed specifically for panoramic photography. In general, these cameras are considerably more expensive than traditional cameras. The development of stitching software was intended to help photographers avoid having to use these expensive cameras when creating VR panoramas. However, some of them offer advantages that may justify their cost to certain VR photographers.

While there are a number of different panoramic camera designs, only the full rotation slit scan camera is truly

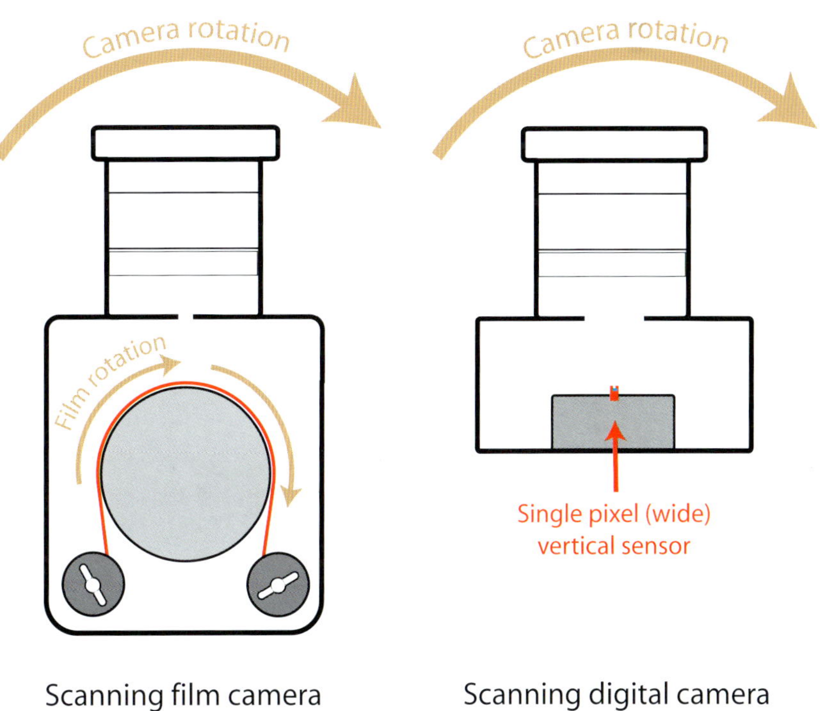

Fig. 10-16 Full rotation slit scan panoramic camera function.

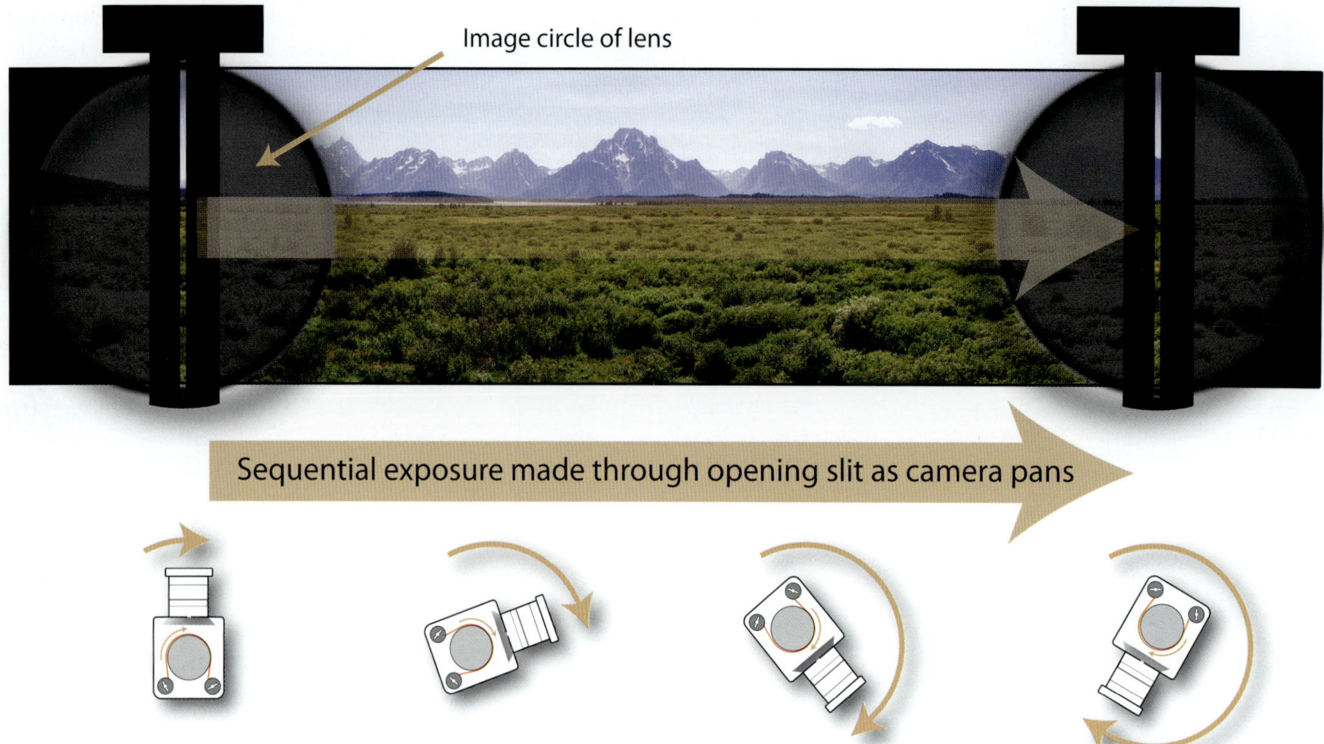

Fig. 10-17 Image recording process within a full rotation slit scan panoramic camera.

effective for capturing seamless 360° views. Full rotation cameras expose the film through a narrow slit behind the lens. As a motor pans the camera in one direction, precision gearing smoothly advances the film to match, resulting in a progressive exposure of 360° or more. Modern digital versions work similarly, except they use a narrow digital sensor to record the image as the camera pans, rather than moving film behind a slit in the camera.

Full rotation cameras provide the ability to capture very high resolution 360° panoramic images. They come in a variety of formats, from those using traditional 35mm film all the way up to the antique Cirkut cameras that used film as large as 16 x 240 inches (imagine a 20-foot long negative)! Most of today's models use either 35mm or medium format (220) film, or a digital sensor of similar height. Shutter speed adjustments are controlled by a combination of the camera's rotation speed and the width of the slit behind the lens.

Using a full rotation camera eliminates the need to stitch multiple images together. These cameras also eliminate the need for a VR pan head, since the panning mechanism is built into the camera itself. More sophisticated systems, such as the Seitz Roundshot Super 220VR and the Panoscan digital camera allow precision control over both exposure and field of view, much like traditional cameras do. They feature variable panning speeds and can even provide exposure compensations *within* the scene, along with the use of interchangeable lenses for varying vertical fields of view.

Less sophisticated rotation cameras may be limited to a single built-in lens, and often employ less precise panning mechanisms. Some are operated by a spring or clock drive mechanism. While effective and lightweight, these do not always pan at consistent speeds. The biggest limitation on the less expensive cameras is their lack of interchangeable lenses, so they are limited in the vertical field of view they offer. Such cameras are generally suitable for exterior views and landscapes, but are often inadequate in tight interior spaces, where larger vertical fields of view are preferred.

Without having to stitch multiple images, the complexities of scanning and digital assembly are significantly reduced. But there are tradeoffs. While you may no longer have to stitch images, you may instead need to scan long strips of film (unless using a digital camera). This requires either expensive drum scanning, or a large format scanner, such as the Epson Expression 10000XL Photo, which can scan film up to 16.5" long. If you use a digital camera such as a Panoscan, Roundshot Digital, Sphereon, or BetterLight, there is no need for scanning, since the panorama originates in digital form.

Digital panoramic cameras are generally more cumbersome to work with than their film-based counterparts, since most require a laptop computer tethered to the camera during operation. This adds more size and weight with necessary batteries and electrical/data cables to run both the camera and the laptop computer. While these limitations may be acceptable for shooting in controlled environments, they present added challenges on remote locations. The added weight of all the supporting gear makes today's digital models less preferred for photo shoots where equipment must be carried or backpacked significant distances. However, this is an individual choice for each photographer. Committed photographers have been known to carry hundreds of pounds of photographic equipment to the most remote corners of the earth in their efforts to make exquisite images.

Digital panoramic cameras have many positive features however, not the least of which is the convenience of a full-digital workflow (you can see your results immediately). There is no film to process or scan, capture resolutions can be extremely high (even greater than offered by large format film), and they usually include sophisticated software for controlling the camera, exposure, and color rendition. All of these make such cameras extremely attractive for panoramic photographers serving high-end clients or who need the best possible image quality, in spite of high prices.

A final advantage of scanning digital cameras is that they can provide pixel-accurate repeatability between successive scans. This allows for precise alignment of multiple panoramas. You can shoot from the same position with different exposures or lighting conditions, and easily blend the images using layers in Photoshop. Such pixel accuracy throughout the full length of a panorama is almost impossible with film-based slit scan cameras.

Traditional photographic printing of long rolls of panoramic film can be cumbersome, and may require special enlarging equipment. Yet digital images of

almost any length can now be printed on commercial presses and large format digital printers. Even low-cost desktop printers, including a number of models offered by Epson, can print panoramic photos up to 13 inches high and 44 inches long.

Shooting a Panorama with a Slit Scan Camera

1) Choose a location within the scene you are shooting that will provide you with interesting foreground subjects throughout the full 360° view.

2) Mount your camera on a tripod.

3) If the camera allows the use of interchangeable lenses, choose a lens that provides a sufficient vertical field of view to adequately cover the scene and its subjects. Full rotation cameras can usually be set to expose more than 360° horizontally. It is a good idea to record *more* than 360° (390°–400° is recommended) in order to assure full coverage and to allow for overlap between the ends. This 30°–40° of overlap may be necessary in order to blend the seam in post production.

4) Level the camera.

5) For cameras with interchangeable lenses, be sure to align the entrance pupil of the lens over the axis of rotation. For cameras with non-removable lenses, the entrance pupil is already aligned as part of the camera design, and no adjustment is possible.

6) Determine the proper exposure for the scene, and set the camera's exposure controls accordingly. A lens aperture of f/8 or smaller will maximize depth of field. The effective shutter speed for the exposure is determined by either the rotation speed or the width of interchangeable slits in front of the film, or by a combination of both. An average exposure for the entire scene is often the best to start with. If you're shooting with negative film, you'll generally want to favor the shadow areas. With transparency film, you should favor the highlight areas. Scanning digital cameras usually have extremely broad exposure latitudes (greater than most films), and allow you to preview your exposure levels on the computer screen in real time.

7) Include a slate of information noting the exposure, focal length, and other pertinent data before or after the full panoramic exposure. Some photographers will set the panorama to be 420° horizontally, and then simply place the slate in the frame for the first 20° – 30° of the exposure. Remove the slate so that this part of the scene will be captured cleanly as the camera comes around again. You'll digitally crop this slate off later, but it's good to have the info attached to the original film or digital file. If the rotation speed of the camera is too fast, you may want to do this as an independent exposure. With digital cameras, some of this data may

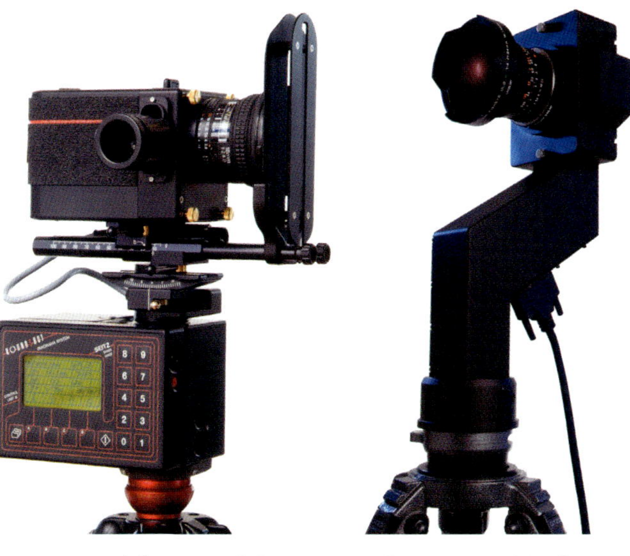

Fig. 10-18 Slit scan full rotation panoramic cameras.

be automatically included in the metadata of the digital file (via the camera's controller software). Even so, many photographers find it useful to shoot a partial pan of a Macbeth chart or other color slate for post production reference.

8) Be sure to check the focus of the lens before shooting (some full rotation panoramic cameras have a focusing ground glass, while digital systems allow for a preview image), as well as rechecking your exposure and the panorama length settings.

9) Start the exposure and move out of the way of the panning camera. For slower rotation speeds, you can simply walk around the camera, staying behind it throughout its rotation. For faster speeds, you may need to position yourself under the tripod or otherwise out of view before releasing the shutter. You might also be able to position yourself as an unobtrusive subject in the scene and trigger the exposure remotely.

10) Write down whatever shooting notes you might want in a notebook after you complete each panorama. These notes should be filed with your processed film or stored digital files.

11) Film cameras will stop rotating when they reach the end of a roll. Be sure the rotation for your last panorama on the roll has been greater than 360° so you have sufficient space to crop or blend the ends together. While there are times when you think you need less than 360° coverage (partial panoramas), it is better to have the full 360° view available, in case either you or the client have a change of heart afterward. Shoot the panorama again on another roll if you didn't get it completely on the first. Some panoramic photographers will simply let their cameras rotate as many times as possible, filling an entire roll of film with the same scene, so that they can then choose any 360° segment they want from the resulting strip of film.

12) Process and scan film (or download digital camera images), and stitch the ends together using your selected VR assembly software. This single stitch of the beginning and end of the panorama will be necessary before you can prepare a 360° panoramic movie from the image. Be sure to instruct your photo lab not to cut the film after they process it. You will need a continuous strip for scanning.

Method 3 – Single Shot Panoramic Systems
There are several lens systems designed specifically for panoramic VR photography, which capture full 360° panoramas in one shot. For the most part, these involve use of a circular parabolic mirror, which reflects the entire 360° view into a ring-shaped image (known technically as an annulus or torus). The resulting image requires a digital conversion so it can be viewed with a corrected perspective. One such example is the GoPano™ from EyeSee360°.

The biggest drawback to such systems is their lower image quality compared to other image capture methods. Squeezing 360° of image data on to a single frame does not allow for the capture of significant detail. The conversion software must interpolate or "fill in" lots of pixel information when converting the annular image into a flat panorama. Also, the surfaces of the mirror are relatively small, so even minor flaws or aberrations, including dust or scratches, have significant effect.

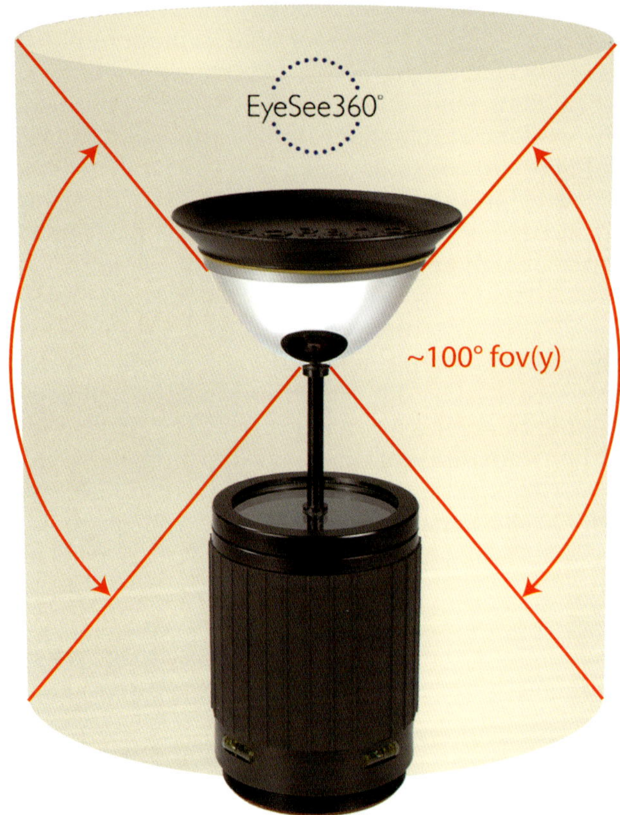

GoPano® parabolic mirror lens adapter

Fig. 10-19 A parabolic mirror lens adapter, such as the Go-Pano, allows for capture of a full 360° panorama in a single shot using a standard digital camera.

One shot systems do have a distinct advantage in situations where movement throughout the scene must be frozen or captured at a single moment, such as with busy crowds or moving traffic. The ability to freeze action may outweigh the lower image quality concerns. There is also no need for stitching sequential source images, so camera and lens alignment problems, as well as movement of subjects in overlap areas between shots, are eliminated.

Parabolic lens systems may represent the most promising design for full motion panoramic video – sometimes

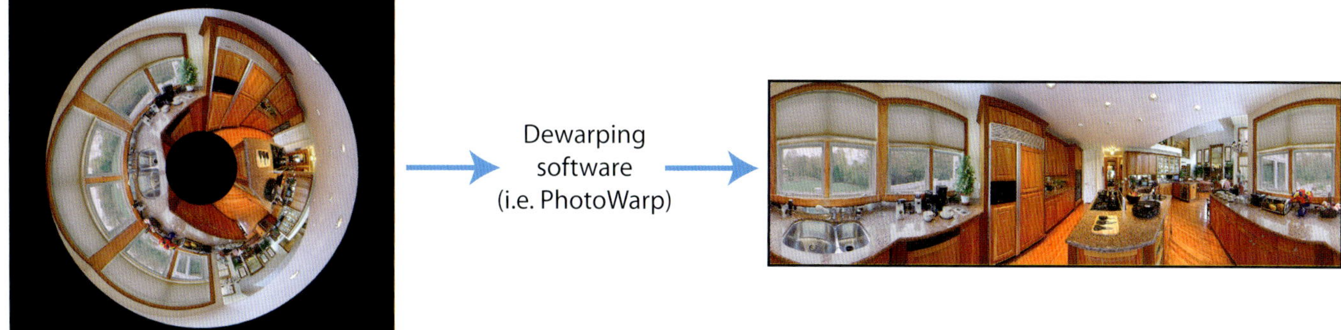

Annulus (flattened torus) image   Flattened single-shot 360° panorama

Fig. 10-20 An annulus or donut-shaped image is captured when using a parabolic mirror lens adapter. It is then transformed, or "flattened" into a cylindrical panorama using dewarping software such as PhotoWarp from EyeSee360.

considered the holy grail of photographic VR. Since they capture a full 360° panorama in a single shot, they can be attached to video and motion picture cameras to capture multiple 360° frames every second. Once these sequences are dewarped or converted, they can yield full motion 360° panoramic video images. Challenges with such video technology include the limitations of current computer processing speeds (necessary for on-the-fly conversions and play back) and bandwidth for delivery of the large resulting files to end users.

Shooting a Panorama with a Single Shot System
1) Choose the location and camera position that you want to shoot from. Try to include at least three subjects of interest in the foreground, spread throughout the 360° view.

2) Mount the camera and lens system on a tripod. The camera will usually be mounted facing straight upward, with the parabolic mirror reflecting the 360° view to the sides.

3) Level the camera.

4) Determine the proper exposure for the scene, and set the camera's exposure controls accordingly. You will probably need to take several light readings from different parts of the scene and average them. Using the camera's auto exposure setting can often yield good results. Follow the manufacturer's recommendations for suggested aperture settings, and adjust exposure via

shutter speed. Since the entire scene is being captured on one frame, there is no worry about banding problems caused by inconsistent exposures between stitched frames.

5) Check to be sure the scene is in focus before shooting.

6) Know what the vertical field of view for your system is and position yourself outside of this before shooting. Common ways to do this are either to crouch under the tripod, or to position yourself somewhere in the scene that is unobtrusive, and fire the camera remotely.

7) Shoot more than one exposure of each panorama, changing the exposure settings (plus or minus up to 3 stops). Do not move the camera between shots. Having multiple exposures of the scene, all identically aligned, is often useful for retouching parts of the scene that were too bright or too dark in the primary image.

8) Be sure to write down whatever shooting notes you need in a small notebook after you complete each panorama. This information should include exposures, location, date, node ID, etc. These notes should be filed with your processed film or downloaded digital files.

9) Process and scan film (or download files from a digital camera), and convert the annular images to flattened panoramas using the lens manufacturer's software. Photoshop retouching or exposure corrections are best done on the processed panorama file, rather than on the original annular image.

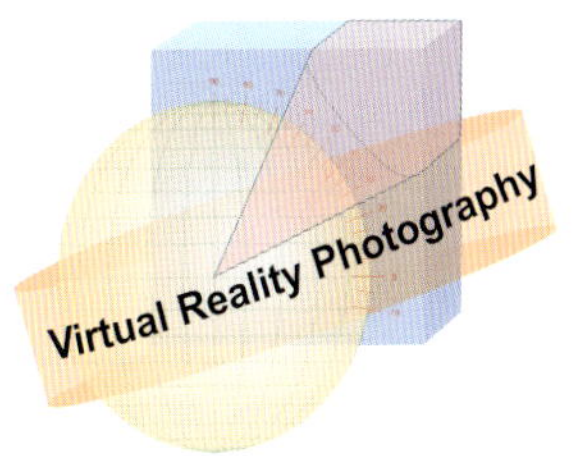

Chapter 11: Cubic and Spherical Panoramas

There are occasions when a cylindrical panorama doesn't offer sufficient vertical field of view for a scene. Imagine trying to show a VR panorama of the Sistine Chapel, or the view over the edge of a cliff, without including the views upward or downward. Many car, boat, and aircraft interiors need to be photographed in their entirety for VR purposes, including views straight up and straight down, where control panels, console details, sun roofs, seats, and other important features may be located.

Spherical and cubic VR technologies come to the rescue in these situations, providing what is known as "360°x180° panoramic coverage.

There are three basic methods for creating cubic and spherical panoramas. They include:

1) Multi-row stitching of overlapping images – an expansion of the cylindrical stitching process, which allows the camera to be tilted up and down during shooting, rather than only leveled at the horizon.

2) Using a scanning camera system with a fisheye lens to capture a complete 180° vertical field of view as the camera pans 360° or more horizontally.

3) Shooting two or more hemispheric images with a true fisheye lens (circular 180°x180° images), and using a fisheye assembly / stitching program to merge the images into a virtual sphere.

Method 1 – Multi-Row Panoramas
Multi-row panoramic photography requires use of a multi-row stitcher, such as PTGui or Autodesk's Stitcher. Traditional stitchers only allow for stitching of a single row of images, and those images must be shot squared to the camera's panning axis (normally centered on the horizon).

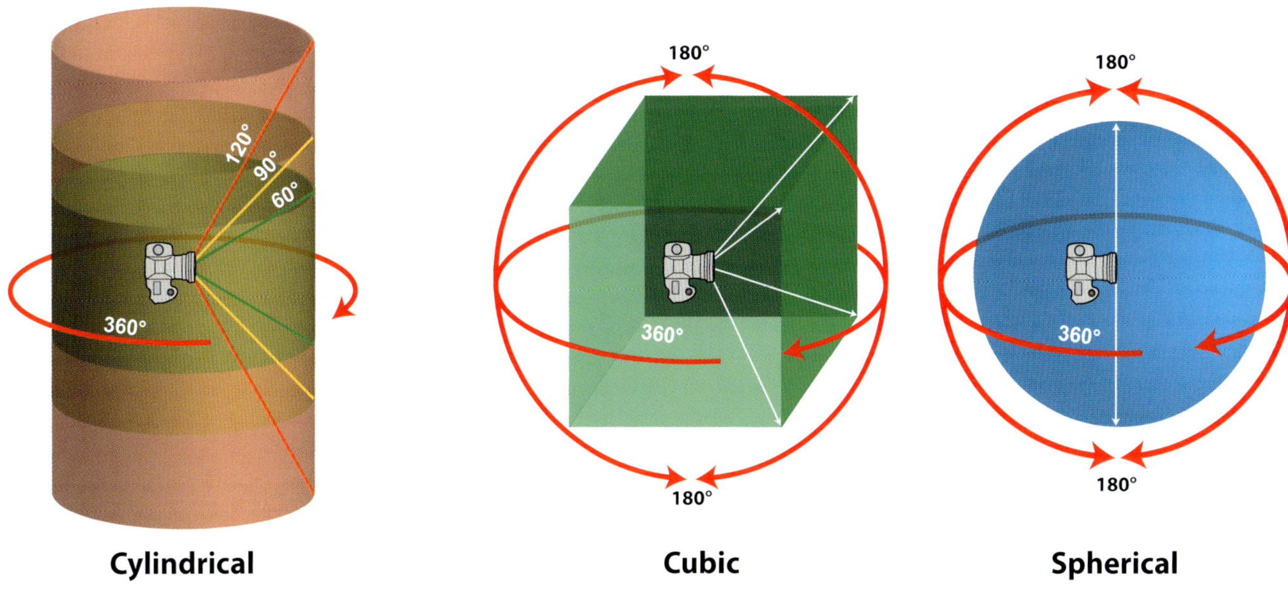

Cylindrical

Vertical field of view is limited by focal length of lens and by height of virtual cylinder.

Cubic   **Spherical**

Cubic and spherical images provide 360° views both horizontally *and* vertically.

Fig. 11-1 A comparison of cylindrical, cubic, and spherical projections. Cubic and spherical projections allow for 360°x180° fields of view.

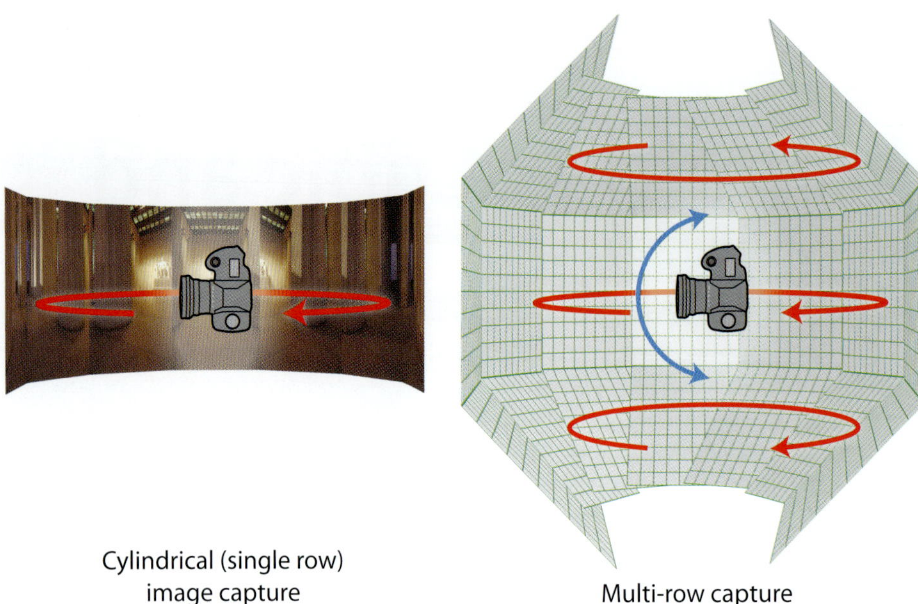

Fig. 11-2 The concepts of single and multi-row panoramic image capture.

can dramatically increase the number of source images necessary for a full panorama, adding significantly to both shooting and post production time.

The advantages of multi-row systems are that more source images provide the possibility for higher quality and higher resolution, plus they make it possible to achieve ultra-wide fields of view using normal focal lengths. This enables photographers with consumer digital cameras and their not-so-wide lenses to create high resolution 360° panoramas with unlimited fields of view.

Multi-row stitchers allow the camera to be tilted upward or downward, as well as leveled on the horizon. They provide for stitching in both horizontal and vertical directions. This lets the photographer increase the vertical field of view of a panorama by shooting additional images, rather than requiring the use of wider focal length lenses.

Obviously, it is important to know whether your stitching software can accommodate multi-row stitching before you start taking pictures, as well as what limitations it might have in terms of the kinds of lenses you can use (some only accept rectilinear or "corrected" lenses, not fisheyes). You should also determine whether there are limitations to the total number of images or rows that your software can stitch. Shooting multi-row panoramas

Shooting Multi-Row Panoramas

Shooting multi-row panoramas is simply an expansion of the techniques used for single-row panoramas.

1) Your camera should be mounted on a tripod with a *multi-row* panoramic VR head. The difference is that the entrance pupil alignment must be maintained as the camera is tilted upward or downward, as well as when it is panned. Older VR pan heads only held alignment through the panning axis.

2) Choose a lens that gives sufficient field of view to adequately cover the scene and its subjects with a minimum number of shots. Most multi-row stitchers today allow the use of fisheye lenses (whether true fisheyes or full-frame fisheyes), but some do not. Be sure

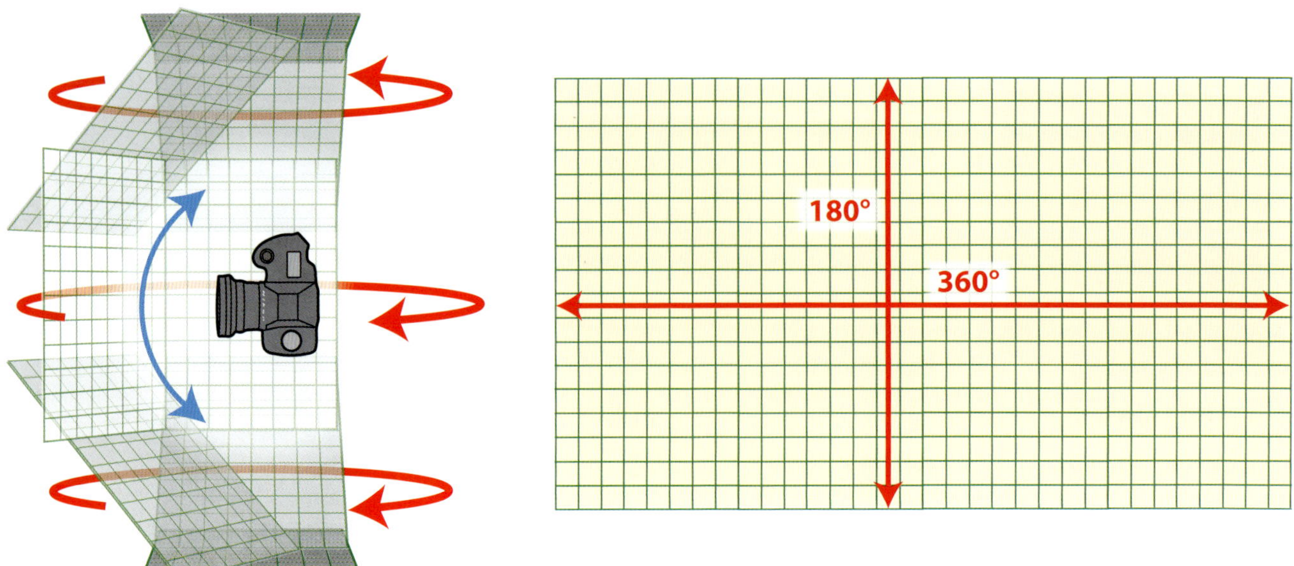

Fig. 11-3 Stitching and assembly of multi-row image sequences can create 360°x180° panoramic views.

to confirm your software capability before choosing a lens for your panoramas. Almost all stitchers can stitch images shot with rectilinear lenses, so these are often the safest choice. Remember that the longer the focal length of your lens, the more images you will need to shoot and stitch in order to complete your 360° coverage.

3) Determine how many photos will be required and the pan increment between each in order to complete the 360° view. It is best to shoot the same number of images for each row, although some stitchers allow for differing numbers per row. For example, if you use an 18mm lens, you will need to shoot at least eight images per row (45° pan increment between images) for 360° horizontal coverage. Three sets of these eight images will be needed – one with the camera tilted 50° downward, one level with the horizon, and one tilted 50° upward, in order to have sufficient overlap both horizontally and vertically *and* to provide full 360°x180° coverage. This means 24 images per panorama.

Note: Depending upon the field of view of the lens you are using, there may be times when you'll want to shoot a single shot straight up and another straight down to provide the views needed for the very top (zenith) and bottom (nadir) of the 360°x180° panorama. The view straight upward can be shot simply by tilting the camera 90° upward while on the tripod rig. However, the view downward generally requires removal of the camera from the tripod and shooting without the tripod in place. Try to keep your feet and other camera support mechanisms (such as the tripod) out of the shot. This "clear" shot of the downward view can also be used to retouch out the pan head and tripod legs that will partially obscure the view in images from the downward facing rows.

4) Level the VR head and camera.

5) If not done previously, align the entrance pupil of the lens on the pan head.

6) Determine the proper exposure for the scene, and set your camera's exposure to manual mode. Shoot every image in a given panorama with the same exposure settings.

7) Shoot a slate frame at the beginning of each node including information on exposure, lens focal length, number of shots per row, and number of rows. Date, location, node ID, film roll number, project name, and copyright information are useful additions.

8) Refocus the lens on the scene and select the starting position for the pano sequence. The middle or horizon row is usually the best one to start with.

9) Shoot the image sequence in its entirety. Keep careful track of what rows you have completed and make sure you are shooting the proper number of shots for each row. It's easy to get distracted and forget where you are in the sequence. Try to be as consistent as possible in your shooting technique. Counting each frame number aloud as you shoot is helpful to keep your attention focused. If you need to change film or digital storage cards while shooting, be sure to shoot another slate at the beginning of the next roll or card so there is no confusion about the image sequence in post production.

10) It may be useful to shoot a blank exposure or a new slate in between rows to serve as a visual marker. While not always necessary, this can be helpful for post production sequencing of the images, particularly when you have shot more than a single row tilted upward or downward.

11) Keep copious notes and file them with your processed film or downloaded digital files. When you are dealing with dozens or hundreds of source images for each multi-row panorama, there are a lot of things that can cause confusion. Complete notes can help resolve many matters for post production.

12) Label your film or digital files accurately. Renaming digital files after scanning or download can help maintain effective organization. For example, images might be labeled with the name of the node, followed by the degrees of tilt and the image number. An example follows, and in the chart below:

Node#_Degrees of tilt_Frame#

13) If shooting film, be sure to instruct your lab not to cut the film when they process it. You will probably want it kept in a continuous strip for scanning, or to cut it into specific lengths for your particular filing methods.

	First image	Second image	Third image	
Horizon row (0°)	**N1_0_01**	**N1_0_02**	**N1_0_03**	**...etc.**
Up 30° row (u30)	**N1_u30_01**	**N1_u30_02**	**N1_u30_03**	**...etc.**
Up 60° row (u60)	**N1_u60_01**	**N1_u60_02**	**N1_u60_03**	**...etc.**
Down 30° row (d30)	**N1_d30_01**	**N1_d30_02**	**N1_d30_03**	**...etc.**

Method 2 – Slit Scan Camera and a Fisheye Lens

Certain full rotation slit scan panoramic cameras can be used satisfactorily with fisheye lenses – but not all of them. Since fisheye lenses generate a curved image, rather than a "corrected" rectilinear one, the vertical position of any given point in the scene relative to the center of the image will move significantly as the camera pans. This is most pronounced toward the top and bottom edges of the image. Unless the slit which the image is exposed through is extremely thin, a panorama will be blurred near its top and bottom due to this projection movement during exposure.

The Panoscan digital camera is one scanning camera that allows use of a fisheye lens very effectively. The active image sensor area on the Panoscan is only a single pixel wide, so it records only the very center column of the projected image as the camera pans. Since fisheye lenses offer a field of view of 180° or more, they can be used on cameras such as the Panoscan to capture full 360°x180° flattened panoramas. These can then be easily converted to cubic or spherical VR movies. This process has a unique advantage of neither requiring stitching nor assembly of multiple source images to form a full panorama. The Panoscan is also capable of recording extremely high resolution images with very fine detail. However, these capabilities come at a price. The Panoscan and other slit scan digital cameras, such as Roundshot Digital and Sphereon cameras are high-end systems with high-end price tags.

Shooting a 360°x180° Panorama with a Slit Scan Camera and Fisheye Lens

Shooting panoramas with a full rotation slit scan camera and fisheye lens is almost identical to the slit scan process with a rectilinear lens.

1) Mount your camera on a tripod and align the pan axis. Note that when using a 180° fisheye lens, the rotation axis should *not* necessarily be aligned with the entrance pupil of the lens, but rather with the front element of the lens where the 180° view axis originates. Consult the user manual for your particular camera for alignment details.

2) The camera you use may require a particular fisheye lens. Be sure to test whatever lens you choose with the camera before using the configuration on an important project or assignment. Again, it is good to set the pan angle for the camera for 390° – 400° in order to assure full coverage and to allow for blending of the ends in post production.

3) Determine the proper exposure for the scene, and set the camera's exposure controls accordingly. A lens aperture of f/8 or smaller will maximize depth of field. Digital cameras such as the Panoscan have extremely wide exposure latitudes – up to 11 stops, which surpasses that of most films. This means that an average exposure reading for the entire scene will probably be sufficient to retain both shadow and highlight details, even in the very high contrast situations. The pixel accurate alignment of the Panoscan between successive scans also allows it to be used for HDR (high dynamic range) compositing of multiple panoramas shot with different exposures.

4) Remember to include a color target and slate with shooting information before or after the exposure. Also, keep good written notes as you shoot, and file them with the recorded images for reference in post production.

5) Level the camera before shooting.

6) Be sure to check the focus of the lens. Reconfirm your exposure and pan angle settings.

7) Start the exposure and move out of the way of the camera

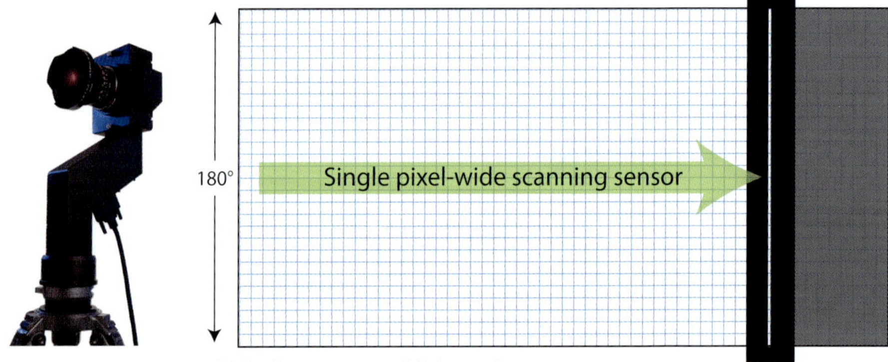

Scanning *digital* camera and fisheye lens

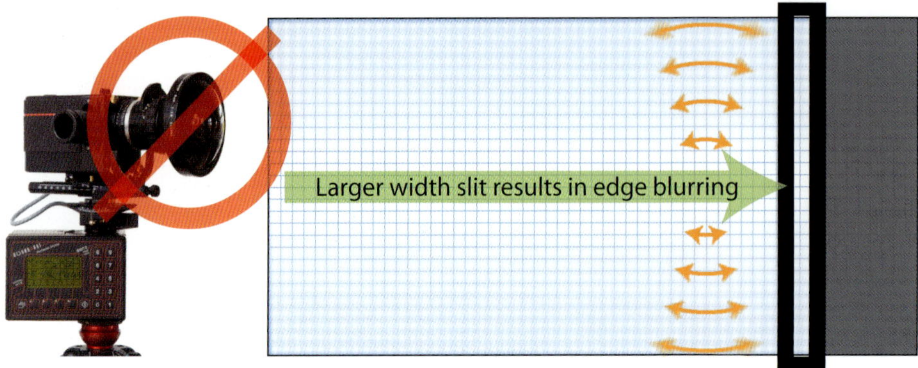

Scanning *film* camera and fisheye lens

Fig. 11-4 Fisheye lenses, in general, can't be used with scanning *film* cameras.

as it pans. The legs of your tripod and the front edge of the support bracket will obscure the view downward to a limited extent. Plan on reconstructing or retouching these areas digitally in post production.

Method 3 – Spherical Fisheye Panoramas

Spherical panoramas can be photographed by shooting two opposing hemisphere images using a film or digital camera with a true fisheye lens. (Remember that a true fisheye lens projects a 180° or greater round image entirely within the camera's film plane or image sensor.) The hemisphere images are then digitally assembled to form a complete virtual sphere with software such as Easypano's Panoweaver.

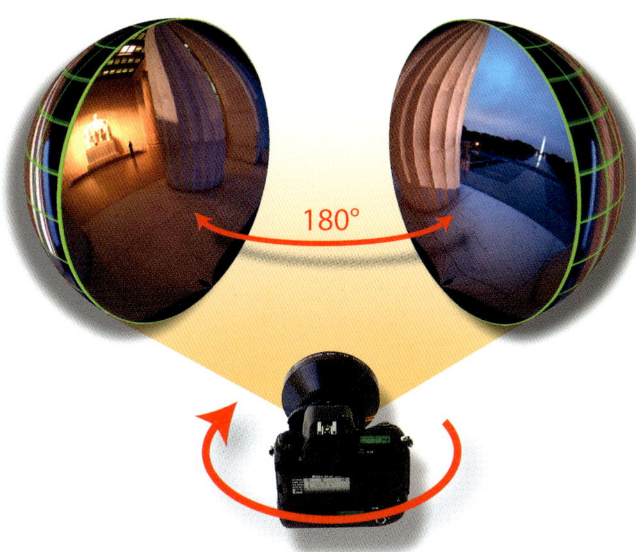

Fig. 11-5 A spherical fisheye panorama can be created by combining a pair of opposing hemisphere images.

If shooting with a full-frame digital or 35mm film camera, the lens used will be an 8mm (or wider) fisheye, providing a circular image covering a full 180° field of view. The best of these lenses is probably the Nikkor 8mm f/2.8 manual focus lens, which unfortunately has been discontinued by Nikon, and is becoming increasingly difficult to find. It is also fairly expensive. At one time, Nikon made a 6mm f/2.8 fisheye lens (also now discontinued) that offered an amazing 220° field of view, actually capturing everything in front of the camera, plus 20° behind in all directions. This lens weighed about 12 pounds and was about 9 inches in diameter. It cost as much as a new car.

For those on limited budgets, Nikon offers two fisheye adapters (models FC-

E8 with a 28mm thread, and FC-E9 with a 46mm thread) for their Coolpix line of consumer digital cameras. These adapters screw onto the front of the existing Coolpix camera lenses, and produce a circular fisheye image of just over 180° fully within the image sensor. Their effect is almost identical to that provided by a true fisheye lens, although image quality can be slightly lower.

One of the problems with fisheye lenses, particularly those of lower quality, is that they can have significant aberrations, distortions, and light fall off near the outer edges of the image. Subtle variations in grinding, polishing and manufacturing of optical systems can also mean that every lens produced is slightly different, even those of the same model produced by the same manufacturer. Thus, one 8mm lens may really be 7.8mm in focal length, while another might be 8.1mm. One may have slightly more than 180° of coverage, while another may have significantly less. For most photography, precise focal length definition is not critical, so manufacturers allow for somewhat broad tolerances in these areas.

Therefore, when shooting two opposing hemispheres, the particular lens you use may not provide absolute 180° views. This means the seam where the two images align may require digital retouching in order to appear smooth.

The Sigma lens company makes an 8mm fisheye lens that costs about one third as much as the Nikkor 8mm. Early versions of the Sigma lens had a number of optical problems, particularly near the image edges, but these have been improved in more recent versions. An even cheaper option is the Russian Peleng 8mm lens, which many new VR photographers are attracted to because of its low price. While a reasonable choice for introductory exploration of fisheye photography, the Peleng lenses have a number of noticeable optical flaws and limitations, which many serious pros find unacceptable.

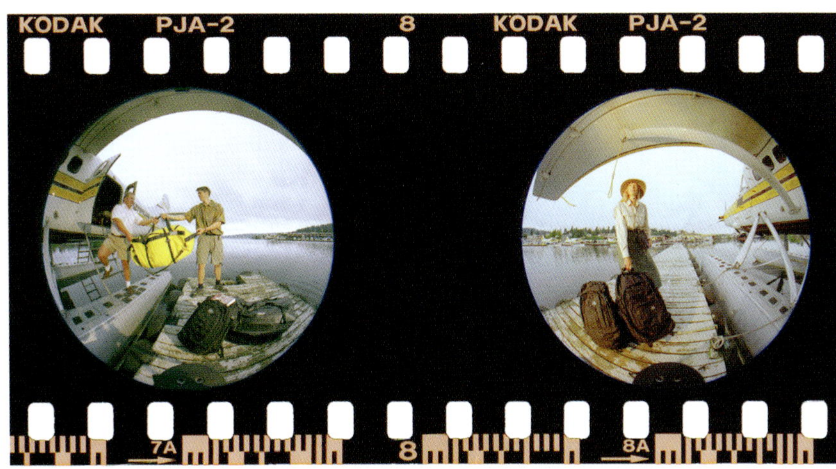

Fig. 11-6 A pair of opposing hemisphere images, as shot on 35mm film with a Nikkor 8mm f/2.8 fisheye lens.

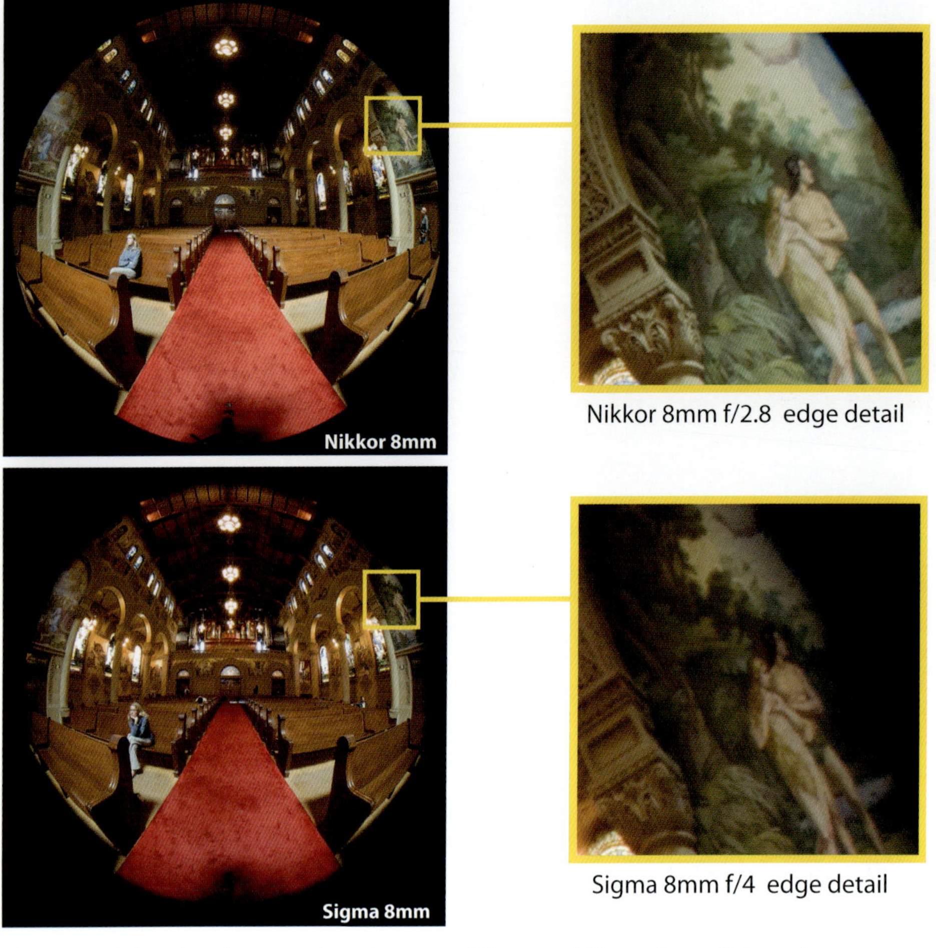

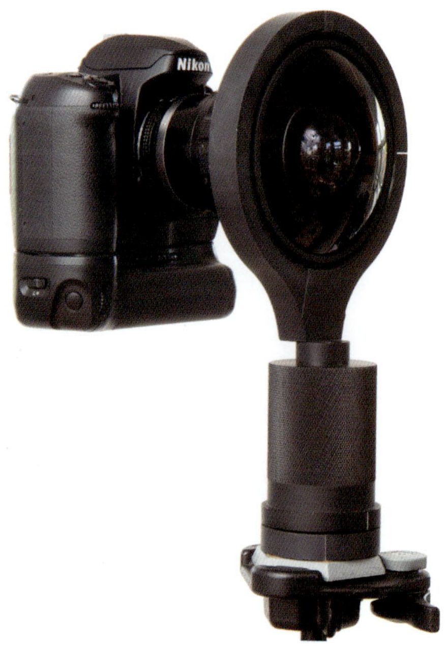
Nikkor 8mm f/2.8 edge detail

Sigma 8mm f/4 edge detail

Fig. 11-7 Edge detail comparison between Nikon and Sigma 8mm fisheye lenses.

One of the apparent advantages of the Sigma lenses is that they consistently provide a field of view of 183° or more, which means there can be reasonable overlap in the seams between hemisphere pairs. Unfortunately, these lenses still tend to have significant light fall off near the edges of the image, which either requires cropping of the image inward (thus reducing the field of view to less than 180°) or assembly of the image pairs with the darker edges visible along the seam. Either way, you may wind up doing a fair bit of digital retouching of the hemisphere seam. Again, individual lenses vary, so one may be better than another in this regard.

Note that the image circles projected by the 8mm fisheye lenses are designed to just fit within the 35mm film frame. The image sensors of some digital SLR cameras are smaller than the 35mm frame and crop off portions of the image circle. This is not a problem for fisheye stitching applications, but may be a problem for VR software that requires the full fisheye image circle in each image for spherical assembly.

Shooting a 360°x180° Spherical Fisheye Panorama

The process for shooting a spherical panorama is reasonably straightforward, and is almost identical whether shooting with 35mm film or a digital camera.

1) Mount your camera with its fisheye lens on a rotator or indexed pan head. You will need to pan your camera exactly 180° between shots for software requiring two-shot or hemisphere pair assembly. Newer applications allow for the use of overlapping three and four-shot combinations for each panorama, where stitching is done, rather than the more precise abutting of two opposing hemispheres in older fisheye applications. Be aware of the requirements and limitations of your chosen software when planning your shoots.

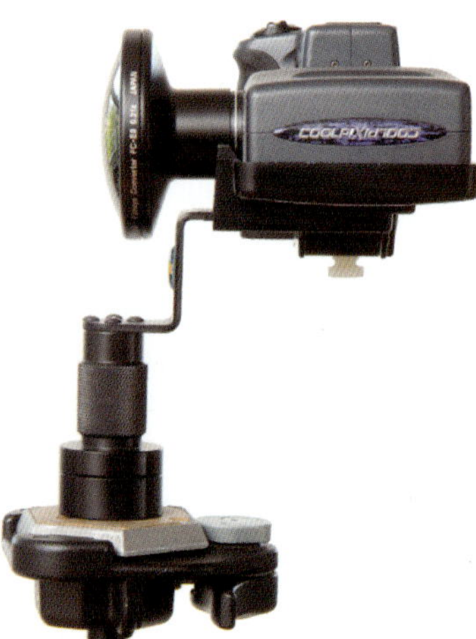

Rotator for Nikon 8mm f/2.8

Rotator for Coolpix & FC-E8

Fig. 11-8 IPIX rotators for Nikkor 8mm and Nikon Coolpix with FC-E8 adapter.

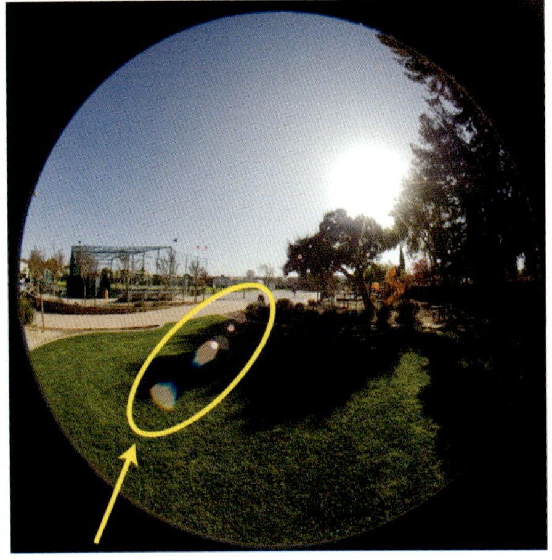

Lens flare results from light off center

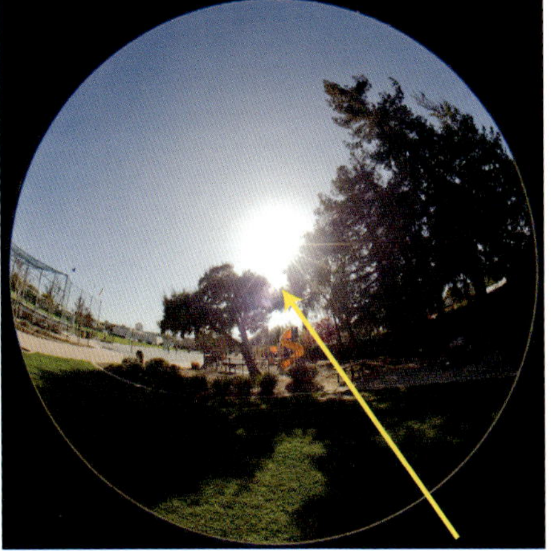

Centered light results in centered flare

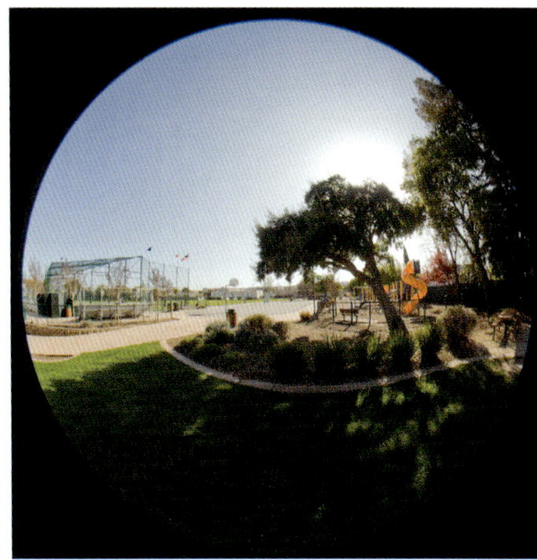

Obscure light source to minimize flare

Fig. 11-9 Fisheye lenses can be prone to lens flare, but this can be controlled with light source positioning within the frame.

2) As with all panoramic photography, an important step is to determine your best shooting position for the scene. Remember to get in very close to the subjects of interest, and make sure that you have several such subjects positioned throughout the 360-degree view. This will compel your viewers to pan, tilt and zoom throughout the image.

As you position the camera and rotator on your tripod, consider where you are positioning the hemisphere edges. Remember that these edges will become the seam between your two hemisphere views. You will want to make sure that there are no moving subjects near these edges, because if a subject overlaps a seam and has moved between the first and second shot, it will either wind up being misaligned or incomplete after assembly.

3) Consider the location of lights or bright areas of the scene relative to their position along the seam. Fisheye lenses are particularly susceptible to lens flare from bright lights, in part because their ultra wide views prevent the use of lens shades and other flare limiting devices. To minimize flare, place the bright light squarely in the center of the shot. Most lens flares appear opposite the center of the image from the light source causing them. Among the things you pay for when you buy more expensive lenses are better optical coatings on the lens elements. These coatings and other quality controls minimize flare and other optical aberrations.

You will need to weigh the placement of bright lighting sources in the center of a hemispheric view against the measurement of consistent exposures between the opposing hemisphere

shots. Exposure settings need to remain constant for both hemispheres so that the seam areas have consistent color and brightness. Otherwise, your post production retouching job can be a nightmare – or you will have to live with a distracting visible seam in your completed spherical image.

If one side of the scene you are shooting is much brighter than the other – for example, you are shooting a room with large windows on one side and dark corners on the other – you will find that your camera meter gives you significantly different exposure readings when facing toward the bright windows than it does toward the dark corners. Choosing the best single exposure for both can

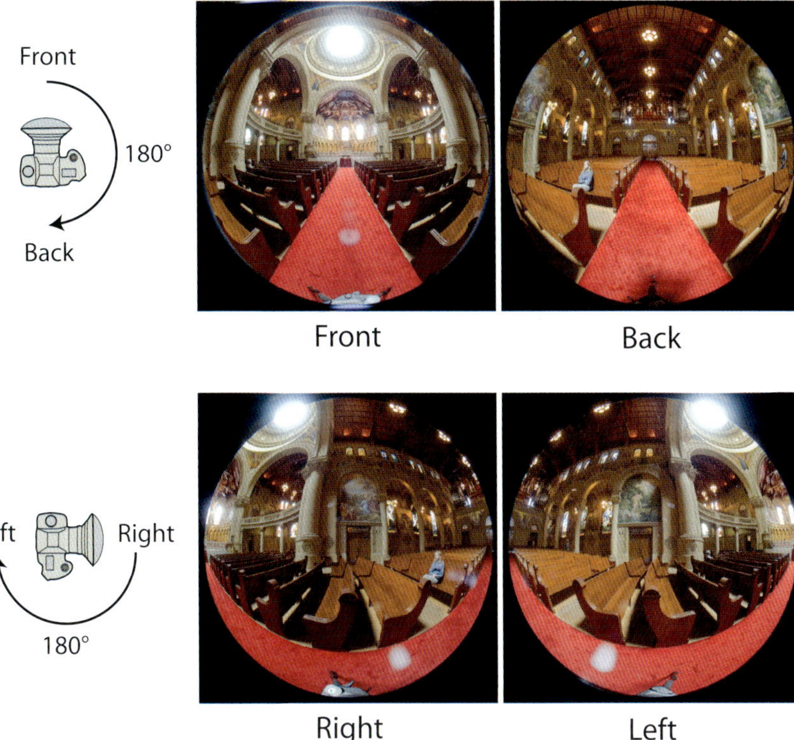

Fig. 11-10 Shooting a second hemisphere pair offset by 90° from the first can provide a post production alternative if lens flare makes one pair unusable.

be difficult, and having the windows fully included in one hemisphere will likely cause flare that will not match the shot from the opposite direction.

In these instances, it may be best to position the camera so that the bright window or other light winds up split on the seam. This way, it may create similar mirror images of the flare and other aberrations might result, and provide a better likelihood of the images matching uniformly.

4) Next, set the proper aperture and shutter speed, making sure the camera is set to manual exposure mode, and lock the exposure setting. Shoot the first hemisphere image. If you are using a two-shot system, rotate the camera 180° on the rotator, and shoot the second (opposing) hemisphere. Keep your hands, feet and other body parts, along with any camera bags or other equipment not belonging in the scene, completely behind the camera for both images. The fisheye lens captures everything in front of the camera, from straight up to straight down and 180° from side to side.

I find it advantageous to have click stops on spherical pan heads every 90 degrees, rather than 180 degrees (it's best to have a precision machinist add these if your pan head doesn't already have them). This allows me the option of shooting <u>four</u> hemisphere images for each panorama, which I tend to do as standard practice. That way, I have a choice of two sets of hemisphere pairs that I can use to assemble spherical fisheye panoramas. If one pair is mismatched because of lens flare or movement near the seam, I have another pair shot 90° off axis from the first, which may work better. One hemisphere pair also serves as a backup for the other. Furthermore, having four images provides me with the option of using fisheye *stitching* software to assemble spherical or cubic

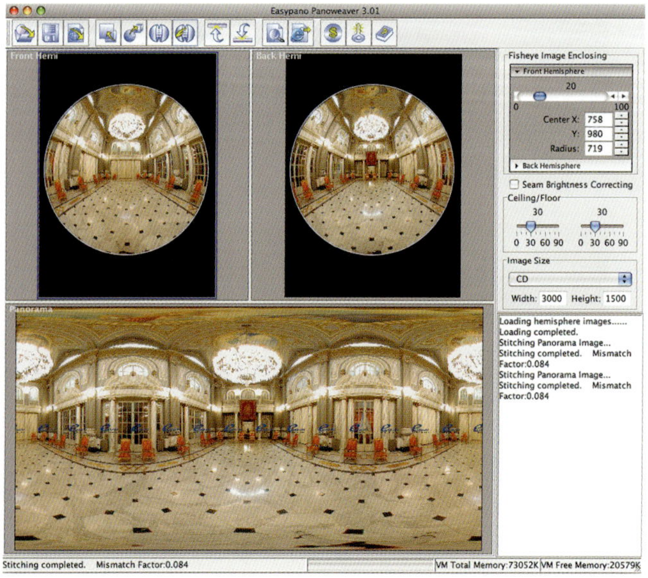

Fig. 11-11 Hemisphere assembly with Panoweaver software by Easypano.

panoramas, since my four source images overlap one another.

5) Once you have shot your hemisphere pairs, you can download and assemble them with your spherical authoring software.

Full-Frame Fisheyes

Spherical and cubic panoramas (360°x180°) can also be photographed effectively using full-frame fisheye lenses, rather than true hemispheric fisheyes. Full frame fisheyes project image circles that are slightly larger than the full frame of your camera or image sensor. Even though the images they produce have the curved fisheye perspective, their images fill the rectangular frame of your camera so you don't see the edges of the image circle like you do with a true fisheye.

Focal lengths for full frame fisheyes are longer than those of true fisheyes. For example, in the 35mm format, Nikon's 8mm lens is a true fisheye that projects a 180° circular hemispheric image inside the film frame. Nikon's *full frame* fisheye for the same format has a 16mm focal length. Its image circle is cropped by the edges of the frame, but the longer focal length magnifies the image more. The 16mm full-frame fisheye offers a 180° (approximate) field of view, but *only across the diagonal*. The horizontal and vertical fields of view are more limited because they are cropped by the frame edges.

Nikon also offers a 10.5mm full frame fisheye for its prosumer digital SLR cameras, which has a smaller image circle to match the smaller size of the Nikon DX series (digital) sensors. This 10.5mm lens offers almost identical field of view coverage on the Nikon prosumer digital SLRs as the 16mm does on the Nikon full frame digital and 35mm cameras. The 10.5mm is *not* designed to be used on 35mm format cameras, however, as it has no manual aperture ring and requires the electronic aperture connection of the Nikon D series cameras.

When photographing panoramas with full frame fisheyes, it is necessary to use fisheye *stitching* applications for assembly of the panoramas (remember that not all stitchers work with fisheye images, so be sure that your chosen stitching application does so before committing to use a fisheye lens for your VR panoramas). Stitching means that you need to have overlap between your images when shooting panoramic sequences.

Using a full frame fisheye, such as the Nikkor 16mm on a full frame or 35mm camera, (or a Nikkor 10.5mm on a Nikon DX prosumer digital SLR), you can effectively capture a full 360°x180° panorama with eight shots. Shoot six images around the horizon (pan 60° between shots), plus a zenith (straight up) and nadir (straight down). These eight shots provide adequate overlap for stitching *and* full coverage in every direction.

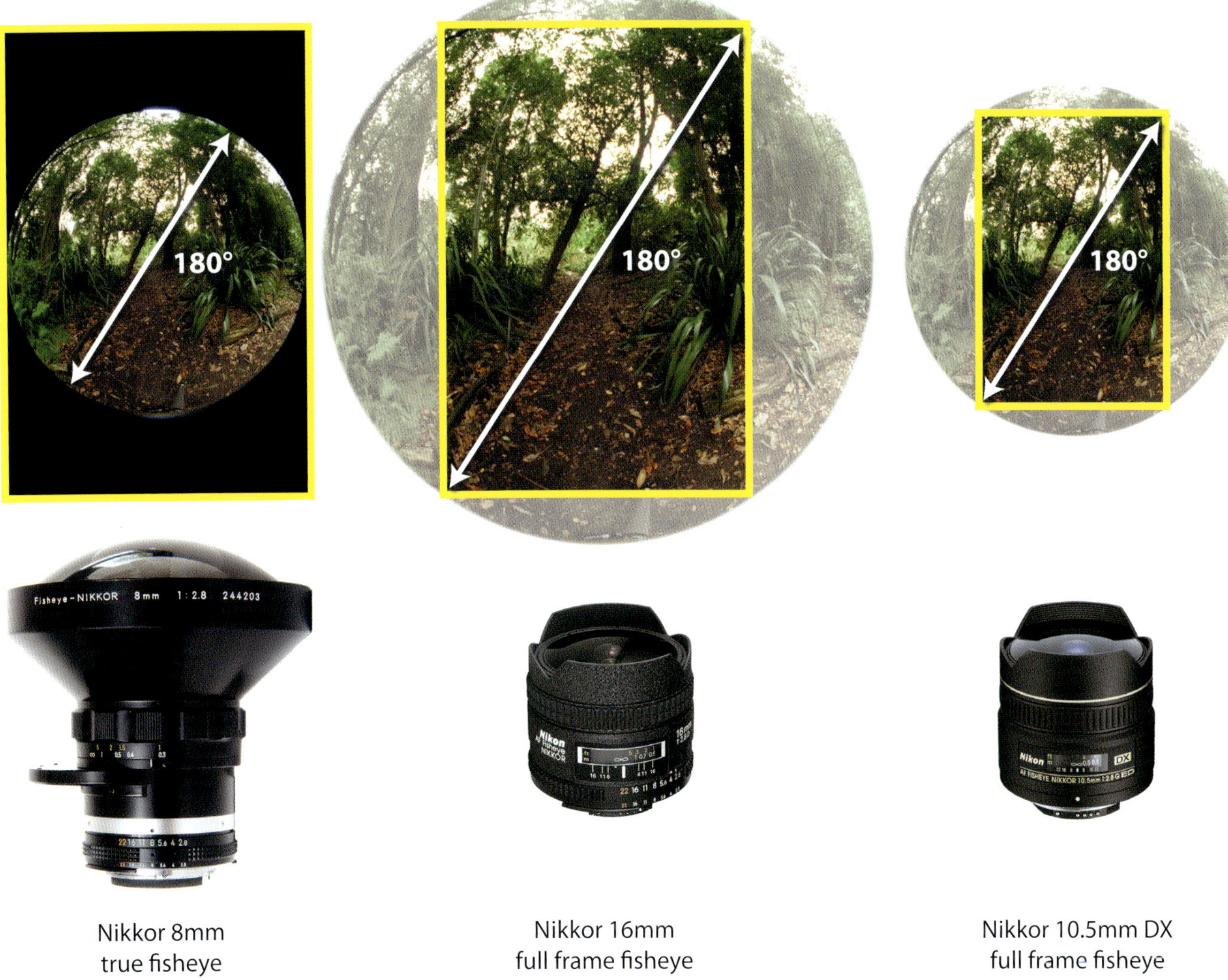

Fig. 11-12 Relative image circles and frame coverage for Nikkor true and full frame fisheye lenses.

Panorama Choice: Film vs. Digital

The film vs. digital question has been around since the earliest days of digital photography. Today, there are compelling advantages to both, particularly as the image quality of digital cameras increase and their prices decrease. As with almost everything else in photography, there are tradeoffs no matter which way you decide. For most VR photographers, panoramic imaging represents only a portion of their work, so the factors that lead them to choose film or digital for their panoramic photography may be a result of the demands from the other types of photography they do.

To help in the decision making process, consider the pros and cons of each listed below. Remember also that digital technologies continue to improve dramatically.

	Film	**Digital**
Field of view	Pro: Full field of view.	Con: Limited field of view for same lenses, except with newer full frame models.
Color balance	Con: Requires matching of film type to lighting, and use of color correction (CC) filters.	Pro: In camera white balancing is generally sufficient for color correction, even under mixed lighting.

	Film	Digital
Exposure latitude	**Pro**: Wide latitude for negative film (7-9 stops). **Con**: Narrow latitude for transparency film (5 stops).	**Pro**: High end (expensive) cameras offer broad exposure latitudes similar to (or better than) negative films. **Con**: Consumer level (less expensive) cameras have narrower latitudes.
Capture speed	**Pro**: extremely fast during shooting. **Con**: Requires scanning for post production.	**Pro**: High end cameras capable of rapid shooting for extended bursts. **Con**: Consumer cameras often have delays between shots while buffered images are being saved.
Resolution	**Pro**: Very fine - depending upon film used. Can be used to create wall sized panoramic prints and show fine detail. Film can be scanned at high resolutions, as needed.	**Pro**: Digital cameras have in some cases have already surpassed the resolution of 35mm film.
Equipment costs (camera, lens, pan head)	Consumer: $750 - $1,000. Professional: $2,500 - $12,000.	Consumer: $1,000 - $2,500. Professional: $2,000 - $10,000.
Film / processing / scanning costs	$5 - $35 / node	(none)
Work flow & post production	**Con**: Film scanning slows down post production speed & adds cost.	**Pro**: Images are digital from the outset – requiring no scanning. Can stitch or assemble on location with laptop computer, if needed.
Portability & durability in the field	Good to excellent.	Moderate to excellent.
Obsolescence period	**Pro**: 35mm cameras & lenses retain value fairly well over 3–5 year period.	**Con**: Digital systems can lose value faster (up to 50% per year).
Slit-scan camera systems (Seitz, Panoscan, Sphereon, etc.)	**Pros**: Can capture 360° images seamlessly and faster than traditional multiple shot cameras, panoramas require no stitching, can provide the highest resolution panoramic imagery. **Cons**: Expensive, difficult to use when supplemental lighting required, film models not capable of fisheye 360°x180° coverage.	**Pros**: Same advantages as film, plus some digital models are capable of fisheye or 180°x360° images. **Cons**: Same disadvantages as film except for 180°x360° coverage.
Single Shot Systems (GoPano, etc.)	**Pros**: Captures full 360° panorama in single moment, can freeze action throughout scene, no stitching required, allows for rapid shooting of images and sequences, including for motion picture and video applications. **Cons**: Low overall resolution, requires specific software for dewarping, hard to visualize resulting image when looking through viewfinder, not capable of 360°x180° views, only global exposure control while shooting.	**Pros**: Same advantages as film. **Cons**: Same disadvantages as film.

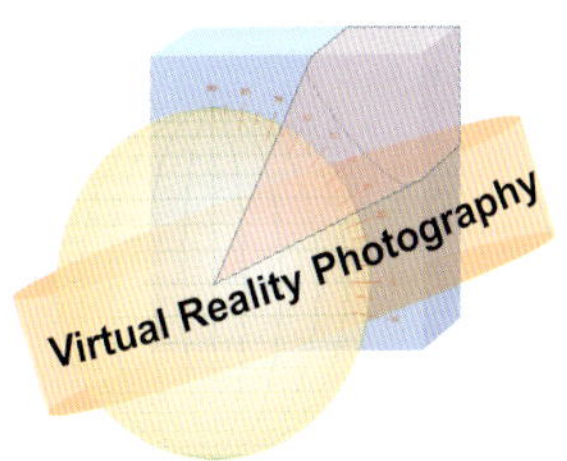

Chapter 12: Panorama Effectiveness

The challenge of panoramic VR photography is to not only create compelling imagery in a 360-degree image, but to do so understanding that it will not generally be viewed in its entirety at a single moment in a VR display environment. A panoramic VR image will usually be viewed within a window on a computer screen, but that window will only display a small portion of the complete 360° view at a time. The photographer must consider the size and aspect ratio of this viewing window, as well as how the person viewing it will navigate within it, looking left, right, up, down, and zooming in or out. All of these will change the composition of the image from the viewer's perspective.

Good VR photographers will plan for their images to be seen in an almost infinite number of ways within a movie window, as well as making those panoramas effective as stand alone print images. Yes, it can be a difficult task to do well, but as they say... if it were easy, everyone would do it.

You must first learn to visualize the complete panoramic image as you're planning to shoot. Then, consider how that panorama will be presented in smaller sections in a movie window. Before shooting, you should spend time looking through the camera's viewfinder and search for the best perspective. Check the views to the side and behind you, in addition to what's in front of you. All these views will be included in the full 360-degree panorama.

Perspective and View

As discussed in **Chapter 3**, perspective is simply the point of view from which the photograph is shot. It involves not only the relative positions of the camera and subject, but also the field of view captured.

Most VR panoramas are photographed using extremely wide angle lenses which maximize the vertical field of view recorded. Shooting multi-row panoramas with longer focal length lenses also results in a very wide field of view. The effective perspective is similar, although resolution can be greater due to the larger number of source images that are combined to make the panorama.

When photographing wide views, the photographer will most often want to be close to subjects in order to make them dominate the overall image and draw the viewer's eye. If a subject of interest does not appear large enough in the

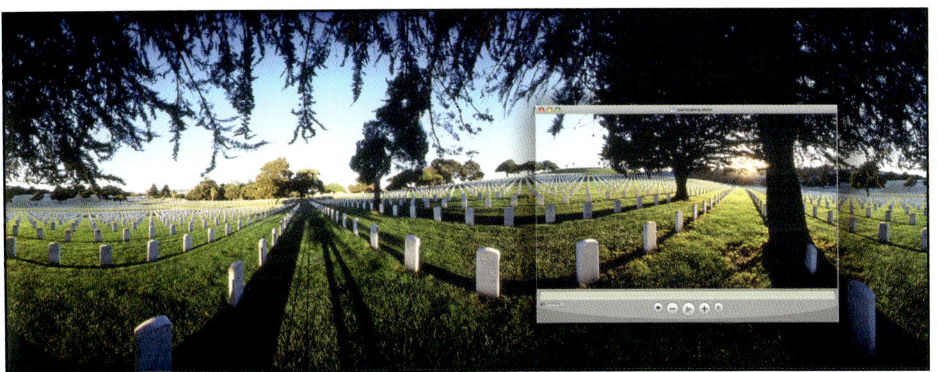

Cylindrical

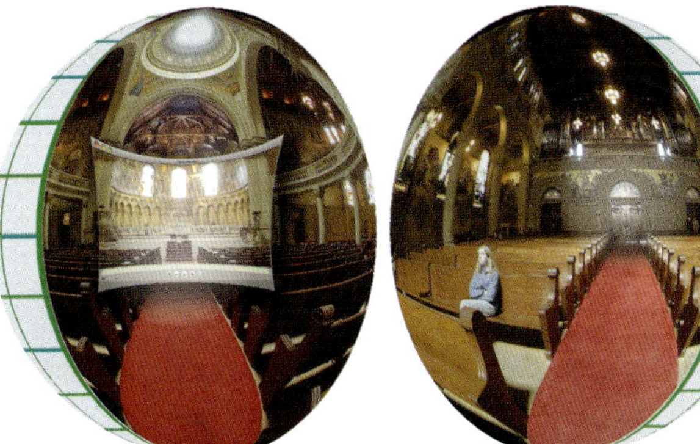

Cubic / spherical

Fig. 12-1 The framing of the initial view in a panoramic movie window should be considered by the photographer when shooting a panorama sequence.

image, it risks being perceived as clutter or distraction within the panorama. Just as traditional photographs usually require a principal or prominent subject, so do panoramic images.

However, VR panoramas often require more than a single subject, since the entire image is not viewed at one time on a computer screen. A panorama that has only a single point of interest will not compel a viewer to look around beyond the initial view. Large expanses of slate gray sky, acoustic ceiling tiles, boring pavement, or drab carpeting, will also offer little incentive for viewers to look up, down, or further around in an interactive VR image.

About only thing worse than having to sit through a boring slide show of someone's family vacation is to have to navigate through boring virtual reality imagery on a computer screen. Since most VR audiences have countless other web sites and media to explore, they will quickly move on if you do not hold their interest. Herein lies one of the great challenges of panoramic VR photography.

When making traditional photographs of a single subject, the photographer changes distance from the subject, or perhaps changes the focal length of his lens to control the prominence of that subject in the image. However, when shooting 360° panoramas, moving closer to one subject often means that you move further away from another. While it is tempting to position your camera midway between and hope for the best, doing so often means that neither subject will be featured well.

Remember the antiquated concept of "f/8 and be there," where photographers simply pointed their cameras in the general direction of the subject and assumed that if they cropped enough of the unnecessary material out of the resulting image, they could find an interesting photograph? This is the trap that many photographers fall into when first shooting panoramic VR.

They place their camera with an ultra-wide lens "somewhere in the middle of a scene" and shoot the panorama. They have little concern over composition, lighting, point of view, location of the subject(s), or the relative perspective of the scene. They worry primarily about camera alignment, exposure, and focus – all important technical concerns, but overlook the equally important aesthetic concerns. A mistaken assumption is if you are in the middle of a scene and you're shooting the entire 360° view around you, that somewhere within

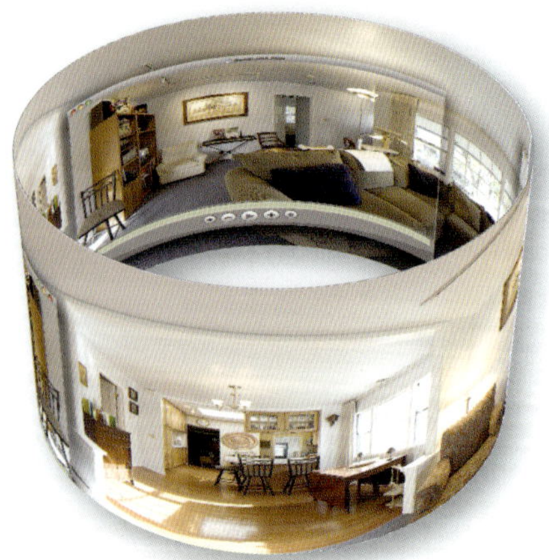

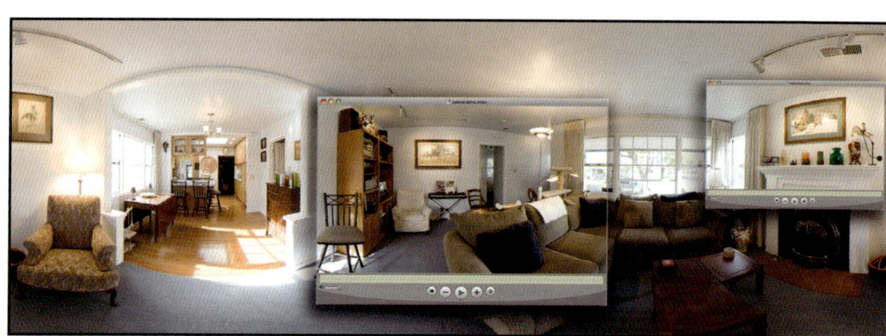

Less interesting – middle of room perspective

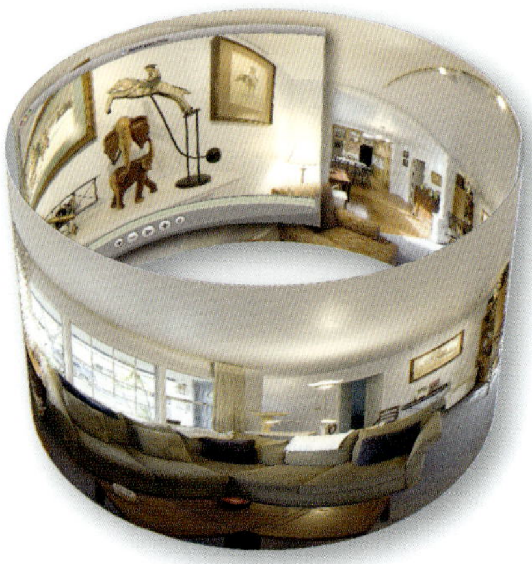

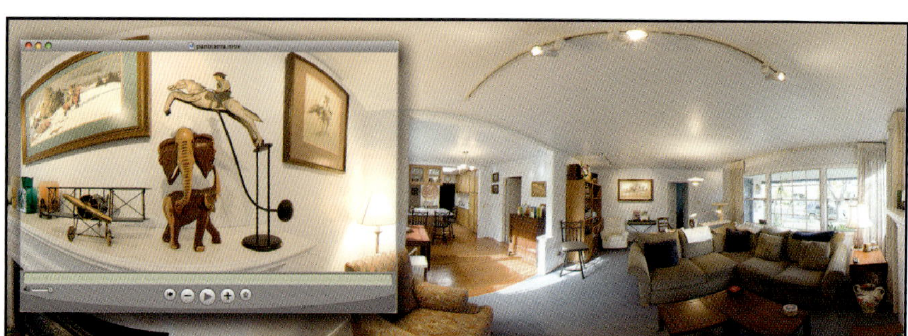

More interesting – perspective close to subjects of interest

Fig. 12-2 The difference between visually boring vs. interesting panoramas can be as simple as changing perspective.

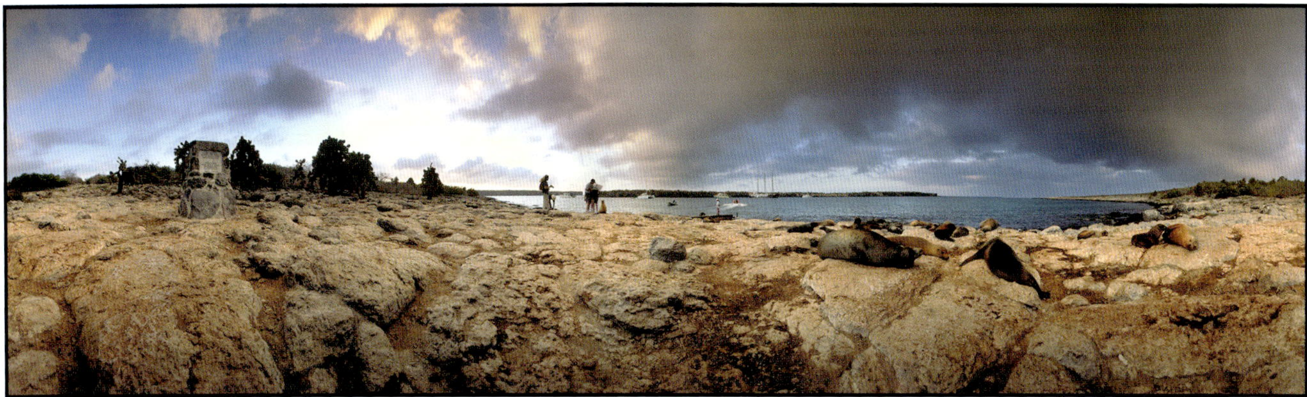
Original 360° panorama

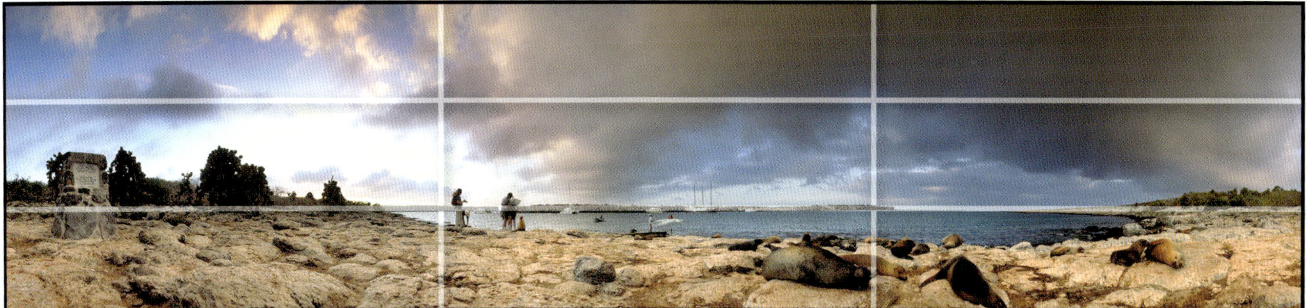
Cropped – applying rule of thirds

Fig. 12-3 Even though some 360° panorama stitching applications require a camera leveled and centered on the horizon during shooting, photographer pre-visualization and post production cropping can yield improved compositions.

that scene, your viewer should be able to find something of interest. This is dull photography, and does little more than to simply document a location. It's "f/8 and be there" all over again.

A good VR photographer must walk around the location he or she is shooting to find perspectives that provide at least two (and preferably three) subjects of interest that are not only prominent in the frame, but which are also distributed throughout the 360° view. This is not always easy to do. It helps to keep your camera with you as you scout a location and to look constantly through the viewfinder as you pan around.

You may have to do a lot of moving about, crouching low or reaching high to find a position within the scene that will provide effective views in all directions. You may need to move people, furniture, or other objects (when acceptable) within the scene in order to make the full 360° interesting. You may also find yourself limited by where the sun or other available lighting appears within the scene. Remember that good photography requires a willingness to work the scene. Simply setting a camera on a tripod and pushing the button doesn't create good pictures any more than starting your car and stepping on the gas gets you to a chosen destination. Knowing your destination and being willing to steer in the right directions, whether you are driving a car or shooting with a camera, are essential.

Spend time planning where to position your camera for the best perspective and view of the scene. The results will be the difference between low quality "snapshot" imagery and a more refined elegance of professional photography.

As you compose the image, also plan for the opening view of the VR movie. This will be the first glimpse your viewers have of your panorama on screen. Give them something of interest that inspires them to navigate within the image – to pan around, to look up and down, or to zoom in for a closer look. As long as there are further subjects of interest, your viewers will continue to explore interactively. And the longer they remain looking at the image, the more valuable that image becomes to both you and your clients.

The success of most web sites or multimedia titles is gauged both by how many people view the content and how long they remain on the site. Compelling interactivity, such as good VR imagery, attracts viewers and keeps them involved. Boring content prompts them to quickly move elsewhere.

Framing and Composition
The technical requirements of many panorama stitching applications stipulate that the series of images must be shot with the camera level and centered on the horizon.

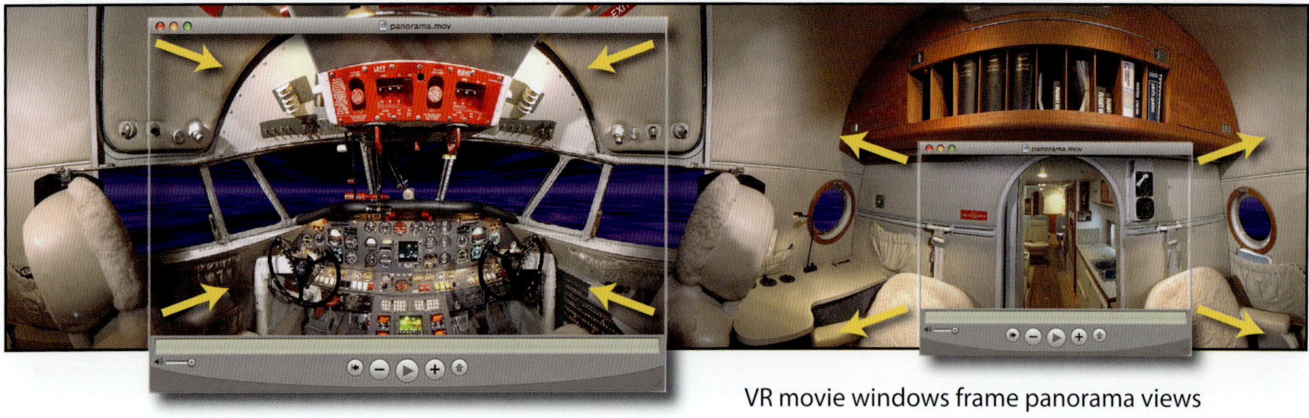

Fig. 12-4 Plan ahead for the composition of the initial movie window you'll want for VR presentation of a 360° panorama.

This unfortunately does not favor good photographic composition, as it's generally better to have a horizon conform to the Rule of Thirds and be positioned above or below the center of the frame.

Fortunately, the panoramic photographer is not limited to this composition restriction when actually presenting the completed panorama, since only a portion of the image will be displayed in a VR movie window at any given time. This allows the photographer to specify better framing and composition in the movie window. Viewers will be able to pan, tilt and zoom elsewhere from this initial view, but the author can at least start them out on the right path visually.

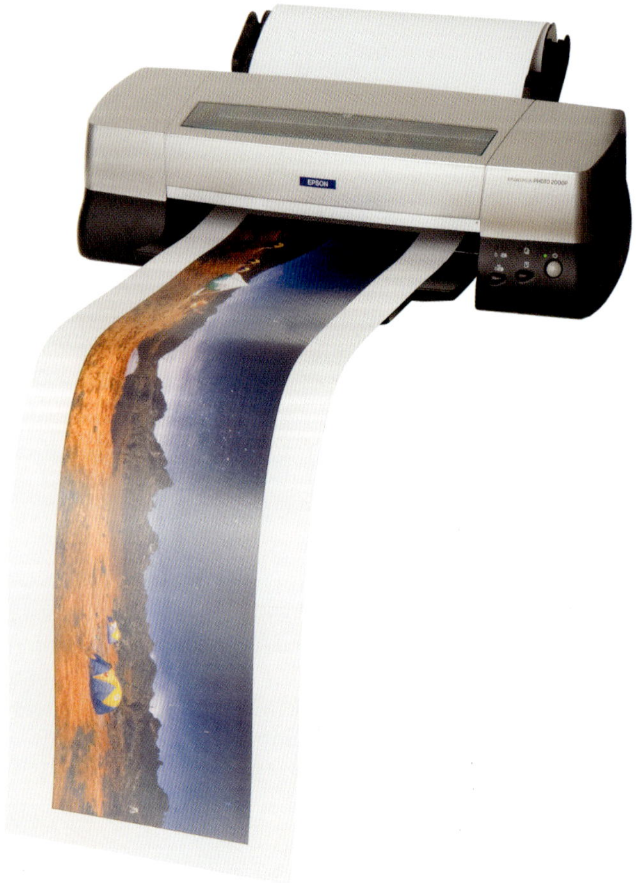

Be sure to include several prominent subjects of interest throughout the horizontal view of the panorama. This provides incentive for the viewer to continue panning around the image. With cubic and spherical panoramas, it is important to include additional subjects or composition elements upward and downward, so the viewer has reason to explore the vertical range of the image, as well. What can be a bit tricky is shooting the panorama so that it is effective both as an interactive movie, as well as a stand alone printed photograph.

The biggest difference here is that a printed image is viewed in its entirety. Such uses include large wall prints, billboards, bus cards (the long horizontal ads on the sides/backs of buses), web site banners, book or magazine gatefolds, motion picture and television backgrounds, museum cycloramas, product packaging, and wrap-around publication covers.

One generally has to shoot the panorama with the camera leveled and the horizon in the middle of the frame for proper stitching. However, the image can always be cropped afterward for better composition as a printed panorama. Note that sometimes a visible horizon line may not actually appear in a panorama, particularly those shot indoors or on locations where the horizon is obscured by other features within the image.

Unless you will be using a multi-row stitcher, it is generally NOT effective to try to tilt the camera on its panning axis for composition control. This can cause even worse problems than the ones you are trying to fix composition-wise. These new problems can be difficult, if not impossible to correct in post production.

Fig. 12-5 Panoramic images can also be made into striking prints using desktop printers such as this one from Epson.

With full 360° panoramas, you can also use the Offset filter in Adobe's Photoshop software to change the

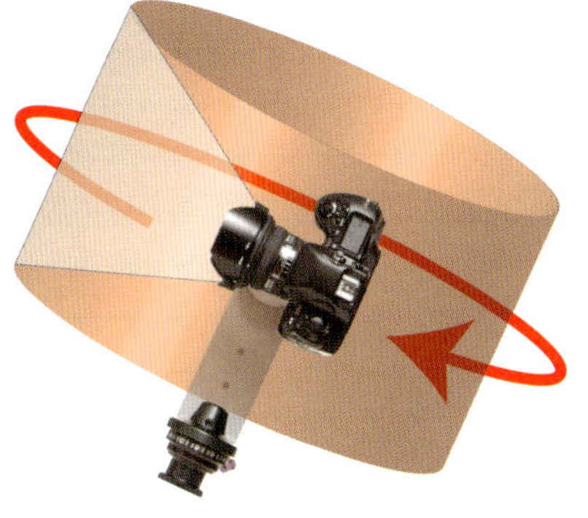

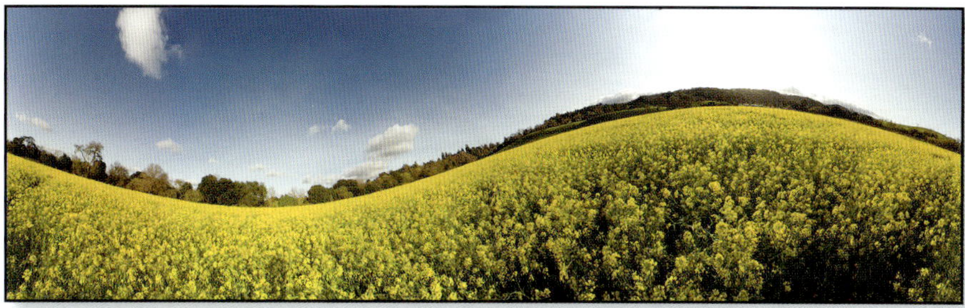

Non-level horizon – camera squared to tilted pan axis

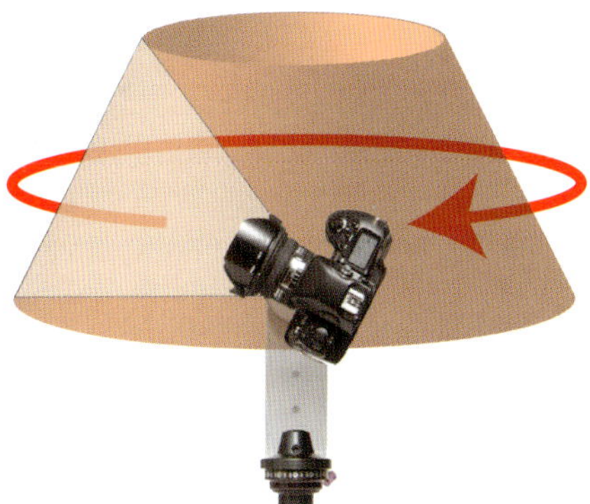

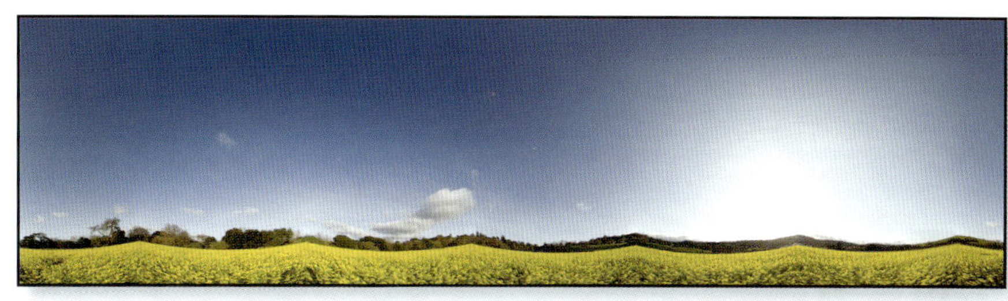

Cupped horizon – camera tilted on perpendicular pan axis

Fig. 12-6 Shooting stitched panorama sequences on non-level pan axes can cause problems for *some* stitching applications.

position of the left and right sides of the image and to position the subjects of interest compositionally to follow the rule of thirds (note that this can only be done with 360° panoramas).

Consistency in Technique

There are probably as many combinations of equipment and techniques for VR photography as there are photographers. Some of these combinations work better than others, but as with all creative endeavors, no single method is best for every situation.

It *is* important to maintain consistency in each technique you use. This means you should develop a systematic procedure for each type of shooting you do. The more consistent you are in both shooting technique *and* equipment use, the fewer problems you will encounter.

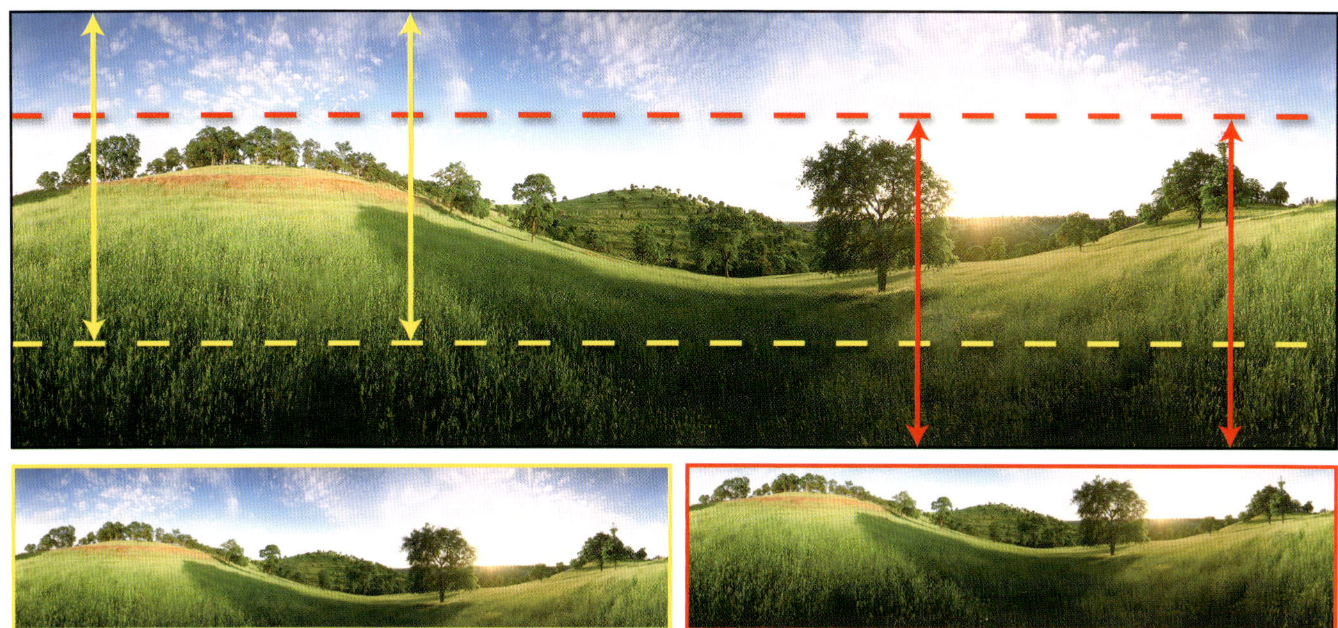

Fig. 12-7 Cropping a panorama after stitching is often a better approach for composition adjustments, particularly for printed panoramas, than shooting the sequence with a non-level camera.

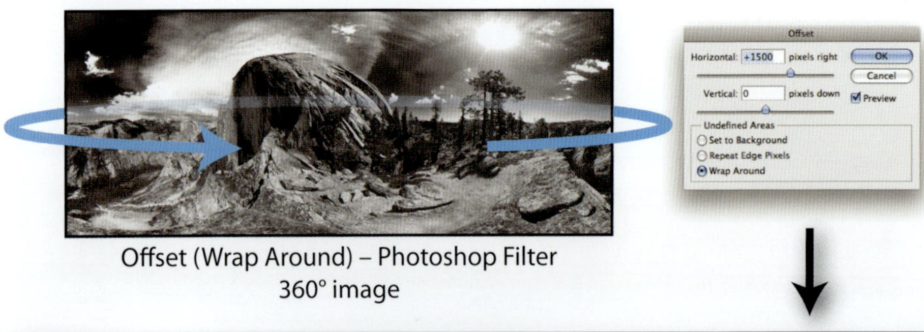

Offset (Wrap Around) – Photoshop Filter
360° image

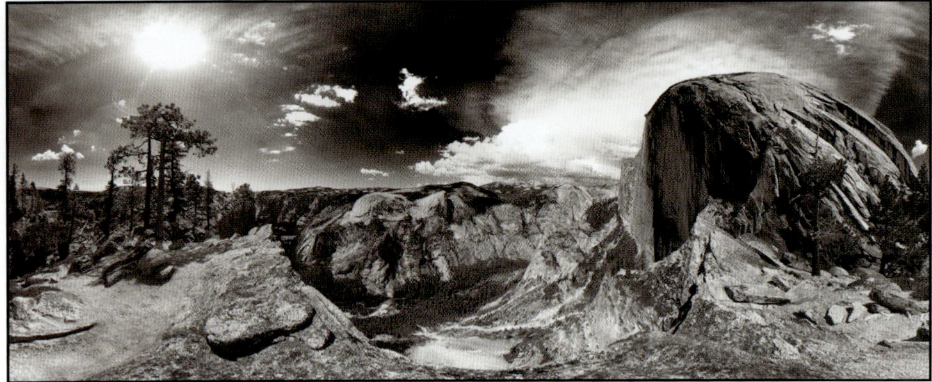

Fig. 12-8 Use of Photoshop's Offset filter is invaluable for adjusting composition of a 360° panoramic image for printing. Note that the ends of the panorama must match perfectly in order for this to work seamlessly.

VR photography is generally far more technical in nature than most other kinds of photography. There are lots of things that can go wrong during the process. Maintaining a consistent approach allows you to better pinpoint where or how problems occur when they do. Problems generally result from something that changed during your process. If your technique has been successful previously, it is very likely to continue successfully if you don't change any part of it.

Of course, every shooting situation is different and you will need to change obvious things like exposure, lighting, camera positions, etc. However, maintaining consistency in the following areas will help you maintain the quality and technical control of your work.

1) Use the same camera and lens combination as often as possible. Many VR photographers only have only one camera & lens that they use for VR, so this is not usually a problem. However, as you add to your stable of equipment, you may find yourself with an increasing variety of cameras and lenses. Be sure to test each combination thoroughly before relying on it for an important shoot. Test every combination throughout your entire process from photography to final VR assembly of the images. Most experienced VR pros shoot 90 percent of their work with one or two camera/lens combinations. Familiarity with these combinations means one can count on consistent results. If you regularly change from one lens or focal length to another, or try different cameras, you may have a difficult time pinpointing where things might have gone wrong when problems arise. Use

different tools when necessary, but remember that consistent results require consistent methods and techniques.

2) Use the same pan head and tripod. It doesn't matter whether you use a commercial pan head such as those from Manfrotto, Kaidan, or Peace River Studios, or whether you make your own. Use whichever one you choose consistently. This provides you with more familiarity each time you use it. Modify your equipment as necessary, but do so carefully and in controlled steps.

3) Use the same film or digital media as often as you can. When shooting on film, choose one or two films that you rely on consistently.   Negative (print) films are generally best, since they offer wider exposure latitudes than transparency films. A relatively slow speed (ISO 100 or less) daylight balanced film will give the best detail and can be used for the majority of your VR photography. A high speed film (ISO 400 or higher) can be useful in low light situations where slow shutter speeds are unacceptable (such as when there is movement within the scene). Remember that with increased ISO film speed comes an increase in grain and lower resolving power.

For digital shooting, you'll want to keep your camera set for the lowest ISO equivalent (light sensitivity) you can. Cameras that allow adjustments of their relative ISO yield more image noise when you increase light sensitivity (a corresponding decrease in image quality). Do a series of tests with any digital camera to find the best combination of settings that provide the best image quality. Then stick with these for most of your panoramic VR work.

4) Maintain consistent exposure and focus as you shoot. With 35mm cameras and lenses, an aperture of f/8 or f/11 is considered optimal, as this provides good depth of field without needing as much light as smaller apertures. Exposure can be adjusted with faster or slower shutter speeds, depending on the brightness of the particular scene you are shooting. Keep both aperture and shutter speed constant throughout a given panorama to avoid banding and noticeable stitching errors in the final image. If you are using an auto-exposure camera, you must set it to manual exposure control before shooting, or lock the exposure for the full panorama sequence.

Lens focus should be kept constant throughout a panorama sequence, as well. Using an aperture of f/8 or f/11 provides significant depth of field when using wide angle and ultra-wide lenses. Changing the focus of a lens actually changes the reproduction size of a subject in the camera, resulting in misalignments and stitching errors in post production assembly. Focusing the lens at its hyperfocal distance, rather than at infinity, maximizes depth of field. Note that the hyperfocal distance for each focal length and lens aperture is different. The chart in Fig. 12-9 provides reference hyperfocal distances for a variety of 35mm lenses. A more extensive discussion of hyperfocal distance is provided in **Chapter 4**.

5) Keep detailed notes for every shoot, including information on the lens (focal length) used, exposure, number and sequence of shots, etc. File these notes with your original film or digital files. Photographing a completed information slate before every node will provide not only color reference data, but also all the information you might need later on in the post production process. You can make your own slates simply by recording your shooting information on a pad of paper and photographing it before each node, or you can use efficient commercial slates such as the VR Photography Slate book, available through **www.vrphotography.com**

Keep your photography process as organized as possible. Write down anything that might be important to remember about the shoot in a notebook as you are shooting. If you are creative, you will invariably try new things. If you haven't kept track of everything with notes that you can refer back to, you may never be able to remember what worked and what didn't, or why.

I find that preparing checklists before every shoot is helpful, as well – not only to make sure I have all the necessary equipment and supplies I might need, but to remember particulars about what shots the client

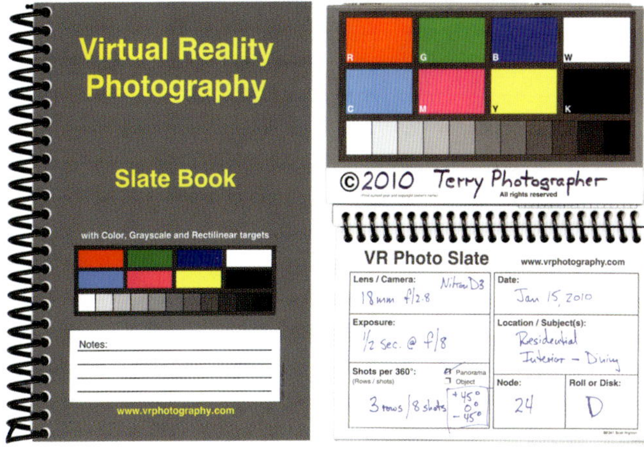

Fig. 12-10 VR Photography slate book.

needs, what techniques might have been discussed, and how everything is supposed to be assembled after I'm finished with the photography.

These notes and checklists should be retained in a project or job file. I keep these filed with the original film or digital images in file cabinets in my office. Other photographers keep them in sequential shoot logs or journals in composition notebooks.

6) Try to shoot the first image of every panoramic sequence facing in a similar direction, and try to align the camera with a structure or action within the scene. This is not so important when using slit scan cameras, but can be valuable when shooting multiple images for stitching.

If you square the camera with the walls in a room interior, the individual images in the sequence may have value as stand alone photographs. Also, it is easier to remember where you are in your panoramic sequence, when you know that your first shot was aligned with the plane of a wall or other dominant subject.

The same principle applies to shooting outdoors. Use the face of a building as your starting direction, and square the camera to that plane. Then start shooting every other panorama that you will be linking to in the same direction. For example, if the first shot of your first panorama is facing due north, it would probably be a good idea to make the first shot of every other panorama facing toward the north, as well. This will help you, or whomever is doing the assembly of your panoramas, orient them properly as they will all be aligned similarly.

Exceptions may be made to this when there is action happening between

Hyperfocal Distances

35mm format equivalent   (Circle of Confusion = 1/1000" or .0254mm)

	f/2.8	f/4	f/5.6	f/8	f/11	f/16	f/22
14mm	11'	7.6'	5.4'	3.8'	2.8'	1.9'	1.4'
15mm	13'	8.7'	6.2'	4.4'	3.2'	2.2'	1.6'
18mm	18'	13'	9.0'	6.3'	4.6'	3.1'	2.3'
20mm	22'	16'	11'	7.8'	5.6'	3.9'	2.8'
24mm	32'	22'	16'	11'	8.1'	5.6'	4.1'
28mm	44'	30'	22'	15'	11'	7.6'	5.5'
35mm	68'	48'	34'	24'	17'	12'	8.6'
50mm	138'	97'	69'	48'	35'	24'	18'

Depth of field increases →

← Depth of field increases →

Fig. 12-9 Hyperfocal distance chart for 35mm format lenses.

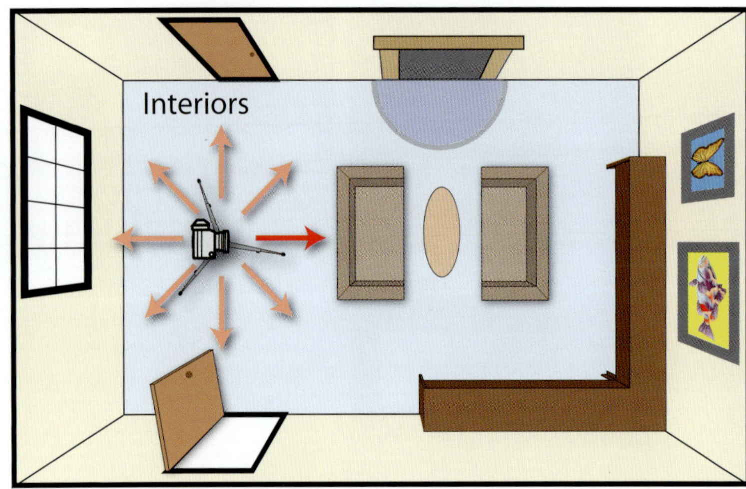

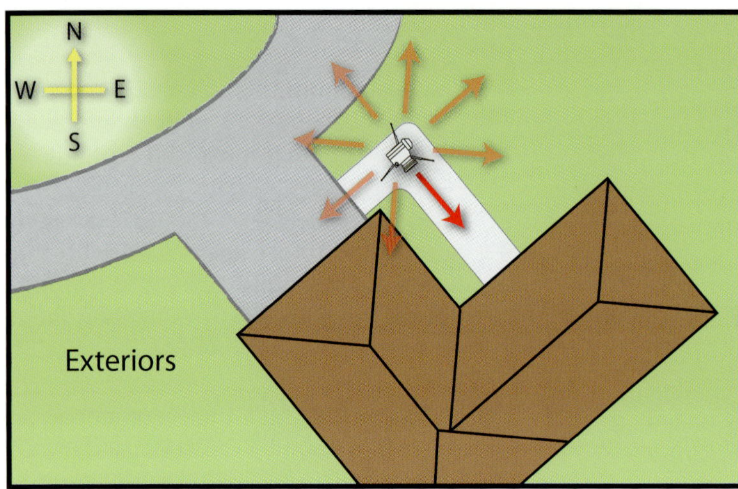

Fig. 12-11 When shooting a series of panoramas, try to be consistent in the orientation of your shot sequences. This will help facilitate assembly and accurate alignment of these panorama scenes in post production.

frames, or when lighting conditions prescribe otherwise (such as minimizing flare). In these instances, orient the shots so that the transition, blend, or seam areas between shots wind up where you need them.

Determining Best Exposure
While it is important to keep exposure constant throughout a panorama, determining the best exposure can be difficult when the light level changes in different directions. For exterior shots, there is invariably some part of the scene in direct sunlight, while other parts are in shadow. Similar differences in light quantity are found in most interior panoramas, particularly when windows or doors are present in one part of a room but not others.

There are several approaches to choosing best exposure. The first is to use an average exposure for the entire scene. This involves taking light readings (either through your camera's internal light meter or a hand held meter) every 90 degrees around the panorama and averaging the results. For example, when facing an open window, your camera may indicate an exposure of 1/250

sec. @ f/8. Turning to the right, you may get a reading of 1/60 sec. (keep the aperture at f/8). Turning another 90° so you are facing a darkened area, you may have an exposure of 1/15 sec. The final quadrant might indicate 1/125 sec. Thus, you have a 4-stop exposure range. Choosing one in the middle (1/60 sec. @ f/8) will be simplest.

Note that if you are shooting with **negative** or print film, you are better off exposing for the shadow or darker areas of the scene (1/15 sec. @ f/8 in the above example). This is because negative films have broad exposure latitudes and they handle *over*exposure well. Exposing for the darkest parts of the image on negative films allows you to capture all the details in the shadows, and the overexposed highlight areas still retain detail on the film.

If you are shooting with **transparency** or slide film, you are better off favoring the highlight or brighter areas of the scene in your exposure. This is because slide film does not handle overexposure well at all. Overexposed details quickly wash out or become solid white. Most slide films have relatively narrow exposure latitudes, so if your scene has lots of lighting contrast, it may be impossible to capture both highlight and shadow details in the same shot. For this reason, negative (print) films are generally the best choice for those opting to use film for their panoramic VR photography.

If you shoot with a **digital** camera, you will have to experiment to find the best exposure setting for each panorama. Every digital camera responds differently to lighting contrast. Some respond better to slight underexposure, while others handle over-exposure better. If you shoot in RAW mode, rather than JPEG, software applications such as Photoshop or the proprietary software program that may have been provided with your camera can extract more exposure latitude from your image data. RAW formats generally require greater storage space and they can slow down the capture rate of your camera, but they can offer significant advantages in post production.

Most consumer quality digital cameras have exposure latitudes somewhere between the performance of transparency and negative films, while high-end professional digital cameras can exceed the broad

Average exposure:
1/60 sec. or 1/125 sec. @f/8

Negative films –
Exposure should favor *shadows*:
1/15 sec. @ f/8

Transparency films –
Exposure should favor *highlights*:
1/125 or 1/250 sec. @ f/8

Digital cameras –
Expose to *slightly* favor highlights:
1/125 sec.@f/8

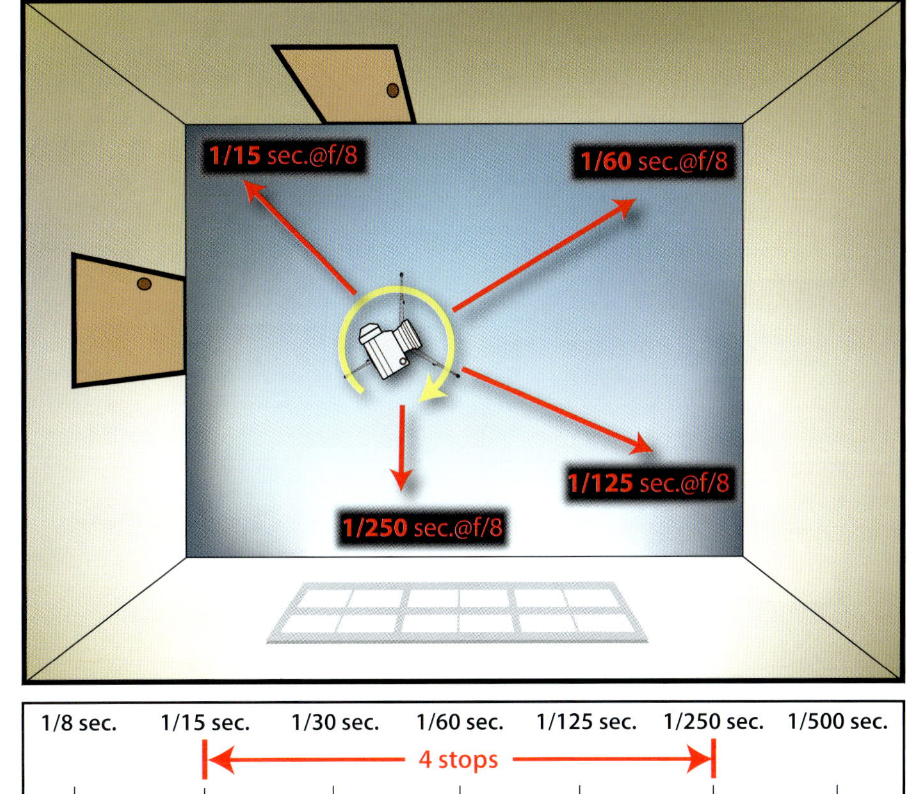

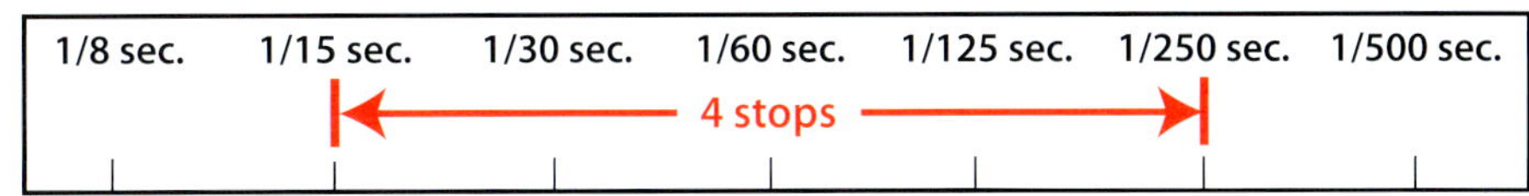

Fig. 12-12 Determining best exposure for a scene requires consideration of its exposure extremes.

exposure latitudes of the best negative films. Of course, when you shoot digitally, you can usually preview the results as you shoot, and you can redo a sequence with exposure adjustments as needed before you leave your location.

Be aware that some panoramic scenes will present you with challenging lighting extremes beyond the exposure latitudes of even the best negative films or high end digital cameras. In these instances, you will probably want to use fill lighting or other more advanced shooting techniques.

Supplemental Lighting

When the exposure latitude of a scene is too broad for your chosen camera or film to capture effectively, then your job as a photographer is to modify or add lighting in order to bring the contrast level within the range of your capture media. In extreme cases, a photographer might eliminate existing lighting and replace it entirely with "artificial" lighting. However, this can be a huge undertaking when shooting panoramic images, as the entire scene encompassing a 360° view needs to be lit artificially. A better option is often to modify the existing light and supplement it as needed. Simpler is usually better.

When faced with too much contrast in a scene, you should consider first whether you can make modifications to existing lighting that will help reduce the contrast. Something as simple as closing the louvers on a venetian blind, or pulling curtains partway across a window, can bring lighting levels into an acceptable range.

The next step might be to turn on all the available lights in a room. This makes the ambient light level in the room brighter, bringing it closer to that of the daylight coming through a window. Note that doing this usually results in "mixed" lighting conditions, where the color temperature of the room light is different from the color temperature of the daylight from the windows. In many instances, this will be acceptable, but in others where exact color reproduction is critical, it may not. In the latter instances, you may have to use color correction filters or gels over one or more of your lighting sources in order to balance the color temperatures.

Remember that the human brain compensates for subtle color differences that our eyes see, so we easily recognize familiar colors and hues no matter whether we see them under tungsten light (yellowish), fluorescent (bluish-green), metal halide, candle light, or any range of daylight. Photographic film and digital media, however, are fixed in their relative sensitivities to color and balanced for specific color temperatures. The most common films are daylight balanced (5000°–5500°K), while others are tungsten balanced (3200°–3400°K). Using the wrong film (or color balance setting on a digital camera) for the lighting type you're shooting under will usually result in an undesired color cast to your images. (For more on color balance and compensation, see **Chapter 5**.)

One of the best techniques for reducing lighting contrast is to use **fill lighting**. Fill lighting is the use of a light, usually located near the camera, to fill in light needed in the shadow areas of the image. This effectively increases the light level in the shadow areas enough to bring out detail when the camera exposure is set for the highlight areas. It reduces a scene's contrast by adding light into its darker areas.

Most often, you will see fill lighting done with an on-camera flash or strobe unit. In fact, many of today's auto-everything cameras have a "fill flash" setting. The camera sets exposure for the level of the ambient light in the overall scene. The flash unit is programmed to put out enough light as the picture is taken to be equal to or slightly less than the ambient light level. Thus the captured image is properly exposed for the ambient light, plus it has needed strobe light filling in the shadow areas.

Fill lighting can be done in any number of ways. It does not require an on-camera flash. In fact, in **Chapter 5** we discussed light quality and learned that it is often best to place lighting off to a side of the camera and subject axis, rather than head-on from the camera. This can be done with fill lighting, too. It is usually most effective to have fill lighting coming from the opposite direction of the main (or key) light in a scene. So, if sun or window light is the key light source in your photo, your fill light might best be positioned on the opposite side of your subject, facing the key light.

This may *seem* hard to do when shooting multiple images for a panorama, but remember that as long as the intensity and direction of your fill lighting does not change too dramatically in between shots, the blending of images in the stitching process can make lighting changes almost unnoticeable to the viewer.

This is a bit more difficult to do when shooting with a slit-scan panoramic camera, as the fill light either needs to remain static within the scene, or move as the camera rotates. Some slit scan photographers add a bracket onto their camera to hold a fill light, so the light rotates as the camera does. This setup also requires the use of a continuous lighting source, rather than a flash, since the panoramic exposure is made in a continuous pan, rather than a frame at a time.

If using a single shot panoramic system, such as the GoPano™, the entire scene will be captured at one instant.

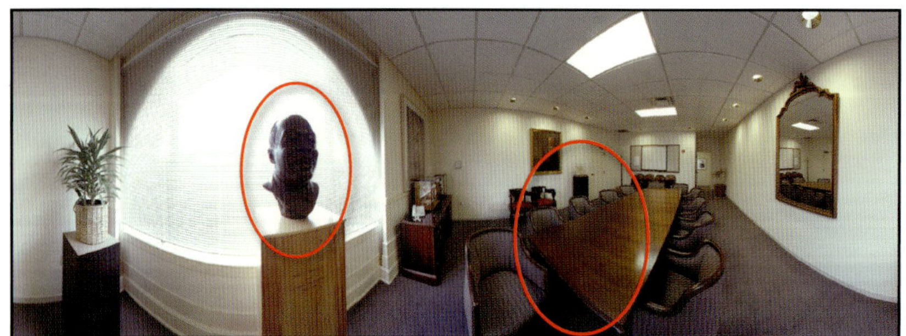

Problem (lighting) areas in panorama

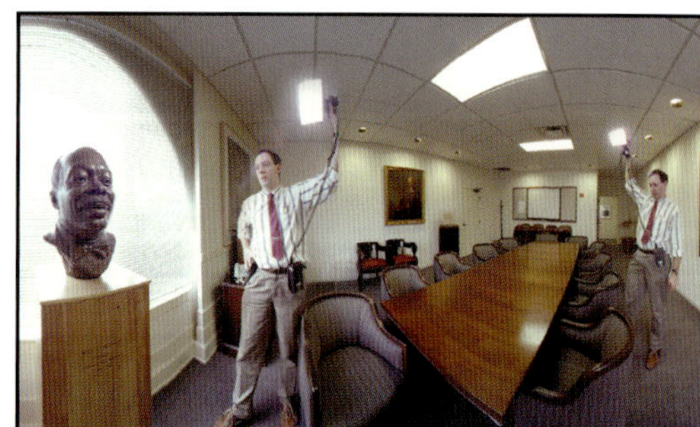

Fill lighting added (out of camera view)

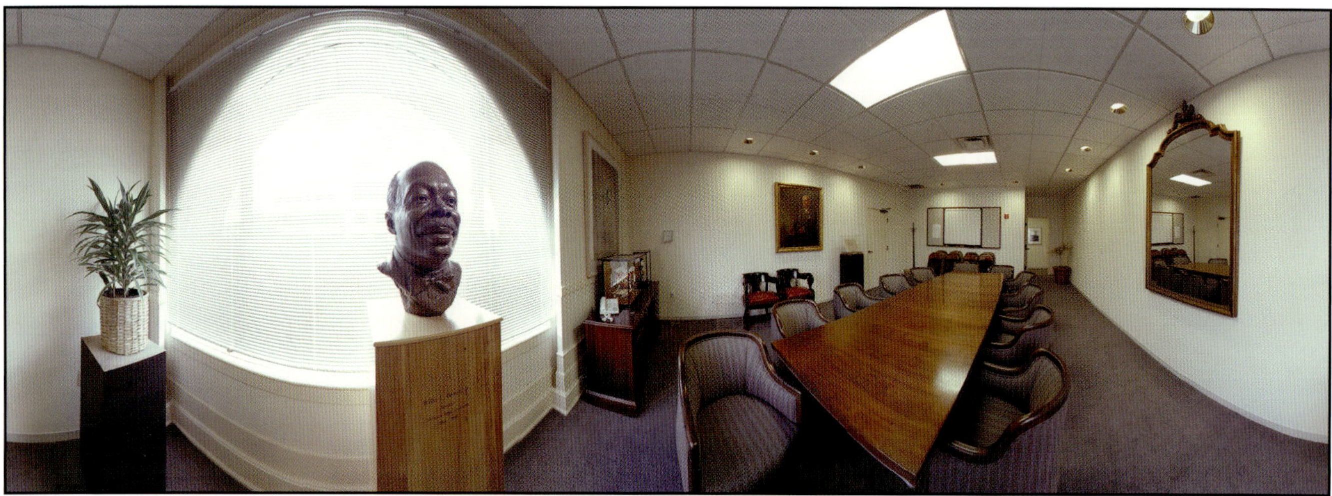

Final stitched result

Fig. 12-13 Fill lighting can be extremely effective in solving light balance problems with stitched panoramic photography.

Therefore, there is no opportunity to move fill lighting during the exposure. This means that any fill lighting you use will have to be positioned directly above or below the camera (outside of its field of view), or hidden within the scene. Your fill lighting will have to cover the entire scene, or at least the full portion of the scene that needs the supplemental light. These one shot systems tend to limit photographers to shooting available light scenes, but creative photographers can find ways to do just about anything with equipment they might have available. Just remember that fill lighting is generally going to be a lot more difficult with the one-shot camera and lens systems.

Fill lighting sources are not limited to on-camera flash, either. A light reflector or white card can be used to bounce the primary light source back into the scene from an off-camera angle. Sometimes a mirror or crumpled sheet of aluminum foil can suffice. Even a flashlight, mini light, or small strobe hidden within the scene can serve the purpose.

Be creative and try different things. Your goal is to bring the lighting levels between highlight and shadows into a closer exposure range, so they can be captured by the film or the media you select *and* are pleasing to the eye.

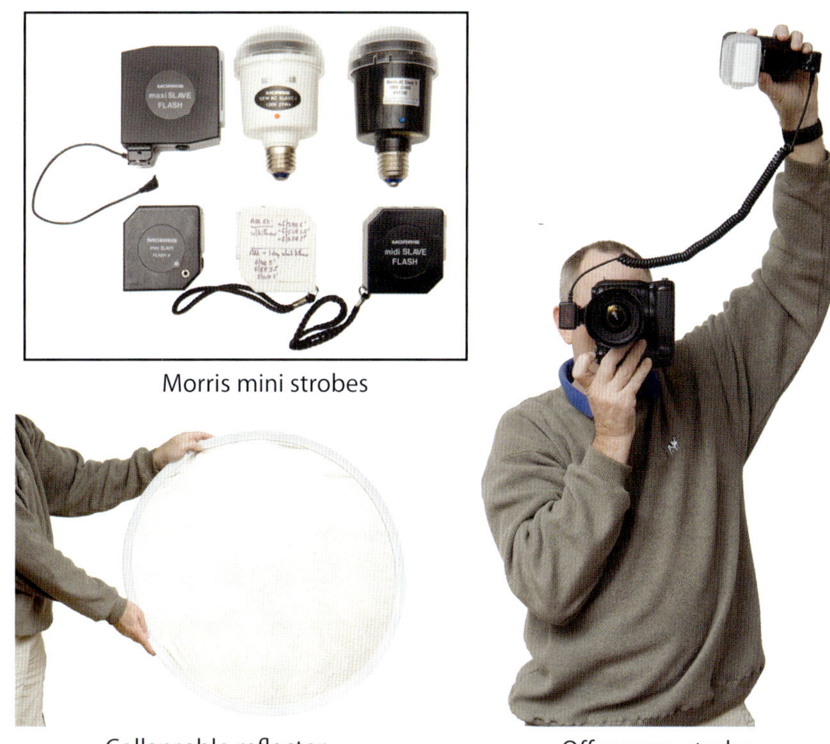

Morris mini strobes

Collapsable reflector

Off camera strobe

Fig. 12-14 Compact fill lighting tools are portable and easy to use.

Generally, it's best to avoid adding so much light that shadow areas are equal in brightness to the highlight areas, because your resulting image will look too artificial. Most photographers find that keeping shadow lighting a half or full stop below highlight intensity maintains a natural look to the scene, but still allows for the capture of good detail in highlight, mid tone, and shadow areas.

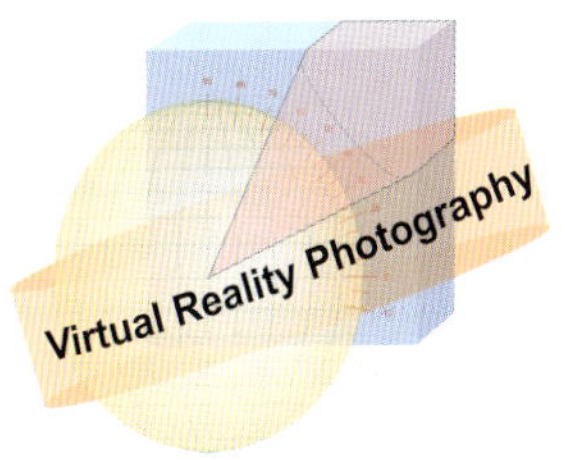

Chapter 13: Planning the Shoot

Good photography doesn't happen by accident. It usually requires good planning and attention to detail throughout. Even breaking news and unexpectedly "found" photographs require that one be sufficiently prepared to photograph them when these moments occur. We often hear others describing an amazing situation or scene they were a part of by saying, "If only I'd had a camera with me... I would have had a prize winning shot!"

What they really *mean* is, "If only I'd had a camera... *and* I had it up to my eye, *and* I had the right lens, focus, and exposure set, *and* I was in a good position, *and* I was able to frame the image well, *and* I had film in the camera, *and* my batteries were charged, *and* the flash went off properly, *and* that the guy in front of me didn't block my view, etc., etc..."

Every form of photography requires some sort of advance planning. Panoramic VR photography generally requires far more than traditional photography. Most interactive multimedia projects require even more than just a single panoramic image. The sequencing, continuity, transitions, effects such as sound, graphics, animations, and user interfaces must be planned ahead of time and coordinated with the photography efforts. VR multimedia projects often require the collaboration of many creators. In this regard, their production is similar to that of a motion picture or television program. They are best approached with a written plan or script

identifying each of these elements and how they will fit together, not only in specific scenes, but in the project overall.

Single Node Projects

The simplest VR projects are those that require just a single panoramic image. These include stand alone feature-type imagery, perhaps of a tourist destination, event, or real estate interior. Sometimes a web site or game developer will use a 360° panorama as an interactive portal for their viewers. On screen, the viewers pan around the scene and can click on a doorway, window, or other "hot spot," taking them to a sequence of related content.

Each position that you shoot a panoramic image from is called a **node** in VR production terminology. Thus, a single node is a single panorama photographed from a given position within a scene.

At first glance, it would seem that you could shoot single node projects with little or no preparation – after all, you really only need to put your camera and pan head on a tripod, and shoot the panorama from somewhere within the scene. This is the approach that many real estate VR photographers take, and they manage to produce perfectly acceptable images for what their market needs. However, the panoramas are generally little more than uninspired documentation of a home interior, and are considered throw away imagery once the house is sold.

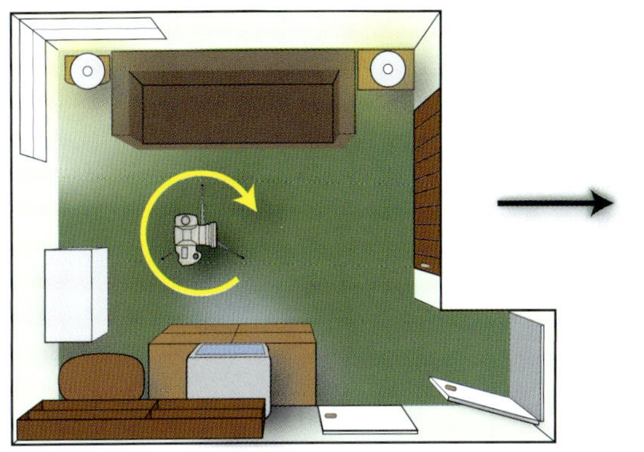

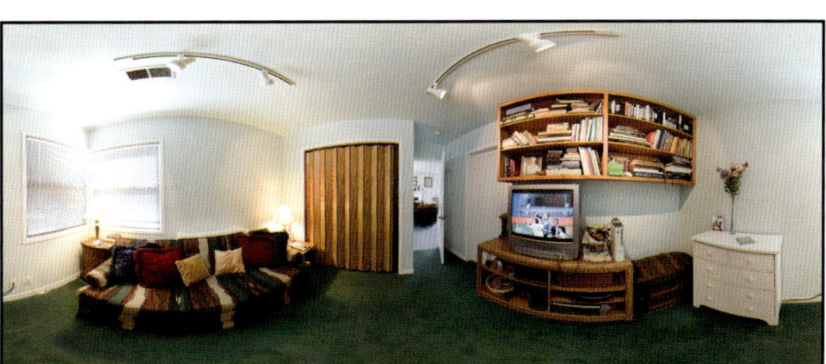

360° single node panorama

Fig. 13-1 A single node is a single panorama, which could represent the entire content of the simplest VR production.

These panoramas are often done with such haste that a photographer may shoot a dozen or more complete home tours in a single day. This volume is necessary for such work, as the real estate industry pays so little for these images – often between $5 and $10 per node.

Most pro photographers, however, care more about the quality of the work they create, and seek to produce compelling, quality imagery rather than throw away documentation. As with any effort, better results generally require more planning and preparation.

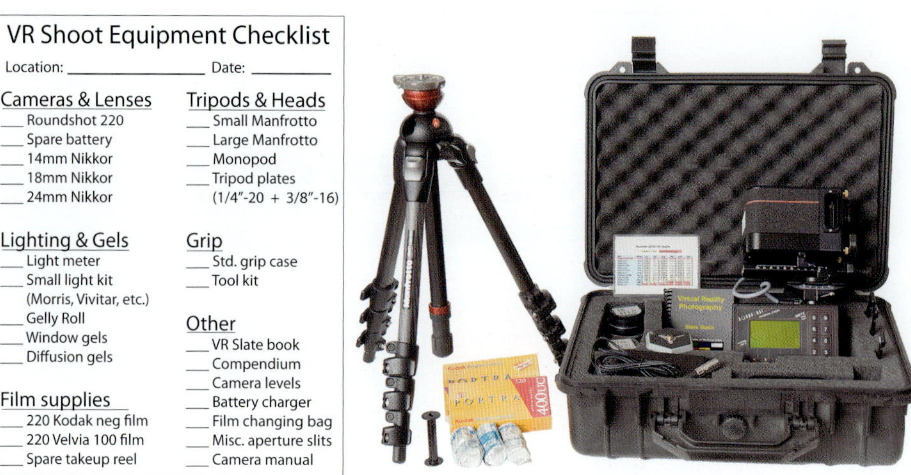

VR Shoot Equipment Checklist

Location: ________________   Date: ________

Cameras & Lenses
___ Roundshot 220
___ Spare battery
___ 14mm Nikkor
___ 18mm Nikkor
___ 24mm Nikkor

Lighting & Gels
___ Light meter
___ Small light kit
    (Morris, Vivitar, etc.)
___ Gelly Roll
___ Window gels
___ Diffusion gels

Film supplies
___ 220 Kodak neg film
___ 220 Velvia 100 film
___ Spare takeup reel

Tripods & Heads
___ Small Manfrotto
___ Large Manfrotto
___ Monopod
___ Tripod plates
    (1/4"-20 + 3/8"-16)

Grip
___ Std. grip case
___ Tool kit

Other
___ VR Slate book
___ Compendium
___ Camera levels
___ Battery charger
___ Film changing bag
___ Misc. aperture slits
___ Camera manual

Fig. 13-3 Equipment checklist and gear for a basic Roundshot 220VR shoot.

Even if you are shooting a single panorama on an assignment, you'll want to make sure you have everything you need for the job. If you can make at least one scouting visit to a location before you shoot, you will be better able to plan for equipment you'll need and how best to approach the assignment. This includes determining the best time of day for natural lighting, or whether supplemental lighting and color correction might be needed. When scouting is not possible, you still need to be prepared for surprises you might encounter.

One of the best ways to prepare is to create an equipment checklist that you go through as you're packing your gear. Even if you only use a single camera and lens for your VR photography, you'll want to have a checklist that reminds you about things like charged batteries, tripod pan head, film/digital media, proper camera function, etc.

Having an understanding before the shoot of what additional content and elements that will be linked to your panorama when published will also help you plan better for the shoot – particularly if you need to create the additional content while you are on location.

For example, your assignment might be to shoot a single panorama of a hotel lobby for a hotel's web site. However, the web designers are planning to add a variety of hotspot links from your panorama, which they may also need content for. These might include an exterior view of the hotel, so that when a user clicks on the front door, they are shown the exterior view. Or perhaps a link will be created to an online registration center when the user clicks on the front desk in your panorama. Clicking on the elevator doors may take the viewer to descriptions and pictures of the various rooms available, while links from other parts of the lobby may take the viewer to images of the hotel's fitness facilities, conference rooms, and restaurants (perhaps even including menus and price lists). Clicking on the concierge's desk might bring up a short welcome video from the hotel manager/staff, as well as information about surrounding attractions. Perhaps the gift shop in your panorama will link to studio product shots of souvenir and hospitality items available at the store.

While you may not be responsible for photographing these additional images yourself, you will need to know what the producers have planned so that when you create your panoramas, you can make sure that these subjects or link areas are appropriately featured in it. These kinds of details may help determine

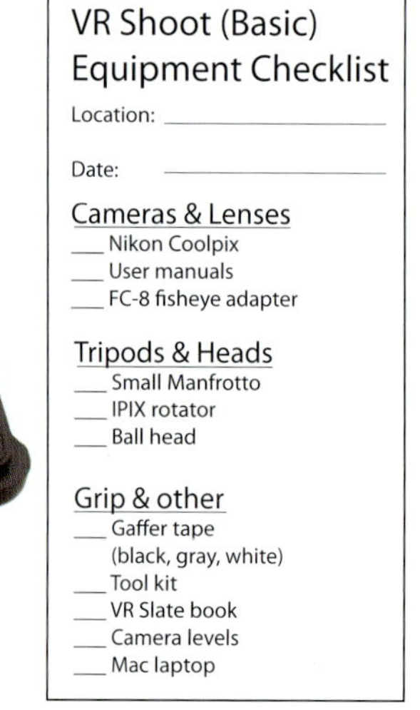

VR Shoot (Basic)
Equipment Checklist

Location: ________________

Date: ________

Cameras & Lenses
___ Nikon Coolpix
___ User manuals
___ FC-8 fisheye adapter

Tripods & Heads
___ Small Manfrotto
___ IPIX rotator
___ Ball head

Grip & other
___ Gaffer tape
    (black, gray, white)
___ Tool kit
___ VR Slate book
___ Camera levels
___ Mac laptop

Fig. 13-2 Equipment checklist and gear for a simple digital panorama shoot.

Technical Note: VR Photography Slate Book

Keeping track of what you've shot, where you shot it, and all the technical information necessary in order to allow proper post production of your panoramas is almost impossible if you don't write this information down somewhere. This is particularly important when you do projects requiring more than a single panoramic image.

Motion picture and television productions always use a slate (usually with a clapper or electronic marker for sound synchronization) placed in front of the camera at the beginning of every take, in order to identify the shot, scene, location, and other technical information that will be needed for identifying or sequencing the footage in post production.

VR photography, with its many variables, can be just as complex, particularly when shooting multiple nodes over many days and multiple projects. A written record of your shooting information can be critical for post production, as well.

A low cost, pocket-sized VR Photography Slate Book is available that allows you to record the information about the shoot. The slate pages and a fold-over color target are photographed under the same lighting conditions as your subject for the first frame of your image sequence. The color target provides a reference for color corrections in post production, and the slate information provides stitching, sequencing, and continuity data. The back of each page can be used for notes, diagrams, and node mapping.

The slate pages can either be removed from the book and kept with processed film or digital files, or they can be retained within the book as a journal of your shoots. The book also includes reference tables for fields of view (fov), hyperfocal distances (for maximizing depth of field), model and property release forms, and a variety of other helpful information.

The VR Photography Slate Book is available from **www.vrphotography.com**

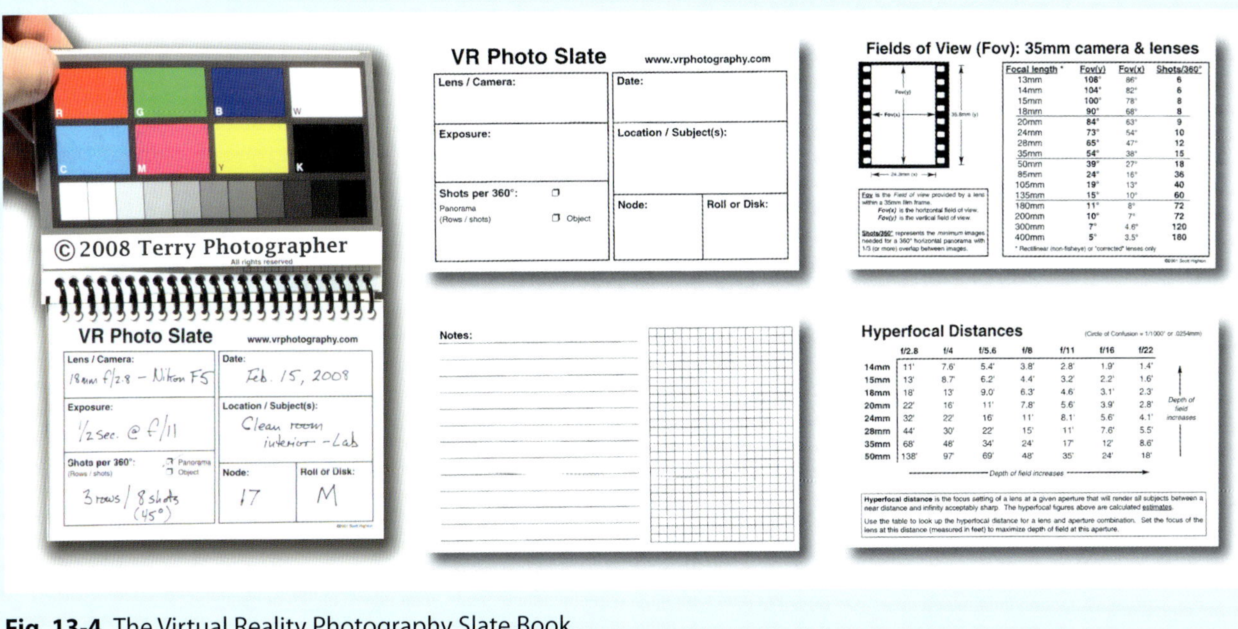

Focal length *	Fov(y)	Fov(x)	Shots/360°
13mm	108°	86°	6
14mm	104°	82°	6
15mm	100°	78°	8
18mm	90°	68°	8
20mm	84°	63°	9
24mm	73°	54°	10
28mm	65°	47°	12
35mm	54°	38°	15
50mm	39°	27°	18
85mm	24°	16°	36
105mm	19°	13°	40
135mm	15°	10°	60
180mm	11°	8°	72
200mm	10°	7°	72
300mm	7°	4.6°	120
400mm	5°	3.5°	180

Hyperfocal Distances

(Circle of Confusion = 1/1000' or .0254mm)

	f/2.8	f/4	f/5.6	f/8	f/11	f/16	f/22
14mm	11'	7.6'	5.4'	3.8'	2.8'	1.9'	1.4'
15mm	13'	8.7'	6.2'	4.4'	3.2'	2.2'	1.6'
18mm	18'	13'	9.0'	6.3'	4.6'	3.1'	2.3'
20mm	22'	16'	11'	7.8'	5.6'	3.9'	2.8'
24mm	32'	22'	16'	11'	8.1'	5.6'	4.1'
28mm	44'	30'	22'	15'	11'	7.6'	5.5'
35mm	68'	48'	34'	24'	17'	12'	8.6'
50mm	138'	97'	69'	48'	35'	24'	18'

Fig. 13-4 The Virtual Reality Photography Slate Book.

where you position your camera, or even the time of day that you shoot. You'll want to know as much as possible about what is needed before you arrive. Then plan your shooting schedule and equipment needs accordingly.

Multi Node Projects

Production demands tend to get exponentially more complicated when you do multi-node projects, where you create multiple panoramas, object movies, and other media, along with necessary links, transitions, user interfaces, and other programming elements. Consider the complexity of producing a video/film program. Add to that all the possible story paths, junctures, and links that become necessary when you make that same program interactive so that the viewer can choose alternate directions at various points along the way. This is effectively what you may need to plan for when you photograph and produce multi-node VR projects.

Let's expand the single-node hotel assignment described previously into a multi-node production. We might replace the various information and still image links with additional panoramas or object movies. For example, when your viewers clicked on the hotel entrance in the first panorama, they would link to another panorama shot from the hotel exterior, rather than just a still photo of the hotel facade. Once in this exterior panorama, they could look around in all directions, and might even be able to click on additional hot spots to move up or down the block. They might even hear ambient street sounds in the background. This exterior panorama must then be linked back to the initial panorama inside the hotel lobby, so viewers can walk back inside on your virtual tour.

Once inside, clicking on a link to the restaurant or gift shop would take them to interactive panoramas inside those spaces, rather than to still images or simple graphics. In the gift shop, clicking on a souvenir item would link to an interactive object movie of that product, showing it from any angle, perhaps with its functions animated. (Object movies are discussed in **Section 3**.)

As you can imagine, the number of links back and forth between each of these nodes, along with the content required for them, increases significantly with each element added. So planning and preparation must be extremely thorough *before* shooting ever begins.

In general, you will want to map the layout of the scene you will be shooting and determine exactly how many different nodes or panoramas you'll need to effectively cover the scene for your viewers. These should be identified and numbered on your layout, along with other links you'll want, and this layout should be used as a guide for your shooting efforts.

Often, you will find that you make changes when you are actually on location. You may discover that you can get away with fewer nodes in one part of the scene, or that you may need more in another. Unless you are working from a written plan, you will invariably overlook one or more critical elements, and that can result in a very costly reshoot.

Continuity

In multi-node shoots, it is important to maintain continuity, which is the consistency between your panoramas and their various links. This means that you'll want to keep lighting and exposure relatively constant, and that you'll need to shoot related nodes under similar conditions. For example, if you shoot your interior nodes with bright daylight views through the windows, you will probably want to shoot the building exteriors during the day as well, rather than at night. Similarly, if the interior panoramas revealed night time views through all the windows, the exterior nodes should probably also be presented as night time views. If you jump too often between different conditions, the changes can be distracting for the viewer.

Of course, it is not always possible to perfectly match lighting and exposure throughout a scene, particularly when the shoot involves dozens or more nodes over multiple shooting days. In these instances, one should plan the photography accordingly. For example, you might be able to shoot the exteriors during "magic hour" light (the hour before sunset or the hour after sunrise)

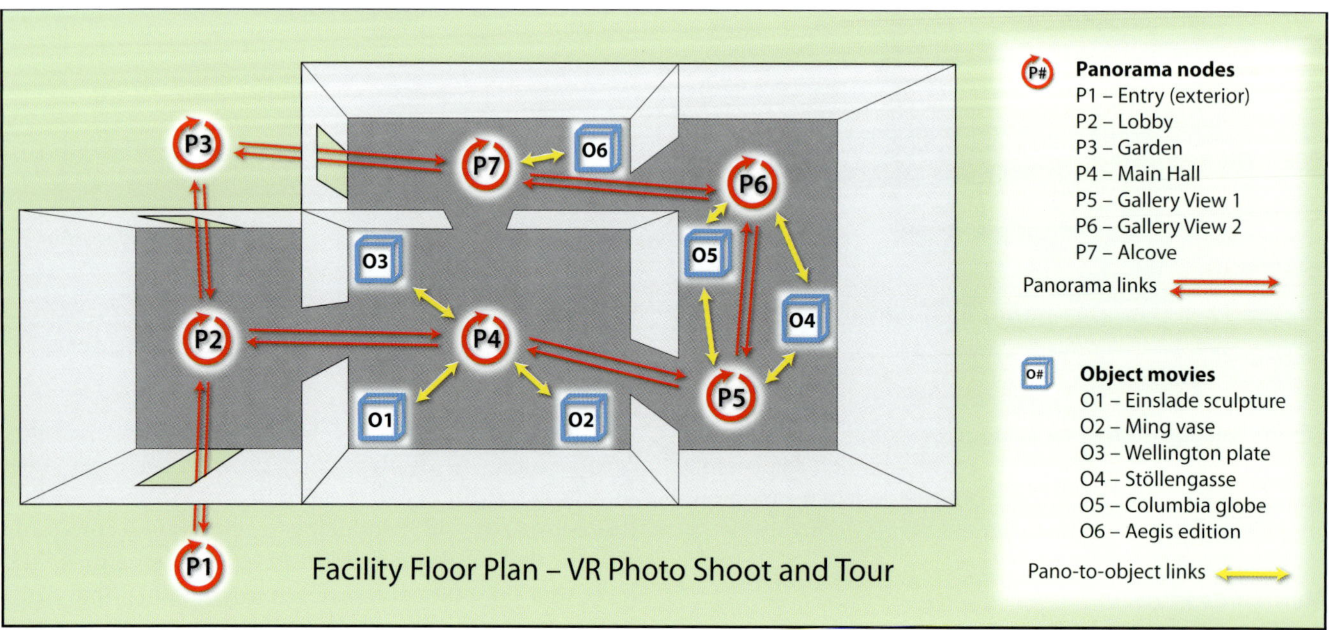

Fig. 13-5 Shooting diagram and floor plan for a multi-node scene with panoramas, object movies, and transitions.

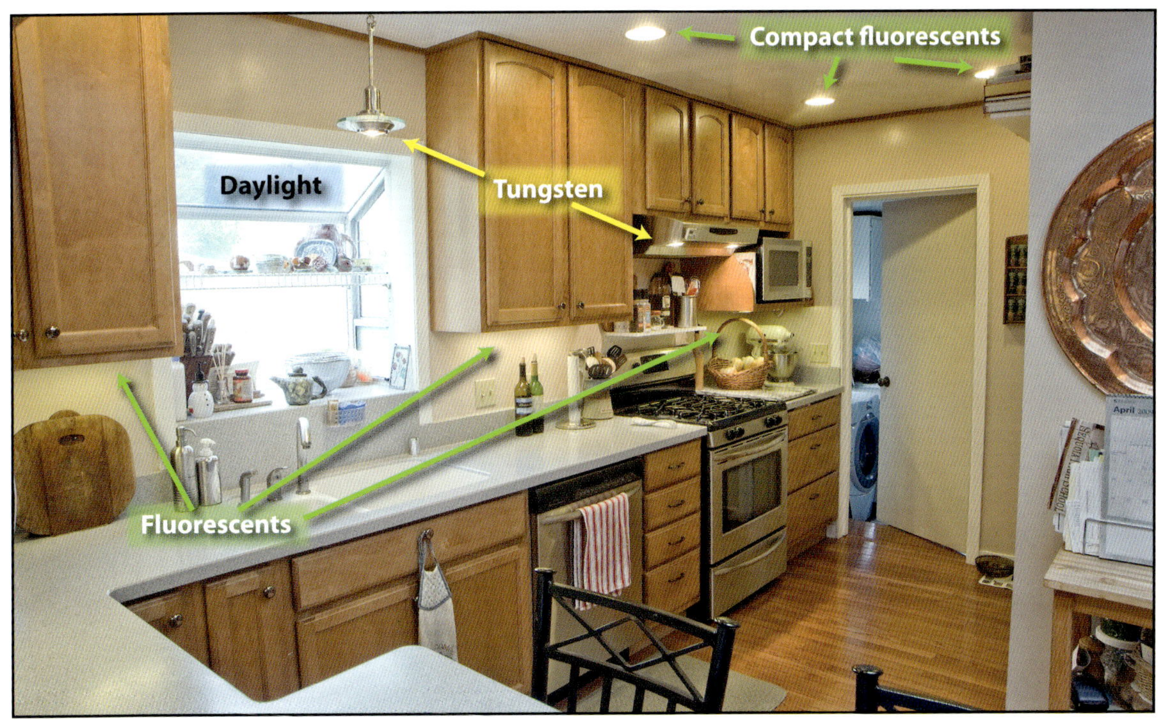

Mixed lighting combinations

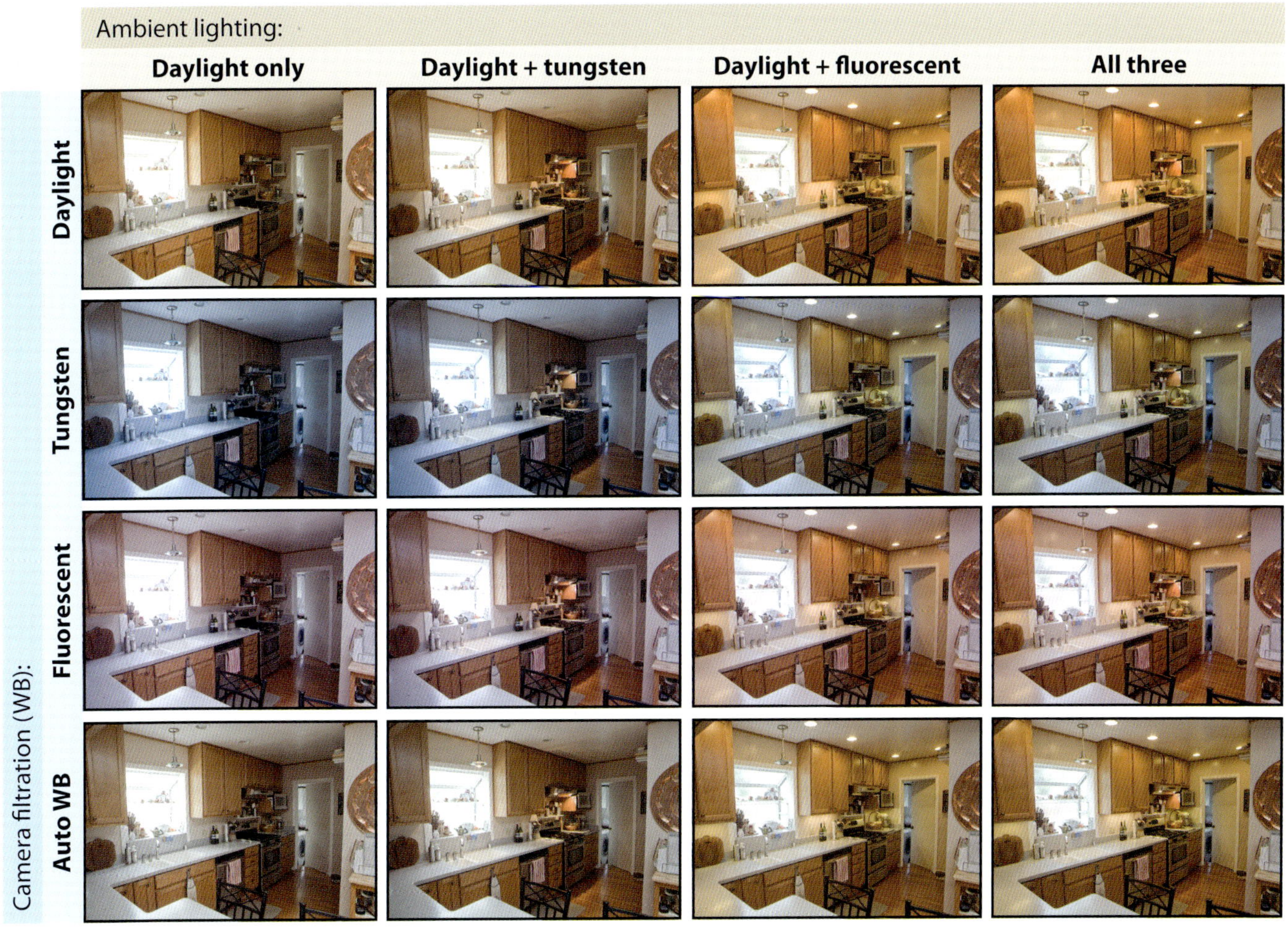

Ambient lighting:

	Daylight only	Daylight + tungsten	Daylight + fluorescent	All three
Daylight				
Tungsten				
Fluorescent				
Auto WB				

Camera filtration (WB):

Fig. 13-6 Comparison chart of common white balance (WB) settings when photographing a mixed lighting environment.

and the interiors that include window/door views during daylight hours. Deep interior nodes, where only artificial lighting is found, can be shot at night, since they won't be affected by daylight or darkness outside anyway.

Consider also how you might transition through a series of nodes with different types of lighting or color balances. If the dominant light in a room is tungsten based, and you filter your lens or adjust your camera color balance for this, any daylight coming through the windows will be rendered far more blue than it should, and may look unnatural. Similarly, if the primary light in the room is daylight coming through the windows and you color balance for this, tungsten lights in the room will appear far more yellow than you might like. (See discussion of Color Balance in **Chapter 6**.)

You can spend a lot of time and money putting color correction gels over windows and interior lights in order to match their color balances, and this may be necessary when color accuracy is critical. However, often if you simply expose and color balance for the *dominant* light in the scene, the "off color" or less dominant light sources may well be perceived as natural by the viewer.

In order to aid the transition from a node color balanced for one type of lighting to a node with another, it is sometimes helpful to add an additional node between them that splits the color balance difference. This makes the change less abrupt for views as they navigate through the tour, and is less likely to call their attention to the lighting change.

How Long Will It Take?

Figuring out how much time to budget for a VR shoot is a skill that comes with experience. While 10 panoramas a day is often used as a rule of thumb by professionals, there are many variables that can skew that figure significantly one way or another. Some low end real estate photographers can shoot 40-50 panoramas in a day (at 8-10 different locations) because they use an automated process and don't worry much about lighting or aesthetic concerns. On the other hand, I once photographed the interior of a NASA wind tunnel, which required three days of preparation and shooting, with a crew of assistants, just to photograph a single panorama. This shoot required extensive lighting and access into normally inaccessible areas, along with close cooperation with NASA staff. We even had to repaint and restore part of the tunnel interior.

This is why it is good to make at least one scouting trip to a location when planning your shoot. It will give you a better chance to anticipate what challenges you might face, and to plan for what equipment you might need. Also, if you are doing the shoot professionally for a client, you will need a solid grasp of the challenges you might encounter up front so you can accurately estimate your service fees.

Other Concerns – Releases and Permissions

There are a number of issues that every photographer should be aware of, particularly if you are doing VR photography professionally.   These issues are often overlooked by those just starting out, because they are

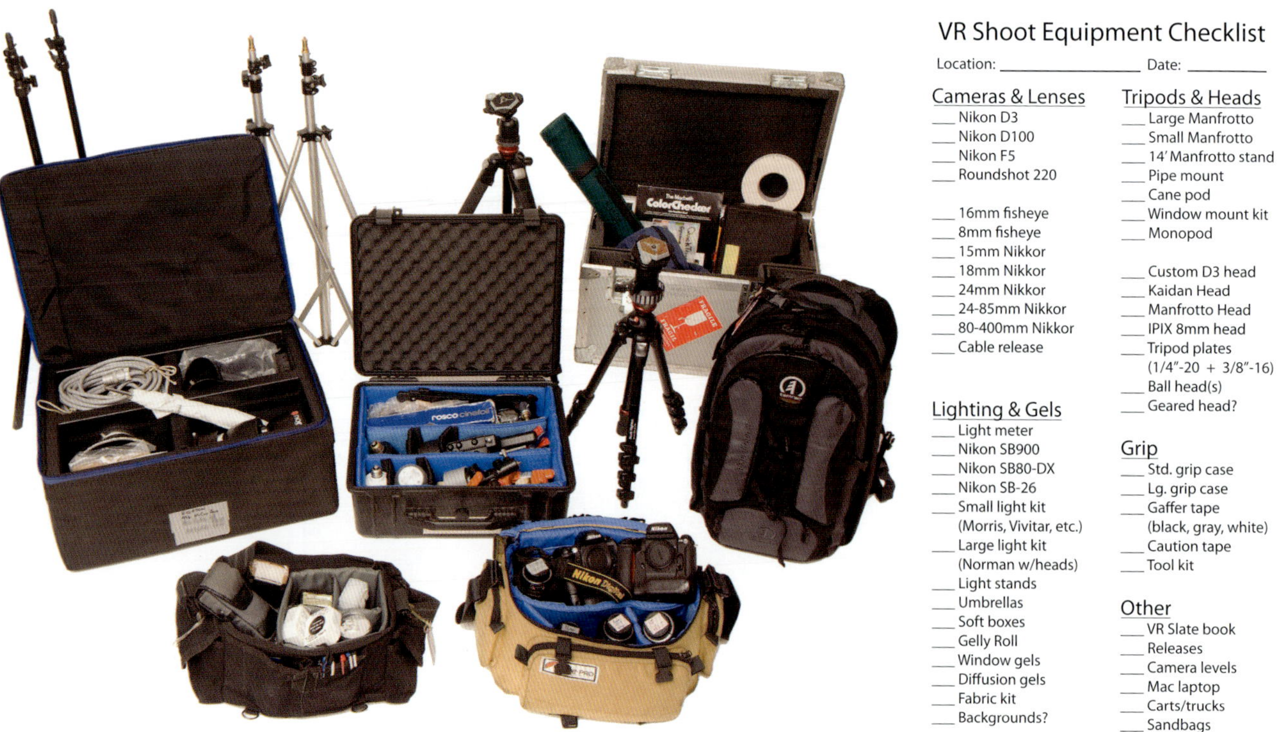

Fig. 13-7 Sample equipment and checklist for a commercial panoramic VR shoot. Note critical equipment redundancies.

Photo Release

I, _________________________________, do hereby grant permission for
Print name
display, reproduction and publication of photographs taken of me on the following
date(s): _________________________________ in any medium. I affirm that I am 18 or
Print date(s)
more years of age and authorized to grant such permission(s).

Signature: _________________________ Date: _________________________

Print name: _________________________ Witness: _________________________

Guardian's Consent (*if under 18*): I am the parent or legal guardian of the above-mentioned individual. I hereby approve the foregoing, and consent to use of the photographs subject to the terms above.

Signature: ____

Property Photo Release

I, _________________________________, do hereby grant permission for
Print name
display, reproduction and publication of photographs taken of my property (described
below) on the following date(s): _________________________________ in any medium. I
Print date(s)
affirm that I am 18 or more years of age and authorized to grant such permission(s).

Signature: _________________________ Date: _________________________

Print name: _________________________ Witness: _________________________

Property Description: (subject, location, etc.) _________________________
____
____

Fig. 13-8 Sample photo (model) and property release forms.

far less interesting than actually making good pictures. But they are no less important to your business.

The first of these is securing permission to photograph your subjects and the locations. This should generally be done *before* you begin shooting, and is best accomplished with a written Property Release or a Photo/Model Release. Laws relating to the need for such releases vary widely from country to country, and even by how the resulting photographs are used. However, the process of getting a signed release forces the photographer to formally engage subjects and property owners by making it clear what his or her intent is in photographing them. The written document helps avoid misunderstandings and possible legal actions later on.

A release can be a simple form that the subject signs authorizing the photographer to publish (or extend publication rights to others) images the photographer creates of the subject during that shoot. Keep in mind that "publishing" is no longer limited solely to print reproduction, but also includes public display and all forms of electronic distribution such as web sites, CD/DVD discs, television, phone transmittal, and even e-mail.

There are times when releases are probably not necessary, such as when you are photographing a public place and when individuals are not visually identifiable. For example, if you are shooting a panorama of a city skyline, it is unlikely that you would need a property release from the owner of every building before you publish the image. Likewise, if there were a crowd of people in your foreground watching a parade, you probably wouldn't need releases from every one of them. However, if you are shooting on private property, it's best to have written permission to publish the work from the owner(s). Similarly, if your images include people who might be recognizable and you plan to publish these images, it is best to secure a photo or model release from those individuals. Be aware that some government agencies that oversee public lands now demand photo permit fees *and* require that you have their written permission

for commercial use of photography done on these properties. When in doubt, check to see what's required before shooting. There's nothing worse than having an important shoot terminated by a park ranger simply because you failed to secure a shooting permit ahead of time. Many times, these permits are available at little or no cost.

Keep in mind that it's almost impossible to absolutely protect yourself against every possible legal threat, so focus on what is practical, and err on the side of caution. Since neither the author nor the publisher of this book are legal experts, we cannot give legal advice. Please consult with a qualified legal professional for advice and recommendations for your own situations.

Safety and Insurance

When you are photographing in either public or private locations, your activities are likely to have an impact on others, particularly as your projects become more complicated. Tripod legs and lighting stands can mar the surfaces they are set on, equipment can fall over, and unsuspecting individuals can trip over your gear. Unfortunately, accidents do happen.

Safety should always be the primary concern on any photo shoot. That includes not only the safety of the photographer and crew, but of everyone else who might be around. This means that the photographer must be constantly vigilant to keep cords and gear out of the way, to make sure equipment cases are not left open or in precarious positions, and that safety equipment, such as orange vehicle cones, warning tape, harnesses, and equipment "keepers" are all used when appropriate. With proper attention to safety both before and during the shoot, accidents can be minimized. This is yet another argument for a preliminary scouting visit before a shoot, so that any safety concerns can be addressed and planned for ahead of time.

Liability insurance becomes a necessity when you work as a photographer professionally. If an accident happens during a shoot, those who were injured or had property damaged may seek to recover damages. Insuring yourself against such claims becomes important, not only to protect your personal and business assets, but those of your client(s), as well. In today's overly litigious society, plaintiffs and their attorneys will seek compensation from anyone even remotely associated with an accident. Since most photographers do not run million dollar businesses, attorneys will also go after the "deep pockets" of the clients we may be working for on the assignment.

Many public agencies in the U.S., including the National Park Service, require that commercial photographers provide a certificate of insurance naming that agency as a co-insured party, before they will issue a permit or give permission for commercial photography to be done on their lands.

Liability insurance policies for photographers are generally available through professional organizations such as the American Society of Media Photographers (ASMP), the Advertising Photographers of America (APA), and the National Press Photographers Association (NPPA), as well as other organizations internationally. Some common insurance carriers can also add riders to personal policies that cover certain liabilities, as well as photo equipment.

Remember however, that proper preparation and ongoing diligence is your best protection. Prevention of an accident is far better than having to deal with the results of one after the fact, no matter how well you might be insured and no matter how minimal your responsibility might have been.

Case Study: The Masco Virtual Showhome

The following case study was written in the late 1990s, only a few years after QuickTime VR was first released to the public. It describes both the shooting techniques of the time, as well as the general approach to planning and photography of a large VR project for a major corporate client – much of which remains applicable today.

In the fall of 1995, the author collaborated with RDC Interactive to photograph and produce a virtual tour CD of a luxury show home in Columbia, MD for the Masco Corporation.

Masco is the parent company of a number of well-known home product companies such as Baldwin,

Delta, Drexel Heritage, and Thermador. For many years, Masco built a multi-million dollar show home near the site of the National Association of Home Builders (NAHB) annual convention to showcase the products of its various companies. During these conventions, Masco would transport attendees to and from the convention hall to the latest show home site, where attendees would walk through the home, see the company's products in place, and pick up printed literature. The costs for doing this every year were significant for Masco.

Terry Beaubois and Greg Miller are the principals of RDC Interactive, based in Palo Alto, CA. They are both professional architects who saw the value of multimedia information design for their architecture clients and the industry in general. They began working with QuickTime VR during its early development at Apple, and had been looking for an opportunity to use it in a major commercial architectural project. They recognized the tremendous benefits that an interactive electronic product could bring to a company like Masco, and after a series of meetings, secured a contract to produce an interactive virtual show home on CD.

The result was the fully interactive, cross-platform Masco Virtual Showhome CD-ROM, produced and delivered by RDC Interactive in a remarkably short period of three months. At the 1996 NAHB

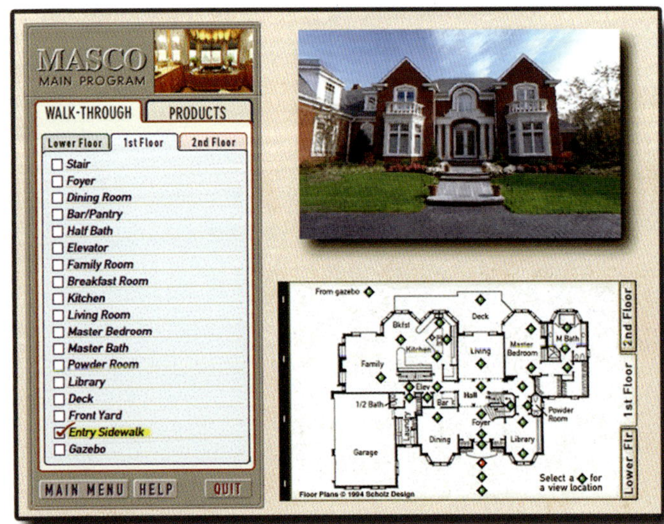

Fig. 13-9 The Masco Virtual Showhome CD user interface.

convention, Masco presented the CD on large projection screens in its booth on the trade show floor. In addition to the interactive VR tour, the CD also contained detailed product information and photographs of Masco products within the home, including a number of VR object movies of such products as door knobs, bath tubs, and sinks. The content was presented within an elegant and intuitive custom user interface designed by RDC Interactive.

NAHB attendees visiting the Masco booth viewed the virtual tour on the trade show floor, rather than having to ride a bus back and forth to a remote site from the convention center, and each of them left with a copy of the CD. Masco saved the costs of printing thousands of traditional brochures, as well as the costs of building another show home for that year's convention *and* transporting attendees back and forth from the convention. Attendees were grateful to have all the Masco product information available electronically on a disc that they took away, and for not having to carry the weight of countless printed brochures and other collateral throughout the convention itself.

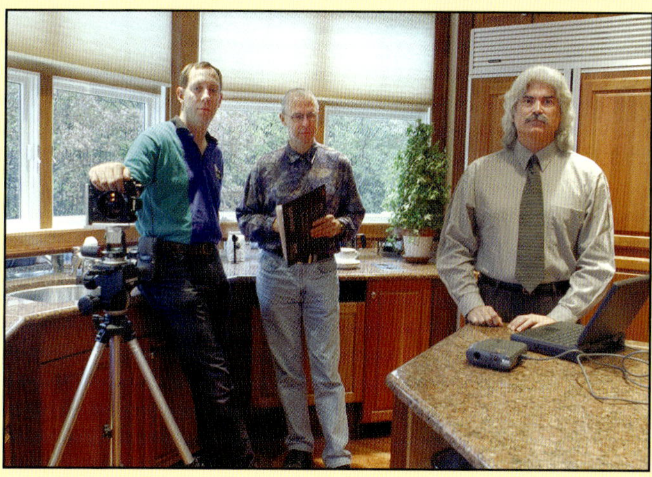

Fig. 13-11 The production team on location (1996): Scott Highton, Roger East, and Terry Beaubois.

Details of the Photo Shoot

I was originally contacted by the folks at RDC Interactive because of my work photographing the Apple Company Store VR tour that accompanied Apple's original QuickTime VR Authoring Tools Suite in 1994. RDC and I had collaborated on a couple of smaller VR projects previously, and it seemed natural for us to work together on the Masco project. RDC was known for its excellent user interface and information design, and I embrace opportunities to work with companies where our talents and skills combine so well.

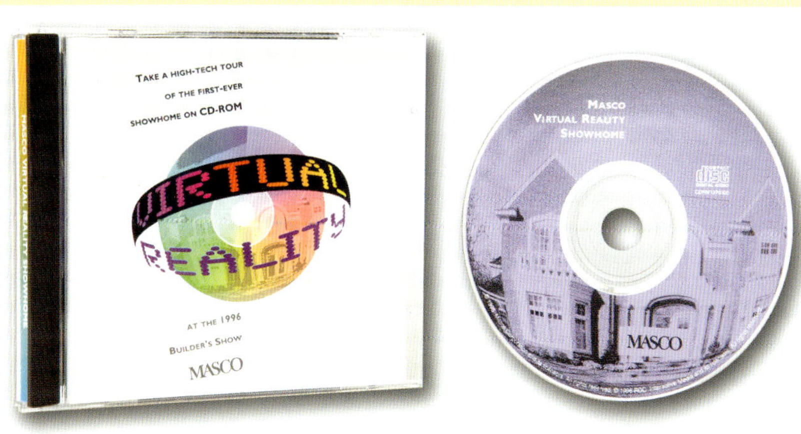

Fig. 13-10 The Masco Virtual Showhome CD.

Masco agreed to make one of their existing show homes in Columbia, MD available for us to photograph several months prior to the NAHB convention. We were given three days to do the shoot. We planned to photograph 61 panoramic nodes, as well as a variety of other sequences (such as a stop-frame animation of the elevator interior as it moved between the three floors of the home). We created a shot list based on the architectural floor plan, which we used to catalog and map the project both during the shoot and in post production. We did not have the luxury of a scouting trip prior to the shoot, but were able to get a few interior photos of the house from Masco, which helped me to better consider the lighting challenges that we might face.

It is estimated that the virtual show home project saved the Masco Corporation about one million dollars that year over their traditional practices of building a new show home and shuttling attendees back and forth.

The Masco CD was intended to serve the company for about six months, but it proved so valuable that it was kept in distribution for several years. Today, it remains one of the premiere examples of successful commercial interactive media ever done.

Masco and RDC demanded nothing less than the high quality look of traditional architectural

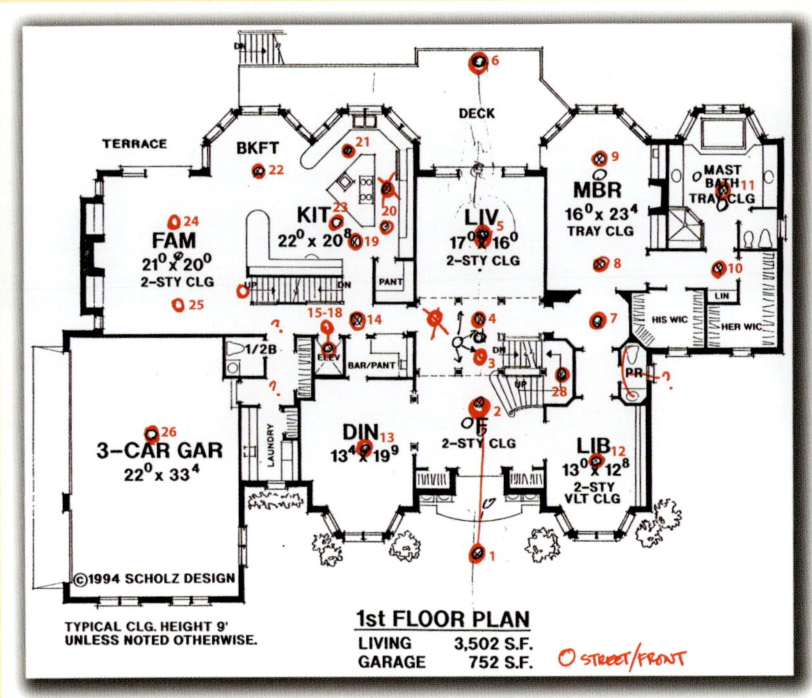

Fig. 13-12 Our shooting diagram for the first floor with each panoramic node mapped out. Note that some nodes were deleted during the location shooting process. Two other floors were similarly mapped in pre-production.

depending upon average light levels for every node. Each panorama required 12 shots, or one every 30°, plus an additional shot of the information slate and color target, which were critical for post production organization and work flow.

I chose an ISO 100 Kodak daylight balanced negative film for maximum exposure latitude, and placed either blue 80A or 80B gels behind the lens to color balance the scene when the predominant interior lighting was tungsten based.

Unfortunately, the weather forecast for the three shooting days was for heavy overcast and rain, but we took advantage of unexpected sunny skies on the morning of the first day to shoot the

photography in the VR panoramas. This sort of work usually requires that interior photographs be shot in a five to 10 minute period surrounding dawn or dusk in order to balance the light levels from the exterior windows with the interior lighting of the home.

However, it was not physically possible to photograph 61 panoramas with this balanced lighting in the three shooting days we had available. Furthermore, it would have been prohibitively expensive (and time consuming) to install neutral density gels over every window in the house in order to balance the exposures manually. Our solution was to digitally composite properly exposed window views into the window areas of each panorama in post production. This was the most cost effective means for solving this problem.

I shot 40 rolls of 35mm negative film (close to 1,200 individual shots) during our three days on location. The panoramas were all captured using a Nikon F3 camera and 15mm Nikkor lens (the widest rectilinear lens Nikon made at the time). These were single-row cylindrical panoramas, as that was all that QuickTime supported at the time. Lens aperture was usually set at f/8, and shutter speed was varied

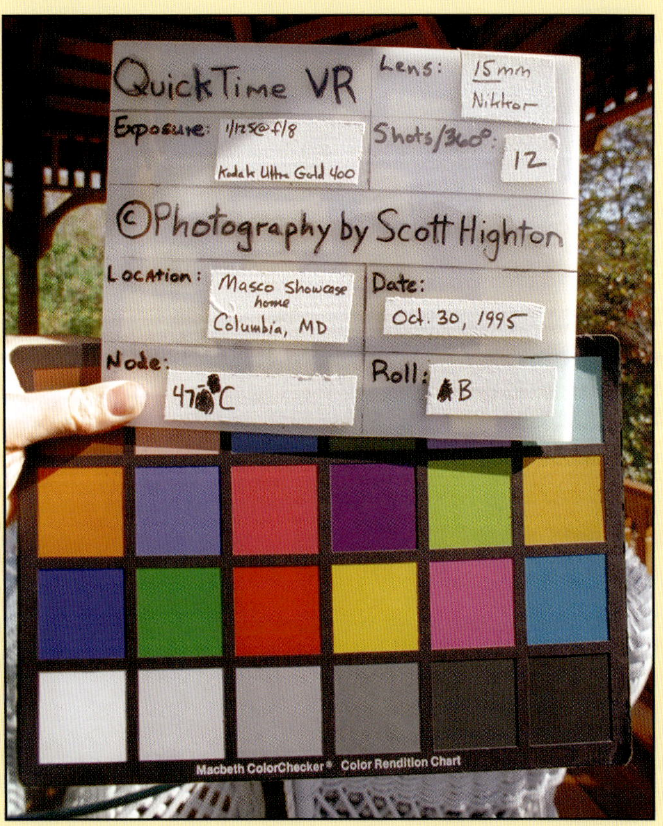

Fig. 13-13 A home made slate and Macbeth color chart were shot at the beginning of each panorama series to aid in post production.

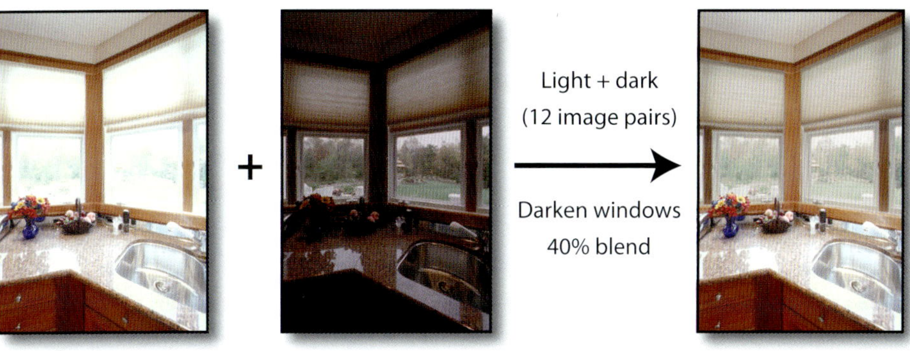

Panorama result

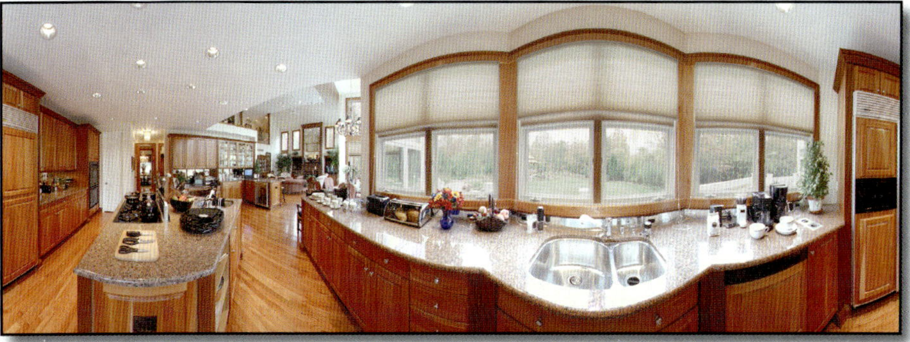

Fig. 13-14 Correcting window exposures required blending and compositing a second set of darkened image scans with the properly exposed interiors.

already had a long term relationship with a local PhotoCD service provider near my office, so they were aware of the unique needs of film scanning for VR production. These included the development of custom film terms and the ability to turn *off* the PhotoCD scene balancing algorithm (SBA). PhotoCD software normally defaults to having SBA on when scanning negative film. The SBA adjusts color balance and exposure for every frame, resulting in nicely exposed individual shots. But this is a disaster for VR

exterior panoramas. The ensuing overcast actually helped us during the remaining days when we shot the interior panoramas, as it kept the exterior light to within about five stops of the interior light levels (during bright mid-day sun, this difference might normally exceed eight or nine stops). The exposure range between exterior highlights and interior shadows remained well within the exposure latitude of the negative film.

A critical element to the success of the shoot was scanning the film for post production assembly. I

sequences, where it is critical to keep exposures and color balance constant for groups of source images for each panorama.

One of the limitations of most film scanners is that they cannot, in a single scan, capture the full exposure latitude that negative film is capable of recording. Therefore, digitizing the full range of exposure data captured by our film sometimes required two different scans – one set for the interior exposures and the second for the much brighter exterior scenes through the windows. We scanned

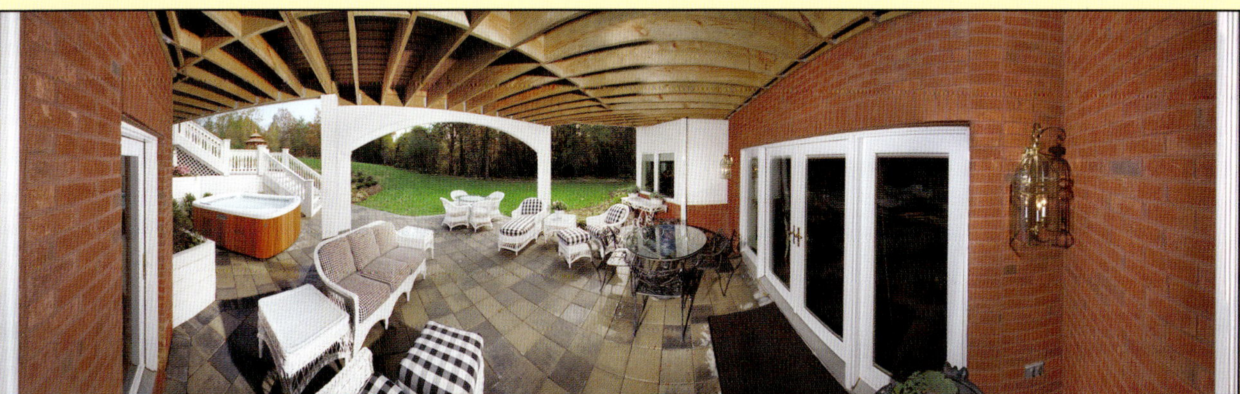

Fig. 13-15 Fill lighting was required for the dark area under the back patio deck in order to balance it with the bright yard exterior. Otherwise, supplemental lighting was kept to a minimum during the shoot due to time constraints.

approximately 1,200 individual frames, and then rescanned about 150 of these at darker exposure levels to adjust window views. The darker scans were then masked and blended into the window areas of the panoramas to make the final images. Using the same frames of film scanned at different exposures allowed for more precise post production alignment when compositing the images than shooting two separate exposures. Every time a camera is touched on a tripod, it is moved slightly, which can result in misalignments and compositing headaches in post production.

While I did take several cases of studio lighting on the shoot, we wound up using very little of it. Most of the panoramas were shot using available light – a combination of exterior daylight and interior tungsten lighting. I did use a portable strobe unit for fill lighting on a few of the panoramas, such as an outdoor patio area underneath an overhead deck. This was necessary in order to balance the lower light levels in the shadows with those of the adjacent hot tub and yard that were in full daylight.

We were fortunate in that the utility areas of the home – such as the garage, laundry room and gymnasium, which were lit with fluorescent lighting, were not included in the shoot list for the project (they did not include Masco Corporation products). I had brought several rolls of fluorescent color correction gel for this type of lighting just in case there was a change of plan during the shoot. Had we needed to photograph these areas, the extensive installation of gels to match the fluorescent *and* tungsten lighting to the daylight balanced film and exterior window light probably would have required another full day of preparation time and shooting.

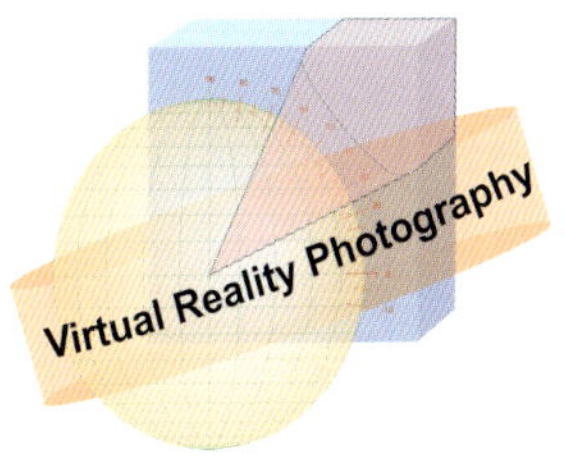

Chapter 14: Advanced Techniques

Once you have mastered the basic techniques of panoramic VR photography, you're likely to want to push your limits and "break the rules" a bit. As long as you have a good technical foundation and understand the mechanics of why things are generally done the way they are, you can build on that experience and try new things. Keep in mind that these efforts will be experimental, and that you may meet with many failures. It is best to test such techniques on your own before counting on them when results are critical or for paid client work.

Varying Exposure

There are times when it might be to your advantage to adjust the exposure between source frames of a panorama, rather than to keep the exposure locked throughout. The instances where this will work are more rare than one might think, and they generally require that there be at least two uniform transition areas along the vertical axis within the complete panorama. Planning for this technique also requires that you have plenty of experience using your chosen stitching software, so you know how it handles blending between source images, and that you can visualize these blends as you shoot.

In general, you will want to avoid varying exposure when you have areas of continuous tone subject matter along the horizontal or panning axis of your panorama.

This would include large expanses of sky, grass, fields, walls, floors, and ceilings, among others. The viewer's eye expects these sorts of areas to remain consistent in both their color and density, and to only vary naturally based on lighting intensity and direction.

Photographing a room interior with bright windows on one side and dark shadows on the other, is a situation where your life could be much easier if you could simply adjust the camera's exposure as you pan. However, when the overall exposure changes, so too do the recorded color densities of the walls, ceiling, and floors, which give an unnatural looking result to a stitched panorama. This is why we usually shoot panoramas with a constant exposure, and either use fill lighting to brighten the dark areas, or make selective adjustments digitally in post production.

However, if there are transition areas that comprise the entire vertical field of view within the panorama, it is possible to make exposure adjustments as you shoot and then take advantage of the blending abilities of your stitching software to make these changes appear natural.

I utilized this technique for several panoramas on the Masco Virtual Showhome project that had extreme contrasts in lighting levels. While this wasn't possible

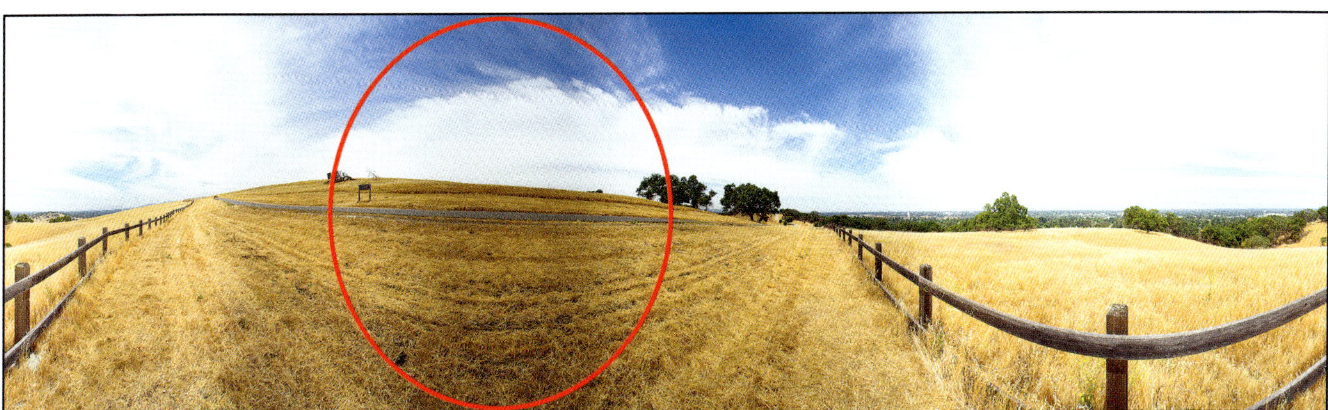

Fig. 14-1 Changing camera exposure during a panorama sequence usually causes distracting light or dark regions in the assembled panorama, as illustrated above. Yet under the right circumstances, intentionally changing exposure settings mid-sequence *can* work to the photographer's advantage.

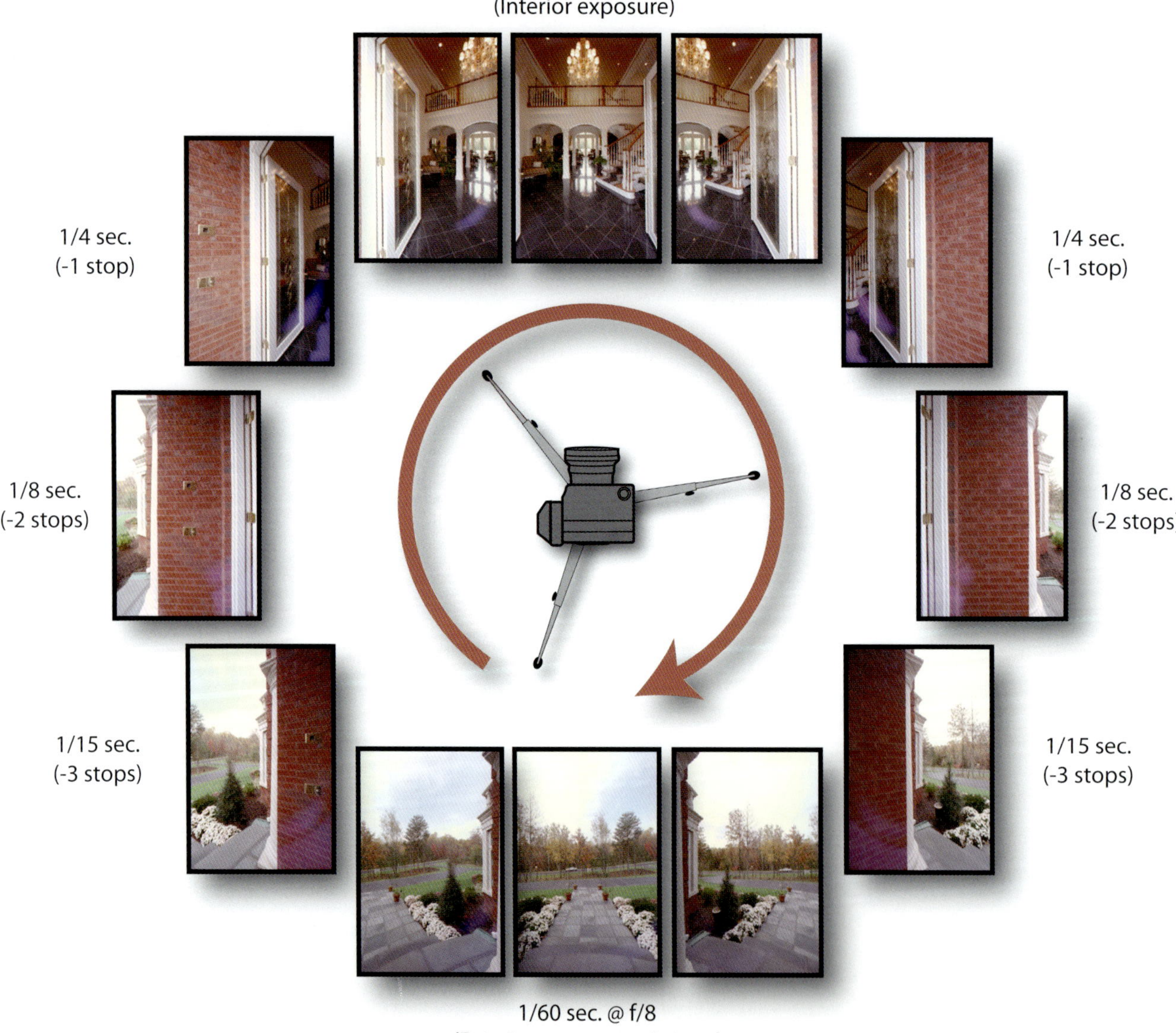

Fig. 14-2 Gradual exposure adjustments through multiple image elements in the above panorama sequence made it possible to make the dark interior and bright exterior of the show home look balanced, even though there was at least a four-stop exposure difference. Shutter speed was adjusted one stop through each of four sequential images on both sides of the panorama, and the stitching software smoothly blended the transition areas.

for every panorama that contained bright window views, it did apply to those that didn't have ceilings or floors requiring constant exposure throughout the horizontal axis. The opening panorama on the CD for the front door entrance shown in Fig. 14-2 was one such example.

In this panorama, the exposure facing the shaded door area was 1/2 sec. @ f/8, while the exposure toward the driveway and front yard needed to be about four stops darker due to these areas being in bright sunlight. The proper driveway exposure was 1/30 sec. (Remember to adjust exposure in a panorama sequence with shutter speed, rather than aperture, because aperture changes can affect the depth of field or focus range). The light level changed gradually from dark to light, so I felt a gradual adjustment of camera exposure could work. However, since this was the first time I tried this technique, I shot two other complete versions of this same node at both the lighter and darker exposures for backup. It would have been unacceptable to tell my client after the fact that I didn't get their opening shot because I was trying an unproven new technique.

The brick exterior walls on either side of the entrance were close enough to the camera that they filled the entire vertical field of view. A gradual blended exposure transition would not call attention to itself. Knowing that I was shooting 12 images per panorama (30° pan increments between shots), I planned to make the four stop exposure change gradually in one stop increments.

This allowed me to plan the panorama's exposures in quadrants of three shots each.

The first quadrant faced directly toward the darker doorway area, so I did these three shots with the same 1/2 second exposure. The next three shots to the right were used for the transition, so they were 1/4 sec., 1/8 sec. and 1/15 sec. respectively. The next three shots were held constant for the bright front yard/driveway exposure of 1/30 sec. Finally, the last three shots reversed the exposure transition with 1/15 sec., 1/8 sec. and 1/4 sec. respectively. The result appeared fairly natural looking when blended together in the authoring software. Further minor tweaks were added in Photoshop before the VR movie was created.

Selective Focus

One of the firm rules about shooting panoramic image sequences is keeping lens focal length and focus constant. Changing focal length or zooming a lens in/out between shots causes obvious misalignment between shots, since the zooming action changes the size (magnification) of a given subject within the frame. When the same subject is a different size in one image than it is in the adjacent shot, alignment errors will result in the stitching process, and these are almost impossible to correct.

However, changing the focus of a lens – even a fixed focal length lens – also causes slight changes in the

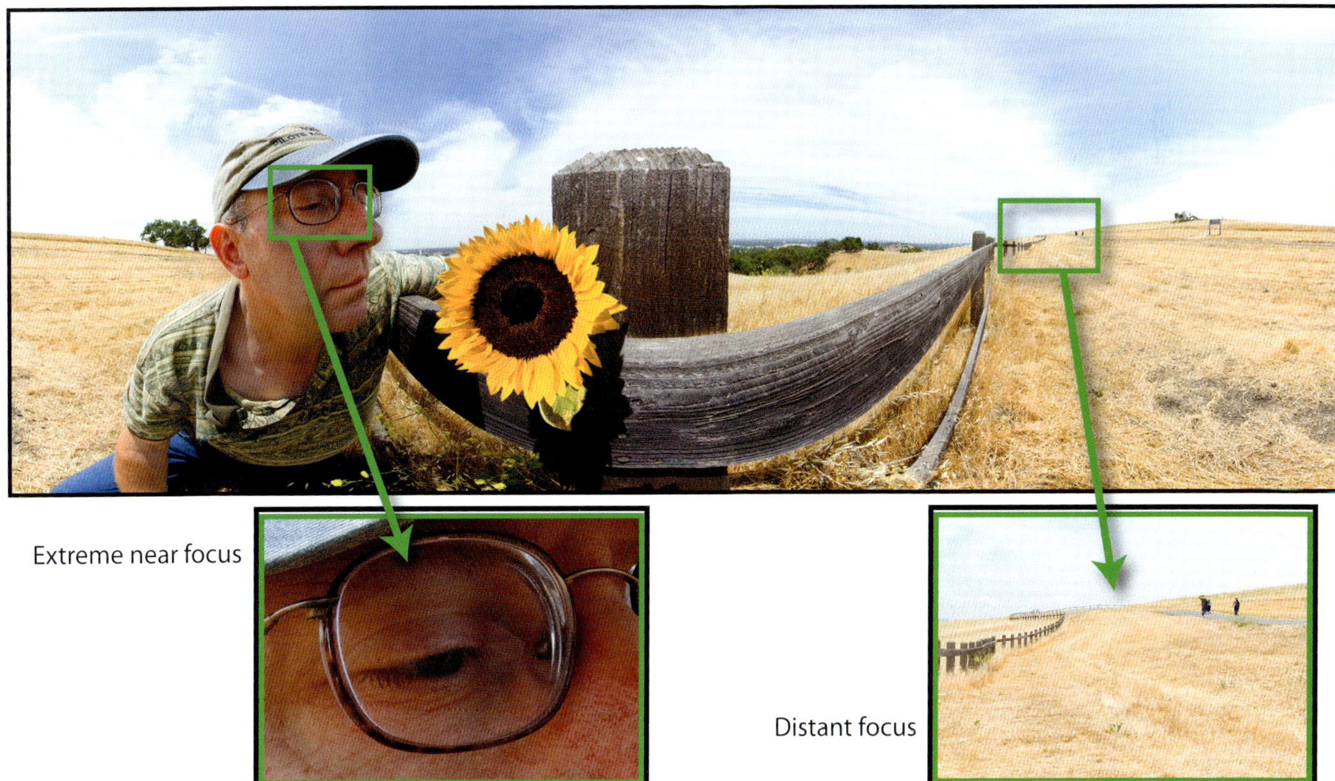

Fig. 14-3 Maximum focus or depth of field in a panorama can be achieved with use of a combination of techniques.

magnification or size of the subject in the frame. This is a more subtle change than that of changing focal length, but it is important to note. The fact that the change is relatively minor works in our favor when we want to take advantage of it.

It is therefore possible to focus extremely closely on one subject within a panorama and have other parts of the panorama focused at infinity, assuming that you can make a gradual transition over several frames between the two. Many software stitchers are somewhat forgiving of slight misalignments between adjacent frames, but they do not handle major misalignments well. If you can spread a dramatic change in focus out over several different stitches, you are more likely to have acceptable results. Also consider that the higher the resolution of your stitched images, the lower the tolerance for alignment errors will be.

When you need to maximize the range of focus in a panorama, it is best to use a combination of techniques described in **Chapter 4**.

> **1)** Shoot with the widest angle (shortest focal length) lens possible. A short focal length gives a greater depth of field at a given focus distance and aperture than a longer focal length lens.

> **2)** Use the smallest aperture possible, since a smaller aperture provides more depth of field than a larger one. Remember that apertures are fractional numbers, so that $f/22$ is a smaller opening than $f/4$. While $f/8$ is often used as a standard aperture for VR panoramas, $f/11$, $f/16$ and $f/22$ can be used when greater depth of field is needed. You'll trade off this increased depth of field with longer shutter speeds, however, in order to compensate for the reduced light passing through the lens.

> **3)** Use hyperfocal distance settings and the hyperfocal guides on most professional lenses to maximize depth of field. Hyperfocal distance is the distance that your lens should be focused at a given aperture in order to keep everything from infinity to a closest distance in acceptably sharp focus.

Only if a combination of the above does not provide an acceptable focus range for your panorama should you consider also adjusting the focus of your lens as you pan.

Compositing Images

Compositing or combining multiple images together to form a photograph that might not be possible in real life is a technique that has become all too common with the ready availability of digital imaging software. We've all seen family portraits where a missing family member was added into the shot later, or juxtapositions of unexpected subjects into a scene for dramatic effect. The same thing can be convincingly done with panoramic shots using tools, such as Adobe's Photoshop or Elements software.

It is important to use caution when employing such devices, however, as they can violate the visual integrity of your photography. Trust, once lost, is hard to regain. If those who view your images assume they are accurate renditions of real environments when they, in fact, are not, then you will have a difficult time convincing viewers that your images are faithful representations of reality in the future.

That having been said, image compositing is a choice to be made for each situation, and in many instances may be perfectly acceptable.

Compositing in VR panoramas is often done for architectural interior scenes in order to balance exposure between bright exterior window views with darker interiors. This was described in detail in the Masco case study in **Chapter 13**. However, it can also be used to correct stitching and blending errors that occur in post production to more accurately represent the reality of the scene.

In 1996, I was invited to join TerraQuest's Virtual Galápagos online expedition as their VR photographer. A crew of about a dozen writers, photographers, technicians, and multimedia experts were sent on a 10-day expedition to the Galápagos Islands in Ecuador to document the wildlife and our experiences "live" on the Web. This was one of the first such projects to use the world wide web as a platform for both interactive education and online broadcasting.

While most of our coverage was based on topside experiences and views of wildlife on the islands, I knew from previous travel to the Galápagos that the underwater world was a critical subject to include in our coverage. The opportunity to shoot underwater VR panoramas in such a precious environment was irresistible. I planned my equipment for the trip accordingly, even though we knew that there'd only be a small handful of opportunities to dive during the busy schedule.

In an early morning dive off Champion Island, it was my intention to find a stable position on a rock outcropping to shoot an underwater panorama of the colorful reef, with a fellow diver included in the image for scale. We found a spot about 40 feet below the surface with relatively clear water visibility. I positioned the weighted tripod, camera (a Nikon F3 in a specially modified Aquatica housing), strobes, and diver in position, and began shooting the panorama sequence.

About a third of the way through my sequence, we were suddenly mobbed by a group of curious Galápagos sea

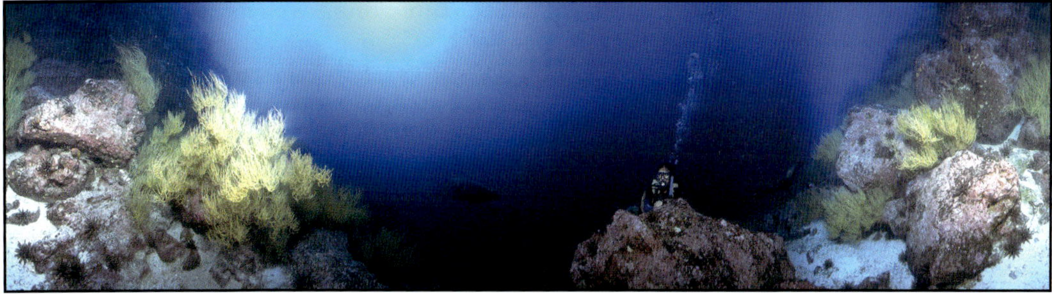

Original 360° stitched panorama from 12 images

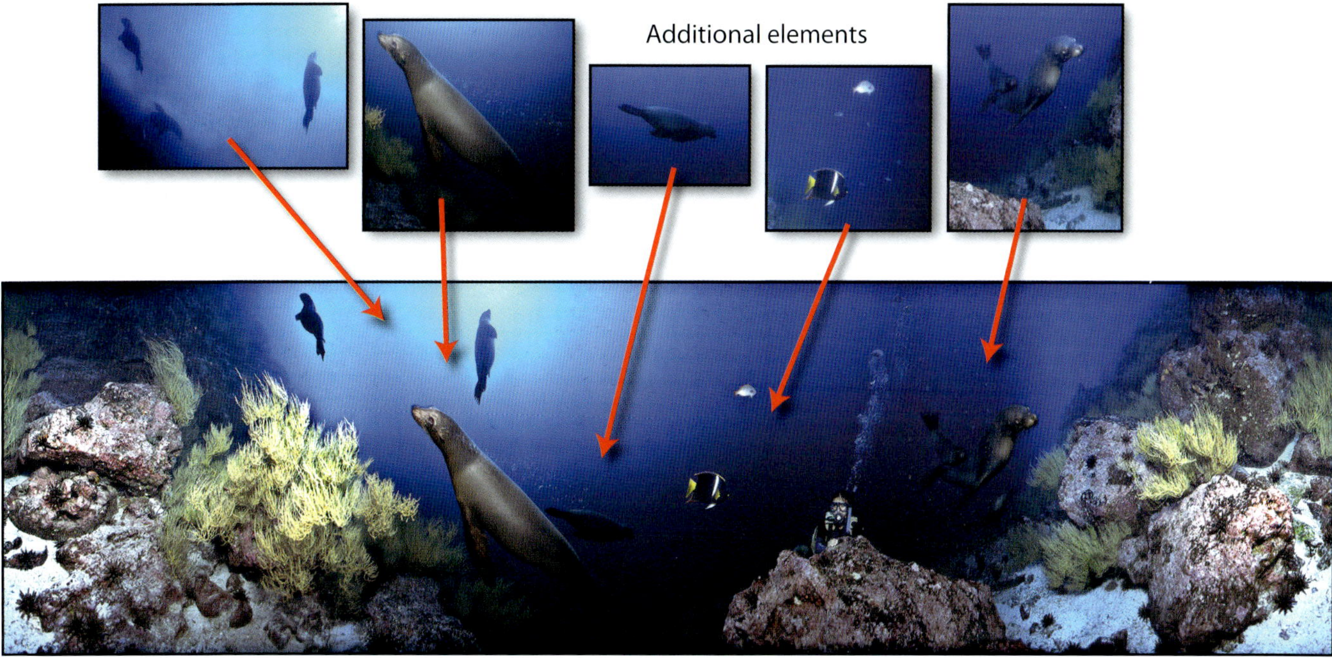

Final panorama result

Fig. 14-4 Compositing elements that were in the scene, but at different times, helped create a more dynamic panorama.

lions, who repeatedly darted in and out of the frame, zooming over, under, and around us at blazing speeds. My initial response was one of annoyance, because they were cluttering up the images of the reef in my viewfinder, and I knew that it would be impossible to stitch overlapping images effectively when a subject was in one frame but not the next. So we sat there for several minutes, using precious air and time, waiting for them to lose interest in us and move on.

Fortunately, they did not, and their apparent lack of concern for my intentions finally brought inspiration. I realized that these playful creatures were, in fact, the essence of the scene I was photographing. They were critical players in the underwater ecosystem I was trying to show. The difficulty was in quickly figuring out how to capture their dynamic nature in a panoramic VR sequence.

I decided that if I could capture the full body of any of these sea lions in a frame of film, that it might be possible to composite their shapes into the completed panorama in post production – to paste the images of the animals into their respective positions on the panoramic background. So while keeping the camera in the same position on the tripod, I waited until one or more of the sea lions swam completely into my frame, and then shot. I continued shooting the panoramic sequence without the animals present in between these others. Sometimes the sea lions were in the foreground, and other times they were more distant in the frame. I wanted a variety in order to provide the sense that we felt when we were with the animals underwater, as they rocketed past us in their play. The trick was to avoid wasting too many shots, as I only had one camera in the water, and it was limited to a single roll of 36 exposure film.

The results were better than I had originally hoped. I had to sequence and stitch the 12 shots without any sea lions comprising the overall panorama, and then put each of the sea lion shots through the stitcher individually in order to properly "warp" them to match the stitched distortion of the completed panorama. Once I had these elements all saved as individual image files, I was able to align and composite them in their respective positions in Photoshop. From there, the final PICT file was saved and taken back into the QTVR Authoring Studio for creation of the panoramic VR movie file. The result was a panorama that accurately recorded the relationships of the sea lions with the reef and underwater environment of the Galápagos Islands. The image has been widely published in both VR movie and print form in the years since.

Underwater and Aerial

There will come a time in most photographers' careers when they will want to try making images in more challenging and unusual environments. Underwater and aerial photography are two typical examples. Both will significantly increase the technical demands and need for safety above the levels required for traditional photography. When you add these elements to the demands of panoramic VR photography, you are creating many new risks.

Therefore, safety has to be established as the utmost priority before embarking on an aerial or underwater shoot. Every decision you make in the water or air must include the question of whether it is safe or not. Proceed slowly and deliberately. Avoid panic at all costs. No photograph is worth dying over. Underwater and aerial environments present a multitude of life-threatening possibilities, particularly to those who aren't adequately prepared for the challenges they present.

Underwater

Scuba diving is a popular sport, and most who discover the joys of diving have a desire to bring back pictures from their underwater adventures. With the availability of low cost, disposable underwater cameras and housings for traditional cameras, it seems simple enough to bring one along for point-and-shoot pictures on a dive. The results are usually mediocre. Divers either give up on the idea of taking pictures underwater or get more serious and pursue better equipment and techniques.

While it takes lots of practice in order to become a competent underwater photographer, there are some basic principles that can get you started.

1) Become a good, safe scuba diver first. Diving, and all the concerns about air supply, controlled ascents, gas laws, and emergency procedures, should become second nature before you add distractions such as exposure, composition, shutter speeds, fill lighting ratios, and equipment protection to the mix. Never dive alone. If

you're taking pictures underwater, you're likely to be working harder and using air faster than your diving buddy. Think about safety constantly, and keep close tabs on each other. It is better to miss a good picture and live to try it again, than to lose your entire future. There are relatively few animals in the ocean that pose a direct threat to human safety. Most diving accidents are caused by poor judgment and failure to abide by general dive safety rules.

2) Water, no matter how clear it might seem, absorbs light. Overall light levels diminish quickly within the first feet of water depth, so available light photography becomes less practical the deeper you go. Additionally, water absorbs light at the red and yellow end of the spectrum faster than it does the blue end, so the deeper you go, the less range of color can be seen with light coming from the surface. This is why underwater scenes almost always have a blue or blue-green color cast. Our brains tend to compensate for this when we see it with our eyes, but photographic film and digital sensors do not. The missing red and yellow wavelengths mean that available light photography will yield primarily blue and green colors below only two to three feet of clear water. Below about six feet, almost all visible reds and yellows disappear. Most photography below these depths will require supplemental lighting, such as underwater flash.

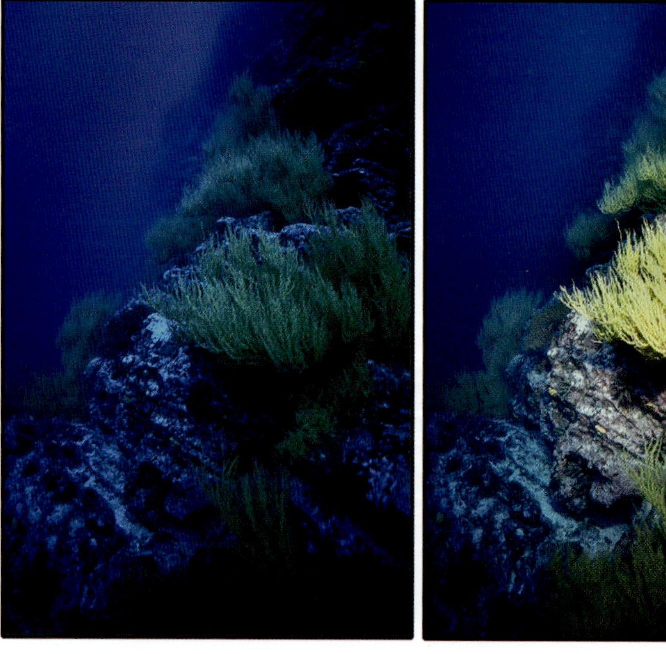

Fig. 14-5 Most underwater photography requires supplemental lighting in order to replace the light (particularly in the red and yellow wavelengths) absorbed by the water itself.

3) Use wide angle lenses and get as close as possible to your subjects. The closer you are, the clearer your subjects will be in your pictures. Remember that water, no matter how clear it seems, diffuses both color and sharpness.

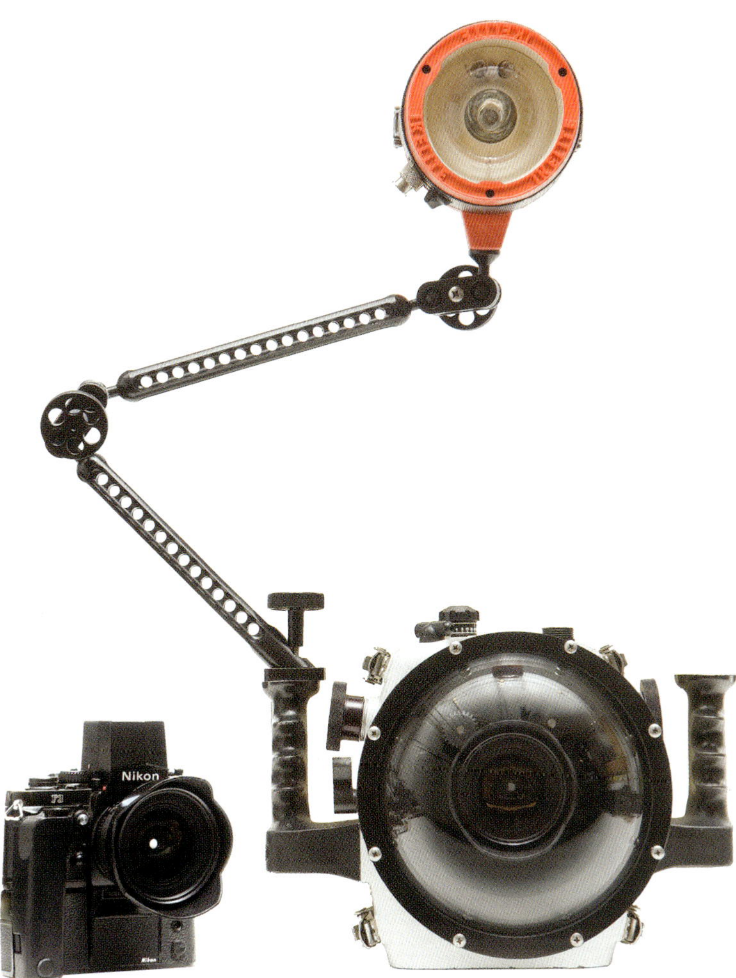

Fig. 14-6 An Aquatica underwater camera housing for a Nikon SLR camera, with underwater strobe mounted on an arm that allows it to be positioned away from the front of the camera lens.

The more water there is between your camera and subject, the worse this becomes. Anything further than about six feet away underwater will be difficult to light with your strobe(s) and will not record well. Remember that the light coming from your strobe has to travel both to the subject and then back to the lens of your camera. Light is absorbed by the water in both directions.

4) Get your underwater lights away from your camera. When the light is positioned next to the camera, the strobe puts a very intense light on the suspended particles in the water immediately in front of the lens, and these record as bright blotches in your pictures – much like falling snow does in winter shots at night. This is called lighting back scatter, and can be avoided by positioning your light(s) away from the front of your lens. Many underwater photographers mount their strobes on extension arms and aim them so that they don't cast any light in the area immediately in front of the lens. This takes a little practice and experimentation with your particular setup, but the effort is usually worthwhile in the long run. While the long extension arms for the light may seem cumbersome topside, remember that most

underwater photo equipment is close to neutral in buoyancy (unless it gets flooded), and is much easier to handle underwater.

5) If you have your camera in an underwater housing and are shooting with a wide angle lens, make sure the housing has a round or dome-shaped lens port instead of a flat port. Flat ports are designed primarily for macro photography, and cause serious refraction problems near the edges of the image when used with wide angle lenses. A dome port prevents most of this, but requires that the lens be properly aligned with the dome's center inside the housing. Use of a dome port usually yields sharper wide angle pictures underwater, but also requires that the lens be capable of fairly close focus. Since the dome interface with the water becomes another optical element in front of your lens, it affects the apparent focus distance of the image. As a rule of thumb, the focus of your lens will usually need to be set at around twice the diameter of the dome itself for distant objects underwater. So if you have a relatively large 8" dome on your camera housing, such as those made by Aquatica for professional SLR cameras, your lens will need to focus to at least 16". The ability to actually see what the camera will record through a single lens reflex (SLR) viewfinder can be invaluable underwater, but putting an SLR camera into an underwater housing is generally neither cheap nor without risk. Cameras and lenses designed specifically for underwater photography, such as the Nikonos system, and many low cost point and shoot cameras, are generally cheaper than a professional underwater housing and the many accessories required to shoot with it underwater.

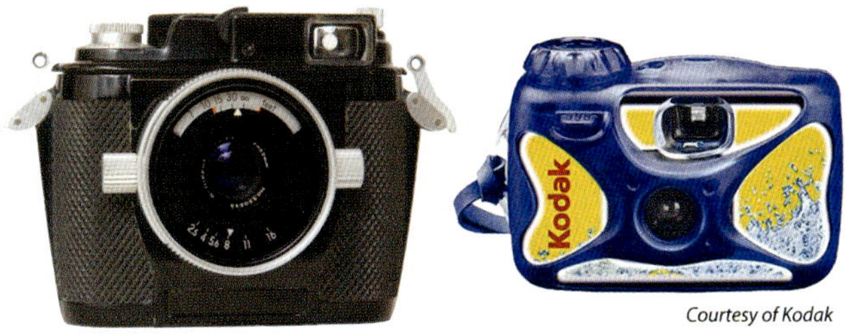

Courtesy of Kodak

Fig. 14-7 Less expensive options for underwater photography include used Nikonos underwater film cameras, as well as disposable one-use cameras.

6) Take care of your equipment. This means testing and changing all the O-rings, seals, and batteries yearly, whether you've used the system or not. Test everything at home before you leave on that dive trip, and leave plenty of time for repairs, if needed. Rinse all underwater

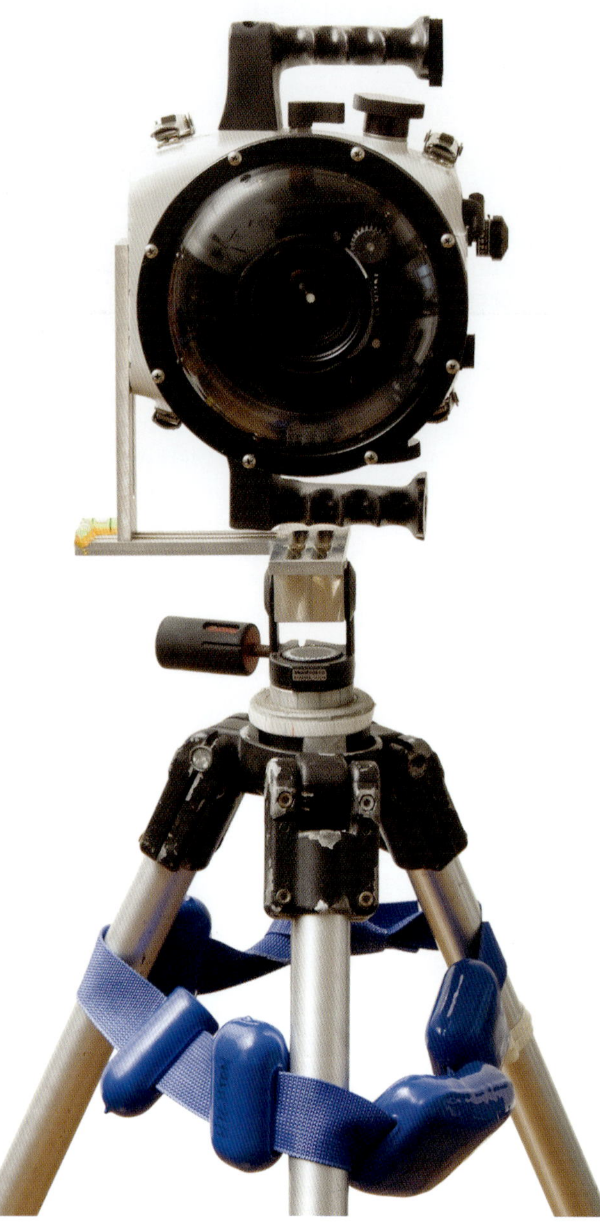

Fig. 14-8 A custom (cylindrical) VR pan head the author built for his underwater camera housing, mounted on a well-used Manfrotto tripod. The diver's weight belt is added to help keep the system firmly in place on the sea floor.

equipment in clean fresh water after every dive, and dry thoroughly before storing. Take your time and be thorough when preparing for each dive. There are dozens of little things that you can forget, any one of which will result in a flooded camera – and most likely the loss of your ability to shoot underwater on that trip, along with expensive repairs. If you *do* flood a camera, it is generally recommended to remove all batteries and flush it thoroughly with fresh water. Depending on how long you are away, keep it stored in water or alcohol until you can get it to a service technician. Consider that it is often cheaper to replace flooded cameras than it is to repair them, so take due care when preparing your equipment for every dive.

7) Use a tripod and pan head underwater for your panoramic photography. Add a couple of diving weights or wrap an extra weight belt around your tripod in order to keep it stable on the bottom. Make sure you level the camera, just as you would topside, and shoot in similar pan increments for the focal length lens you are using. Tripods and VR pan heads made of aluminum will hold up quite well to underwater use, as long as you rinse and dry them thoroughly after each dive. Regular lubrication of the moving and non-aluminum parts (such as bolts, nuts, screws, springs, clamps, etc.) will help prevent rust. I find it best to designate one or two low cost tripods for my underwater use. When their parts start to fail, I don't feel too bad about replacing them (usually by rotating an older topside tripod into underwater duty) and I scavenge the worn out one for replacement parts. These are among the reasons why I have stayed with the Manfrotto line of tripods for most of my career. Many of their parts have been interchangeable from one model to the next. They are also typically of high quality and are relatively low cost.

8) Underwater photography doesn't mean you have to dive deep into the ocean or travel to exotic destinations. Consider photographing near the surface of ponds, nearby lakes, or local tide pools. Remember that most aquatic wildlife can be found at relatively shallow depths, and that the best natural light is near the surface. Take advantage of these facts, and try your preliminary underwater photo efforts in water that you can wade in, rather than that which you have to swim or dive in.

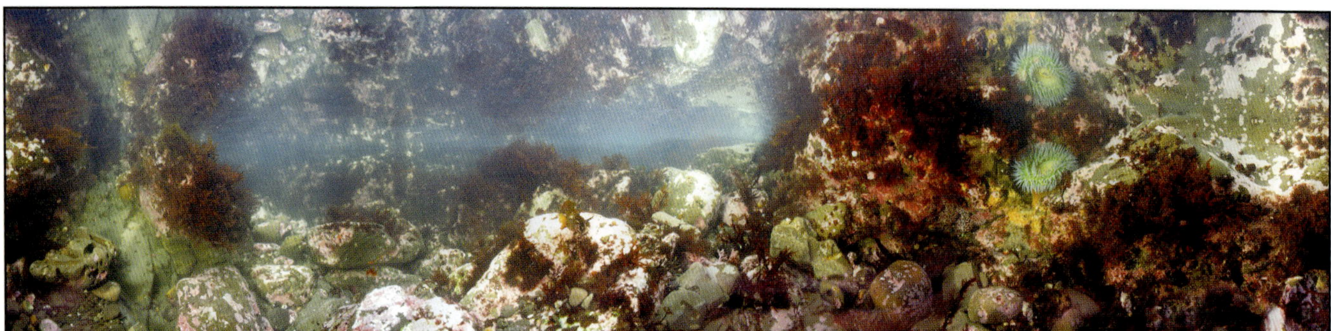

Fig. 14-9 Underwater panoramas don't necessarily require deep dives or scuba experience. This one was shot in a Pacific coast tide pool in only 18 inches of water. The photographer barely needed to get his feet wet shooting it.

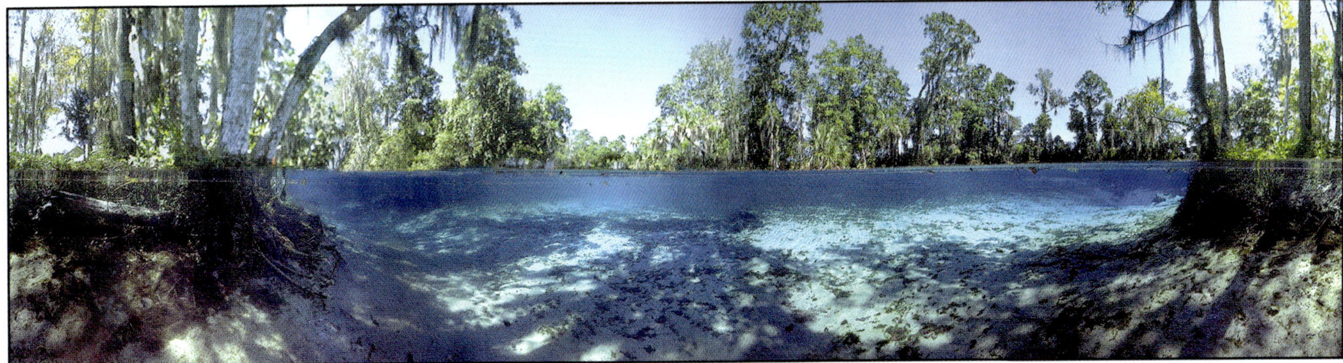

Fig. 14-10 This panorama was shot on a tripod in waist-deep water in a Florida spring, using a split over/under technique.

Aerial

There is something unique about views of our world from above. These are views that most of us don't see terribly often, except through tiny windows of airliners flying at 36,000 feet. Flight in small aircraft only a few hundred or few thousand feet above the ground offers a spectacular perspective that begs to be photographed. Yet much like underwater photography, initial efforts are generally disappointing. Aerial photography presents a complicated set of problems to even experienced professional photographers.

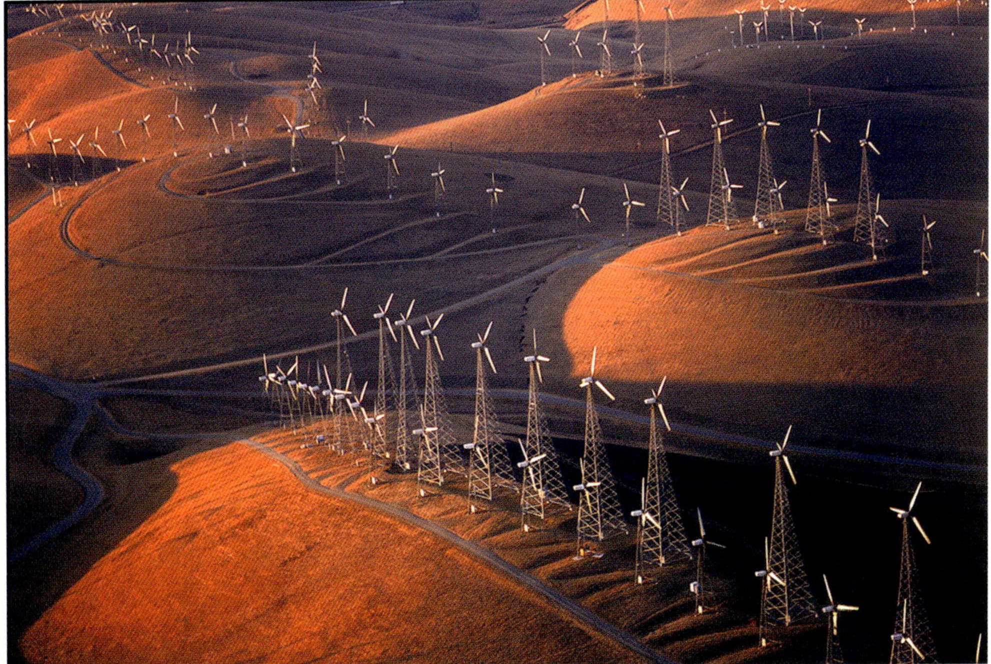

Fig. 14-11 Aerial photography can provide tantalizing images of subjects from a unique perspective which relatively few others ever get to see on their own.

1) The first and primary concern is, once again, safety. Experienced pilots will sometimes feel that they can both fly and take pictures at the same time. While this is definitely possible, doing so is much like shooting pictures while you're driving a car along the freeway. One or both efforts are bound to be a failure. Bad pictures are far preferable to fatal accidents, but both are preventable. You are better off concentrating on your photography while an experienced pilot flies the aircraft. Commercial pilots and small aircraft are usually available for hourly rates at most small general aviation airports. Plan your flight on the ground ahead of time with your pilot. Make sure that everything you want to do in the air is within the limitations of both the aircraft and the pilot who is flying it.

2) The best light for aerial photography is at the beginning or end of the day, when the sun is low and shadows are long. This gives more saturation to colors and is more visually pleasing than the flat, harsh light of mid-day. Getting up early for a dawn shoot can be difficult, and morning fog or haze can often obscure the morning "magic hour" light. Evening or sunset shoots are often preferred, as weather can be observed throughout the day and the go/no-go decision can be made before everyone involved heads for the airport. However, winds in the afternoon are often stronger and more gusty, making the aircraft a less stable shooting platform and giving a bumpier ride.

3) For the sharpest images, aerial photographers choose slow, fine grain films (ISO 50 or less) with high color saturation to help minimize the effects of haze. Digital photographers often choose the lowest ISO speeds their cameras offer. One advantage of aerial photography is that most subjects are on the ground, a significant distance away, so that the focus of your lens will be at or near infinity. Since there is no need for lots of depth of field (everything's the same relative distance from you), you can shoot

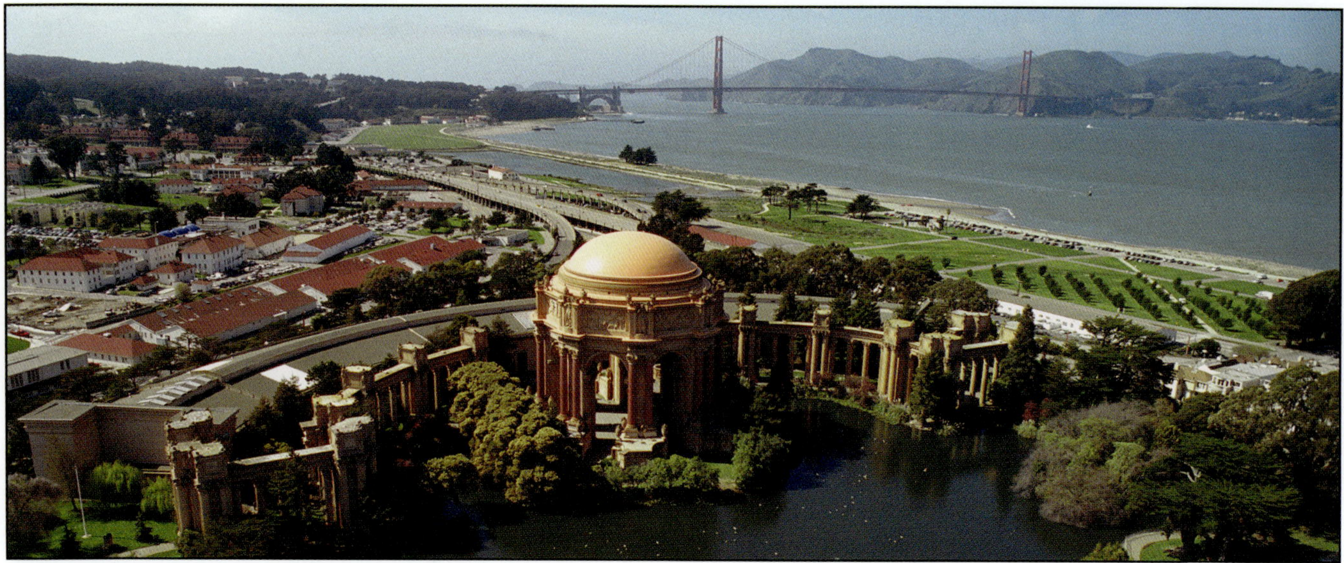

Fig. 14-12 Aerial photography presents a complicated set of problems, even to the most experienced pro photographers. Safety to those in the air and on the ground is the primary concern. The added challenges of panoramic shooting from an aerial vantage point complicate matters even further.

with your aperture wide open and thus maximize your shutter speed. Speeds of 1/500 or 1/1000 sec. should be a minimum, unless you are using a gyroscopic stabilization system or vibration reduction (VR) lens. The high shutter speed is necessary to help prevent the vibrations from the aircraft itself from blurring your images. Do not rest your camera or your hands against the aircraft interior, as that will transmit the vibration directly to your camera. Instead, fully support the camera with your hands and arms, letting it "float" in front of your eye. Your body will absorb many of the aircraft's vibrations, and your pictures will be sharper.

4) Avoid shooting through aircraft windows, which are generally made of strong plastic, but are of poor optical quality. These plastics will degrade sharpness and color quality in your images. A good camera ship should have a removable (or fully openable) window, or even better, a removable door. Things get very loud and windy when the cockpit is open, yet good communication between the photographer and pilot are a must. A seat on the floor next to an open door is an ideal spot for an aerial photographer. This generally provides a wide range of shooting directions, unimpeded by wings, struts, landing gear, or window plastic. Of course, the photographer and any equipment must be harnessed inside the plane. Reliance upon seat belts alone is foolhardy, although necessary on rare occasions. In these instances, be sure to tape the buckles closed with a loop of duct or gaffer tape to prevent accidental opening in flight (but not so thick that you can't rip through it in an emergency). I usually wear a climbing harness clipped with locking carabiners and slings into a hard point inside the aircraft interior when photographing from an open door. I also keep a sharp knife in a protective pouch on my harness, so I can cut myself free in the event that I need to get

out of the aircraft quickly after an emergency landing. Take only the equipment you need on the flight, and be sure to keep all equipment cases closed and harnessed inside the aircraft. A small lens rolling out the door at 500 feet can kill whomever it hits on the ground, or cause serious damage to property. It is also a violation of FAA regulations to drop objects from aircraft over populated areas, and such an accident can cause your pilot to lose his or her flight privileges.

5) Choose the right aircraft for the job. High wing airplanes are generally better than low wings for aerial photography, as the wings are above the fuselage and don't block the view downward toward the ground. Helicopters offer the best unobstructed fields of view and are far more maneuverable than fixed wing aircraft, but they usually come at a significantly higher price. A helicopter can sometimes be held over a given spot in a hover, which allows you to maintain alignment for your rotation when shooting a panorama sequence. However, if you are more than 2,000 feet above ground, a small fixed wing airplane can often be flown in a tight enough circle that you can effectively stitch the resulting images without too many problems. Using a GPS waypoint, it is also possible to fly through the same spot in the air from multiple directions, shooting another image element for a stitched panorama each time.

6) For aerial panoramas, you are often better off using a slightly longer lens than the ultra wide lenses normally used for panoramic VR. A 28mm or 35mm lens will provide more detail than a 14mm or 18mm (remember that your subjects are all pretty far away), and will make it easier to keep wings and landing gear out of the frame. This may require 18-24 shots per 360° panorama, rather than the usual six to 12. Make sure you know the

limitations of your stitching software before you shoot. Generally, you will need to keep the camera level and centered on the horizon as you pan, just as you do on the ground, unless you are using a multi-row stitching application such as Autodesk's Stitcher or PTGui.

7) Critical equipment to bring with you on any aerial shoot includes plenty of film or digital media (shoot as much as you can – flight opportunities are not generally common and can be expensive), warm clothing (100 mph wind blowing by the door or window gets cold even on the hottest summer days, and temperature decreases with altitude), sun glasses or goggles to protect your eyes, and at least one air sickness bag in a readily accessible pocket. You will find that nausea creeps up on you pretty fast when you are in turning or bumpy flights and your eyes are focused in a viewfinder for prolonged periods. Pilots and aircraft owners don't appreciate your decorating their aircraft interiors with remnants of your most recent meal, and you will be assigned the cleanup duties once you are back on the ground. All that wind blowing through the cabin will help ensure that the mess is well circulated. Grab a couple of these air sickness bags out of the seat pocket on your next commercial flight, and put them away in your camera bag for the day you might need them on an aerial shoot.

8) Consider other means of getting your camera into the air, such as hot air balloons, blimps, and even kites. Hot air balloons are very stable aerial platforms and they move relatively slowly. They present great opportunities for aerial panoramas, particularly if you have the freedom to move around in the basket. In fact, they may be the best choice for aerial panoramas using fisheye lens systems, as it is possible to position your camera so that the balloon and basket obscure very little of the view. You will need to be cautious about image alignment, especially if you hand hold your camera. Keep in mind also that the balloon will move with the wind between your shooting of one hemisphere and the next. It will be better to first shoot the view in your forward direction of movement and the view rearward last, as this will provide for some overlap of the ground below between hemispheres. Another disadvantage is that hot air balloons are not as maneuverable as motorized aircraft, so you can't always position yourself over a desired spot on the ground. If you are good with tools and have a bit of creative ingenuity, you might find success building remote camera mechanisms for photography from small, unmanned blimps, kites, or even radio controlled aircraft.

Production vs. Post Production
One of the great benefits of having the array of digital tools available to us today is that many limitations and problems encountered in photography can be fixed in post production. However, this is no excuse for sloppy technique while shooting. It is usually more advantageous to get the best quality possible when shooting, than it is to try to add missing information after the fact. As a rule of thumb, it will require more time and expense to fix problems in post production than it will to do things right in the first place when shooting.

Lighting is one such example. Getting your light quality, relative intensities, and color balance the way you want while shooting is usually more effective than trying to fix problems in post production. However, the costs of doing so should always be weighed against those of making adjustments in post production. While it is certainly possible to make global color corrections in Photoshop, the results are generally less satisfactory than having properly color balanced images in the first place.

As we saw in the last chapter with the Masco project, sometimes the tradeoff between making adjustments in post production, such as filling in window views with properly exposed exteriors, is worthwhile and can actually *save* time or money overall. But don't fall into the trap of thinking that every shortcoming can or *should* be fixed in post production.

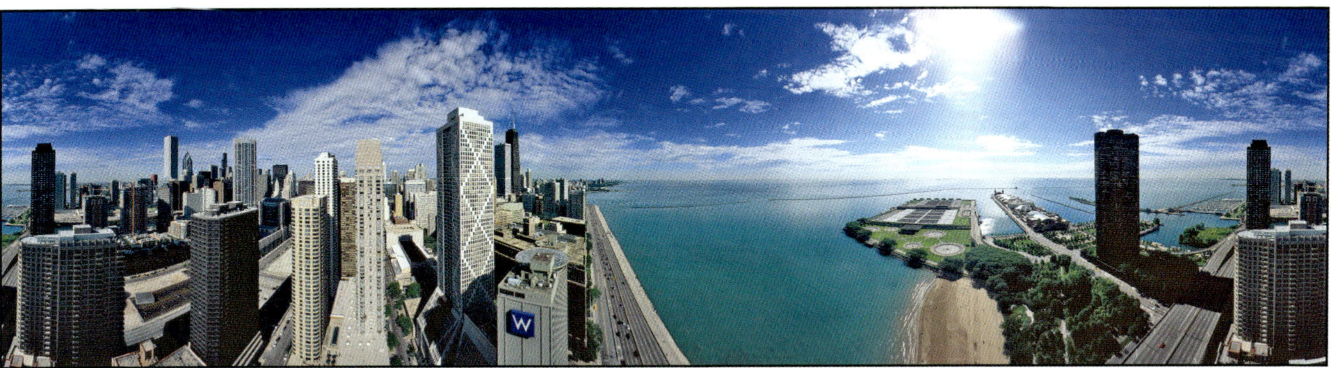

Courtesy Mark Segal, SkyPan International

Fig. 14-13 Chicago panoramic photographer Mark Segal of SkyPan International used a five foot long electric powered radio-controlled helicopter to photograph this panorama 350 feet above the shores of Lake Michigan. His custom slit scan camera rig (film-based) captures two complete 360° revolutions per second, and the rotation speed adds a stabilizing gyroscopic effect to the capture process. This shot was one of a series done at different altitudes for a real estate developer who wanted to show the potential views for a twin tower high rise being planned on Lake Shore Drive.

Failing to keep images sequenced and organized in the field will cause tremendous confusion when you get into post production. Shooting images on a slightly misaligned pan head can make it almost impossible to stitch your panoramas later on, no matter how beautiful the images themselves are. Forgetting to set focus, exposure, or zoom so everything matches between images can make it impossible to get acceptable results, even with an unlimited post production budget.

The bottom line is that you should put as much care into your actual photography efforts as possible, and use your post production time for assembly and minor tweaking.

As a professional VR photographer, I insist on doing both the photography and post production assembly of the panoramas I create. I do this for two reasons. The first is that I maintain full control over the quality of my work. The second is that doing so places full responsibility on my shoulders for what techniques and equipment I use, so I don't find myself able (or wanting) to blame anyone else for something that might not have worked right. Knowing that I'm responsible for the entire process not only gives me more options when I need them in the field, but also means that I make better decisions about production vs. post production while I still have these options available, rather than after the fact.

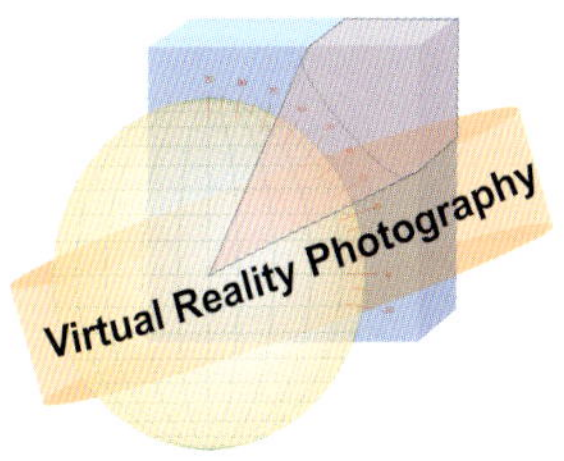

Chapter 15: Related and Support Media

In order to take VR photography to its highest levels, one needs to go beyond photography alone. Virtual reality images are intended to be interactive – to involve the viewers and to fully engage them in the scene. Imagine watching a feature film or your favorite television program without any sound, or going to a web site that contained no links. Imagine the potential of interactive media that contains moving images rather than just stills. Once you have the ability to create the panoramic scenes that are the visual foundation of most VR projects, then you can consider other elements that can be added to make the result complete.

Audio Elements

Audio or sound elements are relatively simple, yet incredibly effective additions to interactive panoramas. They can be as basic as a single track of music or narration, or as complex as multi-track layers with directional sound and hot spot triggered effects.

There are a number of ways to add sound to your interactive panoramas. The easiest is perhaps to simply add a looping audio movie in to the HTML coding of a web page that contains your panorama movie. This can be quite effective for background music or ambient sound. A controller can be included on the page so that the viewer can mute the sound if it becomes distracting, or change its volume.

However, more sophisticated means are available that allow you to actually embed audio tracks directly into your VR movies, so that they will be heard whether appearing on an HTML page or not.

One such software application is CubicConnector (**www. clickheredesign.com.au**). CubicConnector allows you to embed multiple tracks of audio into your VR panoramas and set both their playback levels and sequence. It

even allows you to create directional sound in your panoramas, so that a particular sound is louder when the viewer looks in one direction but fades lower when they pan away. When done well, this makes the panoramic image far more dynamic for viewers, and may compel them to explore the scene and all its elements in greater detail.

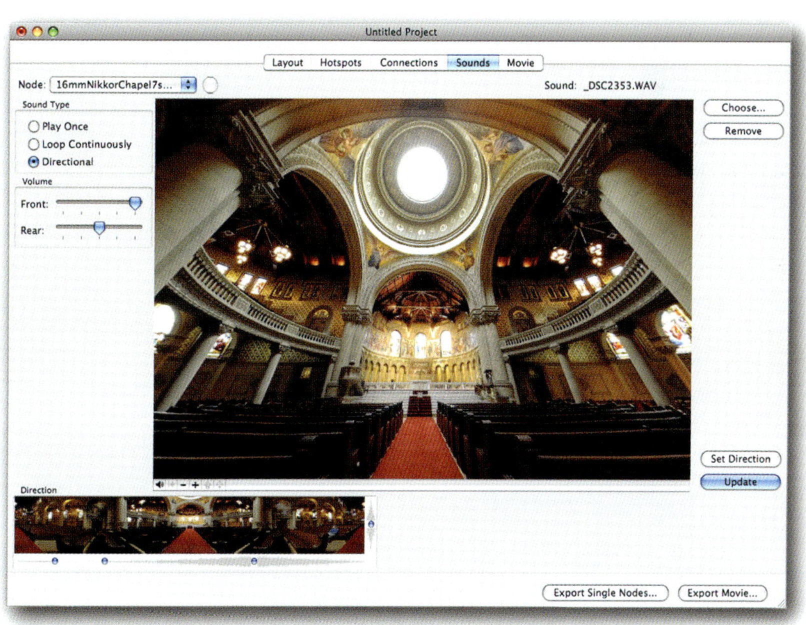

Fig. 15-1 CubicConnector software allows the addition of directional sound to a VR movie.

Recording sound becomes another job to be done on location during your photo shoot. While there are libraries of sound effects and music that are available for commercial use (be sure to secure the proper licenses to reproduce existing music and other recordings in your panoramas), very often you will wind up needing to record both specific sounds or speech, and general background sound (often called "wild sound") on location. For example, wild sound of bird calls, insects, and other sounds unique to the location you're shooting may be critical to record, since these may not be easily found in commercial sound effects libraries. Similarly, background street traffic, the hum of a productive office, or the whir of a particular kind of machinery may only be available if you record it yourself in the field. Even seemingly generic sounds like a babbling brook or rushing water that are often available in commercial sound libraries may not match the scene that you photographed terribly well, and you'll want something more accurate to use.

Recording sound effectively in the field is more complicated than simply holding up a microphone and pushing the record button on a tape deck. As with good photography, it requires the use of proper equipment and knowledge of how to isolate and capture only those elements that you want.

I recommend the use of a digital audio recorder of some sort, and an investment in a decent stereo microphone with windscreen. A good set of headphones is a must in order to adequately monitor the sound you are recording. Don't rely only on a meter or digital readout of the sound levels on your recording deck. You must be able to hear what is being recorded through your deck as you are recording in order to know for sure whether the quality of the sound is acceptable or not.

A good microphone makes all the difference in the world in audio quality, whether recorded on the cheapest portable cassette deck or high end pro studio system. A low quality microphone will invariably produce low quality recordings, no matter how sophisticated the rest of the recording system might be. Fixing bad sound in post production is probably harder than fixing bad photography after the fact. Remember the old adage that if you put garbage in, you'll get garbage out. If you start out with good source material, you'll have more flexibility and less work to do in post production.

When recording in the field, wind blowing across the microphone is the most common problem that degrades sound quality. Even a slight breeze will cause disturbances that sound like static or dropouts. Built-in line filters included with some microphones do very little to mitigate this. An inexpensive foam windscreen that fits over the end of the microphone will protect against some wind distortion, and causes little if any interference with the sounds you want to record. You can make one of these by wrapping a thin piece of open-celled foam around the head of the mike and securing it with a rubber band. Specialized blimps with faux fur covers, that allow recording even in the windiest conditions, are used by professional sound recordists.

As with panoramic photography, recording good sound generally requires that you get close to your subject. The intensity of sound falls off in an inverse square proportion to the distance from its source, much like light does. Thus, if you simply stick a microphone out in the middle of a scene, it's going to capture a little bit of everything but isolate nothing.

The closer you get your microphone to the source of a sound, the greater the relative intensity of that sound will be compared to all the other background sounds, and the more distinctly it will be recorded. The farther away from a sound source you are, the lower its relative volume to the rest of the ambient sounds will be. You want to have your desired sounds well isolated in your recordings so you can adjust their levels precisely in post production mixing. If you want to have a particular bird song available for use in a tranquil meadow panorama, but your recording has lots of ambient city noise in the background, you'll be unable to separate the two. An amalgam of sound will become a distraction in your panorama, rather than a sensory supplement.

When recording location sound, particularly "wild sound" or ambient noises, make sure to record at least 30 seconds (a minute or more is preferable) of good, useable audio. This will give you enough to layer, or even loop, the recording in post production so it won't sound overly repetitive to your viewing audience.

An important, yet often overlooked audio tool is found on many of today's digital cameras with their built-in microphones. These are intended for the annotation of audio comments to specific images as they are being shot. However, their sound quality can be surprisingly good, and they can be excellent tools for recording ambient wild sound when you don't have a dedicated audio deck available.

Fig. 15-2 A basic audio kit including: recorder, stereo microphone, windscreen, and headphones.

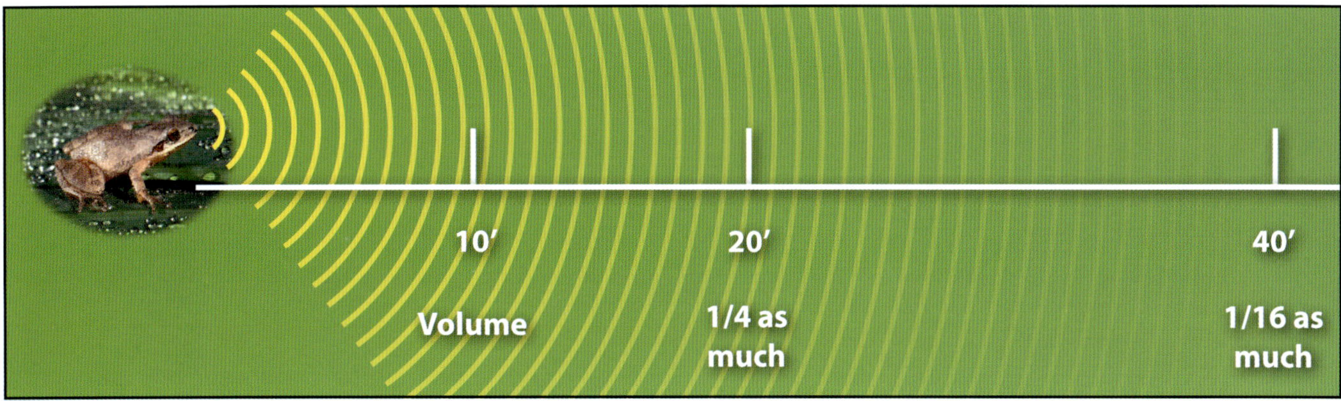

Fig. 15-3 Sound levels diminish over distance in an inverse square relationship, just like light intensity diminishes.

Most digital SLRs limit recording of audio files to one minute or less, but that can be more than adequate. When using these, keep in mind all the rules about protecting the microphone from wind, and getting as close to your sound source as possible.

Supporting Graphics

As discussed in **Chapter 13**, many VR panoramas can benefit from the addition of supplemental graphics and illustrations, either accessed when the user clicks on hot spots within the image, or as adjacent material to a panorama movie window.

One such example is the inclusion of a compass or direction indicator that rotates next to the panorama, showing which direction within the 360° panorama the viewer is facing. Another example is the display of a map or overview of a multi-node scene, where the user can navigate from node to node by clicking on a particular point on the map, rather than via hot spots within each

panorama. Such features can add tremendous function and clarity to panoramic images, so it is wise to consider collecting source materials, such as maps and overview graphics, while you are on location in the field.

As you get more creative and start pushing the boundaries of VR, you may find that you want to include video or other motion graphics within your panoramic scenes. While possible, this is not necessarily an easy thing to do today without considerable programming and post production experience. However, it may be something you want to plan for when you are on location and have the opportunity to shoot the necessary content.

It is possible, for example, to have a full motion video playing within a VR panorama. You might want to do this if you have shot a panorama of a restored movie theater and want to have a short looping movie playing on the theater screen, or perhaps a video image on the screen of a television in a living room panorama.

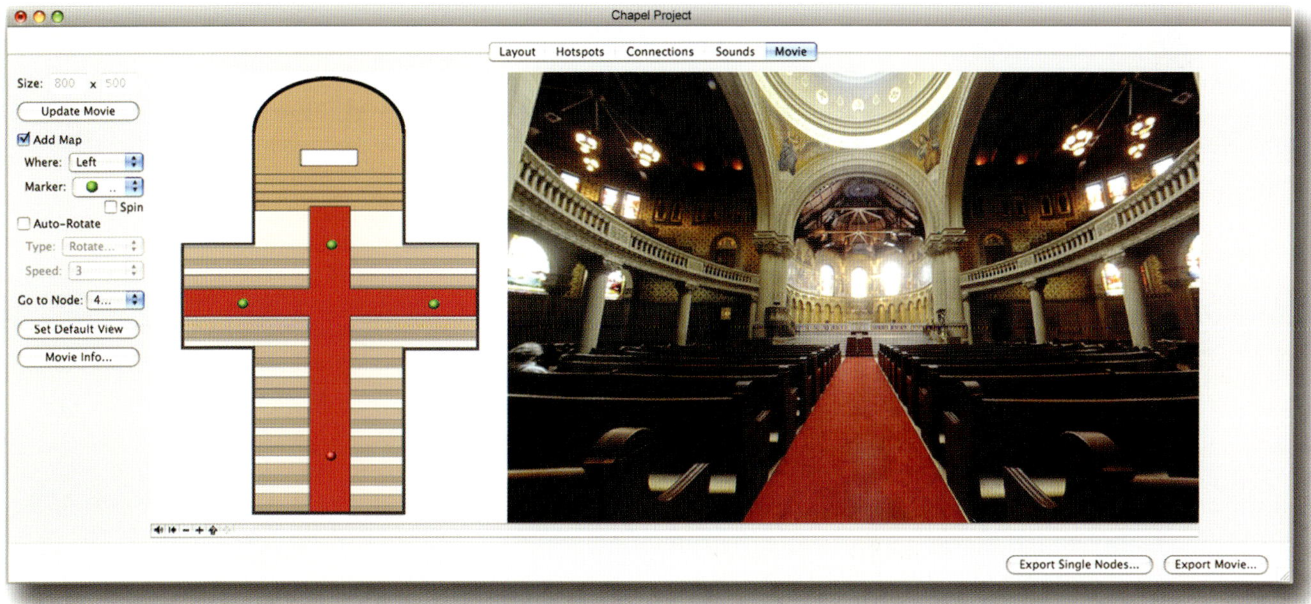

Fig. 15-4 CubicConnector software also allows linking of maps and other reference materials to VR movies.

It is also possible to program moving transitions between panoramas, so rather than your viewers experiencing a sudden jump from one panorama to the next when they click on a hot spot, they see a motion-type transition between the two. While this might be as simple as a zooming effect or a cross dissolve, it could also be as sophisticated as a video shot covering the path actually followed between nodes. You will need to plan for these types of sequences and shoot them while on location so that they match properly with your panoramic images.

Note that these sorts of additions can take considerable time and may not always be worth the effort. But keep in mind that your VR projects may have a life well beyond their immediate purposes, and that the related content that you create may provide significant value in the future. Furthermore, as VR authoring software applications become more mature, assembling such content may be far less labor intensive and you (or your clients) will be grateful for the efforts you made during a shoot to capture source content for such new features.

The Future of VR:
An Interview with Paul Debevec

Paul Debevec is the associate director of graphics research at the University of Southern California's Institute for Creative Technologies (USC ICT), and a research associate professor at USC's department of Computer Science.

His Ph.D. thesis at the University of California, Berkeley presented Façade, an image-based modeling and rendering system for creating photoreal virtual camera motion through architectural scenes derived from still photographs. Using Façade, he led the creation of a photoreal animation of the U.C. Berkeley campus for his 1997 film **The Campanile Movie**. The techniques developed on this project were later used to create many of the Academy Award winning special effects for **The Matrix** motion picture trilogy.

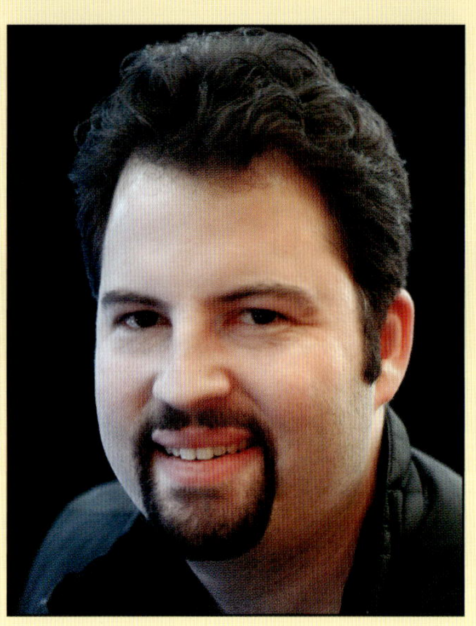

Debevec went on to demonstrate image-based virtual lighting techniques in subsequent animations "Rendering with Natural Light," "Fiat Lux," and "The Parthenon."

He also led the design of HDR Shop, the first widely used high dynamic range (HDR) image editing program. In 2001, Debevec received ACM SIGGRAPH's Significant New Researcher Award, co-authored the 2005 book "High Dynamic Range Imaging," and chaired the 2007 SIGGRAPH Computer Animation Festival. Information about his ongoing virtual imaging research can be found at**: http://www.debevec.org/**

Q: Virtual reality imaging – for most of us – has been limited so far to technologies that either require a series of photographs to be assembled to create a panoramic image, or sequenced around an object **to create an object movie. Explain how your work, which maps photographs or photo-realistic images onto virtual shapes, differs from this, and what you see in the future for both approaches?**

A: QuickTime panoramas and QuickTime object movies are straightforward ways of representing environments and objects more immersively – or three-dimensionally, but they have limitations. With panoramas, you are fixed at a single point, so there's no sense of motion through the scene to make things appear compellingly three-dimensional. You are just really just browsing across a single two-dimensional photograph, even if it does cover the whole sphere. With object movies, there's a true sense of three-dimensionality since you see the object from different viewpoints as you move it around. The problem with object movies is that the jump in viewpoint from one view to the next is usually rather significant, so the motion isn't terribly smooth.

You can make the transitions between views much smoother if you first project the object movie images onto a 3D model of the object. The first time I did this was in 1991 when I wanted to make a 3D model of my Chevette. I took just a few photographs of the car – from above, in front, in back, and the two sides, and then used the outline of the car in these images to volumetrically carve out a basic three-dimensional model of the car. Then, I projected the images out from the camera viewpoints back onto this 3D geometry, and the result was a texture-mapped 3D model that could be seen continuously from any viewpoint; I used this to make an animation of the car flying smoothly toward and then away from the viewer. (See the animation at **http://www.debevec. org/Chevette**).

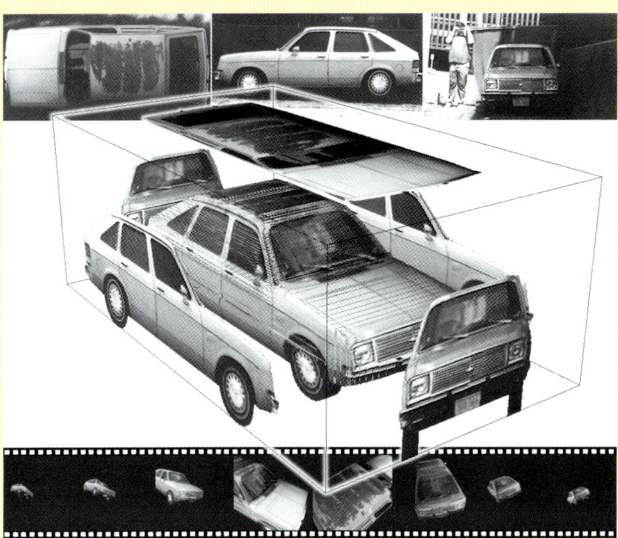

Fig. 15-5 Paul's 3D model of his Chevy Chevette (1991).

Projecting images onto 3D models is also effective for architectural scenes. The "Façade" system I worked on for my Ph.D. thesis made it possible to reconstruct basic 3D models of architectural scenes from photographs using photogrammetry based on geometric primitives. Projective texture mapping – treating the cameras that took the pictures as virtual slide projectors to project the photographs back onto the reconstructed geometry – provided realistic textures. In this work, I was able to improve the quality of the renderings using *view-dependent texture mapping* to cross-dissolves between different texture maps depending on direction of the virtual viewpoint. Thus, when looking at the side of a building from the right, the rendering would primarily use a texture map from that direction, fading to an image from the front if the user navigates to that direction. This helped increase the realism of our 3D model of the bell tower in our computer animation of the Berkeley campus, *The Campanile Movie*. (**http://www.debevec.org/ Campanile**).

For smaller objects, it is possible to obtain the three-dimensional geometry of objects using either a laser stripe scanner or structured light, and the next generation of QuickTime object movies may use such underlying 3D geometry to provide the realism of image-based models with the smooth viewpoint control of traditional CG models.

Q: Can you explain the basics of the VR work and research you do? We have seen the results of this work in high-end feature film visual effects, such as the ground-breaking sequences in the Matrix trilogy. What other industries are using the visual imaging technologies you've helped develop, and where do you see these headed over the next 5-10 years?

A: My group's first successful technology transition was the use of our image-based rendering techniques from *The Campanile Movie* on *The Matrix*. At the SIGGRAPH '97 conference, our film caught the attention of the *The Matrix*'s visual effects supervisor, John Gaeta, as a promising path for creating photoreal 3D backgrounds of real sets to become the virtual backgrounds of the "bullet time" shots. The *Matrix* sequels went even further by leveraging high dynamic range rendering and image-based lighting techniques I developed for our animation *Fiat Lux* (**http://www.debevec. org/FiatLux**) to render and integrate CG cars and digital actors. In both cases, students from my computer animation teams (George Borshukov and H.P. Duiker) went on to apply our technologies to the films, leading to some of the most successful early results in motion pictures.

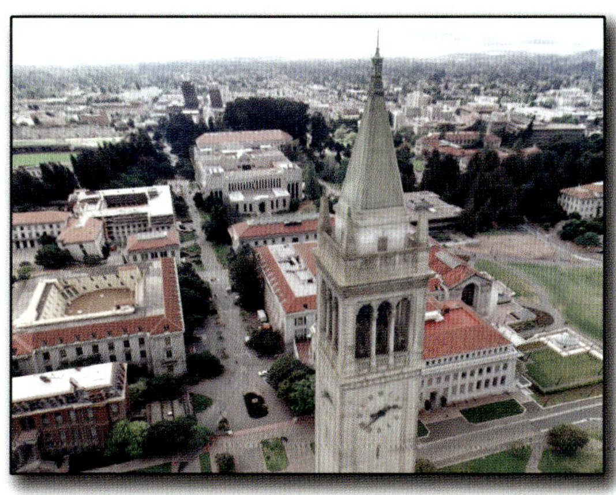

Fig. 15-6 The Campanile Movie, from UC Berkeley.

Much of our recent work focuses on capturing *relightable* VR models using image-based techniques. We have built a number of devices called *light stages* consisting of spheres of strobe lights or LEDs that allow an object to be photographed under all possible incident lighting directions. By scaling and summing the color channels of all these images according to the color and intensity of each direction in a desired lighting environment, we can make the photographed object appear – after the fact – as it would anywhere, lit by any form of illumination. These relightable image datasets can also be mapped onto 3D geometry, allowing the VR object to be realistically shown from any viewpoint in any illumination. This means that you could see what an ancient artifact or a product for sale would look like in natural light sitting on a shelf, or on your own dining room table. Hopefully, we'll see these techniques made available commercially in the near future.

This is done in all possible lighting directions, using high-speed cameras synchronized to rapidly changing LED lighting conditions. Using combinations of view interpolation, light field rendering, and image-based relighting, we can film someone in our studio, and later match both their viewpoint and illumination to place them into essentially any motion picture footage. Other research being done in the area of *computational photography* is presenting simple modifications to cameras, sensors, and lenses – making it possible to change the focal plane of images *after* photographing them, alter the viewpoint in a photograph, or derive a three-dimensional depth map of a scene from a single image.

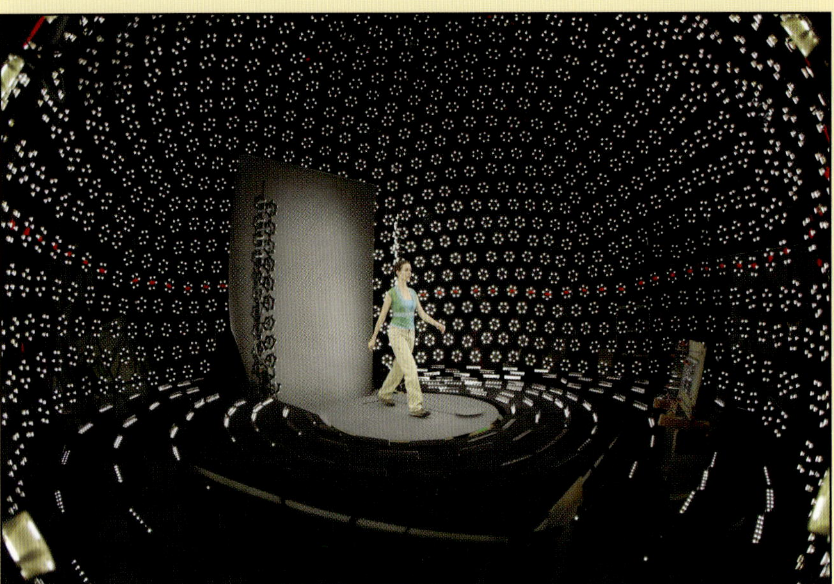

Fig. 15-7 The Light Stage 6, designed for photography of moving subjects, which can then be digitally relighted to appear as though they were lit by *any* form of illumination.

Hopefully, the variety of these techniques will produce technologies that will become available to VR photographers. The pioneering photographers who are early adopters of these techniques will be a big part of this process.

Q: Consider that the automotive industry today has almost completely abandoned traditional photography in favor of high quality, computer rendered graphics, combined with HDR backgrounds. Most consumers can't tell the difference between these digital renderings and traditional high-end advertising photographs. Consumer software programs are now reaching the market that put this power into the hands of consumers – not just skilled CGI artists or technicians. These include Autodesk's ImageModeler, Maya, and others. Automotive photographers in Detroit and Los Angeles have argued that such technologies have made their photographic specialties obsolete. Do you see this happening in other areas of photography and graphic arts, particularly relating to VR panorama and object work?

Q: Are the traditional photographic VR technologies (such as QTVR) and more advanced systems of image mapping / rendering merging together? Do you see image mapping and all the expanded possibilities of it, such as relighting, retiming, resequencing, and even creating new views that were never witnessed by a camera, as an eventual replacement for traditional photographic VR – or perhaps even for traditional photography as a whole?

A: Absolutely – these techniques are all coming together. As an example, the project we've done most recently has used our full-scale Light Stage 6 device to capture full-body human performances, such as walking and running, from a dense array of viewing angles, similar to a QTVR object movie.

A: Our *Fiat Lux* animation in 1999 used HDR image-based lighting techniques to render shiny black dominos into a VR model of St. Peter's Basilica, illuminated by the light I actually recorded while on location. At the time, a few people suggested this could be a good technique for rendering computer-generated cars into photographed environments, and

I've certainly seen this become one of the notably successful applications of the technique.

HDR image based lighting techniques allow computer-generated objects to be lit by the actual light of the environment they are being composited into, and to cast all of the shadows and reflections that they really would if they were actually there. These techniques found their first applications in movie visual effects, where it's important to make computer-generated objects and characters look like they were actually in the scene when everything else was filmed. Automobile advertising has been another successful application, since computer graphics are great for modeling the shape and reflectance of cars. Once you can get the lighting on the model to match a real location, the result essentially duplicates what you would get if you actually photographed the car in that environment. A driving factor behind this process is the utility of producing compelling images of a new car model for marketing before even a single car has been built. Also, the process can be less expensive than transporting a car and a full crew out to a location. The icing on the cake is that the lighting can be modified and augmented *after* being photographed to achieve even finer control of the completed rendering.

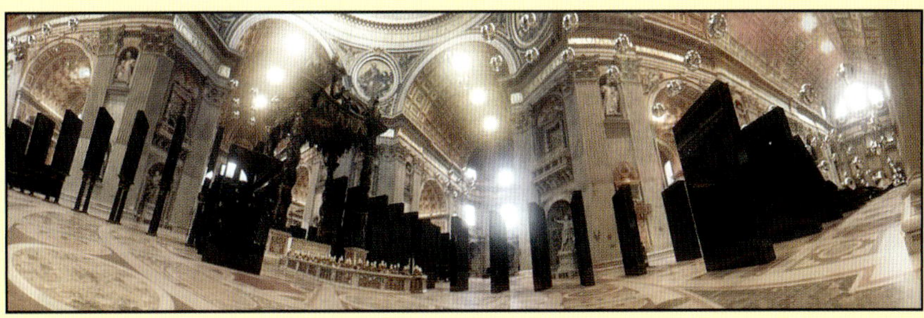

Fig. 15-8 A panorama rendered from Fiat Lux, where image-based lighting techniques were used to combine photos from St. Peter's Basilica with matched lighting computer generated objects (dominos and marbles) to create a photo-realistic animation.

Q: What new opportunities do you see presenting themselves for VR (and traditional) photographers with these emerging technologies? What will it take for these photographers to be successful in business with these?

A: It's my hope that these technologies will allow VR photographers greater artistic control over the images, models, and experiences which they create, and to achieve the results they want more efficiently. Clearly, we will need further development of content delivery systems to view these experiences over the internet, and it's my hope that software developers will create easy-to-use tools that make experiencing the next generation of photoreal, three-dimensional, virtual scenes both exciting and enjoyable.

Part 3
OBJECT VR IMAGING

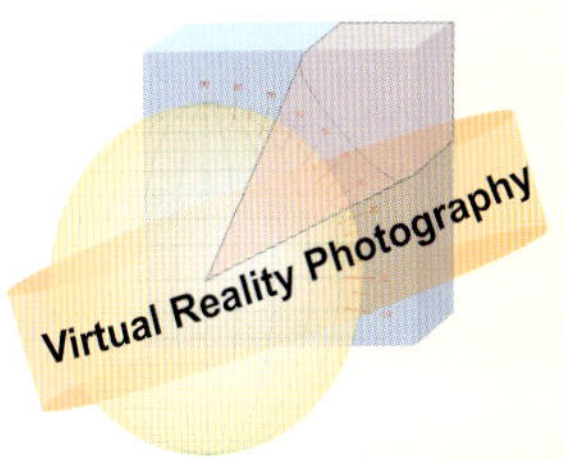

Chapter 16: Object Movie Introduction

Virtual reality photography is not limited only to the creation of panoramic images. Interactive object movies – or image sequences shot of an object from many different angles – are another key element of VR imaging. These sequences, when presented in an interactive viewer, allow the viewer to "virtually" rotate an object and view it from any angle.

While panoramas show the view from a particular location looking outward, object movies are essentially the inverse – where the camera looks inward at an object while moving around it. The result is one of being able to virtually pick up an object and move it around in your hands, viewing it from any angle. Object movies are often used by online retailers to show products, as well as by museum and collector web sites to document artifacts or other physical collections. They are also gaining popularity on auction sites such as eBay, where they provide bidders with a more in-depth look at an item being sold, and often help increase the final sale prices.

An object movie is composed of anywhere from a half dozen to several hundred images surrounding a subject, each taken from a slightly different angle. These images are arranged in a series of linked playback sequences.

Most often, an object will be placed on a turntable and photographs will be shot as the object is rotated in 10° to 30° increments. The more shots you have (the smaller the rotation increment), the smoother the rotation will appear in the playback window. Yet, more images increase file sizes, and consequently, the longer it will take for your viewers to download the movie. Fewer shots yield smaller file sizes (and faster downloads), but playback does not appear as smooth.

Think of object movies as a form of animation, where the viewer has control over the speed and direction of playback. If there is too much movement or change between each frame of the sequence, the movie will appear "jumpy" when viewed. Increasing the number of frames (or reducing the movement between them) makes the motion appear more fluid and pleasing to the eye.

As with many other things in photography, there are tradeoffs among image quality, cost, and efficiency.

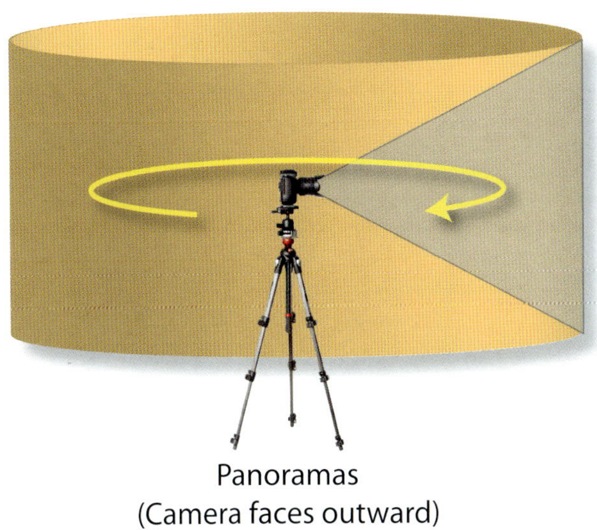
Panoramas
(Camera faces outward)

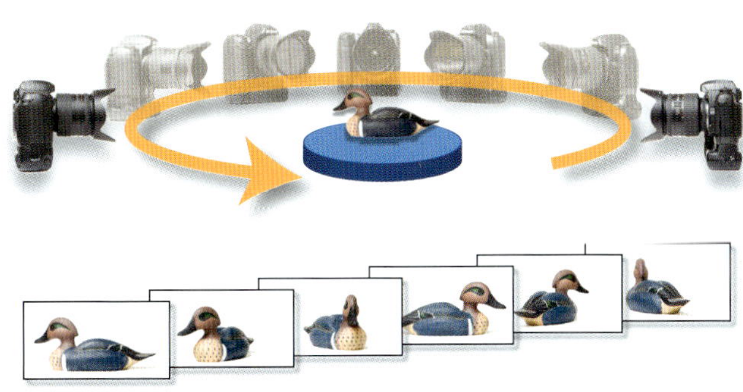
Object movies
(Camera faces inward)

Fig. 16-1 Panoramas represent the view from a camera shooting outward, while object movies are created from a series of images shot with a camera facing inward toward an object.

The job of the photographer or multimedia author is to determine what combinations are most effective for the clients and markets you are serving, as well as the subjects of your work.

Object Movie Tradeoffs

Less	More
Smaller movie window	Larger movie window
Less visual appeal	Greater visual appeal
Smaller file sizes	Larger file sizes
Shorter download times	Longer download times
Fewer images	More images
Jumpier playback	Smoother playback
Less time to photograph	More time to photograph
Less post production	More post production
Lower costs to produce	Higher costs to produce

Fig. 16-2 Function vs. performance for object movies.

For example, let's consider uncompressed file sizes for a color photograph displayed on your computer screen. If the image is 320x240 pixels (4.5" x 3.3" @ 72 dpi, or the size of a small movie window), the uncompressed file size is about 225K. If you *double* both the dimensions to 640x480 pixels), you *quadruple* the file size to about 900K.

Now consider that the most basic object movies contain anywhere from 18 to 36 individual pictures, so you are multiplying the amount of data that your viewer has to download (and that their computer needs to process during playback) by these amounts. While file sizes of most movies are reduced with the application of compression algorithms, the *relative* file size increases correspondingly with increases to the number of frames (total duration) or the dimensions (window size) of the movie.

Practical limits on object movie size used to be more severe than they are today. Back when 28K dial-up modems and 100MHz processors were the norm, it was impractical to distribute movie files over the web unless they were under 1MB in size. It simply took too long for end-users to download larger files, and personal computer processors choked on the data volume when trying to play them. Today, many of these limitations have been overcome with greater bandwidth commonly available through DSL and cable modem connections, along with dramatically higher processing speeds of even low cost personal computers. However, multimedia authors still have to carefully consider file sizes when preparing their VR content.

Planning Your Object Movie

The first thing to consider when planning photography for an object movie is how many perspectives your viewers need to see. The more views needed, the greater the work and costs involved. A minimal approach is often the best. Also, you need to consider whether an object movie provides sufficient added value to the presentation beyond what a single traditional photograph would, in order to warrant the extra resources required to produce and deliver an object movie effectively.

Just as a panoramic photographer can't expect to capture a good VR panorama simply by positioning his camera in the middle of a scene and shooting everything around, neither can an object photographer expect good results simply by putting an object on a turntable and photographing it as it rotates.

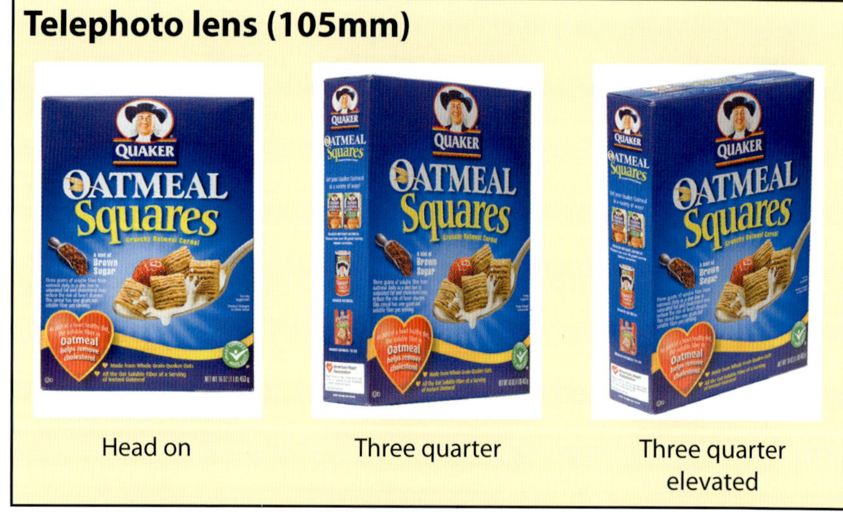

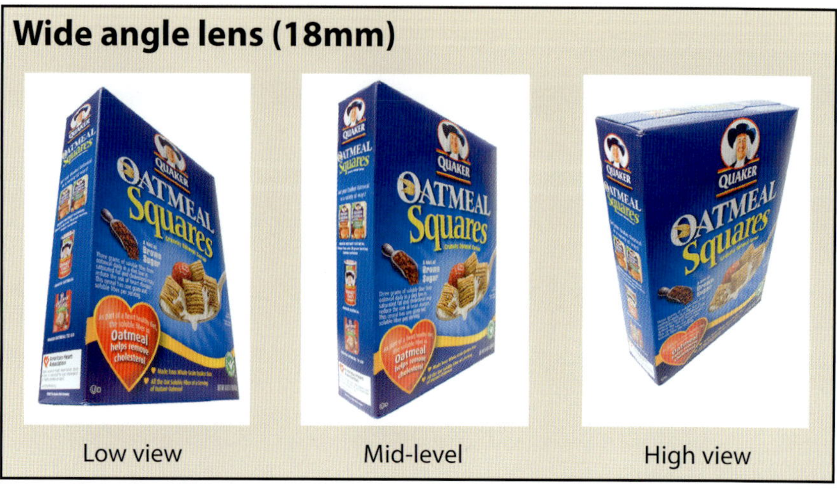

Fig. 16-3 Lens focal length and camera positilon define the view presented.

For decades, professional product and catalog photographers have applied perspective, lighting, and presentation techniques in order to best show their subjects in single photographs. The successful VR object photographer will use many of these same techniques to create effective object movies.

Perspective and View

We'll only briefly discuss these here as an overview for the object photographer. For an in depth look at perspective and view, refer to **Chapter 2**.

The first thing to determine is the best perspective and angle your subject should be viewed from. Is it best seen from a head-on angle, or is it better from slightly off to one side? Perhaps it is best viewed from a position to the side and slightly above, so that three sides are visible at once. Even though an object movie will include photographs from many different angles, you want to start out with a view that shows the product at its best. This will be considered a key frame of the movie, and most often will be the initial view or start of the sequence.

Figure 16–3 shows a number of different perspectives to consider when choosing how you might show an object. Each provides a different look or "feel" to the viewer, and each offers a different impression of the object. These are only a few samples, but they are all a result of combinations of:

- the photographers' choice of viewing position relative to the object
- the focal length of the lens used
- the shooting distance from the object

The first row of images was shot with the camera about four feet from the cereal box using a medium telephoto lens. This tends to keep the scale of closer and distant parts of the object relatively consistent, and renders a visually accurate reproduction. The head-on shot shows only a single face of the cereal box, and while useful for graphic reproduction, does not really give a sense of the dimensionality of the product packaging. When we rotate the object to a three quarter view for the second shot, the viewer can now see two sides of the box at once, providing a sense that it is a three-dimensional object, rather than simply flat art. The third shot shows the same three quarter view, but from a slightly elevated position. This reveals all three dimensions (height, width, and depth) of the package by revealing three different faces of the object at one time.

The second row of images in Figure 16-3 shows the same three quarter view of the product, but we are now shooting with a wide angle lens and the camera much closer to the object. Note how the wide views from a close distance increase the sense of depth and size. This is

because the relative distances between the front and back parts of the package have expanded, and the perspective lines extending from the edges of the box now converge toward perceptible vanishing points. These closer views give an impression that the object is probably larger than it really is. For some subjects, this would be unflattering (wide angle, close views of the human face and body are generally unattractive), while other subjects benefit from the added sense of depth and drama.

Number of Images

Once you have determined the perspective from which to photograph an object, then you need to decide how many different angles to include in your object movie. Remember that an object movie is really just a series of images shot in a stop-motion animation sequence. Changes between frames will result in perceived motion when the series of images are played back in rapid sequence.

Single-Row Object Movies

Rotation increment	No. of frames per 360°	Performance	
90°	4	*Jumpier*	*Smaller*
72°	5	*playback*	*movie files*
60°	6		
45°	8		
40°	9		
30°	12		
20°	18	Generally	
15°	24	acceptable	
10°	36	QTVR "standard"	
5°	72		
3°	120		
2°	180	*Smoother*	*Larger*
1°	360	*playback*	*movie files*

Fig. 16-4 Object movie options for rotation increments.

Therefore, you need to decide what range of movement(s) you want to show for the object. In other words, do you want your viewers to be able to turn it a complete 360° or do you want to limit their views to a smaller range? Next, you must determine how many individual frames you want to subdivide this range of movement into. Using fewer frames results in smaller file sizes, less photography *and* post production efforts, and faster downloads for your viewers. The more frames you use, the smoother the motion in the movie will appear, but the greater the file size and amount of work required to produce it will be.

An early standard for object movies was established by Apple when they developed QuickTime VR. They recommended a 10° rotation increment between frames

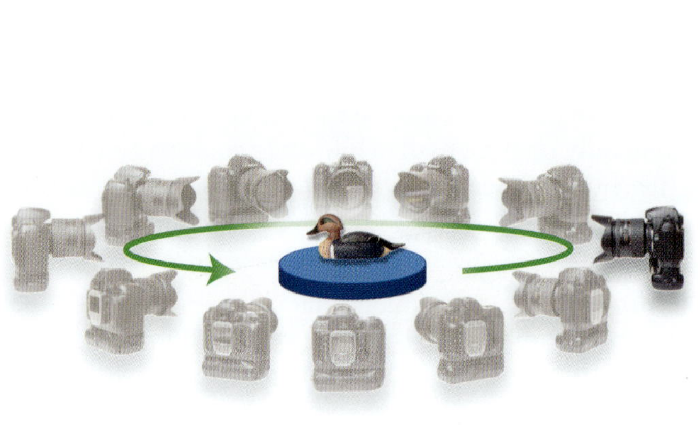

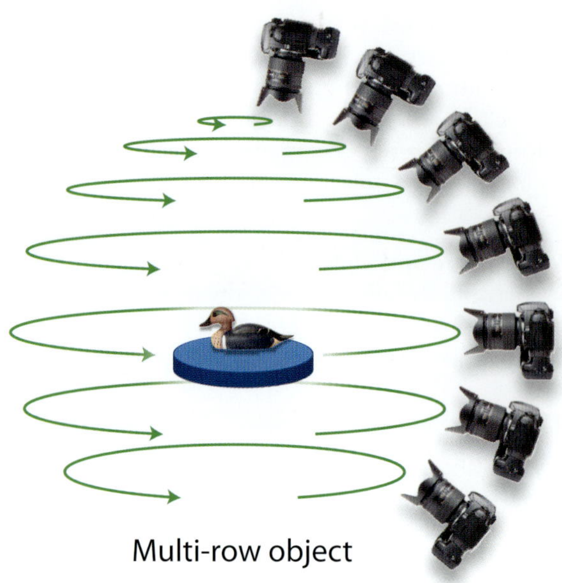

Single row object

Multi-row object

Fig. 16-5 Single row vs. multi-row object movies.

of a QTVR object movie. This means that in order to show the full 360° views around an object, 36 frames will need to be shot (in 10° increments). Apple felt this was a good compromise between smooth playback and reasonable file sizes. Although many other combinations are used successfully, this is still common, and is a figure to be considered for reference purposes.

Single Row vs. Multi-Row
All of our discussion up to this point has been based on a camera shooting from a single level around the object. These are called "single row" object movies, because they are made up of a series of images shot around the object from a single "row," much like a row of seats in a theater or stadium might surround the stage at a single level.

There are times however, when you'll want your viewers to be able to view the object as it rotates *and* from levels

above or below. In such cases, you'll need to repeat the initial row of camera positions from different vertical levels. The results of such combinations are known as "multi-row" object movies.

Once again, it is generally much easier to place an object on a turntable and rotate it in front of the camera than it is to move a camera around the object. The effect is similar, in that you can photograph the object from numerous angles, but when the object moves and the camera remains stationary, it is far easier to maintain consistent image alignment, lighting, and background control between shots.

The camera will still need to be moved to multiple levels when shooting multi-row object movies, but use of a turntable for object positioning is preferred. Maintaining consistent alignment while moving the camera vertically around an object, combined with the demands of

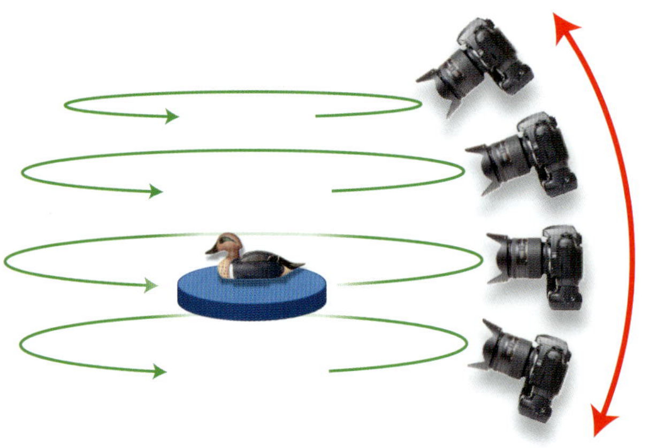

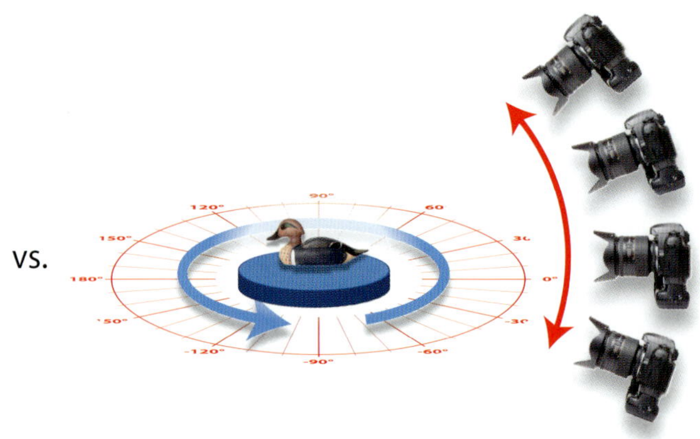

Camera rotates around object

vs.

Object rotates on turntable

Fig. 16-6 It's generally simpler to rotate an object in front of the camera, than to rotate the camera around the object.

maintaining lighting and background consistency, are what makes multi-row object movies so much more labor intensive than their single row counterparts.

Consistency and alignment between images are among the most important concerns for successful object VR photography. Remember that you are essentially creating a stop-motion animation sequence. It is critical to have both camera and object mounted on stable support mechanisms so that they remain consistently aligned as they move. We'll discuss shooting techniques and tools specific to object photography in **Chapter 17**, but consider these alignment concerns as we explore object movie interactivity in this chapter.

Multi-row object movies involve far more images than single row movies, so more shooting, along with additional post production and assembly efforts are required. Remember that each frame of the movie will probably need a similar amount of retouching or Photoshop work. Even if you only need to do one or two minor tweaks to an image, you will multiply that work by as many images as your object movie includes.

For a single row object movie shot in 10° rotation increments, you'll have to retouch and assemble 36 individual images. If you shoot this as a multi-row movie with four rows, you'll have to deal with four times as many images (4 x 36 = 144 images). If you expand this movie to include rows every 10° vertically from straight above to directly below the object (imagine "north pole" to "south pole"), you'll wind up with 19 rows of 36 images each, or 684 total images.

There are very few commercial products that benefit from presentation of "pole-to-pole" object movies (showing the object from every level above and below its center). Most often, showing an object from only a few levels will suffice to give the viewer an "all around" sense of the object, and will save significantly on both file sizes and production efforts.

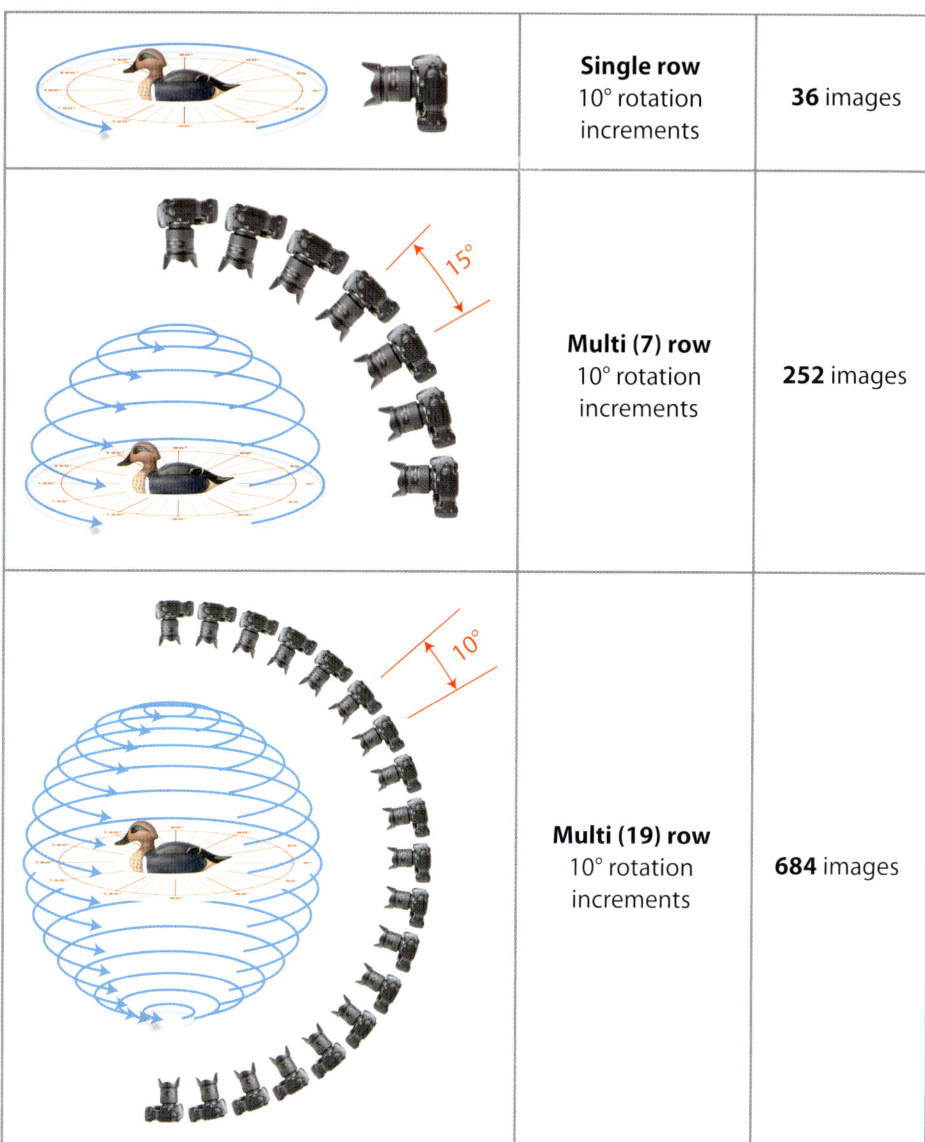

	Single row 10° rotation increments	**36** images
	Multi (7) row 10° rotation increments	**252** images
	Multi (19) row 10° rotation increments	**684** images

Fig. 16-7 Increasing the number of rows for a multi-row object movie significantly increases the number of photographs and post-production time required.

production efforts. Some VR producers will limit the number of rows that they shoot by making the vertical increments larger than the rotational increments, or by including only views from "above the equator."

Consider the production of a multi-row object movie that only shows views of the object from its equator (0° vertical level) and above. If photographed in 10° increments, both rotationally and vertically, this would require 360 individual images (10 rows x 36 images per row).

Alternately, you might consider increasing the increment between vertical rows to 15° or 30° (while keeping the rotational increment between shots at 10°) in order to further reduce the number of photos you'll need. A 15° vertical increment would mean you'd only need seven rows of 36 shots (at 0°, 15°, 30°, 45°, 60°, 75° and 90°) totaling 252 images. A 30° vertical increment between rows would result in only four rows (0°, 30°, 60° and 90°) for 144 images. Or you may find that you only need two or three vertical rows to present the necessary dimensionality of the object effectively.

As a VR photographer and object movie author, you have full control over how you present the movie and how many images (i.e. how much work) will be required. You may find that you prefer to use smaller degree increments between shots, and therefore will require more images. If you wanted a 1° increment between shots both in rotation and vertical directions, you'd wind up with an object movie requiring over 65,000 individual images – impractical from both production and viewer perspectives. You will have to explore these options for yourself by preparing test sequences, and then choose your object movie structures based on file size, smoothness, and range of motion needs of your particular project.

Remember that file size will be dependent upon the number of images or frames in your object movie (shots per 360° of rotation multiplied by the number of rows), along with the pixel dimensions of those images and the compression algorithm, used to prepare the movie.

Compression

Unfortunately, there are no magic formulas used to predetermine exact file sizes for completed object movies. This is because post production movie compression plays such a big part in minimizing the file sizes, and there are so many different compression algorithms available. These include common algorithms such as photo jpeg, video, and an increasing array of others. Comparative testing and accumulated experience will lead you toward the best tradeoffs between acceptable quality and minimal file sizes.

To get recommendations on good starting points for object movie compression, I turned to my friend and colleague John Greenleigh, who is one of the leading VR object photographers in the world. John runs Flipside Studios (www.flipsidestudios.com), based in Emeryville, California. John created almost all of the QTVR object movies of Apple products for Apple over many years.

A good starting point for object movie compression, according to John, is **photo jpeg** – set at a level of 60 or above. **Sorenson** compression, while highly praised for linear movie distribution, tends to cause color fringing in object movies, particularly with subjects photographed against contrasting backgrounds.   Photo jpeg seems to work well for almost all subjects and shooting styles, whether images include dark, light or colored backgrounds, and high key or low key lighting.

One very important tip to note is that when using solid backgrounds, whether white, black, or any color, the more uniform the background is, the more efficiently the compression algorithms work. Many object VR photographers will go in to each frame of a movie sequence and replace the photographed background with a similar "pure" color in Photoshop. While a photographed background may *appear* to be a single, continuous color to our eyes, there are actually thousands of small variations present that compression algorithms wind up trying to preserve. Therefore, if you can replace every background pixel with a consistent single color, the file compression difference can be significant – reducing the movie down to as little as one third of its original file size.

Even with higher bandwidth internet connections such as DSL and cable so common today, most commercial web sites seek to keep their content file sizes as small as possible. Many choose to offer two or more versions of the same material for their viewers – a smaller file (usually lower resolution) for viewers with slow connections, and a larger file for those with higher bandwidths. For multi-row object movies, the largest files are best kept to a size of 2MB or less, while smaller single row versions are often targeted between 300K and 600K.

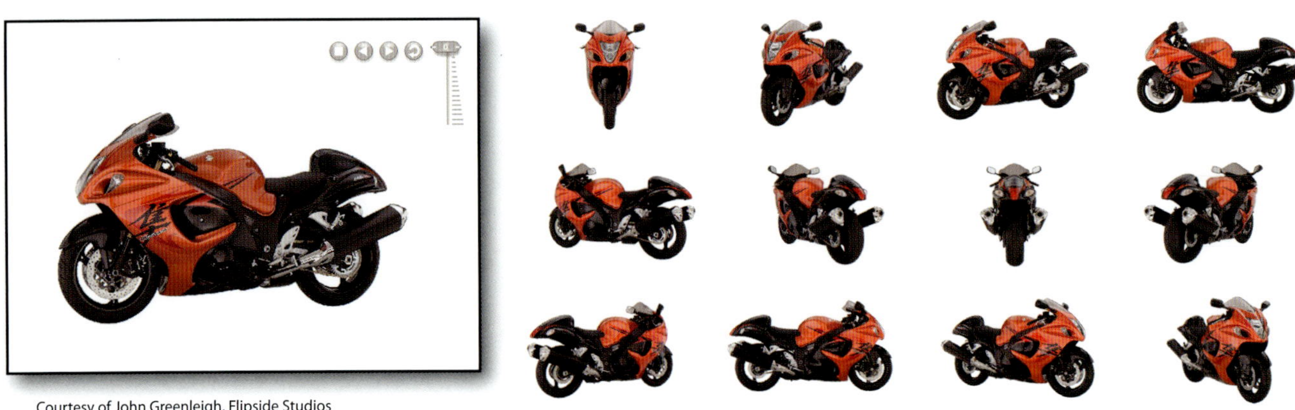

Courtesy of John Greenleigh, Flipside Studios

Fig. 16-8 John Greenleigh of Flipside Studios photographed and produced this Flash-based object movie of the Suzuki Hayabusa (the fastest production motorcycle in the world) for the Suzuki web site.

VR Toolbox's QTVR authoring software (www.vrtoolbox.com) actually offers an on-the-fly compression window, which lets you preview how your object movie will look under different compression settings, as well as an estimate of the resulting file sizes.

In recent years, John reports that clients have started favoring Flash versions of object movies, rather than the original QTVR (QuickTime VR) format. Even though QuickTime is an industry standard, not every user on the web has QuickTime installed. Many clients now tend to prefer the use of Flash for animations and other interactive media, since these can be viewed on just about any web browser without requiring the user to download and install an additional plug-in. However, as web standards evolve further, the preference for Flash presentation may well give way to more universal (i.e. less proprietary) technologies, such as HTML 5.

The good news is that it makes little difference in the actual photography of an object sequence whether it is

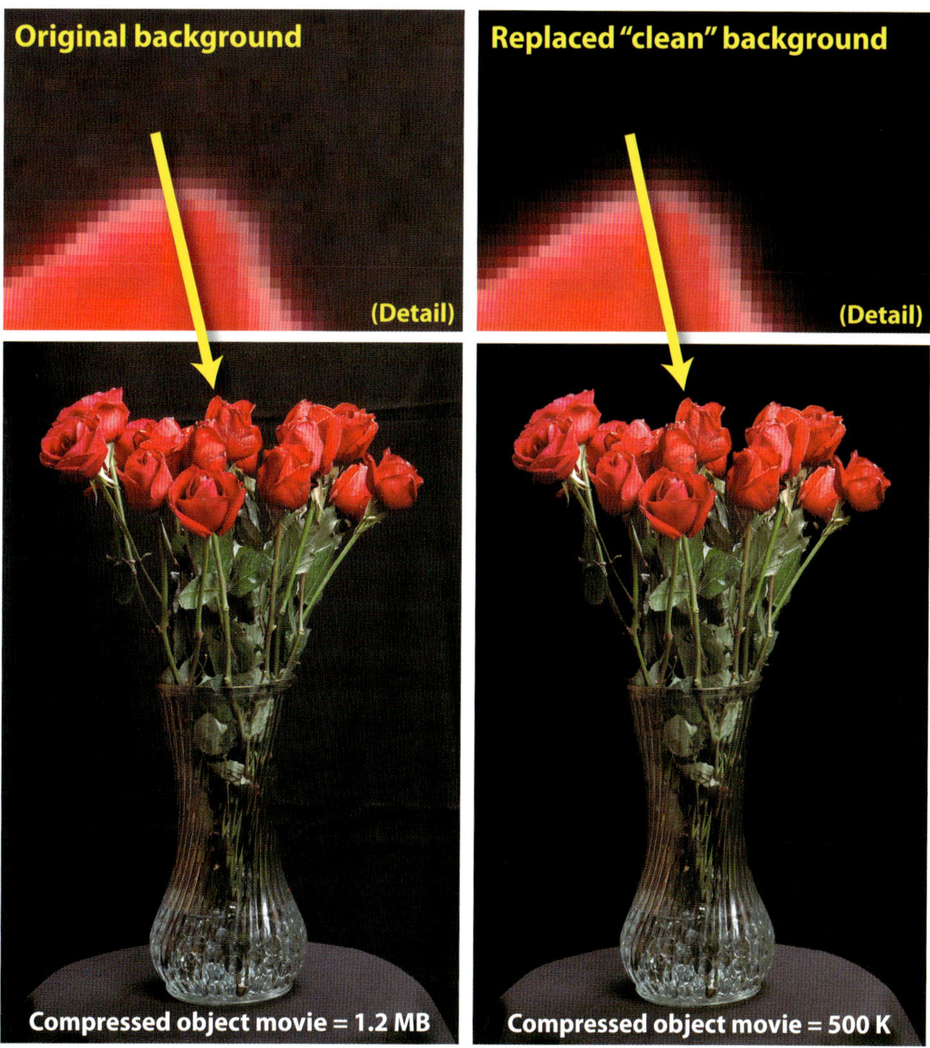

Fig. 16-9 Replacing photographic backgrounds with similar single color backgrounds during post production can yield significantly better file compression.

presented in QuickTime VR or Flash. You still want to make sure the camera and object are consistently aligned, exposure and white balance are held constant, and that backgrounds are replaced with "pure" colors when possible in order to more efficiently compress file sizes.

John recommends the following. "For the Flash spins, we now save each image using Photoshop's 'Save for Web' function, and usually go with JPG High at Quality 65. This can reduce each 200K image to 95K. However, this level of compression also tends to alter the color and contrast, so we often need to make a set of images with the color adjusted specifically to be saved for web."

John finds that only a handful of his commercial VR clients desire multi-row object movies any more. The desired effect of showing their products from many angles can usually be accomplished by combining a single row movie with thumbnail links to traditional still photos, or even animations, that show product features in action. The costs of creating single row object movies, along with the necessary bandwidth needed for delivery,

are significantly lower than those required for multi-row movies. In fact, single row object movies consisting of only 12 or 18 frames, rather than the previous standard of 36, are becoming more common today, primarily due to the desire for small file sizes.

Remember that with object movies, the window size in which you choose to present the movie relates directly to the resolution and the resulting file size of that movie. A 640x480 pixel movie creates a file about four times the size of a 320x240 pixel movie, because the resolution and window are four times as large (2 x height x 2 x width = 4x). For this reason, a 320x240 pixel window or a close equivalent, tends to be the standard for commercial object movies on the web, although that is changing as higher bandwidth becomes ever more common.

However, you and your client(s) will need to determine what is best not only for your subject matter and delivery formats, but for the markets your content will serve. Ultimately, it will be your collected experience that will guide you.

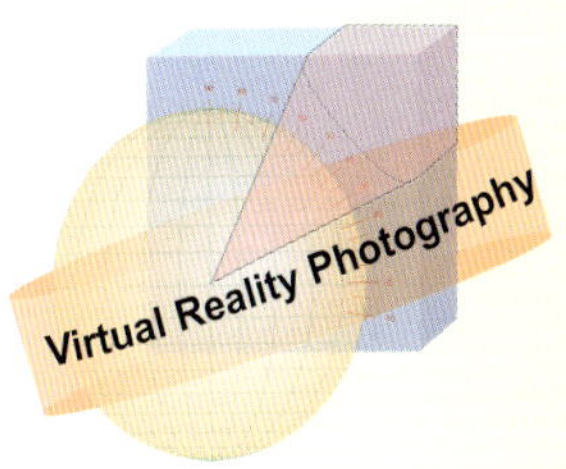

Chapter 17: Equipment and Technique

In theory, capturing images for object movies is as simple as putting an object on a turntable and taking a series of photos as the turntable is rotated. However, to photograph object movies well, we need to more carefully consider our technique and even the kind of equipment we choose for shooting them. Our choices do not necessarily have to be expensive or complex – indeed some of the best work is done with the simplest approaches – but we do need to understand the basic principles necessary for success.

As mentioned in the last chapter, object movie photography is really little more than stop-motion animation, where one creates a series of still images with slight movements between frames. When these images are played back in rapid sequence, they give the perception of motion to the viewer. However, this perception can be completely ruined if the animation technique is inadequate.

Consistency and Repeatability

The most important requirements for successful object movie photography are consistency and repeatability. Consistency applies to keeping exposures, color balance, focal length, and focus constant throughout an image sequence, and repeatability applies to the ability to move the object (or camera) in incremental amounts between shots, as well as the ability to *return* to those positions repeatedly as needed. The absence of any of the above will result in unintended variations between shots, and their less-than-smooth playback as a movie.

The foundation of good object movie photography is being able to keep everything as consistent as possible while changing only intended elements between frames.

Shooting single row object movies can be as simple as placing your object on a turntable and shooting it from a fixed position (your camera on a tripod). Multi-row movies get significantly more complicated, as you

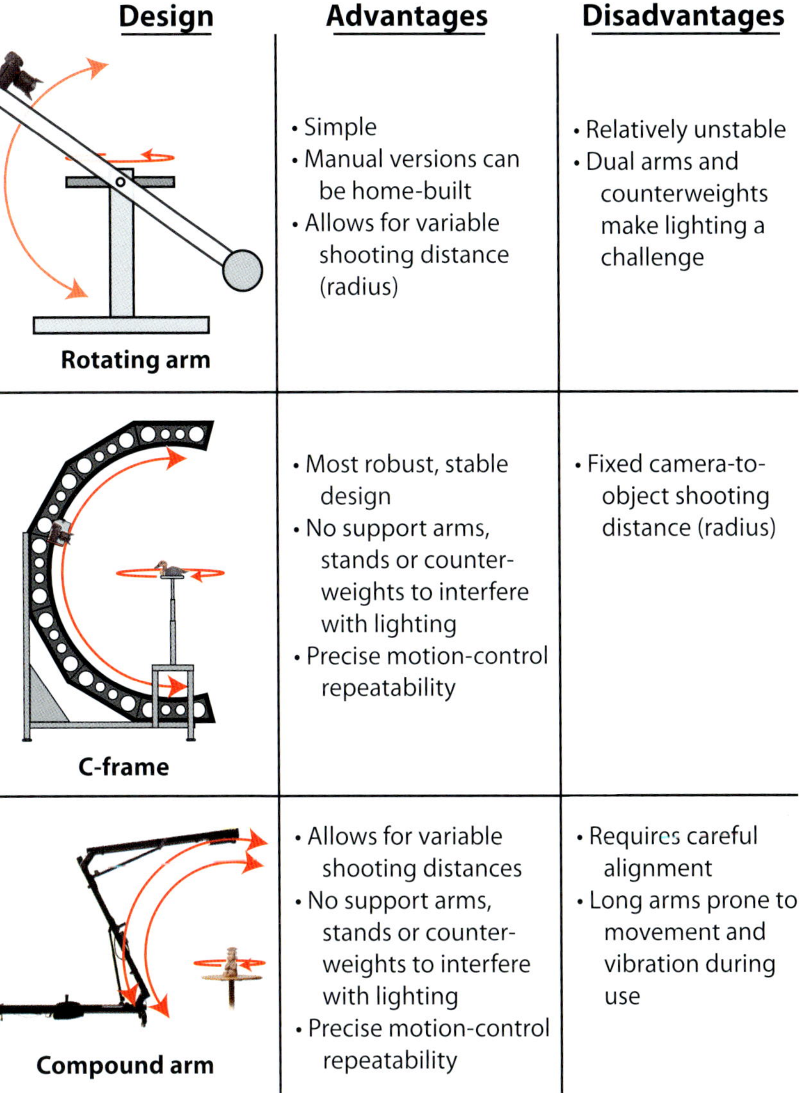

Design	Advantages	Disadvantages
Rotating arm	• Simple • Manual versions can be home-built • Allows for variable shooting distance (radius)	• Relatively unstable • Dual arms and counterweights make lighting a challenge
C-frame	• Most robust, stable design • No support arms, stands or counter-weights to interfere with lighting • Precise motion-control repeatability	• Fixed camera-to-object shooting distance (radius)
Compound arm	• Allows for variable shooting distances • No support arms, stands or counter-weights to interfere with lighting • Precise motion-control repeatability	• Requires careful alignment • Long arms prone to movement and vibration during use

Fig. 17-1 The three primary designs for today's multi-row object rigs.

generally need to maintain the same shooting distance and alignment between camera and object as the camera moves above and/or below the object while it turns.

Specialized camera rigs for object photography are available from companies such as Kaidan, Corybant West, and Peace River Studios. These rigs help maintain alignment between camera and object, and are designed for photography of multi-row object movies, although they can be used for single row movies, as well.

There are three basic designs for multi-row object rigs. Each has its own strengths and weaknesses. Your choice will depend upon your priorities in terms of cost, frequency of use, and the types/sizes of objects you plan to shoot. Multi-row object rigs are relatively expensive and their movements are often computer controlled. Photographers need to carefully consider how much use they'll have for such a rig before deciding upon its purchase, due to both price concerns and the relatively large sizes of these rigs. A creative individual with a little mechanical ingenuity can often figure out how to build a manually operated rig using low cost parts from a hardware store. The difficulty with such home built systems however, is maintaining repeatability of camera and object positioning.

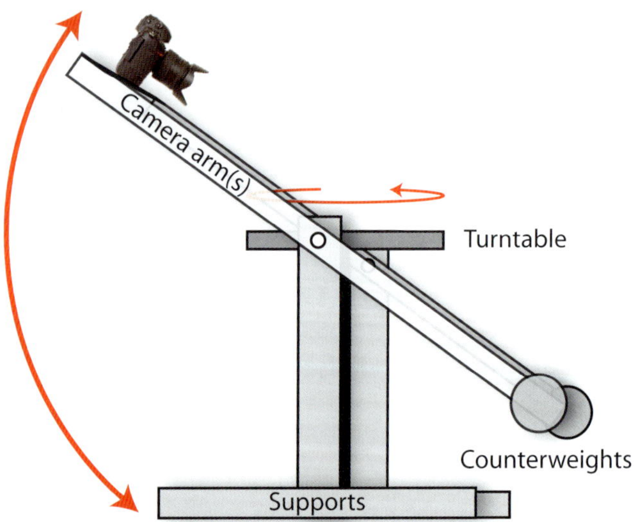

Fig. 17-2 Rotating arm object rig.

The first type of object rig is a **rotating arm** design. The camera is attached to a cross piece supported by one or two counterweighted arms that rotate (tilt) vertically. This allows for vertical camera positing at equal distances from the object, while the object itself is rotated on a turntable in front of the camera. The height of the rig (and the axis of camera tilt) is set by raising or lowering the support stands. Alignment is often difficult, as improper counterweight balance or slight differences in the support stands can cause the rotation axis to be skewed somewhat, or to introduce a misalignment into

the camera support cross piece. Another disadvantage to this design is that the support arm(s) limit the possible positioning of lighting and can create undesirable shadows or reflections on the object as the rig tilts up and down.

There are several advantages to this design, however. The first is that it is probably the simplest mechanically, and can be home built from a variety of photographic lighting and grip products available at pro camera & hardware stores. It is also the only design that can be effectively operated without electronic motors or computerized controls. Furthermore, it allows adjustments of camera-to-object shooting distances simply by changing the position of the counterweighted support arms. This gives the photographer a broader selection of lens focal lengths and perspectives to use when shooting objects of varying sizes.

Commercial rigs of this design (with electronic motion controls) are currently available from both Kaidan (www.kaidan.com) and Peace River Studios (www.peaceriverstudios.com).

The second rig design is based on a large **C-frame**, which functions as a vertical track on which the camera is raised and lowered. The semi-circle or C-shape allows the camera to be moved 180 degrees vertically, from directly above to directly below the object, while maintaining a constant distance between the camera and object. The object is positioned on a turntable centered at the midpoint of the C-frame. Rotating image sequences can be shot from multiple levels.

One of the great advantages of this design is that it does not have moving support arms that get in the way of lighting setups, or that cast shadows like the rotating arm rigs. This gives the photographer far more freedom in lighting, as the camera track is supported primarily from below and behind the camera's axis of movement. The C-frame is probably the most stable of the three designs, and is least affected by incidental bumps to the rig during shooting.

The biggest disadvantage to this design however, is that is that is only allows a single shooting distance (or radius), which is determined by the arc of the rig itself. Therefore, larger objects must be photographed with wider lenses and smaller objects must be photographed with telephoto lenses. This limits the photographer in perspective choices for multi-row object sequences. Also, the largest objects you can shoot are limited to sizes smaller than the radius of the rig.

Kaidan (www.kaidan.com) is currently the only manufacturer offering a commercial product of this design with their Meridian C-60. The C-60 has a shooting radius of about five feet.

so the photographer effectively has as much flexibility and control over lighting setups as he or she would with traditional studio photography – and that is a major plus for those creating high quality object imagery.

These rigs do require some calibration. Both leveling and alignment need to be fairly precise before shooting. They are generally quite large, and require a good sized studio space to use effectively. They are also very sensitive to any extraneous motion. Because their design includes multiple long arms interconnected into an articulating system, they require a fair bit of "settling" time in between movements of the camera in order to dampen vibrations. If they are accidentally bumped during a shooting sequence, it is best to restart the sequence entirely, rather than try to rematch the original alignment and camera positions.

Assuming that the rig is kept stable during the shoot, the fact that it is computer controlled is a great advantage. Shooting a multi-row object sequence can be preprogrammed and fully automated. Additionally, the camera can be returned precisely to any position that might need to be shot again as necessary, such as when a lighting flare from the object requires correction of one or more frames.

Currently, the only manufacturer offering rigs of this design is Corybant West (www.corybantwest.com) in Santa Cruz, CA.

These and other computer-controlled object rigs are a necessity for large volume and production-type shooting of object movies. A computer controls both the rotation of the object turntable and the vertical positioning of the camera, while also remotely triggering the camera for

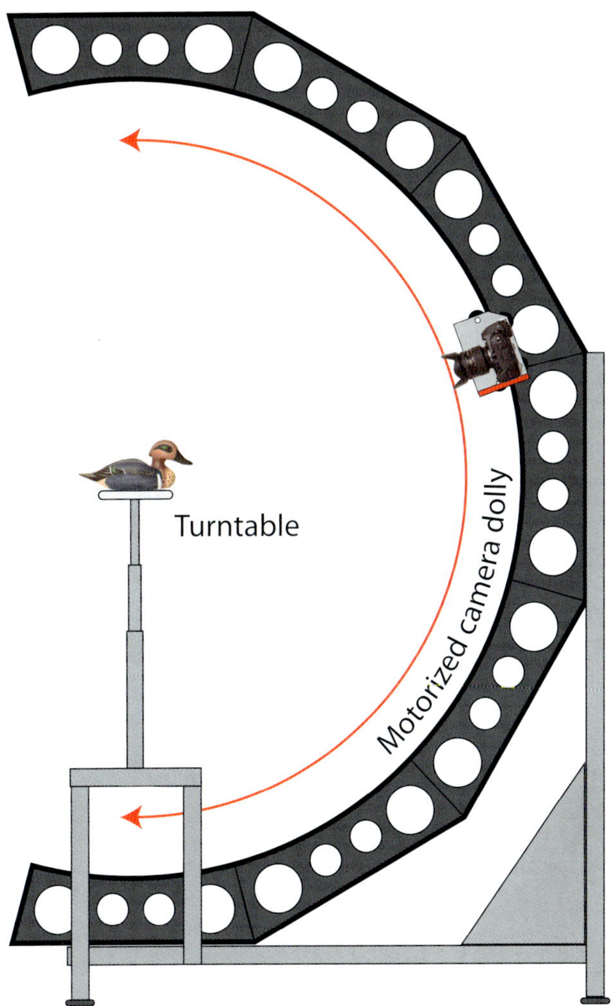

Fig. 17-3 C-frame object rig.

The third design is a compound, articulating arm rig, which is the most sophisticated and versatile of the current rig designs. These systems are entirely computer controlled, and the computer calculates the needed angles for the rig's folding arms in order to position the camera accurately throughout a wide variety of shooting radii. This offers the photographer almost unlimited choice in lens selection, as the rig can follow small or large arcs, or even be programmed to move a camera along oval or other non-circular vertical tracks. This is a simplified form of a full motion control rig as used by special effects studios for motion picture work.

As is the case with the C-frame design, the articulating arm system is only supported from behind the camera, leaving space in front of and beside the object for lighting and other equipment. There are no moving support arms in these positions to get in the way,

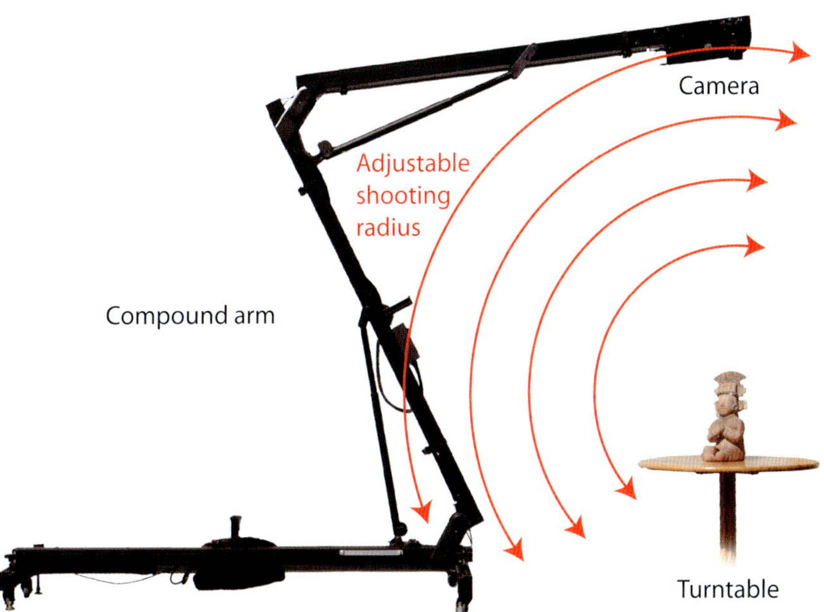

Fig. 17-4 Articulating arm object rig.

each exposure. Some of these systems can even be set up so that the images are automatically downloaded from camera to computer for post production and final movie assembly. This sort of automation makes high volume production possible for environments such as museum/ artifact documentation, electronic catalog production, and commercial product photography.

Camera Equipment

Object movie sequences can be shot with almost any camera or format, whether film based, digital, or video. However, remember that precise alignment between images is critical in minimizing post-production assembly time and allowing smoother playback. Digital or video cameras are generally the best choice for object movie photography. With these cameras, the image sensor remains in a fixed position with no movement between exposures relative to the rest of the camera. If the camera position is kept constant, the image alignment remains constant.

In a film camera, the film must be advanced between each frame in order to expose a new section of the roll. While this movement itself has little, if any, impact on the relative position of the camera, there are many small inconsistencies that result in the framing of each image on a film roll. For example, a 35mm camera might advance the film roll anywhere between 38mm and 39mm between shots. This one millimeter difference is negligible for normal photography, where you will probably crop within the edges of the frame anyway. But for capturing object sequences, the slight change will result in a jumpiness or jitter between images, and will require extensive realignment in post production to smooth out. Of course, these misalignments are further exacerbated when film is scanned or digitized, as it is almost impossible to consistently align each frame within a scanner. The process of loading and unloading each roll of film from a camera when it is mounted on a rig also causes some camera movement.

To aid in the post production alignment of such image sequences, it can be helpful to place reference or control points within the scene during your photography. These can be simple things such as small push pins or adhesive dots placed in the stationary foreground or background of your object. These can be used as reference marks for the realignment of each frame in post production, and can then be retouched out of each image before exporting the completed movie. If your object is rotating in front of the camera on a turntable, you'll want to make sure these reference points are *not* attached to the turntable or the rotating object, so they don't move when the object or camera moves.

When shooting automobiles or other large objects without a turntable, photographers will often mount a small ball onto a suction cup, which they then position on top of the vehicle directly above the axis of rotation. As the camera moves around the vehicle, the ball is used as a reference point to match the alignment of each frame, and is then removed in post production retouching. Some photographers have even attached laser pointers to their cameras to help them more accurately align each shot with this reference spot. This is a very useful approach when you have to move your camera around an object (instead of rotating the object on a turntable in front of the camera) without some sort of motion control system.

The best approach for consistent image alignment however, is to shoot with a digital camera from a fixed position, and have the object rotating independently in front of you. The image sensor in a digital camera will remain in a constant position between shots as long as the camera doesn't move, and the downloading of images can be done directly into your computer without having to physically open (and possibly move) the camera to remove film. Digital capture also provides immediate feedback for the photographer on exposure, composition,

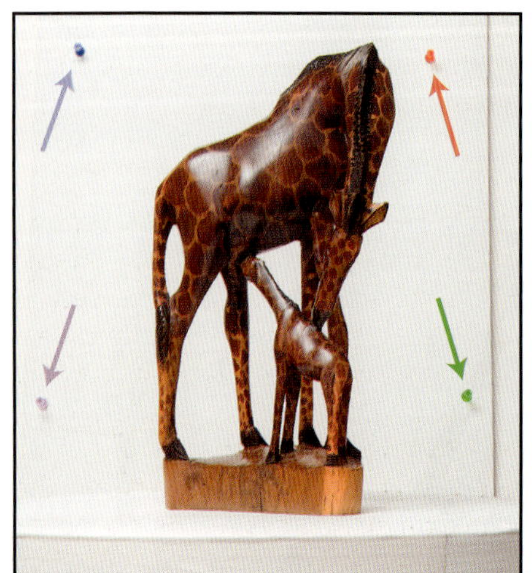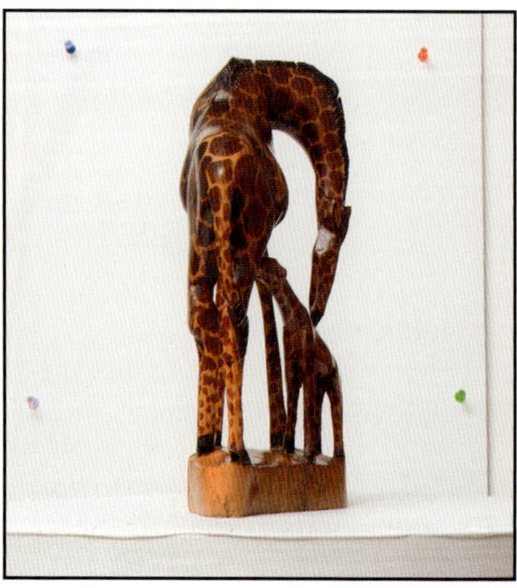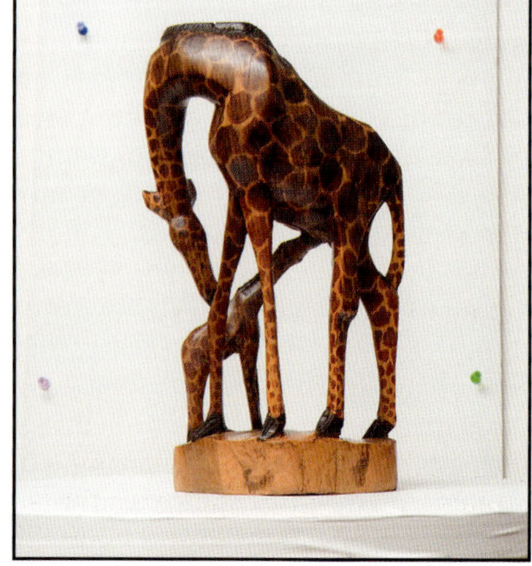

Fig. 17-5 Reference markers, such as push pins, on the object background can be used as post production alignment points. These can then be removed during the background replacement process.

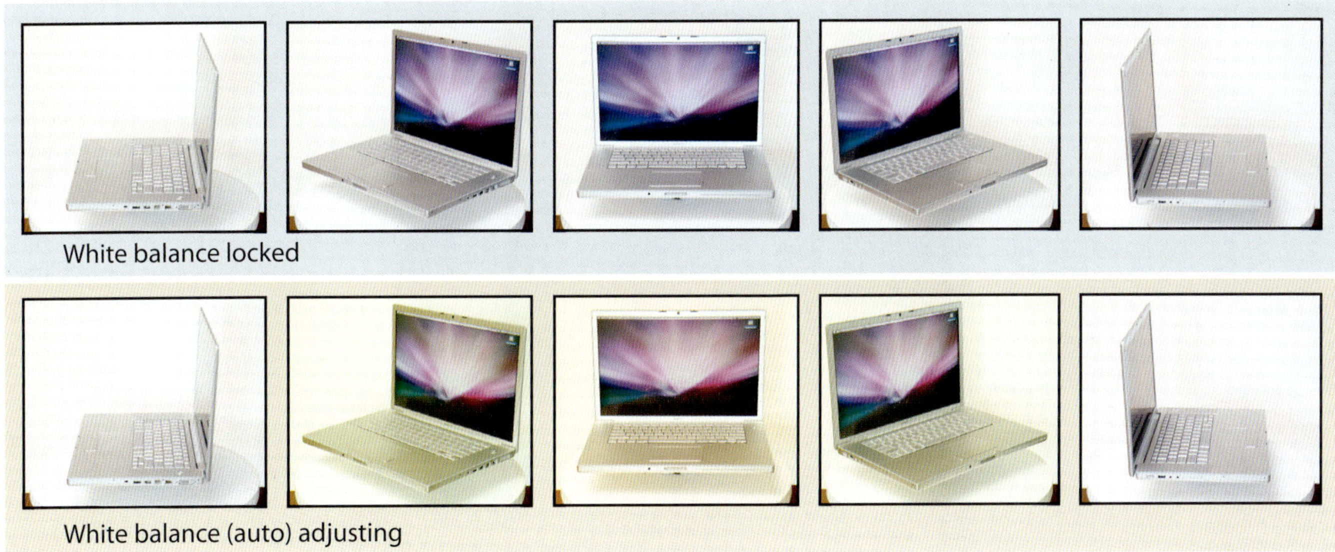

Fig. 17-6 White balance and exposure settings should be set to Manual throughout an object movie shooting sequence.

alignment and color balance, so when errors occur, you can reshoot the necessary frames while everything on set is still locked.

Before high quality digital cameras became so affordable, object movies used to be shot using video cameras. This required a video capture board in your computer, and software applications that would allow you to select specific frames out of each video sequence. Unfortunately, resolution was limited to about one megapixel – the limit for most video cameras of the day. Today, even the cheapest digital still cameras provide higher resolutions than high end professional video cameras, so digital cameras have become the preferred choice for most object photographers. Furthermore, most digital cameras now allow direct download of their image files either through USB, Firewire, and wireless connections, or via removable memory cards.

When choosing a digital camera for your object photography, keep in mind the need to maintain consistency between images. It is imperative to use a camera that has manual exposure control, manual white balance, and manual focusing. The automatic settings for these features, which are standard with most consumer digital cameras, are of great benefit for most other photography, but they cause endless problems when shooting object sequences. Having your camera automatically readjust exposure in the middle of an object sequence because one side of the object you are shooting is lighter than the other, will result in the entire sequence being unusable. Such will also be the case if your lens automatically changes focus as the object rotates, or the white balance readjusts. If you cannot turn off these automatic features, you will never get smooth or consistent results in your movies.

Therefore, the lower end auto-everything digital cameras are often *not* the best choice for object photographers. Look toward the prosumer or professional models when you are buying, and test to make sure that the one you choose will work the way you expect. Bear in mind that some manufacturers claim to have manual settings on their digital cameras, but this may only involve limited manual adjustment of the camera's automatic features, rather than true manual control.

Lens Selection (Focal Length)
Lens choice for object photography will depend a lot upon the subject you are shooting, the limitations of the object rig you'll be working with, and the perspective that you want for the object.

Using a wide angle lens with the camera close to the subject tends to present a distorted, yet imposing view, much like we see when we use a wide angle lens to photograph a tall building from street level. Shooting the same subject from further away, but using a longer lens, provides a more natural and realistic view. This relationship applies to shooting objects of almost any size.

VR object photography is most often used to present three dimensional objects for commerce. In general, these products are best shown with as little perceived "distortion" as possible. Therefore, photographers tend to choose longer focal lengths and longer shooting distances to make these subjects look natural. Of course, there can also be advantages to using other perspectives and lens choices depending upon the feeling that the photographer wants to impart. However, using longer lenses with their accompanying narrower fields of view can also simplify lighting and composition demands.

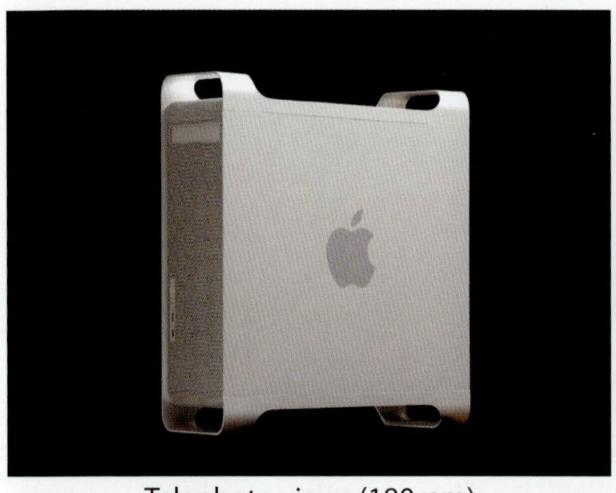
Telephoto views (180mm)

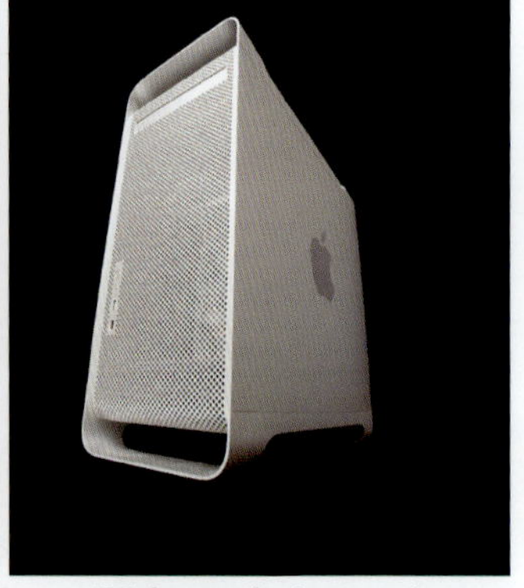
Wide angle (18mm)

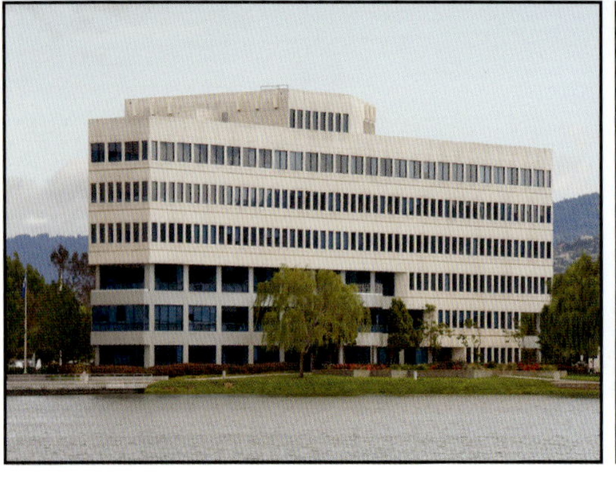

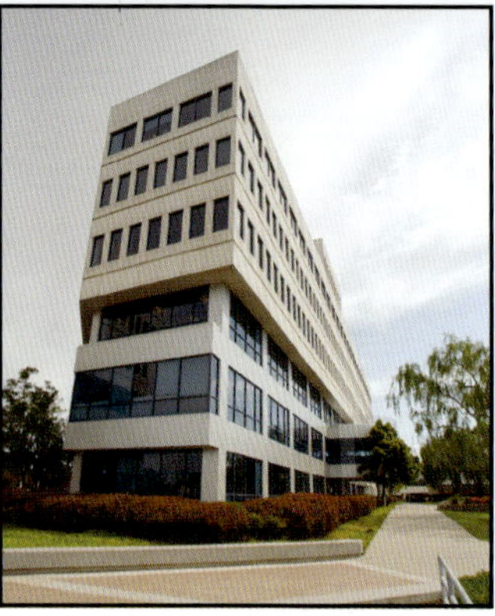

Fig. 17-7 The combination of lens focal length and camera position can make significant differences in the appearance of an object. These choices by the photographer affect how the product will ultimately be perceived by viewers.

Centers of Rotation

While it may sound obvious, properly centering an object on your turntable is a step that is often overlooked. For most objects, the physical center of the object should be positioned directly over the axis of rotation of the turntable itself. If not, the object will appear to wobble or rotate off center in the final movie.

Certainly there can be exceptions to this, such as when you are shooting more than one object (such as a pair of shoes) or when your object has an unusual or asymmetrical shape. In these cases, you may want to choose an approximate center of the object grouping, or a center of balance, as the alignment position for your rotation axis.

It's a good idea to physically mark the center of your turntable so you can identify this rotation point. A small mark with a permanent pen, or an adhesive dot will usually do the trick. Most of the time, your object will cover this mark and it will not show in your images, but having it as a reference point will help you properly align and center your objects before shooting.

Once you've done this, it is also helpful to manually rotate the turntable while looking through the camera's viewfinder. As the object turns, you can often tell whether it feels "off center" visually, and adjust its position accordingly. It is far better to do this before you start shooting, than it is to discover that the rotation of the object seems off balance after you've finished the entire production process.

With larger objects, it may be difficult to visually align the physical center of your object with the mark on the center of your turntable. In these cases, the use of a carpenter's plumb (which can be purchased at low cost from most hardware stores) suspended from the ceiling can help. Before placing your object on your turntable, hang the plumb line through a hook from the ceiling, and then center your turntable directly below it. Now you can raise the plumb line high enough to place your object underneath. If you center the object under the plumb, it will also be centered on the turntable.

Similar alignment methods can be done using low cost laser pointers and other tools. Visit your local hardware store and browse through the aisles. You'll be amazed at how many items you can find that can be of use in your object photography efforts. Be creative.

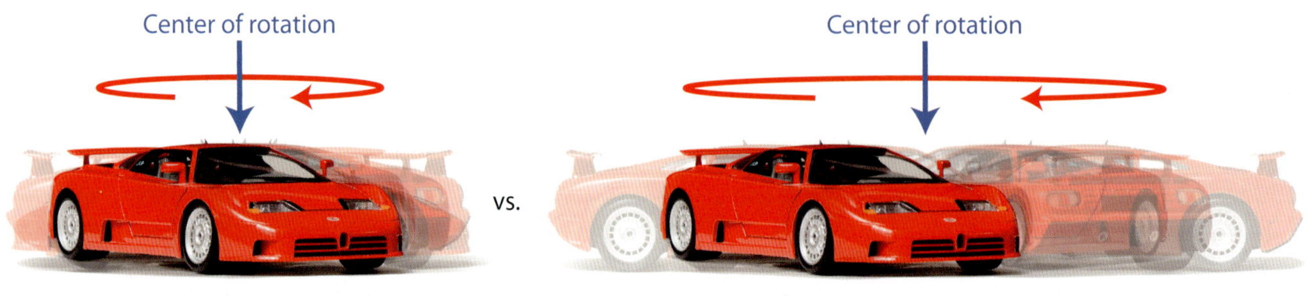

Fig. 17-8 The point about which an object is rotated should be selected carefully when aligning an object on a turntable.

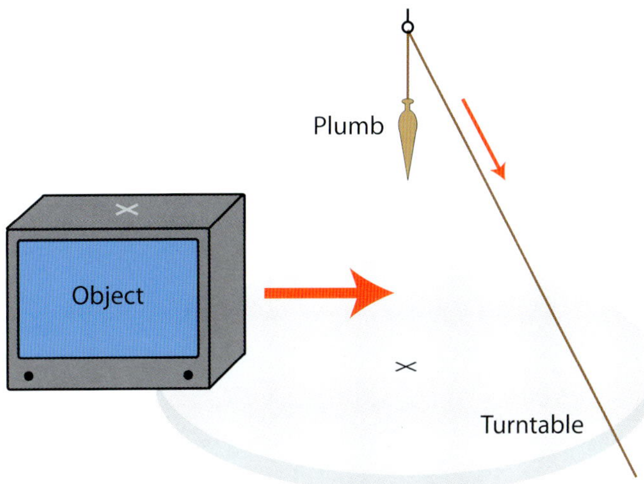

1) Center turntable under plumb
2) Raise plumb line
3) Position center of object under plumb

Fig. 17-9 Centering an object on a turntable.

Building Your Own Object Turntable

Turntables for object photography need not be elaborate nor expensive. They simply need to be large enough to adequately support the kinds of objects you will be shooting, and to have some sort of indexing system that allows you to rotate them in the degree increments that you require.

First, let's consider the turntable mechanism itself. Then we'll explore ideas for accurately indexing its rotation.

Your local hardware or kitchen supply store is often the best place to look for low-cost turntable mechanisms. You may find something perfectly suited for your object photography in an existing lazy susan or kitchen cabinet insert. For example, Rubbermaid (www.rubbermaid.com) produces several different sized plastic lazy susans. These can be

bought for about $15 at popular houseware stores, and are anywhere from 10 – 14 inches in diameter. They are ideal for photographing small objects. Simply mark the rotation increments you desire on the outside edge of the turntable. Rotate the turntable by hand, aligning each marked increment with a fixed reference point between shots.

For a more heavy duty approach, check your local hardware store for turntable or lazy susan mechanisms, which are comprised of two thin metal plates sandwiched around a ball bearing raceway. These mechanisms come in several sizes, the largest of which is about 12 inches in diameter, but they hold up to 1,000 pounds of weight. You can usually find them for less than $20.

Next, go to the plywood section of your hardware store for pre-cut table rounds. These are available in either plywood or finished white Melamine™, and come in diameters ranging from 24" to 60".

You can mount one table round to another, or simply mount the one you want to use as your turntable to a piece of plywood or other surface. Keep in mind that one of these surfaces will need to have an off-center hole

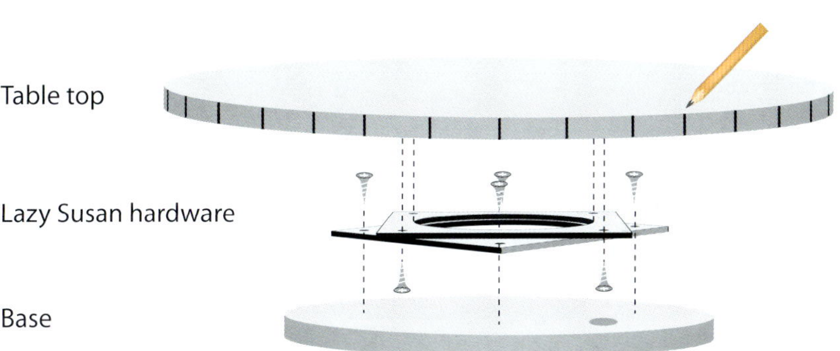

Fig. 17-11 Assembly of a hardware store lazy-susan mechanism between two precut plywood or Melamine table rounds.

drilled into it in order to allow screwdriver access to the back side of the other. This will allow you to attach the two surfaces together from the inside. It is best to plan your construction so that the hole is drilled in what will become your base piece, so that the actual turntable surface will be the solid one.

You will also want to make sure you properly align the center of your turntable top with the center of the turntable mechanism before permanently attaching them together. Otherwise, your turntable will "wobble" or rotate off center. You may find it useful to drill a very small hole or otherwise mark the exact center of your turntable before assembling it. This will provide not only a reference point for alignment during construction, but will help you visually center your objects when you are shooting. Note that this hole will usually be covered by your object, so it will rarely be visible in your images.

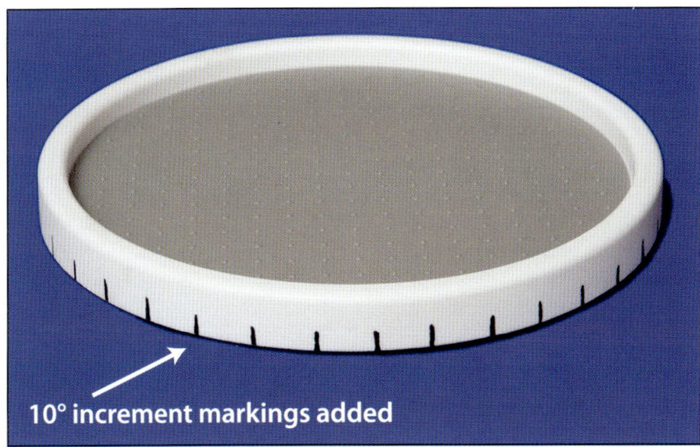

Fig. 17-10 Low cost turntable from a kitchen supply store.

Finding the true center of a large round piece can be a bit of a challenge, but there is a fairly simple geometry technique that will help. First, make sure you choose a table top that is truly cut to a round shape. In my experience, many of the plywood rounds found in hardware stores are cut somewhat unevenly.   The finished table tops, such as those made from Melamine™, are often better.

To find the center of your round table top, you will need draw two pairs of arcs from the edge of the table toward the center. (Do this on the bottom or non-visible side of your table top, unless you are planning to paint or cover it later.) This can be done using a piece of thin wire with a pencil attached at one end and a push pin attached to the other. The length of wire between the two should be just a bit longer than the radius of your table top, and the wire should be attached as close as possible to the points of both the pencil and push pin. You will be using this combination as a drawing compass, and you want to keep the distance between the attachment point (pushpin) and the pencil point constant.

Insert the push pin into the wood at some point along the very edge of the table top. Keeping the wire taut by gently pulling on the pencil, draw an arc across the opposite side of the table top circle. Now remove the push pin and reposition it on the opposite side of the table, making another arc in the opposite direction. These opposing arcs will intersect at two points. Using a ruler or straight edge, draw a straight line between these intersections. This line will pass through the center of your table top.

Repeat this procedure by drawing another pair of arcs roughly perpendicular to the first, and draw another line between their intersections. You now have two straight lines that intersect at (or very close to) the center of your table top. If you want to be sure, you can create additional arc pairs at different angles and confirm that the lines between their intersections pass through the same center point , as well. This is not a precision compass and you may wind up with some variation in where these lines cross, but you can at least get a close estimate to your center using this method.

Melamine table tops are durable, smooth and usually come in a bright white finish, all of which make them excellent choices for turntable surfaces. Of course, you can paint plywood any color you want, or simply drape colored fabric over a turntable surface when you are shooting. Some photographers have even sewn custom fabric covers with elastic "waists" that can be easily

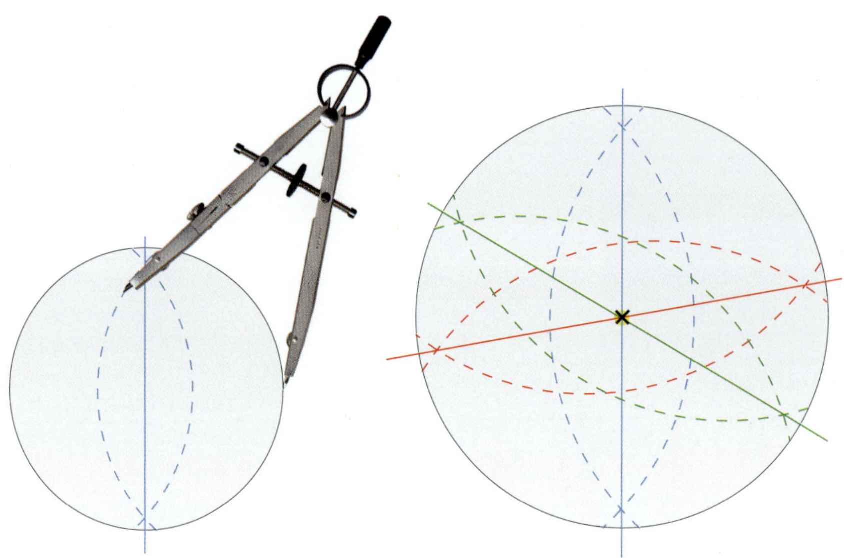

Fig. 17-12 Finding the center of a round piece.

interchanged over their turntables for different shooting backgrounds.

Once you have your turntable put together and turning smoothly, you'll need to find a way to mark rotation increments on it. There are several techniques that you can use.

The first involves temporarily taping a protractor to the exact center of the table, and extending the degree markings out to the outside edge of the turntable. If you drilled a small hole in the center of your table, you can stick a pin in it to anchor a wire or string that you can pull to the edge of the turntable. Mark whatever increments you'll need. Every 10 degrees is usually sufficient for most object movies, but if you think you might need smaller increments in the future, now is probably the time to mark them when you have everything set up. You may also find that marking different increment sets with different colors can be helpful (such as red for every 30°, blue for every 15°, and black for every 10°).

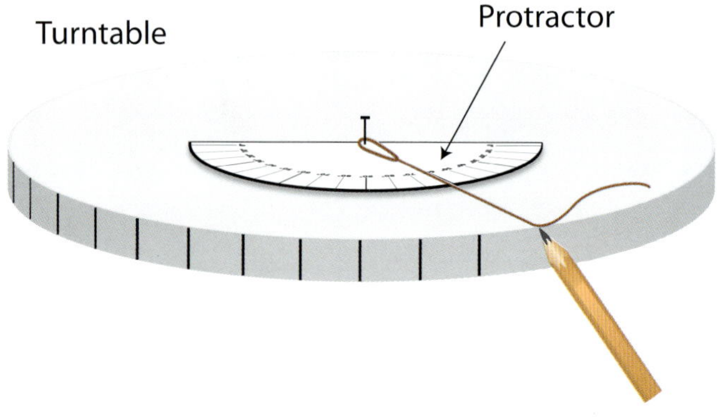

Fig. 17-13 Marking rotation indexes with a protractor.

A second method involves taping a piece of ribbon or a long strip of paper around turntable's outer edge. Make sure it is wrapped tightly, and then cut it so it is exactly the length of the turntable's outer circumference. Now remove the ribbon or paper and open it up flat.

Next, start folding it into halves or thirds, creasing it at each fold to get the combination of equally spaced sections that you desire. Fold it in half once, and you'll have two 180° increments. Fold it in half again and you'll have four 90° increments. Figure out how many increments you want and then calculate the number of folds you'll need to get that figure.

For instance, 36 increments of 10° each would require that the ribbon be folded into 36 sections. Calculate how many times you need to multiply two and/or three together in order to get 36. In this case, you'd multiply by two and three twice each (2 x 2 x 3 x 3 = 36). For each time you multiplied by two, you'll fold the ribbon in half. For each time you multiplied by three, fold the ribbon over itself in thirds. Thus, for 36 segments of 10° each, fold in half twice and in thirds twice (it doesn't matter what order you do the folds in, as long as the total is the same).

Once finished, unfold the ribbon and wrap it again around the outside of the turntable. Everywhere you see a fold or crease, make a corresponding mark on the turntable. While this may not be an absolutely precise method of dividing your turntable's circumference, it gets you close enough for most purposes without having to deal with fractional inch or centimeter calculations.

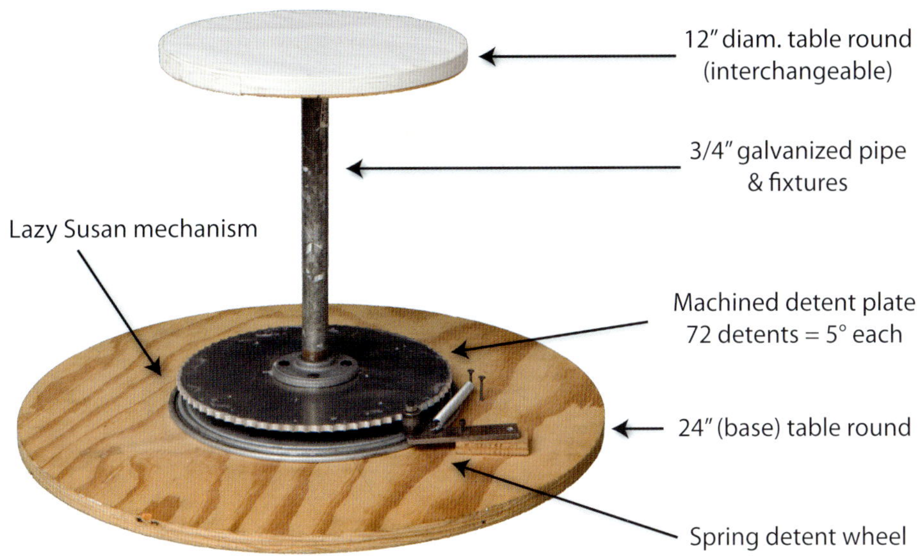

Fig. 17-14 The author's home made manually indexed object turntable.

Once you have your turntable divided into rotation increments, you'll need to create some sort of an index or reference point against which to align the marks when shooting. This can be as simple as a stationary mark that you put on the base (non-rotating) section of your rig, or a pushpin or sticker that you press onto a spot near your table's edge. All of these markings will need to be retouched out of your shots if they are visible, so some photographers choose to position these reference points on the back of their turntables or beyond the camera's field of view. Be creative in how you do this.

Of course you can get quite elaborate if you want, and come up with mechanical systems that provide click-stop increments for your turntable's rotation, or even include motorized drives. However, for most object work, a simple turntable with consistently repeatable positioning is all that will be necessary. As you expand into higher volume production work, or need more precision and flexibility in your shooting system, you'll probably want to transition from your home made rig into one of the commercial rigs like those offered by Kaidan, Peace River Studios, and Corybant West.

Chapter 18: Object Lighting

Most object photography is treated, from a lighting perspective, like traditional commercial product photography. The photographer tries to find the best way to present the product visually. The shape, size, color and surface textures of the object being photographied will greatly influence what sort of lighting design is required to show the product to its best advantage.

VR object photography is often more difficult to light than traditional still photography of the same subject, because the object you are photographing will have to be captured from multiple angles while the lighting has to appear consistent between. This is necessary to avoid a perceived jumpiness between images when viewing them in rapid sequence if exposures or shadows change between them.

It is a good idea to review the basics of photographic lighting in **Chapter 5** before proceeding on to the controlled studio or product-type lighting challenges presented with object photography. You'll want to first understand lighting balances, the different quality of light provided by different light sources, and how to modify the quality, quantity, and color temperature of light.

Background Choices

Before shooting any object movie sequence, determine what the background for your object in the movie will be. Neutral backgrounds, such as black or white, are the most common choice as they do not distract from the object itself, and are generally the easiest to retouch in post production. Remember that object movies are composed of multiple individual images – anywhere from a dozen to several hundred or more – and any retouching that is required for one image is likely to be needed for all the rest. When shooting these images, it is important to do the best job you can of lighting the object and maintaining a clean looking background. A seemingly innocuous Photoshop correction needed for a single image becomes a major chore when it has to be repeated dozens or hundreds of times.

A black background is usually the easiest to shoot against, and generally requires the least post production work. Of course, this also depends upon the color

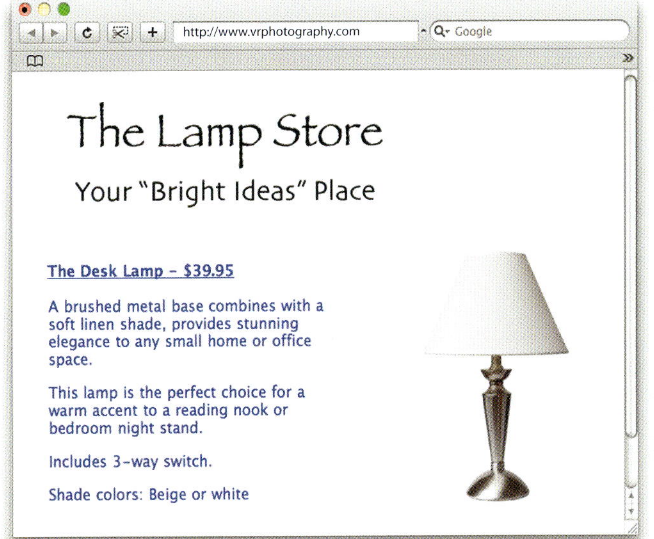

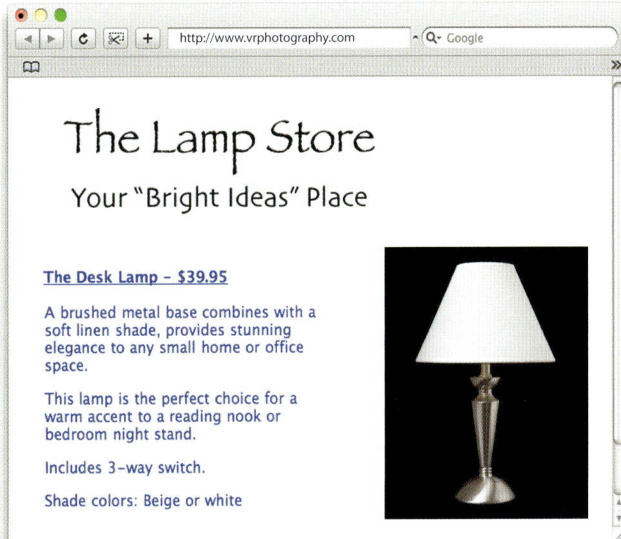

Fig. 18-1 The same object photographed on white and black backgounds, for display on a simple web page.

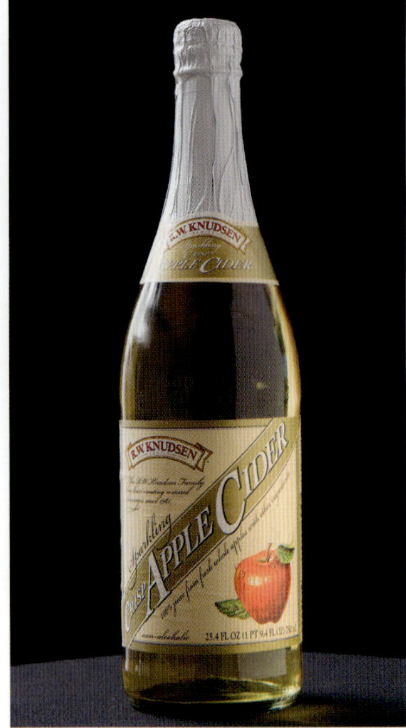
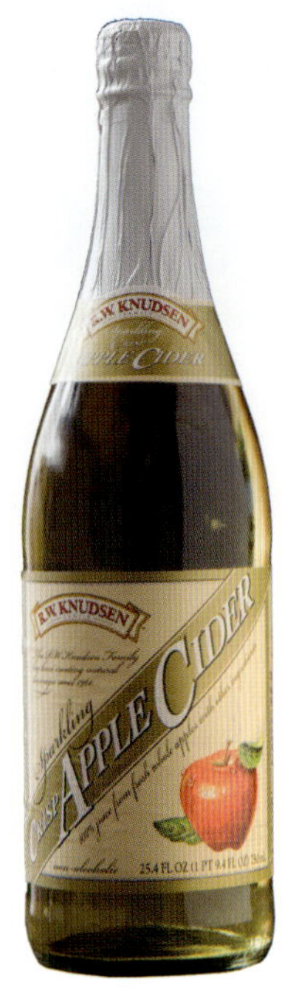
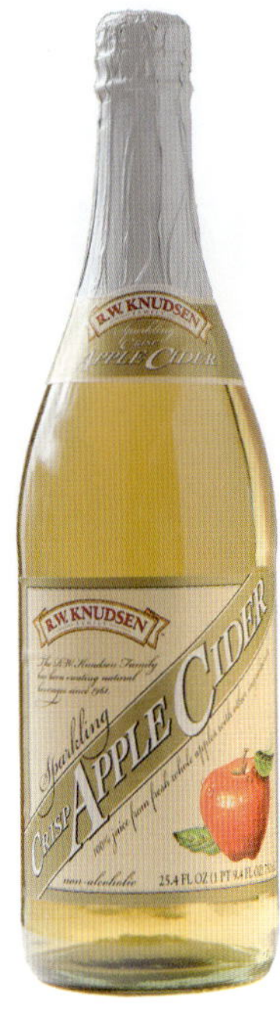

Originally shot
against black

Background digitally
replaced with white

Originally shot
against white

Fig. 18-2 Trying to change a background in post production doesn't always work well. It's better to plan the proper background and lighting while shooting so that the product looks more natural in its final publication or presentation..

certainly possible to change a background color after the fact, but again, consider the amount of post production work that will probably be involved. Depending on the lighting, opacity, and reflectivity of the object, it may not look right with a background color different from what it was shot against, even if you have the post production time and resources to make the change in every image.

There are also techniques, such as blue or green screen photography, that allow for more straightforward stripping in of alternate backgrounds. These are used extensively in film and television production for special effects, or to make it appear as though a studio newscaster is in front of a location background. Blue/ green screen photography requires very careful lighting of the colored background so that it has no shadows or highlights, and is of even brightness. After the images are captured, the blue or green color is stripped out of each image and replaced

and reflectivity of the object you are shooting. A black telephone or a very dark sculpture is going to be difficult to visually separate from a similarly dark background (although it is possible). Likewise, a white coffee mug or electrical switch plate may too easily blend in with a pure white background.

While black backgrounds are often the easiest to work with, white backgrounds seem to be the most common. This is due to their visual "cleanliness," which provides a more positive image for a commercial product, as well as the fact that they can be easily matched to the pure white backgrounds used on most web pages. This can help maintain clean designs for web sites that use object movies. Yet this is simply a style preference.

Background color should be discussed and clearly specified with a client before you begin shooting any object VR project. It is

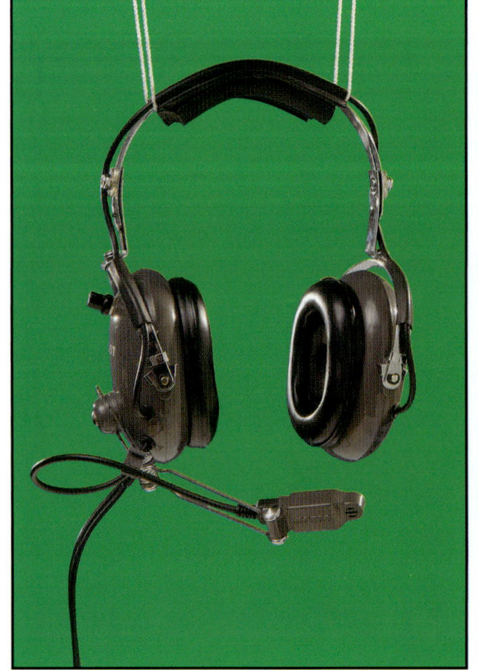
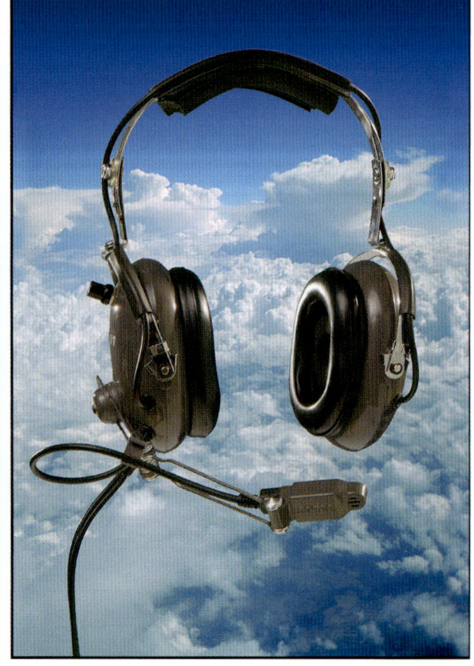

Fig. 18-3 Green screen processes allow for straightforward removal or replacement of backgrounds. This can be useful for object VR sequences, but significant care is required for proper lighting of the screen and the object(s) being photographed.

with the chosen background. When lighting for blue/green screen work, it is important to keep the reflected blue or green background light from washing onto the object you are photographing. Otherwise, that part of the object will also be removed with the rest of the colored background.

Separate the Object and Background

When first attempting to photograph an object, most photographers will simply place the object on a turntable, add lighting, and take the pictures. The light(s) used to illuminate the object also light the background. While this can be done if you are in a rush and not too concerned with the quality of your results, you will find you have more control over your lighting if you separate your object from your background and light the two independently. This requires more shooting space to do successfully, but the resulting control over how everything looks is far greater.

Distancing your background from your object provides a number of advantages:

1) It allows you to light the object and background independently, so adjusting your object lighting has little effect on your background light. With a white background, for example, you can keep the background bright while independently adjusting the object lighting.

2) When trying to achieve a very dark or black background, distancing the object lights from the background material, such as black fabric, means that less light reaches it and the darker it will be (remember the inverse square reduction of light intensity from **Chapter 5**). Again, changing the positions of lights illuminating the object has little effect on the amount of light illuminating the background when the two are kept far apart.

3) The added space between object and background offers room to insert a back light or other light control device behind the object and in front of the background.

4) A larger distance between object and background means that the background will be less in focus than if the two were close (assuming the same lens aperture and focal length). This helps to visually isolate the object from its background.

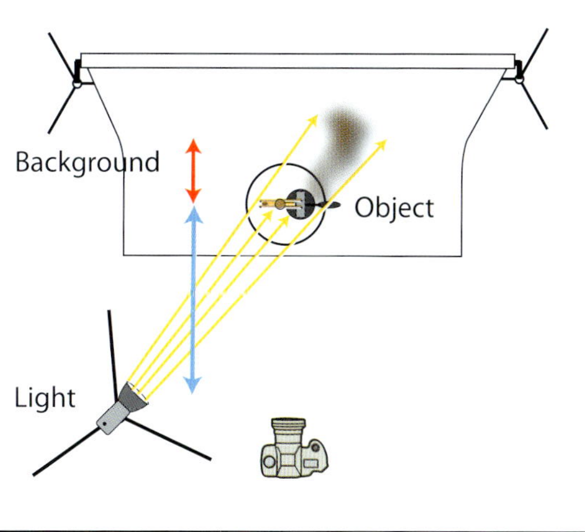

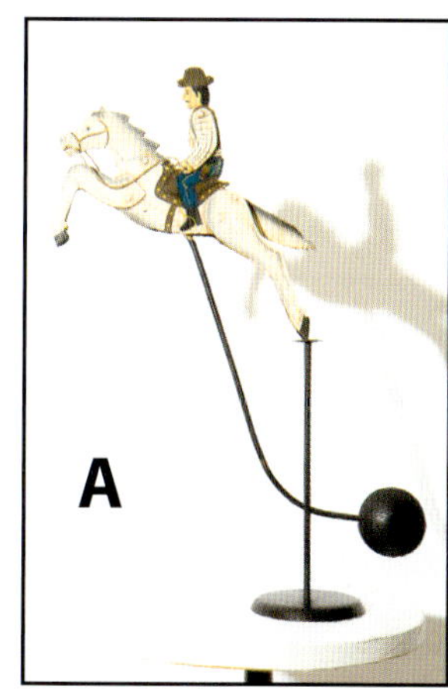

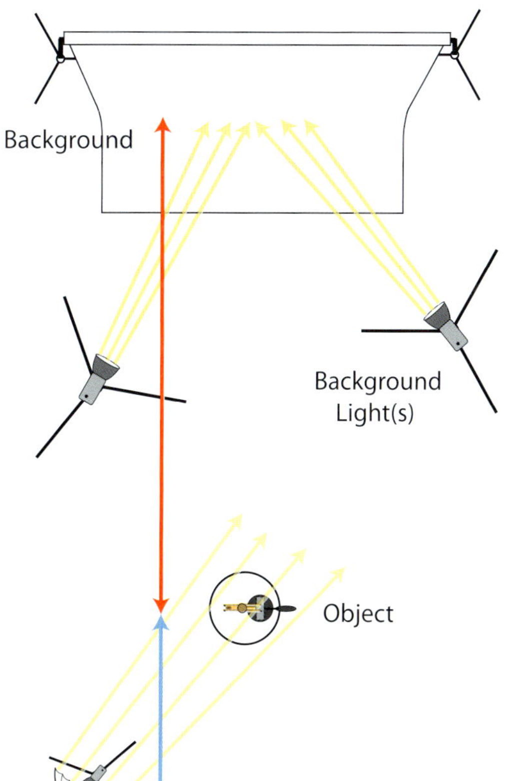

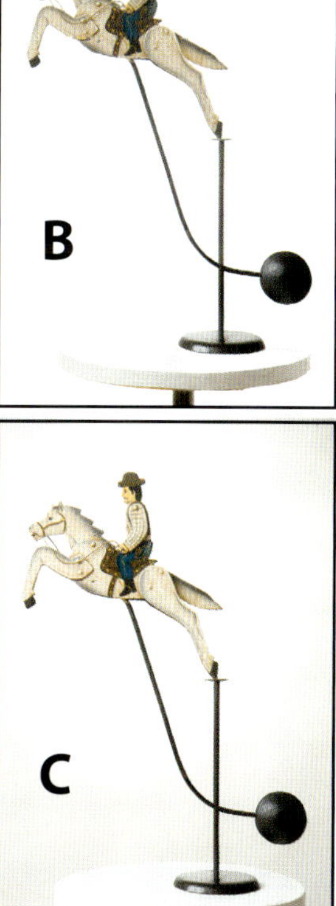

Fig. 18-4 Putting adequate space between an object being photographed and its background allows independent lighting of each, and minimizes light spill between them. This allows for more precise lighting control overall, as in results B and C.

Basic Lighting Approaches

Experienced studio photographers are always trying to develop new approaches to lighting product shots that will set their work apart from the countless other product photos we see every day in magazines, billboards, and on our TV screens. Unique lighting styles result from the creativity and technical abilities that a photographer develops over time. However, a few basic approaches to product photography lighting can carry both professional and non-pro photographers a long way when doing object VR.

The first and easiest approach is to simply use soft lighting. A single diffuse light source is often enough to show a product or object clearly and evenly, without casting harsh shadows or without producing significant reflections on the object. Remember that the object will be rotated as you shoot the VR sequence, so you'll want to use a lighting setup that will require minimal (if any) adjustments as the object turns or new surfaces are revealed that reflect light back toward the camera.

The easiest way to diffuse a light source is to aim it at a white wall or ceiling, and let the light "bounce" onto the object indirectly. Try the following for yourself. With your digital camera, make two photographs of an object. Shoot the first with a single light on a stand to the side of your camera, pointed directly at the object. This bare bulb type of light is very harsh and directional, leaving strong shadows on your object. For your second shot, keep your camera and light in the same positions, but aim the light upward toward the ceiling and let it bounce off of the ceiling back on to your object. Adjust your exposure accordingly (there's now less light hitting the object), and compare the results. The soft or bounced lighting will generally be more flattering.

There are many other tools available for diffusing light in photography.   One that has perhaps been around the longest is the lighting umbrella.   These umbrellas look very similar to traditional rain umbrellas, except that lighting umbrellas have a light or reflective surface on the inside of their domes. They are mounted on the front of a strobe or other light source, which is pointed away from the object being photographed. The umbrella reflects and scatters light back onto the subject.   Different types of reflective materials are available, and umbrellas come in different sizes, so there are many options for how much diffusion is provided. The advantages to using umbrellas are their relatively low cost and their ability to collapse for storage. Since they are attached directly to your light source, they can also be aimed, much as the source light itself can.

Another light diffuser commonly found in photographers' studios is the "soft box." These are lightweight, fabric covered frames (supported internally with flexible poles, much like a tent), which attach to the front of a light source. The sides of these boxes are made from an opaque black fabric, which prevents light from shining where it's not wanted, while the front is a translucent material that the source light shines through. There are often baffles inside, which serve to further soften the light and to even its intensity.

Soft boxes come in a tremendous variety of sizes and shapes, from small units designed for hand held strobes, to huge units 40 to 60 feet long requiring a dozen or more studio strobe heads (these are often found in studios specializing in high end automotive photography). Soft boxes take longer to set up and break down than lighting umbrellas, and they're usually more expensive. But many photographers prefer them for shooting reflective objects. Their advantage is that their visible surface is smooth and uninterrupted, so when they are seen reflected in an object, they don't include distracting umbrella ribs. Soft boxes also come in a variety of shapes and sizes, from thin strip lights for very narrow soft lighting control, to the more traditional rectangles, and even ovals or domes. Umbrellas are invariably

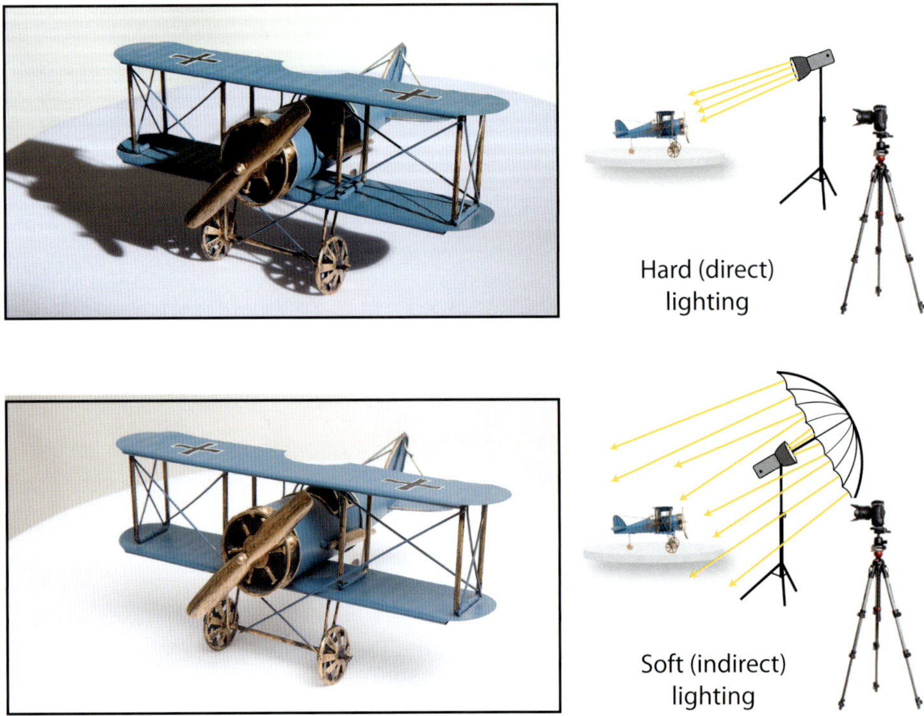

Fig. 18-5 Comparison of hard vs. soft (diffuse) lighting.

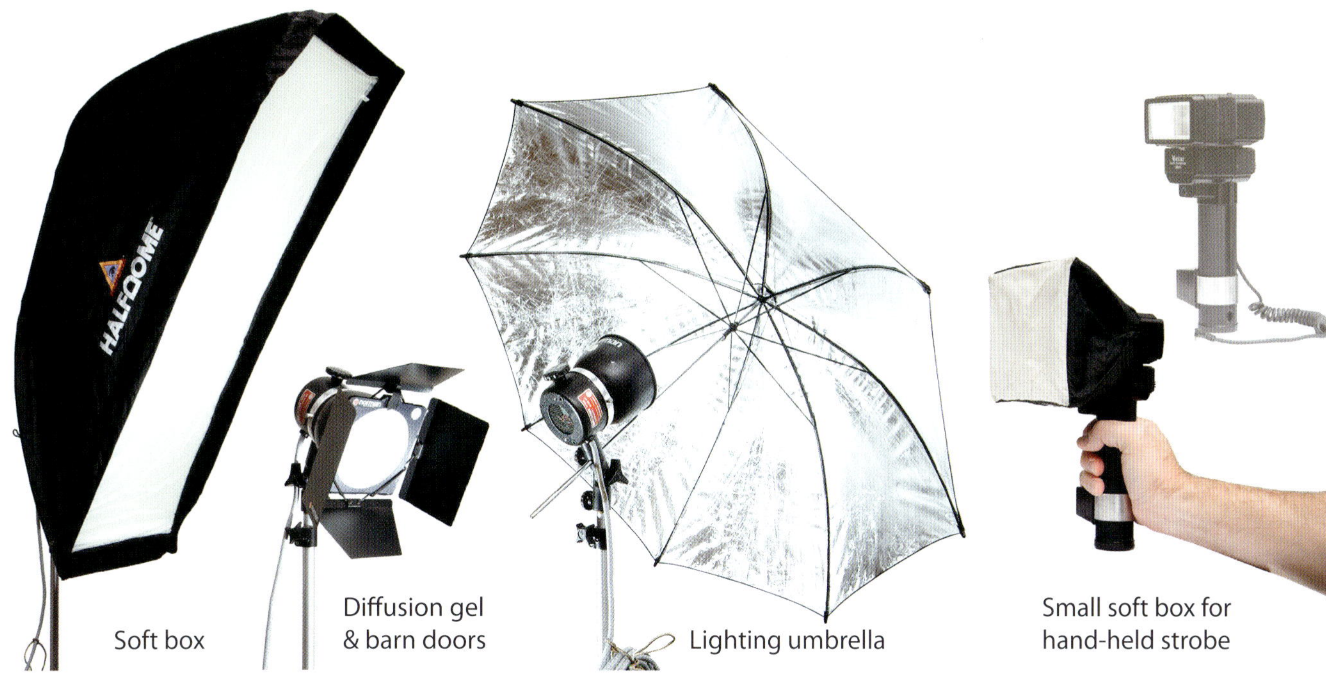

Fig. 18-6 A variety of diffusion tools are available to help soften the light output from photographic lights.

round in their shape, and when used to light highly reflective subjects, can show a defined umbrella pattern in reflections, which can be distracting.

A single large, diffuse light can be used to photograph many objects effectively. You may even find that this approach is satisfactory for shooting objects on a plain white background without needing to light the background separately. In fact, this is the sort of lighting setup that many of the companies who prepare online auction items for eBay and other sites use. It's quick, simple, and relatively effective visually, although there's little inspiration to it. As the object is rotated in front of the camera, there are usually few reflections or flare problems to worry about.

Expanding the Envelope – Multiple Light Sources
While soft lighting can be useful for showing a product clearly and cleanly, it often lacks visual punch. However, even a single soft light, when used at an angle off axis from the camera, can provide some sense of drama with contrast between highlight and shadow. Yet, you'll want to avoid falling into a rut of lighting everything with soft, diffuse light, as it can make your work boring.

At some point, you'll want to start using multi-light approaches, not only to keep things interesting, but to better illuminate the products you're shooting. As you start using less soft lighting, you'll encounter stronger highlights and harsher shadows, which create greater contrast.   Hard lighting sources often more make exposure balance more difficult than soft light sources.

Many photographers find it best to use a combination of hard and soft lights for products in a studio or controlled lighting environment.

Keep in mind that the use of multiple light sources does not necessarily require the use of multiple *lights*. As discussed in **Chapter 5**, a light source can be a reflector, painted wall, mirror, window, or the sun. Anything that brings light onto your subject, whether directly or indirectly, can be considered a light source.

There are three principal terms that we use to describe light sources in product-type lighting – *key light*, *fill light* and *back light*.

A **key light** is the primary light source used to illuminate an object you are shooting. A **fill light** is a secondary light source, generally illuminating the object from its shadow side (opposite the key light), which "fills" in the shadow areas somewhat. It is generally less bright than the key light. A **back light** is a light that illuminates an object from the back (or opposite side of the object from the camera), and provides highlights that help distinguish the contours and edges of the object.

A fourth type of light often used in object and studio work, is known as the background light. This may be one light or many, but is used to illuminate the background behind the object being photographed. When using multiple light sources for an object shoot, remember that you'll have more control over your lighting if you put some distance between the object and your background, and light the two separately. This will help avoid your object lighting spilling onto your background, plus you can more easily control the intensity, color and shape of your background light without it affecting your object lighting.

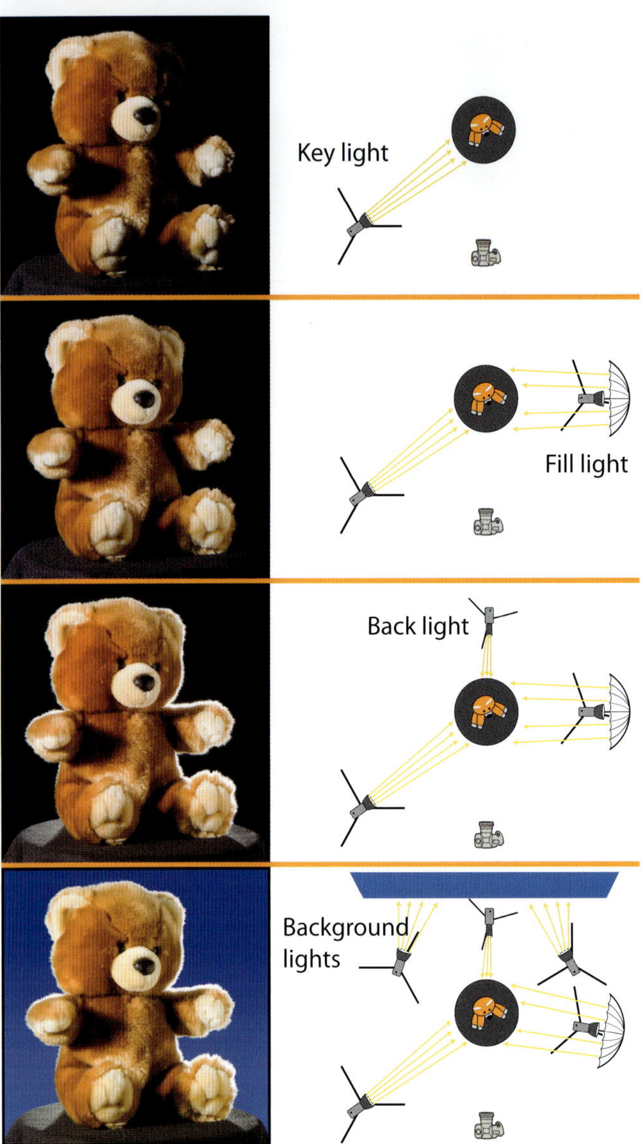

Fig. 18-7 Additional lighting sources can be used to help accentuate elements of an object being photographed.

Lighting Control Tools

Good studio photography requires the ability to control light – to control its quality, its quantity, its color, and how it falls upon your subject. There is an old joke that trying to control light is like to trying to give a cat a bath... it's possible, but there are quite a few challenges involved. In spite of all this, for almost 150 years, photographers have found ways to control light so that their cameras, film, and today's digital media can record it well.

When we modify a light source, we are generally changing some combination of its quality (hard vs. soft), intensity (brightness on the subject), direction (the angle from which it strikes the subject), shape, and color.

Quality and Diffusion

Quality of a given light is most often controlled by diffusion material or its reflection off of another surface before reaching the subject. A bare bulb inside a polished reflector will provide very hard light, creating well defined shadows and high contrast. That same light, bounced off of an umbrella, reflector, or shined through diffusion material, will provide a much softer quality of light that more evenly illuminates a subject, reducing both contrast and shadow definition. Diffusing a light in this way also reduces its intensity, so a corresponding increase in camera exposure must usually be made.

Intensity

The brightness or intensity of light reaching a subject from a given light source depends on several things. These include the brightness of the light source itself, its distance from the subject (remember the inverse square rule from **Chapter 5**), and how much is absorbed by lighting control devices placed between the light source and the subject.

The films or digital sensors in our cameras need a minimum amount of light to effectively record an image. However, we have the freedom to increase or decrease the intensity of light striking our subjects, because our cameras have controls (aperture, shutter speed, and ISO) that allow us to compensate for different light intensities and still make proper exposures.

If the amount of light on our subject is increased, we can use our camera controls to *decrease* the exposure a corresponding amount. Likewise, if the subject or scene becomes darker when we block light with light modifiers, we can *increase* the camera's exposure to compensate. A complete primer on exposure can be found in **Chapter 3**.

Object VR photographers will generally use a combination of light modifiers and light-to-subject distances to balance light the way they want on their subjects. Remember that even though we can adjust *overall* exposure with our cameras' exposure controls, we still need to control the *relative* intensities of our light sources to create a desired look for our subjects. Adjusting the intensity of individual lights lets us keep highlight and shadow levels within the latitude of the film or digital media we are using.

The use of a professional photographic light meter can help photographers understand how much modification of a light source (whether changing its distance from the subject or with addition of light modifiers) can change the relative intensity of that light on the subject. A light meter will provide a quantitative numerical measurement of the light level on the subject, either in lumens or in f/stops. You can shield a light meter from other lights so that it only measures the amount of light

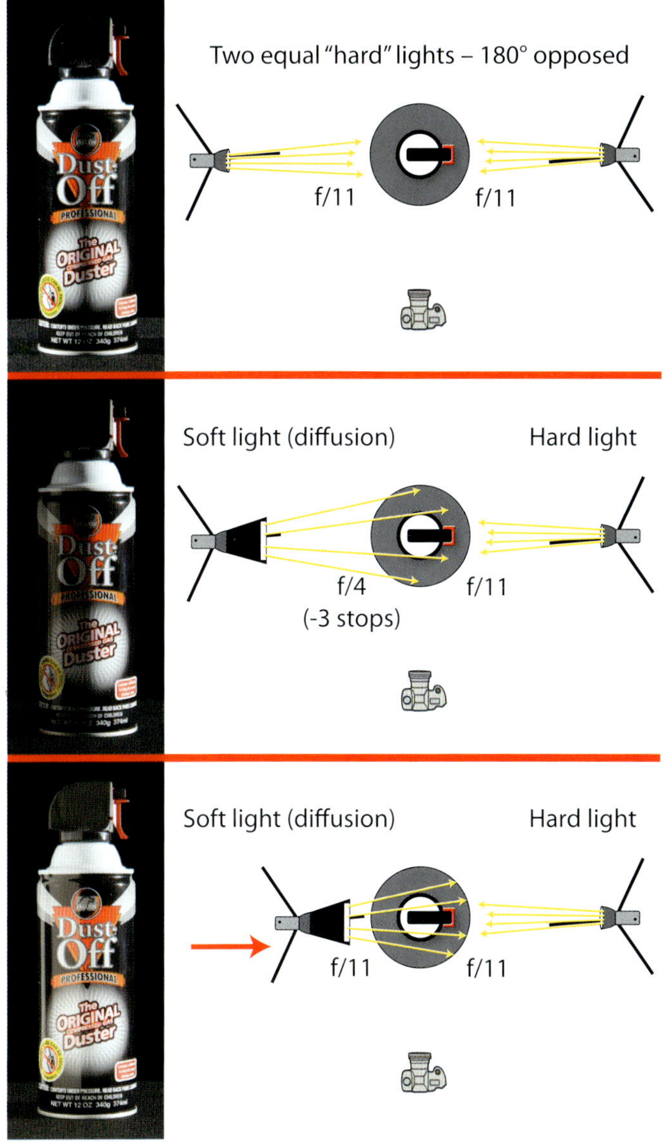

Fig. 18-8 Object lighting can be controlled with diffusion and distance.

Light-to-Subject Distance Adjustments	
To make a light:	**Move it:**
1/2 stop brighter	**16%** closer (84% of original distance)
darker	**19%** farther (119% of original distance)
1 stop brighter	**29%** closer (71% of original distance)
darker	**41%** farther (141% of original distance)
1-1/2 stops brighter	**40%** closer (60% of original distance)
darker	**60%** farther (160% of original distance)
2 stops brighter	**50%** closer (50% of original distance)
darker	**100%** farther (200% of original distance)
3 stops brighter	**65%** closer (35% of original distance)
darker	**180%** farther (280% of original distance)
4 stops brighter	**75%** closer (25% of original distance)
darker	**300%** farther (400% of original distance)

Figures are based on point (hard) light sources. Diffuse (soft) light sources *usually* perform similarly.

Fig. 18-9 Inverse square control of light intensity.

coming from a single light source at a time, in order to better understand the balance and ratios of multiple lights on an object.

Direction (Angle)

The direction or angle from which light strikes a subject has a tremendous impact on the overall look of that subject. When we talk about lighting angles, we usually refer to the direction that the light strikes the subject *relative* to the camera position. A "front" light comes from same direction as the camera is from the subject (the front), while a back light strikes the subject from its back side relative to the camera. Side lighting comes from one side or the other of the subject – on an axis perpendicular to that of the camera-to-subject axis.

The direction of a light determines where highlights and shadows will occur, and has perhaps the greatest influence on the aesthetics and overall rendition of the subject. Front lighting provides even illumination, but also reveals little depth and texture of an object, as shadows fall behind the object and are not visible to the camera. Back lighting reveals little detail because most of the subject seen from the camera is in shadow. However, back lighting can also be very dramatic, providing a brilliant outline of an object with visual separation from the background. At its extreme, back lighting creates

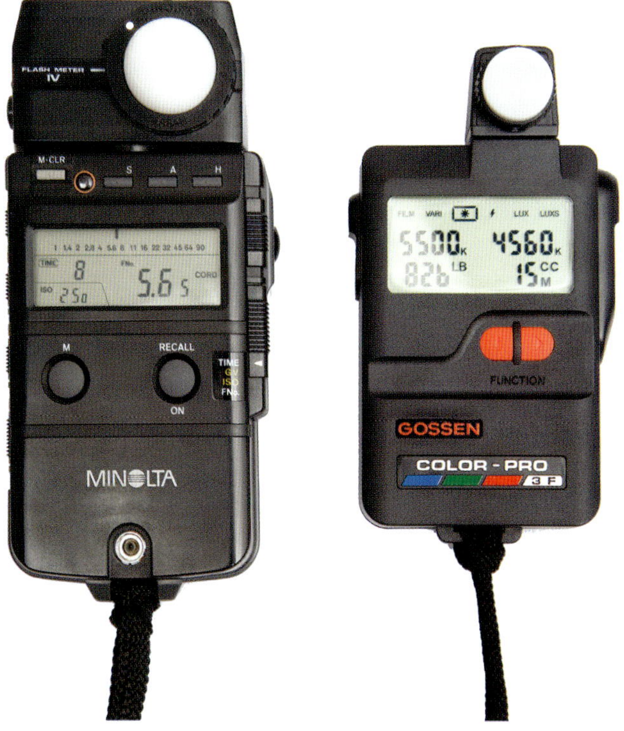

Fig. 18-10 A hand held light meter (on left) measures light intensity (both ambient and strobe), while a color meter (right) measures the color temperature of light and offers recommended filtration to correct the color balance.

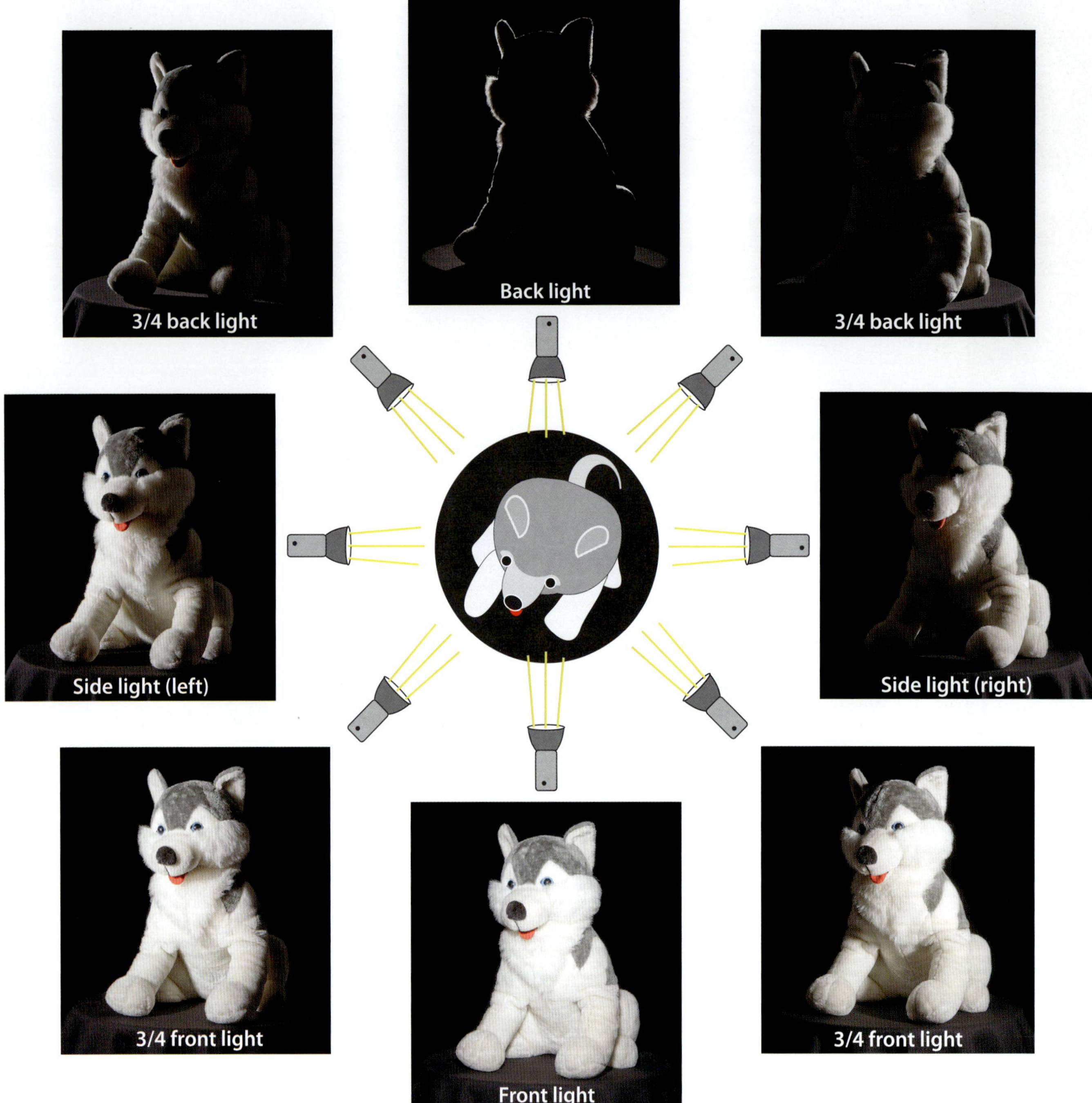

Fig. 18-11 Comparison of different lighting angles from a single light source. Note the changes in texture and shadow.

a silhouette effect, which is why it is generally used in combination with another light to fill in the shadow areas and reveal some details. Side lighting creates both highlights and shadows visible to the camera, which reveal a subject's depth and texture most effectively.

In addition to front, back, and side lighting, we should also consider vertical positioning. A light positioned above the subject would be referred to as an overhead or top light, while one coming from below is often called bottom lighting or "lighting from below."

When considered relative to the camera-to-subject axis, top and bottom lighting are little more than a vertical variation of side lighting. However, they provide a marked difference in overall look of a subject. Overhead lighting seems most natural to us, as most of our visual experiences in life are dominated by overhead light sources. When we are outdoors, sunlight comes from the sky overhead. When we are indoors, most of the light in our homes and offices is from overhead lighting fixtures. Most object and product photography is done with an overhead light as the key light source, since this looks the most natural. However, placing the key light

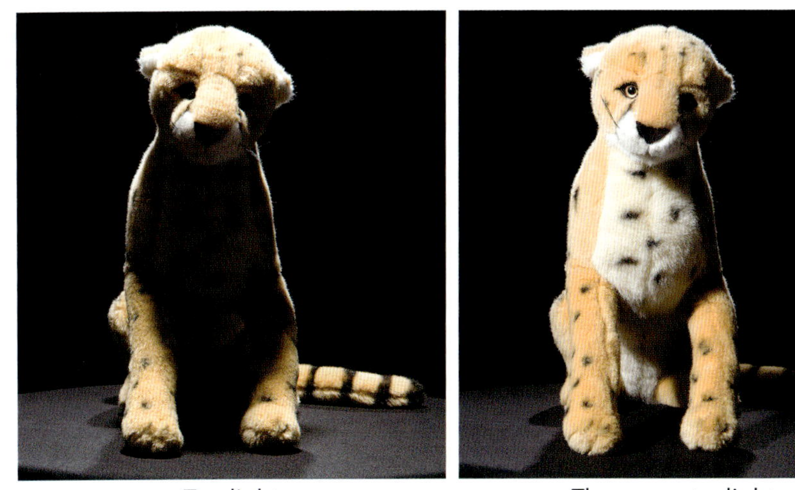

Top light   Three quarter light   Bottom light

Fig. 18-12 The vertical angle of a light is also a factor in the look and feel of how an object is rendered in photographs.

in what is known as a three quarter position, or partway between front and side, as well as elevated somewhat, often provides a pleasing combination of overhead and side lighting.

Bottom lighting is unusual, but can be used for dramatic effect. It can also very quickly become overused. Think back to the classic Hollywood horror films and how they made monsters and other bad guys look scarier by lighting their faces from below. Remember also how, as kids, we'd to make ourselves look scary for story telling by shining a flashlight onto our face from below. Bottom lighting lends a sense of the surreal to your subject. While this is not always appropriate, it can be used for effect at times. Keep in mind that lighting from below can be difficult in a studio or object photography situation, as there may be very little room below an object to position lights. Often, the turntable or support structure holding the object will block most light coming from below. If you want to shoot an object with bottom lighting, you may need to create a custom turntable or support mechanism made of clear plastic or some sort of grid material that will allow light to pass through.

Shape and Color
The shape of a light is generally controlled by the use of lenses, mirrors, snoots, scrims, flags, and other materials that either focus or selectively block parts of the light. There are countless tools available for doing this, and one of the best ways to learn about them is through experimentation. As with most creative endeavors, there is no single best way to light a given subject for your photography. Try different tools and techniques, and keep detailed notes on your efforts so you can repeat those that are successful. The ability to be consistent, and to produce the results that you want, are keys to successful object photography.

Don't fall into the trap of believing that you'll need that latest top-of-the-line lighting equipment. You can learn a great deal with a couple of spring arm desk lamps, or even low cost flood lamps and reflectors, plus a variety of home made light modifiers. (Warning: when working with any sort of "hot" lights, such as high intensity tungsten bulbs, be aware of the heat they generate. Do not attach paper, cardboard, or plastic modifiers directly to these lights, as they can easily catch fire.) Use a variety of materials found around your home to adjust the shape and quality of your lights. Examples include: aluminum foil, makeup mirrors, white bed sheets or other pieces of fabric, shower curtains, translucent plastic bowls, cardboard (white for reflecting, dark for blocking light), clothespins, etc.

Once you've experimented a bit, visit a pro camera or lighting supply house to see what else might be available. Many of these tools are considered to be

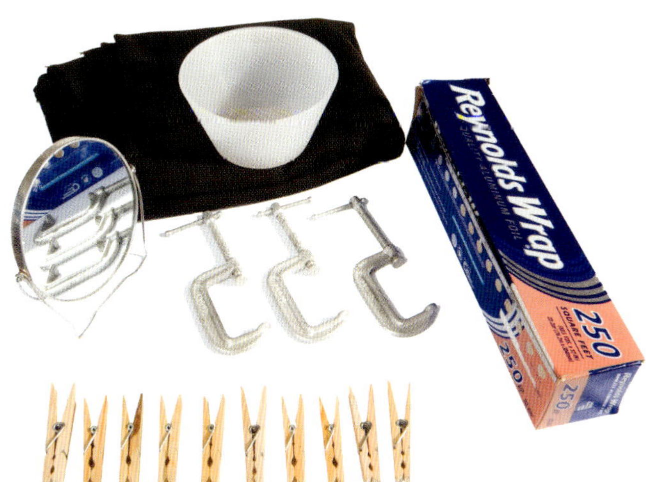

Fig. 18-13 Low cost items found around the typical home which can be used as effective lighting control devices, particularly for smaller products.

"expendables" and are relatively low cost. These include special heavy duty black metal foils, heat resistant diffusion and reflection materials, gaffer's tape (available in white, black and a variety of colors – gaffer's tape doesn't leave a sticky residue like duct tape or masking tape), and of course, color gels.

Colored gels come in a variety of sizes, from small swatches that you can sometimes find in free sample books, to larger sheets (about 20"x24"), or even 25-foot long rolls. These are available in seemingly infinite colors with tints from intense to subtle. They are also available in specific color correction shades that allow you to match the color temperature of tungsten and fluorescent lights to that of daylight, or of daylight to tungsten and fluorescent color temperatures. These gels can be cut to size and placed in front of a light source to change its color. They are often reusable. A single 20"x24" sheet usually costs between $5 and $15, but you

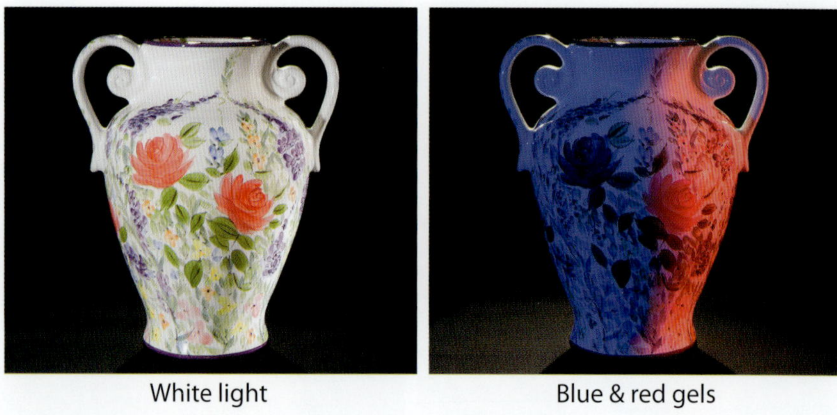

White light   Blue & red gels

Fig. 18-15 The use of colored gels over light sources can add interesting effect, but can become trite or overdone if used too often.

can also buy them in variety packs with a lower cost per sheet.

For modifying the color of small camera mounted strobe units, I find that gels cut directly out of the small sample books are often sufficient to cover the entire strobe head. These are a convenient way to keep a variety of colors at my disposal at very low cost.

Lighting gels can be used on almost any light source. They can be added to windows, desk lamps, studio strobes, or even high intensity HMI par lighting used on Hollywood film sets. Often, a slight change of color can give a whole different look or feel to a subject. In general, you'll want to use colored gels sparingly for object photography. But sometimes, a splash of color can help bring a bit of life to an otherwise boring subject.

Remember that adding a colored gel over a light source reduces the light's intensity. Darker colors remove more light than lighter colored gels. You'll find light transmission data for professional lighting gels in the documentation sheets that accompany the sample gel booklets. Be sure to check your camera exposures and adjust your lighting ratios accordingly after adding (or removing) gels to your lights.

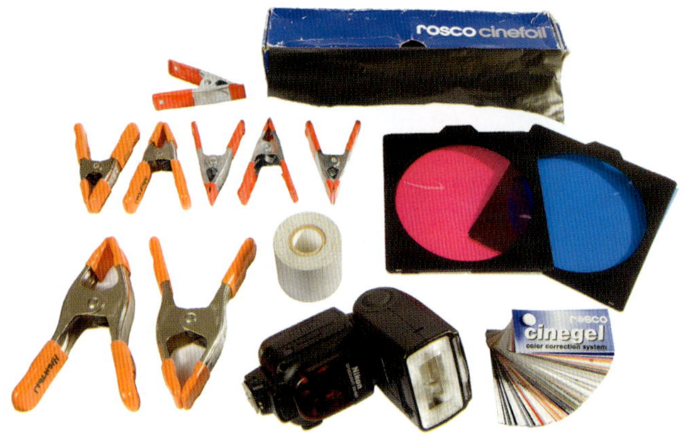

Fig. 18-14 A combination of pro lighting equipment and tools from your local hardware store can provide tremendous flexibility in lighting control for reasonable costs.

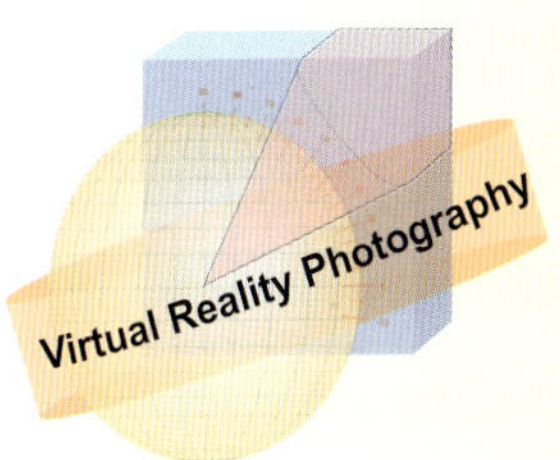

Chapter 19: Advanced Object Techniques

After mastering basic object movie authoring techniques, many photographers find themselves compelled to stretch their creativity, and seek more challenging uses for object movies. The following are but a few examples intended to help inspire development of your own techniques and approaches.

Consider the structure of an object movie and how it is navigated interactively by viewers. Object movies are little more than a series of still photos viewed sequentially, although there can be a variety of different paths available between these images depending upon the structure of the movie and how many images it contains. Think of the design of an object movie as a grid of images, where the viewer's path can move in multiple directions. A single row object movie is the simplest form of this, as there is only one path that the user can navigate. The images form a linear sequence, which may be viewed at any speed forward or backward, depending upon whether the user moves their mouse to the right or left.

Normally, this structure is used to show the rotation of an object. As the user moves their mouse to the right, the object rotates to the right in the movie window. When the mouse is moved to the left, the object rotates to the left. (Note: some authors prefer to reverse these controls, depending on whether they want to give the user the impression that they are controlling the movement of the camera around the object, rather than the object's rotation. When assembling your object movies in post production, try both methods. You may prefer one or the other depending upon the type of subject you're presenting.)

Rotation of an object is usually done for a full 360 degrees, with the last frame looping back to the first frame for a continuous rotating effect. However, most authoring applications allow you to choose whether you loop the playback or not. If you don't loop, the movie stops when the user reaches the last frame in either direction. This is a handy approach to take when you are unable to photograph all the way around an object, or where there are sides of the object that you don't want to show.

If you are creating a complete 360° loop, you will need to determine the proper amount to rotate the object between shots. To determine this, simply divide 360° by the number of shots you want to use. For example, if you want only eight shots, you would divide 360° by eight to get a 45° rotation between images (photos would be done with the object turned 0°, 45°, 90°, 135°, 180°, 225°, 270°, and 315°).

If you want to provide a smoother playback experience for your viewers, you might use 24 or 36 frames instead. Twenty four shots would require a 15° rotation increment (360° ÷ 24 = 15°), while 36 shots would require a 10° increment (360° ÷ 36 = 10°). Remember that the more images you shoot (the smaller your rotation between shots), the smoother your movie's playback is likely to appear. However, this performance comes at a price, as you will shoot more images, will have to process and assemble them all, and the resulting file sizes of your movies will be larger.

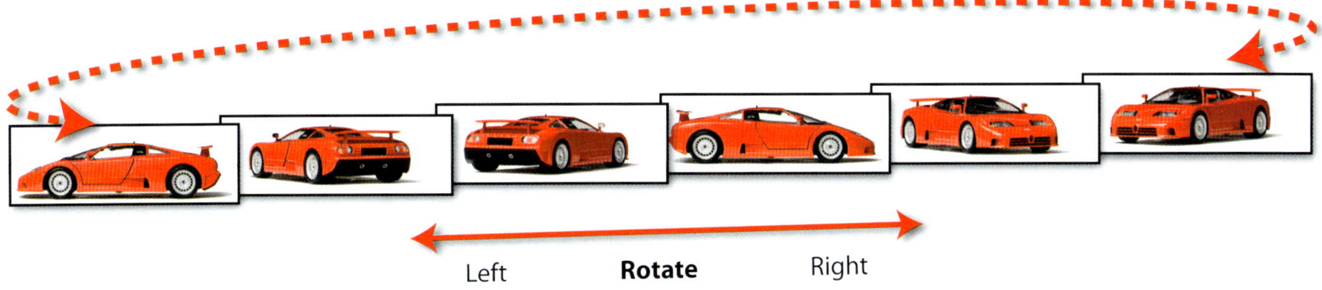

Fig. 19-1 The traditional single row object movie presents a series of views sequencing the rotation of an object 360°.

Fig. 19-2 An object movie structure can also be used to show passage of time, as in this time lapse sequence of sundown at a nuclear power plant in Crystal River, FL.

Time Lapse

Object rotation is not the only element that should be considered for incremental changes in object movies. The creative photographer will find many other uses for this interactive format.

One such example is to record changes to the condition of the object, or even the lighting upon it, such as in time lapse photography. Keep both the camera and object in their same relative positions, but record a sequence of images such as clouds moving across the sky or the sun setting. Then, sequence these in an object movie so that the viewer can scroll forward and backward through the time period recorded. For a time lapse of a sunset, you might not want to loop the beginning with the end of the movie. However, if you've captured a sequence of an entire 24-hour period, it might work very well to loop it so the viewer transitions back to the beginning of the day again. Your decision on whether to loop the movie will depend upon whether the first and last frames of your movie are similar enough to avoid the appearance of a sudden "jump" or change when the viewer crosses them.

Multi-row object movies add a second dimension to the playback and navigation paths. Rather than providing only the forward and backward navigation of a single-row linear movie, they provide the ability for the viewer to move forward / backward through multiple rows of images, as well as across those rows.

The most common use of multi-row object movies is to show rotation of the object with one axis, and movement of the camera above and below the object with the other. This way, when the user drags their mouse side-to-side in the movie window, the object rotates left and right. When dragging the mouse up and down, the view changes to

positions above and below. Both horizontal and vertical rotation can be done independently – or in combination – as the viewer desires.

Yet, the second axis can be used in other ways beyond simply changing vertical perspective. Consider the possibility of using vertical rows to show some other change to the object, such as color variation.

Let's say the product you're shooting comes in four different colors. Perhaps you've chosen to rotate the product through 360 degrees with 24 frames (15° rotation

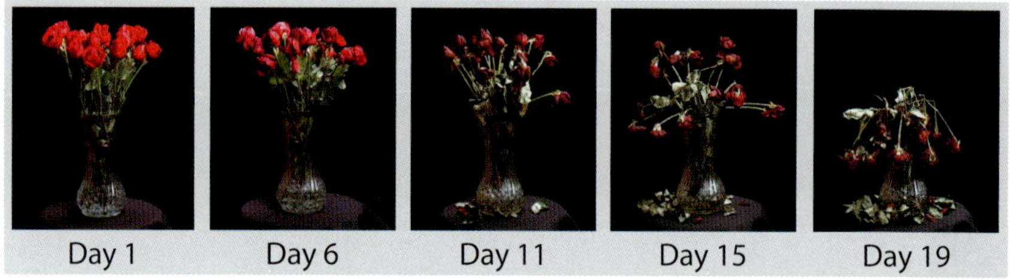

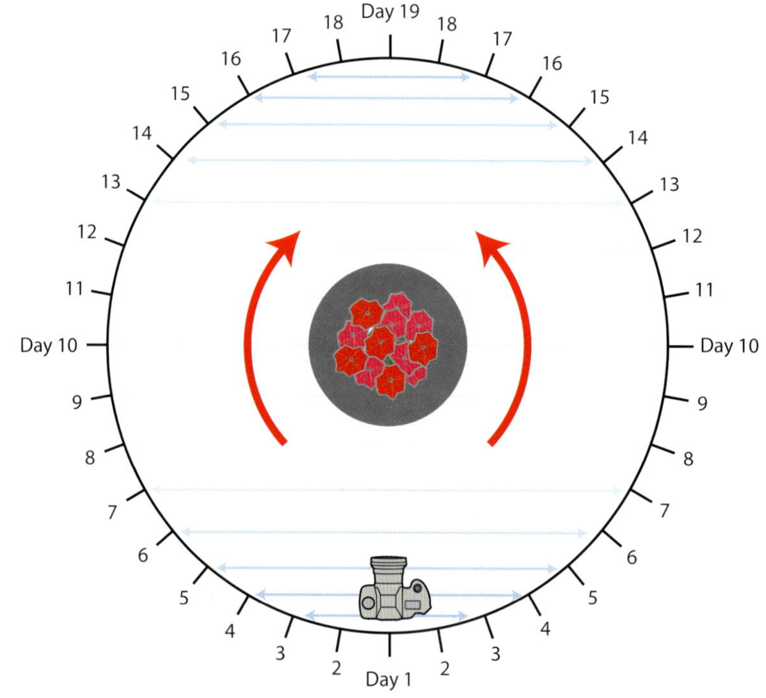

Fig. 19-3 This time lapse object movie of flowers wilting was shot over a 19 day period where camera, lighting, and object could remain fixed in place.

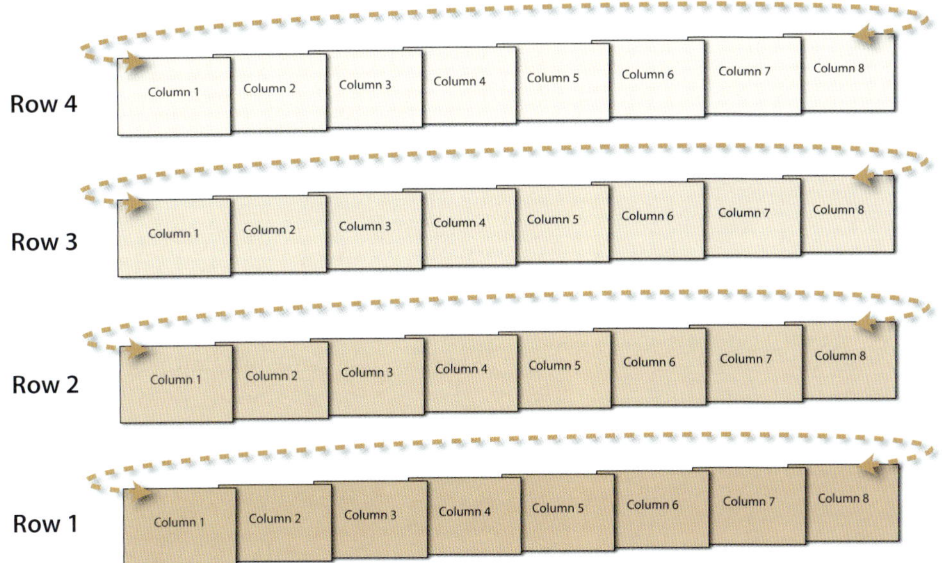

Fig. 19-4 The traditional multi-row object movie structure, generally used to show a rotating object from multiple levels.

need for your movies will increase geometrically as you add rows, demanding not only more production time (and cost), but yielding correspondingly larger file sizes for your movies.

Multiple rows can also be used to show feature variations for a product. For example, if your subject is a car, you could shoot multiple rows showing the doors open and closed, the lights on or off, or even a multi-row sequence of a convertible top being put up and down. If you are photographing a computer or piece of office equipment, you could use extra vertical rows to show the opening of access panels or the addition of optional accessories.

between each shot), so you will be creating a single row of 24 frames for each color variation. Keeping the camera and turntable in the same positions, you can substitute each subsequent colored object, and shoot another row of 24 images. Do this for all four colors that the product comes in. (Note that sometimes it might be easier to make color adjustments to the 24 original images digitally in post production, rather than to actually reshoot each one while maintaining identical camera and product alignment. Such decisions will depend on your skills with Photoshop and other masking tools, and whether you are more comfortable doing production vs. post-production work.)

Your result will be a matrix of four rows of 24 frames each for your object movie. You would assemble these so that when the user moves their mouse left or right, the object rotates side to side, but when they move their mouse up or down, they scroll through the four different color variations. Certainly, you can include more or less variations as needed. For example, if the product came in 32 different colors, you could include 32 rows of 24 frames each. Remember that the number of images you

You could get even more creative by combining multiple elements into the different rows, including tighter & wider views (zooming in or out), daylight and night time lighting (great for glow-in-the-dark products), or combinations of all these. Remember to make your changes gradually between frames, in order to keep the playback and end-user experience a smooth one.

Animation Loops

If you really want to complicate things, consider adding animation loops to some or all of the views you present in an object movie.

This could be useful, for example, if you were photographing a computer from multiple angles, and you wanted to include an animated logo on its screen. For those views of the computer where the screen was visible, you would shoot little sequences (perhaps 3-5 frames each) of the logo animation, which would then be

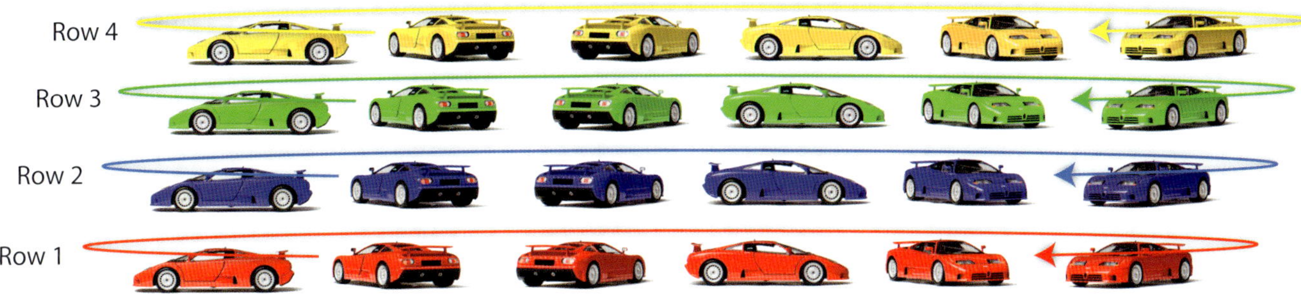

Fig. 19-5 Using the multi-row object movie structure to show color variation of an object as it spins.

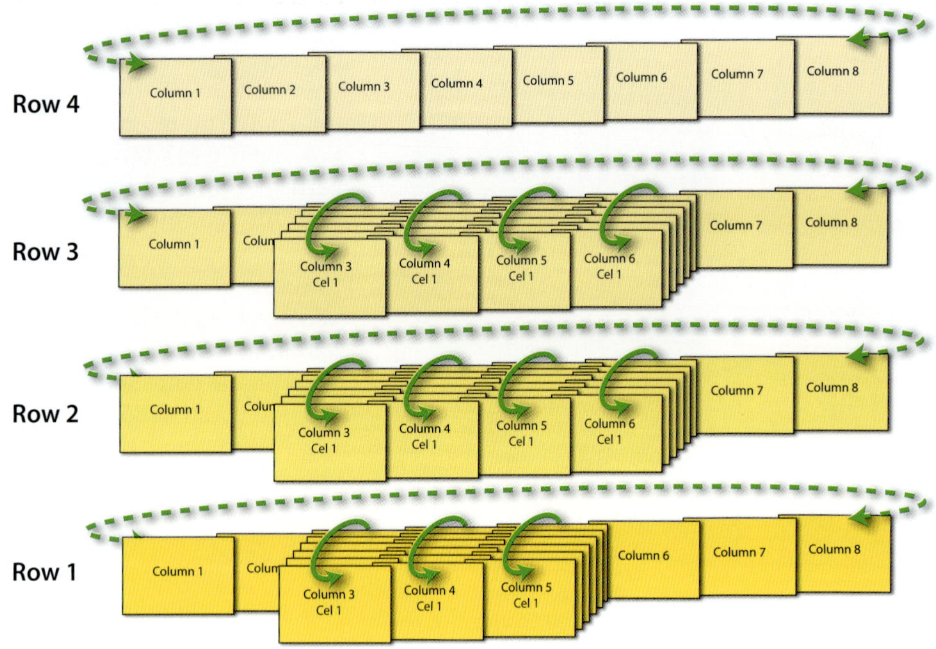

Fig. 19-6 Animated loops can be added as a third dimension to object movies.

Most of these subjects can't be easily moved. Even if they could, you'd probably have a tough time finding a turntable large enough to hold them. The solution is to move the camera around the object.

This is where your shooting technique becomes even more critical. Camera alignment and positioning relative to the object must remain consistent, so it is important to find ways to keep the camera on a track about the object.

The simplest approach, at least for vehicle-sized objects, is to attach a tape measure or line to the center point of your object. Determine the distance your camera needs to be from the object based on the lens you are using. This distance will be the radius for the camera circle around your object.

programmed into the assembly of your object movie. A simple way to think of this structure is the addition of a third dimension to the navigation paths available in your movie.

Again, when planning for such features, consider the number of images that will be required, along with the sizes of the movie files your viewers may need to download. For example, a single row object movie might contain only 18 images. A multi-row object movie might multiply that by six (for six different rows of the same 18 rotation positions) totaling 108 images. If you then added a simple four-frame animation to each of those views, you'll wind up with over 400 photos. That's a lot of work to make a single object movie. If you are considering such endeavors, you will recognize the value of programmable or automated object rigs.

Very Large Objects

OK, admit it. Your creative juices have started flowing, and you're finding yourself thinking about ways to make object movies of exceptionally large things... like trucks or trains, airplanes or boats, perhaps even buildings, islands, tracts of real estate, or scenic wonders of the world.

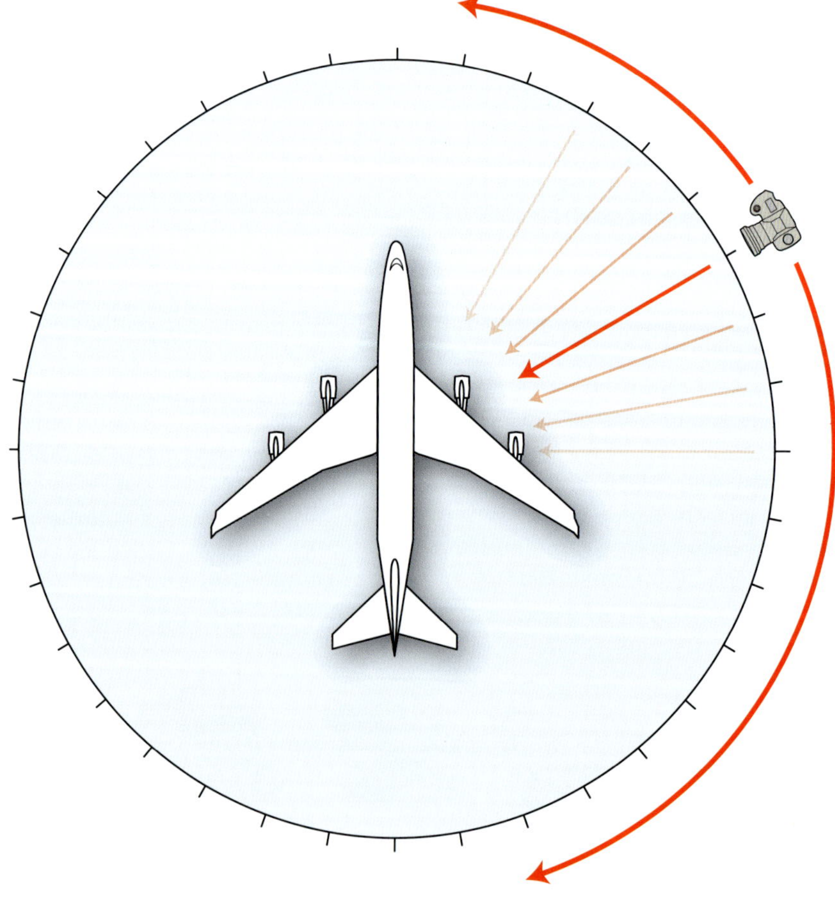

Fig. 19-7 Photographing very large objects as object movies generally requires moving the camera around the object, rather than using a turntable. This requires careful alignment of the camera and determining each shooting position accurately.

Technical Note:
Positioning Points on a Circle

You can use the power of geometry to gain accuracy in determining your shooting positions on a large circle. Rather than relying on a visual reference from a small protractor, where even the slightest error will be magnified by the size of your circle's radius, you can calculate the straight-line distance between points on your circle with the following formula:

distance = 2 * r * sin (a / 2)   where **r** = radius of circle, and **a** = angle (in degrees) between positions

Example: Using a 100′ radius circle, and a 20° angle between shots, the straight line distance (chord) between shooting positions would be:

distance   = 2 * 100 * sin (20° / 2)

= 200 * sin (10°)

= 200 * .1736

= 34.73 feet, or about 34 feet, 9 inches

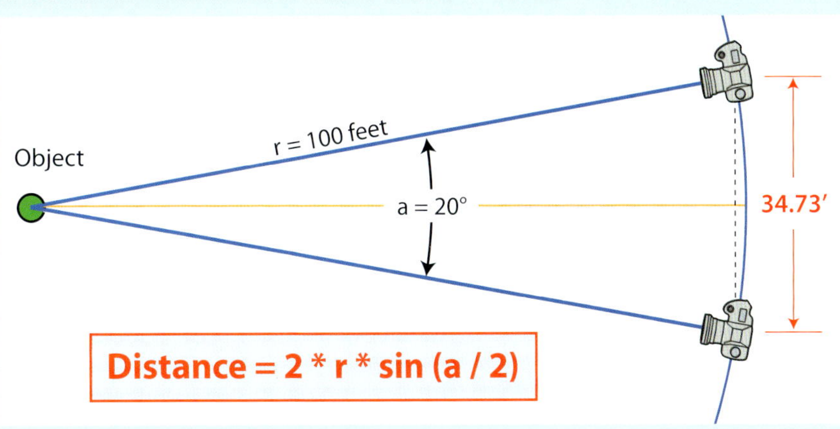

Fig. 19-8 If you know the radius or distance between camera and the center of your object plus the angle desired between shots. you can calculate the distance between shooting points around your object circle.

Pulling this line taut, scribe a circle on the ground surrounding the object. Next, mark shooting positions depending on the number of shots you want for your object movie (36 shots = every 10°, 24 shots = every 15°, 12 shots = every 30°, etc.). You may find it handy to have someone else assist you by holding a protractor at the center point, and calling out the chosen degree angles as you scribe the circle. Use unobtrusive adhesive stickers or small natural objects (stones or small sticks stuck into the ground) as your markers to help minimize the need for post production retouching. Remember that these markers will probably be in view as you shoot from the opposite sides of your object.

Another method for determining your shooting positions is to mount a low cost laser pointer onto an indexed panoramic tripod head. Position the head on a tripod where the center of your object (or shooting circle) will be, and level it. Set the shooting detents on the head for the angle you want between shots, and attach the laser level. The laser can now be used as a precise indicator of the radials that your shooting positions will be on. Using your tape measure or fixed distance line, you can now measure out from your object center to mark the precise positions for your camera on each radial. It helps to have a large white card or other visual target for the laser to reflect off of. This will help you better identify where the laser is pointing as you move large distances from it.

Of course, whenever you are using or working around lasers, be sure to protect your eyes properly, and avoid shining the beam directly into your camera or lens. Also, make sure that it doesn't shine into the eyes of anyone around you, nor toward aircraft that might fly overhead (there are serious criminal penalties for shining a laser at an aircraft in flight, even if done by accident).

Aerial Object Movies
What if the object you need to shoot is so large, or the areas surrounding it are inaccessible, that you cannot effectively photograph it from the ground -- no matter how well prepared you are to measure precise angles and distances? If you are shooting real estate properties, major landmarks, or other large structures, you might need to take an aerial approach.

Technical Note: Aerial Photo Tips

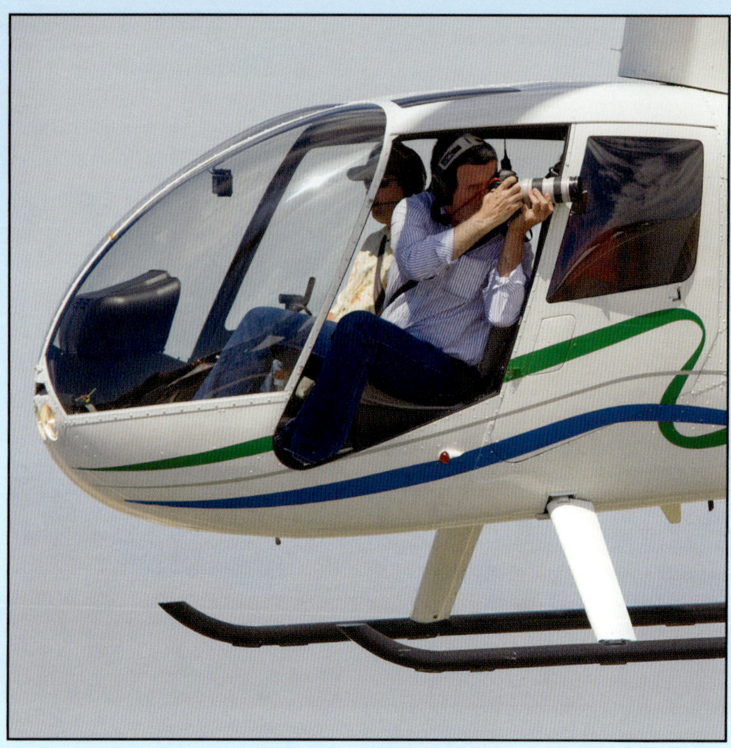

Fig. 19-9 Photography from an aerial platform brings its own unique perspectives, and unique challenges.

1) Safety! Safety! Safety! All decisions about an aerial shoot should be made with safety as the utmost concern. If something doesn't feel right, or you're even the slightest bit concerned about whether it's safe, delay or cancel your shoot until you have it planned better. Aviation accidents almost always result in significant property damage and/or personal harm (including death). Most accidents are **not** the result of a single cataclysmic failure of some sort, but rather a sequence of small things going wrong that sometimes build quickly into disaster. If little things are going wrong, take corrective action immediately. Don't hesitate to abort the flight if even if a single issue is causing you concern. Better to live and come back another day.

2) Hire an experienced pilot to fly while you shoot pictures. (Even if you are a pilot yourself, you should still have someone else fly the plane when you are shooting.) Good photography and good flying both take 100 percent of your concentration. Trying to do both at the same time means both

will probably suffer. Plan and discuss the entire shoot with your pilot before you ever set foot in the aircraft. Explain exactly what you're trying to do and what situations you specifically want to avoid. Ask for the pilot's advice on how best to accomplish your goals, and remind him/her that if you ask them to do anything unsafe or that they are uncomfortable with, they should be willing to tell you "no."

3) Find out if you can remove the passenger-side door from the aircraft before flight, or whether a window can be fully opened. The plastics used for windows and canopies on most aircraft are far from optical quality, and will seriously degrade your images. Opening the window or removing the door will mean there is nothing but air between your lens and your subject.

4) Secure *everything* inside the aircraft. Opened doors or windows, combined with sometimes bumpy rides and 100+ mph winds outside, tend to draw unsecured items out of the aircraft. All cameras and lenses should be stowed in a camera bag, unless they are in your hands for shooting. All bags should be kept closed and strapped to a seat so there's no chance of them falling out. Make sure your camera's strap is secured around your neck so it doesn't fall if it slips from your grasp. As bad as it seems to lose an expensive camera and lens accidentally, objects like these falling from an aircraft can result in death to anyone they hit on the ground. There are very serious liability issues resulting from objects dropped from aircraft, whether by accident or not.

5) Secure *yourself* inside the aircraft, as well. If you are sitting next to an open door of an aircraft in flight, you should be firmly held inside by a harness or other restraint attached to a hard point (or the frame) of the aircraft. If you use only a seat belt, wrap a thin loop of tape over the buckle to keep it from accidentally unclipping as you move around. Do not overdo this tape, however. While you want to prevent the buckle from unclipping accidentally, you also need to be able to tear through it quickly in the event of an emergency after landing. Be sure to test both the tape's security and your ability to get out of it before you leave the ground.

6) Try to keep your camera and lens inside the aircraft when shooting, so that no part is blowing in the air outside. This will result in less movement and sharper pictures. Shoot with the highest shutter speeds you can, again to minimize the effects of camera movement. Don't worry about using small apertures for great depth of field. Most ground-based subjects shot from the air are sharp at (or near) infinity focus distance. For aerial work, a fast shutter speed is generally more advantageous than increased depth of field. Shoot with your lens aperture open fairly wide.

7) Avoid touching or resting any part of your camera on the aircraft frame. Engine vibration will be transmitted via the airframe directly to your camera, and reduce image sharpness. Use the natural shock absorption of your body and arms to insulate the camera from such movements. Battery powered gyro stabilizers, which attach to the tripod socket on the bottom of your camera, can often be rented from pro camera shops, and can further stabilize hand-held photography from aircraft and other moving vehicles.

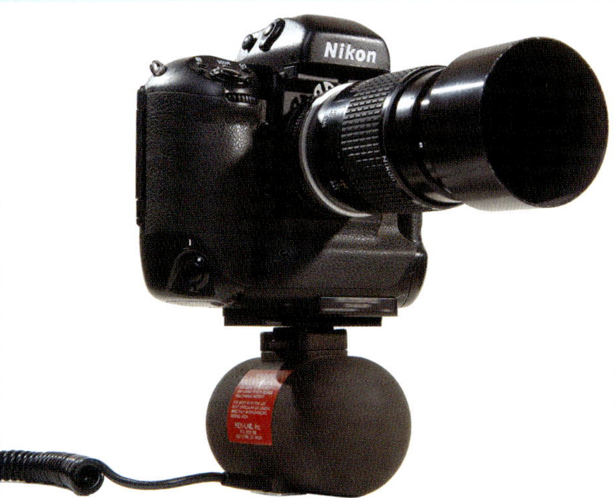

Fig. 19-10 Kenyon gyro stabilizer for hand-held shooting from aircraft, boats, and other moving vehicles.

8) Carry an air sickness bag in a readily accessible pocket. It's easy to become nauseous by looking through a camera viewfinder for prolonged periods in a moving aircraft, particularly while doing turns or other maneuvers. There's no shame in getting air sick (it happens to the most experienced aerial pros). However, you want to avoid making a mess inside the aircraft. Remember that high winds blowing through the aircraft via the open window or missing door will blow anything loose throughout the cabin, including remnants of whatever meal you last ate that might not have stayed inside your stomach. These contents will find their way into every nook and cranny of the aircraft, as well as over all occupants and equipment that might be exposed. An air sickness bag is an excellent alternative to hours of cleanup after your flight.

9) Try to shoot when the light is interesting. You'll have to deal with aircraft, pilot, and weather availability when scheduling your flights. But the hours immediately after sunrise or before sunset will provide the most visually appealing light. Consider also that the calmest air is generally encountered in the mornings. As the day progresses, convection currents and winds aloft increase, resulting in rougher flights and greater difficulty in keeping the aircraft on a specific track and cameras stabilized. Mid-day light often yields a fairly flat appearance for ground-based subjects photographed from the air. Overcast days are generally *not* recommended for aerial photography.

10) Avoid using longer telephoto lenses or shooting from too long distances. The air near the earth's surface has a surprising amount of material suspended in it, which serves to diffuse light. While hardly noticeable at what we often think of as long distances on the ground (100 – 200 feet), it is exacerbated at the longer shooting distances common to aerial photography. Ask your pilot to fly you as close to your subject as is both safe and legal (often 500 to 2,000 feet), as opposed to trying to photograph your subject from a mile or more away in the air. Being closer reduces the amount of smog and haze you'll be shooting through, and also allows you to use shorter focal length lenses, which have the added benefit of reducing the blurring effects of any camera movements.

Aerial photography has its own set of unique challenges. The most important concern however, is safety – not only for yourself, your pilot, and aircraft, but for those on the ground below.

Once you've committed to an aerial approach, you'll need to determine what camera positions will be necessary around your object, as well as how to successfully get to

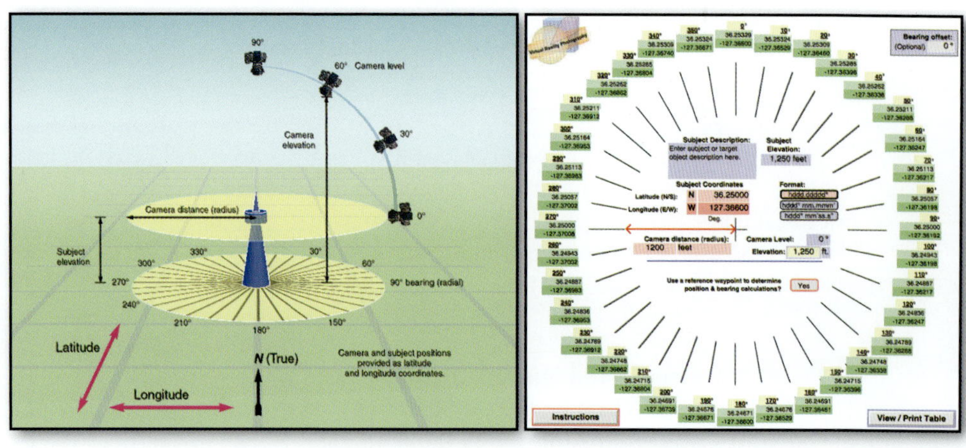

Fig. 19-11 The GPS Object Photography Calculator from www.vrphotography.com

them. One of the choices you'll need to make is whether to use a helicopter or fixed wing aircraft to get to these positions.

Helicopters generally cost three to five times as much to rent as fixed wing aircraft, so budget limitations are always a concern. Depending upon your location in the U.S., you might find a small fixed wing aircraft with four seats (such as a Cessna 172 or 182) with pilot for $150/hr. while a small helicopter with two seats (such as a Robinson, Enstrom, or Schweitzer) with pilot will probably be closer to $350/hr. Keep in mid that with any aircraft rental, you'll pay for the flight times getting to and from your shooting site, as well as the time you spend on station taking pictures. Many experienced aerial photographers refuse to fly photo missions in small, single engine piston helicopters like those mentioned above, insisting on the greater safety and redundancy of twin engine or turbine powered helicopters. Unfortunately, these aircraft, such as a Hughes 500 or Bell Rangers, usually rent for $700 and more per hour. Rates are generally far higher for aircraft outside of the U.S.

Helicopters have the advantage of being able to fly very slowly or to even hover in a fixed position. They also tend to feature less restricted fields of view from their cockpits than do traditional airplanes. However, they are not necessarily the best choice for aerial object photography.

A fixed wing aircraft can be flown in a very smooth circle around a point (your object) by a good pilot, leaving you the job of maintaining camera alignment and taking the photo sequence at your chosen intervals. Even if that circle is not perfectly round, as long as the airplane ends its path in the same place as it started, the object sequence will loop smoothly. I find it useful to have an assistant come along during aerial object shoots to watch the gyro compass on the aircraft's instrument panel and to call out our 10 degree turn increments as a cue for my next shots (assuming I'm doing 36 shots around the object).

Since your photography from the air is invariably going to be hand held, plan for significant post production time to tweak the alignment of each image. This will be necessary whether you are flying a circle in a fixed wing aircraft, or stopping to hover and shoot at each position in a helicopter. Hovering and shooting will take more time (thus costing more money), and most helicopters induce quite a bit more airframe vibration when in a hover than in forward flight, thus increasing the risk of blur due to camera movement. Again, remember to use the highest shutter speed you can in order to minimize the effects of vibration and camera movement. Set your focus at or near infinity and shoot with your aperture wide open. Some photographers tape the focus ring on their lens in position so they don't change it accidentally. Be sure to turn off the autofocus mechanism if you are shooting with an AF system. Depth of field is not usually a concern when you are farther from your subject, such as when shooting from the air.

Determining where your shooting positions should be over long distances, whether in the air or on the ground, remains a challenge. But there are tools available that can help.

One example is the GPS Object Photography Calculator, available online from the Virtual Reality Photography web site: **http://www.vrphotography.com**

This calculator allows you to enter the latitude and longitude coordinates of almost any point on earth, and to enter a shooting radius of your choice. It will calculate 36 GPS waypoints (latitude and longitude coordinates) surrounding your target. This information can then be used with a handheld GPS unit, or entered into the autopilot system of your aircraft, as a series of waypoints on a GPS track or route. The calculator also allows you to find waypoints and altitudes for circles of different heights above the object for multi-row aerial movies.

Synchronized Multiple Cameras

One of the more stunning applications of object movie technology is to freeze action, such as a person jumping in the air or a bird in flight, and to show that same moment from a variety of different perspectives. Imagine an object movie of a springboard diver, suspended in midair, which shows that same frozen-in-time moment from many different angles. This would allow the viewer to see the diver from any angle – an effect made popular in motion picture and television production after captivating audiences in the 1999 film *The Matrix*.

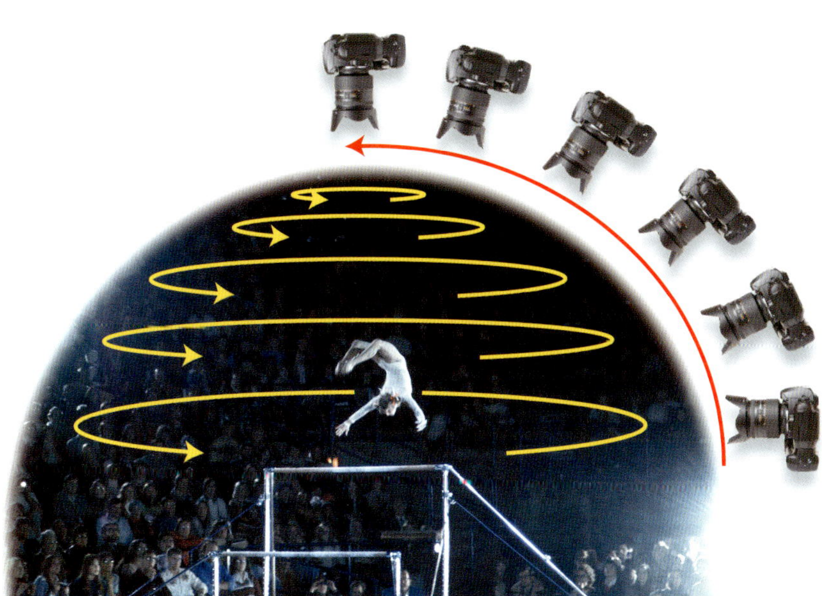

Fig. 19-12 Freezing objects in motion for object movies usually requires multiple synchronized cameras and lenses – one set for each shot needed in the sequence.

Unfortunately, creation of this effect is generally quite expensive, as it requires a large number of matching cameras and lenses, all aimed and focused at the same spot, and synchronized to fire at the same moment. For some of these "Bullet Time" sequences in *The Matrix*, over 120 matching cameras and lenses were required. Extensive digital post production was also involved to make sure that the alignment, color, exposure, and the composited backgrounds of every image matched.

Certainly such "frozen moment" object movies can be done with fewer cameras, but whether you employ six or 60, you'll still need to make sure they all match. Digital cameras are the preferred choice, as they eliminate the need for film scanning. Which ever cameras you choose must allow for manual exposure control and white balancing, in order to avoid each camera making its own subtle adjustments.

The creation of most VR object movies today requires that individual photographs be taken from each viewing position around the object. This involves shooting many images and considerable post production time.

However, as the pace of technology advances, other options are becoming available.

One of these is called image mapping, or image modeling. The process involves shooting a small handful of images from a few angles around the object (at least two, but rarely more than a dozen). Then, using sophisticated image mapping software, the images are calibrated with one another on a computer and a virtual 3D model of the object is generated. The photographic images are then mapped onto the surfaces of the virtual 3D model, creating a fully interactive photo-realistic rendering, which can be viewed from any angle or exported into a variety of 3D formats, including object movies.

One commercial software application that does this is ImageModeler from Autodesk, currently available for both Mac and Windows platforms.

Use of such applications could minimize the challenges of shooting precisely aligned images of large objects, such as aerial views, or for frozen in time action sequences. These programs offer the possibility for a photographer to shoot fewer perspectives initially, and to digitally render any needed views with precise virtual alignments later on.

While this would certainly make life simpler from the photography and production end, it creates the potential for significant additional work on the post production end. Such software applications still require an author to define the virtual 3D shapes for the images to be mapped on. However, as technologies advance, more of this process will probably become automated.

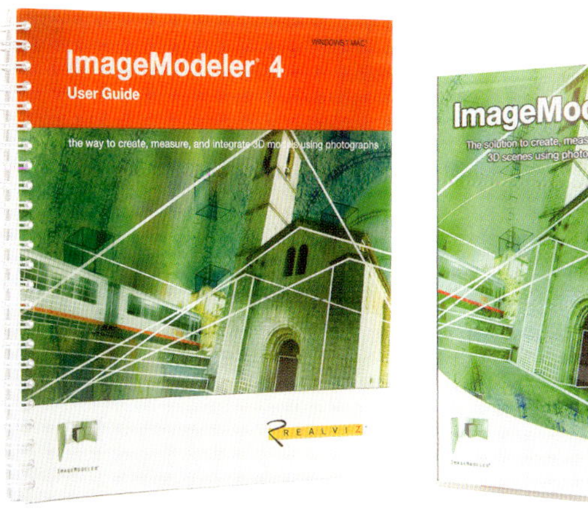

Fig. 19-13 Autodesk Image Modeler software.

Part 4

BUSINESS PRACTICES

> *"Opportunity is missed by most people because it is dressed in overalls and looks like work."*
>
> **– Thomas Edison**

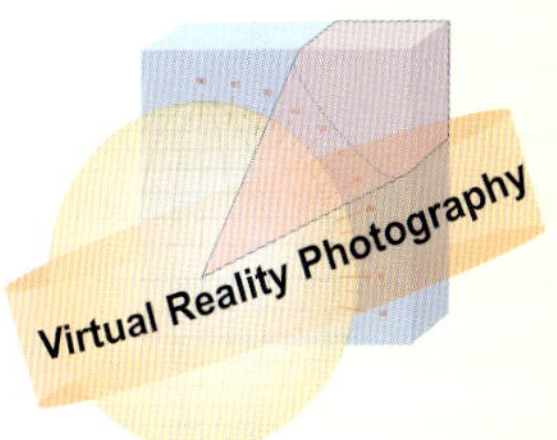

Chapter 20: Rights and Value

Whether you are a full time professional photographer, multimedia author, or part time hobbyist who hopes to make enough income from your VR work to pay for some of your equipment each year, you need to understand the basics of how the businesses of photography and other intellectual property authoring are run. Everyone wants to be paid a fair value for the work they create, particularly when that work provides significant value to a client.

The business model upon which most creative industries are based is that of licensing work for specific usage, as opposed to selling the rights and ownership of that work outright. As an independent author creating a photograph, you can license the usage of that photograph to many different clients over time, earning licensing or usage fees from each of them. Thus, a single photograph can potentially earn its author many thousands of dollars in fees from dozens of different clients over the life of that image.

Similar business models are used in literature, music, entertainment, and other industries, where creative content and intellectual property are licensed for limited use over and over, rather than being sold outright for a single price. Examples include the purchase of a software application or music recording, where the fee you pay is proportional to the license that is extended for your use of the content. If you buy a typical music CD, you receive a limited license for your own personal use of that music. Likewise, you receive a personal use license for most software you buy. If you need to have the software available for many computers (or seats) in a business, you purchase a more expensive "volume" or "seat" license – even though the intellectual property (lines of computer coding) may be virtually identical to the personal use version. Similarly, if you want to use a music track from a pop album for your company's latest radio or TV ad, you need to buy a synchronization or broadcast license for that use in addition to what you may have already paid for the recording itself. It's exactly the same content, but it is being licensed differently.

It is this sort of ongoing stream of licensing fees and royalties, sometimes as small as pennies per use, that allows creative authors such as photographers, musicians, writers, filmmakers, and software developers to earn income from their work throughout their careers. Consider that some of these creations can take years to produce, as in the case of image collections, books, films, and software applications. Authors need to be able to rely on continuing income streams from past work in order to survive financially while they create new work. Additionally, the content they create during their lives can generate licensing income for their families and heirs long after the author has died.

It is this principle of generating a continuing stream of income from the creative content and intellectual property that is the foundation of creative work today. VR photographers should consider the same approach with their work. Obviously, if you know you are creating once in a lifetime VR image sequences, it would behoove you to make sure you retain the rights to that work in order to be able to license those rights repeatedly in the future. However, even with run-of-the-mill commercial work, such as low cost real estate tours, consider the potential value of such work decades from now. While most of these panoramas are considered by clients today to be "throw away" content after the house is sold and the images have served their immediate purposes, they may find renewed life or value in the future, either for what might be considered "retro" products, or for historic purposes.

I know one photographer, now in his 90s, who photographed various unknown socialites at society events in the 1930s and 1940s for what, even at the time, was very little money. Most of his subjects were not important enough to even be published in the local newspapers back then. Yet over the years, he retained ownership of the negatives and the rights to his work. Today, he regularly sells prints of these unknown socialites and debutantes as limited edition fine art prints. These gallery sales earn him thousands of dollars apiece.

You often don't know what photographs or other creative works will be of value in the future, so it is unwise to just give ownership or all rights away to clients who will likely dispose of the images after they've used them for their immediate purposes. Always consider the potential long-term value of your work. Ninety percent of it may forever be worthless outside of your personal files, but it's almost impossible to accurately predict which 10 percent will yield future payments. Keep this in mind before you agree to copyright or ownership transfers to clients.

There are times when selling all rights or ownership of your work is appropriate. In the United States, current copyright law provides for this under both work for hire contracts and employer-employee relationships. However, these types of agreements should provide other tangible compensation to the author, such as employee benefits and long term employment. This is value in place of the potential ongoing revenue streams for the author. Of course, both copyright and employment laws vary around the world, as do individual contracts between authors and their clients.

Value and Licensing of Photography
Photography, by its very nature, is easily copied. Digital technologies make high quality copying and publishing of photography as easy as pushing a button. So whether you have the first copy or the millionth, it can be of equal quality to the original.

Since photography is so easily reproduced, most publication photographers charge fees for usage based on the value that a client receives from the work. Licensing fees are different for most every client, depending upon the specific usage planned. Cost factors specific to the photographer are also factored into pricing and valuation.

Photographers must maintain an orderly system for assigning value to their images, assuring themselves a reasonable profit, while not creating unfair exposure to those securing the reproduction rights. The control of the right to reproduce an image is one of the fundamental rights granted by copyright law. That right was given to copyright owners so that they could profit from their work, and thus be motivated to create more work. The connection between reproduction rights and profitability has been recognized since the days of the very first laws governing such rights in the late fifteenth century in Venice.

Usage is usage. Greater usage of a photograph by a client means the client is receiving greater value from that image. The photographer or author should be compensated accordingly. A small usage by a client, such as a small print run of a limited distribution collateral piece, will command smaller usage fees than will a larger use or combination of rights licensed, such as those for major print and electronic advertising campaigns.

For many years, the only way to reproduce or publish photography was through paper and ink printing processes. Reproduction rights were generally licensed with clearly defined terms specific to the printing industry. However, the overwhelming penetration of video, personal computers, and the internet into traditional publishing markets in recent years has meant that few publishers are exclusively print-based any more. In fact, most markets for VR have little need for usage rights *other* than electronic media.

When licensing VR content to clients, it is crucial to understand and clarify the usage rights that you are licensing. Most large media corporations have boilerplate-type contracts that they ask their content suppliers to sign. These often specify the licensing (and sometimes the complete *transfer*) of **all** electronic rights.

As increasing amounts of content are delivered in electronic form, the scope of the phrase "all electronic rights" becomes even more extensive than the overly broad phrase "all print rights" was in traditional print media. Just as print rights are licensed by specific usage (example: "one-time, non-exclusive, North American consumer weekly newsmagazine rights for XYZ Publication, circulation not to exceed 100,000 copies"), so too should the licensing of electronic rights also be specified in such detail.

The term "electronic rights" can include many existing print rights, plus the rights for electronic media uses. These may include all electronic media in existence today, as well as those that might be developed in the future.

For clarity, we will use the following definitions:

Media – tangible means for distributing an image. Generally there are three types of media:

   Print – on paper or other tangible printed material

   Electronic – digital or analog data distributed via a variety of electronic media

   Film – Celluloid based material

Application or **Product** – a particular vehicle within a given medium (magazine, annual report, promotional brochure, billboard, video, software program, CD/DVD, web site, etc.)

For photographers, print and electronic media offer broad opportunities for publication. However, these opportunities are quickly diminished if the reproduction rights are not carefully defined, controlled, and priced. Most photographers would not license "all print reproduction rights" to a client unless there was a very high fee. Print rights include magazines, books, encyclopedias, posters, brochures, etc. In keeping with that logic, it is unwise to license "all electronic reproduction rights" without similar limitations or appropriate compensation.

While an image licensed in print might normally be used in only one application, an electronic application using that same image can be served up in many different forms. It is not uncommon for a successful web or online product to end up as a CD, DVD, or multimedia product, and vice versa.

> **Reproduction Rights Rule #1:**
>
> *Never license a broad scope of media rights unless you are receiving compensation consistent with that scope.*

Value of Content

The value of visual content in electronic media is perhaps far greater than it ever was in the traditional print market. Audiences have come to expect more visual information in electronic publications, so the demand is higher. Although electronic and print markets frequently overlap, they should always be considered distinct and separate, especially when licensing rights or usage. Electronic media are not replacements, but rather, extensions of traditional print markets for photography. Therefore, the additional demand for images in electronic media effectively increases the overall value of photography. In the case of VR photography and its interactivity, primary publication markets are almost exclusively electronic. While single images from both object and panorama movies can quite effectively be used in print media, it is the interactivity that they offer in display on an electronic screen that yields their most potential.

Determination of the values for visual content depends upon a variety of factors. However, two principles of business never change.

1) **Compensation should reflect the value of the image(s).**

2) **Value is relative for different uses and different clients.**

In the publication market (whether print or electronic), image value is based on specific factors. These are:

Competition: What level of competition exists? What is the availability of similar images from other sources? If images are unique and exclusive, they should command better fees.

Novelty: Novel (new) images are those which have a new look and have not been seen by the market at large.

Freshly produced images are generally more valuable than those that have been available to the market for a while. Innovation by style, technique, and artistry also adds value.

Importance: The intended size, placement, and repeated use of an image in an application increases value. The relative volume of images also indicates importance. If a photograph is the sole image appearing in an application, it is usually more valuable than if it were only one of 100 or more.

Distribution Volume: Circulation, press runs, discs pressed, and on-line accesses all influence value. Generally, the greater the distribution, the greater the value.

Application Market: Each application has a market. Examples of specific markets include consumer, trade, institutional, not-for-profit, and corporate. Generally, the larger the market an image is used in, the greater the value. The exceptions to this are in niche market applications, where great selectivity is exercised. Here, the importance of an image is even greater, since the goal of niche marketing is maximum impact on a small, select group. In short, every web site hit or viewing of the content can have high value, since that web page has been specifically requested by a user. This is in contrast to the hundreds of pages that might be printed and delivered in a magazine or book, but of which only a small handful might be looked at by a reader.

Term of Use: The longer an image or application is in use by a client, the greater the value it provides.

Risk Factors: Liability is a good example. Images used in applications requiring a model or property release (advertising, promotion, trade, etc.) are riskier to publish than editorial images. Even the best releases are contestable and subject to interpretation. A given release can be inadequate if it prohibits image alterations or additions. This increases risk to photographers (for their clients' misuse of their images). Other risks can include physical risk required to create the image in the first place, as well as the risk of the work being devalued by publication in certain media like clip art or royalty free systems. Increased risk generally commands increased fees to the author.

Obviously, assessing value combines a little bit of both science and art. One can numerically determine specific size, placement, number of copies, and similar statistics. Risk can be assessed to some degree based on the use and the terms of releases. However, the level of competition and the novelty of an image are unsure things. Assessing the value of these is somewhat of an art. It requires that the photographer or multimedia author learn how a given user values the image – and that's something that many clients are unwilling to share as it can weaken their negotiating position.

Pricing and Compensation Structures

Electronic media are simply modern forms of traditional publication, which have evolved far beyond the scope of print media. Pricing usage for any publication, be it electronic, print or otherwise, should reflect both past and future valuation. Rights granted should be on a "one-time" basis whenever possible, unless the fees earned are far higher than traditional base fees.

Compensation for visual content is usually based upon the following structures or combinations thereof:

1) Flat fee – the photographer is paid a single, fixed amount for the use of his or her photograph(s). The broader the license or the more usage extended, the higher the fee will generally be. If the usage goes beyond the original license, additional fees must be paid. This is often the simplest arrangement for both photographer and buyer.

Examples: A panoramic VR movie is licensed for a 1/4 page display for three months on a corporate web site for a fee of $650. If the image is displayed for six months instead, the fee might be $910. In print media, an image might be licensed for 1/4 page, one-time, non-exclusive use in a consumer weekly magazine, with a 3,000,000 maximum circulation for a fee of $350.00. If the final usage is 1/2 page instead, the license fee might increase to $500.

2) Structured tier fee schedule – a schedule of fees agreed upon between the photographer and client. The photographer's fee increases when distribution of the product reaches certain levels, such as the number of online accesses, the number of CDs pressed, or the number and sizes of each broadcast.

Example: A VR panorama is presented as the opening page on a commercial travel disc, on a non-exclusive basis (meaning that the photographer can also license the image elsewhere during the same period), with publication rights extended to the client for one year.

> Up to 5,000 copies produced – fee is $1,000.
>
> 5,001 to 7,500 copies – $250 is added.
>
> 7,501 to 10,000 copies – $150 more is added.

In this case if the client produces 5,000 copies or less of the disc, the photographer is paid $1,000. If an additional run of 1,500 is made (totaling 6,500), the photographer is paid an additional $250. If an additional press run is made <u>after</u> the one year term of the license is complete,

the subsequent licensing fees revert to the starting point of $1,000 for the first 5,000 or less copies. This is to encourage the client to license all their desired usage up front. While a client might choose to license usage on a "pay as they go" basis, it generally costs more.

3) Percentage of sales fee – the photographer receives a percentage or a stipulated amount for every sale. This could be a fee based on the selling price of every disc, publication, or book, or it could be a stipulated amount for every download or access to an application. Frequently, this would be in *addition* to a base or guaranteed minimum for the usage. In this approach, the photographer can accept the risk of a small return if the client's product is not successful, yet share in the reward if the product succeeds.

Example: A 180° panorama is reproduced as a 16"x30" commercial poster for a 12 percent royalty on net sales, before taxes and delivery fees. The posters might sell in a retail outlet for $14.99 with a wholesale price of $7.00. Under a 12 percent royalty, the photographer receives 84 cents per unit sold (.12 x $7.00). The photographer might negotiate a $1,000 minimum guarantee, paid as an advance against the first 1,190 units sold (1,190 x $.84 = $1,000). Additional 84 cent royalties would then be paid to the photographer for every unit sold after that.

4) Per unit (produced or sold) fee – the photographer's fee is based upon a fixed payment per unit produced or sold (units *produced* is the preferred method).

Example: A single photograph is one of several dozen included in a full screen slide show on a non-profit DVD for a fee of $.03 per disc pressed, with license extended for the copyright life of the product.

In this scenario, each image would be valued at three cents per disk. If the volume of discs initially pressed is 10,000, the fee is $300. As more disks are pressed, the total fee increases. Generally, in such an approach, the fee per unit decreases in steps as the volume increases. In such a case, the payment at the 50,000 unit level might be reduced to one cent per disc.

When it comes time to extract the value of images in an actual transaction, all the foregoing theory must be applied in short order. To do that, photographers have traditionally taken different approaches, depending upon whether the images licensed are generated on assignment or are selected from a library of existing (stock) images.

Assignment pricing is often complex, and the basis of such pricing varies. Advertising, editorial, corporate, and architectural photography each have their own pricing peculiarities. However, licensing of stock photography has become more standardized over the years, although the markets for stock imagery have changed dramatically in the last decade due to an increasing abundance of low-cost clip art and royalty free image sources.

Day Rate Against Usage
There are a variety of photography pricing models available, each having its own advantages and flaws. At times, it may seem like every professional photographer uses a different pricing system. Some use sophisticated pricing software and reference tables, while others seem to randomly pull prices out of a hat. Some simply accept whatever their client offers to pay – which is not a terribly good method for remaining in business long.

An ideal system that provides a similar pricing method for both assignment and stock photography has long been desired. Such a model was created and published by the American Society of Media Photographers (ASMP) in the late 1990s. The model is based on the concept that a fee for a given usage should remain constant for a photographer, whether created via assignment or stock (previously created images). For stock licensing, the usage fee alone would be the primary billable amount (research and other stock fees can also be added). For assignment work, the photographer's creative fee or day rate would be applied as a *minimum against the usage fees.*

This is similar to the traditional editorial magazine model of a day rate minimum applied against a published space rate. The photographer is guaranteed a minimum day rate for an assignment, but if the number and size (space) of photos published, combined with the magazine's space rate, are greater than the day rate total, the photographer gets paid the higher space rate.

The Day Rate Against Usage model applies this principle to **all** licensing of photography, whether assignment or stock. If the photographer's creative fee or day rate for an assignment is greater than the combined usage fees, then the creative fee or day rate total is used as a minimum. If the value of the usage exceeds these, then the photographer bills for the larger usage amount.

For example, a photographer might charge $1,500/day (plus expenses) for a 3-day corporate shoot, totaling $4,500. If the client only used a few of the resulting images for a small collateral piece, the usage fees might only add up to $2,800. In this case, the $4,500 total day rate would be applied against the $2,800 usage total, and the photographer would bill the client $4,500 (plus expenses).

However, if the client wanted the images for trade show displays, corporate identity campaigns, and multimedia uses (on a web site or CD-ROM), the usage fees might easily total $20,000 or more. In this case, the usage total would exceed the day rate or creative fee minimum, and the photographer would bill the client for the usage amount. Obviously, all this needs to be agreed upon with a written Assignment Confirmation or contract prior to the photographer ever starting the assignment.

Again, the advantage of this system is that the different licensing fees a photographer sets for each type of usage can be applied identically to both assignment work and stock sales.

Among the first steps in this process are calculation of fair fees for each type of usage that the photographer might license – and determination of a discount structure for clients desiring more than a single usage. While some photographers may not feel it appropriate to discount usage fees for volume, the more common practice in the industry seems to be that photographers do offer volume licensing discounts.

There are a number of commercial pricing references to consult as a starting point for determining your own usage fees. You can also talk with other photographers to help you determine fees based on your particular types of photography and business needs. Once you've established a set of base figures, you can calculate all other fees and adjustments when usage changes, such as when clients change reproduction size, distribution, duration, and quantity of photos licensed.

For most of these variables, simple square root and inverse square relationships can be used to calculate relative prices. (Note that these are calculations most photographers are already familiar with through exposure and lighting relationships.) To illustrate the concept, let us consider some typical photography uses.

Example: A photographer might set his or her base rate for a particular usage at $200 for a 1/4 page reproduction. Doubling the reproduction size to 1/2 page would increase the fee by the square root of two (1.414), totaling $283. Quadrupling the size to a full page would increase the fee by the square root of four (= 2) to $400. Halving the size to 1/8 page from the original 1/4 page would reduce the fee by the square root of .5 (= .71) to $141. A minimum fee, such as $125, could also be specified, as well.

			(Base)					
Reprod. Size:	1/16 p.	1/8 p.	1/4 p.	1/3 p.	1/2 p.	2/3 p.	3/4 p.	1p.
Fee:	$100	$141	$200	$231	$283	$326	$346	$400

Fig. 20-1 Inverse square pricing for reproduction sizes. In this example, base price for calculations is 1/4 page @ $200.00.

This can also be applied to changes in the license term or duration.

Example: A photographer might set a base fee for corporate web use of a 1/2 screen VR movie at $1,000 for three months. Doubling that term of use to six months would multiply the fee by 1.414 (the square root of 2) to $1,414. A one-year license would cost $2,000 (the duration of the base term is multiplied by four so the price doubles).

			(Base)						
Term:	1 mo.	2 mos.	3 mos.	4 mos.	6 mos.	9 mos.	1 yr.	1.5 yrs.	2 yrs,
Fee:	$577	$816	$1,000	$1,155	$1,414	1,732	$2,000	$2,449	$2,828

Fig. 20-2 Inverse square pricing for license duration. In this example, base price for calculations is 3 months @ $1,000.00.

Note that usage specifications can be changed in combination, as well. For instance, if you were to double the term (duration) of use, as well as the reproduction size and the number of languages licensed, you would be effectively multiplying the usage by a factor of eight. The fee would therefore increase by the square root of eight, or a factor of 2.83.

One of the great advantages of this system is that you can set your base fees using any usage combination that you want, and precise usage needed by your clients will be calculated consistently. Each photographer should set their own base fees depending on their particular business structure, experience, and market demand for their work. The relationships between increasing and decreasing usage factors remains completely consistent and predictable – which is of benefit to both photographers and their clients. This system provides mathematical logic to usage fees, and allows for precision pricing, even down to an exact number of copies distributed, if so desired.

Circulation or distribution changes are calculated differently than the previous usage factors, since large adjustments in circulation don't affect usage fees as much as similar changes elsewhere in usage. A slightly modified formula – the square root of the square root (fourth root) of the circulation difference – would appear to more accurately reflect today's usage-fee-to-circulation ratios.

Example: A photographer sets her base fee at $500 for 10,000 copies of a photo reproduced 1/4 page in a corporate brochure or magazine. Doubling the circulation to 20,000 would multiply the usage fee by a factor of 1.19 (the fourth root of 2) to $595. If the circulation was increased by a factor of 16 to 160,000, the usage fee would be doubled to $1,000.

			(Base)						
Circulation:	1,000	2,500	5,000	10,000	20,000	50,000	100K	160K	250K
Fee:	$281	$354	$420	$500	$595	$748	$889	$1,000	$1,118

Fig. 20-3 Modified pricing model for circulation. In this example, base price for calculations is 10,000 copies @ $500.00.

Finally, this pricing system allows for consistent discounting of license fees for multiple photographs and/or for multiple types of usage. Multiple photos and uses involve an inverse square (1 divided by the square root) relationship between the number of images and/or uses, and the adjusted fees calculated for each.

As an example, consider a client wanting to license multiple photographs. The first image would be licensed at the photographer's full fee for that usage. The second photograph would be charged at 71 percent of its calculated fee (one divided by the square root of two = .71). The third image would be charged at 58 percent, and the fourth would be at 50 percent, etc. This same relationship is also used when more than one usage might be desired.

Example: A calculated usage fee is $500 for one image. The total fee for five images used at the same size, distribution, etc., would be $1,617, resulting from the sum of the discounted fees as follows:

Image # (usage fee):	1/Sqrt(x)	Disc. Fee	Total fee
First image ($500 fee)	100 %	$500	= $500
2nd image ($500 x .707)	70.7 %	(+) $354	= $854
3rd image ($500 x .577)	57.7 %	(+) $289	= $1,143
4th image ($500 x .5)	50.0 %	(+) $250	= $1,393
5th image ($500 x .447)	44.7 %	(+) $224	= $1,617
6th image ($500 x .408)	40.8 %	(+) $204	= $1,821
7th image ($500 x .378)	37.8 %	(+) $189	= $2,010
8th image ($500 x .354)	35.4 %	(+) $177	= $2,187
9th image ($500 x .333)	33.3 %	(+) $167	= $2,354

Fig. 20-4 Cummulative inverse square pricing structure for multiple images. In this example, base price for calculations is a license fee for one image at $500.00.

Note that some photographers do not feel it is appropriate to discount fees for multiple uses or images, and would simply charge first image and/or usage fees for each. In the above example, this photographer would multiply the single image usage fee ($500) by the number of images (5) to total $2,500, rather than the volume discount shown above of $1,617.

If the mathematical relationships described here are more than you want to deal with, a basic pricing calculator incorporating them all can be download from the Virtual Reality Photography web site:

http://www.vrphotography.com

Copyright and Ownership of Work

Copyright is often perceived to be a complicated subject, requiring legions of lawyers and complex registration processes. While copyright law *can* be complex and infinitely variable throughout the world, the actual principle of copyright is quite simple – it is the right to copy something. In many countries including the U.S., copyright is automatic and vested with the author at the moment an original work is fixed in some tangible form (such as on film, paper, or digital media). Determination of which person or entity is the actually the author involves both contractual terms and the specific copyright laws of your country. But usually, it is the author or current copyright holder who controls all the rights for others to copy that work.

The most precious thing that an independent photographer creates during his or her professional career is the body of work that he or she produces. However, that work will never even have the possibility of providing a full return to the photographer if it is given away in pieces over the years. This is essentially what happens when you give up the copyrights or ownership of your work to clients.

Copyright is an *intangible* asset, yet it is an asset of significant value that can be leased, licensed, or sold. All of the pricing examples presented in this chapter are based upon the photographer retaining copyright ownership of their work and licensing usage (permission to others to reproduce or copy that work for specific publications, sizes, quantities and periods of time). There can, however, be instances where photographers find themselves needing to transfer the ownership of their copyrights. In such cases, determining the full value of the image(s) and copyright is critical, so that the photographer can be compensated appropriately. In these instances, the photographer should be aware of the following:

• The buyer is placing great importance on the image(s), since they want the copyright.

• The image(s) will *never* produce additional revenue for the photographer from this or any other client. That lost revenue is value for which the photographer should be compensated in the copyright transfer transaction.

There are two common arrangements for structuring photographers' fees when copyright title transfers are involved.

1) Assignment of copyright ownership – generally, an undesirable arrangement for photographers and other content creators, since it involves a complete transfer of image ownership to the buyer. The creator will lose control over the quality and use of their work, and will be unable to earn any future income from royalties, residual sales, resale, or stock licensing of the material. It is also possible for photographers to discover that they are competing against their own work, if the purchasing client sells the images to a stock agency or decides to market the images as stock themselves. There can be occasions when assignment of copyright is necessary, but generally, the needs of most clients can be satisfied through broad usage terms and written guarantees by the photographer not to resell the material to competing clients. In the rare event that a copyright assignment is truly necessary, the photographer should negotiate an appropriate fee to compensate for all future income that he or she will be unable to earn from the material.

Example: a photographer whose fee for a specific package of limited rights is normally $1,500 per day, might have a quadrupled or quintupled fee of $6,000 or $10,000 per day for copyright assignment work.

2) Work for Hire – Under a work for hire, the photographer or author not only loses the copyright to the work from the moment he or she creates it, but also loses all rights to authorship. This includes loss of the right to be identified as the author of their work. Additionally, photographers cannot recapture their copyright after 35 years, a right they retain in the U.S. when they transfer or assign it, as described above. In any situation where ownership of the copyright is absolutely required by the buyer, photographers should arrange a transfer or assignment of copyright, at a rate which fairly compensates them for the entire value they are giving up, rather than agreeing to a work for hire.

Unfortunately, work for hire terms are increasingly being demanded in corporate contracts, even when there is little need for them. However, under current U.S. copyright law, work for hire must be agreed to in writing _before_ the work has begun. Work for hire terms cannot be demanded after the fact, nor can payments for work already begun be withheld until work for hire terms have been agreed to.

> **Reproduction Rights Rule #2:**
>
> _Photographers and authors should carefully consider the long-term value of copyright before agreeing to transfer ownership of that copyright to another party._

Copyright Protection

Digital and electronic technologies have made it far easier than ever before to copy photographic images. High quality scanning, image capture, digital reproduction devices, and even simple web downloading, have resulted in a greater risk of image appropriation or theft for the owners of copyrighted material. Images should generally be protected through the use of watermarks, encryption, pixel-embedded copyright notices, and other effective protection technologies. These techniques should be used on all electronic files. Don't assume that simply because you are distributing images in "low res" formats that they cannot be used for commercial gain by others. Even the smallest files can be easily interpolated with readily available software to yield reproduction quality images today.

Physically protecting a photograph from unauthorized reproduction is a task separate from copyright protection. The majority of unauthorized reproductions are "innocent infringements" – usually the result of some confusion by the client over usage licensed from the photographer or content provider. For this reason, photographers should request that clients destroy (or return to the photographer) all copies, scans, separations, film, or digital files made from the photographer's originals after the license terms are complete.

It is also important for photographers to actually register their copyrights with the U.S. Copyright Office. While copyright protection in the United States is automatic from the moment an image is fixed in a tangible form (such as on film or digital media), legal expenses and punitive damages (up to $150,000 per violation) can only be collected if the copyright has been registered with the Copyright Office. Non-registered images are still protected by copyright, but only actual value of the usage can be pursued in court.

The process of registering copyrights is fairly straightforward, and can be done for both unpublished and published images. Copyright registration is viewed by many content creators and authors as a reasonably cheap form of insurance. For registration details, contact the U.S. Copyright Office at:

http://www.copyright.gov

Multimedia Background

The vast majority of virtual reality imagery is published today in what are often referred to as "multimedia" applications. Electronic multimedia publication represents a merger of two major production industries – traditional print publishing and motion picture/ television. Both have relied for decades on independent contractors and content providers. For the print industry, this included writers, photographers, illustrators, and editors, while the film/TV industry also included actors, producers, directors, musicians, voice over talent, set designers, crew, and countless others. The two industries, however, evolved separately in their approach to acquiring content.

The traditional print publishing field has long regarded content from outside (non-employee) sources as material licensed for specific use. This is a foundation of most independent photography businesses, as well. Photography done on assignment for a client is generally owned by the author and licensed for specific uses to the client.

The film/TV industry however, is far more complex. Even the simplest production requires a camera operator, audio technician, and an off camera interviewer or producer, at minimum. Most productions require many more people, and are thus considered collective works. Through necessity, production companies hire their crews, including photographers and cinematographers, under work for hire arrangements. Contribution to a collective work, as well as contribution to a motion picture or audio-visual work, are categories enumerated in the Copyright Act as qualifying for a work for hire – primarily due to the demands of the film/TV industry.

Multimedia has brought a merger of these traditional print and film/TV industries, along with a conflict between them regarding rights licensing. This has resulted in two different models for multimedia content acquisition. Multimedia producers coming from the traditional print industry generally adopt a book publishing model, and are willing to license specific uses, including royalty payments to photographers and other content providers working on assignment. Producers coming from the film and television side tend to offer a flat fee for the work *and* expect to own all rights to the material created under work for hire agreements.

Both models have advantages, although few of those advantages are for photographers or authors under the film/TV model. Ownership of content is a primary asset in the expanding electronic market place. Large media conglomerates have repeatedly and publicly stressed the importance of content ownership and its value to their stock holders as the industry has expanded in recent years. Again, photographers should fully recognize the long term value of their copyrights before negotiating fees and agreeing to transfer ownership of those copyrights to other parties.

Moral Rights

Moral rights, which are different from copyrights, give creators the right to control attribution (credit) and the integrity (alteration) of their work. Moral rights protect both the integrity and paternity of an artist's original work. These rights provide a level of sanctity to original creations. Unfortunately, in the United States, there are no moral rights currently provided to images made for publication. Only fine art works, created for exhibition, and for which 200 or fewer copies will be produced, are eligible for moral rights protection in this country.

Generally, the way to enforce your moral rights is through contracts governing the licensing and use of your work to your clients. There are two contractual terms that provide for this – photo credits and alteration limits.

Photo credits are a key part of the compensation photographers receive for any display of their work. The inclusion of a photographer's credit and/or copyright notice is fairly simple both in electronic and print publications. For visual creators, credit lines accompanying published images provide name recognition. They are a key element of one's professional reputation. Readily visible copyright notices also serve to remind the viewing audience that the images are protected under copyright law. The ease with which images can be copied today makes the issue of photo credits more important than ever for *all* media. Inclusion of published credits and copyright notices should always be a point of discussion in any licensing or usage negotiation.

It doesn't do a photographer any good to have his or her work seen by millions of people if those people can't identify the work as having been created by that photographer. Readily visible credits and copyright notices make the difference. Proper attribution of authorship also aids in the protection of images in countries beyond the U.S., which have a greater concern and stricter laws governing moral rights.

Example: Many photographers require that their fees be tripled when their photos are reproduced without proper credits. This is done primarily for editorial usage. It is important to stipulate this up front in written contract terms, however.

Alteration – A photographer might wish to allow a client to alter his or her work where such alteration is customary – such as in advertising use, or to restrict alterations where they are taboo – such as in news reporting. Regardless of whether or not one will allow alteration of one's work, *always insist on* **indemnification** from the client if the work undergoes any alteration. Appropriate contractual language for dealing with credit and alteration can be found in an extensive online Licensing Guide published by the American Society of Media Photographers (ASMP) at:

http://www.asmp.org/tutorials/licensing-guide.html

Conclusion

Photographers are visual communicators, content providers, and copyright owners. We have the responsibility serve our clients' changing needs with a complete grasp of the value that our work, skill, creativity, and services bring to those clients. We must fully comprehend the converged electronic and print markets before we can adequately license our work for publication with complete fairness to both our clients and ourselves.

Talk with your clients. Talk with each other. Learn together. The expanding media and electronic technologies bring a world of opportunity for everyone.

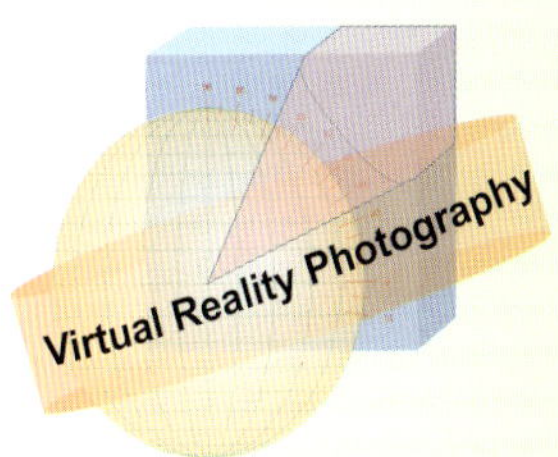

Chapter 21: Pricing and Estimating

The importance of reproduction rights and their value, as discussed in **Chapter 20**, cannot be overemphasized. Copyrights and rights licensing are the very foundation of successful photography and other creative businesses. Once you understand the value that your work provides to your clients, and the fact that this value can be ongoing and generate a continuing stream of income, then you are well on your way to establishing a viable and profitable business.

However, the next step is determining how to price your services, or what to actually charge clients for your work.

Pricing should be based upon three major factors:

1. Your individual cost of being in business along with your costs of providing that service/product (including your profit).

2. The value your creative work provides for the client.

3. What prices your market will bear.

The first step in figuring out what to charge is to determine your actual costs of being in business. These are costs such as rent, insurance, advertising, promotion, utilities, professional memberships, office supplies, capital expenses (computers, peripherals, cameras, lenses, printers, etc.), insurance, vehicle costs, subscriptions, business education, travel, salaries (including your own), and most importantly... profit (without profit, your business cannot grow).

Don't confuse your salary (or the amount you take from your business for your personal use) with profit. They are completely different. Profit is the gain your business realizes when it is taking in more money than it is paying out. Profit is the money that you put back in to your business to help it grow. Salary (whether for yourself or others) is an expense for your business.

Next you must estimate a realistic number of working days you expect to be able to bill to your clients in a year. A good way to do this is to look at your totals in previous years. Divide your average total (often referred to as the "cost of doing business," or **CODB**) by the number of days you actually bill to clients in a year. The result is your *minimum* billing rate per day for your services.

Note that when you estimate/bill a client for VR work, you'll usually bill them for your daily rate, *plus* all job expenses (including markups), such as film, processing, media, travel, lodging, equipment rental, digital services, assistants, shipping, etc.

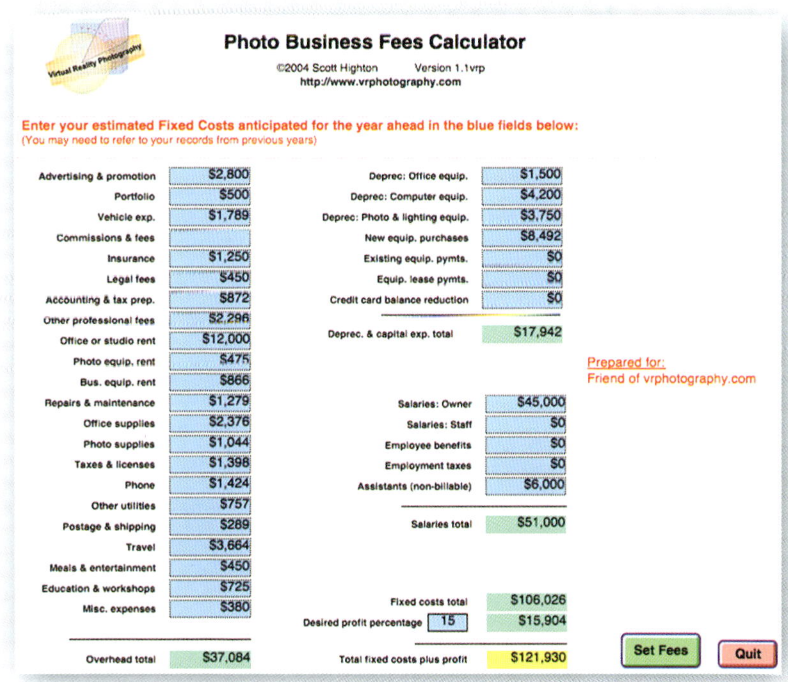

Photo Business Fees Calculator

©2004 Scott Highton   Version 1.1vrp
http://www.vrphotography.com

Enter your estimated Fixed Costs anticipated for the year ahead in the blue fields below:
(You may need to refer to your records from previous years)

Advertising & promotion	$2,800		Deprec: Office equip.	$1,500
Portfolio	$500		Deprec: Computer equip.	$4,200
Vehicle exp.	$1,789		Deprec: Photo & lighting equip.	$3,750
Commissions & fees			New equip. purchases	$8,492
Insurance	$1,250		Existing equip. pymts.	$0
Legal fees	$450		Equip. lease pymts.	$0
Accounting & tax prep.	$872		Credit card balance reduction	$0
Other professional fees	$2,296			
Office or studio rent	$12,000		Deprec. & capital exp. total	$17,942
Photo equip. rent	$475			
Bus. equip. rent	$866			
Repairs & maintenance	$1,279		Salaries: Owner	$45,000
Office supplies	$2,376		Salaries: Staff	$0
Photo supplies	$1,044		Employee benefits	$0
Taxes & licenses	$1,398		Employment taxes	$0
Phone	$1,424		Assistants (non-billable)	$6,000
Other utilities	$757			
Postage & shipping	$289		Salaries total	$51,000
Travel	$3,664			
Meals & entertainment	$450			
Education & workshops	$725		Fixed costs total	$106,026
Misc. expenses	$380		Desired profit percentage 15	$15,904
Overhead total	$37,084		Total fixed costs plus profit	$121,930

Prepared for:
Friend of vrphotography.com

Set Fees   Quit

Fig. 21-1 A photo business fees calculation form listing all expenses of being in business. Divide the total by your number of days of expected work to get minimum day rate. A free calculator is available at: **http://www.vrphotography.com**

Once you have your minimum rates determined, then you need to consider the value or usage that the client will be receiving from your work, and price that value appropriately. A client making *greater* use of your images and therefore receiving greater value, pays higher fees than a similar client making less usage and therefore receiving less value from those same images. Usage fees are generally added onto professional photographers' shooting rates, although many photographers simply include them in the overall rate quoted for a specific job. The important thing to remember is that a client's usage greatly affects the fees the photographer charges.

For example, a client using your images for a large scale international advertising campaign, including magazine ads, billboards, interactive kiosks, CD-ROMs, web sites, television ads, and trade show displays, will receive far more value from your work than if they were only producing a short run facilities brochure and using it on their web site for a year. Authors charge (and clients pay) for value provided. Therefore, you either add usage fees separately or factor them in to your overall rates.

It is critical to price your creative service and usage fees based on the needs of <u>your</u> business, rather than on what a client tells you they want you to charge (or what they offer to pay). Clients will often come to creative authors and say "we want you to provide us with X,Y and Z, and we can pay you this much." Too often, authors will say "OK," thinking that any work at any price is better than no work. The problem is that your prices and fees are now being set by your client(s), whose sole responsibility is to look after their own interests, not yours.

How many of us would walk into a car dealer and say "I want to buy the latest Mercedes or BMW, but I can only pay you $500?" Do you think they'd jump at a chance to give you the car, even though it would mean a loss to them? Do you think they believe that any sale is better than no sale? Would your local plumber or electrician let you tell them what you'll pay for their services? Real business people will tell you what they charge and then let you decide whether you want to hire them or not. Consider whether your landlord or mortgage banker would accept you telling them "I love the house, but I am only going to pay you 30 percent of what you would normally charge for it..." Why on earth would photographers or other creative authors even consider allowing clients to determine our prices in this way?

The fees you charge in your business should never be based upon what someone else charges in theirs, because each of our individual businesses are different, even though we may be providing similar products or services. One photographer's shooting rate may be higher than a competitor's because he has a greater overhead to cover, or she may live/work in a more expensive region. One of them also probably has more shooting days than the other for which they can bill in any given year.

Inexperienced photographers will often fall into the trap of thinking that they should charge by the photograph or VR node, rather than by the day or the job. This is a very dangerous way to price VR services, whether you are doing only the photography or both photography and post production.

Consider a classic example where you are hired by a company to shoot a dozen VR panoramas of their facility. After an initial review and scouting trip, you determine that you can probably shoot 3-4 of these panoramas per day (including necessary lighting, subject availability, etc.), and you estimate the shoot will take three shooting days plus two travel days. You divide the estimated costs by the number of panoramas (nodes) needed, and come up with a per node price, which the client agrees to. Everything sounds good so far. Unfortunately, when you arrive for the shoot, the weather is horrendous, the facility is under renovation and the access you were assured of is not readily available. There may also be other conditions requiring that you shoot a great deal of extra material taking far more of your time, which will also require countless additional hours in post production. Guess who gets left holding the bag for all these added costs? You do, because you agreed to a per node cost, rather than fees based on the amount of work involved.

Furthermore, you might have received approval from your client for fees based on your creating 12 or more nodes, and you priced each panorama lower because of the volume of work. However, during the shoot, the client changes their mind and decides that they really only need three or four panoramas, or that they need to cut the budget and now want to cut out some of the work. Thus, your five day project drops to one day, yet you are still held to a low per node price, with the added problem that you may have already turned down other work, which keeps you from making up the lost income. While this may sound far fetched to those without much business experience, it happens all the time.

Therefore, it is better to charge a day rate (you can usually estimate that you'll be able to create a certain number of images per day), a job rate, or a day rate combined with a creative fee so you're covered when events beyond your control change the situation. Most experienced photographers will charge for usage in addition to their creative/day rate (based on the value their work is providing to the client) and even specify a minimum that will be charged in the event the project is scaled back or canceled by the client. Of course, all of this needs to be clearly spelled out in your paper work and contracts with clients before you begin any work.

Put It In Writing

Many photographers unnecessarily worry about presenting contracts to a client requiring client signatures.

They worry that this will somehow seem threatening to the client. There's no reason for this, however. Remember that you can't even get the oil changed in your car without first signing a 1-2 page service contract. Written contracts (with signatures) are not threatening to clients. Rather, these documents clearly define up front what the understanding of your agreement is. It is far better to disagree over specific clauses in a contract and correct them before starting any work, than it is to argue over disagreements in court and try to collect payments after the fact, particularly without a written contract in place.

There's a wise saying that a verbal contract isn't even worth the paper it's (not) printed on.

The paper trail you should provide for every client includes the following (in the order used):

1) A written **Estimate** (including all fees, terms, and conditions)

2) An **Assignment Confirmation** (including fees, terms, and conditions, _and_ requiring a client signature)

3) An **Invoice** (including the same terms and conditions, with fees reflecting the actual work done)

4) A **Delivery Memo** (reiterating all above, specifying exactly what is being delivered to the client, what usage is licensed, _and_ requiring client signature).

Examples of these are provided on the VR Photography web site – **http://www.vrphotography.com**

Being Profitable vs. Market Pressures

No one will ever run a successful business by undervaluing their work. Yet discussions on a number of web forums often include comments from photographers saying that it's all well and good to talk about earning several thousand dollars for a day of photography, but that there's no way that they could ever command such rates in their local market. This is often followed by an earnest explanation of how they can charge $125 to $250 per delivered panorama and still make a decent income through high volume work. It's important to note that most of these individuals don't stay in business too long, but they are regularly replaced by other new voices who have bought into the same misconceptions.

Charging low prices in the hopes that you'll generate high volume only serves to make you work that much harder and go out of business that much sooner. In my opinion, charging $125 to do a VR shoot is not "low end"... it's little more than inviting a client to throw away their money.

Photographers (along with web designers and other authors) often talk about what their local market will bear when trying to justify low prices. It's a trap that has resulted in the failure of far too many businesses. If your local market won't buy your services at a fair price (fair to BOTH your clients and your business), then the business owner needs to consider other markets or other services.

A successful business charges rates based on what it costs for the owner to stay in business -- NOT what he/she _thinks_ clients want to pay. General Motors doesn't sell new cars for $995 because that's what most of us would _like_ to pay. They sell cars for $10,000 and more because that's what it costs to run their business – including design and manufacturing costs, delivering cars to market, paying employees, covering leases and mortgages on their facilities, insuring themselves against liability... and most importantly, making a profit.

A VR photographer or multimedia producer must do the same thing. You have to fully understand your Costs of Doing Business (CODB) – how much you spend on rent (mortgage), utilities, advertising, promotion, business licenses, salary (including what you pay yourself), insurance, taxes, equipment purchases (like computers, cameras, VR rigs), maintenance, depreciation, software, ISP and web hosting services, phone(s), office supplies, car or truck expenses, portfolio development, insurance, etc., etc. Most importantly, you have to add the profit you require each year (remember, without profit, your business cannot grow). Then, you divide this total by the number of billable days that you expect to work in the year (i.e. days when someone is actually paying you for your services) to arrive at a minimum daily rate you need to charge EVERY billing day. This represents your overhead or CODB, and is what you need to charge simply to keep your doors open for business.

Then you add the direct costs of doing a particular shoot or project, which you pass on to your clients (with a markup). This includes things like film, processing, scanning, digital media, retouching time, assembly and production, rental equipment, mileage, permits, assistants, travel costs, insurance, shipping, and other delivery services, etc.

Even the busiest independent photographers consider they are doing well when they approach 100 billable days of work in a year. Generally, for every day you are actually shooting, you'll spend another two days (non-billable) in preparation or in post production and follow up. That accounts for 300 days a year. Add to that the time needed to deal with running your business (accounting, taxes, advertising, client calls, preparing direct mail, e-mail and web site issues, communicating, maintaining and testing hardware/software & other equipment, filing, registering copyrights, working on portfolios and other new work, etc., and there's not a lot of time left for more important things like weekends, vacations, and personal or family time.

Now, let's assume you manage to become one of the busiest photographers around, and actually invoice clients for 100 days of work in a given year. You would yield a gross income of $12,500 per year (plus direct expenses) by charging $125 per day (or per shoot). This is considered poverty level income in the United States, and doesn't even *start* to include any of the overhead or other business expenses you have to subtract to yield your net income.

Next consider the busy 100+ day photographer who earns $400 – $500 per day for his or her work. (For several decades, this was the range of what professional magazine photographers earned for their editorial photography assignments). This would yield a gross income of $40,000 to $50,000 per year, which doesn't sound so bad. But again remember that this would only be the case if you were among the busiest and most in-demand professionals. Now consider that your business expenses and overhead costs will probably eat up between 40 and 70 percent of your gross income. That means that your net income will probably be between $12,000 and $30,000 for the year. This could be pretty hard to live on in the United States, especially if you have a family to support.

Now imagine yourself as a photography client. If you were looking for a capable professional, would you trust your corporate image to someone who doesn't believe his/her own work is worth any more than a few hundred dollars a day? While most clients would love to get great value for a cost well below its worth, we all understand that we usually get what we pay for. If Mercedes or BMW actually sold their new cars for less than $1,000 in today's market, would you believe that you were truly getting a high quality luxury automobile, or would you question whether it was even a vehicle you could rely upon for transportation at that price?

A number of companies in the VR industry have tried offering VR services for $100 - $250 per shoot. These have been most commonly found in the low end real estate market. The photographers they hire to do their shooting are often high school students or part-time hobbyists hoping to make some extra spending money. They often do the work with little more than what are described as "drive by shootings" (from the old practice of real estate agents who literally photographed properties from a car window as they slowly drove by). Most photographers who care about their professional reputations seek to distance themselves from this quality of work (and pricing) as much as possible.

Working on Spec

Many underemployed photographers have fallen into the trap of thinking that they can make money by shooting assignments for free and then hoping that a client will pay for the work after the fact. This is called working on spec (or speculation), and is an extremely effective means for going out of business quickly. How many shoots can you afford to do without getting paid, and why would anyone else want to pay you up front for your work if they know you'll do it for free, and that they'll only have to pay you if they decide they really need the result? Most will probably say to themselves, "Let's see what we get from this guy who'll do it free... then we can hire a professional to do it right."

That doesn't really help your business at all. Most clients don't want to have to deal with the annoyance of doing a shoot twice, so once they've had this experience, they'll more likely pass over the "free" photographer and go directly to a professional who will do the job right the first time.

Royalty Free (RF) or Clip Art

Selling images as Royalty Free (RF) or Clip Art devalues one's work even further. Once any business has proclaimed that their product or service is of little value (because they offer it free or at low cost, such as RF), they'll be hard pressed to ever shake that reputation. It's a mistake that most businesses and photographers never recover from.

In the early 1990s, clip art photography was offered by some of the large stock photo agencies as a low-cost alternative to the standard of controlled image licensing. The stock photo industry saw licensing incomes decline dramatically as so many new sources of imagery entered what had once been a lucrative market. The stock agencies, and many individual photographers, believed that they could increase their declining revenues by selling low cost images in high volume.

Today, a decade and a half later, the stock photo industry is in shambles, and stock photography is effectively a commodity, bought and sold at the lowest prices. As a commodity the only thing left by which to differentiate the suppliers is price. Stock photographers often make only pennies per stock image sale, and few, if any, are the individuals who can make a living from stock photography alone. For the most part, the industry is dominated by a handful of major agencies, most of which were started as side businesses by billionaires who'd made their fortunes in other industries.

Estimating

The process of estimating and pricing a photographic assignment has been described as both an art and science. In reality, it takes a bit of both, but for the most part, it is done using only some basic math.

The first thing you have to start with is an understanding of what your costs of doing business (CODB) are, as was discussed earlier in this chapter. Once you know this and you know the minimum fee you need to bill each day you work, then you can move on to determining how much time a particular job will require and what additional expenses will be necessary.

You will need to estimate how many days of work the job will require (remember that you have preproduction and planning days, actual shooting days, possible travel days, and of course post production and assembly/delivery days. From these, you will calculate the appropriate creative and production fees, including a mechanism by which your time is paid if the requirements demanded by the shoot are changed beyond the scope of your control. Also included should be usage fees reflecting the client's actual use or value received from your creative work. Again, some photographers will roll all these into a single fee that they present to the client, either as a daily rate or as an overall creative fee for the assignment, while others will separate them out and identify them individually.

The next step is to determine the actual expenses that you will have for doing the shoot and delivering the results to the client. These include things like film and processing costs, digital media, scanning, printing and electronic archiving expenses, mileage, meals, travel expenses, assistants, expendables (lighting gels, gaffers tape, replacement light bulbs/flash tubes, etc.), and equipment rentals. These are billed to the client on top of the creative, production, shooting and usage fees, as they are considered direct costs for the particular shoot. Most photographers include markups on these expenses, just as other service industries do.

It is important to present specific and clear details, particularly of the contractual terms, in your written estimates, as the actual shoot will rarely turn out to be what was originally expected. Thus, it is important to specify what your rates and fees are in the event critical elements of the shoot change during the process. These changes often occur because the client's needs are altered or because unexpected surprises (outside of the photographer's control) arise. For example, if you are delayed by weather conditions, or perhaps the subject is unavailable for shooting once you arrive on location, it is important to specify how the resulting additional expenses will be billed to the client. Similarly, if the shoot takes significantly *less* time to complete or can be done far more efficiently than you specified in your estimate, you might want to be able to pass some of these savings back to your client.

Case Study: Estimating a VR Photo Shoot

We asked four leading virtual reality photographers to prepare estimates for the same VR project, so that we could compare not only their approaches, but also their pricing and contractual terms. All were presented with a written Request for Photography, which was modeled on projects and assignments done by each of them in the past.

Both the client and the project in this case were fictitious, but the resulting estimates were prepared as if this was a real project.

The results are presented on the following pages. They reflect the different markets that the four photographers work in, as well as their different approaches to licensing, fee structures, and how they actually shoot such assignments.

VR Photography invites select photographers to participate in such pricing exercises every few years in order to help educate the VR community about changing business practices and markets. We encourage other photographers to freely discuss their pricing and business approaches with each other, as well.

Compare the following estimates submitted by our panel of photographers. Some charge a flat rate per panorama or object movie. Others include a time factor or day rate to allow for complications that invariably arise during any location shoot, and which demand significantly more work or effort than originally planned. Also, look at how usage value is incorporated.

Consider the post production and assembly costs for the finished movies. Some of the photographers included these in their per-movie totals, while others itemized them as separate charges. Look at other itemized costs, such as whether state sales taxes are being collected (sales tax requirements are different for every state), and whether the photographer charges for liability insurance (often required by clients).

Request for Photography

The Crotalus Museum is a non-profit natural history education institution located in the foothills of Stunning State Park near (your local major city). Founded in 1978, we offer over 30,000 square feet of natural history exhibits, along with a 320-seat theater, and conference facilities. We host a select number of university researchers annually, and we operate an award winning natural history educational outreach program to schools and civic organizations throughout the state.

We are seeking to contract interactive photography services for a major update to our museum's web site and educational programs.

Initially, we will need a series of panoramic and object VR movies of our museum facilities to use in a virtual online tour. At this time, we'll need between 12 and 16 360-degree panoramas, along with about 15 object movies of select display items. We will also need still photos of our museum facilities for our promotional use in advertising, brochures, and trade publications.

Our contracted photographer will need to work directly with our in-house graphic design staff, as well as our outside (contracted) web design studio to coordinate formats and technical specifications.

After the initial assignment is completed, the Crotalus Museum may choose to further engage the photographer for ongoing documentation of Museum displays, including additional object movies and promotional photography.

The Crotalus Museum is a 501(c)3 non-profit organization, which relies on donations from the public and museum admission fees for funding. All donations, including in-kind services, are welcome and may be tax deductible.

Thank you for your interest and consideration of this project.

Deadline for receipt of proposals is **June 30**. Photography is expected to begin in July or August. For further information, contact:

Roger Rattler
Development Director
The Crotalus Museum
E-mail: crotalusmuseum@highton.com
Phone: (650) 592-5277

A client will always consider the bottom line price when choosing a photographer, but their choice will not necessarily be the cheapest one. Other factors will also be considered, such as the quality and style of each photographer's work, his or her industry reputation, and even their personality and professionalism.

Written estimates provide clients with insights into how you, as a photographer, work. Put yourself in the client's position when reviewing the following estimate submissions and consider what elements would be important for you. Does an estimate show attention to detail? Does its structure leave you (the client) open to surprises or added costs? Are the fees reasonable? Is the photographer open to negotiation if your budget can't accommodate their price – and does their estimate give you the sense that redefining the scope and usage of the desired work could effectively alter the bottom line to meet your needs?

Estimate Summaries

Photographer	Total Cost	Notes
Tim Petros Gyroscope Interactive Photography www.gyrovr.com (Los Angeles, CA region)	**$37,175.00**	Tim's estimate had the highest bottom line total at $37,175. He charges $650 per panoramic movie (shoot and assemble), and $765 per object movie. Additional still photography is charged at a flat day rate of $1,650/day. Tim's higher cost for photo assistants ($350/day) reflects the higher going rates in California (and particularly his proximity to Los Angeles), but he expects to need and assistant for 15 days of shooting *and* post production. Insurance is listed as a line item cost passed on to the client. For these fees, Tim provides unlimited use of his images to the client, but for a period of three years. Any use beyond that requires an additional license (and presumably fees paid) by the client.
Scott Highton Virtual Reality Photography www.highton.com www.vrphotography.com (San Francisco, CA region)	**$31,936.51**	Scott didn't specify a per-panorama or object movie price, but rather, used a day-rate structure, estimating that all the work could be photographed in five days. At $1,750/day, that works out to an average of about $350 per movie – just for the photography. Post production and assembly of each movie is Itemized additionally at ($450 per panorama, $750 per object movie). Scott charges the same $350/day for photo assistants as Tim, but only includes them for actual shooting days, not post production work. Scott's bottom line price comes in below Tim's, because Scott didn't specify additional costs for the extra traditional stills requested. His day rate structure allows for this to be added, if these photos can't be shot during the five days of the planned VR shoot. Scott also itemizes insurance costs, as well as California sales tax. Usage provided is for broadly defined advertising and promotion purposes (non-transferable) for a term of three years.

Photographer	Total Cost	Notes
Jook Leung 360VR Photography www.360vr.com.com (New York, NY region)	**$15,000 to $20,000 (plus additional services)**	Jook provided an estimate with a non-specific bottom line, but gave an expected high and low range for the photography and post production. Additional expenses were itemized and fees listed, but not added to the bottom line total. This helps Jook's estimates appear lower to a client than the final invoices are likely to be, and may give him an advantage in some instances, as it's harder for the client to really compare the expected bottom lines. He does specify $500 per panorama and $600 per object movie. Jook uses a day-rate of $1,200/day for additional still photography, and charges $200/day for assistants (optional, but recommended for on-site shooting days). Usage provided is exceptionally broad – for unlimited exclusive use by the client in perpetuity. That means that the client will never be required to pay additional licensing fees for any use they (or their assigns) make of the work, and Jook also agrees to secure this client's permission before licensing his photographs from this project elsewhere.
Pat St. Clair St. Clair Photo Imaging www.stclairphoto-imaging.com (Rochester, NY region)	**$15,785.00**	Pat's estimate was the lowest of the four photographers. Part of that is attributable to the region where he's based (Western New York), as well as his emphasis of keeping costs low by using available lighting on location and not needing assistants. He specifies $500 per shot and assembled panorama, and $400 per object movie. Pat's estimate lists very few itemized specifics. It appears to be both all-inclusive and easy to understand. Pat plans for seven days of shooting, and proposes to extract the additional still photos the museum wanted from the source images used to create the panoramas and object movies. Usage extended is unspecified in scope – meaning that it will be assumed to be unrestricted, but is limited to a term of three years.

The actual estimates received are shown on the following pages. Thanks to each of these photographers for their willingness to share this information.

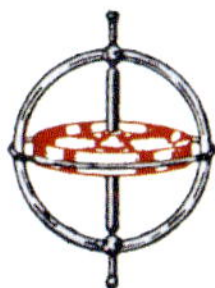

Gyroscope Interactive Photography
29139 Hillrise Drive
Agoura Hills CA 91301
ATTN :TIM PETROS

818-706-1231
tim@timpetros.com

COST ESTIMATE

Roger Rattler
The Crotalus Museum

No: 5564
Date: 1 July, 2010

(650) 592–5277

Job Description
Interactive photography of The Crotalus Museum interiors, facilities, and artifacts on Museum premises, for use in a virtual online tour: 12-16 360º panoramas, and approximately 15 interactive object movies. Additional traditional still photography for use on website, advertising, brochures, and trade publications.

Usage License
This license shall be valid for a period of 36 months and shall cover publication of the Work in the following media only: Unlimited Media. Any use of the Work by the Client after 36 months shall require a separately negotiated license.

Terms
Estimate is valid for 15 days from the date of issue. Fees and expenses quoted are for the original job description and layouts only, and for the usage specified. Final billing will reflect actual expenses.   All rights, including copyright, remain the exclusive property of Gyroscope Interactive Photography until invoices are paid in full.

Fees

1 Crew Meals @ 375.00 ea.	375.00
15 Photographer's Assistant (days) @ 350.00 ea.	5,250.00
1 Post Production/VR Authoring (Revisions and additional retouching) @	550.00
1 Pre Production (Meetings, pre-production prep.) @ 450.00 ea.	450.00
16 QTVR photgraphy, retouching, authoring (VR panorama production) @	10,400.00
15 QTVR photgraphy, retouching, authoring (VR objects) @ 765.00 ea.	11,475.00
5 Still photography (days digital still photography) @ 1,650.00 ea.	8,250.00
1 Travel (& misc. expenses) @ 250.00 ea.	250.00
Fees total:	**37,000.00**

Insurance

1 Liability (Insurance) @ 175.00 ea.	175.00
Insurance total:	**175.00**
Estimate Total	37,175.00

Signature________________________ Date_________

Fig. 21-2 Estimate from **Tim Petros**, Gyroscope Interactive Photography, for the Crotalus Museum shoot.

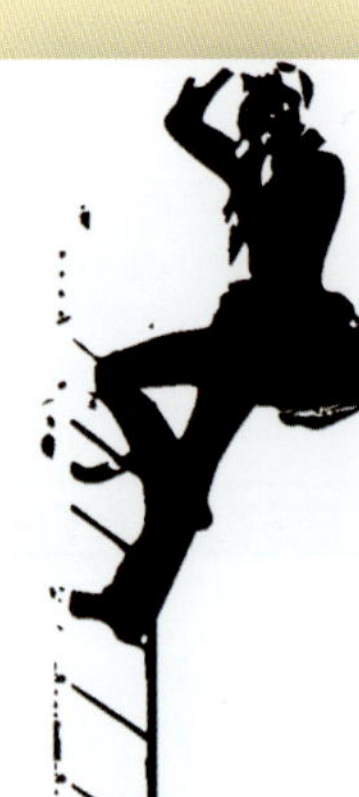

Photography by Scott Highton

Virtual Reality   ·   Interactive Media   ·   Photojournalism   ·   Motion Pictures/Television

(650) 592-5277   www.highton.com

June 30, 2010

Roger Rattler
The Crotalus Museum (Client)
123 Sidewinder Road
San Jose, CA 95000

Cost Estimate

Assignment Description:

Virtual reality (VR) photo shoot of Crotalus Museum in San Jose, CA, of approximately 12-16 360-degree panoramas and 15 object movies. Crotalus Museum to provide necessary access (whether during normal or non-business hours, as needed), models and releases, as well as space to set up in-house studio for photography of objects. Crotalus Museum will provide assistance and accepts full responsibility for security and transport (positioning) of Museum display objects for photography.

Usage extended is for Crotalus Museum advertising and promotion for a period of three (3) years (ending July 31, 2013), and is non-transferable. All other rights reserved. Any use of the images must be accompanied by a ©2010 **Photography by Scott Highton** photo credit. This credit must include hot link(s) to: **http://www.highton.com** when images are used on the Internet or any applications with Internet access available.

Quantity	Service/Product	Unit price	Price
5	Photographer's day rate	$1,750.00	$8,750.00
5	Assistant (per day)	$350.00	$1,750.00
12	Panorama stitching VR movie assembly	$450.00	$5,400.00
15	Object movie assembly (single row only, 18 shots each)	$750.00	$11,250.00
1	Supplies, filters, gels, expendables, etc.	$500.00	$500.00
1	Crew meals and expenses	$350.00	$350.00
1	Insurance	$250.00	$250.00
150	Estimated mileage	$0.75	$112.50
2	Digital delivery (per CD or DVD disk)	$35.00	$70.00
8	Still photo editing & post prod. (per hour)	$100.00	$800.00

Subtotal	$29,232.50
CA sales tax	$2,704.01
Total	$31,936.51

35 percent deposit required prior to start of work.
Deposit due: **$11,177.78**

Terms: Balance due within 10 days of Invoice date, 1.5% interest/month thereafter.

Copyright and ownership of all images held solely by photographer.

No license or usage granted until licensing/usage payments received in full.

Any use or reproduction must be accompanied by the following credit:

©2010 Photography by Scott Highton

Web reproduction must include photo credit hot link to: **http://www.highton.com**

Cancellation notice of 3 days or less may result in minimum 50% charge.

996 McCue Avenue   San Carlos, CA 94070-2525   USA

Fig. 21-3 Estimate from **Scott Highton**, Photography by Scott Highton, for the Crotalus Museum shoot.

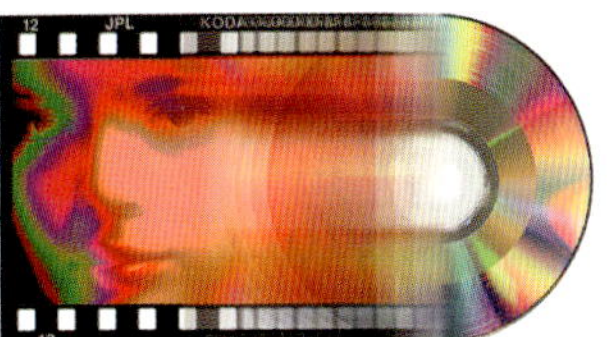

**JOOK LEUNG
360VR PHOTOGRAPHY**

Digital photo-illustration and
360 degree panoramic photography

282 Brookside Avenue
Cresskill, New Jersey 07626

mobile: 201 679 6177
email: jook@360vr.com
www.360vr.com

June 30, 2010

Reply to RFP Estimate:

A unit pricing for 360 degree panoramas delivered in a QTVR mov or Flash swf file is $500. each. This includes the photography, editing and post production to make Web ready files. Add $100 for another output option.

Resolution is 6000 pixels minimum with basic html/xml files to allow Web hosting for client review which is included. Estimate 2-3 days to complete on site photography for the panoramas. Client may have to schedule non-consecutive days while museum is closed to public or there is scheduled exhibit maintenance by other departments.

Unit pricing for object movie photography at 20 degree intervals (18 positions and single row) with no background editing is $600. each for small objects that can be rotated on a turntable. Set lighting to illuminate objects may be needed. Choose QTVR or Flash format. Add $125. for both formats. Resolution for each frame at 3000 pixels is reduced to 600-800 pixels for Web delivery. Estimate 2-3 days to complete on site photography for object movies depending on scheduling coordination with museum staff and any security procedures.

Total minimum 4 days on site, two weeks post production: Range of costs:
Low: $15,000
High: $20,000

Edited/retouched stills photos: $250. each (3000 pixel resolution - 10 inches at 300 dpi)

Additional photography will be quoted at $150/hour. ($1200. day rate)
Additional retouching/editing will be quoted at $100/hour.

Fig. 21-4 Estimate (page 1) from **Jook Leung**, 360VR Photography, for the Crotalus Museum shoot.

Cancellation fee for each shooting day (less than 24 hours notice): $600.

Travel, lodging, meals: estimate $100/day for local travel and meals.

Photo assistant: optional but recommended while photographer is on site: $200/day

Discounts: A 10% discount is offered if client agrees to give the photographer a photo credit next to every image used.

Rights granted: This is not work for hire but photographer will agree that client has perpetual exclusive rights and photographer will not re-market original or any derivative works without permission of the client. Photographer does retain the right use his work for self-promotion purposes.

Deposits: an advance of 25% is requested to reserve the services of the photographer and begin preproduction planning.

Terms: 50% due upon completion of client review, balance due on receipt of assets with final invoice.

Consult rate and additional post-production is $100/hour.
On site consult rate is $150/hour.

This estimate is good for 90 days.

Thank you for this opportunity to provide this estimate of our services. Please contact me for any additional information or other questions.

Jook Leung
Jook Leung 360VR Photography

Web: http://360vr.com
Email: jook@360vr.com
Mobile: 201-679-6177

Page 2

Fig. 21-5 Estimate (page 2) from **Jook Leung**, 360VR Photography, for the Crotalus Museum shoot.

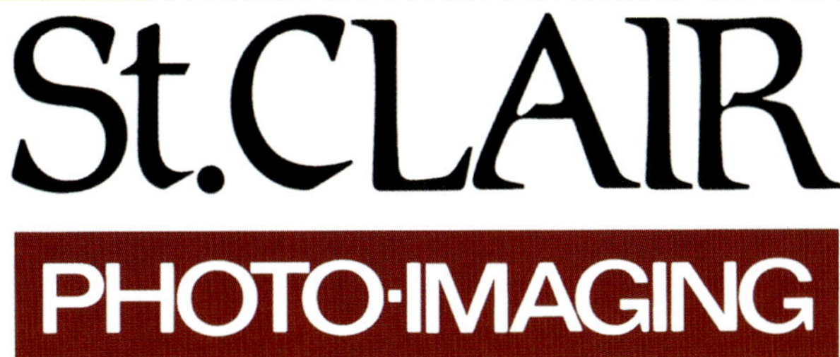

St.CLAIR
PHOTO·IMAGING

June 30, 2010

Roger Rattler
Development Director
The Crotalus Museum

RE: Request for Estimate

Dear Roger,

Thanks for including St. Clair Photo-Imaging in your request for estimates, I appreciate the opportunity to bid on this exciting project for The Crotalus Museum! You'll find my estimate attached, but first allow me to comment on the unique approach I'll take for your project.

First, let me assure you I fully appreciate your nonprofit status and all that it implies. I realize your funding is limited, yet your mission is unique and exciting and demands rich media to tell your story as it deserves to be told. There are things both you and I can do to keep the costs down and the quality high!

From my side of the equation, I bring years of experience with high-end available light photography. I've made it an art form, and have worked hard at systematizing my approach. What this means to you is that my work will have very high image quality, yet I work alone and use virtually no lighting gear . . . that works towards keeping the costs down. I've sent you links to several other projects I've done . . . you can expect the same quality level on the work I'd do for you.

Additionally, some of the still photography for collateral use can be generated from the 360° pans, possibly all of it. That, too, will work to keeping the costs down. Once we see what we have from that source, then we can plan additional still photography as needed.

Copyright for the work remains with St. Clair Photo-imaging, and The Crotalus Museum will have usage rights for three years as part of this pricing. I will also archive all new photography and guarantee it's availability for those first three years.

If you wish to proceed, I'd suggest an initial meeting where I'd meet you and your team, and we'd brainstorm our approach. Following that meeting, we should do a joint walk thru of your facilities where we can delineate the shots that will best represent The Crotalus Museum, both 360° pans and object movies.

Best Regards . . . hope to hear from you soon!

Patrick A. St. Clair
Owner, St. Clair Photo-Imaging

89 Citation Dr. Henrietta, NY 14467 • (585) 359-0730 • FAX(206) 350-0519

Fig. 21-6 Cover letter from **Pat St. Clair**, St. Clair Photo Imaging, for the Crotalus Museum shoot.

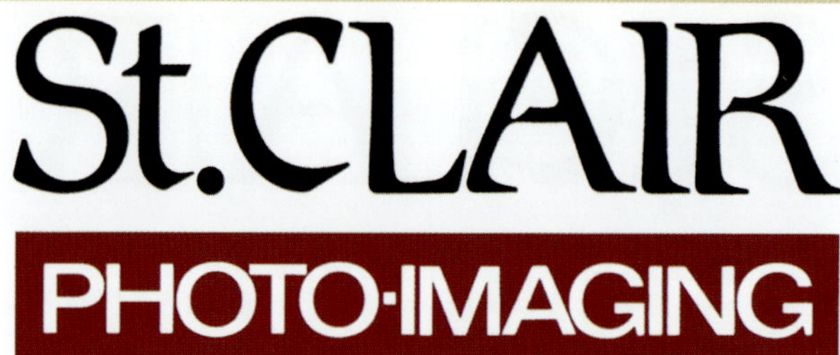

ESTIMATE:

Date: June 30, 2010
Client   Roger Rattler
            Development Director
            The Crotalus Museum

Purchase Order #:   Estimate for Interactive Photography
                      Equipment Rental

Terms: Net due 30 days from invoice date. Past due accounts will be charged 1.5% per month.

<u>Description:</u>

For the sake of this estimate, the project is defined as fifteen 360° cubic interactive panoramas, fifteen single row interactive object movies, and 30 still photos, five from object movies, and 25 extracted from the interactive panoramas. With no delays on the client's side, the project will require seven days of photography onsite, with another seven days for post-production. Moving artifacts for object movie photography will be the responsibility of museum staff.

The panoramas will be shot using advanced available light photographic technique, including exposure blending.

The object movies will be shot on site in a natural setting in the museum (as opposed to an off site studio environment). Minimal lighting gear will be used, and the museum background will be in soft focus to provide clear visual separation from the object itself. Doing it this way will eliminate the time intensive masking that would otherwise be necessary. One high res still will be shot of each object at the same time and setting as the object movie shooting.

Archiving all files and three year's usage of images are included.

Fifteen 360° interactive panoramas, photography & authoring	$ 7,500.00
Fifteen single row object movies, 36 steps, no masking	6,000.00
Extract twenty-five 3000 x 2000 pixel still frames from 360° pans	625.00
Consumables and three years archiving	225.00
Ten per cent contingency	<u>1,435.00</u>
Estimated Total	$15,785.00

Patrick A. St. Clair
Owner, St. Clair Photo-Imaging

89 Citation Dr. Henrietta, NY 14467 • (585) 359-0730 • FAX(206) 350-0519

Fig. 21-7 Estimate from **Pat St. Clair**, St. Clair Photo Imaging, for the Crotalus Museum shoot.

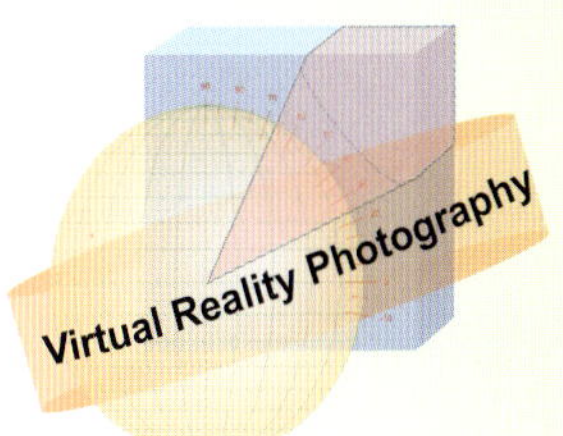

Chapter 22: Negotiation

Negotiation is a process of conferring, bargaining, or discussing in order to reach an agreement. It is done in almost every business around the world. It is done between governments and heads of state. It is done between children and their parents. It occurs at one level or another almost daily within each of our lives.

Any time we are asked to do something, or when we desire something from someone else, there is likely to be at least a minimal negotiation involved. When you ask a clerk in a store if you can get two pairs of shoes at a discount over the single pair price, or when you tell your kids that they can have ice cream for dessert if they finish their dinner, you have engaged in a negotiation process. Negotiation is something we all practice regularly, even if we are unaware we are doing so. It is not a hard thing to learn, and most of us do it naturally.

However, negotiating *well* is an art, which involves quite a bit more than issuing ultimatums that serve only the interests of one side. Much as a good deal is one where the interests of both parties are met, good negotiation is the process of finding solutions that satisfy the interests of those parties. The idea is to *balance* the various interests and reach an agreement.

Negotiation is relatively easy when both sides have common interests or compatible needs. It becomes more difficult when those interests are in conflict, or when one or both parties are not terribly concerned with the needs of the other.

As a photographer in business, you will find yourself having to negotiate to some degree with almost every client. Negotiation will commonly occur over your fees, what rights or usages are involved, how long it will take to do the job, where and when you will shoot, what expenses will be charged, how long it will take for your invoice to be paid, how your work will be credited, and even what files or image formats you will deliver.

Your client will have specific needs for many of these, while you as the photographer may have others. The negotiation process, and more specifically *your* job as a

negotiator, is to find a way to satisfy everyone, so that *your* needs along with those of your client are met.

Obviously, not everyone comes to the table with the same power to negotiate. If you are dealing with a company on a project that lots of other photographers are qualified to do, you probably won't have as much negotiating leverage as the company that is hiring will. This client may have dozens of your competitors to choose from, so they have more options available to them. However, if you offer a unique set of skills or capabilities that the client is seeking, then you will have far more leverage in the negotiation process.

With this in mind, let us consider some of the basic principles of negotiation:

1) Good negotiation involves finding solutions that meet the needs of **both** parties.

2) The most powerful tool in any negotiation is the word "no."

3) You cannot negotiate a good deal unless you have the ability to walk away from a bad one.

While one would hope that all our business deals would involve clients whose interests are supportive of ours, such is rarely the case in real life. More often than we'd like, a client's demands may be in conflict, or even damaging to our own business needs. If we can't afford **not** to do the job, then we will probably have to accept the job under the client's terms, rather than our own. If we cannot afford to walk away from a bad contract, we are in a weak negotiating position.

As you develop your business, keep in mind that you will be better able to negotiate *good* deals if you can keep your business both solvent and unique. If you are financially solvent, you will be better able to walk away from deals that aren't good for you. If your business is unique, offering a variety of services or skills that few of your competitors can match, then you will be sought out by clients who need those services – rather than being just one option of many from which they can choose.

This is why the most powerful word in any negotiation is "no." When a potential client tells you they only have a few hundred dollars in their budget for a job, and they need to own all the copyrights and images you will create, your best response is a polite "no." You can explain why their offer is unacceptable, and present a counter proposal if you want, but you have to be willing to say "no" in order to even consider suggesting a better one. You have to be confident in the skills and value you provide and then be willing to stand by your convictions as you negotiate.

The ability (and willingness) to walk away from the deal if it doesn't deliver what you know you are worth is a key to negotiating a good deal. As a professional photographer, you'll probably walk away often. Many established pros expect to win only a small percentage of the jobs they are asked to estimate or bid on.

Keys to Successful Negotiating

Keep a proper mind set when you negotiate – remember that you are negotiating for your own salary, the food you need to put on your family's table, the roof over their heads, and the very life blood of your continued business. You wouldn't give up any of these just because someone else was looking for a bargain. Negotiate like your business survival depends on it – **it does**.

Many photographers find it helpful to keep a list of capital expenses and their monthly overhead costs in plain sight next to the phone in their office. That way, they have these right at hand when negotiating fees over the phone. This helps remind them of the expenses they have to pay and what they need to earn. If you are reminded about the new computer, software, camera, or an exotic lens you need, you are more likely to maintain your priorities in your negotiation.

Consider also the different media and mechanisms you have at your disposal by which to conduct negotiations. Generally, negotiating over the phone is the best, because you can do so from an environment in which you are most comfortable – your own home or office. This also provides you with access to your computer files and other records, which may be useful should you need to look something up quickly.

When talking with a potential client, I find it useful to look at the client's web site while I am on the phone with them. This gives me a sense of their size and professional image, as well as details of the type of business they are in. It also helps me to better understand and discuss their needs. Of course, *they're* often looking at my web site at the same time, which gives them a better idea of the quality and style of the work I do. We can direct one another to specific pages or links on our sites. I can show them examples of similar work that I've done for other clients, while they can direct me to concepts that they

need fulfilled on theirs. This process helps us establish a rapport and understanding of each other's interests, and leads us into a negotiation process from more evenly balanced positions.

E-mail is another means for negotiating, although it still seems impersonal enough that most people prefer the phone instead. E-mail has an advantage in that the discussion is documented in writing. Even after a phone discussion, it is a good idea to summarize the decisions made and send them to your client via e-mail for their confirmation. This gives them a chance to respond with any corrections or additions, and helps clear up any misunderstandings early on. There is a definite advantage for both parties to have a written record to refer back upon later.

Many people prefer to negotiate in person or face to face, rather than by phone or e-mail. This provides a more personal connection, and can be to your advantage if you are a "people person." However, it can also work against you, particularly if you meet at your client's business. The client or their representatives wind up negotiating on their own home turf, and you can more easily become their prey, rather than their partner. It is also easy for them to bring other people in on the negotiation process, which can further intimidate you as an outsider on their turf. There's a psychological advantage to conducting business in your own territory. However, the savvy photographer can use this to his or her advantage by presenting himself or herself as the unique outside expert that the company absolutely needs as a partner for the project under consideration. A lot of your own presentation ability comes down to simple attitude and confidence. When you have this, the turf you're negotiating on becomes less relevant.

The good news is that with today's busy corporate schedules, most business deals begin with either phone conversations or written correspondence. The process moves on to face-to-face discussion after an initial relationship has been established. In fact, it is not unusual in our increasingly wired world, for business relationships to be forged without the parties ever meeting in person.

This is actually the norm today for many photographic assignments. Clients today often contact a photographer near the city or location where images need to be shot, and everything is arranged by phone, e-mail, or fax. The photographer shoots the images and delivers them electronically. Contracts and invoices are sent electronically, and a payment is made in return. Many businesses even do their invoicing and payments electronically, using bank transfers, credit cards, or other online systems.

Characteristics of a Good Negotiator

In order to be a successful negotiator, you need to be able to do the following:

• Be a good listener. You should be willing to understand the viewpoints and perspectives of your client. You must hear what they have to say, and you must ask questions that will help clarify what their needs and perspectives are.

• Be able to make decisions. Nobody wants to negotiate with someone who doesn't have the ability to make decisions. Think about how distasteful it is to spend time negotiating with a sales person at a car dealership, only to have them tell you that they can't approve the deal on their own, but have to take it to a manager. Try to negotiate with the people who can actually make decisions. Make sure *you* can make decisions on your end, so your client doesn't face the discomfort of thinking they're dealing with an indecisive negotiator.

• Keep your word. Once you have made an agreement, or say you will do something, be sure to fulfill that commitment. Trust is essential in any relationship, whether business or personal. A client that knows she can rely on you is one that will be willing to return over and over again. However, it only takes one instance of lost trust to ruin any relationship.

• Clearly articulate your position. Don't assume that your client knows about your business needs. If you don't make your needs clearly known early on, they will likely not be included in the negotiation process until after it is too late.

• Be creative and be flexible. As a photographer, creativity is a core element to your business. Use this same creative ability to come up with solutions and compromises that mitigate the differences between your client's and your own positions.

Offer Options

Many times, you may find it advantageous to present several options to a client for their consideration. Clients will often like the fact that you are providing them choices of contract terms, approaches, and/or pricing for your services, while others that you may be competing against are only offering them one.

Given a single option, a client will probably feel it is a take-it-or-leave-it proposition. If this is indeed what you have to present, then you may not have a choice. However, if your service or pricing has some leeway in it, you may want to indicate this to the client. Don't simply change your prices for no reason when negotiating. Always try to exchange value for value. If the client needs a lower price, reduce the usage you are offering. Perhaps a reduction in the amount work required for the

assignment could correspond to lower fees. Similarly, if a client is willing to commit (in writing) to a larger volume of work, you might be willing to discount your rates somewhat for multiple days of photography.

Offering your client more than one option gives them a choice. One of these will usually seem more attractive than the other. Three options gives them more of a choice than only two. One of these three will usually be perceived to be the least desirable. The second will either be seen as the lesser of two evils, or as an undesirable extreme to the first. That leaves the third to be perceived as the best option, or as a good compromise between two less desirable extremes. Three options gives the client a sense that they are truly being offered choice. You are essentially leading them into a negotiation process.

So if two is good and three is better, why not present four or more options to give the client even greater choice and improve your odds of landing the contract? Unfortunately, offering more than three options generally makes a proposal too confusing, and the client may wind up more attracted to your competition because their proposals require less study and consideration.

Of course, not every situation demands the preparation of multiple options for the client. You need to use your judgment. However, being willing to offer more than just one contract possibility indicates your desire to craft an agreement that works for everyone. It helps foster continued dialog, and hopefully leads to a contract for the job.

Making Negotiation Work

Once a negotiation has begun, remember that you are negotiating because the client is interested in you. You are offering something that they want. They may tell you that they can get a better deal from another photographer, but understand that they are talking with you because they value something you have – experience, reputation, creative ability, unique qualifications, technique, equipment, reliability – perhaps even your personality. If they thought a competitor of yours was better, they'd be negotiating with him or her instead.

They want to work with you. It's your job to help make this happen by negotiating an agreement that meets both the needs of your business and those of the client.

If the client presents you with a take it or leave it proposition (assuming that it is unacceptable to you), be willing to explain what your problems with their offer are *and* be willing to present a counter offer. This can often open the door to negotiation of a supposedly non-negotiable deal. Asking *why* they need the things they are demanding will help you understand better what their concerns are, and can help you craft a reasonable compromise. Furthermore, asking a client "why" often forces them think a bit deeper about what their needs truly are. If they can't explain the particular need well, it may be because they are unsure of it themselves. Consequently, they may be willing to negotiate that point to a greater degree than they originally indicated.

Let's consider a situation where a client demands ownership or a "buyout" of the copyrights to your work. Note first of all that the term "buyout" is vague and ill defined – and should not be agreed to in a written contract. A transfer of copyright is more specific (see **Chapter 23** for details about copyright). Basically, when a buyout is requested, your client wants to completely own the work you create under contract for them.

For photographers and other authors, the body of work you create over your professional life has significant value, since the rights to reproduce and display that work can be bought or sold repeatedly. There is tremendous potential value to your work, no matter how mundane or simple a given image might seem at the time it was created. Therefore, if you agree to give up your rights to your work by transferring copyright to a client, you are giving up all future income you could ever earn from that work, as well as the right to even be identified as its author. In order to ensure adequate compensation for this lost value, photographers usually charge significantly higher fees when a copyright transfer is involved.

The client generally doesn't want to pay more than they have to, and the photographer generally doesn't want to give up rights of authorship or ownership of their work. This is where negotiation can be furthered by asking the client questions, such as "Why do you want/need a copyright transfer?"

The answers will likely include one or more of the following reasons:

- The client requires it of all their vendors – usually mandated from corporate legal departments or executive offices.

- Proprietary concerns – the client doesn't want to risk having their proprietary processes and/or intellectual property held by others outside of their control.

- Competition – the client doesn't want to see the images they paid to have created accidentally appearing in a competitor's ads or publications.

- The client isn't really sure at the time how they might need to use the work in the future, and they don't want to find themselves being held hostage by a photographer over unreasonable reuse fees later on.

This is where you explain the needs of your business, including building a body of work, generating an ongoing stream of revenue from licensing of your work over time, serving the current and future needs of your clients, etc. Then, offer possibilities for contractual terms that can eliminate their concerns and serve the needs of both your businesses.

For example, you can address concerns about costs of future licenses by offering to create a reuse fee schedule for every usage that they might want to consider in the future, which you will adhere to should they seek additional licenses later on. Keep in mind that you should also put a time limit on these rates (several years is usually adequate, but be sure that this meets your client's needs first). One advantage to this is that it forces the client to consider all the possible uses they might have for the images, and gives you a better handle on the value your work may be providing to them.

Rarely does a client ever use your work in all the ways they think they might at the outset of an assignment. So it is often to the client's advantage to license future rights only as needed – sort of a pay-as-you-go program. That way, they're not paying for rights up front that they may never need or use. Most photographers will offer a discount on multiple rights or uses if they are purchased up front, such as when the original assignment is confirmed. Think in terms of a rental car contract, where it's cheaper for you to pay up front for a two week rental than it is to pay for one week, and then add six more days – one day at a time – on to that. On the other hand, if you're reasonably sure you're only going to need the car for 3-4 days, there's no point in contracting for a month long rental, even though the average cost per day is lower with the long term discounts. It doesn't make sense to pay for more than you need.

It helps to explain to a client that if they really need to have a transfer of copyright, you'll need to charge them a fee that corresponds to every possible usage they might make. Why on earth would they want to pay for rights that they will never use? As a respectable business person, you want to make sure that they are getting fair value for their money when they hire you, so you help guide them toward the most cost effective means of working with you. Photographers who are willing to do copyright transfers often charge anywhere from three to 10 times their normal shooting rates for such assignments, since they give up any possibility of future income or licensing fees from that work, as well as rights of authorship.

Some clients build image libraries from work that photographers have shot for them, and market these images as their own stock (often in competition with the photographer's own stock licensing efforts). Clients can do this when they have secured a copyright transfer from the photographer, and are under no obligation to share any of the licensing royalties derived from these images, since the photographer has given up ownership of his or her copyrights.

One very good alternative to a copyright transfer demand is to offer the client unlimited use of your images for a fixed term. This term might be one year, five years, 10 years, or more – or even unlimited use *in perpetuity*. The longer the usage term, the higher the fee will generally be. This approach is often a good way to address the concerns of clients who really have no firm idea of how they *might* want to use your photographs in the future, but want to keep all their options open without having to get back in touch with you years later. The client can keep copies of the images in their files and use them at will, while the photographer maintains ownership and control of the copyrights with the opportunity to license other usage rights elsewhere. (Remember that you should *never* license usage of images created for a client to a direct competitor. This is a breach of good ethics, and can also lead to serious legal problems.)

With traditional film photography, there was always some question over whether the photographer or the client would retain the **original** negatives or transparencies (this was usually negotiated for each client). However, with today's digital technologies, a copy of a digital file can be just as perfect as the original, so it really doesn't matter who retains which one. In practice, the photographer will generally keep the original film or camera raw files, while *copies* of the scanned, retouched, or digitally assembled results are retained by the client. Most VR clients are unconcerned with original film or camera files, and are usually only interested in the final panoramas and object movies assembled by the photographer.

Having been in business in the same location for almost 25 years and maintaining files of every professional shoot I have done during that time, I can explain to clients that they are generally far more sure of being able to locate images kept in *my* files than they are if the original film is kept in their offices. With corporate reorganizations, staff changes, and relocations happening so frequently in today's business world, the likelihood of images being lost, misplaced or even destroyed is far higher in *their* corporate environment than it is in my office, where my business is focused solely on the creation and preservation of these images. On more than one occasion, when I have agreed to let a client retain possession of original images, the images have been inadvertently lost during an office move or staff change.

In one particularly painful instance, *all* of the original film and high resolution scans from the very first commercial QuickTime VR project ever done – the original Apple Company Store tour – were ordered destroyed by a short sighted manager during an office move. These historic images were deemed old and outdated by the manager, who was more concerned that they no longer represented the company's current product lines and were taking up space in their files, than about the historic value of the images. Even though the original film and high res scans included both copyright notices and author identification, no one involved with the decision bothered to contact the photographer, and the materials were apparently destroyed within two years of their creation.

Client concerns about images being used by competitors, or about proprietary information, can generally be alleviated with the use of contractual terms such as exclusivity and embargoes.

Before negotiating such terms, it is important for photographer and client to understand that with constantly changing technologies of our modern age, proprietary information usually becomes public knowledge in a very short time. Once a product is released onto the market, most details about its design, manufacture, and construction become quickly known. Many products are discontinued or replaced with newer models within a year, or might even be rendered obsolete during that time. Keep this in mind as you negotiate the duration of embargoes or exclusivity clauses in your contracts.

An exclusivity clause could stipulate that your client has the exclusive right to use the images you've created for a given period – perhaps six months or a year. That means that you will agree not to license these images to *any* other entity during this period (possibly including display on your own portfolio or web site). Once the stipulated period is over, you can market the images as stock. Generally, the longer the client maintains exclusive rights, the greater the licensing fee. Often, exclusivity is needed by a client only until their product has been released or a particular event has occurred. Afterward, it might even be to their advantage to have you marketing your images to outside publications, as it increases the publicity and exposure they receive. This becomes a win-win situation, where the client receives additional promotional value from hiring you as their photographer while you earn added licensing income from your work.

An embargo clause would specify that you agree *not* to license the images to specific corporations, publications or other entities for a given period. These generally will be direct competitors of your client. Most photographers and their clients consider it bad form to *ever* license images shot on assignment for one client to a direct competitor. Doing so will likely assure that you don't work for the original client again. Furthermore, the second client will be unlikely to hire you for future work, because you now have a track record of licensing images shot for one client to a competitor. Remember how important your professional reputation is in your business dealings, and do your best to maintain your integrity.

Embargo clauses are most often found in news and magazine contracts where the publisher wants to make sure that the images they are licensing appear only in their magazine until their next edition is released (usually within one week or one month). They simply want assurance that they will be the first publication to carry the images. Once they have gotten the scoop on their competitors, they are relatively unconcerned whether their competition publishes the "old" images. As more publications move to online and web distribution, we may see similar demands for VR content. An embargo clause can often be an attractive option for clients who initially request a copyright transfer. A one week or one month image embargo toward competitor publications (or corporations) can be a lot less expensive for the client than an exclusivity deal or copyright transfer, and leaves the photographer with many more options for re-licensing the work elsewhere later on.

For example, let's say you were hired to shoot aerial images of a major waterfront project in your city for an engineering firm. While you were shooting the assignment, you photographed some natural disaster that happened, and it turns out that you have the only images of this major news event from your unique aerial perspective.

If you had signed a copyright transfer agreement, you would not be able to do anything with these images without getting a written license to do so from your client. Basically, you wouldn't own the work, so you'd have no say or control in where it could be published or to whom it could be licensed (or for what price).

If you had agreed to an exclusivity clause, even though you still retained ownership and copyright to the images, you could not license the images anywhere else until the term of that exclusivity had expired. Thus, you would miss out on possibly significant licensing fees from news publications clamoring for the unique coverage you had of the event.

If you had agreed only to an embargo of the images to your client's specified competitors or other entities, you would be perfectly free to license these images concurrently to the news publications, which will generally pay far more for "fresh" news coverage than stories that happened days or weeks earlier.

Of course, such occurrences happen rarely, and many assignments will generate imagery that will only be of use to the original client hiring you. Consider the needs both you and your client might have over the long term. If you ever feel any doubt that a client might be concerned about licensing work you shot for them to another party, it's a good idea to contact them just to make sure. It's always better to turn down a potential stock sale and keep an existing client happy, than it is to lose a client by breaching your contract or trust with them.

Keep in mind that you'll often will have no idea of when or how your images from any assignment might become valued in the future, nor even *which* images will be marketable and which will not. Giving up ownership of any image without appropriate compensation can be very short sighted and something you're likely to regret later.

Negotiating Fees

One of the first things clients often ask a photographer is how much they charge or what their assignment rate is. This is one of the ways that clients qualify photographers to see if they will even be worth considering for the job at hand. If the client has only a few hundred dollars in their budget for photography, they probably won't want to waste time negotiating with a photographer whose minimum rate is in the thousands or ten thousands of dollars. Similarly, if the client is looking for a very high end polished result, they probably won't want to interview countless new or inexperienced "wannabes" fighting for a chance to shoot the job for a few hundred dollars.

However, even on the highest paying jobs, price often remains a concern. Clients generally don't want to pay any more than they have to, so negotiation of fees is inevitable for almost every job.

If you've gone through the exercise of accurately determining your cost of doing business (CODB) and setting your rates as described in **Chapter 21**, you will not only know how much you need to charge in order to remain profitable, but you will also have confidence in whatever fees you quote to the client in your initial estimate.

Therefore, any negotiation of your fees has to involve potential changes to the job description or how the job will be performed. You cannot claim that a job is worth $10,000 one day, and then admit that it's only worth $7,500 the next. From the client's perspective, it looks like you were simply padding your original estimate, rather than charging a fair and proper fee from the outset. None of us likes to work with vendors or contractors who intentionally overcharge us just to see if they can get away with it – and it doesn't help your professional reputation to be perceived by your potential clients that way.

It is certainly possible to lower your fee for a particular job when a client needs it, but a fee reduction should always correspond to a reduction in the value of the services or work you are providing to the client.

Perhaps you've found a way to reduce the amount of time the job will take, or to reduce the expenses involved. Or perhaps you've been able to reduce your fees based on a reduction of usage rights that are being extended to the client. Perhaps you can trade non-cash value from the client, such as copies of their final product that you can use for your own promotions, and which you are willing to accept to offset their cash payments to you. The important thing is to trade value for value. If the client needs a lower price, they have to accept less value, as well. If they need greater value, they have to pay more for it.

Again, this is where being willing to say "no," or being able to walk away if you need to, is so important in negotiating. When you are confident in the value of your work, you will find it much easier to hold your ground and negotiate agreements that are fair to yourself *and* your client.

An old photographer friend used to claim that when he quoted a fee on the phone, the first thing he wanted to hear was his client falling out of their chair in shock. The last thing he wanted to hear was the client quickly saying, "OK, that's great," because it meant he had set his price too low. He maintained that one could always reduce a price during the negotiation process, but you could never get away with increasing it after you'd quoted an initial price that was too low.

While there is certainly some real life practicality to this, it is not necessarily a good approach to business, I think, as it implies that you are willing to take advantage of your clients when you can get away with it. That sentiment will ultimately come across either during the negotiation process or over the longer term of your business together, and trust will be lost. Consider whether you would want to enter a business relationship with someone whom you felt wanted to take advantage of you. Remember that your potential clients will be considering their relationships with you in the same way.

You are much better off being forthright and honest – charging fair fees for the value you are providing, and maintaining a high level of integrity. The best business relationships are built for the long term. You'll want your clients to look back at their first contracts with you as positive experiences – without feeling like you tried to take advantage of them. You'll want them to be interested in returning to work with you again.

On the other hand, you don't want to charge less than what your work is worth on the mistaken assumption that it will enamor you to your client. This will do little more than diminish the potential income and value of your business. If you constantly under price your services or product, you risk damaging not only your future earning potential, but the rest of the market in which you work, as well. Be fair. The best business deals are those in which the interests of **both** parties are served. Your job as a negotiator is to bring forward fees, terms, and agreements that do this.

Of course, there will be times when the party on the opposite side of the table will try to take advantage of you, and may not have the same goal of reaching a deal that serves both parties' interests well. Obviously, your first priority is to look after your own interests, and this is where the power of the word "no," along with the ability *and* willingness to walk away, are so important.

No deal is usually better than a bad deal. Yet, forceful and confident communication can often turn a potential bad deal around. If you are willing to stand your ground, you may be able to bring negotiation back to a point where the interests of both parties can be adequately served. Understand also that you may reach an impasse, and a good agreement may be unreachable.

This happens. Be willing to move on. There will be other opportunities. You are generally better off spending your time pursuing opportunities with better potential than the ones where you fight tooth and nail over every detail.

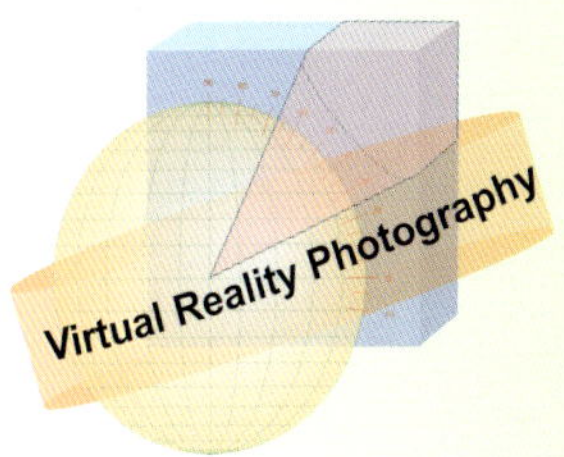

Chapter 23: Legal Concerns

Disclaimer:

This book, and this chapter in particular, should in no way be perceived as a legal guide or as legal advice. If you have legal questions or need legal advice, please contact a qualified attorney specializing in your particular area of concern. The following information is offered by the author solely as a reference for contract terms that a professional photographer might encounter. It is based only upon the author's experience, and may not necessarily apply to situations encountered by others.

When you enter into any business, an unfortunate fact of life is that you must deal with legal matters. Legal concerns will usually arise sooner, rather than later. Legal processes and litigation are a part of life in the business world, and you are much more prepared if you at least have a basic understanding of the legal terminology that you may have to deal with. Understanding these terms can, in fact, help *avoid* expensive litigation in your businesses.

You will likely to encounter these terms in client contracts, loan applications, purchase or lease contracts, and even business license applications when you set up your office or studio. You'll want to be familiar with them when preparing your own contracts, agreements, releases, permission forms, and other documents for your own clients, as well.

One important reminder:

Put every agreement in writing!

In a legal conflict, a verbal agreement is worth little more than the paper it's printed on (which is non-existent). A good written agreement, signed and dated by both parties, clarifies the understanding and provides a tangible record of what is expected by all concerned. It is the best tool you have to avoid going to court in the first place, as well as the strongest evidence to support your positions if you have to go there. Written contracts are a fact of life today in everything from using credit and debit cards, to having the oil changed in your car.

The following terms and definitions are not a complete list by any means, but are a selection of some you may encounter in the business of photography. *Note that the definitions presented here are only representative of laws and practices in the United States, and may not apply in other countries.* An extensive online library of terms and their definitions related to the photography industry is available through the Picture Licensing Universal System (PLUS™) Coalition at:

http://www.useplus.org

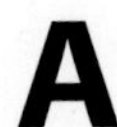

A

Advance

Payment made prior to actual sales occurring, such as in book publishing, when a photographer or author is paid an amount of cash up front, sometimes before work is even begun on project. Such advances are generally applied against royalty payments due for actual sales after publication.

For assignment photography, an advance is either a flat fee or a percentage of the total estimate the client pays the photographer before work begins. This helps cover up-front expenses the photographer will incur in preparing for and completing the shoot. Since clients often take weeks or months to pay invoices, the advance payment helps the photographer avoid serving as an interest free bank for the project until such time as payment for the final invoice is received.

Advertorial

Presentation of advertising or promotional information in what appears to be editorial form.

"Paid Programming" is one form of advertorial found in the broadcast industry – programs that are meant to look like news or feature shows, but which are merely program length advertisements, whose purpose is only to promote a commercial product or service, or to raise money.

In newspapers and magazines, advertorials are ads or advertising sections designed to look like editorial content, but whose purpose is to promote or sell commercial products and services.

Even though advertorials are designed to look like bona fide editorial content, licensing fees for advertorial use should generally be charged at advertising rates, rather than significantly lower editorial usage rates.

Agent, Agency

A party empowered to act for or represent another's interests.

A photographer's agent or representative will often handle marketing, sales, and contract negotiation with clients for that photographer. A stock agency will market and license photographers' stock imagery to clients. An advertising agency will generally represent the interests of its corporate clients, designing advertising and promotional campaigns, and hiring technical and creative parties – such as photographers, designers and production firms – to do much of the work involved.

Agents and agencies generally charge commissions for their services, based on minimum fees, expenses (plus markups), and percentages of the sales or media buys that result.

Agreement

A written or oral arrangement between parties regarding a course of action or a relationship.

Amendment(s)

Any change(s) or addition(s) to an agreement.

Ancillary / Corollary Rights

Extensions to the main or primary rights that add usage for supporting products.

Example: While a primary usage might be for publication in a textbook, picture book, or commercial web site, ancillary or corollary rights would include use of the same materials in student guides, instructor guides, educational software, or in-house intranets.

Arbitration

When a presumably neutral party is chosen to hear both sides of a dispute and to come to a decision to resolve it.

Arbitration is generally far less expensive and less involved than legal action through the courts, so it is often specified as a clause for dispute resolution in many contracts. *Binding* arbitration requires that both parties accept whatever decision is reached by the arbitrator without further recourse.

Assign / Assigns

The transfer of a claim, right, or property to another. An assign or assignee would be the recipient of such rights or property.

Photographers will often encounter such terminology in client contracts specifying that the client will not only receive certain rights to the photographer's work, but that the client may also assign those rights to others (assigns or assignees), including other companies owned by a client parent company, or a variety of outside publications if the work is intended for publicity and promotional use.

Such terms may also be included in contract clauses related to the survivability of an agreement, should one or more of the parties involved cease to exist.

Assignment (i.e. Photography Assignment)

Content (photographic or other) produced under a contract or agreement, or assigned for an author to produce, and involving client specifications on what the final product should be, or perhaps even how the work needs to be done.

Details of a client's usage of the work should be spelled out in an assignment contract or license agreement.

Assignment Confirmation

A written document that specifies agreed terms of an assignment and gives approval to the photographer or author to proceed with the creation of the specified work. The photographer should insist that the client sign and return this document *before* beginning any work, in order to have written confirmation that the client wants the work to happen and has agreed to pay the photographer for it.

Audience

The number of people, or a description of the various groups that will see a publication or use a product. For print publications, this is often measured with a combination of circulation, distribution, and estimated numbers of viewers/users per copy. For electronic publication, this might include the number of copies distributed, screenings, views, or web hits/downloads.

Author / Authorship
Generally, an author is the actual creator of an original, copyrightable work. For legal and copyright purposes however, this can be reassigned to another entity, such as an employer, or to a client under a work for hire contract. In these instances, the employer, or the company that the work is being produced for, owns the right of authorship, and the individual who actually created the work may not necessarily even be identified as its author.

B

Bid
A document provided by a photographer or contractor to a client that specifies a fixed fee for a specific work or product to be produced. Bids are generally provided on a competitive basis with other photographers or service providers who are seeking the same assignment from the client.

A bid differs from an estimate in that both the photographer and client are locked into the exact terms, conditions, job description, and fees quoted. If the job takes more (or less) time, or the expenses involved are higher (or lower) than anticipated, the client is obligated to pay exactly the amount of the bid. Likewise, the photographer is obligated to produce the specific work or product described for the specified fee.

Any adjustments to the job description or pricing after a bid has been offered and accepted (outside of variance amounts specifically described in the bid), must be agreed to by both parties via a written Job Change Order. Otherwise, either party can legally hold the other to the original terms of the bid

When preparing a competitive bid, it is important to make sure that you and the other vendors you are bidding against are bidding on the *same job description and details*. Consider these details carefully and ask lots of questions so you can anticipate any difficulties or challenges that may come up as you do the work, and which may cost you more time or money. Factor all these in to your bid. Keep in mind that the client will most often choose the photographer or vendor providing the lowest or second lowest bid.

Many photographers avoid making job bids, preferring to present Estimates instead. Estimates allow for more pricing flexibility when the demands of the assignment change while work is underway.

Breach
Any violation of one or more terms, promises, or conditions specified in a contract or law. Unlicensed reproduction of copyrighted material would generally be considered a breach of copyright law. A client's failure to pay an invoice amount within the specified time agreed in a contract would be a breach of that contract.

Buyout
A broad, poorly-defined term sometimes used by clients to describe a transfer of copyright from the author (or creator) to the client. Its use should be avoided in contracts, as it is so vague. It is better to describe specific rights that are being transferred, or to specify a complete transfer of copyright when necessary. A transfer of copyright means that the original author or copyright owner is giving up all rights to their specified work, including the right to license or sell that work in the future, or even to be known as its author. Therefore, it is important to command a significantly higher fee from the client, as the original author will lose all possibility of future licensing fees from that work. Note that there is a difference between transferring ownership of copyright and ownership of the physical media (such as the film or canvas that the image was created on).

C

Cancellation
Termination of a contract or agreement, generally before all of its terms or conditions have been fulfilled. Many contracts have cancellation penalties prescribed within. One such term might be found in a photographer's Estimate or Assignment Confirmation, where a charge of 50 percent of the total estimate may be incurred by the client if the assignment is canceled within 48 hours before it was scheduled to begin. This is to compensate the photographer for the time, planning and expenses incurred in preparing for the shoot, and for the other work he or she may have had to turn down during this time from other clients.

See also: **Kill (Fee)**

Change Order
A written form that specifies agreed changes to a contract or bid, and corresponding fees or price adjustments. Change orders should be signed by the client. They serve as a legal amendment or change to the original bid or contract.

Circulation
Generally refers to the number of copies of a periodical that are printed and distributed each issue. For electronic publications, circulation usually refers to the number of individual viewers downloading or viewing the publication's content each issue.

Clause
A specific article or provision of a document or contract.

Clearance(s)
Pertaining to usage rights and permission to use copyrighted material. When rights have been cleared,

or clearance is provided, it means that the client has successfully obtained a usage license from the copyright holder.

Clip Art

An older term referring to content or material that could be used on a royalty free (RF) basis. Clip art discs containing collections of images, illustrations, and other visual content could be purchased at minimal cost and the content could be used for many purposes without the need to secure additional rights or pay additional fees beyond the purchase price of the original disc.

The term "clip art" widely fell out of favor because of its early association with low cost, low quality content, and today is more popularly known as "royalty free" (RF) content. Its opposite is "rights managed" content, wherein specific rights for specific usage must be secured from the copyright owner prior to every use.

Collateral

A fairly broad term used to describe a variety of advertising and promotional publications, such as brochures, catalogs, flyers, post cards, editorial, and information pieces, both in print and electronic form – usually produced by a company or their ad agency to supplement primary advertising efforts. Most of the brochures, flyers, promotional discs and other information materials that one might receive at a trade show or industry seminar would be considered corporate collateral.

Collective Bargaining

Negotiation between organized workers, usually members of a labor union, and their employer(s) to determine wages, hours, rules, and working conditions.

Collective bargaining is generally prohibited for independent contractors in the U.S., as they are not considered employees.

Collective, Collective Licensing

A collective is usually a reference to a number of individuals or entities acting as a group. Collective licensing is an alternative to the traditional stock agency, wherein a group of photographers or other authors are legally allowed to set licensing and usage fees for their work. (In the U.S., non-employee contractors are generally prohibited from any efforts to standardize fees or pricing for their services by the U.S. Deptartment of Justice and restraint of trade laws.)

Collective Work

For copyright purposes, a work that is created by multiple authors. Examples include an issue of a magazine or other periodical, an anthology, or encyclopedia in which a number of contributions – each of which may be copyrightable themselves – are assembled into a collective whole.

Commercial Transactions

Uses involving an exchange of goods and/or services for financial gain. A commercial use of a photograph would be when a client uses an image to either directly make money, or gain commercial value, or perhaps to promote *another* product or service for the purpose of financial gain. "Commercial" is also a common term used to describe an advertisement appearing on television, radio, or in other media.

Commercial Misappropriation

The use or appropriation of another's property for commercial purposes without their consent.

Commission

A payment to a representative, agent, individual, or agency, generally based upon a percentage of gross or net sales. A commission can also be set as a flat fee per transaction or item sold. A lawyer who works on commission receives a payment based on a percentage of the judgment awarded by a court or a negotiated settlement. A photographer's representative or agent working on commission will generally receive a percentage of the fees billed to the photographer's client(s) as a result of the agent's efforts.

Commissioned Work

A work created by an independent photographer or author to the specifications of a customer or client. When a client hires a photographer to shoot a particular image or set of images, the resulting work is a commissioned work. So too is the work resulting when an artist is hired to create a painting or sculpture by a client.

Compendium Rights

A compendium is a short, complete summary. Compendium rights are rights for usage of copyrighted works, which may include photographs and other graphical arts, within a compendium.

Compensation

Value received in exchange for value provided (or lost). This may be a negotiated fee, an in-kind product or service, or a unique and valued access or privilege. A photographer may receive hundreds or thousands of dollars from a client as compensation for the work he or she provides. A model or property owner may receive compensation in the form of a fee, or even copies of the photographs the photographer created using their likeness or property. Similarly, an airline may offer you an upgrade in your seating or service in compensation for a delay or inconvenience they may have caused.

Compilation

A work composed of materials from multiple sources. The individual source materials, as well as the compilation, may be independently copyrightable. Compilations can also include collective works. In the music business, a "compilation CD" might present the "Best of" performances of a single artist, or a collection of songs from a variety of other albums. In photography, compilations could include "The Year in Pictures" issue of a weekly newsmagazine, or a body of work from a photographer or group of photographers published in print or electronic form.

Composite

An image that is made from the combination of other images or visual elements. Merging a subject or foreground image with a different background, or digitally replacing the head of one person onto the body of another with digital image processing tools such as Photoshop™, results in a composite image. There can be both ethical and legal issues that arise from this practice, depending upon how the resulting images are presented or used.

Confidentiality, Confidential

Generally implying information that cannot be shared with others, or which must be held in confidence. Photographers often run into confidentially clauses or non-disclosure agreements (NDAs) in contracts with corporations that need photography of unreleased products or proprietary facilities and processes. It is important to respect these agreements, as even the largest corporations can literally be put out of business by the inadvertent release of proprietary information or intellectual property to their competitors. Often, such clauses and agreements will expire with the public release of the product in question, but in other instances (such as photography of a manufacturing process or facility), the confidentiality must be maintained for many years, if not decades. Each contract is different. Be sure that you are very specific with your clients on the details for each one.

Consideration

Value provided to one party by another as part of a contract. Due consideration might be a monetary fee, photo credit, a promotional web link, copies of the resulting publication, or combinations of these and more. Photographers often provide aspiring models with copies of photographs for the models to use in their portfolios as consideration for their modeling work.

Contract

Any legally binding or enforceable agreement between two or more parties (people, businesses, organizations, or other entities). Contracts generally involve the exchange of product or services for monetary or other value, although they can involve almost any sort of agreement. Contracts can be actual, implied, written, or verbal. Written contracts are almost always preferred, because they provide documents that specify the understanding and agreement between the parties. Written contracts are far more useful if disputes arise after the fact, and are far more reliable than verbal or non-written contracts when a dispute escalates to legal action.

Contributor

An author or artist whose work is published as part of a collective work.

Cooperative, Co-op

An enterprise collectively owned and operated for mutual benefit. Photographer's cooperatives can be a viable means for compatible photographers to join together in order to market and sell their stock imagery, or to generate assignment work.

In advertising cooperatives, advertisers or agency clients can pool their resources to secure greater market exposure than they might individually.

Copies

Reproductions or likenesses of another object or item. For copyright purposes, an original photograph is known as the "original." Any reproduction of that original is referred to as a "copy." Copies can be exact reproductions, reasonable facsimiles, renderings, or even loose interpretations referenced from an original or another copy.

Copyleft

A controversial, non-legal term used to describe licensing arrangements that permit the copying, modification, and distribution of creative works (primarily software) as long as those doing so do not keep others from also having the right to freely copy, modify, and redistribute these same or derivative works. Copyleft is a play on the word copyright.

See also: **Creative Commons**.

Copyright

The exclusive right to publish, reproduce, distribute, adapt, perform, and/or sell an artistic, literary, dramatic, or musical work. In its simplest terms, copyright is the right to copy or distribute copies of an original work.

In the U.S., copyright is automatic and vested with the author the moment that a work is fixed in a tangible form, such as when it is captured on film, written on paper or digital media, or recorded to tape or disc. (Exceptions to this are under work for hire agreements and employer/employee relationships.) Photographs, illustrations, designs, text, musical compositions, performances, motion pictures, video, and audio recordings are all examples of work that can be copyrighted. Copyright laws vary significantly around the world, however.

Copyright itself is a tangible asset, from which almost unlimited licenses for use can be bought or sold. Copyright carries the potential for being tremendously valuable. Ownership of the physical manifestation of a photographic image, whether original negative, transparency, fine art print, or digital master, is different from ownership of copyright. A copyright owner has the exclusive right to publish or copy the work, or to extend licenses to others to do so. While an individual may own a very expensive fine art print, or even a recording of a musical performance, he or she may not legally copy or publish that work without first securing a license from the copyright owner.

The duration of copyright is currently prescribed by the U.S. Copyright Office as extending from the moment the work is created and fixed in a tangible form until 70 years after the author's death.

Copyright Infringement
Any violation of the exclusive rights of a copyright owner.

Copyright Notice
Any notice that informs that a work is copyright protected. Inclusion of a copyright notice is *not* required to protect a copyright, but is useful in minimizing unintentional or "innocent" copyright infringements.

Under U.S. copyright law, proper formats for displaying copyright notice are as follows:

> © 2010 Author Name
>
> **Copyright 2010 Author Name**
>
> **Copr. 2010 Author Name**

Some international conventions still stipulate the addition of the phrase "All rights reserved". It is believed that the following format is perhaps the most widely accepted internationally:

> © **2010 Author Name, All rights reserved**

Copyright Registration
While copyright is automatic from the moment a work is fixed in a tangible form, successfully defending against infringements (in the U.S.) is more likely if the copyright has been registered with the U.S. Copyright Office. If a copyright has *not* been registered and an infringement occurs, the copyright holder will be limited in court to collecting actual damages suffered as a result (including the profit made by the infringer in their copying or distribution of the work). However, if the copyright *has* been registered within time limits specified by copyright law (currently within three months of the work's creation, or any time prior to the infringement occurring), then the copyright owner can also collect legal fees and statutory damages (currently up to $150,000 per infringement). Many photographers and authors look at the small cost of registering a basic copyright as cheap insurance, especially since the Copyright office allows bulk registration of many images for a single registration fee. For specifics on copyright registration and varying fees, consult the U.S. Copyright Office's web site at:

> http://www.copyright.gov

Copyright Transfer
The exchange of ownership of a copyright (and all rights therein) from one party to another. Some clients may demand ownership of copyright for work they assign to independent photographers or other authors. It is generally advisable for independent authors to resist such demands, as the author will lose all control over use of their work, as well as the potential for future licensing fees. However, there may be times when compensation is significant enough to warrant turning over copyright to the client. In such cases, a copyright transfer is preferred over a work for hire arrangement, as a copyright transfer allows the original author to recapture the copyright after 35 years. Under work for hire agreements, there is no provision for recapture of copyright.

Copyrighted Work
A work protected by copyright. Defined by the U.S. Copyright Office as: "Original works of authorship fixed in any tangible medium of expression." These include the following:

> **1)** Literary works
>
> **2)** Musical works
>
> **3)** Dramatic works
>
> **4)** Pantomimes and choreographic works
>
> **5)** Pictorial, graphic, and sculptural works
>
> **6)** Motion pictures and other audiovisual works
>
> **7)** Sound recordings
>
> **8)** Architectural works

Ideas themselves cannot be copyrighted. Only the expression of ideas in tangible forms are eligible for copyright protection.

Covenant
Any agreement or contract, whether in written or verbal form. The term "covenant" is often used in legal documents or in contract language generated by large corporations and legal professionals.

Creative Fee
A fee charged by a photographer or author for their work effort. Creative fees vary tremendously based on the experience, capabilities, creativity, knowledge, and expertise the author brings to the job. They can also include factors such as the amount of work involved, the location where the work is done, the time commitment involved, risk, and market influences. Creative fees can either be combined with day rate type fees, or charged in addition to these, depending upon the author and the work involved. Normally, creative fees only cover the creative effort provided by a photographer or author. Expenses and other costs incurred in producing the work are usually charged additionly.

Creative Commons
A non-profit organization devoted to making the creative works of authors more widely available for others to legally use and share. Creative Commons (CC) encourages authors and creators to offer less restrictive limits on their work than what are imposed by traditional copyright protections, in order to foster new creativity and opportunities for others to build upon such works

more freely. A series of licenses – ranging from the "all rights reserved" of traditional copyright, to "some rights reserved" – and all the way to putting work completely into the public domain, are defined and supported by Creative Commons at their web site:

http://www.creativecommons.org

While not usually appropriate for photographers and other authors who are trying to earn income from their work, the Creative Commons approach can be of value to many seeking to collaborate or build upon the works of others.

See also: **Copyleft**.

Creator

Any individual or entity who creates, or has created a work. For copyright purposes, the creator is the actual author of the work, unless the work is created under a work for hire agreement or under an employer/employee relationship, in which case the creator (and initial copyright holder) is the author's employer.

Credit

Text or notation identifying the author of a work. Photo credits are best included adjacent to the published photo, on the same page, with large enough type to be both legible and noticeable, and preferably including proper copyright notification. Example:

© 2010 Author Name

Photographer and author credits should be included in all publications and productions, whether print, electronic, or other media.

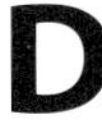

D

Damages

Injury or harm to a person or property, resulting in a loss of value. In a legal sense, there are three primary types of damages a court can award. Actual damages are the actual values that were either lost by one party, gained by another, or a combination thereof. Statutory damages are penalties that can be imposed based on violations of law or legal statutes, such as copyright laws. Punitive damages (also known as exemplary damages) are those awarded to a plaintiff beyond the actual loss, imposed as punishment for the defendant's wrong.

Day Rate

A fee or fees charged by a creator for a single day's work of a particular type. In the past, day rates were used by photographers more frequently than today, as most photographers now use pricing models where they charge a creative fee, plus usage, plus expenses. A *minimum* day rate is still something independent creators calculate internally to help determine their creative fees, however.

Day rates traditionally varied depending upon the type of work a photographer was doing, and were applied against the clients' usage of the work.

For example, a photographer shooting editorial images for a magazine might charge an editorial day rate of $500 – $750 per day as a minimum against the space rate the magazine pays for publication of the resulting images.

That same photographer might charge anywhere from $1,250 to $2,000 per day for corporate photography, such as for corporate brochures, web sites, and annual reports. The increased fees reflect the increased value or usage that the client receives from their use of the images.

For advertising photography, that same photographer might charge $2,000 to $3,000 per day. The day rate is one of the underlying foundations of the more commonly used creative fee today. All other expenses for a shoot are generally charged to the client *in addition* to the day rate or creative fee.

Today, day rates remain common in work for hire situations such as in the motion picture industry, where photographers and other authors are hired to help create a collective work. In such instances, the creative artists are hired on a daily or hourly basis, with copyright and ownership of that work belonging to the client. Such projects are generally long term and provide steady employment over many weeks or months.

Defamation

An attack or injury to one's reputation and/or honor via the use of false or malicious statements. In spite of freedom of speech rights guaranteed by the U.S. Constitution, defamatory material (including photography) is prohibited by law in all 50 states. If defamation is in written or tangible form, it is referred to as *libel*. If it is spoken or in oral form, it is called *slander*. Photographers should be cautious in the use of digital manipulation to alter the reality represented in their photographs, as well as in the written captions published with their images, as combinations of both can result in defamatory or libelous exposure.

Delivery Memo

A written document providing a physical description of an image or group of images being delivered to a client, along with a description of the terms and conditions of how that work may be used. A delivery memo also outlines the responsibilities of all parties involved. Delivery memos should generally be signed by the client, acknowledging receipt of the work and agreeing to the associated terms and conditions. However, many photographers and authors include a clause stating that "objection to these terms must be received in writing within X days, or they are deemed accepted by the client..." This provides some protection to the photographer in case the client (either intentionally or inadvertently) does not return a signed copy of the delivery memo.

Derivative Work

A work that is based on (or derived from) one or more already existing works. A derivative work is copyrightable if it includes what copyright law calls "an original work of authorship." A derivative work must be different enough from the original to be regarded as a "new work" or must contain a substantial amount of new material. The new material must be original and copyrightable in itself. The copyright in a derivative work covers only the additions, changes or other new material appearing for the first time in the work.

Just because you are creating a derivative work does not automatically give you free rein to use or incorporate others' work at will. Permission (a license) to use the copyrighted work of others is still generally necessary before creating a derivative, or else you risk violating the copyrights of those whose work you are using.

Distribution

Generally, a reference to the geographic area where a product will appear or be distributed – as in a specific country or region. Examples might be Spain, Europe, or Latin America.

Distribution Rights

The rights to distribute a product or work in a defined geographic region. Distribution Rights are different from Language Rights, as they are specific to geographic region. For instance, Spanish Language Rights provide for the publication of a work in the Spanish language, whereas Distribution Rights will limit the availability of that work to Spain, Mexico, or Latin America as a region. The two are often associated with one another, even though they are distinct.

Distributor

An agent or entity that distributes products to consumers or dealers. Book and magazine distributors generally catalog, warehouse, market and sell printed products from multiple producers, either purchasing the product at a discount and selling for a profit, or by taking a percentage of the sales price.

Document / Documentation

Written or printed material which contains information providing proof of something. In a photographer's business, documentation of business agreements should include Estimates, Assignment Confirmations, Invoices, and Delivery Memos, along with Model and Property Releases, letters of agreement, contracts, and even e-mail correspondence. Notes from meetings or phone conversations, as well as notebooks and journals, can also provide documentation for legal purposes, but are often considered less desirable because they do not necessarily represent the mutual understandings between two or more parties that a signed contract would.

Domain

One or more networked computers that share a common communications address on the World Wide Web. Accessed via a Uniform Resource Locator (URL), such as **http://www.vrphotography.com** – the domain name in this instance would be "vrphotography.com"

Domain names are assigned by a number of sanctioned registrars for ICANN (Internet Corporation for Assigned Names and Numbers), and must be unique.

See also: **Public Domain**.

Duplicate

Any copy of an original. In photography, duplicate transparencies are copies of original film images, often sent out to clients for reproduction or publication. This helps protect a valuable original from loss or damage by allowing it to remain in the possession of the author while duplicates are sent to clients and potential clients for their use or consideration.

Internegatives and copy negatives are also created from original film or images for subsequent reproduction or printing. Analog copying introduces some loss of quality between an original and a duplicate because of both the need to use an optical copy system and the fact that a film image is being copied onto a second piece of film. Today, digital copies or duplicates of original digital files can be exact reproductions of the digital data (ones and zeros), so every copy can be a precise match and of equal quality to the original.

Duration (License)

The length of time that a license or agreement is in effect, or, the length of time that a part of a contract is applied. A license for a client's use of certain images on their web site might be for a duration of three months, or perhaps one year. Broadcast video licenses might include a maximum number of airings within a three-year term. These examples describing a time period are specifying a license duration.

Rather than accepting a request for copyright transfer by a client, a photographer might counter offer with a license for unlimited use in perpetuity (i.e. an unlimited duration). This gives the client freedom to use the image(s) in any way they like for as long as they want, but allows the photographer to maintain ownership of their work and copyright.

E

Edition

In book publishing, the size, style, or form that a book is published in (i.e., hardcover, paperback, pocket edition, etc.), or any of the versions of a textbook or reference book that are periodically revised (i.e. the third edition), or the total number of copies of a book that are printed from the same plates published around the same time (i.e. an edition of 5,000 copies).

In magazine, newspaper or periodical publication, editions are any version of the various regular issues published, such as the Sunday edition of a newspaper, or the year-end Year In Pictures edition of a weekly news magazine, or even a special edition published to commemorate a certain landmark event or subject.

In multimedia or broadcast usage, the date and/or time in which a program is transmitted or made available for audience viewing is considered the edition, such as the "Six O'Clock Evening News," or the March 25, 2010 online web posting.

Editorial Use

Use of specified content as a part of a bona fide news, information, or educational presentation, rather than for commercial purposes. Payment rates for editorial usage of photography are generally far lower than for commercial or advertising usage. Editorial space in publications and broadcasts is generally made possible by money earned from the sales of accompanying advertising time or space.

A recent trend is toward the presentation of advertising or promotional information in editorial form, often called "advertorials." Licensing fees for advertorial use generally will more closely match those of advertising use than editorial, because advertorials are essentially a disguised form of advertising.

Electronic Commerce (E-Commerce)

The buying and selling of commercial goods or services, combined with the transfer of funds or other assets, via online, electronic, or digital means.

Electronic Rights

An overly broad term that literally means the right to use a work in any and all electronic media. This could include television and radio broadcast, satellite transmission, web content, computer files, and all forms of digital media, electronic signage, digital projection, etc.

It is all too common for client contracts to specify an extension of "electronic rights" by the photographer or other content providers, when all that are really needed are rights for specific media, such as "six-month corporate web site use" or "up to four e-mail promotions to XYZ Corp. clients prior to December 15, 2010."

Use of the broad term "electronic rights" for limited usage licensing is just as vague and open ended as using the term "print rights" for printed media licensing. Usage licenses should be specified in as much detail as possible, and fees charged based on the values of the specific usage being extended. General descriptions such as "print rights" or "electronic rights" are inclusive of *all* such uses, and generally wind up costing the client far more than they are willing to pay for the specific rights they truly need.

Embargo

A restriction or restraint upon sales or trade. In photography contracts, embargoes are used to specify a given period and/or markets in which the author agrees not to sell the work in order to give the client an advantage of original or exclusive use. Such an embargo might specify that the photographer will not license use of an image to any third party until after the initial client has first published it, or perhaps for a period of one to six months. The client may also request, or a photographer offer, an embargo against licensing the image(s) to any other entity in the same market (whether geographic or trade-specific) for a given term.

Employee

A person hired by a business, firm, or individual, to work for wages or salary. In the U.S., there are important copyright and tax consequences related to the hiring of an individual as an employee. For copyright purposes, an employee does not own the work created for his or her employer, but is entitled to all benefits (both short and long term) available to employees, including tax withholding, workers compensation, vacation accrual, retirement, advance notice of termination, etc. Independent contractors are not generally considered employees, although they may be treated as such via contract terms. Work for hire or "work made for hire" is a contractual term that is often used by employers to gain the advantages of an employer/employee relationship (such as ownership of copyright) without the costs or obligations of hiring individuals as employees. For this reason, independent photographers should be wary of entering into work for hire agreements.

End User(s)

Member(s) of the targeted audience that a publication or product is produced for. In the magazine industry, the subscribers or readers of a publication are considered the end users. In the software industry, end users are individuals who purchase or use the software product for its intended purpose. On the web, individuals browsing a particular site in order to make use of its tools or information are considered its end users.

Errors & Omissions (E&O)

A clause or policy included in some insurance contracts that protects the insured against liabilities such as invasion of privacy, copyright infringement, libel, slander, defamation, unauthorized use, etc. E&O insurance is usually an added rider or policy (at additional cost) to general production or liability insurance policies, which provides coverage against liabilities incurred as a result of inadequate (or missing) model and property releases, license agreements, or other permissions for use. While this (and any other insurance policy) does not *eliminate* the possibility of legal action being taken against an author or producer, it does offer some level of protection against such actions when they occur.

Estimate

An approximate calculation of the probable cost of a piece of work, made by the person or entity proposing to do the work. In photography, an estimate is one of the four essential written documents a photographer provides as a paper trail outlining an agreement with each client for each work (Estimate, Assignment Confirmation, Invoice, and Delivery Memo). An estimate can be broad or specific in its description of costs and work involved, and is generally expected to be within 10-15 percent of the final invoice amount, unless significant changes are required (and agreed to by the client) for the work or work product during its production. An estimate differs from a bid in that a bid is a firm price for which a product or work is agreed to be produced (no matter if it costs more or less for the photographer to do), while an estimate is an approximate calculation, subject to reasonable change.

It is generally advisable to get a client signature on an Estimate or Assignment Confirmation indicating an agreement to the terms and price(s) set forth for the job, *prior* to beginning any work on that job.

Exclusive

The granting of an exclusive right, or the inclusion of an exclusivity clause in a contract, providing privileged use of the described image(s) to the named client. Provision of an exclusive license to one client prohibits the photographer or author from licensing similar rights to third parties during the described term of exclusivity.

Exclusivity can be defined as broad or specific. For example, the granting of "exclusive reproduction rights for a period of one (1) year" provides the client with the right to be the sole publisher of the licensed image(s) during the specified one-year term. The photographer cannot license the described image(s) to any other party for use or reproduction during that time. However, if the photographer were instead to license "exclusive North American print periodical rights for a period of three (3) months," then the client would be the sole North American magazine that could publish the work during that term. The photographer, however, could license the image(s) for reproduction in books, web sites, billboards, or other media during this same period, as the exclusivity granted to the original client is limited only to print periodicals.

Generally, the greater the degree of exclusivity a client receives, the higher the license fee will be. The greater exclusivity limits the earning potential for the images by the photographer from third parties during the term of exclusivity, so the photographer will generally charge more to the exclusive client in order to make up for the resulting lost potential income.

A "non-exclusive" license is one in which there is no exclusivity included.   When a photographer extends a non-exclusive license to a client, the client has no guarantee that the image will not appear in other media or publications, and the photographer is free to license the image(s) elsewhere at any time.

F

Fair Use

There are certain forms of reproduction of copyrighted works that do not necessarily constitute copyright infringement. Fair Use is a doctrine (section 107) under U.S. copyright law that permits the use of copyrighted materials without permission of the copyright holder.

Fair use includes criticism, comment, news reporting, teaching, scholarship, research, and even parody, although other factors are considered, as well. These include:

1) the purpose and character of the use (including whether it is for commercial use or nonprofit educational purposes),

2) the nature of the copyrighted work,

3) the amount and substantiality of the portion copied in relation to the copyrighted work as a whole, and

4) the effect of the use upon the potential market for, or value of, the copyrighted work.

The distinction between "fair use" and copyright infringement may be unclear and not easily defined – often requiring legal action and a court decision on the particular case in question.

Other exempted uses can be defined through legal statutes that permit the copying of copyrighted work without permission of the copyright holder in situations where serving the public interest outweighs any harm that might result for the copyright owner.

First Rights

The rights to be the first to publish an image or work within specified media or territories. For example, the granting of "first North American print periodical rights" provides the licensee with the right to be the first print magazine in North America to publish the image(s).

Flat Rate (Fees)

A fee structure that some photographers use for pricing their assignment work. A certain fee is charged to the client for the work, no matter how much time or effort winds up being necessary on the part of the photographer. This fee will likely be different for each assignment, but some photographers will keep such a fee constant for a given client over multiple assignments or projects. Generally, this flat fee is inclusive of only the photographer's normal creative and/or licensing fees.   Production expenses incurred for the project, such as film, processing, digital file preparation, media, assistants, models, permits, etc., are usually billed to the client in addition, and generally with a markup.

Flat Rate (Licensing)

A single fee charged to a client for their broad and relatively unrestricted usage of an image (or collection of images). This is often done as a form of royalty free (RF) licensing, although it may be more limited.

For example, a collection of images might be licensed to a client for their unrestricted future use for a single flat fee (specifying that the license is nontransferable). The same fee would be charged to another client for their unrestricted use, as well, even though the actual use and reproduction of these images may be completely different for each client.

Another variation would provide more limited use to a client for an image or collection of images. In this instance, the photographer might license unlimited use of the image(s) to a client for a period of one year for a flat fee. The fee would be the same whether the client made extensive or minimal use during the license period.

Freelance
A term used to describe a creative artist, not under contract for regular work, whose work and/or services are sold to individual clients or buyers.

Frequency
How often publication is made. For example, the frequency of a weekly newsmagazine would be once per week or 52 times per year. A monthly magazine would have a frequency of once per month or 12 issues per year. A corporate annual report would be once per year, although related collateral materials might be more frequent.

For electronic or web distribution, frequency can refer to either the number of times a given file in downloaded from a web site, or how often the content of that web site is changed significantly.

Fulfillment
The satisfaction or completion of the requirements and/or terms of a contract, thus bringing it to its conclusion.

Also, a term used to describe the successful distribution and delivery of a product to its users. A software publisher that needs to deliver its product to its clients, might use a "fulfillment house" – an independent firm whose sole business is to take orders and/or ship the ordered products out to buyers for other companies.

A photographer might also use an online digital lab to fulfill print orders. The online lab will likely handle the taking of the orders, collecting of the fees, the making of the prints, and the mailing or shipping of them to the client(s). This online lab or fulfillment house keeps a portion of the proceeds from each transaction and forwards the balance on to the photographer or the photographer's account.

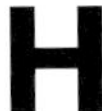

Hold Harmless
Terminology used in contracts and agreements wherein one party accepts full responsibility, while releasing the other party from potential liabilities. A Hold Harmless clause is more commonly known as an Indemnification clause (see Indemnity).

A photographer might encounter such a clause if he or she is seeking permission to shoot in potentially dangerous locations or situations. The property owner may be willing to extend permission for the photographer to do so, but will want to be held harmless from anything bad that might happen while the photographer has access. Thus, the photographer may be asked to sign a release including

a clause that holds the property owner harmless from any accidents, loss, or damages that might occur.

Hourly Rate
A per hour fee charged for photography or other services. Some clients will ask photographers for their "hourly rate" when they believe that the photo shoot should take only a short time, and they don't want to pay a photographer's full or half-day rate. However, few assignment photographers charge hourly, or even half-day rates, due to the fact that very few assignments really ever take much less than the better part of a day. Even if you're actually shooting for an hour or less, you still have all the prep and travel time, setup & packing of your equipment, downloading, film processing, digital image processing, post production assembly, and other tasks that take significant additional time for each shoot. Furthermore, if you are committed to a particular shoot, even though it may only be scheduled for an hour or two, you are generally unable to accept other work during the rest of your normal work day, because you cannot risk being late or missing the second job if the first one goes long. For these reasons, charging an hourly rate for assignment photography is generally not a good practice for photographers.

Impressions
The number of copies printed or produced. In marketing and advertising, can also be used to indicate the number of individuals or targeted audience members reached.

Imprint
In the publishing world, an individual brand, or a particular division of a publishing company.

Incorporate, Incorporation
To combine or join with something already formed. Example: incorporation of photographs into a book or web site is the inclusion of them in the existing book material.

Also, to combine or organize into a legal body, or corporation, that acts as an individual entity.

Indemnify / Indemnification / Indemnity
To protect against, to exempt from, or to compensate for loss or damages.

Photographers will frequently encounter Indemnification clauses in contracts from corporate clients, where the company is asking the photographer to indemnify the corporation against damages resulting from the photographer's activities related to the shoot, as well as the photographer's failure to get proper releases or other permissions. While the photographer should be vigilant in his or her attention to safety and the protection of property, as well as be responsible about getting releases, etc., agreement to most indemnification terms also means that the photographer may be obligated to defend the corporate client against lawsuits related to the shoot or the client's use of the photographer's images, even if the legal actions are without grounds.

Photographers are not in business as insurance providers, so agreeing to provide indemnification to the client for anything outside of the photographer's direct control *could* be disastrous to the photographer's business.

Therefore, photographers should carefully limit their indemnifications to only those elements which they can fully control.

Furthermore, indemnification should work both ways – where the client also agrees to indemnify the photographer against the *client's* misuse of the photographer's work (such as publishing an unreleased photo resulting in a lawsuit by the subject or model), or against losses during the shoot resulting from the client's actions (improper safety equipment available, inadequate facility maintenance resulting in injury or damage to the photographer's equipment, etc.).

When faced with blanket indemnification demands on client contracts, photographers should consider crossing out such clauses, or negotiating fair and balanced terms that specify appropriate responsibility for each party to the agreement.

Independent Contractor
A person or company, not an employee, contracted to do a given task, or to work for a given period according to his or her own methods.

There are a wide variety of tests used by various government entities (including the IRS, state tax agencies, workers compensation agencies, and even copyright law – all of which may be different) to determine whether an individual qualifies as an independent contractor or not. These tests consider whether the contractor provides his or her own tools and equipment, does the work in their own place of business, works for more than one client, does the work independent of client supervision, and chooses when to do the work.

In general, independent contractors do not receive employee benefits (such as vacation accrual, sick days, retirement, health insurance, severance, etc.). However, unless otherwise agreed, independent contractors generally own the copyrights to the work they produce, licensing usage of these works to their client(s).

It often costs a company less to hire a photographer as an independent contractor, rather than as an employee (since they don't have to pay benefits), so there has been increased pressure from corporate accounting offices to do this in recent years. However, many of these companies don't like the fact that they won't own the copyrights to the photographer's work this way. Clients often try to get around this by hiring independent contractors under *work for hire* agreements, which means that the entity hiring the contractor owns the copyrights to the work produced, rather than the photographer or author who created it.

Photographers should be cautious of such agreements. Most independent contractors try to avoid work for hire agreements unless they are appropriately compensated. When negotiating, remember that your client is saving significant costs in not having to hire you as an employee, including health insurance, workers' compensation, employer Social Security contributions, and all the vacation, retirement, sick time, and severance benefits they might have to provide if you were an employee.

Industry
A particular branch of large scale business and productive enterprises.   Examples might include: tourism, manufacturing, communications, aviation, transportation, construction, publishing, etc. Most photographers will find themselves drawn to serving certain industries, and will become specialists in these areas.

Infringement
A violation of a law, agreement, or right. Photographers will most often encounter this term when referring to copyright infringement – wherein one party has violated the copyright(s) of another. Other rights may also be infringed upon (meaning trespassed or violated) by photographers, such as a subject's right to privacy or their right of publicity (use of their name or likeness without permission).

Infringements of these rights can often result in legal action, which can get very expensive very fast, and should be avoided. Just as photographers have every right to be upset when our copyrights are infringed by others, so too should we expect our subjects and fellow authors to be upset if we infringe upon their rights.

Innocent Infringement
A legal defense often used in copyright cases wherein the accused infringer claims they were unaware of that the material they copied or used was copyrighted. Photographers can minimize the likelihood of such defense being successful by making sure that copyright notices are included with any publication or distribution of their images, and that copyright information is embedded in the metadata of every digital image file. This not only helps inform potential users that your work is indeed copyrighted, but also makes it more difficult for infringers to successfully claim they were unaware of the copyright.

Insertions
The number of times a given image is used in a single publication over a period of time or over multiple issues of that publication.

For example, if a particular photograph is used to accompany the text of a story in a monthly magazine, and is also used on the Contents page of that same issue, that would be considered two insertions. If that same photo was then used again to help illustrate another story in a subsequent issue of the magazine, that could be considered a third insertion.

Usage licenses may be worded so that they extend reproduction rights to the client for (up to) a given number of insertions in the publication during a set time period. Obviously, the more a photograph is being used or published, the greater the value the client is receiving from its use, and the greater the fee paid to the photographer should probably be.

Insure / Insurance

A contract to pay (or be paid) money in case of loss (of life, health, equipment, property, or other value).

Photographers often pay an annual premium to an insurance company to issue a policy agreeing to protect the photographer against claims or damages resulting from the photographer's liability, damage to others' property, or loss/damage to the photographer's own property. Liability coverage is often required by clients and property owners in order for a photographer to work on their premises.

Equipment coverage pays the photographer for the value of photo or business equipment that may be lost or damaged. Premiums – or the costs of such insurance – usually correlate directly with the value and coverage provided by the policy.

When buying insurance, it is important to consider the limitations and exclusions of the policy, in addition to the value of the coverage. For example, some equipment policies will pay for lost or stolen equipment at its replacement value, whereas others will only pay an amount based on the depreciated value of the equipment at the time it was lost. Similarly, some policies will not cover equipment stolen from a vehicle if the vehicle was unlocked or there were no signs of forced entry.

It is important to carefully review and understand what coverage, limitations, and exclusions are specified when comparing prices and purchasing insurance coverage.

Intellectual Property

Ideas and expressions pertaining to perceptions or relationships that are unique and often of value. Examples include copyrights, patents, trademarks, and trade secrets.

A photographic print, or even an original piece of film containing a developed photograph, is tangible physical property. However, the image that is recorded on that film is considered intellectual property. It is the image, not the physical piece of film or photographic print, which is copyrightable and considered to be intellectual property.

Other intellectual properties might include a sequence of words that make up a book or article, the design of an illustration or graphic, or the lines of computer code that comprise a software program.

International

Pertaining to distribution and relationships between or among more than one nation.

International Rights

Authorization or license to use a work outside of its country of origin. Such rights are usually limited to a specified territory or geographic region, and should not be confused with "World Rights" or specific "Language Rights."

Internet / internet

(Capitalized) The connection of world wide computer networks used as the foundation of the World Wide Web. The Internet was developed originally for the exchange of data and information between universities and corporate research departments. Its use required command line interfaces. However, with the advent of the World Wide Web and popular web browsing software around 1990, the Internet became a more user-friendly system where users could access text, graphic, and multimedia information more easily via HTTP or HTML protocols. The term "Internet" is often used interchangeably with "World Wide Web" (or the "Web") today.

(Lower case) Any set of computer networks interconnected with one another.

Use of the term "Internet" or "World Wide Web" in a licensing contract can be overly broad. Rather than licensing "Internet use" or "Web use," photographers and authors should try to be more specific in their descriptions.

Example: "Photographer extends a one-year license to (client) to display up to six (6) images on (client's) World Wide Web site. Display must include photographer's copyright notice and credit adjacent to each image, with corresponding link(s) to the photographer's own web site: http://www.yourwebsitehere.com. License is nontransferable."

Intranet

A privately maintained computer network accessible only by authorized individuals, most often employees of the company that owns it.

Invoice

One of the four essential documents that should be used for every photographer/client business transaction (Estimate, Transaction or Assignment Confirmation, Invoice, and Delivery Memo). An invoice is the actual bill for fees and expenses that is sent to the client for payment. The invoice should also include the terms and conditions that the photographer and client agreed to in the Assignment Confirmation. This serves as further written documentation of those terms.

Issue

All copies of a publication produced for a given date or period, such as a day, week, month or quarter. For a daily newspaper, the issue would include all copies of that newspaper published on a given day, including various local editions. For a weekly newsmagazine, a particular issue would include all copies and editions published for that week.

K

Kill (Fee)

A fee paid to photographers and other independent authors, when a project is canceled. Kill fees are generally paid by magazines or other publications after the author has completed an assignment, but the magazine decided not to publish it (killing the story). This is done to help compensate the author for the work they were contracted for but which was not used.

Many publications pay independent photographers a day rate against a space rate. The photographer is paid an agreed rate per day for shooting the assignment, but if the publication decides to use a lot of images or publishes them in larger sizes, the photographer receives additional compensation based on the space his or her photographs take up on the page(s). This is why photographers are often willing to accept what are generally considered to be low daily shooting rates from editorial magazine clients, because they understand that they will be compensated further if the magazine editors really like their results and feature more of their images in the publication.

A kill fee helps provide the photographer or author with at least a percentage of the potential income they lose due to a client's decision *not* to use work created on the assignment. However, kill fees can also be negotiated even if an assignment is killed before it begins, and the photographer has invested time and money into preparing for the shoot (or turned down other paying work because of the scheduled assignment).

L

Language Rights

The right to publish a creative work for distribution in a given language, not to be confused with Distribution Rights, which involve license to publish and distribute the work in particular countries or geographic regions. The two are often combined when licensing a work for publication.

Example: English language rights involve the publication of a work only in the English language. However, distribution rights will limit what countries or regions are included, specifying whether publication and distribution will include North America, Great Britain, South Africa, or even perhaps, an English edition in a non-English speaking country.

Liability / Liable

A legal obligation to make good on any loss or damage that occurs in a transaction. To be liable means that one is responsible, usually for some undesired result.

In accounting terms, a liability refers to a debt of a person or business on a financial balance sheet.

Libel / Libelous

Defamatory content printed or recorded in tangible form that causes damage to the reputation or honor of another. There are a number of defenses against libel, not the least of which is truth. If a published image or statement is indeed true, then it may not be libelous, even though its publication or presentation might be damaging to the reputation or honor of the subject.

License / Licensing

Formal permission to do something. The licensing of reproduction rights for a copyrighted work should always be done with a written agreement that clearly details the specific rights being extended and any restrictions or limitations on those rights.

Licensee

The person or party to whom a license is granted, or who is the recipient of such license.

Licensor

The person or party granting a license.

Limited Rights

Rights that are restricted in their scope or intent. Most licenses for reproduction and use of creative works are limited to very specific terms, as opposed to "unlimited rights" or "unlimited use," for which there are no limits or restrictions.

Local

The area of a city, county, or other small geographic region. Photographers on assignment may choose not to charge clients for travel expenses, such as vehicle mileage, when work is limited to a local geographic area. Otherwise, mileage and other travel charges might apply.

Local distribution is used to describe the circulation area of a newspaper or other publication, when confined to a city or other limited geographic area. A larger circulation area would be described as regional distribution, while national distribution would specify circulation throughout an entire country.

A local area network (LAN) is a term used to describe a group of computers connected to each other via Ethernet or wireless systems, usually within a single building or complex.

Loss / Loss Fee

The damage or disadvantage caused by losing something.

A loss fee is an amount charged or paid as compensation for the loss of something of value, such as an original photograph. While professional photographers' organizations, such as the American Society of Media Photographers (ASMP) have established loss fees for original film images in the neighborhood of $1,500 each, courts will also consider other factors when determining awards in lawsuits seeking loss fees. These include the nature and uniqueness of the lost images, the earning potential and track record of the photographer's similar work, where the responsibility for the loss lies, etc.

One of the great advantages of digital photo technologies is that exact digital copies of original photographs are routinely delivered to clients, rather than irreplaceable original slides or negatives. This virtually eliminates the risk of a client losing an original image, since master files generally remain in the photographer's possession. This obviously is a welcome benefit to both photographers and clients.

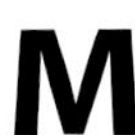

M

Marketing

A broad term describing a collection of processes used to move goods and/or services from producer to consumer. These can include advertising, public relations, promotion, and sales efforts, among others.

Photography clients will sometimes request a rights license for "marketing efforts." Photographers can be fooled into believing that this license is of lesser value than others, such as advertising, when in reality, "marketing" usage encompasses a wide variety of such rights, and should probably cost the client more than just specific advertising rights or public relations use.

Media Buy

The amount of money spent by an advertiser for the collective advertising space and time in all media for a given project or promotion.

Advertising and other agencies often base a portion of the fees they charge to their clients (the companies for which they are creating advertising and promotions) on a percentage of the total cost of the media buy. Hence, the more ad space or air time that the client buys for their promotions, the higher fee the agency earns.

The size and amount of a client's media buy is a good representation of the value the client will be receiving from the work created for use in these media, and can be useful information for photographers and other independent authors in understanding value the client places on their work.

Medium (Media)

A system or channel of communication, information, or entertainment (plural is "media"). Examples include print media (newspapers, magazines, brochures), and electronic media (television, radio, world wide web, e-mail, phone, CDs & DVDs, etc.).

Many media overlap these two main categories today. Newspapers and magazines commonly publish both print and electronic versions of the same content. Many television productions offer not only broadcast distribution of their programs, but also home video versions (videotape or DVD), online supplements (world wide web), and even print publications, such as books or transcripts. Billboards and bus cards (the large advertising cards found on the sides and backs of most city buses) are now presented in both printed and electronic form.

When licensing usage of photography or other content, it is important to define specific media for which the content can be used by the client. In general, the greater the usage or media being licensed, the higher the fee charged.

A broad description on a license, such as "electronic use" would generally command a far higher usage fee than would a more specific description, such as "... display on the opening or index page of (client's) web site, sized at 640x480 pixels or less, for a period of 30-days, ending no later than (date)."

Model

A person depicted in a photograph, or one who poses for an artist, image maker, or audience. Professional models are generally compensated for their efforts. However, any individual whose likeness appears in a photograph or other visual work is considered a model for legal purposes.

When an individual appears and is recognizable in a photograph that is intended for commercial use, whether a professional model or not, a signed model release should be secured. In today's increasingly litigious society, model releases are advised even for noncommercial uses of photographs in which recognizable individuals appear.

Model Release

Written permission from a person whose likeness appears in a photograph or other visual work, for their likeness to be used for commercial purposes. There are many "standard" model releases available from professional photographer, artist, and legal organizations.

Most photographers find it convenient to keep printed model or photo release forms in their camera bags so they can secure written permission from people appearing in their photos at the time the images are created.

Moral Rights

Moral rights give creators the right to control attribution (credit) and the integrity (alteration) of their work. These rights provide a level of sanctity to artists' original creations. Moral rights give an author the right to always be identified as the author of their work, whether done under work for hire or not, as well as control over modifications of that work by others.

In the United States, there are no moral rights currently provided to images made for publication. Only fine art works, created for exhibition, and for which 200 or fewer copies will be produced, are protected by moral rights in this country. These rights vary significantly by country, and are generally far more favorable to authors in Europe.

Multimedia

Technically defined as the presentation of information via two or more media formats, such as text and photos, or photography and sound. Common usage however, is to describe electronic publications that include a wide variety of formats, such as a web site or CD/DVD that includes text, still photos, video footage, music, narration, and links to other similar content that allow for user interactivity.

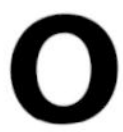

National

Pertaining to the entirety of a single country. A license for national usage or national distribution would allow for publication throughout an entire country, including across state lines, but not across national borders or into neighboring countries.

Negotiate / Negotiation

The process of conferring, bargaining, or discussion in order to reach an agreement. At its best, negotiation provides agreements that serve the best interests of all involved parties.

Non-disclosure Agreement (NDA)

An agreement specifying confidentiality, usually required by the party that is hiring an independent contractor to work on a project or program. NDAs can range from being very specific about what sorts of information must be held in confidence, to quite broad.

It is important to read and fully understand the requirements of an NDA before signing it. Some can be so broad that they prohibit the contractor from even revealing to others that he or she is working with a company, while others specify confidentially only for a limited time and about specific information.

See: **Confidentiality**.

Non-Exclusive

The opposite of exclusive. A non-exclusive license to publish an image or other work gives the licensee the right to publish the work as specified, but also allows the copyright owner to license the work to other parties concurrently. Non-exclusive licenses are generally more common than exclusive ones, depending upon the particular market one is working in.

Work created on assignment for a client generally is provided with a right of exclusive use by that client until after its initial publication or completion of the license term. However, existing work, such as stock photography, is more often licensed on a non-exclusive basis. Non-exclusive licenses are by far most common in traditional and multimedia photography (except for assignment work), and are usually assumed unless exclusivity is specified in a written contract.

Non-Transferable

When rights extended to one party are prohibited from being transferred or conveyed to another.

If a photographer licenses "non-transferable" rights to one client, such as an architectural firm, then that client cannot legally give permission to other parties for use of the work. These would include architectural magazines, contractors, city planning commissions, or others who might also be involved in the project, unless authorized by the photographer.

Non-transfer clauses are used by independent photographers and authors to limit use of their work to the original party to which they are licensing it. If your original client was acquired or taken over by another entity, a non-transfer clause could help limit the use of your work to only that original client, and not its new owner.

O

One-Time Use

A right to publish or use a work only once, as described in a license or contract agreement. One-time use would allow a magazine to publish a photograph in only a single issue or edition, although there might be many thousands of copies of that issue printed and distributed.

Option

A description of rights and their respective costs that will be both guaranteed and available in the future.

A photographer might license rights to a client to publish a feature story including the photographer's panoramic images for a certain fee, but also offer an option to the client to use the same images in a multimedia product for an additional fee. The client could reuse the work and pay the additional fees, but may instead opt not to, and not have to pay the extra fees.

Original

That from which subsequent reproductions or copies are made. For film, it is a master negative or transparency exposed in camera by the photographer. With digital photography, it is the file created in the camera (often in a RAW format), which records an image in a tangible form.

With film technology, each copy or reproduction is slightly different from the original, usually involving a loss of color fidelity, exposure latitude, sharpness, etc., so ownership and long-term protection of the original film is a critical concern, especially to the photographer. With digital technologies, a copy of a digital file is essentially as perfect and exact as the original. So it is possible for both the photographer and client to have digital files that are exact copies, therefore easing the concern of where an original file resides and whether it might be damaged during shipping or client handling. It is recommended that photographers and clients back up (duplicate) their digital image files regularly, so that the equivalent of a Second Generation Original (SGO) is always available in case of loss or damage to the original camera file or the media it is recorded upon.

Orphan Works

Copyrighted works whose owners are difficult or impossible to identify and/or contact. An inability to contact copyright holders of orphaned works prevents other creators from being able to use these works in any way, even though the copyright owner might be willing to allow this if they could be identified and contacted.

With an "orphan" designation, a copyrighted work still retains all the protections of copyright law, but provides none of the opportunities for licensing or use. The U.S. Copyright Office and the U.S. Congress are currently working on solutions for this dilemma.

Ownership

Legal right of permanent possession.

It is important to note the difference between ownership of a photograph and ownership of its copyright, both of which have value.

In the U.S., the author of a work is generally the owner of the copyright to that work, meaning that he or she is the one who controls licensing of the rights to others to copy, reproduce, or make commercial use of that work. However, ownership of the work itself, such as an original negative, transparency, print, painting, sculpture, recording, or book, may reside with some other entity, such as a client.

A client may possess and own physical photographs or prints created by a photographer, which they may be entitled to sell to another party. But without ownership of the copyright, or a license from the copyright owner, they cannot duplicate or use the photographs commercially.

This is an important distinction to note when preparing photographer/client contracts, as ownership of one does not necessarily include ownership of the other.

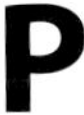

P

Page Rate

A fee charged or paid based on the size that a photograph or ad is reproduced on a publication's page.

For example, a magazine might charge an advertiser $100,000 to include a full page ad in a given issue. A half page ad might cost $60,000, a quarter page ad $35,000, etc.

That same magazine may offer assignment photographers a day-rate-against-page-rate agreement, where the photographer is guaranteed a minimum day rate to shoot an assignment, but may receive more if the magazine features lots of the resulting images on its pages.

Let's say that this magazine has an editorial page rate for photography of $300/page (note that this is considerably less than what the magazine charges advertisers to buy a page of ad space). A photographer is given an assignment and is paid $600/day for one day of shooting. When the story is published, the magazine features 2-½ pages of the photographer's images. The total space fees would be $750 (2.5 x $300/page), so the photographer is paid the higher amount for the space vs. $600 assignment (per day) fee.

Paper Trail

A collection of documents (either printed or electronic), relating to an agreement to do a given job or project.

For photographers and their clients, this should include four documents at minimum: an Estimate, an Assignment Confirmation, an Invoice, and a Delivery Memo.

Others include (as necessary): Model and Property Releases, Permissions or Licenses from third parties, Change Orders, Contract Amendments, as well as correspondence, shooting notes, phone notes, personal conversation notes, e-mails, and any other documentation for the project.

Such paper trails are essential for photographers to keep for future reference, particularly when questions arise regarding contractual terms, shooting techniques, financial records, or should some sort of legal action occur. Written documentation and contracts carry far more weight than verbal recollections do in court. Written contracts can also help keep disagreeing parties from ever going to court in the first place.

Party / Parties

Individuals, groups, corporations, or legal entities which are defined and identified in a contract or legal agreement.

Paternity Fee

A fee charge for failure to credit or attribute the authorship of a creative work, such as a published photograph.

Generally, paternity fees must be stipulated in a contract or written agreement in order to be enforceable. For many years, these have been accepted for editorial publication of photography (editorial content in newspapers, magazines, etc.), where a penalty for omission of a photographer's credit was a tripling of the photographer's shooting fee.

Such penalties are important because the identification of the author of a published work is critical in order for that author to be recognized and able to attract additional future work from the audience of that publication.

However, in non-editorial publication, such as advertising and some corporate communication, the inclusion of author credits is less standard due to the higher fees paid to authors from the outset. Therefore, paternity fees or penalties for missing credit lines are far less common.

Periodical

Any publication that is issued less frequently than once per day. Common examples are weekly, biweekly, monthly, and quarterly magazines, as well as online publications at similar intervals.

Permission(s)

Agreements and licenses from holders of copyrights, patents, trademarks, or other rights, granting the right of reproduction or use of their work and/or likenesses. A signed model or property release is a form of permission to use the model's likeness or owner's property in a published work. But generally the term "permissions" is used to describe copyright and other intellectual property use agreements.

Perpetuity
Forever, or for an indefinite period.

Example: a license to use something in perpetuity has no time restriction. It can, in effect, be used by the licensee under the terms described in the license forever.

Personal Use
Usage only for private purposes unrelated to business or commerce. This generally excludes reproduction or publication of the work, although in some instances, such as software and personal music licenses, making a single copy of the work for backup purposes *might* be acceptable.

Pick-Up Use
The additional use of a work by the same end user in a different project, program, title, or issue.

Placement
The position, location, and size of an image within a publication.   Prominent placements might include the front and back covers, centerpiece, or gatefold, etc.

Product placement is a reference to the inclusion of a commercial product or trade icon within a photograph, motion picture, or television program. This might include a particular brand of beverage featured within a scene, or a logo or aircraft of a particular airline displayed as part of a travel sequence. Depending on the market and target audience of the image/program, product placement can command significant fees from product manufacturers, who gain advertising and promotional value from having their product appear in a popular medium or production.

Keep in mind however, that most such commercial products are also protected by copyright and trademark laws, and should only be placed within a scene with owner permission and via written agreement. The companies that produce these products usually strive to exercise control over how their products are displayed and how they may be perceived by their public. They may feel it detrimental to be perceived in a context of association that the photographer or image producer creates, and may have cause to seek compensation for damages through legal action.

Therefore, product placements within commercial imagery should be done via mutual agreement.

Portal
A web site or URL that serves as a common entry point via links and connections to other online content and web sites. Search engines such as Google and Yahoo are common examples of portals, as too are subject specific sites such as the Virtual Reality Photography web site at:
www.vrphotography.com

Presentation Use
Use of a work as part of a speech or meeting to convey concepts and information to an audience. This may also include its use in printed handouts or online notes and summaries that may be distributed in conjunction with the presentation. Presentation use generally does <u>not</u> include any other reproduction or distribution rights. These rights should be negotiated additionally as needed.

Example: a lecture is being recorded, and the recording will be sold, broadcast, or distributed on the web. These additional publications of the lecture recording would require an additional license from the basic lecture use. Also, additional publication license would be needed if the lecture is used as a part of a magazine article or book chapter in which the licensed work was included.

Press Kit / Media Kit
A collection of images, articles, press releases, interviews, transcripts, and other multimedia materials that are distributed to the press and other media outlets for the purposes of promoting a particular company, project, product, publication, or event.

When a client asks a photographer for use of their images in a press kit or for "press distribution", it means that the images will be intended for publication in as many newspapers, magazines, and other publications (including online and broadcast media) as possible. The client is seeking to maximize what amounts to unpaid advertising or publicity through free distribution of this content to these media outlets.

From a photographer's perspective, your work is likely to see wide publication and distribution, but generally without your credit and without further compensation to you. Furthermore, the various media outlets that your work is distributed to are likely to file your images in their archives, where they might be drawn upon to accompany future stories that have little, if any, relation to the company or project you originally created them for.

Unless the photographer is able to arrange for specific contract terms that provide control over required photo credits, or limitations on where and when the images may be published (including by the press and other third parties), then the photographer is likely to lose most control over future licensing and rights restrictions for this work. These considerations should be factored in to the fees charged for work licensed for press and media kit distribution.

Price Fixing
Direct or indirect joint action with a competitor that may have the potential to influence market prices. Federal law prohibits either individuals or businesses from monopolizing, or attempting to monopolize markets for goods or services.

For example, a group of independent photographers or members of a trade association who agree to standardize their fees in a given market, may be in violation of federal and state antitrust laws (restraint of trade, price fixing, unfair competition, and trade practices). Penalties can be severe.

Such laws are intended to help promote healthy competition in the market place, and to minimize or prevent the growth of monopolies which could otherwise stifle fair competition.

This does *not* necessarily mean that photographers cannot discuss their pricing strategies or rates with one another – but rather, that they cannot collectively agree to charge what the others do for the same services or products.

In fact, open discussion of business practices and education among photographers is encouraged by many trade associations under the concept that an informed and knowledgeable competitor is often the best type of competitor to have.

See also: **Restraint of Trade**.

Profit
The sum remaining after all costs (both direct and indirect) are deducted from the income of a business.

Sole proprietors should not confuse salary, or the money they take from their business for personal use, with profit. A business owner's salary is an expense that is included with all the other expenses of running the business when calculating profit or loss.

Profit is the amount that remains after all expenses are deducted from income, and is generally a source of funding that can be put back into a small business to help it grow.

Promotional Use
Use of an image to promote a product, service, or publication. Promotional images might be included in advertorial publications and press kits (although advertorial use is generally considered to be a form of advertising, and thus advertising-type fees generally apply). "Promotional use" is often used interchangeably with Public Relations (PR) and Publicity use.

Proprietary
Belonging to a proprietor or private party. Proprietary information includes material or information held under patent, trademark, or copyright by an individual or company.

Photographers and other independent contractors hired by such companies may be required to sign *non-disclosure agreements* (NDAs) covering their work and involvement with these companies in order to protect the techniques, processes, systems, and intellectual property (or other proprietary information) that they gain knowledge of during their work.

Public Domain
As pertaining to creative works, the absence of copyright or patent protection – meaning that the work can be used freely by all.

Creative works generally enter the public domain upon expiration of their copyrights – currently 70 years after the author's death (in the U.S.) , or if the work failed to meet requirements for copyright protection. (Patent protection usually expires 17 or 20 years after initial filing.) Creative works can also enter the public domain with a deliberate surrendering of the copyright(s) by their creator.

Most works created by the U.S. government automatically and immediately enter the public domain, as they are created through taxpayer funding and therefore, belong to the people. Authors working under contracts with government entities should be aware of such copyright stipulations when drafting or signing government contracts.

Public Relations (PR)
Coordinated efforts made to establish and/or maintain public awareness of a commercial service or product. "Public Relations (PR) usage" of photography or other creative content is extremely broad in scope, possibly including advertising, publicity, granting of unlimited third party uses, etc , and should generally be more narrowly defined in licensing terms.

See also: **Publicity Use** and **Promotional Use**.

Publication
The printing and/or distribution of multiple copies of a work. For copyright and other purposes, "publication" can include electronic distribution, such as e-mail, web sites, online, or public broadcasting, unless specified more narrowly.

Publicity Use
The use of a work for the purposes of bringing notice of a person, place, product, or cause to the public . "Publicity Use" is a very broad licensing term, which can be interpreted to include many other related and unrelated uses, depending upon interpretation.

See also: **Public Relations**, **Promotional Use**, and **Press Kit**.

Publish
To make publicly known, or to issue a work in printed or electronic form.

Punitive Damages
Also known as exemplary damages, are awards made to a plaintiff beyond the actual loss incurred. Punitive damages are imposed by a court as punishment for the defendant's wrong.

Purchase Order (PO)
A form or agreement issued by a company or its representative promising to pay a prescribed amount in exchange for a certain service or product.

Many companies will not make payments to their suppliers or vendors without a purchase order signed by an agent of the company and the vendor or supplier.

Photographers and other independent authors should be aware that most corporate purchase orders contain a great deal of fine print in addition to the description of fees and services to be rendered. This fine print can include hidden terms such as copyright transfers, indemnification clauses, liability waivers etc., that the vendor might not normally agree to. Therefore, it is important to *carefully read and understand* every part of a purchase order before signing it.

If there are clauses, terms, or conditions presented as part of a purchase order that are in conflict with the photographer's own contract or agreement, it is common practice to cross out and initial the conflicting terms on the client's purchase order, and to clearly indicate that in the event of a conflict, the terms of the photographer's contract will override those of the purchase order.

It is not uncommon for a corporate client to fax only the front page of a PO to a photographer or other vendor for signature, without including all the fine print clauses that appear on the back or subsequent pages of the original. Therefore, it is recommended that you sign (and modify, if needed) only the hard copy originals of any purchase order presented to you by a client, so that you are sure of having the complete document.

R

Redress

To set right, rectify, or remedy, often by making some form of compensation.

A photographer, model, or client may have a right to redress from another party due to loss, damage, or other liability resulting from that party's action (or inaction).

Regional

Pertaining to a geographic section of a country, often including multiple states.

Example: a photographer might license use of images to a publication for distribution in the southwest region of the United States, or "the wine country of northern California."

Rejection/Approval Rights

Any rights given to an individual or entity allowing them to reject or approve the publication or use of a work.

In some instances, an author will retain such rights when licensing his or her work to others in order to help maintain the integrity of that work. This would be done to control editing or in the case of photos, cropping, retouching, or sizing for reproduction. Some public figures may also request the right of approval/rejection for publication of photographs taken of them before agreeing to pose or sit for the photographer, in order to control and protect their public image.

Release (model or photo)

A document signed by a person or subject appearing in a photograph granting permission for their likeness to be used in that photograph for commercial or other specified purposes. In the case of a minor (a person not yet of legal age), the release must be signed by a legal guardian.

Such releases are generally secured by the photographer, and authorize the photographer to extend permission to other parties for commercial use of the images the photographer creates of the subject.

Release (property)

A document signed by a property owner or authorized representative granting permission for photographs of their property to be used for commercial or other specified purposes.

Release(s)

Any document that extends permission for a work to be published, broadcast, displayed, shown, or put into circulation.

In some contracts, a release clause may be used to stipulate a release of responsibility (or liability) by one party to another, or perhaps to give up any claim to rights or ownership that may be in question.

Remainder

Extra or leftover copies of books and other publications, that typically are sold at greatly reduced prices.

Many book publishing contracts specifying royalty payments to an author are based on the quantities of the book that are sold, but specifically exclude those copies sold as remainders because there is little, if any profit made from such sales.

Renewal Rights

Permission to extend or renew an existing license for a work. This may be included as an option in the original license, or provided as a new license near expiration of the original license.

Example: a client may license one-year, corporate web site publication of a series of VR panoramas for $10,000, but also want the option of extending that license if they want/need to after the one year has passed. The photographer or author may include the renewal rights and stipulate renewal fees in the original license agreement, or may issue a subsequent license renewing the original agreement terms and fees, depending upon the needs of both parties.

Repeat Use

Multiple or repeated placement of the same image or work in a given title, program, project, or issue of a publication.

Example: the same photograph is used on the cover, table of contents page, and in a featured article in a single issue of a monthly magazine.

Represent, Representative

To act or stand in place of, or to be an agent, proxy, or substitute for. Also, to present a likeness, portrayal, or depiction of.

A representative or agent may negotiate for and represent the interests of an individual, company, or other entity. Some photographers are represented by agents for assignment work or for stock photo licensing. Most photographers will encounter agents representing the corporations or other entities that they wind up doing work for. These may be art buyers from advertising agencies, or creative directors and other employees of the client itself.

Whenever possible, it is most efficient to conduct negotiations with individuals who have authority to make decisions for the client's company, rather than representatives who must take your proposals to other decision makers.

Reprints

Printed materials which are reproductions or reprinted copies of original publication materials.

Magazines frequently offer reprints of articles to subjects or clients that might have been featured in these articles. This is a profit center for magazine publishers and reprint companies, and the reprints are used by the magazine clients for promotional use.

In general, reprinting of articles and photographs for third party use is licensed separately. Independent authors normally charge additional licensing fees for the added usage.

Reseller

A party which buys goods or products from one or more suppliers and then resells them to others, generally at a profit. Those who sell products or goods on consignment are also considered to be resellers.

In the publishing world, brick and mortar book stores, along with online outlets, are considered to be resellers, as they buy (or sell on consignment) books and other publications at a discount from publishers, and resell them to the public or their own clients.

Restraint of Trade

An action or condition that tends to prevent free competition in business, such as the creation of a monopoly or the limiting of a market.

While laws vary from country to country, independent photographers may violate restraint of trade regulations by agreeing with one another to set or standardize prices and fees they charge to their clients, whether done intentionally or not. Independent photographers and other authors should be very cautious about inadvertently agreeing to charge common prices or fees when discussing business practices with one another.

Unions, on the other hand, are generally allowed to negotiate and set fees for their members. This is allowed because unions represent employees, rather than independent business people.

A cooperative or co-op structure in the U.S. allows for benefits similar to union negotiation for independent business owners.

See also: **Price Fixing**.

Restriction(s)

Any limitation specified in a contract, agreement, or license.

Example: An insurance policy may provide coverage for loss or damage to a photographer's equipment, but may have restrictions that exclude coverage in war zones, or for theft of equipment from unlocked vehicles.

Retention (Holding) Fee

A fee charged to a client for holding or retaining a work longer than the agreed time period.

Holding fees were far more common before digital technologies became readily available, when a client's holding on to original film for an extended period effectively prevented the held images from being marketed or licensed elsewhere. Today, a copy of a digital file can be just as perfect as the original, so multiple copies of an image can be in front of a potentially unlimited number of different clients around the world simultaneously.

Furthermore, original source images are now usually kept in the photographer's own files, while digital copies are sent out to clients. Thus, there is little risk of losing potential income because an original image is being held by a client.

Returns

Magazines, books, and other printed publications that are distributed to resellers or other retailers, but which are not sold. These unsold copies are often returned to the wholesaler, distributor, or publisher, who may issue credits for them to the retailer.

Reuse

A second or repeated use of an image other creative work.

Example: a client may initially license use of a photograph for display on their company web site for a period of one year. The subsequent addition of trade show display, printed brochure, or any other use beyond that specified in the original license agreement would be considered a reuse, and would generally involve additional licensing fees.

Revenue

The total monies earned or received before subtracting expenses. Often referred to as gross income.

Revision(s)

Major revision - any modification to a work involving changes to five percent or more of the content (including both words and images).

A *minor revision* is a modification of a work involving changes to *less* than five percent of the content (words and images).

Revocation

A cancellation, repeal, or annulment of an agreement, license, rights, or clause of a contract.

Right of Privacy

A broad right inferred by the U.S. Constitution, and extolled as "a right to be left alone." This includes certain freedoms from government intrusion into private lives, as well as intrusions by others, including the free press.

It is for such reasons that photographers shooting photographs of people for publication are well advised to secure the permission of their subjects in the form of a written model or photo release.

Such documentation is evidence that the subject has agreed to release – at least to a limited extent – their right of privacy during the photo shoot.

Right of Publicity

The right of an individual to prevent unauthorized use of their name, likeness, or other recognizable aspects of their persona (such as their voice, etc.) for commercial purposes.

This right varies considerably under differing state laws, and may not even exist in some. It is a part of right to privacy laws in some states, while others specify it under laws relating to unfair competition.

It is most often invoked by recognizable public figures whose personal or professional image has been damaged by unauthorized use, or where others may have gained some advantage.

This right may or may not survive the individual after his or her death, although there has been an increasing tendency in recent years for the estates and heirs of deceased public figures to seek and be granted continued protection of this right of publicity.

As with right of privacy concerns, a signed model or photo release is essential in order to document your subject's permission to reproduce, publish, or otherwise use their likeness as it appears in your photographs.

Right(s)

A claim, power, title, privilege, or interest in a given property (whether tangible or intangible), such as a copyright.

For creative works like photography, rights for an almost unlimited number of uses may be extended, licensed, exchanged, and bought/sold. When an author or owner of a work grants a license for a particular use of that work

to another party, they are considered to have licensed a right for the use.

Rights can be exclusive or non-exclusive. An exclusive right means that only the party holding that right can exercise it. A non-exclusive right means that the party holding the right can exercise it, but identical or similar rights may be held and exercised by others concurrently.

Right To Assign / Right to Transfer

A contractual term that allows the licensee or rights recipient an ability to grant the rights they've received for use of a work to other parties.

Rights Managed / Rights Protected

A creative work for which licensing is controlled and specified for each use, and for which exists a detailed and accurate licensing history.

Many photography clients require that their image suppliers have this sort of information, particularly about stock images being considered for use, since it may be important for the images chosen to be guaranteed *not* to appear (or have appeared) in a competitor's products and promotions, or because some level of exclusivity is required.

Rights managed or rights protected content generally commands higher licensing fees, and is often of higher quality than unmanaged content such as that sold as clip art and royalty free (RF) material.

Royalties / Royalty

A percentage of sales revenue or an amount per unit sold, which is paid to an author or rights owner of a work by a publisher or user of that work.

Royalty agreements are common in book publishing, where authors are often paid an advance fee for creating the book content. This advance is applied against their royalty earnings from eventual sales of the book.

Example: An author may contract to write and/or photograph a book for a $7,500 advance against a 10 percent royalty. (Royalty payments are usually based upon the publisher's discounted price to its distributors and resellers, rather than the cover price of the book.) If the publisher earns $15.00 for each book, a 10 percent royalty is $1.50 per book. Therefore, it would take sales of 5,000 books to cover the advance paid to the author (5,000 x $1.50 = $7,500). If more than 5,000 copies are sold, the author receives an additional $1.50 royalty per book. But if less than 5,000 copies are sold, the author retains the full advance, but receives no further royalty payments until sales surpass the advance total.

Royalty Free (RF)

A term applied to images and image collections that are sold on disc or by subscription, which offer extensive, almost unlimited usage for a single fee. The images are generally mass marketed, and few efforts are made by the copyright owner to accurately track usage history.

These image collections are generally of lower quality than rights managed imagery, and are frequently sold in high volume at low cost. They are also known as "Clip Art."

RF imagery usually comes with limited restrictions on how it can be used. For example, these images usually may not be published as pornography nor resold to others. RF content has historically carried greater risks for end users – including sometimes limited accountability for necessary model and property releases.

S

Sampling
The taking or copying of a portion of one work for the purposes of using it in another.

Some artists have a misperception that sampling, if done below a minimal level, is acceptable both ethically and under copyright law. This is completely wrong. Copying *any* portion of a copyrighted work, no matter how small, can be a violation of copyright law. Such copying or use requires the permission of the copyright holder.

If you are going to create an original work, be sure to make that work completely original.

Search Fee
A fee charged by image library owners or their agents for the efforts necessary to find a selection of images to a potential client's specifications from an image library. The fees are generally used to help distinguish bona fide stock photography clients from those who have little interest in – nor budget for – actually licensing usage rights, as well as to compensate the library owners for the time and effort of researching and fulfilling such requests.

Frequently, these search fees will be applied toward licensing fees that may result. In these cases, if the client actually does buy a use license, the search fee is effectively waived.

While search fees were very common at one time, they have become less so in recent years after several major stock photo agencies dropped them entirely. The availability and widespread access to online image libraries has also shifted the burden of extended searching to the client.

Seat License
A usage license, most often used for computer software or digital applications, that is specific to a group whose members are all given access to that software.

An example would be a 50 seat license, where the software is licensed for use by up to 50 individuals on 50 different computers within a company or among its contractors.

Photographers are likely to encounter this in both software that may be provided to them for use by their clients, or from clients who are producing multimedia content, which they plan to license in this way to *their* clients.

Second Serial Rights
The right(s) to republish a portion of an already published work, such as a book, in a magazine, or periodical.

Secondary Rights
Generally considered as "small" rights, such as photocopying and xerography. Fees for such rights and usage are so small that they would fall into what is now termed a "micropayment" level (pennies or less per instance), but the collective volume of secondary rights usage is considerable. Fees for such usage are generally collected by Collecting Societies via blanket licensing agreements.

Secondary Use
A lesser of two or more uses. For example, if a panoramic image was being used as a double page spread in a magazine, but also as a section header on a table of contents page, the larger spread would be the primary use, while the smaller header would be the secondary use.

Site License
Used primarily for computer and other digital software applications, a site license is a license that allows for an unspecified number of users at a given location or site. Site licenses are often purchased by corporations, who need to have every employee and contractor using the same software application and version throughout the company. Site licenses are generally used for larger groups than might more effectively be covered by a seat license.

Slander
The making of false statement(s) via spoken word that damages the reputation or character of another person. Slander is differentiated from libel in that slander is done via spoken word, while libel is done in print or published form.

Space Rate
Rates that are paid either by an advertiser to a publisher, or by a publisher to an image provider, based upon the amount of space that an ad or image occupies on a printed page.

A full page ad will generally cost an advertiser significantly more to run in a magazine than a 1/4 page ad, because it takes up more space. Similarly, a photographer who is being paid a space rate will receive more compensation if the publisher runs her photo over an entire page than she would if it only appeared on 1/3 page.

Note that the rates advertisers pay for ad space are significantly higher than what photographers and other content providers are paid when their work is published at a similar size in the same publication.

Space rates or similar fee structures are also used for some electronic media.

Spec (Speculation)

Work that is done for a potential client without any guarantee of payment or acceptance.

There are tremendous risks for photographers and other authors who take on speculative work offers, as they may wind up completing the work as prescribed by the client, but have no assurance that the client will necessarily accept the work or pay them for it.

Accepting a spec assignment is effectively giving up any negotiating power you might have with a potential client, as you take on all the responsibility for creating the work to their specifications, but agree that they have no responsibility to compensate you for your efforts unless they choose to do so after the fact.

Statutory Damages

Penalties that can be imposed by a court based on violations of law or legal statutes, such as copyright laws.

Stipulated Damages

An amount agreed upon for compensation to one or more parties for specified breaches of contract by the other party. Such stipulated damages are generally specified in terms of a contract.

Examples: Stipulating a fee of $1,500 for the loss of *each* original transparency or negative by a client, or a tripling of the license fee when an editorial client fails to include a required credit line with a published photo.

Stock

Preexisting images that are available for licensing. Stock photography may be created on speculation by the photographer or author anticipating a future market for such imagery, or may result from past assignments that the photographer has done for clients and for which their are no exclusivity requirements restricting the photographer's licensing of the images elsewhere.

Stock photography is often licensed by individual photographers, as well as by large and small agencies representing the imagery of multiple photographers.

Sublicense

A license for use extended to a third party by a party that is not the primary rights holder of the work.

Example: A photographer licenses an image to a publishing company or a news agency, which then sublicenses the image to its member publications for their use. Note that licensees must have the permission of the rights owner in order to legally issue sublicenses.

Submission

The offering of photographs or other works to a potential user, publisher, or agent for their consideration.

It is generally advisable to include a delivery memo or other written agreement with an image submission, specifying terms and conditions for the recipient's use or consideration of the work, and requesting acknowledgment of the work's receipt and acceptance of both the work and the terms.

Subsidiary Rights

Rights commonly specified in book publishing contracts that cover usage beyond the initial publication of the book in print form. These may include, electronic and audio book versions, motion picture and television rights, as well as performance and merchandising rights.

Supplementary Work

A work that is supplemental, in addition to, or supporting of the primary work being licensed or published.

For a book or a major story in a periodical, supplementary works might include, introductions, forewords, illustrations, photographs, tables, indexes, and appendices, among others.

Supplier

One who provides products or services to others. Photographers, stock agencies and other image providers are considered as suppliers to their clients.

Survive / Survival / Survivor(s)

A contractual term used to specify that certain portions (or all) of an agreement will continue to be applicable, even after the period or other terms of that agreement expire.

Survivors are individuals or parties with legal claim to the rights and property of a person who dies or a company that goes out of business.

T

Termination

The conclusion of an agreement or contract. Termination may be done by mutual consent, or by failure of one party to live up to the agreed terms prior to the scheduled completion date.

Terms (and Conditions)

The collection of statements, points, or clauses that document the understandings between parties in a contract or agreement.

Terms and conditions are the qualifications and restrictions included in a licensing or contractual agreement.

"Term" is also used to describe the duration of an agreement.

Example: "The license term is for a period of three years."

Territory

A defined geographical area in which a work will be published, broadcast, or distributed. A usage license that defines a territory may also include language restrictions.

Example: "English language broadcast rights throughout North America," or, "Northern California Spanish language publication rights."

Third Party/Parties
Any party outside of the principal parties involved in a contract or agreement.

Total Exclusivity
Usage that is made available to only one party, and no others. If a licensee is granted total exclusivity to a work by a licensor, the licensor cannot license the work to any other party during the specified term.

Trade Secrets
Confidential processes, mechanisms, formulas, and information that can provide competitive advantage, which are owned by individuals or companies, and which are not generally known nor easily discovered by others.

Trade secrets are generally considered to be a form of intellectual property.

Trademark(s)
A name, symbol, or other distinctive mark that identifies a product or company. U.S. trademarks must be registered with the U.S. Patent and Trademark Office (USPTO), and their use is restricted to the given trademark's owner, manufacturer, or licensees.

The ™ annotation, used in the following manner: Company™ or Product™, designates that the name or term preceding it is a trademark. The use of the letter R in a circle following a company or product name, as in Company® or Product®, means that the trademark has been applied for and registered with the USPTO, but not yet approved.

A service mark is a trademark that is used to identify a service, rather than a product or company, and is designated with an "SM", rather than a "TM" annotation.

U

Unauthorized Use
Any use of a work that is done without the permission or authorization of the owner.

Uniform Commercial Code (UCC)
A set of regulations that have been adopted, at least in part, by all 50 states of the U.S., which are intended to help standardize the ways in which commercial business is transacted, including sales and licensing – such as when a photographer sells a photograph, licenses a stock image, or is contracted to create images on assignment.

Breaches of contract and disputes over contractual matters can be handled under the UCC in state courts, whereas copyright disputes must necessarily be heard in federal courts, since copyright laws are federal laws. This difference can be a tactical element when a photographer or other visual artist finds it necessary to file legal action, particularly if the cause for the action was possibly both a copyright violation and a contractual breach.

Unlimited Use / Unlimited Rights
A license granted for use of creative work without limitation or restriction. Note the difference between a license extending unlimited use to a client, and one that extends "all rights." The granting of "all rights" is effectively a transfer of copyright and ownership of the rights to the work, meaning that the author or original owner of those rights no longer owns them.

Whereas the granting of "unlimited rights" gives the recipient the right to use the work without restriction, but the author or original owner still retains the copyright, and can continue to license use of that work to others.

URL
Abbreviation for Uniform Resource Locator, which is commonly used to describe the online address for a particular page or site on the World Wide Web. For example, the URL for the Virtual Reality Photography web site is:

http://www.vrphotography.com

Usage / Use
The combination of details that describe how an image or creative work is permitted for use to a client. These details are generally spelled out in the license agreement:

Example: "One time, non-exclusive North American consumer magazine publication, in XYZ Weekly, not to exceed 1/2 page reproduction and circulation of 650,000. All other rights reserved."

V

Variance
A term used in estimates and contracts to describe an amount of variation that may be acceptable in accompanying prices or fees. In many instances, a 10 percent variance is considered acceptable. Therefore, if the final amount due from a job is within 10 percent of the estimated amount, the invoiced amount may be acceptable.

Note that variances are generally only acceptable for work involving estimates, rather than bids, since a bid is an agreement to produce a defined work result for a specific cost.

Waive / Waiver
To give up or forego a right, claim, or privilege to which one is legally entitled. A waiver is an agreement, generally in written form, to do this.

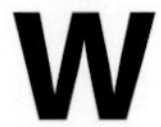

Warranty / Warranties

A guarantee or assurance of something having to do with a contract or sale of a product.

Example: a photographer may provide a warranty to a client that she has secured signed model releases for all recognizable persons appearing in a series of photographs submitted to the client for their use or publication. If the photographer's warranty proves to be false later on, the photographer may become liable for damages incurred by both the client and the models due to the client's resulting use of the images.

Example: a product manufacturer offers a one-year warranty to the buyer that the purchased product will remain functional and free of defects during normal use. Should the product fail, the manufacturer will assume responsibility for the product repair or replacement, or will refund the buyer's money.

Work

For copyright and contractual purposes, a term to describe the tangible product or material produced. For creative authors and artists, this can include any copyrightable material such as photographs, illustrations, multimedia, written documents, software code, digital data, musical compositions, recordings, paintings, sculpture, etc.

Work For Hire (Work Made for Hire) or WFH

An agreement wherein a work is created for an employer or a client, and the copyright is owned by the employer or client, rather than the person who actually created the work.

Creative works, such as photography, which are done by employees within the scope of their employment, are generally considered to be works for hire. Thus, ownership of the copyrights to such works belongs to the employer.

Independent authors and contractors automatically own the copyrights to the works they create, unless they contractually agree to a transfer of copyright or agree *in writing* to work for hire. Work for hire agreements are being increasingly demanded by large corporations, who want the benefits of having an author work as an employee, but don't want to be saddled with the overhead and other expenses of hiring such an individual as an employee (continuing salary, benefits, vacation, retirement, medical, unemployment, tax withholding, Social Security, etc.).

In short, work for hire is a great deal for the client, but a terrible deal for the author.

There are, however, certain requirements on how work for hire must be secured from independent contractors. Both parties must sign a written work for hire agreement *before* the work is begun, and the work being done must be commissioned as a contribution to a collective work, motion picture, audiovisual work, translation, supplementary work, compilation, instructional text, test or answer material for a test, or an atlas.

For photographers, the categories that work for hire agreements tend to fall into most often are contributions to a collective work such as a magazine or periodical, or contributions to an audiovisual work, such as a web site or other electronic publication.

Work for hire contracts must be executed *before* the work actually commences, and are generally unenforceable if presented by a client after the fact, particularly if accompanied by a threat to withhold payment until the agreement is signed. If no signed work for hire contract exists, then the photographer, author, or other independent contractor who created the work automatically owns the copyright to that work.

World Rights

A license to use or reproduce a work throughout the world.

Such a license may be restricted by other terms or limitations, such as the length of time (or term) of the permitted use, or what languages it may be published in, or particular purposes for which it may *not* be used, such as pornography, promotion of gambling, smoking or alcohol products, or any sublicensing or transfer of agreed rights to others.

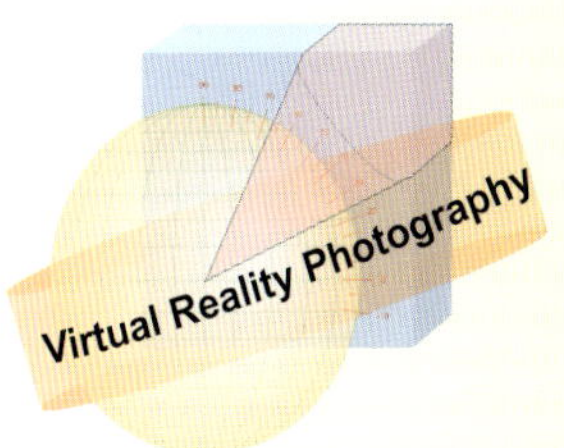

Chapter 24: Business and Marketing Strategies

Professional photographers all face the challenge of finding clients and getting hired by them for a fair rate. VR photographers are no exception, but in addition, they need to be able to convince their clients why VR might be a better approach than traditional photography or illustration. As VR photographers, we need to be able to explain the advantages of an interactive view – whether panoramic or object – over the use of traditional still photos for a given client's needs.

The first step in this process is to identify the types of clients and industries that can benefit from the use of VR. These might include tourism, travel, corporate training, education, instruction, lifestyle & entertainment (clubs, restaurants, etc.), real estate, high end & luxury products (automobiles, aircraft, boats), and cataloging (museums, historical artifact collections, online retailers), among others. Consider also the relative value of panoramic or object movies to each of these. Keep in mind that most interactive VR content will be displayed electronically, whether on a web site or video screen. There are many commercial uses for printed versions of panoramas or object movie frames, as well.

Next, identify those market segments and those individual clients for which you already have connections. Even if you have no experience creating commercial VR imagery, you can often use your existing access to specific markets and clients to create sample work. If you already do work for the boating industry, or even if you just happen to have a few friends who own nice boats themselves, take advantage of this access to shoot some sample VR portfolio pieces.

You might also consider shooting test VR material on a traditional commercial shoot if you have the time, and then show the results to your client. You want to stimulate your client's excitement about the possibilities for using VR (and hiring you to create it) for future projects. It is generally much easier to generate interest in new services through your *existing* clients and contacts, than it is to start from scratch trying to sell new clients, who are unfamiliar with your work or the potential of VR imagery.

After you've identified these potential markets, you'll have to determine whether they will accept the fees you need to charge in order to remain profitable. You must go through the process of calculating your cost of doing business (CODB), as described in **Chapter 21**, so you will know the *minimum* fees you need to earn every shooting day. If for example, your CODB is $500 per day or more, it is unlikely that you'll be able to consider the real estate VR market, where a photographer might make only a few hundred dollars on their busiest day. Again, it's usually better to start out trying to sell your VR services to a market that you're already familiar with, and then gradually expand your reach from there.

Next, you'll need to identify specific contacts – individuals at companies in these markets who are the actual buyers of photography and photo services. These people are generally found in the marketing departments of large corporations, with titles like Art Buyer, Producer, Designer, or Creative Director. Smaller companies, including advertising agencies, web design firms, and multimedia production houses, usually have people with similar titles who make similar decisions about hiring photographers and other content creators.

It is perfectly acceptable to call a company that you are interested in working with and to simply ask who is responsible for their hiring of independent photographers and multimedia authors. If you haven't done this before, it is easy to feel intimidated by the idea of speaking to people who may control millions of dollars worth of creative budgets each year, and who already work with dozens of high profile professionals.

However, understand that creative directors and art buyers at even the largest companies are constantly on the lookout for new talent – after all, it is their job to provide a constant supply of fresh, innovative work to *their* clients. They want to hear from you and to see what you have to offer, particularly if it is high quality work. It is rare that they will come looking for you, since they already have so many authors coming to them. Therefore, you have a far better chance of developing a professional relationship by making the first move yourself.

Often, a phone call introducing yourself and asking if you can send them some promotional materials (printed collateral, an e-mail with a link to your web site, etc.) is all it takes. Keep in mind that most of these people are quite busy, and probably won't have time to meet you in person. Don't be disappointed if you can't get a portfolio appointment. Your initial goal is simply to get your work in front of them somehow. Once you've done that, let your work speak for itself. That's what they're most concerned about anyway. There's no point in wasting your time or theirs with an in-person meeting if the style or quality of your work doesn't match what they're seeking.

Developing a personal list of potential clients and contacts takes time – and your list will change continuously. Not only will your own business change, but many of the contacts you make along the way will change their jobs and locations, as well.

Set up a simple database on your computer to keep track of them all. Include fields such as name, company, address, phone, fax, e-mail address, web URL, and some sort of space for your contact history or other notes. Make sure you date everything, as it will become harder to keep track of when you were last in touch with each contact as your list grows. I actually include two date fields in my client database, one to specify when the initial contact was made, and the second to indicate when I last updated my information for that contact. You'll waste a lot of time and postage sending out promotions to a list that hasn't been updated within the previous year, as many of the people on that list may well have moved on to other positions during that time.

There are companies that create and maintain professional lists of photography buyers, which they offer commercially for rent or lease. You'll pay a small fee for each name or contact they provide, and they'll deliver the information either as a data file, or on printed labels for your promotions. Some of these companies will even do the mailing of your brochures or flyers for you, again for a fee. The advantage to using these services is that they are constantly updating their lists, and often include a number of contacts that you might not readily find on your own. The disadvantage is that these are not personal contacts you have initiated yourself, so the recipients of your promotions may have no prior knowledge of who you are. Thus, your work can easily get thrown into a file to be lost among the hundreds of other promo pieces received from other photographers via such list services.

While list services can be useful for some photographers, most find it better to create their own personal lists. It is far more effective to make your own contacts with potential clients. Phone them and introduce yourself. Leave a message if they're not there, and follow up again later. Confirm that they are indeed a person who hires photographers or licenses stock photography like yours. If they are not, then ask them who in their company does this, and follow up with that person. Once you reach a valid photo buyer, ask if you can put them on your mailing list for occasional brochures and announcements. Also ask if you can send them information by e-mail (be cautious with e-mail, as it quickly becomes an annoyance if overdone).

As your business develops, you will also start receiving queries from potential clients who found you through your advertising, promotions, web site, or even referrals from others. Make it a habit to ask every one of them how they found you (this helps you track the effectiveness of your advertising and promotion efforts), and if you can add them to your mailing list. Do this even if their needs and your services are not necessarily a match for the project they've called you about. The fact that they've already expressed an interest in your work makes them much more likely to become a future client than most of the "cold" call targets that you instigate on your own.

As you develop your list, plan ahead for what types of promotional materials you'll want to send. Keep in mind that *potential clients will need to be exposed to your name* **between six and 10 times** *before they start remembering it.* That means you have to have a strategy for repeatedly exposing them to your name and work.

There are many ways to gain this exposure, some of which are more cost effective than others. In general, these should be used in combination for the greatest impact.

Web Sites
For photographers today, a professional web site is an *essential* element of marketing and promotion. The web is now the primary source used by clients looking for assignment photographers and stock imagery. If you don't have a web site where potential clients can see your work and contact you easily, then you are missing out on what is probably the most effective marketing and promotional medium available.

The great thing about a web site is that you can set one up and operate it for relatively little cost, and you can update or add to it at any time. For a VR photographer, there is no better way to show your work to potential clients, since the interactive nature of your VR imagery is best displayed on a computer screen. A web site also means that clients anywhere in the world can look at your work at their convenience. There are no portfolio shipping costs, no risk of loss or damage to film and print samples, and no expensive preparation of portfolio pieces. Potential clients can review your work anytime and anywhere they have an internet connection.

A professional web site should have its own domain name – something memorable like **vrphotography.com** or **smithpanoramas.com**. This tells potential clients that you are serious enough about being in business to register your own domain name (which costs $35 per year or less), rather than using free space provided by large internet service providers such as AOL or Yahoo. It's fine to post your family photos for personal use under a URL like **www.aol.com/freegallery/bobspictures.html**, but when you're trying to present yourself as a respectable business owner, it's better to present your work under a domain like **www.bobsphoto.com**. When you register a domain name, choose one that will be descriptive and easy for your clients to remember (shorter names are better). If you can get a domain name that matches the name of your business, it will make it easier for people to identify and find you on the web. For example, if your business name is Bob's Photography, you might want to register and use **bobsphotography.com** as your domain name, if it's available.

Next, you'll want to design your web site so that it communicates clearly what you do. Show your best work and enable potential clients to easily contact you when they want to utilize your products or services. There are a number of widely available software applications for designing and building your own web sites. If you have basic design skills and are willing to take the time to learn these programs, you might be well off doing it yourself. If not, hiring a professional web designer is often money well spent. If you have a very limited budget, start small and expand your site's scope as your business grows.

Make sure you only show your best work on your web site, and be sure to include high quality examples of the kinds of work you are hoping to be hired for. If you want to shoot motorcycles and automobiles, it won't do you much good to show mostly food photography on your web site. If you're hoping to attract clients that want object movies created of their kitchen products, it doesn't do you much good to present only scenic outdoor panoramas, no matter how stunning they might be.

Remember that the overall impression you give to a potential client looking at your web site will only be as good as the weakest image you show. Make sure that every image and every VR movie you present is the very finest you can do. If in doubt, leave it out. You're better off displaying a small number of exquisite work samples, than including many lesser quality pieces that your best work gets lost in.

Update your web site regularly. If there is new work posted on it from time to time, people will come back to look at it repeatedly. Every time you post new material or make a significant change, send an announcement out reminding your list of clients and potential clients about who you are, and giving them yet another exposure to your name in the process.

Also, take the time to submit your web site to the major internet search engines. Google, Yahoo, and others all have sections on their web sites where you simply enter the URL for your site's home page, and the search engine "spiders" will crawl every page linked through your entire site, cataloging and indexing them. Then, when people using these search engines make a request for keywords that have been identified with your site, the search engine will provide them with appropriate links to your web pages. If you are designing your own web pages, be sure to learn about keywording and metatags so you can use these effectively in attracting search engine traffic.

Printed Materials
Among the most cost effective printed promotions you can create are custom postcards (these can often be ordered from online printers for about $99 for 500 copies). Mail out a new one to prospective clients every two or three months. Some photographers will send these out as frequently as every four to six weeks, particularly if the cards follow a theme or visual sequence. Be sure to include information about your web site and its URL on all your promotions, so potential clients will know where to go to see more of your work in detail.

Magazine or source book reprints are another form of printed promotion that you can mail to prospective clients. Let's say you were fortunate enough to have several pages of your work featured in a major magazine article. Contact the magazine and find out if you can order reprints of that article. Reprints feature only the article itself, not the entire magazine. Many magazines offer reprint services specifically to serve the companies whose products have been featured in their publications. There are usually fees involved, but you may also be able to negotiate this when accepting magazine assignments or licensing usage of your work. Note that getting your web URL included in your magazine and other photo credits whenever possible can also help bring additional traffic to your web site.

Source books are large format advertising books, printed annually, in which photographers and other creatives purchase pages for the display of their work. The source book publishers distribute these books free to thousands of qualified art buyers and creative directors throughout the country. Usually included with the price of each advertising page are reprints of that page, which the photographer can send out for their own promotions in addition to the distribution of the book by the publisher.

In general, advertising in source books is expensive, and there is no guarantee that you will get any work as a result. Most photographers feel source book ads should only be done in *addition* to other promotional efforts if one has the money available (pages generally cost thousands of dollars each), but should *never* be done as one's primary promotional vehicle. It is much cheaper, and generally far more effective, to have a series of promotional cards or brochures printed promoting your work, and to mail them out on a regular schedule to a small, carefully targeted audience. The dramatic increase of web use in recent years may well contribute to the obsolescence of printed source books in the future, as most clients looking for new photographers or stock imagery now use the web almost exclusively for their searches.

E-mail

E-mail has become a standard for modern communications, both in business and our personal lives. However, e-mail also comes with its drawbacks, not the least of which is the amount of spam or junk mail that we all have to put up with.

While e-mail provides an immediate means of getting information out, it is generally only useful when the recipient is willing to receive it. Unsolicited e-mail, no matter how beneficial or informative, will always have a risk of being perceived as spam. At best, it may simply be filtered out by your intended recipients' e-mail software. At worst, it will be perceived as an annoyance – and this is *not* the impression you want to leave with potential clients.

Therefore, you should probably avoid using e-mail for solicitation of new clients, unless you already have established some other contact with them and they have expressed their willingness to hear from you via e-mail. Most certainly, do not ever attach large files to your e-mails without prior permission from the recipient, as you risk further aggravation when you tie up their e-mail box and storage space.

E-mail is a great method for following up and staying in touch with people you're already connected with, but is a very risky proposition for soliciting new clients. Use it carefully and judiciously.

Social Networking

Social networking web sites, such as Facebook, Twitter, Linked-In, and others, have become quite popular in recent years. Many photographers feel that participation in one (or many) of these should be included as an element of their professional marketing and promotion. Others argue the importance of having a personal web log, or blog, as a way to keep clients interested and informed about their business. The latest wave of marketing gurus seem to feel it important to do them all.

While social networks are here to stay, they can easily cause more damage to your business and its reputation than value they might add. They must be used very carefully.

Keep in mind that anything you post on the web is likely to remain there for a long time. It will be archived and will probably be accessible to anyone and everyone for years to come, even if you remove or delete it from the site you posted it to. When you post a personal comment to a social networking site, even if it's completely unrelated to your business, eventually it is likely to become identified with your name or business through the databases of web search engines.

If you post a comment about an experience working with a particular client or art director (good or bad), eventually that comment may be read by that client, even if you posted in on a personal web page or social networking site. Such posts might also be read by other clients considering you for future work, who may find concern with how you "publicized" a previous client relationship. Your words can come back to haunt you. Many corporations have strict rules relating to employee use of social networking sites for just such reasons, and horror stories abound about employees losing their jobs as a result of personal comments posted to social networking sites.

What you write will be available for future employers and potential clients to read when they're doing online research into your business. It's all too easy to lose a job offer when a potential employer reads comments posted to your web log (blog) or social networking pages about previous employers, clients, or your personal life.

If you choose to participate in such sites, or to publish your own blog, be professional about it. Treat these with the same care that you would any other promotional media. In general, it is best to be benevolent and positive when you write, and supportive of those in your online communities.

Too many photographers fall into the trap of thinking they should include a blog on their web site so that clients can "get to know them" more personally. Yet these photographers forget that maintaining an effective blog requires that you regularly post new and *useful* information in order to draw readers back. This becomes a major chore and demand on their time. So they wind up posting pointless drivel about their personal lives or favorite sport teams when they can't think of anything else to write. This presents an unprofessional image to clients, and ultimately damages the reputation of both the photographer and his or her business. Face it, nobody beyond immediate family or friends will care about what you ate for dinner, how happy or sad you are in your current relationship, or how disrupted your life is.

If you regularly have something important or useful to say, take advantage of the social networking media. Otherwise, it's probably better to abstain. Remember the old saying, "It is better to be silent and thought a fool, than to open your mouth and remove all doubt."

Posting to certain social networking sites can also deprive you of potential income. Read carefully the "Terms of Use" that you must agree to in order to participate. Many of these networks require your agreement to grant almost unlimited use to anything you post on their site, including your copyrighted photographs, art works, writings, videos, sound recordings, etc. That means they can use your work for their own advertising, promotions, and even extend use of this work to other parties without any compensation to you. Read their Terms of Use carefully, and make sure you fully understand the implications before joining such networks or posting content to them.

CDs and DVDs

For many years, VR photographers found it advantageous to send out CDs and DVDs of their work to prospective clients. This was appropriate when web bandwidth was still fairly limited, as file sizes of VR movies were prohibitive for transmission and downloading. However, now that most everyone has access to the wider bandwidths of DSL and cable modems, it is easier and more economical to present portfolio and promo materials on a web site than it is to format, produce, record, label, and ship a CD or DVD.

There are still occasions when a CD or DVD can be useful, such as when a client has requested a large volume of work for review, or when delivering a collection of images from an assignment shoot. But overall, portfolio presentation is more cumbersome this way.

You are probably better off devoting the money and effort that you would have spent producing a high quality portfolio CD or DVD into further developing your web site, and then sending out post cards or other printed reminders to potential clients directing them to your web site. Again, a web site can be constantly updated, and you can provide enough depth of content that prospective clients can browse as little or as much as they like before contacting you about work.

Many people are reluctant to load a CD or DVD into their computer anyway, particularly if it comes to them from an unknown source. The concern over inadvertently installing a virus or other destructive application is serious. CDs and DVDs also tend to get lost or filed away, with no one knowing what content it contains. This renders your expensive promotion useless. It's better to have a printed brochure or card, that includes a sample image or two and the photographer's URL, to physically remind clients about what kind of work you offer, and where to go to see more of it. If they like what they see, they'll bookmark your site, and return to it again and again

Letters

In today's fast paced world of e-mails, voice mail, and web sites, it's easy to overlook the value of an old-fashioned business letter. Because so much of our modern day communication is done electronically, a personalized business letter, printed on quality stationery, is a relatively unique and classy thing to receive. Put yourself in your prospective client's position and imagine having to sort through a hundred or more e-mails each day, or needing to look at several dozen different web sites.

Then a day comes when a personalized letter on real stationery arrives in your mail box. It stands out from all the other clutter of bills, junk mail, periodicals and coupon packets. You open it first, pleased to discover that it contains something you value – the possibility of a new creative collaboration. (Of course, it will also reference a web URL and e-mail address, so you can further explore the work of this potential creative partner.)

This personal letter is unique, and will at least in some way stand out from among all the other electronic demands for your attention. As a photographer hoping to develop a client relationship with an art buyer or creative director, that is *exactly* what you want to happen.

Letters cost more to send than e-mail, but that adds to their uniqueness. Any time you send out promotional materials, be sure to include a personalized note to the recipient. This gives your client (or potential client) a sense that they are important to you, and that you're willing to take the time necessary to communicate personally, rather than treating them like they are only one name from a mass mailing list of hundreds.

Referrals

Perhaps the most successful promotions photographers can utilize are referrals, or recommendations from existing clients to potential future clients. If you can get satisfied clients to sing your praises to others who might be looking for someone with your talents and abilities, then you have found perhaps the best form of promotion possible.

This is one of the reasons why it is so important to stay in touch with past clients. Even if they don't have work for you any more themselves, they may be willing to refer you to their peers and associates. Some photographers find it useful to join their local chambers of commerce or service organizations just for such purposes. These can give you a chance to meet and socialize with other business owners in your community. That can help them think of you first when they have the need for a photographer, rather than looking through other resources for someone as yet unknown to them. Again, the benefits will vary depending upon the kinds of work you do, as well as the size and nature of your local business community, but it's certainly something to consider.

Photographers should also look to their communities of fellow photographers for referrals. When one photographer gets a client call for a project that he or she is unable to do, he or she will want to refer that client on someone else whose work they are familiar with and whom they know will do a good job. This allows the first photographer to continue to serve the needs of their client (by referring them to someone who will do a good job), as well as to do a favor for a fellow photographer (who hopefully might return this favor in the future).

Such fellowship and professional camaraderie can be found with membership in photography trade associations, such as the American Society of Media Photographers (ASMP), Advertising Photographers of America (APA), and the Professional Photographers of America (PPA). Membership in these organizations usually costs several hundred dollars per year. Fees are high because these groups are geared primarily toward working professionals. The International VR Photographers Association (IVRPA) is an association dedicated specifically to virtual reality photographers. They have a much lower annual dues structure, and welcome both professional and no-pros alike.

Advertising

Advertising can take many forms, including ads in your local paper, yellow page listings, display ads in trade magazines, showcase directory ads, and of course, paid links or banner ads on web portals and search engines. The selection of advertising opportunities is huge.

The most important thing about advertising is to remember what your target market is, and to spend your advertising budget effectively. It doesn't do much good to spend thousands of dollars for an ad in a general consumer magazine when general consumers are not your target market. Likewise, buying a display ad in your local phone company's yellow pages doesn't do much good unless you are offering services whose clients use these yellow pages to look for suppliers. If you are seeking corporate and business clients, you are better off focusing your advertising dollars on business-to-business media, rather than general consumer media.

Consider the value you will receive for the money you will spend, and be sure to carefully track the results when you do place ads. Always ask potential clients contacting you where they found out about your business, and note this in your files. At the end of each year, and particularly before you sign contracts for additional ad placements, review the results from your past advertising efforts. Before committing to a new advertising opportunity, get in touch with existing advertisers who offer similar services to yours, and find out whether they feel their efforts have been worthwhile.

Remember that a single ad does not usually generate much response. An ad campaign, which puts your name or company information in front of potential clients repeatedly, will help them remember you better. You are better off buying multiple smaller ads over many issues of a print or online publication, than you are sinking all your advertising budget into a one-time promotion.

Take advantage of free and low cost listings in local or regional directories, as well as opportunities to have your work (with you clearly identified as the author) included in promotional efforts by other parties. Again, be creative, and make your advertising budget go as far as possible, no matter how big or small it might be.

Portfolio Presentation

While photographers' work is increasingly reviewed via the web, there are still times when a photographer will be asked to meet in person with a prospective client, and to present a physical portfolio. For VR photographers, a physical portfolio might include a book of panoramic prints, enlarged transparencies in custom mounts, laminated reprints of published work, or an interactive presentation on the photographer's laptop computer.

It is important when making personal presentations to follow certain protocols.

The first is to limit the samples of work you show to between 12 and 20 images. (You can have more available, but only bring them out if the client asks for more.) Experienced creative directors and art buyers can usually tell within the first few images whether a photographer has the style and capabilities that they are seeking. Don't overwhelm them by insisting on showing the best of everything you've ever done in your career. Select your portfolio images based on the type of work this client will probably want you to create for them. Again, it doesn't do much good to show a stunning portfolio of aerial scenics or underwater wildlife to a client who needs highly stylized macro photography of computer chips. Similarly, it doesn't do much good to show VR object movies of athletic shoes to a tourism client who needs panoramas of their resort facilities.

When presenting your work, resist the urge to give a running commentary about each image. Let your work speak for itself. Most clients like to have a chance to look at each image in your portfolio at their own pace, and to do so without being incessantly bombarded with information about how difficult the shot was, what camera or lens you used, or how early you had to get up in the morning to capture the great light.

When a prospective client is looking at your work, force yourself to be quiet. If they have a question, let them ask it, then offer your response. Speaking too much implies that you are nervous and insecure. Clients are generally looking for someone confident and capable who they can rely on to produce the work they need. Don't worry if they flip through your images very quickly, even without

Case Study: Landing the First Commercial VR Photo Shoot

In 1994, I was hired by Apple Computer to photograph a VR tour of the original Apple Company Store at their headquarters in Cupertino, CA. The material was to be used for demonstration purposes and sample content in the initial release of Apple's QuickTime VR Authoring Tools Suite. It was the first commercial use of QuickTime VR, done by the company that invented the technology, and was used to introduce QTVR to the world.

The process by which I was chosen as Apple's first outside VR photographer is a good example of the somewhat unexpected ways in which photographers can be selected by major clients.

It was around 8:30 on a Friday evening when the phone rang in my home office. Normally, I try to leave my business concerns well behind by this hour, but this night, I happened to hear the phone through the open door to my yard, where I had been enjoying the evening with my family. I was tempted to ignore the call, thinking that it was probably an unwanted sales pitch or a wrong number.

However, I answered it, and it turned out to be from the QuickTime group at Apple. They were looking to hire a photographer for an unnamed, yet-to-be-released project (which they couldn't tell me anything about), and were conducting interviews the following Monday. We scheduled a time and, as I do with all new clients, asked how they found my name and contact information. The project manager answered that they found it in a listing I had placed in a *four-year old* film & television directory for our region, which was the most recent copy they had on their office shelf.

When I arrived for my appointment Monday afternoon, I met two members of the development team. I had close to 20 mounted enlarged transparencies in my portfolio – a professionally bound leather case embossed with my name and logo. They looked at the first photo, started to pick up the second one, and then got into a relatively vague description about the project (they couldn't reveal details until I signed a non-disclosure agreement – *after* being offered the job). We talked for about 20 minutes, and I gave them each a business card and a printed promo piece showing several of my images. I was discouraged that they had never even looked at my work, beyond that first image.

A week later, I got a call that they wanted to hire me. We negotiated a contract, and in a few more weeks,

I did the shoot. It was the beginning of a long and mutually beneficial business relationship, which gave me an opportunity to be one of the pioneering VR photographers in the industry.

At one point during the shoot, I asked the project manager how they came to choose me from among all the other photographers they had contacted. His responses revealed how the creative process often functions in a large corporate environment.

He said they made all their calls on the Friday evening I described above. They were under a strict development deadline. If a photographer they called didn't answer his or her phone that night, they didn't even bother leaving a message, since they needed to complete all their interviews the following Monday. It was just lucky that I happened to be within earshot of my business phone.

Then he said that during the interview, I actually listened to what they had to say, rather than telling them how I thought they should be doing their project. They liked that I was interested in the technology they were developing and didn't come in with preconceived notions about what they were trying to do. They also liked the fact that I had some digital imaging experience (digital was still fairly new back then). Even though I wouldn't be responsible for any digital work on this project, they felt my experience would at least give me a better appreciation of what their software engineers were trying to accomplish in our collaboration.

Finally, I asked him how they possibly could have chosen me as the best photographer for the job, when they only looked at one image in my portfolio. He said I was the last photographer they interviewed that day, and by the time they got to me, they were absolutely sick of looking at photographers' portfolios. They had one photographer who brought close to 100 tear sheets and samples of his work, and insisted on showing every one of them. Apparently, all they had to do was to see one image to know that I possessed the competence and professionalism they needed for the job. After the other interviews they had done, that was all that was necessary in order to make their decision.

While not every client seeking a photographer will work this way, it's surprising how often getting a job is a matter of merely being in the right place at the right time, and being sufficiently prepared to seize an opportunity when it arises.

seeming to consider each one individually. Experienced creative directors and photo editors are usually quite good at sorting through hundreds or even thousands of images at a time, and are very efficient at evaluating good photography quickly.

If a prospective client doesn't have much experience with VR and you are presenting samples of your work on a computer, it can be helpful to show them how the mouse or track pad is used to navigate around the first few images. Then, let them proceed on their own if they'd like. Having such work available on your web site also allows them to peruse it at their leisure, and to forward your URL on to others in their company who might be interested.

Finally, after making a portfolio presentation in person, it is important to offer what is commonly referred to as a "leave behind" – some sort of printed piece that reminds the client of your work and how to contact you. These can include promo cards, brochures, and reprints, among others. With some basic page layout software and a good desktop color printer, you can even create custom leave behinds for individual clients (make sure you bring several of each, in case you wind up meeting with more than one person from that company). Also, remember to offer a business card to everyone that you meet with, and be sure it includes your phone number, e-mail address, and web URL.

For a time, it was considered a necessity for a VR photographer to have a demo CD to leave behind with prospective clients after every presentation. These were often complicated and costly to produce. In recent years however, these have fallen out of favor, since it is so much more efficient to show such work on your web site. CDs generally wind up thrown away or lost in some file cabinet anyway. Today, it's better to simply direct clients to your web site. Some photographers even set up custom pages for particular clients in order to show specific portfolios or results of client assignments.

Staying In Touch With Your Clients

Your combined contact and client list may well be the most valuable asset your business owns, as it is the key to your potential income. Like other assets, it can appreciate or depreciate over time. Take good care of it by maintaining it constantly, and it will increase in value. Let it sit idle or unused for too long, and its value will decrease.

Update your contacts regularly. Art buyers and other creatives tend to move from job to job with alarming frequency. Try to stay in touch with them when they do. When new creative directors come into a job, they usually bring their own supplier and resource lists. When they're looking for a photographer, they tend to first seek out those that they've worked with before,

rather than looking up the ones their predecessors may have relied upon.

When one of your clients makes a change to their personnel, you need to quickly establish contact with the *new* art director, so that he or she becomes familiar with who you are and the kind of work you've been doing for their company. You may need to send them your promotional materials or schedule a meeting, just as you would to introduce yourself to a completely new client.

It's also important to keep in touch with the previous art director after he or she moves to their new job or company. They may wind up doing similar work, and may be in a position to hire you again. You want to make sure they remember you. Keep them on your mailing list and update their contact information.

Most photographers today are chosen by clients because of the photographer's proximity to the subject or location where the client needs photography. Gone are the days when photographers were hired to shoot extensive international campaigns, traveling from country to country in order to bring a consistent look or visual style to a project. Today, it is far more economical for clients to hire a local photographer in each city. This saves them significant costs of expenses and travel fees for photographers' time spent on airplanes or waiting in hotels. It's a fact of life in how corporations and publications work today. Photographers have to adapt.

Clients will generally search for local photographers using the web. They may use popular search engines such as Google and Yahoo, or they may use an online professional directory such as ASMP's Find a Photographer. Referrals from other photographers are also common. Many professional photographers regularly get calls from clients of fellow photographers, because of a conflict with the first photographer's schedule or because the current project needed the work shot in a different location than where the first photographer was based.

In such situations, good photographers will often refer the client to an associate that they know and trust in the needed location, knowing that the favor will probably be returned. There was a time when such an action might generate a small referral fee, but this is rarely done today. If you are fortunate enough to be the recipient of such a favor, a note of thanks to the referring photographer, perhaps accompanied with a token gift certificate of some sort, is a nice gesture of appreciation. Remember that your network of contacts and friends in the industry should not be limited only to clients or potential clients alone.

A truly successful network branches into many different areas of one's life, and when nurtured carefully, can lead to happily blurred lines between clients, associates, peers, and friends.

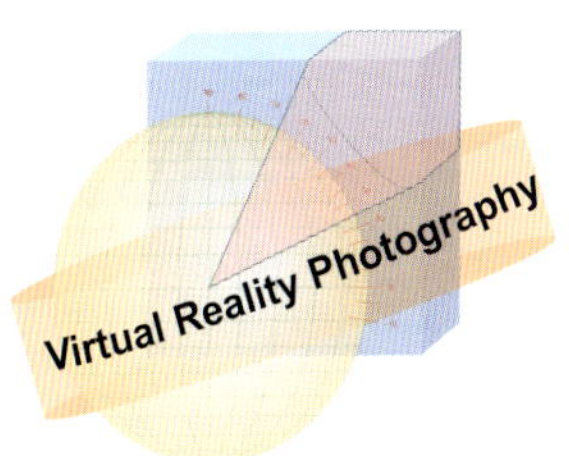

Index